The British in India

Humphrey Trevelyan, Political Agent in central India, greets Bhawani Singh, the young Maharaja of Chhatarpur, at the latter's investiture in 1942.

The British in India

A Social History of the Raj

David Gilmour

FARRAR, STRAUS AND GIROUX | NEW YORK

Farrar, Straus and Giroux
175 Varick Street, New York 10014

Copyright © 2018 by David Gilmour
All rights reserved
Printed in the United States of America
Originally published in 2018 by Allen Lane,
an imprint of Penguin Books, Great Britain, as
The British in India: Three Centuries of Ambition and Experience
Published in the United States by Farrar, Straus and Giroux
First American edition, 2018

Library of Congress Cataloging-in-Publication Data
Names: Gilmour, David, 1952– author.
Title: The British in India : a social history of the Raj / David Gilmour.
Description: First American edition. | New York : Farrar, Straus and Giroux,
   2018. | Published in Great Britain in 2018 by Allen Lane, an imprint of
   Penguin Books, as: The British in India: Three Centuries of Ambition and
   Experience. | Includes bibliographical references and index.
Identifiers: LCCN 2018026606 | ISBN 9780374116859 (hardcover)
Subjects: LCSH: India—History—British occupation, 1765–1947. | British—
   India—Social life and customs. | British—India—History.
Classification: LCC DS463 .G53 2018 | DDC 954.03/5—dc23
LC record available at https://lccn.loc.gov/2018026606

Our books may be purchased in bulk for promotional, educational,
or business use. Please contact your local bookseller or the Macmillan
Corporate and Premium Sales Department at 1-800-221-7945, extension
5442, or by e-mail at MacmillanSpecialMarkets@macmillan.com.

www.fsgbooks.com
www.twitter.com/fsgbooks • www.facebook.com/fsgbooks

1   3   5   7   9   10   8   6   4   2

To Ramachandra Guha and Sujata Keshavan

– and of course for Sarah

Contents

List of Illustrations

Frontispiece: Humphrey Trevelyan meets the Maharaja of Chhatarpur, 1942 (© British Library Board/Bridgeman)

1. *The 'Earl of Abergavenny'*, by Thomas Luny (© British Library Board/Bridgeman)
2. *Madras Landing*, by C. Hunt (© National Maritime Museum)
3. Steamers in the Suez Canal (Hudson Collection, CSAS)
4. Calcutta: Government House and the Esplanade (private collection)
5. Old Court House Street, Calcutta, *c.* 1865 (Samuel Bourne/ Hulton Archive/Getty)
6. The Residency, Bangalore (private collection)
7. The Mall, Simla (© British Library Board/Bridgeman)
8. Christ Church, Lucknow (private collection)
9. Victoria Terminus, Bombay (Courtesy of Special Collections, University of Houston Libraries)
10. James Skinner, by Ghulam Husayn Khan (© British Library Board/Bridgeman)
11. Richard Wellesley, Earl of Mornington, by Robert Home (© British Library Board/Bridgeman)
12. Sir Charles Trevelyan, by John Fonceca (© British Library Board/Bridgeman)
13. Sir James Rivett-Carnac, by Henry Pickersgill (© British Library Board/Bridgeman)
14. Lockwood Kipling with his son Rudyard (© National Trust/ Charles Thomas)
15. John Beames, 1858 (© British Library Board/Bridgeman)
16. Sir Alfred Lyall (© British Library Board/Bridgeman)

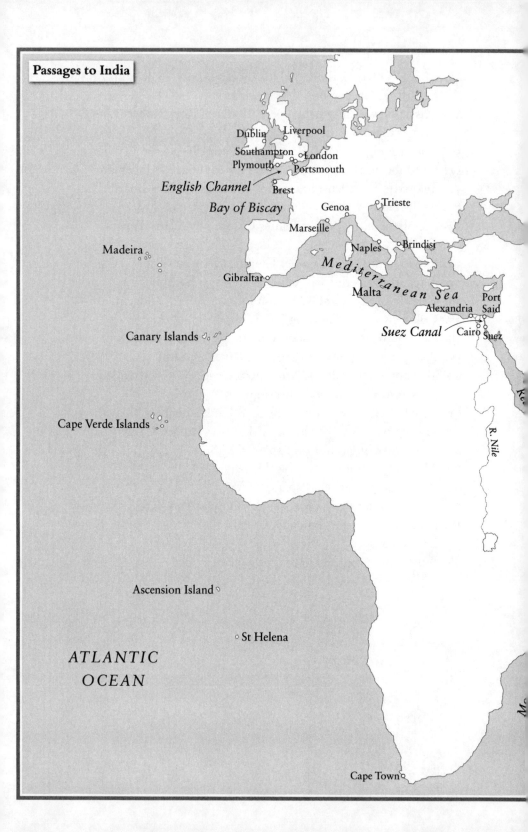

Passages to India

Dublin
Liverpool
Southampton
Plymouth
London
Portsmouth
English Channel
Brest
Bay of Biscay
Genoa
Trieste
Marseille
Madeira
Naples
Brindisi
Mediterranean Sea
Gibraltar
Malta
Port Said
Alexandria
Canary Islands
Suez Canal
Cairo
Suez
R. Nile
Cape Verde Islands

Ascension Island

St Helena

ATLANTIC
OCEAN

Cape Town

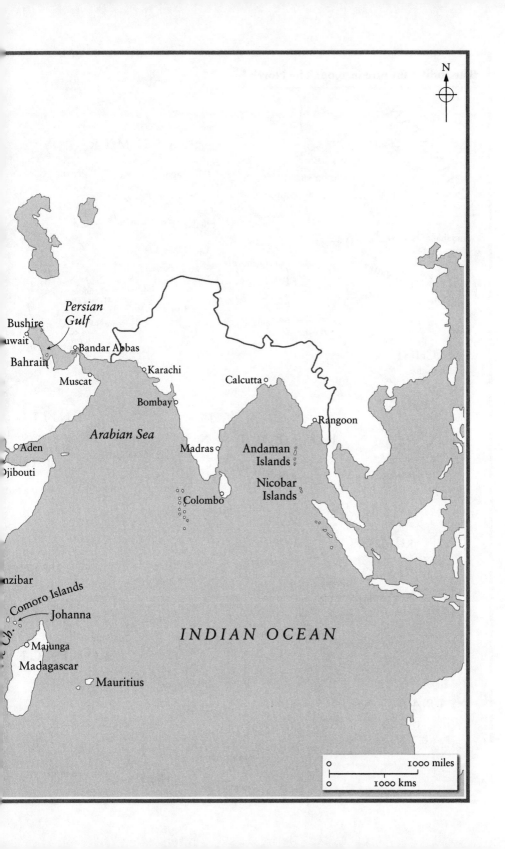

N

Persian
Gulf

Bushire

uwait

Bahrain

Bandar Abbas

Karachi

Calcutta

Muscat

Bombay

Rangoon

Aden

Arabian Sea

Madras

Andaman
Islands

Djibouti

Colombo

Nicobar
Islands

nzibar

Comoro Islands

Johanna

INDIAN OCEAN

Ch.

Majunga

Madagascar

Mauritius

1000 miles

1000 kms

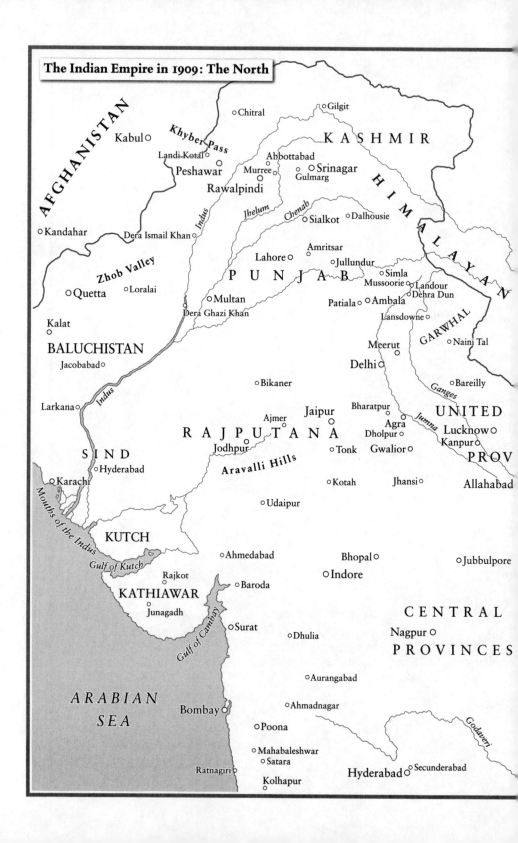

The Indian Empire in 1909: The North

AFGHANISTAN

Chitral
Gilgit
Kabul
Khyber Pass
KASHMIR
Landi-Kotal
Abbottabad
HIMALAYAN
Peshawar
Murree
Srinagar
Rawalpindi
Gulmarg

Kandahar
Dera Ismail Khan
Jhelum
Chenab
Sialkot
Dalhousie

Zhob Valley
Lahore
Amritsar
Jullundur
PUNJAB
Simla
Mussoorie
Landour
Quetta
Loralai
Dehra Dun
Multan
Patiala
Ambala
Kalat
Dera Ghazi Khan
Lansdowne
GARWHAL
BALUCHISTAN
Meerut
Naini Tal
Jacobabad

Indus
Delhi
Bikaner
Bareilly
Larkana
Ganges
Bharatpur
UNITED
Jaipur
Ajmer
Agra
Jumna
Lucknow
RAJPUTANA
Jodhpur
Dholpur
Kanpur
Tonk
Gwalior
PROV
SIND
Aravalli Hills
Hyderabad
Kotah
Jhansi
Allahabad
Karachi

Udaipur

KUTCH

Mouths of the Indus
Ahmedabad
Bhopal
Jubbulpore
Gulf of Kutch
Indore
Rajkot
KATHIAWAR
Baroda
Junagadh
CENTRAL

Surat
Dhulia
Nagpur
PROVINCES

Aurangabad

ARABIAN
SEA
Bombay
Ahmadnagar
Godaveri

Poona

Mahabaleshwar
Satara
Ratnagiri
Hyderabad
Secunderabad
Kolhapur

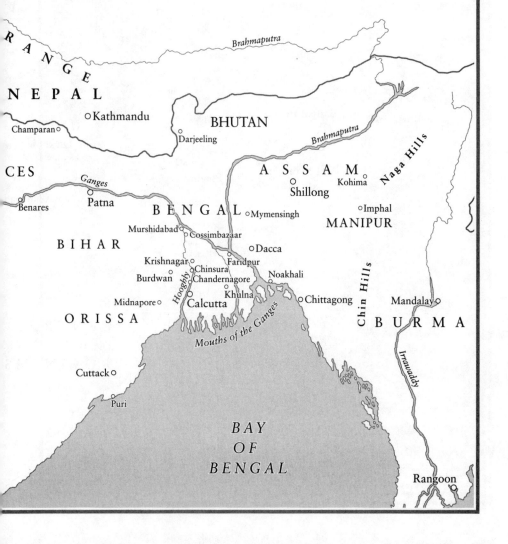

T   I   B   E   T

R A N G E

N E P A L

Champaran○

○Kathmandu

BHUTAN

Darjeeling○

Brahmaputra

Brahmaputra

Naga Hills

A   S   S   A   M○

Kohima○

Shillong

CES

Ganges

Benares○   Patna○

B E N G A L   ○Mymensingh

○Imphal

MANIPUR

B I H A R

Murshidabad○   ○Cossimbazaar

○Dacca

Krishnagar○   ○Faridpur

Burdwan○   Chinsura○/Chandernagore○

○Noakhali

Chin Hills

Midnapore○   Khulna○   ○Chittagong   Mandalay○

Hooghly

Calcutta   BURMA

O R I S S A

Mouths of the Ganges

Cuttack○

Irrawaddy

Puri○

*BAY
OF
BENGAL*

Rangoon○

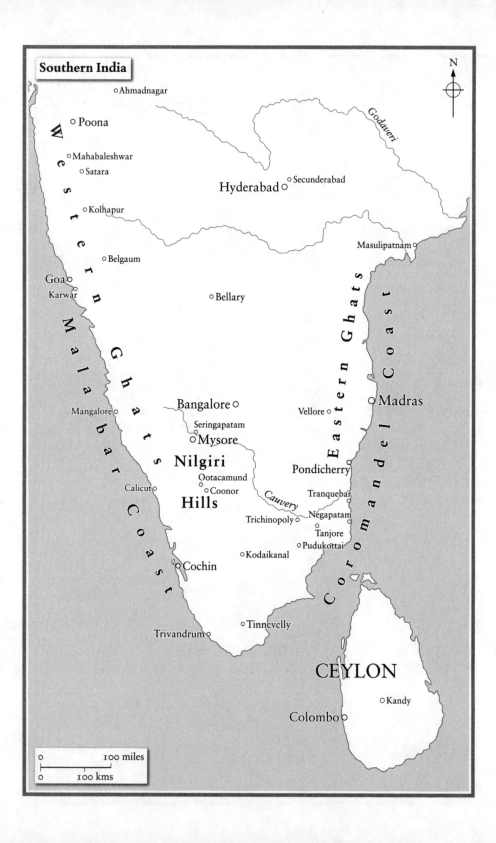

Southern India

N

Ahmadnagar

Poona

Mahabaleshwar
Satara

Hyderabad   Secunderabad

Kolhapur

W e s t e r n   G h a t s

Belgaum

Masulipatnam

Goa
Karwar

Bellary

E a s t e r n   G h a t s

M a l a b a r   C o a s t

Mangalore

Bangalore

Madras

Vellore

Seringapatam

Mysore

Nilgiri

Pondicherry

Ootacamund
Coonor

Calicut

Cauvery

Tranquebar

Hills

Negapatam

Trichinopoly

Tanjore

Pudukottai

Kodaikanal

Cochin

C o r o m a n d e l   C o a s t

Tinnevelly

Trivandrum

CEYLON

Kandy

Colombo

| o | 100 miles |
| o | 100 kms |

Acknowledgements

In the thirty years since I began research in the archives of British India, I have accumulated debts to many archivists and librarians as well as to individuals who have conserved the letters and diaries of their ancestors and who have generously allowed me to study them. Most of the research for this book was done in the Centre of South Asian Studies in Cambridge, the Imperial War Museum in London, the National Army Museum, the National Library of Scotland, the Nehru Memorial Library in Delhi, the Bodleian Library and Balliol and Oriel Colleges in Oxford, and above all in the old India Office Library, which moved across the Thames to become the Oriental and India Office Collections of the British Library and is now called the Asia, Pacific and African Collections. I would like to thank the staff of all these institutions. I am also grateful to the British Association for Cemeteries in South Asia (BACSA), not only for its work on the preservation of British burial grounds but also for its compilation of cemetery records, its publication of recollections of the Raj, and its excellent journal, *Chowkidar*, edited by Rosie Llewellyn-Jones.

Many people, some of whom are alas now dead, encouraged me to use the papers and documents in their possession. They include Denis Blakeway, Roger Bramble, Richard Calvocoressi, Anne Chisholm, the Earl of Crawford and Balcarres, Tam Dalyell, Wendy M. Davis, Richard Dawkins, Martin Fearn, Antoinette Galbraith, Patsy Grigg, Francis Hamilton, the Marquess of Lansdowne, Lady Alexandra Metcalfe, Sara Morrison, Nigel Nicolson, Jean Phillips, the Marquess of Salisbury, Helen Shaw Stewart, Xan Smiley, Bridget Swithinbank, Anne Tatham, Judy Urquhart, Audrey Verity and Ben Watson. My thanks to them all.

Many other individuals, in Britain and in India, have helped me in diverse ways, and for their assistance I would like to thank Ram Advani, Antony Barnes, Richard Bingle, David Blake, Mark Brayne, Margaret Cassidy, Alec Cobbe, Charles and Monika Correa, Sunanda and Sumita Datta-Ray, Keshav Desiraju, Patric Dickinson, Sir Stephen Egerton, Lord Egremont, Lawrence Fleming, Alan Gordon Walker, Major Humphrey Gore, Sir Max Hastings, John Hemming, Caroline Jackson, Subinda Kaur, Kate Kee (Trevelyan), Susanna Kerr, Sujata Keshavan, Sunil Khilnani, Rosie Llewellyn-Jones, Arvind Mehrotra, Nandini Mehta, David Morton Jack, Brigitte Nix, V. C. Pande, Jane Pomeroy, Phillida Purvis, Shashi Sen, Geetanjali Shree, Anne Stephens, Richard Symonds, Gina Thomas, Lord (Hugh) Thomas, Riccardo Tomacelli, Deirdre Toomey, Sriram Venkatakrishnan, Charles Vyvyan, and Tim and Erica Watson.

The historians Judith Brown, Ramachandra Guha and Srinath Raghavan have each read the entire manuscript, and so have my wife, Sarah, and my son, Alexander. I am grateful to them all first for the undertaking and subsequently for their wisdom and advice.

Gillon Aitken, a child of the Raj, was my agent for many years until his death in 2016. He gave me much encouragement for this book, as did his partner in the firm, the wise and supportive Clare Alexander. Once again I have been very fortunate with publishers on both sides of the Atlantic. At Penguin the incomparable Stuart Proffitt has been an inspirational editor, Ben Sinyor and Richard Duguid have overseen the publication process with cheerful efficiency, and Sarah Day has been a copy-editor both intuitive and precise. At Farrar, Straus and Giroux the book was accepted by the wonderful Elisabeth Sifton, my editor for many years, and was subsequently handled with enthusiasm and skill by Laird Gallagher. My thanks to all.

As usual I have relied heavily on Sarah and my children for their support during a book which has taken an inordinately long time to research and write. The decision of three of my children to have babies during the month scheduled for the final chapter may have delayed the book a little, but it added to the gaiety of life and helped preserve the sanity of the author.

The British in India

Introduction

A few years ago the Scottish comedian Billy Connolly was surprised to learn that he had Indian ancestors. Appearing on the BBC television programme *Who Do You Think You Are?*, he was hoping to find out which country his great-grandmother Florence had been born in, Ireland or Scotland. In fact, as he soon discovered, she was born in India, in Bangalore, the daughter of Daniel Doyle, a labourer from County Wicklow who had enlisted in the British Army as a youth and was sent to India in 1856. For a few years in the south her father's career had prospered. From a rifle regiment he was transferred to the Royal Horse Artillery, a more prestigious unit, where he received three 'good conduct' medals and was promoted from gunner to corporal. Yet that, alas, was the high point of his career. To the amusement of his irreverent great-great-grandson, Daniel's name was soon appearing repeatedly in the Regimental Defaulters Book; his misdemeanours were unspecified but seem to have consisted chiefly of violence and drunkenness. Eventually he was court-martialled and reduced to the ranks, and in 1866 he was admitted to hospital in Bangalore suffering from diarrhoea, dysentery, alcoholism and syphilis.

Salvation for Doyle came three years later with his marriage, after which his army report rated him as 'regular, good and temperate'. The agent of this remarkable transformation was his wife, Margaret, the daughter of John O'Brien, another Irish soldier in India, a private in the Madras Fusiliers whose regiment had been sent north to help counter the Rebellion of 1857.* O'Brien was part of the relief force that

---

* The events of 1857–8 have been called many things, including 'The Indian Mutiny', 'The Sepoy Rebellion', 'The Great Uprising' and even 'The First War of Indian

I

arrived too late to save the British in Kanpur (Cawnpore) although it did manage to reach the besieged city of Lucknow. Badly wounded in the shoulder during the conflict, O'Brien decided to retire on his pension to Bangalore. Although the subsequent Doyle-O'Brien marriage might have seemed a purely Irish union taking place in a tropical ambience, this was not in fact the case. As the registry records demonstrate, John's wife, Matilda, was an Indian girl who at the age of thirteen converted to Christianity a month before her marriage. Billy Connolly's reaction to the news that he thus had Indian forebears and probably – given that Matilda had several siblings – a large number of Indian cousins, was both charming and bemused. Although the comedian still felt he was a 'Glaswegian, Scottish person' – large, white and hairy – he was 'very proud and happy to be part Indian' as well.[1]

As Connolly's story suggests, much of Britain's relationship with India, especially at a personal and popular level, has very quickly been forgotten. One cannot help wondering why his maternal grandmother, to whom he was very close, never told him that her own grandparents had lived in India and that her mother had been born in Bangalore; if she had been ashamed to admit her Indian ancestry, she could have left that bit out. The story also indicates how much of the British-Indian relationship, again at a personal level, was accidental. Most British people did not go to India to conquer it, govern it or amass a large fortune there. When Daniel Doyle enlisted in the 3rd Battalion of the 60th Rifles, he did not know that he would be sent to India and spend half his active life there as a soldier who would never be called upon to fight a battle. Like private soldiers, many British women and children lived in India by accident, without having chosen to do so; chance or unexpected circumstances had brought them there. If we look merely at Connolly's own profession, the theatrical, we find a good number of future actors living fortuitously on the Subcontinent: a list of those who were born in India, or went to school or spent parts of their youth there, would include Vivien Leigh, Merle Oberon, Norman Wisdom, Lindsay Anderson, Spike Milligan, Tom Stoppard, Felicity Kendal and Joanna Lumley, many of whom will appear later in this book. If we

---

Independence'. Although it was usually called 'The Mutiny' by contemporaries and later generations of the Raj, 'Rebellion' strikes me as more accurate and less of an anachronism.

examine an even smaller profession, that of writers, we find that Thackeray, Kipling, Saki, Orwell (and Orwell's second wife, Sonya) were all born in India.

The British in this book lived in India from shortly after the death of Queen Elizabeth I until well into the reign of Queen Elizabeth II, a span of some three hundred and fifty years. Life for them was very different – and was led very differently – in diverse ages, just as it was in Britain. For nearly three-quarters of that time British settlements – and later possessions – were administered by the East India Company (EIC); for the last ninety years of the Indian Empire (1858–1947) they were under the direct rule of the British government. All divisions by 'period' are artificial and prone to generalization, but perhaps one can divide Britain's time in India roughly into thirds. The first (and largest) had its share of war and violence, especially on the west coast, but was mainly a matter of small enclaves concentrating on trade. The second, stretching from the 1740s to the 1850s, was a period of conquest and expansion during which the East India Company, one of several rival European entities, emerged to become the paramount power in India. The third (and shortest), ending in 1947, was an era of consolidation and subsequent withdrawal. Yet even these divisions would need to be divided into contrasting subdivisions. As at home, the behaviour of the British in India was very different in the Regency period from what it was in the more earnest years of the early Victorians.

The different eras can of course be divided in other ways, culturally and sociologically as well as politically and militarily. Some British historians have periodized the empire in terms of British attitudes to India and the Indians. Roderick Matthews, for example, has marked his compatriots' 'mental journey' with 'milestones marked Greed, Scorn, Fear and Indifference', a division that sounds harsher than his work subsequently suggests.[2] An older historian, Clive Dewey, has divided the centuries of British rule into 'five oscillations', the attitude of 'friendship' (working with Indian agents and institutions) alternating with the 'Gospel of Uplift' or exhortation to 'improve' (telling Indians what was good for them and then trying to enforce it).[3]

I would not dispute that these and other divisions are useful. Most eras have a zeitgeist and sometimes seem to have more than one. Yet human beings remain individuals under whatever pressure they are subjected to and whatever wider forces they are caught up by. At

Oxford in the early 1970s I was lucky enough to be taught by Richard Cobb, a great historian of Revolutionary France who claimed that he had 'never understood history other than in terms of human relationships'.[4] I might not go as far as that but I do believe that British behaviour in India owed as much to individual characters, ambitions, scruples (or lack of) and personalities as it did to any zeitgeist or contemporary framework of imperialism. Thirty years ago, while doing research into the life of George Curzon, I came across British members of the Indian Civil Service (ICS) and soon realized that they were not the monolithic bunch depicted in fiction and film, obdurate, unimaginative men with brick-red faces and moustaches. They were above all individuals trying – as Cobb would have recognized – to deal with the eternal problems of human behaviour and relationships.

This work is primarily a book about individuals. It deals with large groups of people – with soldiers, with foresters, with missionaries, with numerous others – but the emphasis is on how the individual reacted to his or her Indian experience. Cobb's tendency to write about people on the margins of the Revolution used to annoy French colleagues and provoked one of them to complain testily at a conference, 'Prostitutes do not make history.' Prostitutes may indeed not change the fates of nations, but they belong to history and therefore deserve the attention of historians. In this book I have of course written about viceroys and governors, bishops and commanders, but I have also given space to men and women at different levels of society, even if they didn't 'make history'. Like Cobb, I believe that they deserve at least to be recorded and to be given human proportions.

This, then, is not a book about the politics of the British Empire, still less a discussion of whether that empire was good or bad; inevitably it was both, in a myriad of different ways. I am not seeking to make judgements or to contribute to any debate about the virtues and failings of imperialism. I am chiefly interested in the motives and identities of British individuals in the Indian territories of the empire,* in who these people were and why they went to India, in what they did and how they lived when they got there, and in what they thought and felt about their

---

* It is therefore not a book about the Eurasians (in the twentieth century known as Anglo-Indians), people of British-Indian descent who would deserve a book of similar size for themselves.

lives on the Subcontinent. I believe that writers of social history should attempt to write impartially about customs and behaviour even when we find them abhorrent; we should look at them in the context of their time and not from the vantage point of a usually smug present. From childhood I managed to resist the exhortations of uncles and grand-fathers to go hunting and shooting, but I have tried to write about 'blood sports' in India without prejudice against them. Some readers may feel that I have given too much space to spearers of boar and pur-suers of jackal, but pig-stickers, like prostitutes, are a part of history.

As British people continued to live in India long after Independence in 1947, I have had to decide at what point to end this book. I have chosen the mid-1960s, when most of the 'stayers-on' had left or died and before the hippy 'invasion' had really begun. Perhaps I was influ-enced by my own very limited experience of hippiedom. In my 'gap year' in 1971 I went to India with a couple of friends, three eighteen-year-olds travelling overland and camping in the open without apparent danger in Turkey, Iran, Afghanistan and Pakistan. Kabul was a sort of junction for the new invaders. The real hippies stayed there a month, until their visas ran out, strumming guitars and smoking hashish before deciding whether to go south to the beaches of Goa or east across the Gangetic Plain and then up to Nepal. As it was mid-April and the heat was mounting, we set off for Kathmandu.

On our return from Nepal to India we stayed at Dehra Dun, in the foothills of the Himalaya, where I had an introduction to a remarkable woman, Vijaya Lakshmi Pandit, who invited us to stay at her home for a few days. The sister of India's first and greatest prime minister, Jawa-harlal Nehru, Mrs Pandit had been ambassador to the Soviet Union and the United States as well as high commissioner to London; she had also been a politician and president of the General Assembly of the United Nations. Although she was now in her seventies and had retired from political and diplomatic life, she remained passionately interested in those subjects and did not conceal her disapproval of the current prime minister, her niece Indira Gandhi. I fear that my friends and I were not good company for her. Suffering from a mild form of dysen-tery, we were rather tired after six months 'on the road', and our formidable hostess was clearly not impressed by the sight of fledgling hippies lounging around her drawing room, ineptly fingering a guitar or patting a Nepalese tom-tom. One day she strode impatiently into the room, gestured dramatically at the view through the window and exclaimed, 'The Englishmen I used to know would have climbed that mountain before breakfast.' I appreciate her point now rather more than I did at the time; such men doubtless were a different breed. Remembering Mrs Pandit with gratitude, I have decided to end this book with Britons who climbed the Himalaya before breakfast.

Oxfordshire, January 2018

PART ONE

ASPIRATIONS

I

Numbers

The association of India with riches has a long literary history. Andrew Marvell imagined his coy mistress finding rubies on the banks of the River Ganges, while Alexander Pope endowed his 'Goddess' in *The Rape of the Lock* with a 'casket [of] India's glowing gems'. Earlier, and more earthly, Shakespeare's Falstaff envisaged Mistress Ford as his East Indies and her well-filled purse (or rather, her husband's) as his 'exchequer', and the same playwright compared Henry VIII's lustful enjoyment of Catherine of Aragon to having 'all the Indies in his arms'. The Subcontinent's riches had a more melancholy effect on Othello, who, suddenly contrite after murdering his wife, likened himself to 'the base Indian' who threw away a valuable pearl. In the generation between Shakespeare and Marvell, oriental jewels dazzled a courtier of Charles I, the Earl of Denbigh, who brought sacks of them from the East in 1633 and commissioned Van Dyck to paint him in his smart Indian pyjamas.

Speaking at the Crystal Palace in 1872, Benjamin Disraeli admonished his Liberal opponents for attempting to 'effect the disintegration of the Empire' by claiming 'there never was a jewel in the crown of England that was so truly costly as the possession of India'.[1] Disraeli's meaning was slightly altered by other people so that the phrase 'jewel in the crown' – or sometimes 'the brightest jewel in the crown' – came to refer to the Indian Empire not as an expensive possession but as a precious, glamorous and prestigious one. Paul Scott, a perceptive witness of the last years of British India, called the opening novel of his *Raj Quartet, The Jewel in the Crown*, while in the 1980s Granada Television adopted the same name for its magnificent production of the quartet.

India shone most brightly in the British imagination after 1876 when Disraeli, by then prime minister, gratified Queen Victoria's wish to be made Empress of India. Memories of the Rebellion of 1857 had receded, the recent opening of the Suez Canal had made India seem closer, at any rate in time, and photographers were sending home exotic and uplifting glimpses of life in the East, of maharajas and elephants, of railway bridges spanning vast rivers, of intrepid district officers in sola topis seated under a banyan tree dispensing justice to a benighted populace. The British public grew avid for books with titles like 'My Life on the Frontier' or 'Forty-two Years in Bengal'. It had begun to recognize India's value to Britain, especially as a source of imperial pride, and in economic terms too, for the Subcontinent absorbed much of Britain's overseas investment, notably in the age of railway construction. It also became aware of India's growing military significance, how Indian troops had contributed to the establishment of British paramountcy and how the Indian Army was now being deployed to help the empire on expeditions to Persia, Africa and the Far East. Such interventions may seem insignificant compared with the role played by Indian soldiers in the world wars of the twentieth century, but at the time they were important. The sense of India's value to Britain was conveyed by George Curzon, the last Victorian viceroy of India, when he wrote, 'While we hold onto India, we are a first-rate power. If we lose India, we will decline to a third-rate power.' On another occasion, in Birmingham Town Hall, he told his audience that the loss of empire would reduce Britain to the status of 'a sort of glorified Belgium'.[2]

Plenty of people were at hand, in Parliament, in the universities and in India itself, to justify the conquest and acquisition of vast territories thousands of miles away on another continent. The British, it was often argued, should *not* feel guilty about being invaders, because India was always being invaded (though usually from the north-west, through the Khyber Pass, rather than from the sea, whence the Europeans had come): India was what V. S. Naipaul called in the 1970s 'a wounded old civilization', 'a land of far older defeat'.[3] Nor should the British worry about being foreigners because Indian dynasties were often foreigners to their subjects and because the inhabitants of the Subcontinent were also foreigners to each other: a Bengali in Bombay was as much a foreigner as a Welshman in Rome. A 'Native of Calcutta,' argued Sir John Strachey, a formidable provincial governor in Victorian India, was 'more of a foreigner to the hardy races on the frontiers of Northern India than an Englishman' could be.[4] In any case, insisted Strachey, Britain's role in India was primarily benevolent, at least by then: it resembled a guardian or trustee working for the good and the improvement of the native inhabitants. According to William Hunter, an historian and civil servant, the British had rescued the Subcontinent from the chaos caused by the decline and disintegration of the Mughal Empire, and their rule was now 'wielded in the joint interest of the races'; without it, India would quickly be torn apart by antagonistic forces, both racial and religious. What India needed, declared Sir James Stephen, a jurist and friend of Strachey, was Englishmen to rule with the qualities of their ancestors, 'the masterful will, the stout heart, the active brain, the calm nerves, the strong body'. With similar arrogance the viceroy Lord Mayo told Sir Henry Durand, whom he had just appointed lieutenant-governor of the Punjab, 'Teach your subordinates that we are all British gentlemen engaged in the magnificent work of governing an inferior race.'*[5]

Before he began his career as a novelist, Paul Scott served in the British Army in India and then Malaya at the end of the Second World War. In Malaya he felt homesick not for England but for India, and on his return home to suburban north London he realized, as he recalled thirty years later, that 'India was also my home. It is difficult to describe but I think in a curious way India in those days was every English person's home, even if it had not been visited. Because we ruled it and benefited from it, it contributed to our well-being and upbringing. It was mysteriously in our blood and perhaps still is.'[6]

As this passage implies, India could dominate the imperial imagination even of people who did not go there. And the numbers of people who *did* go were remarkably few. In the second half of the nineteenth century millions of Britons left their islands to begin new lives overseas. More than a million went to Australia and New Zealand; another million went to Canada and southern Africa; and over 3 million, the majority of them Irish, emigrated to the United States. Yet at the end of that century the

---

* Durand unfortunately had little opportunity of doing so. On New Year's Day 1871, shortly after taking up his post, he was killed when his elephant charged at an arch too low for his howdah. A year later Mayo also died, murdered by a convict in the penal settlement of the Andaman Islands.

entire British population of India – that is, the territories later consisting of India, Pakistan, Bangladesh and Burma (now Myanmar) – numbered no more than 155,000, far fewer than the inhabitants of Newcastle at that time and about a fifth of the size of the Glaswegian populace. Many of them, moreover, had not chosen to go there, including, most obviously, children born on the Subcontinent as well as thousands of soldiers who had enlisted in York and Dublin and elsewhere without knowing that their regiments would later be sent out to India.

It was as if the British, at almost every level of society, were proud to have India as their jewel but did not want to spend much time admiring the object: it was just nice to know it was in the bank and to be able to boast about it. The monarchy was the chief exception to this. Although Queen Victoria, Empress of India, never went east of Berlin, she cared passionately about her Indian subjects, especially the two classes she was acquainted with, visiting maharajas and her own servants. Her grandson toured India as George V, and he, his father and his eldest son also went there as princes of Wales. The higher aristocracy was by contrast indifferent. Apart from the Duke of Buckingham, who was governor of Madras in the 1870s, no peer who had inherited a dukedom or a marquessate stooped to govern either of the Indian provinces he could aspire to (Bombay and Madras),* even though such places were surely of a size and importance worthy of patrician proconsular attention. (In 1900 the population of the presidency of Bombay was 25.4 million and that of Madras 38.6 million, while that of Great Britain was 38 million.) Politicians too were reluctant to concern themselves with India: debates in the Victorian House of Commons often emptied the Chamber and led to a stampede towards the tea room. Even those hoping one day to govern India from Westminster and Whitehall were unwilling to visit it, although Curzon went there twice as a young man because he hoped to be viceroy on his way to becoming foreign secretary and prime minister.† No future prime minister before Clement Attlee travelled to the Indian Empire at any stage of his political career, although the future Duke of Wellington went there as a colonel of

* See below, pp. 104–7.
† He succeeded only with the first two of his ambitions. After Bonar Law's retirement in 1923, Curzon was sure he would be chosen to succeed him as prime minister, but George V preferred Stanley Baldwin.

infantry in 1796, and Winston Churchill followed, a hundred years later, as a subaltern of hussars.*

Even men whose duty it was to administer India from London were disinclined to acquaint themselves with the territories associated with their work. Arthur Godley, a wily and phlegmatic bureaucrat, spent twenty-six years running the India Office in Whitehall without ever visiting, or showing any inclination to visit, the place to which he had dedicated his career. This attitude was imitated by a number of his officials. E. C. Winchester joined the India Office as a junior clerk in 1878 and retired from it forty-two years later as a staff clerk. Outside office hours, India seems to have played no part in his life. He occupied his spare time, no doubt agreeably, playing the organ and composing church music, including nine chants for the *Te Deum laudamus*.[8] Another curious example was John Maynard Keynes, a young man interested in a vast range of subjects that did not happen to include India. After passing the civil service exams in 1906, he joined the India Office because it was prestigious, because it had short working hours and because his preferred ministry, the Foreign Office, would have sent him abroad, far away from his friends in Cambridge. Twenty months later he resigned to become a university lecturer and later a fellow of King's, his beloved Cambridge college.[9] In the meantime he had acquired sufficient interest in the Subcontinent to make it the subject of his first book, *Indian Currency and Finance*.

The India Office was a government department presided over by a secretary of state. Its precursor was East India House in Leadenhall Street in the City, which was staffed by officials of the East India Company until 1858 when the Government of India Act transferred the

---

* Attlee himself was reluctant to go, nervous that his work on the Simon Commission to India (1928–9) might debar him from office if Ramsay MacDonald came to power in 1929 (as it temporarily did). He was soon absorbed by the Subcontinent and became the most knowledgeable of all prime ministers on the subject.

Churchill went to India forty-four years before he became prime minister, but apparently he was even then aspiring to the post. One day in the late 1890s the master of the Ootacamund Hunt was bringing home his hounds when he was accosted by an unknown cavalry officer, smoking a cigar on horseback, who told him he proposed to leave the army, enter Parliament and eventually become prime minister. It was Lieutenant Churchill of the 4th Hussars.[7]

Neville Chamberlain also visited India before he became an MP. He was a businessman in Birmingham, manufacturing metal ship berths, at the time of his travels in 1904–5.

administration of India from the Company to the Crown.* East India House had certain similarities to its successor, among them the ease with which its employees were able to separate their jobs from their interests and pursue parallel careers, often literary ones, without the distraction of visiting India or even thinking about it outside the office. Charles Lamb, essayist and critic, entered the accountant's office as a clerk in 1792 and spent his entire working life in Leadenhall Street. So did Thomas Love Peacock, the poet and novelist, who retired in 1856 as chief examiner of correspondence after thirty-seven years at East India House. His successor in the examiner's office was John Stuart Mill, who also spent over thirty years in the building, although his particular outside interest was philosophy.

Men who allotted their free time to writing about almost everything other than India might understandably be reluctant to visit the place. But the same excuse cannot be made for James Mill, the philosopher's father, an impatient and bad-tempered figure unable to appreciate the humour of his easy-going colleague Peacock. Yet another head of the examiner's office, Mill had written his very long *History of British India* before establishing himself at East India House. Although he had never been to India and knew no Indian languages, he had considered himself equipped to write a history demonstrating the barbarism of the Subcontinent, its peoples, cultures, customs and religions. Many British officials in India regarded the work as offensive and ignorant, yet it enjoyed extraordinary success in Britain and became an important text at Haileybury, the college in Hertfordshire where civil servants of the East India Company were trained. The historian Macaulay, who believed the answer to India's problems would be the anglicization of its leading classes, regarded Mill's efforts as 'the greatest historical work which has appeared in our language since that of Gibbon'.[10] Yet *The Decline and Fall* would surely not have been quite so great if its author had never been to Rome.†

• • •

* The Regulating Act of 1773 and William Pitt's India Act of 1784 had already diluted the powers of the East India Company, giving ultimate control of its activities to a cabinet minister known as the president of the Board of Control.

† Another remarkable absentee from India was Max Mueller (1823–1900), a German scholar and naturalized Briton who became a fellow of All Souls and a professor of philosophy at Oxford. The foremost Sanskrit scholar of his age, he translated Vedic scriptures

Established by royal charter at the end of Queen Elizabeth's reign, the East India Company was by 1615 trading on India's west coast at Surat and on its eastern shore at Masulipatnam. The two settlements there were followed over the next four decades by some thirty others, known as 'factories', in the south-east of the Subcontinent and in Bengal on land belonging to the Mughal emperor or to various local rulers. The factory at Madras, built in 1640 on the Coromandel Coast, was the first territorial possession of the Company. A later one was Bombay, which King Charles II acquired as part of the dowry of his Portuguese wife, Catherine of Braganza, and which he then leased to the EIC for ten pounds a year. By the end of the century the Company's most important factory had been founded on the River Hooghly in Bengal and was known as Calcutta. Although these three places became great imperial cities, they cannot be seen as part of a nascent empire at that time. They were just three among a considerable number of European settlements and not in any way pre-eminent. Down the Coromandel Coast from Madras were French Pondicherry, Danish Tranquebar and Dutch Negapatam; up the Hooghly from Calcutta were Danish Serampore, French Chandernagore and Dutch Chinsura.

The Company's servants were carefully graded and salaried, from Writer (the most junior) to Factor and thence to Junior Merchant and Senior Merchant. Their lives were both isolated and restricted. The gates of the factories were shut at night, and their inmates led a collegiate life, dining communally until the eighteenth century, their routines presided over by a governor (or agent) and his councillors, titles that sound grander than their job descriptions: the 'second in council' was in fact the book-keeper, the 'third' the warehouse-keeper. For decades the settlements' populations could be counted as often in scores as in hundreds. Even when the number crept over the century mark, the mortality rate often cut it back again: in Bombay in the year 1700 there were fewer than a hundred Britons. Madras at that date had only slightly more: ninety-five men, eleven widows and eight 'maidens'. The males were divided between Company servants, other traders known as 'free merchants', a few 'seafaring men' and a handful of guards; there were also a chaplain and a surgeon. By 1740

---

and wrote a much-lauded book called *India: What Can It Teach Us?* Yet apparently he did not think that an actual visit to India would teach him anything.

the settlement had a British civilian population of 168 plus a company of soldiers in a garrison of some 300 men consisting mainly of 'topazes' or Indo-Portuguese.[11]

The British population of India expanded from the middle of the eighteenth century as a result of military success and the consequent extension of the Company's trade and administrative opportunities. The EIC at that time was competing not so much with the fratricidal Mughal dynasty (whose members suffered three generations of extremely low life expectancy) but with rivals disputing the imperial spoils, notably French colonists and Indian princes. France's capture – and brief tenure – of Madras in 1746 resulted not only in the creation of Britain's Indian Army but also in the arrival of royal troops from England. A new battleground had been found for an ancient rivalry. Although the Company raised its own forces to counter the traditional foe, these would not have been enough to win the contest without support from home. Several regiments were sent out during the Seven Years War (1756–63) and several more, half of them Scottish, to combat Indian enemies in the 1780s. As the Company's control reached beyond its main settlements into Bengal and in the south into the Carnatic, the numbers of British soldiers in India increased from a few hundred in the 1740s to 18,000 by 1790. Even so, they remained a small number of men spread over a vast area. Most of the troops involved in the acquisition of territory in the Mysore wars (between 1767 and 1799) and Maratha campaigns (between 1775 and 1818) were in fact Indian soldiers (known as sepoys) led by British officers.

The wars against the sultans of Mysore and the Maratha princes brought the Company such extensive new territories in southern, western and north-central India that by the time of Queen Victoria's accession (1837) it ruled nearly half of the Indian Subcontinent and exercised indirect control over much of the rest through treaties with native rulers. Yet there were still then only 36,000 British troops in India. Wars in the 1840s in Sind and against the Sikhs in the Punjab, followed by the annexation of several subordinate states, including Jhansi, Nagpur and Oudh (later known as Avadh), increased the Company's holdings still further so that at the time of the Rebellion they amounted to some two-thirds of the Subcontinental landmass. Until 1857, however, British troops were outnumbered by Indians fighting on their side in a ratio of about one to six: 40,000 to 230,000. It was only after the scare – and surprise – of the Rebellion that the decision was made to adopt a safer ratio of one to two. In 1863 there were 62,000 British soldiers in India (as against 125,000 Indian troops), a figure rising to some 74,000 in 1891. With them in the later year were about 11,000 wives and children.

The British civilian population also increased, especially in Bengal (known as the Lower Provinces) and the contiguous area of the Upper Provinces, later to be separated and known as the North-Western Provinces and subsequently (after British power had extended even further to the north-west) as the United Provinces of Agra and Oudh. Before the Battle of Plassey in 1757 there had been fewer than 80 civil servants in Bengal; by 1774, 238 were needed to deal with the extensions to the Company's responsibilities in the province. In 1820 Calcutta, which had by then established itself as the capital – the home of the governor-general – had over 4,000 British residents. Yet the gender imbalance in Bengal was glaring. It was reckoned that there were sixteen British 'male inhabitants of respectability, including military officers', to every British woman.[12]

The numbers of British civilians in India grew much more slowly than the military. Excluding those employed by the EIC, there were only about 1,500 of these 'non-officials' in 1815, growing to some 2,000 by 1828. There would have been rather more if the Company had not vetted men applying to go out and excluded those it considered dangerous or otherwise unsuitable. The EIC's primary concern was trade, and it did not wish to admit anyone to its dominions who might disrupt or jeopardise that activity. Until 1813 Christian missionaries were specifically excluded because they could be expected to cause trouble with their zeal and their enthusiasm for conversion. Settlers were also regarded with disfavour – almost uniquely in the British Empire – because there was little room for them in a thickly populated country farmed for centuries by its inhabitants. Planters of indigo, the blue dye, were permitted, though they were initially not allowed to own land, and small numbers of lawyers and businessmen were allowed to operate, especially in Calcutta. Yet even by 1850, long after the Company had been forced by the government in London to accept missionaries and ease restrictions on land ownership, there were only some 10,000 British people unconnected to the EIC or the military in the whole of India.[13]

The following decades saw this non-official population grow to 46,000 by 1861 and to 70,000 ten years later. The growth was concentrated in the tea-planting areas of the south and the north-east, in certain industrializing areas in the Ganges Valley, and in 'railway colonies' throughout the Subcontinent: by 1891 British 'railway servants' and their families living in India numbered more than 6,000. Kanpur (Cawnpore) on the Ganges, a village ceded to the Company in 1801, began its British existence as a frontier army camp, always a promising terrain for enterprising tradesmen. The presence of the military and the building of its cantonment rapidly encouraged numbers of tailors, shopkeepers, glove-makers and wine merchants to arrive and set up business. A rum distillery, essential for the British troops, was soon built, followed by other important amenities of home life: a theatre, a racecourse and, as one English visitor observed, some 'extremely handsome' assembly rooms. The British town was virtually destroyed – and its inhabitants were massacred – in the Rebellion, but Kanpur recovered after the coming of the railway in 1859. Industries proliferated, especially textile mills, shoe factories and engineering works, and attracted a skilled workforce from Scotland and the north of England. The first provincial town in India to acquire trams and electricity, Kanpur was soon hailed as 'the Manchester of the East'. Yet its British population in 1901 was literally village-sized, just 463 people, or about one-thousandth of the inhabitants of Lancastrian Manchester.

When describing and enumerating the British population of India, the imperial authorities used categories and terminology that could sometimes be confusing: in the gazetteer of Madras, for example, British police officers were merely listed as 'non-Asiatics'. For most of the period of imperial rule, the British living in India were known as Anglo-Indians, while people of British-Indian descent were called Eurasians. In 1911, however, these terms were officially changed, the Eurasians becoming the new Anglo-Indians, although this term, which may have seemed more respectful (and was what they themselves wanted), was in fact less accurate because large numbers of the community were descendants of Portuguese colonists from Goa and Cochin. For their part the Anglo-Indians were now classified as Europeans, although this too was not quite accurate because their numbers included missionaries from Canada, Australia and the United States.

The Indian censuses, which began in 1871 and were repeated each decade until 1931, used such perplexing and unspecific designations as 'foreign Christians' and 'non-British Europeans and allied races', which included both Americans and Armenians. 'British-born' was also an unhelpful category because it excluded those born at sea on the way out (176 in the 1881 census) as well of course as those, far more numerous, born to British parents living in India. The censuses could be misleading in several other ways as well. The volumes of 1901 indicated that there were 4,000 fewer British males than there had been a decade earlier, but this was because Lord Curzon had temporarily sent nearly 7,000 British troops from India to fight the Boer insurgents in South Africa. More puzzling was the revelation that the German population in the province of Bombay had almost doubled over the same decade, rising from 333 to 658. The enumerators could only conclude that there must have been an unusual number of German ships anchored in Bombay and Aden (then administered by the Bombay government) on the day of the census and that their sailors had come ashore and been included in the count.[14]

The census of 1901 calculated that India contained 169,677 Europeans, helpfully adding that 'ten Europeans in every eleven are British subjects'. Discussing the remaining 14,986, it reported that 'most of those owing allegiance to other flags are either missionaries or members of foreign trading firms'. In fact their occupations were a little more varied than that. The British always had a weakness for French chefs, dressmakers and hairdressers, numbers of whom duly made their way to India, and similar predilections encouraged Italian hoteliers and confectioners to try their luck in Simla and Calcutta; even the Bengal Club, which seldom welcomed foreigners, appointed as its steward an Italian restaurateur, Signor Ressia, who changed his nationality in time to avoid being interned as an enemy alien in 1940.[15] Apart from its visiting sailors, Germany also provided senior officials in the Forest Department as well as engineers at the Jamshedpur Steel Works. A further category of European residents consisted of employees of the Calcutta consulates of Austria-Hungary, Belgium, Denmark, France, the German Empire, Greece, Italy, the Netherlands, Portugal, Spain, Sweden-Norway and – in line with the definition of European – the United States.

The figure of 155,000 British in 1901 remained fairly constant until the beginning of the Second World War. The ratio of men to women was about five to two, mainly because of the number of unmarried soldiers, though the proportions had become slightly more even by the time of the last census in 1931. There was no difference in the balance of the sexes among children and not a great deal among people over the age of fifty; it was in the age groups in between that males dominated. As for religious identities, two-thirds of the British in India were Anglicans, one-fifth were Catholics (mainly Irish soldiers) and one-eighth were either Presbyterian Scots or English and Welsh non-conformists.

The censuses give a rather distorting impression of the distribution of British people in India because they include figures for the military. In 1900 the Punjab (then including the north-west frontier) figures as the province most populated by the British only because it contained the garrisons of Ambala, Mian Mir, Jullundur, Sialkot and Peshawar. The largest concentrations of British civilians were in the great cities of Calcutta and Bombay. In 1901, 11,591 of them lived in Calcutta, sometimes known as the second city of the empire (after London), alongside a million Indians. Apart from Bombay, with about the same number, and Madras, with 4,228, the civilian populations of the other cities could be measured in their hundreds: 818 in Delhi (not yet the capital), 562 in Agra and, as we have noted, even fewer in the Manchester of the East. With such a small client base, few British stores were persuaded to set up shop in India. There were Spencer's in Madras and a handful of Army and Navy Stores in Bombay, Calcutta and Karachi, but India did not have enough potential customers to tempt firms such as Selfridges or J. Lyons to go east.

If we subtract from the 1901 total of British people in India the numbers of soldiers together with their wives and children, and if we also remove the figures for the main cities and larger provincial towns such as Rangoon, Lahore, Karachi and Lucknow, we find some 40,000 people scattered over an area about the size of Europe (without Russia). So sparsely were they spread that many Indians seldom saw an Englishman unless they happened to live in a city or near a barracks. Administratively, India was divided into some 250 districts, with an average size greater than Norfolk and Suffolk combined, that were themselves divided into subdivisions. The British population of a district headquarters, known as a civil station (and usually shortened to 'station'), might consist of the district officer (in most places known as the magistrate and collector), the judge, the civil surgeon, the superintendent of police, two assistant magistrates plus perhaps a couple of wives with whatever children these might have under the age of eight. If a railway line went through the district, there might be a station master; if the area was wooded, there might also be a forestry official; and if the land was in an irrigated zone, an engineer or two would live close by ready to repair the banks of canals washed away in the monsoon. Yet unless the station was also a large town or a railway junction, or it housed a barracks, or it was in the Hills and was used as a resort in the hot weather, that was what a newcomer could expect in the way of compatriot company.

Life in the districts was by any standards a lonely existence, with little for their occupants to do except their work and whatever field sports enthused them and were available. From the 1870s they could go to the British 'Club' but often – when officials were on tour or their wives were in the Hills or in England – there were not enough members around to make a four at whist or play doubles at tennis. And in the subdivisions the solitude was sometimes total: a young man by himself, perhaps thirty miles from his nearest fellow countrymen, and with thoughts of suicide often unnervingly close. One frontier official, stationed in the mountains of Burma, lived among only two other people who spoke English, his Burmese office clerk and an Indian doctor.[16] For many wives the loneliness was even more unbearable, because their husbands at least had work to do and had chosen a career that they knew would take them to India. A woman usually had little choice. Meeting an official or an army officer who was on leave in England, someone usually older than her and desperate to find a wife before he returned to his post, she soon learned that accepting his proposal entailed being dragged away from her home and family and – whether the wedding took place in Britain or India – into a combination of hurried marriage, cursory honeymoon and (before or afterwards) a long and uncomfortable voyage. These experiences were often followed by further uncomfortable journeys, by train and bullock-cart, before she arrived at a remote outpost of empire, usually a barely furnished bungalow with many insects and little sanitation, a place where she would have found life very limited and boring had she not been shortly to give birth to her first child in extremely primitive conditions. Viola Bayley, who had been brought up in Sussex, married a member of the Frontier Constabulary just before the Second World War and found it 'a fairly

THE BRITISH IN INDIA

traumatic experience to start married life' in the district of Hangu near
the Khyber, a place where 'one hardly ever saw a Pathan without a
rifle'. She soon discovered there was nothing to drink except tea with
goat's milk and little to eat except 'tough old roosters' or 'lumps of
barbecued fat from the tails of biblical sheep'. As the district officer and
his wife were on leave, and as the wife of her husband's Indian superior* was in purdah and spoke no English, there was not a single
woman she could talk to. Besides, as she had had as yet no chance to
learn Pashtu, she could not even communicate with her husband's servants. No wonder she tried to console herself with an Alsatian puppy.[18]
In India British women found themselves living in a foreign and very
distant country whose inhabitants outnumbered them by a ratio of
7,000 to one. It is not surprising that they sometimes felt lonely, scared,
beleaguered – and rather cross.

---

* The 'Indianization' of the higher ranks of the Indian Police began after the First World
War. By 1946, 30 per cent of senior officers (assistant superintendents and above) were
Indians.[17]

2

Motivations

REPAIRING THE FORTUNE

'No man,' declared Horace Walpole in 1783, 'ever went to the East Indies with good intentions.'[1] The remark of that witty and mischievous aesthete could not have been made fifty or a hundred years later, but at the time it was almost true (as it would also have been for men going to the West Indies). Many of his British contemporaries went to India with the intention of either making a fortune or retrieving one they had squandered or lost in some other way. 'Shaking the pagoda tree' was a phrase much used – a pagoda in this sense denoting a gold or silver coin – to describe a fortune falling into grateful hands, and it carried the implication that the pagodas might be gathered easily and without excessive scruples.

This was a very eighteenth-century incentive, and the risks as well as the rewards were far greater then than they subsequently became. A man's voyage from London took between five and seven months during which his ship might be blown to Brazil before it could return east, round the Cape of Good Hope and then head into the Indian Ocean to the west of Madagascar. Throughout this time the voyager was aware of the dangers of shipwreck, pirates and, in times of war, attacks by enemy ships, usually French. Once he had arrived at Madras or Calcutta, he had to survive such further hazards as cholera, dysentery, typhoid and malaria, as well as avoid death caused by heatstroke and other ailments that resulted from Englishmen behaving carelessly in the Indian climate. And then he had to make his fortune, look after it sensibly and take it home with him, facing the same risks he had run on the way out. 'Shaking the pagoda tree' did make fortunes for quite a number of men, but for many more the enterprise ended in death or disappointment.

Joseph Fowke was an archetypal eighteenth-century figure, a civil servant in the East India Company whose wife was the daughter and sister of other civil servants. Going to India in about 1736, he had made enough money by the middle of the century to return to England and work in partnership with his brother-in-law, who was still in India trading in diamonds. Although the Company offered him the governorship of both Bengal and Madras, he made such excessive demands about his salary and his powers that he failed to obtain either post. A few years later his wife died, some of his investments failed, and he took up gambling with such dire results that in 1771 he went back to India to try, without success, to recover his fortune. His contemporary George Pigot, who did accept the Madras governorship and held it throughout the Seven Years War with France, also felt the need to return to India in his mid-fifties chiefly to repair the damage caused by his extravagance in England. Reappointed to his old post in 1775, he was, however, soon outvoted, deposed and imprisoned by the members of his Madras Council, and after a few months he died in captivity.

Restlessness at home and a desire to return to India, for financial or other reasons, was quite common in the late eighteenth and early nineteenth centuries, even though those who went back knew that they were effectively losing a year of their lives in the double voyage. Sir John D'Oyly retired from the EIC in 1785 and spent six years as an MP for Ipswich, but his 'declining fortunes' persuaded him to return in 1803 to India, where he died fifteen years later from an illness apparently caused by 'an inordinate use of the hookah'.[2] Sir John Malcolm did not even have the consolation of a parliamentary seat. After failing to become governor of Bombay, he came home to England, bored himself for five years behaving as a country gentleman, and then returned to take up the governorship he deserved in 1827. One of the most successful 'nabobs', men who had acquired great fortunes in India, was Sir Francis Sykes, who had made enough money on his first venture to buy an estate in Yorkshire and obtain a coat of arms. Yet in 1764 he decided to return to India, and in five years he amassed a still larger second fortune that enabled him to purchase estates in Dorset and Berkshire as well as the 'pocket boroughs' of Shaftesbury and Wallingford, both of which elected him to Parliament.[3]

A generation younger than Sykes, William Hickey was dispatched to India by a father exasperated by his indolence, dishonesty and extravagance; he later admitted that in 1763 he had left Westminster School 'most deservedly in high disgrace'. In Calcutta he led a pretty rackety life, his 'propensity' for drink and women unabated, but he managed to run a successful practice as a lawyer in the city. Yet it is as a candid memoirist that he is now remembered. Disarmingly aware of his own shortcomings, Hickey was a sharp chronicler of the defects of contemporary wastrels obliged to join him in his Indian exile. John Royds had 'formerly . . . possessed a handsome estate in Yorkshire, but by living rather too profusely had injured it so much as to make it necessary for him to leave England, and like many others in similar situations, try what Asia would do for him'. Major George Russell had inherited no such estate but had made 'a very handsome fortune' building army barracks and 'other public edifices' in India, which he had 'squandered away at the gaming-table in England', obliging him to return to India 'to endeavor to acquire a second independence . . .'[4] One of Hickey's old schoolfriends, Colonel Cooper, had also spent too much time at the gaming-table. At a dinner in Calcutta for Westminster Old Boys,

> we sat next each other, and during the dinner he told me that having had a cursed hard run of bad luck at the hazard table through a whole winter [in England], he lost, not only his cash, but everything he could raise money upon, and was ultimately reduced to the dire necessity of selling his company in the Guards in order to discharge his debts of honour; that being thus completely ruined in point of fortune, he had availed himself of an offer of a friend in the India direction to send him out a cadet to Madras . . .[5]

Most of the retrieval attempts recorded by Hickey ended in failure and often in death. 'Mr Cator, a man of large independent fortune' who had lost much of it 'in some unsuccessful speculations', was 'induced to return to Bengal' but was killed before he got there when his ship was attacked by a French privateer.[6] General John ('Handsome Jack') St Leger needed to leave England because, after spending a dissipated decade as 'groom of the bedchamber' to the Prince of Wales (later the Prince Regent, later still King George IV), he was virtually bankrupt; he died near Madras in his early forties, 'seized with a convulsion fit'. Another victim of the prince's profligacy was Colonel Henry Aston, a fine cricketer and a friend of Arthur Wellesley, the future Duke of Wellington. Returning to India after living too lavishly in the company of the future monarch, Aston was forced to fight duels with two subordinates and was killed by one of them; on his deathbed he bequeathed his fine grey horse Diomed to Wellesley.

Many young men, unlike Aston and St Leger, did not go to India voluntarily but because their fathers forced them to do so. On his voyage out Hickey encountered a young cadet who 'like me had been somewhat profuse and dissipated, which made his family think it prudent to send him out of England . . . in order to get quit of a set of dissolute companions . . .' He also found an 'unhappy parent' who had managed to obtain an Indian cadetship for a son who had committed 'some atrocious acts that endangered his neck'. Another 'dissipated London dasher', who had 'run through an independent fortune', accepted 'like many other spendthrifts' a commission in the EIC to escape 'his creditors' attacks'. A majority of such cases terminated badly. In Madras Hickey met six London acquaintances all 'ruined by boundless extravagance which [had] compelled them to abandon their native shore'. One of them, a wastrel in the Guards called O'Hara, had been so badly in debt that his father had got him an EIC cadetship, 'then the last resource of ruined profligates'. In India he became a captain but died soon after. Two other former officers in the Guards also died, 'sacrifices to the climate of India', while a fourth soldier, this time a Light Dragoon, was killed in the wars against Mysore.[7]

Unluckier young men than this collection of dissolutes and prodigals were two sons of the actress Mrs Jordan by the Duke of Clarence (the future William IV). George and Henry FitzClarence, aged twenty and seventeen respectively, were two of the twenty-two officers of the 10th Hussars who in 1814 complained to the Prince Regent about the behaviour of their commanding officer in the war against Napoleon. As punishment the boys were court-martialled, dismissed from their regiment and ordered to spend at least four or five years in India, the elder in Calcutta, the younger in Madras. Henry, who had suffered a pretty miserable childhood, serving in the navy and then the army from the age of eleven, fell ill on hearing of his mother's death in 1816 and died in India at the age of twenty. George survived long enough to return home, become a colonel and be ennobled as the Earl of Munster; but he shot himself before he was fifty. Their younger brother Frederick went voluntarily to India in 1852 when, despite never having taken part in a military campaign, he was appointed commander-in-chief of the Bombay Army; he died two years later, still without having fought a battle.[8]*

The custom of exiling family 'black sheep' – or 'unruly spirits' as they were sometimes euphemistically known – did not end with the Regency. Sending errant youths to the colonies survived into the stories of P. G. Wodehouse, where two of Bertie Wooster's cousins are dispatched by their Aunt Agatha to Africa. Early in the twentieth century a despairing English parson hoped to reform his son by making him work in a tea garden in Assam. But as the youth spent his time pursuing the female tea-pickers, the manager sent him to the head office in Calcutta, where his Assamese quarry was replaced by Eurasian girls. Declining to attend the office with any regularity, he soon found himself without a salary and so decided to fund his way of life by stealing bicycles, which he did with considerable success – nobody suspected the young sahib could be a thief – until he was finally caught in the act and imprisoned.[9]

Other 'black sheep' were more content, or at least more resigned to their situation, especially if they were financially dependent on their father or some other family member who had forced them into exile. One traveller in a remote area of Burma came across a peer's son managing a small rubber plantation where he lived with his Burmese wife and their two children. He never discovered what the man had done to earn him 'expulsion from his manorial home', but he learned that 'his exile was perpetuated by a regular sum of money payable only on condition that he remained at the other end of the earth'.[10] Another 'gentleman' was reduced to keeping a lighthouse on the River Hooghly downstream from Calcutta. Walter Lawrence, then a junior civil servant, was accompanying his sick chief downriver in search of sea air, when 'a wild-looking Englishman' came out of the lighthouse and snarled at him. On returning to Calcutta, Lawrence made inquiries: 'Born to a good property in Worcestershire, squandered on the turf, he

---

* The only FitzClarence to enjoy India was their sister Amelia, whose husband Viscount Falkland was governor of Bombay from 1848 to 1853. She travelled in India and the Middle East, her sketchbook at the ready, and wrote engagingly of her experiences in her memoir *Chow-Chow*.

was shipped off to Australia with a few hundred pounds, speedily lost at the Melbourne races: then a berth on a steamship trading to India, which he soon lost. Lastly, work in the lighthouse service.'[11]

Some expatriates recognized that they had deserved their fate and so took themselves into exile; for them there would be no return home, or at least not for a number of expiatory years. Born in Guernsey in 1815, Mauger Fitzhugh Monk trained as a solicitor in Plymouth, but at the age of twenty-two he abandoned his family, fled to India and enlisted in the Bengal Artillery under the name of Fitzhugh O'Reilly. His subsequent letters to his father, apologetic and sometimes self-abasing, refer frequently to his dissolute and inebriated past, but this was evidently not the sole cause of his flight: according to one theory, he exiled himself under a false name in order to escape his creditors. For years Monk in India tried to reassure his family that he was a reformed man – 'now a bottle of brandy lasts me a month' – but he did not for a long time envisage a return to Guernsey. After two years he bought his way out of the army and became successively – but rarely successfully – a schoolmaster, a hotelier, a businessman and a horse-breeder. In the hill station of Mussoorie he met and married Bessy Lewin, whose paternal grandfather was a London rabbi and whose maternal grandmother was Eurasian. Like Mauger, her father, Benjamin, had left England 'under a cloud' and enlisted as a soldier in India (also changing his name, from Levi to Lewin), although in his case, according to his daughter Hannah, he had 'left his home having got into trouble over a girl'. Poor Bessy and two of her children died within five years of the marriage, after which Mauger, as Hannah recalled, was so distraught he wanted 'to marry every third girl he met'. Although virtually penniless, he now, at the age of thirty-four, married a fifteen-year-old girl and set off for Calcutta, at last, after a twelve-year absence, intending to return home. He died, unexpectedly, on the way to Meerut of 'the bursting of an aneurism', four months after his marriage to Ann Weller. The gender imbalance being what it was among the British in India, widows seldom retained their status for very long. At the age of sixteen Ann married her second husband.[12]

Such histories might suggest that the British who went to India were motivated only by greed, fear or a desire to evade responsibility at home. Yet even in the period of 'bad' intentions that Walpole was observing, there were hard-luck stories of men travelling to the

Subcontinent for perfectly decent motives and without any desire to fleece its inhabitants. Men might lose their jobs or property in England not because they had drunk or gambled them away but for reasons of ill health or bad luck or a lawsuit that had unfairly gone against them. Johann Zoffany, that most amiable of painters, had been enlisted as an artist on Captain Cook's second voyage to the South Seas in 1772 but, for reasons outside his control, he was not able to sail. Needing to recoup money he had invested in the plan, he sold the contents of his country house – including his horse, his 'fowling-piece' and his wine cellar – and accepted a commission from Queen Charlotte to go to Florence to portray the Grand Duke of Tuscany's art collection, the 'Tribuna of the Uffizi'. Evidently misjudging the tastes of the queen and her consort, King George III, he produced a wonderful picture, packed with sexual innuendoes about British gentlemen on the Grand Tour, that lost him his royal patrons and (coupled with his extravagance) impelled him to seek commissions as far away as Bengal and Oudh. According to his fellow artist Paul Sandby, he expected 'to roll in gold dust', and his six-year sojourn in Calcutta and Lucknow was both lucrative and enjoyable. Yet the climate was quite wearing for a man in his fifties, and he returned to London, as Walpole observed, 'in more wealth than health'.[13]

It is remarkable how many financial disasters of the eighteenth and nineteenth centuries occurred because people put all their assets into a single investment: a bank that failed, a business that went under, stocks in a railroad company that crashed, a plantation where the crops were destroyed by drought or some other calamity. Henry Cunningham, born a century after Zoffany, was a successful barrister and journalist in London who put all his money into a tea business, but his partner absconded with the capital, thus causing his bankruptcy. Seeing no alternative but to go out to India, Cunningham endured a tedious voyage – 'devouring execrable food [and] learning Hindustanee' – before taking up the post of advocate and legal adviser to the government of the Punjab.[14] For the next twenty-one years he worked on the problems of Indian law and administration, becoming advocate-general in Madras and a judge of the High Court in Calcutta. He also acquired a knighthood and enough local experience to write several books, including *Chronicles of Dustypore* (1875), the first real novel about British life in an Indian district. He and Zoffany are two of the few people mentioned so far who embraced their Indian adventure and made a success of it.

Most of the young men who went to India as 'black sheep' or 'repairers' of fortune were English, and they usually came from the southern parts of their country. There are few Scots, Welsh or Irish among the wastrels and spendthrifts that populate Hickey's memoirs, and not much sign of Tyneside or the Yorkshire Ridings either. The English of the period were richer than the other islanders, and if they had more fortunes they also had more opportunities to lose them, especially if they were army officers in fashionable regiments, stationed in or near London, close to the smart racecourses and near also to the clubs, gaming-tables and whorehouses of the capital. Young Scots were as keen as anyone to make a fortune in India, but they usually started from scratch without having to atone for past follies. The East India Company, wrote Sir Walter Scott, was 'the Cornchest for Scotland where we poor gentry must send out younger sons as we send our black cattle to the South'.[15] The advantages of the Union with England were pretty obvious to those keen to participate in the imperial enterprise. Not that many thought of themselves – at least not before the nineteenth century – as imperialists with duties and a mission. They were chiefly interested in making money and then retiring to 'enjoy *otium cum dignitate* at home'. As one young Scot admitted on his departure for India, he hoped to come back before he was forty, 'free and independent like a gentleman and able to enjoy myself, my family and friends in the manner I could wish'.[16]

Not all Scots were so brazenly ambitious. Many were simply looking for jobs that were not easily available to young men without funds or influence at home. George Darling, a farmer's son from the Borders, became a surgeon on ships sailing to India only so that he could make enough money after a couple of voyages to establish a medical practice in London.[17] Others went east because there was no room for another son in the family firm in Scotland. Alister Macrae, the younger son of a timber merchant, thus went out to Burma in the 1930s and, with numerous other Scots from Glasgow and Dumbarton, made his career with the Irrawaddy Flotilla Company.[18]

Landed estates in Scotland could seldom support large families and often did not even manage to cater for the laird and his heir. They were frequently in debt and in need of funds from outside, from other parts of Britain and from overseas. Three Campbell brothers who joined the civil service in India were members of a family from Fife so impoverished that all their great-uncles had gone to seek their fortunes in America or the Ottoman Empire.[19] The Johnstones of Westerhall, lairds from Dumfriesshire, also embraced the opportunities of empire in different hemispheres. The seven brothers who grew up in southwest Scotland in the 1720s and 1730s had careers so various and varied that three of them went into the East Indian Company, four of them became MPs, and five of them lived at times in the American and Caribbean colonies. Of the three EIC employees, one died at the age of eighteen in 1756 in the incident subsequently known as the 'Black Hole of Calcutta', another sold water from the Ganges to pilgrims who could not reach Benares, and the third (John) became one of the richest and most notorious nabobs of all.[20] Such far-flung careers were not limited to families of the gentry trying to break out of centuries of enforced thriftiness in picturesque but unfruitful glens. According to their chronicler, the Lindsays of Balcarres, one of Scotland's oldest aristocratic families, 'were for many years [in the late eighteenth century] almost strangers in Europe'. Two brothers were in North America, two more had been fighting in India, a fifth was in the Royal Navy (he drowned off St Helena), and a sixth (an employee of the EIC) was trading in elephants on the borders of Burma.[21]

Most landed families in Scotland had less wide-ranging ambitions. Instead of wishing to sample and compare the opportunities offered by Bengal and Jamaica, they focused on their particular problem – usually the debts of their ancestral estates – and then selected one place (India or elsewhere) as their solution and salvation. The estate of Ardvorlich on Loch Earn in Perthshire had belonged to John Stewart's family for 300 years, and its owner (the 12th laird) was determined to rescue it from insolvency. Born in India but educated in Britain, Stewart had returned to India as a Company cadet and later flourished as an industrialist in Kanpur. He stayed over thirty years on the Subcontinent and managed to save his ancestral home by setting up a harness and saddlery factory so successful that in the 1880s it was supplying all the leather equipment for the British armies in Asia.[22]*

Not all Scottish landowners could hope or desire to become

---

* The family was still living at Ardvorlich in 2018.

industrialists. But they could supplement rents from encumbered or unproductive estates by receiving salaries as proconsuls abroad; and by doing so they could save money by temporarily shutting down their large, draughty and over-staffed houses. The eighth Earl of Elgin needed jobs abroad because his father had nearly bankrupted the family by remodelling the family home near Dunfermline, and by bringing the Parthenon Marbles to England and selling them for much less than he had spent on acquiring, transporting and preserving them. Elgin duly served as governor of Jamaica and governor-in-chief of British North America before becoming viceroy of India in 1862, a post also attained by his son, the ninth earl, in 1894. The trajectory from what was later called the governor-generalship of Canada to the viceroyalty of India soon became a familiar one for noblemen in rather straitened circumstances. Lord Dufferin held both posts in the 1870s and 1880s, as did his fellow Anglo-Irish peer Lord Lansdowne, in the 1880s and 1890s. In 1807 a financial shortage had encouraged Gilbert Elliot, first Baron Minto, to become governor-general of India, and he had returned home six years later as the first Earl of Minto. A century later, his great-grandson, the fourth earl, emulated him by accepting the same post, after following the now customary precedent of first serving as governor-general of Canada.*

A DIAMOND AND PAGODAS

Thomas Pitt was an 'interloper', a word used in the seventeenth century to describe an independent trader infringing the monopoly charter of the East India Company. Sailing and trading to and from India from 1674, he made such a nuisance of himself that the EIC arrested him in 1683 and later fined him. Yet Pitt was wealthy enough to pay the fine, buy an estate near Salisbury and instal himself as MP for Old Sarum, the most notorious of all the English 'rotten boroughs', one still without any resident voters when it was abolished by the Reform Act of

---

* From 1773 to 1947 the head of the Indian government was the governor-general. In 1858 he was given the additional title of viceroy to symbolize the fact that he was now the representative of the sovereign. Lord Canning, who was the first viceroy, preferred it to the older designation, and his successors were usually referred to as viceroys, although 'governor-general' remained their only statutory title.

1832. Eventually the Company decided it would be easier to have him on its side, going as far as sending him out to its settlement in Madras as governor in 1697. There he stayed for over ten years, making even more money than before but living an embittered and uncomfortable existence on the Coromandel Coast. As a later resident of the city observed, the hardships of life in India were not then 'tempered . . . by mails, Hills, Clubs, polo, golf, tennis, dances, newspapers, magazines, ice, and tobacco'; it was a cramped and unenviable exile, one 'to be borne with no better distraction than squabbles in Council, an occasional duel, and the constant danger of war'.[23]

Pitt went to Madras without wife or children except his eldest son, who after a few years returned to England. He preferred to be by himself because he was quarrelsome and bad-tempered, his body tormented by gout, and from afar he could rail against the 'hellish confusion' of his 'unfortunate and accursed family'. There was he in exile, he wrote furiously home, working hard to make money for a family that was so mad and useless that his chance of happiness already lay 'blasted by an infamous wife and children'.[24] His chief consolation had been the acquisition, in somewhat dubious circumstances, of a massive 400-carat diamond which in 1717, after long negotiations on his return, he sold for an astronomical sum to Philippe, Duke of Orléans, the Regent of France.* With the money he was able to buy several more estates in the West Country and consolidate the fortunes of a dynasty that came to dominate British politics later in the century: his grandson William Pitt, later Lord Chatham and later still known as 'the Elder', also sat for Old Sarum in the House of Commons. It had been a spectacular career and, as defined by its own ambitions, a great success, one that presaged the achievements two generations later of the nabobs, so called and so mocked for living like 'nawabs' on their return from India, vulgarly flaunting their riches and buying seats in Parliament. Managing to forget how his grandfather had created the family wealth, Chatham assailed the nabobs in 1770 as 'men without connections, without any natural interest in the soil . . . importers of foreign gold

---

* It adorned the coronation crowns of Louis XV and Louis XVI, and was later inserted by Napoleon I into the pommel of his sword. The emperor's second wife, Marie-Louise, took it into exile, but it was returned to France by her father, the emperor of Austria, and set in the crowns of the restored Bourbons and of Napoleon III. Since 1877 it has been on display in the Louvre.

[who have] forced their way into parliament by such a torrent of corruption, as no private hereditary fortune can resist'.[25] *

Diamonds were not the usual means of making fortunes. Europeans had gone to Asia to find spices, but as these in India were inferior to those found further east, they had had to substitute other goods to trade in. In India Englishmen were soon making fortunes in indigo, grown and processed for dyeing, and saltpetre (potassium nitrate), necessary for the making of fireworks and gunpowder; they were also able to make sizeable profits from salt and opium. For the British at home the most visible and tangible products of Indian trade were fabrics arriving at the London docks such as calico, silk and finely woven muslin from areas around the Brahmaputra River. Merchants could make large sums of money from calculating the size of the British appetite for such things. Jane Austen confessed in 1811 that she had paid seven shillings a yard for some 'check'd muslin'.[26]

Until the end of the eighteenth century almost all the Company's civil servants were traders as well as administrators; they might preside in court, maintain the peace and collect the revenue, but they were private merchants as well. So were many of the EIC's soldiers, surgeons and, indeed, chaplains. The historian of the Johnstones of Dumfriesshire has recorded the various occupations of John, the family nabob: 'a merchant in bales of cloth, an officer in the Company's army, a political or intelligence officer, a specialist in the procurement of bullocks, a civil servant, a merchant in the inland trade in salt ... a contracted revenue officer ... and a high administrator of the land revenues of the Mughal empire'.[27]

Their victories against Bengali armies at Plassey (1757) and Buxar (1764) gave the British in the region a novel sense of security, emboldening them to live in country houses instead of cramped fortifications. Combined with the Company's expanding powers and responsibilities in Bengal, these successes also encouraged them to believe that rapid fortunes could now be made from a few vigorous shakes of the pagoda

* Another interloper with an interesting legacy was Elihu Yale, a predecessor of Thomas Pitt as governor of the settlement of Madras. His autocratic behaviour and infringement of EIC regulations persuaded the Company to dismiss him in 1692, and a few years later he retired to Wrexham in Wales. Dying in London in 1721, he would probably have been forgotten had he not given some books and a few bales of goods to a school in Connecticut that eventually became Yale University.

tree. British administrators and Residents* at the courts of Indian princes were well placed to take advantage of the new climate, especially if they were able to acquire a monopoly or two for themselves. One Resident at Lucknow had a local monopoly in saltpetre; so did a Resident at Benares, who also had one in opium. Such opportunities disappeared when the Company took salt, saltpetre and opium under its control in the 1770s, but there remained many other goods for individuals to trade in. Incomes could also be augmented by taking a percentage from activities such as tax-farming or revenue collection. According to William Hickey, the post of Resident at the court of Murshidabad was 'the most lucrative in the company's service' because 'a considerable portion' of the allowance the Company paid to the nawab 'always stuck to his fingers'.[28]†

Of the many ways in which John Johnstone had assembled his fortune, the most notorious was his acceptance of huge 'gifts' from the Muslim nawab of Bengal. For fifteen years after Plassey the British were the power brokers in Bengal, able to make, break and discard rivals for the throne and the high offices of state. Candidates were thus prepared to pay vast sums for their military and political support: Robert Clive received an extraordinary total of £234,000 from the new nawab for his victory at Plassey (and much more later on), yet years afterwards, when accused of corruption in Parliament, he replied that he had been 'astounded' by his 'moderation'.

Like the civil servants, the Company's military officers received low official salaries which they were able to augment by other means. One of these was 'batta', an allowance meant for officers on campaign, although in the 1760s – the most corrupt decade of British India – all officers were managing to draw double *batta* even when they were in barracks.[29] Fifty years later, officers were only receiving 'half-*batta*', but even this made an enormous difference to their earnings. The pay of a colonel in garrison was £37 and ten shillings a month, but he also received £25 in 'tent allowance' and £93 and ten shillings in 'half-*batta*'.[30] Other ways of enrichment were army contracts and the

---

* See below, pp. 179–85.
† From 1765 the EIC controlled the revenue of Bengal and thus effectively turned the nawab into its pensioner. By the time Hickey was writing, the 1780s, his stipend had already been much reduced.

commissary system, by which men could supply provisions to British soldiers and take a cut of several rupees per man. According to Hickey, the 'paymastership' of a large body of troops was 'considered the most lucrative situation a person could be placed in'.[31] Such practices may have been tolerated, but outright swindling and embezzlement usually were not. Company officials constructing forts or a barracks could not easily get away with charging for materials that had not been used and for workers who had not been employed.[32]

Princely gifts were for military officers, as well as for civil servants, the quickest way of making a large sum of money. Soldiers were rewarded for victories and other services by those nawabs of Bengal supported by the Company. They also had the chance of prize money when the wealth of a defeated foe was seized and distributed after a battle. Arthur Wellesley received £4,000 for his capture of Seringapatam in 1799, enough to make him a more acceptable son-in-law for the Pakenhams in Ireland, who had earlier scorned the penniless officer as a suitor for their daughter Kitty. One commander-in-chief in India, Lord Combermere, who as Stapleton Cotton had been with Wellesley at Seringapatam and later in the Peninsular War, gained a spectacular £60,000 in prize money from the siege of Bharatpur in 1826, but then lost nearly all of it – together with his other savings – in the collapse of Alexander's Bank in Calcutta in 1832.[33]

Until near the end of the eighteenth century the Company's policy towards its civil servants was to pay them very little but allow them to benefit from large unofficial 'perquisites'. Even though gifts from the now poorer and much less powerful nawabs dried up in the 1770s, officials continued to make money by doubtful methods until the EIC, pressed by the British government, clamped down on corruption, ordering them not to accept bribes and forcing them to give up their commercial activities in exchange for a proper salary. Yet enterprising souls irked by these and other restrictions found plenty of scope in parts of India beyond the Company's frontiers. Many made a good living as mercenaries for warrior chieftains in western and central India. Others, more peacefully inclined, were welcomed at Arcot, where the nawab employed eight European doctors and surgeons, including Sir Paul Jodrell MD FRS who, following a request from the ruler to George III, resigned as physician at the London Hospital to work at his court. Perhaps the most attractive place for Europeans was Lucknow, capital of the nawabs of Oudh, a dynasty that combined patronage of the arts with reckless generosity and a decadence in living arrangements that was to prove fatal to them when India became Victorian. Their city enticed numerous artists, including Zoffany, who spent two and a half years there, and George Duncan Beechey, who in the 1830s was appointed painter to the court. Employment for Europeans in Lucknow was not always guaranteed, especially if their sponsors died or fell from favour before they arrived, leaving them stranded on the Gangetic Plain without a job; one professor came all the way from Cambridge only to discover that the new college to which he had been appointed principal would not after all be built. Most supplicants, however, were treated well, and they were often granted large and comfortable houses to live in. Engineers were particularly welcome: one of them, Captain Duncan McLeod, was earning a salary of £150 per month as an architect at a time when his Indian master mason was getting only fifteen shillings and a captain in the EIC armies or a British regiment received a mere £15 a month before allowances. Another recipient of Lucknow's munificence was Captain James Herbert, like McLeod an EIC officer, who was appointed astronomer by a nawab so keen 'on promoting divers enlightened arts and sciences' that he decided to build an observatory.[34]

By 1830, noted the French traveller Victor Jacquemont, there were 'no longer huge fortunes to be made' in India although salaries there could still be very large.[35] The days of 'Diamond' Pitt and 'Moderation' Clive were over; the pagoda tree, when shaken, no longer showered its coins upon the adventurous and avaricious. Men went out to India, as they continued to do for the next century, to make their careers and enjoy a higher standard of living than they would probably have obtained at home, but they did not go to amass the riches that had been required to buy estates in the shires and seats in the House of Commons.

In Calcutta, observed the perceptive Jacquemont, people were not there to 'enjoy life' but to 'earn the wherewithal to enjoy themselves elsewhere'.[36] Yet here things were also beginning to change. Men now tended to see India less as a short-term opportunity to make a fortune and more as the principal arena of their working lives, a place where they would have to stay in order to gain the promotions and pensions that would allow them to bring up a family and retire in comfort to the villa in Eastbourne or the town house in Cheltenham. And India certainly offered the cheap labour and inexpensive building materials that enabled them to live in spacious houses with plenty of servants. Families that would have been unable to keep a horse and groom in England could afford two of each in India.

Men often embarked on an Indian career with feelings of reluctance and nascent nostalgia because it inevitably entailed long separations from parents, siblings and indeed everyone else, except those choosing the same destination, whom they had never met. But they calculated that the rewards would probably be worth the sacrifice, especially if some sense of duty was encouraging them to go. Proby Cautley was a pupil at Charterhouse, apparently destined to follow his father and grandfather into the Church. Yet when his father died in 1817, leaving the family short of money, the boy decided to leave school and prepare for an Indian engineering career that would give him the opportunity to send money home to his mother. In his case he seems to have made the right choice for himself as well as his family because he had not shown much interest in the Church and he lived to become one of the great engineers of British India, his canals irrigating large areas of the Gangetic Plain.[37]

As the British population of India expanded, job opportunities outside the army and the administration increased as well. All sorts of professions that had not been required before the 1750s could now be exercised, especially in the larger towns and the army cantonments. British families now needed hatters and hosiers, drapers and booksellers, coach builders and accountants, policemen to protect them, piano tuners to tune their pianos, taxidermists to stuff panthers and other animals shot in the jungle and soon to be displayed as rugs on the floor or trophies on the wall. Undertakers came out from Britain to bury their compatriots, billiard-table makers came out to cater for a new fashion, brewers and distillers arrived to set up their businesses in the most profitable places, usually in a hill station or near an army barracks.

In the second half of the nineteenth century the railways in India offered thousands of British men employment as drivers, shunters, firemen, plate-layers and inspectors. Industry enticed engineers, fitters and weaving masters to come out and work in the jute mills, cotton mills and other factories in Bengal and the North-Western Provinces, while the tea gardens of the south and the north-east required increasing numbers of planters to run them; Calcutta alone housed the offices of over fifty tea companies. From the 1890s the nascent oil industry offered employment in the north-east, in the Burmah Oil Company and the smaller Assam Oil Company, and later in Burmah-Shell, a joint operating company for India. Women too began to travel out for work. Since the seventeenth century they had been going to India almost exclusively as daughters, sisters, wives or wives-to-be, but now they could emigrate with aspirations to follow a profession of their own, usually as teachers, nurses, doctors or missionaries.* The period also saw a great increase in commercial activity, in a proliferation both of banks and of managing agencies, which were the quintessential form of running businesses in British India.† National Grindlay's Bank expanded in logical sequence, starting in Calcutta and Bombay in the 1860s, going down to Madras in the 1870s, diversifying in all other directions in the 1880s (Delhi, Karachi and Rangoon), and opening up in Kanpur in the 1890s. *Thacker's Indian Directory* provides printed evidence of the rapid growth of both commerce and industry. It is in fact so crammed with lists of professions and companies and employees, so fat with addresses and advertisements for innumerable goods, that one gets the impression it represented the population of a large European country. Yet the 'non-official' British inhabitants of India – excluding those attached to the army or the services – all these people doing all these jobs and spread all over the Subcontinent, they and their families amounted to scarcely 70,000 souls.

SPECIES OF ZEAL

Lord Cornwallis, who was governor-general of India from 1786 to 1793, pursued two policies that – for good *and* bad – irrevocably altered the tone and nature of British government on the Subcontinent. His decision to exclude Indians from all senior positions in the army and administration naturally widened racial and cultural divides and helped foster British attitudes of haughtiness, aloofness and superiority

* See below, pp. 65–71.
† See below, pp. 100, 515.

towards the subject peoples. Yet his insistence that civil servants of the East India Company should live on their salaries, give up private trading and resist proffered bribes helped create a civil service that became widely regarded as incorruptible and just, one that even Indian nationalist newspapers would later regard as 'absolutely above suspicion' and 'the high water mark of morality in the public service of the country'.[38]

The Company's servants had once been merchants and accountants, adding up profits and bales of goods. Later they had combined executive duties with private commerce, but now the civil servants among them were to be administrators only, primarily concerned with the welfare of the people they governed. Richard Wellesley, who became governor-general five years after the departure of Cornwallis,* amended and intensified the process of transformation: 'no greater blessing,' he believed, could be 'conferred on the native inhabitants of India than the extension of the British authority, influence and power'.[39] The young Englishmen now coming out were to see themselves as imperial rulers, the new Romans, magistrates and judges impartially imposing the rule of law. Subsequent generations were taught to discard notions that Indians should live according to the ancient customs if these were held to be idolatrous, benighted or – at any rate in Christian terms – evil. Their work assumed the character of moral obligation, not just on practical matters such as digging canals and irrigating land and preventing the Indians from starving, but on such apparently 'immemorial' customs as child marriage, widow-burning and female infanticide.

The creed of imperialism mutated in the course of the nineteenth century, but the 'calling' continued to inspire young men to go out to India until the First World War and beyond. Irony and irreverence are common to all eras, and even believers may have smiled at Lord Milner's assertion that imperialism had 'all the depth and significance of a religious faith', that its meaning was 'more moral than material'.[40] Yet they would have responded easily to the romantic view of a fictional character in John Buchan (himself a member of Milner's 'kindergarten' in South Africa) who thought the beginnings of imperialist feeling were sensual and immediate: they meant 'getting the sense of space into your

* He was also the predecessor of Cornwallis, who returned to the post in 1805 but died two months after his arrival in India.

blood'.[41] This was the mood that inspired one schoolboy to take the exam for the Indian Civil Service (ICS) so that he could 'go to India and ride about the countryside administering justice and being the father of my people'.[42] As a retired civil servant concluded his memoirs in the 1870s, 'It is ennobling to a man's character to feel that . . . he is working, not for himself, but for the good of large numbers subject to his administration. Notwithstanding red tape, the personal power of civilians for good or evil is very great indeed.'[43]

In 1855 the civil service in India was opened to competition: young men were now recruited because they had passed a set of difficult exams, not because an uncle or a friend of their father on the board of the EIC had nominated them for a place. After 1873, when the British Home Office adopted the same method, a young man often passed into both services and then had to make a choice, one that was widened later when he could also pass – as Martin Fearn did – into the Sudan Political Service and the Colonial Office.[44] At the beginning of the twentieth century John Hubback, who later became governor of Orissa, chose India because it offered him the 'prospect of an outdoor life and . . . early responsibility', whereas Whitehall would confine him to a desk and lengthy subordination.[45] The important phrase here is 'early responsibility'. A man who had just graduated from Oxford might have to run a subdivision consisting of a million people in 2,000 square miles with the help of a few Indian assistants and policemen. Many such men thus experienced what one Victorian official described as 'the joy of feeling that one is working and ruling and making oneself useful in God's world'.[46] They recognized they had the chance to do good, the power to reduce poverty by encouraging peasant farmers to use the new dispensaries, to fertilize and irrigate their ancestral fields. As John Christie observed of his fellow recruits in the 1920s, 'most of us believed that we were following a vocation not just a career'.[47] Not all ICS officers felt this, and many of those who did so in their youth became sick and sullen and disillusioned later on. Yet enough remembered the dream and retained the zeal to record what had driven them on during their decades of service.

> To lead life-giving streams to thirsty fields, to foster mighty forests, to build roads and bridges, to minister to the sick, to spread the light of learning, to dispense justice, to maintain peace and order, to strive for

the welfare of hundreds of thousands, perhaps millions of people – these are tasks which by their mere fulfillment provide ample recompense for any hardships that may be involved in their performance.[48]

British administrators might imbue their work with a sense of mission, but only during the middle decades of the nineteenth century were any number of them propelled by missionary fervour in a religious sense. These men usually had an evangelical background, led intensely religious family lives and believed their work in India was even more of an obligation to God than a duty to their country and its empire. Some of the officers responsible for the 'pacification' of the Punjab after the Anglo-Sikh wars believed that the British had been given India by Providence and that it was their duty to convert its inhabitants to Christianity. Their most Evangelical member, Herbert Edwardes, once assumed the voice of God at a missionary meeting in London to tell his listeners that He had given India 'into the hands of England' with 'the best thing a man can have – the Bible, the knowledge of the only true God', yet the British had 'neglected the charge I [God] gave you' and were now ruling it for themselves.[49] His view, however, was a minority one from a particular period. Most later officials would have agreed with Rudyard Kipling that the duty of the British in India was to 'save bodies and leave souls alone'.[50] Christian attempts at conversion only provoked native unrest and thereby complicated the work of the civil servants. The young Mohandas Gandhi was one of many who found it difficult to 'endure' the behaviour of missionaries standing near their school, holding forth and 'pouring abuse on Hindus and their gods'.[51]

The East India Company had from the start distrusted religious missionaries. The directors wished their Indian subjects to have 'the undisturbed enjoyment of their respective opinions and usages' which should not be interfered with by the British or 'molested by others'; missionary preaching, pamphleteering and other behaviour was 'in the highest degree detrimental to the tranquillity of the British dominions in India'.[52] During the eighteenth century the Company had limited the Christian pastoral presence in its territories to its own chaplains and had succeeded in excluding missionaries altogether, forcing some British ones who had come out to operate from the Danish settlement at Serampore in Bengal. But pressure from the Evangelical movement in Britain had become intense, and at the renewal of the EIC's charter in

1813 Parliament insisted that not only should the Church of England be properly constituted with a bishop and a hierarchy in India but religious missionaries also must be allowed in. William Wilberforce, the tireless campaigner against slavery, claimed that the Christian conversion of India was even more important than the abolition of the slave trade. His son Samuel, Bishop of Oxford, took up the cause with an eloquence that inspired men to join the Church Missionary Society, the Evangelical wing of the Church of England, and go out to India. One of them was Thomas Valpy French, who went to India in 1850, came back to England after the Rebellion and then returned in 1862, leaving his wife and eight children behind; they could not compete with his desire to convert Muslims. Despite persistent ill health French rose to become Bishop of Lahore, preaching in Hindustani in one of the aisles of his cathedral, yet at heart he was a missionary, at his happiest wandering around Kashmir or the north-west frontier on a mule. In 1889 he resigned his bishopric and went home, but once again England and his family could not keep him. The following year he sailed to North Africa and went to the holy Muslim city of Kairouan where, dressed as a mullah, he preached beside a mosque, handing out bibles from the folds of his burnous. Later he moved to Cairo and then, sick and emaciated, to Muscat, where in 1891 he died, preaching to the end, in the desert. In the words of his great-granddaughter, the novelist Penelope Fitzgerald, he was 'a saint, holy in the noblest sense of the word, and as exasperating as all saints'.[53]

Until the proliferation of medical missions at the end of the nineteenth century, missionaries seldom had complex motives for going to India. Most of them were motivated by compassion for the 'heathen', a desire to save souls and a sense of duty to 'propagate' the Gospel. According to a (now missing) inscription in a cemetery in Peshawar, Roger Clark left Cambridge and in 1859 went out 'to teach the natives of India the word of God', but he died on the frontier three years later, aged twenty-eight, 'in great joy and peace trusting in Jesus and thankful to the last that he had been a missionary'.[54] Such men often received their calling at an early age and never wavered in their commitment. One future member of the Bible Churchmen's Missionary Society heard his call at the age of twelve when sitting in a church in Liverpool listening to a missionary who had just returned from Greenland; he later spent most of his career in India's Central Provinces, travelling home via the Holy Land.[55] Cecil Tyndale-Biscoe felt that his calling had come even more directly from above; looking back at his youth in old age, he could now 'see plainly how God was preparing me for my steeplechase in Kashmir'. His route there, however, was indirect. When Frederick Temple, then Bishop of London, told him he was such an ignorant fellow that he was 'only fit to teach the blacks', Tyndale-Biscoe applied to join the Church Missionary Society, offering himself for work in central Africa. But on discovering that he had twice suffered from heatstroke even in England, the CMS wondered whether he should go to Persia or north-west Canada; eventually it decided to send him to Kashmir, where he went and ran the society's school for half a century.[56]

KINSHIP

Most British families had little or no connection with India during the period that their country dominated the Subcontinent. Yet a substantial minority had links that were not only 'vertical', lasting for several generations, but also 'horizontal', encompassing siblings, cousins and webs of in-laws. Members of such families often had their careers decided for them by kinship links and histories. One early-Victorian soldier recalled that since infancy he had been 'inoculated' by his mother, his great-uncle and 'sundry parchment-faced gentlemen, who frequented our house, with a sort of Indo-mania'. Members of his mother's family had flourished for more than a century in the shade of the pagoda tree and its 'fructiferous powers', and though those powers had 'sadly declined', India still tempted him with its 'sunny clime – the luscious mango – the huge jack – the refreshing guava – and, above all, the delicious custard-apple'.[57] Destiny propelled him into the army in India.

The appeal of consanguinity was especially strong in the military. L. C. Dunsterville, the 'Stalky' in his friend Kipling's eponymous stories, felt he had no option but to follow his ancestors into the army: quaintly proud of his surname's anagram ('never sit dull'), he consequently became, like his father and grandfather, a major-general in the Indian Army. Other men felt ancestral compulsions that were still more illustrious. What alternative career lay open for Valentine

Bambrick when his father had fought at Waterloo, one uncle had charged with the Light Brigade, and the other had fought in India at the Siege of Bharatpur? John Prendergast boasted of a military ancestry that went back at least to 1066: 'The Prendergasts had always been soldiers – in any case since the time of the Conqueror . . .' Born in a military cantonment and brought up in earshot of military bands and the sound of the 'Last Post', he and his family always assumed he would go into the Indian Army. He did.[58]

There was sometimes too an inevitability about the careers of 'Civilians', as members of the Indian Civil Service were known. With Indian traditions on both sides of the family – Scottish and Irish – John Christie was urged to take the ICS exam by a schoolmaster because 'India, I suppose, was written on my forehead.' His contemporary James Halliday also felt he had to go to India in some capacity – his childhood thoughts had been as a sapper or a gunner – because India was 'implicit' in his family and its history, and his father had died of a heart attack while hunting jackals near Bombay; James passed into the ICS in 1925. Another entrant from that period, Hugh Richardson, confessed that he was 'impelled towards India by heredity', by an array of ancestors, uncles and cousins who had preceded him in the army and other services. Yet another Civilian of the time, Humphrey Trevelyan, was persuaded to go to India after his cousin, the historian G. M. Trevelyan, suggested he should follow in the footsteps of his great-uncle, Charles Trevelyan, who had been a controversial governor of Madras in the mid-nineteenth century.[59]

Filial loyalty was sometimes so strong that young men might decide on an Indian career even if they had little idea what they wanted to do except work in the land where their dead fathers had spent their careers. H. E. Shortt, who had been born in India in 1887, was prepared to consider any career as long as it was Indian – the Forest Service and the Bengal Pilot Service were two options – before he decided on the Indian Medical Service. A generation later, Bill Tydd entered the Indian Police and asked to be posted to Burma, although he recognized the province was 'regarded as the backwater of India', because he wanted to be where his father had served thirty years before. Yet sometimes filial loyalty was enforced and accepted only with reluctance. Eric Tyndale-Biscoe, the son of the missionary whom God had prepared for the Kashmir steeplechase, had read agriculture at Cambridge and was intending to become a farmer in New Zealand when he was 'waylaid en route by his father' and persuaded to become the deputy principal of his school in Srinagar; later he set up a prep school of his own there for the sons of British officers who could not return to Britain during the Second World War.[60]

Marriages in India often took place between a young man in the services, either civil or military, and the daughter of a senior figure in the same services or, less frequently, of a planter or a businessman. The offspring of such a union were thus born and raised on the Subcontinent and, although they might be sent to school in England, they often regarded India as their real home and the country to which they would return as young adults without contemplating a career anywhere else. 'Both sides of my family had served in India for more than a century' is a typical sentence on the opening pages of memoirs recording a life on the Subcontinent. These traditions clearly explain the apparent lack of imagination in choices of career displayed not only by men succeeding their fathers and grandfathers in the same profession but also by siblings following their older brothers one after the other into the same job. If a director of the EIC such as Sir Robert Campbell had four sons, the chances were that all of them would acquire Company posts in India. When Alexander Wynch became governor of Madras in 1773, his five sons divided themselves between Company jobs in the civil service and the Madras Army. Often there was not even that divide. Allen Thornton Shuttleworth, who began his Indian career in 1855 in the Company's Naval Service, was an interesting figure who transferred to the Forestry Service, served as a famine officer in western India and established the first lifeboat service on the Bombay coast. Yet the notion of so varied a career seems to have appalled his seven sons, all of whom passed through the Royal Military College of Sandhurst at Camberley. Five went into the Indian Army, one joined the British Army, and the seventh only failed to get into either because of his weak eyesight.[61]

Other families such as the Dennys had five brothers in the Indian Army, though in their case the uniformity was broken by a sixth, who joined the Indian Police, a seventh who served in the Public Works Department and a sister who successively married two civil servants. But there was no diversity at all among the ten Battye brothers. All of them, known as 'the Fighting Ten', joined the Indian Army and fought in various campaigns in China, in the Rebellion, in Afghanistan and on the north-west frontier. Only Richmond, the second youngest, seems to have regretted choosing the military career that led him to become an officer in the Gurkhas; he would have preferred to be a missionary doctor or a farmer in Tasmania. In the event he turned out to be almost a pacifist, and before he was killed in the Black Mountain Expedition of 1888 he prayed that none of his six sons would enter the army and be compelled to kill human beings. Yet all of them became combat officers except one, and even he joined the army as a medical officer; it was in that capacity that he had to witness the sight of a younger brother's corpse being carried past him during the Gallipoli fighting in 1915.[62]

The army was the career that most often 'ran' in families, sons copying fathers as well as youngsters following their older brothers into the same regiment, which, especially in the case of the Indian Army, acted as a sort of extended clan. Boys also often aspired to follow their fathers into the ICS, if they were bright enough to pass the exams, and naturally men who had built up companies or nurtured a plantation provided opportunities for sons to work in them and eventually take charge of the business. The career least likely to attract descendants was that of the missionary. The life was hard, the work was not usually remunerative, and satisfaction from the job, at least if measured by the number of converts made, was often limited and disappointing. It is striking how often children and grandchildren of missionaries in India decided to live in the country of their birth yet chose more worldly careers themselves. The descendants of Joshua Marshman, a Baptist missionary, went into history, forestry and the Indian Army; the missionary's son became the *Times* correspondent in Calcutta.[63] A similar diversity characterized the Rice family. Benjamin, the patriarch, lived half a century in Bangalore on behalf of the London Missionary Society, devoting nineteen years to *re-translating* the bible into the Kannada language. His son, another Benjamin, inherited enough scholarly zeal to become a schoolteacher, headmaster of the High School in Bangalore and later inspector of schools in Mysore, but his grandson Harold opted for a practical life as an engineer, cheerfully building roads and railways for the maharaja of Mysore.[64]

Paternal desires and filial ambitions were mostly in harmony, but there were some unavoidable disagreements. Sometimes parents persuaded reluctant sons to go to India, and sometimes they were defied. The Rivett-Carnacs were a prominent family whose members served in

British India over three centuries. Yet John, born in 1838, committed the heresy of telling his father that he personally did not wish to go: he had been 'much taken with the blue-and-gold coats of the attachés' he had seen in the capitals of Europe, and his ambition was to don such garments as a British diplomat rather than wear rough jackets and sola topis in the jungles and deserts of India. His father initially accepted his wish but changed his mind when he heard that the system of patronage in the EIC was about to be abolished. He had already acquired two Company nominations for his younger sons, but these would now be useless for them because the boys were too young to qualify before abolition. John succumbed to paternal pressure and was thus condemned to wear a lot of rough clothes in his years as cotton commissioner in the Central Provinces, opium agent in Benares and special commissioner in the Bengal Famine of 1874. His heart, however, was clearly not in the profession, and he sometimes irritated his colleagues with his 'grand talk' about the peerage and 'his dilettante antiquarianism'. Yet he had the compensation of later appointments as private secretary to the viceroy and ADC to the commander-in-chief that gave him frequent opportunities to wear fancy coats. So did his retirement job in England as ADC to Queen Victoria.[65]

Richard Temple, a cousin of Rivett-Carnac, had a somewhat similar conundrum. Educated at Rugby, where he idolized the headmaster Dr Arnold, and in line to inherit a baronetcy and an estate in Worcestershire, he had planned to stay in England and enter politics. Yet his father's second marriage required economies at home and incomes for his children. As members of Parliament did not receive salaries until 1911, Temple joined the ICS and was in time awarded several of its most senior posts, including the Residency at Hyderabad and the lieutenant-governorship of Bengal. Following a successful career, he managed, like his cousin, to indulge his youthful passion in retirement. After resigning the governorship of Bombay to contest – and lose – Worcestershire for the Conservatives in 1880, he was subsequently elected for Evesham five years later. Yet like other retired civil servants from India, he became a political bore, failed to 'add to his reputation in the House of Commons' and, according to the *Dictionary of National Biography*, was 'heard with impatience' by fellow members. The magazine *Punch* persistently caricatured the pomposity of a man who cultivated the appearance of Napoleon III and who admitted that the inspiration for his work – 'administration conducted with immense energy in a gigantic sphere' – had been Napoleon I.[66]

A good lesson to be learned from parliamentary careers like Temple's was that aspiring politicians should go into politics when young and not spend thirty-three years in India getting increasingly out of touch with what was going on in Britain before going home to irritate constituents and fellow MPs with long-winded speeches about the Russian threat to Persia. One young man, educated at Winchester and New College, Oxford, avoided making this error despite the encouragement of his mother, Adelaide. His father and godfather had been in the ICS, several ancestors had been soldiers in India, one grandfather was a retired colonel in Cheltenham and the other was consul-general in Shanghai. Although her husband had died in Burma at the age of forty-five, and although an ICS career would mean she would seldom see her son, Adelaide pressed him to join the service and was distressed by his determination to avoid it.[67] Why she thought he would be tempted by a career that had left him without a father, who had died when he was nine, is not clear. At any rate Hugh Gaitskell defied his mother, entered Parliament, became leader of the Labour Party and would almost certainly have become prime minister had he not died in 1963 at the age of fifty-six.

Another category in the parent–son–Indian triangle consists of youths who went to India because they were desperate to get away from their families in Britain. In the 1850s Henry White King went to India (after joining the Indian Medical Service) to avoid a 'harsh stepmother'; his brother George followed suit.[68] Sixty years later, John Morris had a similar reason: the lack of affection at home made him determined 'to get away from the family at all costs, no matter where'. 'Where' turned out to be the Western Front in the First World War and afterwards the Indian Army in a Gurkha regiment. His motivation may have been complicated by the realization that he was 'a true invert' and that he could feel 'true contentment only when surrounded by people of an alien culture'. Although he eventually allowed himself to be seduced by a Gurkha servant – and 'thereafter I knew my pleasure lay in the East' – he was really not suited to the military life. True contentment, at least in a professional context, lay with retirement posts as a lecturer in a Japanese university and controller of the BBC Third Programme in London.[69]

Decisive splits within families over an Indian career were much less frequent than resolutions by discussion, persuasion and compromise. A father, a godfather and a headmaster might suggest that the same boy should become an academic, a barrister or an Indian civil servant, but these were at any rate serious professions, and negotiations seldom ended in ructions. One breakdown nearly occurred when Richard Burton, who wished to join the Indian Army, was ordered by his father to remain at Oxford and become an academic. Only after a British army had been wiped out in Afghanistan in 1842 did the parent relent and, recognizing the need to defend the empire, unbelt the £500 needed for his son to purchase a commission, go to India and eventually become one of the great explorers of the Victorian era. A gentler debate took place between R. C. B. Bristow, who was born on India's north-west frontier in 1900, and his father over which army the boy should join. While the parent favoured the British Army, his son was attracted by the land of his birth and wished to join an Indian regiment. A compromise was eventually reached, with the father making the greater concession. Young Bristow was allowed to go into the Indian Army provided he 'applied to join a Gurkha regiment, for in India to [his father] Gurkhas were the nearest approach to British soldiers'.[70]

THE LURE OF THE ORIENT

India's chief allure for Europeans of the eighteenth century was its wealth and the chance of getting their hands on some of it. Yet there were other ways beyond trading, bribery and profiteering of achieving this. One lucrative route was to become a mercenary for an Indian prince, train his army and lead it into battle against his rivals. European officers had been fighting for the Mughal imperial armies in the seventeenth century, but their numbers increased over the next hundred years as Maratha chieftains competed to grab territory from the disintegrating empire. One consequence of France's Indian defeats in the Seven Years War was the large number of French officers roaming about the Subcontinent looking for employment. Indian soldiers might fight individually as well as Europeans, but as units they almost invariably fought less well unless trained on European lines and officered by foreigners. Princes such as Scindia of Gwalior and Ranjit Singh, the

Sikh 'Lion of the Punjab', owed much of their military success to the ruffians and swashbucklers of France and other European countries who, like *condottieri* in medieval and Renaissance Italy, hired out their skills and their (often temporary) loyalties.

When war broke out between Marathas and the East India Company in 1803, some of these adventurers sided with the British. Other Europeans were already with the EIC, such as the Saxon John Francke, who, on finding himself penniless in Basingstoke in 1775, felt compelled to enlist as a Company soldier, later rose to the rank of major, and fought with Wellesley at the siege of Seringapatam. Men like Francke illustrate the fluidity and complexity of national feeling and identity in pre-Romantic times. Hanoverian soldiers, whose German 'elector' was also the king of England, fought alongside the British in the second half of the eighteenth century and were more dependable than Swiss troops, who were apt to desert to the French side in the decade before the Seven Years War. Yet later Swiss companies, sent by the Dutch to defend Ceylon, had few qualms about transferring their allegiance to the British when the latter took over the island; they too fought with Wellesley at Seringapatam. Like Francke, who retired to Trichinopoly after acquiring a Russian wife and two Indian mistresses, European soldiers of fortune often had little incentive to return to their continent of origin: some were content to remain in the Company's service, sometimes ending up in command of a regiment and staying in India for the rest of their lives. Aron Lissenburg, a Dutchman, arrived in India during the Napoleonic Wars, made himself a British subject, joined a Madras regiment and became the progenitor of three generations of soldiers in the Indian Army.[71]

In the Romanesque church of San Frediano in Lucca a marble monument commemorates Lazzaro Papi, physician, poet, historian and *colonello per gli inglesi nel Bengala*, apparently in command of 4,000 lancers. Italian soldiers of fortune were quite common in India. Edoardo Tiretta, a Venetian adventurer who had been a friend of Casanova and a fencing-master in Paris, sailed to India as a common soldier on a Dutch ship and ended up as the civil architect to the East India Company and surveyor of streets and buildings in Calcutta. The Angelos from Livorno, who had been persuaded in London to change their name from Tremamondo ('Shake the world'), worked in India in several combative capacities; gravestones in the cemetery of Christ Church in Mussoorie record the deaths of two Angelo brothers, one in the Burma Police, the other in the Gurkha Rifles, who were sons of a general in the Bengal Artillery.[72] One man of distant Italian origins who considered going to India was Napoleon Bonaparte, who in 1795, before his Italian campaigns, told his brother Lucien he was thinking of joining the Company's army so that he could 'return in a few years a rich nabob, bringing some handsome dowries for my three sisters'.[73] In the end the sisters acquired their dowries through their brother's conquests in Italy, his gifts to them including the duchy of Guastalla, the grand duchy of Tuscany and the kingdom of Naples.

A good number of British adventurers served in the armies of Indian princes, especially children of British-Indian marriages whom the reforms of Cornwallis had denied commissions in the Company's forces. One of them was James Skinner, the son of a Scottish father and a Rajput mother who fought for Scindia until his 'half-caste' skills were recognized by General Lake, who in 1803 asked him to raise a force of 'irregular' cavalry: usually known as Skinner's horse (though at times also as the 1st Duke of York's Own Cavalry), it became the finest cavalry regiment of the Indian Army and remained part of the armed forces of independent India. Other British mercenaries in Scindia's employment included Joseph Harvey Bellasis, who 'in a rash moment' joined up with the maharaja after losing his wife and failing to make a fortune as a speculator in indigo; although he died fighting for his new master in 1799, the rest of the Bellasis clan remained loyal to the Company and the British Crown for nearly three centuries.[74] One adventurer with more fluid loyalties was George Thomas from Tipperary, probably a deserter from the Royal Navy, who served several Indian chieftains before carving out a principality of his own north-west of Delhi. He was a skilled soldier, and more chivalrous than most of his fellow mercenaries, but he was eventually outnumbered and defeated in battle by Scindia's Marathas. Although his English had lapsed in favour of Persian and Hindustani, he hoped, after the loss of his territories, to return to Tipperary, but he died at Berampore in 1802 on his way to Calcutta.

Not all adventurous men went to India for combative or pecuniary motives. In each generation young men travelled out simply for the sake of adventure; as Rudyard Kipling put it in 'Mandalay', they had "eard the East a-callin". According to his family's chronicler, Robert Low was 'loafing on a lawyer's stool in Edinburgh when in 1771 he heard the call and upped and offed to join the Madras Army'. Unlike most spontaneous adventurers, he returned eleven years later with enough money to buy an estate in Fife.[75] The contrast between the prospect of office drudgery in Britain and the vision of an active life abroad is a recurrent theme and incentive in the history of British involvement in India. Arthur Clay went into the ICS in 1862 because he wanted to do something more exciting than join the family printing firm, Clays of Bungay.[76] His contemporary, E. C. Cox, was equally gloomy about his opportunities in England, which seemed limited to the choice between clergyman and schoolmaster, so he set off to join his brother as a tea planter in India. On arriving in Calcutta, however, he learned the 'upsetting' news that his brother had abandoned tea to join the Indian Police, where Cox, after spells as a teacher in Darjeeling and a political agent in Kolhapur, eventually joined him.[77] Although he himself retired in due course to London, content to be throwing snowballs at his son in Kensington Gardens, younger men were often keen to leave the capital for ever, dreading the prospect of commuting, the 8.15 from Surbiton, the dingy hours of desk work, and the perennial smog and pollution. Arthur Godden, the father of the novelist Rumer, abandoned London at the age of nineteen for a career in a steamer company on the rivers of Bengal.

Sporting possibilities provided another enticement for those despondent about the idea of metropolitan careers in Britain. Every region in India had game birds and animals to shoot at, and middle-class men without much chance of being invited on to the grouse moors of Langholm or Bolton Abbey could pursue game in a gentlemanly style on the Subcontinent. Charles Kincaid's father had so 'fired [his son's] blood with tales of shooting orang-utans in Borneo' that all he 'wanted to do was to go out [east] and start shooting too'; he joined the ICS in 1891 and was soon aiming his gun at duck and snipe near Karachi. His contemporary, W. O. Horne in Madras, was equally blunt about his motives for joining the service. As he had 'strong open-air tastes, a love of all sports [and] a whole-hearted detestation of desk work', he planned to join the Indian Army until, on discovering the pay was less than he had hoped, he opted for the ICS. Recruits with Horne's ambitions were a rarity in the twentieth century, although Lord Halifax, a former viceroy, does not seem to have realized it: as late as 1939 he was encouraging

Oxford graduates to join the service by outlining the prospects of 'plenty of shooting and sky black with duck'.[78]

The army was a more natural home for hunters and shooters than the ICS: its officers had more leisure, they had greater access to horses, and they lived in a world pervaded by the atmosphere of the chase. Field sports were very much in the mind of Hilary Hook when in the 1930s he was thinking, not very seriously, about his future. He was still resisting his mother's hortation to go to Oxford prior to joining the Sudan Political Service when he read Yeats Brown's *Bengal Lancer*, a book which made him want to go to India to shoot tigers. In 1938, on completing his training at Sandhurst, he joined the Royal Deccan Horse intent not on dangerous soldiering but on what he called 'artful abuse of His Majesty's time'. In a television documentary made in 1987 after his return from Africa, where he had retired, Hook confessed that he had not joined the army because he was 'devoted to fife and drum. I joined the military so I could play polo, go pig-sticking, shooting, hunting and have a jolly time with a lot of jolly fellows.' His candour on camera, and the charm with which he expressed it, caused the BBC switchboard to be jammed by admirers and led subsequently to invitations to 'phone-ins' and 'chat-shows' and offers of marriage from women he had never met.[79]

Many men became soldiers through family tradition and because they had never thought of becoming anything else. Yet they still had to decide which army to join. And just as Simla and a district might seem more tempting to an aspiring civil servant than a ministry in Whitehall, so might Peshawar and the north-west frontier appeal to an ensign more than repetitive journeys between Aldershot and Salisbury Plain. Despite the opportunities for sport provided by a career in the Indian Army, years spent in the same barracks in India were bound to be boring, yet officers were able to take time off from their regiments by going on a staff course or attaching themselves to 'irregular' units on the frontier. Those who hankered after a social life could apply to become ADCs to a lieutenant-governor, when they would spend their days at Government House arranging dinners, balls and garden parties. And those who preferred military excitement could volunteer for foreign assignments when on leave in England. In 1834 Lieutenant William Beatson of the 54th Native Infantry joined the British Auxiliary Legion to fight the Carlists in Spain and later, as a major, he organized irregular forces for the Turkish Army – the 'Bashi-Bazouks' – before he took part in the Heavy Brigade's charge at Balaclava.[80]

Openings for officers of the British Army in India belonged to a higher and even broader league: they could be sent anywhere from China and Ceylon to Canada and the Caribbean. William Colebroke, for example, joined the Royal Artillery in 1803 and served for fifteen years in India, Ceylon, Java and the Persian Gulf; thereafter he turned administrator and, while remaining a soldier (he was eventually made a general), became successively lieutenant-governor or governor of the Bahamas, New Brunswick, the Leeward Islands, and Barbados and the Windward Islands. His contemporary William Gomm also switched continents. After fighting in the Peninsular War and at Waterloo, he became commander-in-chief of Jamaica and then of Mauritius before in 1850 he reached India, where he was styled 'Commander-in-Chief of all the Queen's and Company's forces in the East Indies'. An earlier holder of this last post, Lord Combermere, enjoyed a still more varied career for, in addition to a West Indian governorship and service in the Mysore and Peninsular wars, he became commander-in-chief in Ireland; like Gomm, he ended his career in his nineties as Constable of the Tower of London.

Officers in British regiments may have had little say in their postings to India, but if, when they were there, they acquired a taste for the Subcontinent, they could transfer to the Indian Army and remain there. Many did so at the end of the First World War, including William Slim, who joined the Gurkhas and directed the reconquest of Burma in the second global conflict. So did the Australian 'Bas' Holmes, who fought with his fellow countrymen at Gallipoli, the Somme and Passchendaele but was so impressed by the Indian troops he encountered in France that he joined the Indian Cavalry, served on the north-west frontier and retired in 1946. Olaf Caroe was seduced by India when his regiment, the Royal West Surrey, was sent out in 1914. Attracted to the East since childhood by Kipling's *Jungle Books*, and susceptible to the 'insistent call' of 'Britain's Indian "adventure"', he was so happy to be there that after the war he took the civil service exams and chose the ICS ahead of the Treasury in Whitehall. The best parts of his subsequent career were spent on the frontier, wallowing in what he called 'the strange fascination in living among the Pathans'.[81]

Sport, which was by far the most popular kind of leisure in British

India, was sometimes a factor in a man's decision to leave a British regiment for an Indian one. In 1936 Robbie Barcroft transferred from the Cheshire Regiment to Skinner's Horse so that he could raise a pack of hounds to hunt jackals at Ambala; after Independence he retired to Kenya and raised another pack there.[82] But a more common motive was financial. Indian Army officers were paid better than their British Army counterparts, and the cost of living (including the cost of sport) was much cheaper in India than in England. Many aspiring officers, such as Claude Auchinleck, a future commander-in-chief in India, realized this as cadets and so went straight from Sandhurst to India. Bernard Montgomery had the same intention, but unlike Auchinleck he passed out of the college too low to gain a place in the Indian Army and was consigned to the Royal Warwickshire Regiment (which fortunately had a battalion stationed at Peshawar) instead. The availability of family funding was often the decisive factor in the choice of army. Vivian Stevenson-Hamilton was hoping to join either the Black Watch or the fashionable 12th Lancers, but when his uncle refused him the required allowance, he joined the 4th Gurkhas instead.[83] Some men learned only from experience that they could not afford to remain in a good British regiment in peacetime. One subaltern who did join the 12th Lancers was William Birdwood, another future commander-in-chief in India, but he found it so expensive to live with his fellow officers that he soon left it for the 11th Bengal Lancers, whose uniform of blue turban, blue kurta and scarlet cummerbund much appealed to him. The 'smartness and general appearance' of Indian units also appealed to L. C. 'Stalky' Dunsterville, who even in India 'found it impossible to continue the financial struggle in a British regiment with an allowance of only £100 a year'. After going to Lahore to visit Rudyard Kipling, his old schoolfriend, he began to study Urdu and soon exchanged the Royal Sussex Regiment for the 24th Punjabis.[84]

Childhood memories sometimes inspired young men to look to India for a career. Wondering what to do with their lives, they might remember old prints on the sitting-room wall, a sketch of the Agra Fort, brass elephants on the mantelpiece or a tray from Benares brought back by a great-uncle who recounted his adventures with tigers in the jungle or 'wild tribesmen' on the frontier. Publications might also fuel their imagination, especially the Victorian picture books which liked to portray the India of the south, the country of lagoons and palms and paddy fields, of red soil and white sand and dark-skinned smiling 'natives'. The narrator of Tennyson's poem 'Locksley Hall', whose father died in the Maratha Wars, pined for 'yonder shining Orient' and its 'breadths of tropic shade'; he yearned to be there, his 'passions cramp'd no longer', and 'take some savage woman' who would rear his 'dusky race'. Although the poet may have inspired others to travel to the Orient, he did not inspire himself: Tennyson never went near either India or the Crimea, the graveyard of his Light Brigade. And 'Locksley Hall' may have acted as a deterrent anyway, because halfway through it the narrator realized that he did not after all want to 'herd with narrow foreheads' or be 'mated with a squalid savage'. 'Fifty years of Europe,' he concluded, were better 'than a cycle of Cathay'.

Children's stories have often left a permanent imprint on the thoughts and behaviour of their readers. Ian Hamilton, who went to India with the Gordon Highlanders in the 1870s, admitted that his 'whole attitude' to his 'bearer' (manservant/valet) was coloured by having been forced as a child to read Mrs Sherwood's *Little Henry and His Bearer*, a tale which ends with Henry dying and Boosey his Indian bearer converting to Christianity.[85] The seafaring novels of Captain Marryat prompted youths to join the Royal Indian Marine, just as the fiction of Flora Annie Steel encouraged girls as well as boys to take part in Britain's Indian 'adventure'. Yet by far the most influential and inspirational writer in the last sixty years of British India was Rudyard Kipling.

Born in Bombay on the penultimate day of 1865, young 'Ruddy' spent five and a half years in India before he was taken to England with his young sister Trix and left there for eleven years of schooling. In 1882 he returned to the country of his birth to work as a journalist on the *Civil and Military Gazette* in Lahore, where his father was then curator of the museum and principal of the Mayo School of Industrial Arts. Displaying a precocity that astonished and sometimes exasperated his contemporaries, he had his first book of poems (*Departmental Ditties and Other Verses*) published when he was twenty, and his first collection of stories (*Plain Tales from the Hills*) two years later. From then on he was regarded as an unofficial – and indeed unwitting – recruiting agent for three generations of British boys who were inspired by him to go to India. When in old age Philip Mason was asked why he had joined the ICS in 1928, he simply replied 'Kipling'. Not only had the stories, which as a child he had known almost by heart, given him a 'romantic desire' to go to India; 'with their strong sense of commitment to duties usually unpleasant and often dangerous', they had inspired him to go and carry out those duties himself.[86]

Kipling's own sympathies were with the soldiers rather than the civil servants; his fictional portraits of the latter are not always very flattering. Yet his work evidently had a special resonance with candidates for the ICS. One of them, W. H. Pridmore, remembered how Kipling had 'cast his spell' through his prep school headmaster's readings from *Kim*, and 'the magic persisted . . .' Another, Roger Pearce, had no Indian connections and was reluctantly planning to follow his father into his country flour mill when he read Kipling and was inspired to take the ICS exam. When his contemporary Herbert Thompson went out in 1922 as a civil servant to Madras (which Kipling neither visited nor wrote about), he admitted that his 'only general source of information about India lay in the works of Rudyard Kipling, all of whose books' he had read. Yet a further ICS contemporary, Maurice Zinkin, confessed that no one in his family had ever been east of Suez and that his own knowledge of India was confined to *Kim* and *The Jungle Book*. In this he was matched by his future wife, Taya Ettinger, a daughter of 'White Russian' parents brought up in France. As a child she had memorized *The Jungle Book* in her own language, reading and re-reading about Mowgli and the death of Akela without ever realizing that 'Kipling was not French like Jules Verne . . .'[87]

Kipling's appeal went far beyond educated youths aiming for the ICS: one officer in the Indian Police recalled how it had permeated his entire generation at school. Most people read Kipling when they were children, but Arthur Hamilton only discovered him in hospital after he had been wounded in the First World War; he was mesmerized and, as soon as he had recuperated and been demobbed, he applied to the India Office, studied forestry at Oxford and went out to the Punjab (the province the writer had known best) as an official of the Forest Department.[88] Yet the attraction was not limited to men wishing to join the army or one of the services. Whatever racial assumptions and imperialist feelings he may have had – and which he shared with most of his generation – Kipling's love of India was unquestionable, and he communicated it in a way that was accessible to all. His impact on Ernest Hartley was such that in 1905 the twenty-two-year-old abandoned his middle-class background in Yorkshire for a job as a junior exchange broker in a firm in Calcutta. He did not achieve great things there, and his name might not have survived in print had he not become the father of the actress Vivien Leigh, who shared his love for Kipling.[89]

The writer's influence did not cease when his admirers arrived in India. Indeed it often followed them around so that they felt they already knew the Seonee, the location of the *Jungle Books* (another place Kipling had never visited), and they recognized the Himalaya because they had experienced them through *Kim*.[90] On arriving in India for the first time, Philip Mason 'became aware of a sensation almost of coming home', remembering 'the scents of dust and spices' from Kipling. Stevenson-Hamilton of the 4th Gurkhas had an almost opposite reaction. Posted to the north-west frontier, he was frustrated to be living in a place so far from anywhere described in *Kim* or the *Plain Tales*: he wanted to experience the India he had 'read about in Kipling but which [he] had never seen'.[91] Luckily he was soon able to wangle a transfer into the heart of Kipling country as an ADC to the governor of the Punjab, based in Lahore in the cold weather and in Simla in the summer.

Some devotees, like the doctor Ernest Bradfield, were always looking for opportunities to follow in their hero's footsteps, to bustle through the bazaars of Lahore or travel the Grand Trunk Road like Kim and the Lama.[92] Other men might even decide to change their careers in order to experience the India they had read about. H. R. Robinson, a young officer in the Indian Army who was hoping to experience the 'colourful glamour of the East', became so depressed by the heat, the desert and the stony hills of Baluchistan that his 'soul thirsted' for something else. He looked at the map, saw the Bay of Bengal and recalled the 'cleaner, greener land' of Kipling's 'Mandalay'. So he got himself transferred to Burma, was seduced by the charm of the country and its people, and became in turn a policeman, a frontier officer and a Buddhist mendicant. Unfortunately he also became an opium addict and spent all the money he had – and some he did not have – on his addiction. On being arrested for trying to abscond without paying his debts, he grabbed his pistol and tried to kill himself while reciting Kipling's lines from 'The Young British Soldier'.

> When you're wounded and left on Afghanistan's plains,
> And the women come out to cut up what remains,

Jest roll to your rifle and blow out your brains
An' go to your Gawd like a soldier.

But that, as Kipling was fond of saying, 'is another story'.[93]

Schools and schoolmasters were among the agents most actively involved in promoting the idea of Indian careers for boys. Children born in India were often sent to prep schools near Eastbourne or elsewhere on the Sussex coast, and their nostalgic talk about the warmth and colours of their birthplace could inspire a classmate from greyer and colder climes to imagine a life in the East. Later a headmaster might outline the potential for service and adventure, a life guarding the frontier or building railways and canals, or governing a 'backward' people with vigour and benevolence. A boy then might go to a public school such as Cheltenham College, where the imperialist spirit was so pervasive that dissidents and even the lukewarm would be considered shirkers. The old Haileybury, the college of aspiring civil servants before competition, closed down in 1857 but, reborn as a public school in 1862, it retained much of the ethos of its predecessor. Boys there read about Indian careers in the school magazine and boarded in houses named after illustrious governors of the Indian provinces. It might seem ironic that Haileybury's most illustrious pupil was Clement Attlee, the man who as prime minister ended the British Empire in India, but one could argue that in 1947 the statesman was in fact exemplifying the college ethos of service and imperial responsibility.

Recruitment was not of course always as planned or as predictable as the statistics for 'imperialist' schools such as Haileybury and Cheltenham might suggest. A lot of careers were almost accidental, caused by a chance meeting or an overheard remark. Stanley Batchelor aspired to be a Catholic priest and was so brilliant a scholar that he was expected to become a cardinal: he only applied to join the ICS in 1889 after Cardinal Manning told him he was not fitted for the priesthood because his 'doubts' were too strong.[94] John de Chazal was an idle student at Bristol University with no sense of vocation when in the 1930s he met a cadet at the Hendon Police College. This incidental meeting made him consider a police career, but it was only the discovery that there were sixteen vacancies in the Indian Police and just six at Hendon that persuaded him to try for India.[95] If such careers were the result of mere luck, others were caused by ill luck, although they might have fortunate outcomes. Frederick Fryer was looking forward to an army commission his uncle Charles had promised to arrange for him, but a sudden quarrel between his father and his uncle scotched the expected commission; forced to look elsewhere for a career, Fryer joined the ICS in 1864 and did well enough to end up as lieutenant-governor of Burma.[96] Even more unlucky was August Peter Hansen, a Danish sailor who nearly died of fever in Calcutta in 1904; on recovering in hospital, he discovered that his ship had sailed without him, leaving him sick, stranded, penniless and unemployed. Like Fryer, however, he made the most of his misfortune, taking advantage of his unplanned stay in India to join the police and then the customs department and later chronicling his life in a manuscript that was published after his death, *Memoirs of an Adventurous Dane in India*.[97]

FEMALE VOCATIONS

In 1883 a seventeen-year-old girl called Mabell was worrying about her matrimonial prospects. As she later recalled,

> Unless a girl was quite exceptional – which I was not – her fate was decided by her first impact on society. Anyone who failed to secure a proposal within six months of coming out could only wait for her second season with diminishing chances. After the third there remained nothing but India as a last resort before the spectre of the Old Maid became a reality.[98]

As far as her own future was concerned, Lady Mabell Gore was fretting unnecessarily. In her 'coming out' year she rejected two proposals in her first 'season' and then accepted a Scottish peer, the young Earl of Airlie, whom she married in 1886. Yet her fears about the need to look for a husband in India would have resonated with other girls of her generation, though not often with those of her own class. One of the notorious images of British India is 'the fishing fleet', which conjures up a gaggle of girls at the ship's rails salivating at the prospect of dashing young officers – just as one of the cruellest of phrases is 'returned empties', with its overtones of masculine jeering – used to describe girls unable to attract a mate even in a society with so many unmarried men.

There is a good deal of myth about 'the fishing fleet'. As Maud Diver, who was born and brought up in India, wrote in her book on British women on the Subcontinent, 'more than half the Englishwomen in India today [1909] have spent their girlhood and early childhood in the country itself which, in most cases, means that they have been sent "home" at the age of seven or thereabouts, returning at seventeen'.[99] They were thus returning to the country of their birth, usually to be reunited with their parents or to stay with an elder brother stationed in India. Madge Green and Lucy Hardy both went out early in the twentieth century to look after their brothers, one in the ICS, the other an officer in the mountain artillery with a pregnant wife. Like many other girls, in India and elsewhere, Lucy met her brother's friends and fellow officers and married one of them.[100] Yet for such girls marriage was often not the immediate priority; they were returning to reconnect with their family and their background. M. M. Kaye, the future novelist, was typical of many women born in India who loved their childhood there, hated their years of 'exile' at school in Britain and longed to return 'home' to the Subcontinent. Her father, Colonel Cecil Kaye of the Indian Army, was happy in his retirement in England, but he agreed to take another job in India simply to please his wife and two daughters, who all wanted to go back. Although in her thirties Molly Kaye married an officer in the Indian Army, she never thought of herself as one of the 'fishing fleet' because she was 'one of the India-born, and therefore one of the elect, coming home'.[101]

It is true that there were a good many Mrs Bennetts eager to marry off their daughters and aware that India contained a lot of bachelors, some of whom (especially in the ICS) were both well paid and well pensioned; a civil servant's widow was guaranteed £300 per annum for life. Yet it is also true that ICS officers rarely married girls of the 'fishing fleet'. They were much more likely to meet their future wives before they went to India (which would entail years of separation and a very long engagement), or on their first furlough ('long leave' in Britain after eight years in the job) or among the daughters of officers and civil servants already living in India.

'Disappointment in love' was another reason for persons of both sexes to go to India, though here the motive was to get away from a lover rather than to go looking for one. In 1893, at the age of twenty-two, Pamela Wyndham was sent to India to get over her infatuation with Harry Cust, a Tory MP and archetypal 'bounder'. Although her 'indiscretion' was in fact physically innocent, that of a fellow exile at that same moment was not: her future sister-in-law, Lucy Graham Smith, was also in India, 'recovering' from an adulterous relationship with the ubiquitous Cust.[102] Temporary exile to the Subcontinent was not, however, a guaranteed success. According to the biographer of Lord Dufferin, the viceroy's son Freddie Blackwood was sent there 'to escape one romantic entanglement [but] had to be sent back to escape another'.[103] In the 1920s Charles and Madge Gooch tried to persuade their daughter Marguerite to forget her infatuation with Awdry Cole, a man in his forties, by sailing with her to India from Tilbury. But the girl never reached her destination. The adventurous Cole, wearing a false beard, had also boarded the boat, and at Marseille he persuaded Marguerite to leave the ship and elope with him.[104]

India could be a good place for women to 'start again' after an unhappy relationship in Europe. During the First World War the nurse Sarah Round had become engaged to a Serbian officer; when he jilted her, she decided to forget him by setting off for India, where she ran a dispensary near Bombay for twenty-seven years.[105] At the end of her first marriage, the artist Kay Nixon went out to make a new life in the Subcontinent in 1927: having made her career as an illustrator of Enid Blyton's stories, she expanded her field by drawing for the *Times of India*, providing animal posters for Indian State Railways, and painting pictures of the horses of maharajas.

In its early days the East India Company had found it impossible to devise a consistent and coherent policy about women in its settlements. Men being what they are, women were obviously needed, but of what sort, what race and what religion? And who was going to pay for them? In the seventeenth century, worried by the danger of Catholic 'contagion', the company preferred its employees to marry Indian women rather than the daughters and sisters of Portuguese colonists. Later in the century it sent out numbers of young women from England, though this was expensive, especially if it had to ship them home again without having found a husband. In any case very small numbers of people were at that time involved. Women would have had to be pretty desperate to face a long and dangerous journey, the prospect of death or disease on arrival, and the uncertainty of a marital future anyway.

The situation changed in the late eighteenth century, although the sea voyages remained just as long and almost as grim. There were many more and much richer men around and, at least in Calcutta and Madras, the chances of a reasonably comfortable and civilized life. William Hickey recorded how a Mr Donaldson, 'a needy tradesman' from Scotland, was so delighted to have 'one of his girls well disposed of in India' that he quickly sent off two more to stay with their newly married sister. In 1793 Hickey reported 'a great importation of new ladies' to Calcutta, all dressed in the 'no-waist' style he regarded as 'preposterous' and 'unbecoming' because it made them look pregnant. Yet their number apparently included five daughters of a resident baronet and five of a general, 'all very fine, showy and dashing women', who each married quickly and 'very advantageously' except 'the oldest' daughter of the baronet, who 'capriciously' refused 'a profusion of suitors' before returning to England and marrying someone there.[106]

Most parents and grandparents were usually pleased when their daughters and granddaughters found a man in India whom they wanted to marry. Yet some sabotaged a romance either because they were too possessive or because they found the suitor unsuitable. Lewis Bowring, an ICS officer, was one of several men attracted by a general's daughter who 'sang like a bird', 'rode like an Amazon' and 'won all hearts'. Yet none of the hearts appealed to her angry and resentful father, and in consequence she never married.[107] Another sad case, though one eventually with a happy ending, was that of Anne Becher, who wanted to marry Henry Carmichael-Smyth, a young officer who had fought in the Second Maratha War. Her grandmother, however, decided he was not a good match – he was the son of a London physician – and, after first forbidding Anne to see him again, later informed her he was dead. The poor girl was then sent out to India to find a more suitable man, which she dutifully did, marrying Richmond Thackeray, a senior Civilian, in Calcutta in 1810 and giving birth to William Makepeace, the future novelist, the following July.*[108] Two years later she met Carmichael-Smyth unexpectedly – and traumatically – in Bengal; two years further on, Thackeray died; and two more years later, Anne finally married her first love.[109]

High casualty rates in European wars were an obvious incentive for

* The grandmother might not have thought Richmond more 'suitable' had she known that he had an illegitimate daughter, Sarah, with his Eurasian mistress, Charlotte Rudd.

girls to join the 'fishing fleet' to India. Their numbers certainly rose after the First World War, and they seem to have increased during the Napoleonic Wars as well. In fact there appears to have been something of a glut at the beginning of the nineteenth century: at one Calcutta dinner party a number of girls about to become 'returned empties' complained that potential husbands preferred to keep Indian mistresses rather than have British wives. In Madras, a generation later, the situation was still unpromising: there were so many 'new arrivals' that girls who had once dreamed of 'a mansion and park in Hampshire' were now being forced to 'lower their hopes' and accept 'some Lieutenant Colonel with a liver perforated like a sieve or colon almost brought to a full stop'.[110]

Matters seem to have improved in the 1840s, at least in Bombay, where Lady Falkland, the wife of the governor, described 'the arrival of a cargo of young damsels' as 'one of the exciting events' marking the start of the cold weather season and leading to some fairly rapid betrothals.[111] Another trough in the damsels' fortunes came after 1868, when the opening of the Suez Canal reduced the voyage from Bombay to England to three weeks and gave men more opportunities to go home and pick a wife in Britain. Yet girls still came to stay with their families and their friends, and they continued to meet men who could be persuaded to marry them. Potential brides on occasion even arrived with potential mothers-in-law, who, after achieving their objective, went back to England to fetch another daughter.[112] And even in times such as the early 1920s, when supply might be thought to exceed demand, girls could adapt and, by 'lowering their hopes' from 'a good regiment', succeed in finding someone from somewhere less glamorous. According to John Morris, the gay Gurkha officer, a girl without either looks or a private income who was 'aiming too high' could 'nearly always ... fall back upon either the Ordnance or the Indian Army Service Corps'.[113]

In 1715 a Mrs Pack arrived in Bombay to become the first matron of a British hospital in India. Other women were to follow her – as matrons, midwives, doctors and nurses – to Independence and beyond, though not in any great numbers until the end of the nineteenth century. In 1885 Lady Dufferin made the most worthwhile contribution of any vicereine when she established the National Association for Supplying

Female Medical Aid to the Women of India. British women on the Sub-continent did not need female doctors and nurses – men were trained to look after them – but Indian women, secluded in zenanas or otherwise barred from the company of unrelated men, did. Hariot Dufferin, egged on by Florence Nightingale in England, understood that what these women needed were doctors, nurses, medical schools to train them, and hospitals and dispensaries. By 1914 her association had become so popular and so successful that it had treated 4 million women.[114]

British women came out in increased numbers during the First World War, working for the Queen Alexandra Military Nursing Service, and in the Second, serving in the Red Cross and the Women's Auxiliary Corps. Many others, often dispatched to India by such organizations as the Church Missionary Society or the Friends Missionary Committee, were already working in fields far from the city hospitals and the main nursing services; by the end of the nineteenth century a majority of missionaries in India were women.[115] Anna Louisa Evans, a Quaker sent out in 1886 to run an orphanage at Hoshangabad, remained in India until her death sixty years later.[116] Women like her often lived in remote areas, assisting tribal mothers with childbirth, eye disease and any other kind of ailment. One missionary doctor in Sind might specialize in training *dais* (hereditary midwives), trying to persuade them to be more aware of hygiene and to remove their numerous bangles when delivering a baby. Another, in mountainous Waziristan, might become a specialist in plastic surgery because sometimes husbands in the Afghan borderlands liked to punish wives suspected of infidelity by slicing off their noses, thereby making them too ugly to attract any man again. In the 1930s a Miss Davis was working in the slums of Bombay, running the Children's Remand Home for waifs and strays and abused children. In the same period Miss Margaret Clark was spending the best years of her life – in the words of her obituarist – 'rescuing little girls destined for a life in temple prostitution in southern India'. The refuge she worked in had started as a small rescue hostel founded by a Church of England evangelist and eventually became a community of 900 people with its own doctors, dentists and teachers.[117]

Before the end of the nineteenth century many girls had decided to study at the London School of Medicine for Women or later at British universities in preparation for a career in India. They knew that they were likely to find better professional opportunities on the Subcontinent than in their male-dominated profession at home. Ruth Young graduated from St Andrews in 1909 and, after working for decades in medical colleges in Ludhiana and Delhi, she died in Edinburgh aged ninety-nine in 1983.[118] But many of her colleagues never came home. Dr Alice Marval, who had trained at London, died in the plague of 1900 while trying to cure sufferers of the disease in Kanpur; Dr Ethel Cousins, with a first-class degree from Oxford, died of heart failure when working for a sanatorium run by the Church of Scotland in Almora.[119]

Other graduates of the new women's colleges at Oxford and Cambridge became prominent in social work. some going from the Universities Settlement in east London, known as Toynbee Hall, to found the University Women's Settlement in Bombay. Maisie Wright, a graduate of Newnham College, Cambridge, went to Bombay in 1928 and quickly immersed herself in the training of Indian social workers. Her routine included running a children's play centre on Wednesday afternoons in the Beggars' Home in Nagpada and giving sewing lessons on Saturday mornings to the inmates of the Women's Block of Bombay Jail. She also thought up schemes for her students to dissuade their neighbours from such antisocial habits as spitting on stairways or out of windows on to people walking below; if they made friends with them by asking to see their saris, they could then ask them to use municipal bins instead of throwing their kitchen rubbish on to the street.[120]

A small number of women were sufficiently enterprising to work for Indian employers. On their disapproving 'fact-finding' Indian tour of 1911–12, those indefatigable Fabians Sidney and Beatrice Webb found 'three English lady doctors . . . engaged in hospital and dispensary work' in the princely state of Bhopal, where the ruling begum – a member of an impressive matriarchal line – had 'practically adopted the English Midwifes Act . . .'[121] Another rather rare occupation was that of 'companion' to a lady from an Indian princely family. Several years before E. M. Forster went to Dewas in 1912 as tutor to its maharaja, a Mrs Cooper was working there as 'reader and instructress' to both of its ranis.

One other unusual ambition for a Victorian lady was to set up her own school in India. Perhaps it was not very strange for two widows already on the Subcontinent to set up a preparatory school in the Khasi Hills in 1841. Yet the case of Annette Ackroyd, happily living in Worcestershire, is decidedly odd. In 1871, at the age of twenty-eight, she embarked on learning Bengali prior to going out to India to establish a non-denominational school ('of the strictest theological neutrality') for Hindu girls in Calcutta. Her chances of success were quite hopeless. Nobody wanted her: not the government nor the Christian missions nor even the inhabitants of Bengal, who did not regard the education of their daughters as one of their priorities. Her school failed and closed, though not before she had married a serious and admirably liberal member of the ICS. She and her husband, Henry, were to become the parents of an even more remarkable liberal figure, William Beveridge, the author of the 1942 report that shaped Britain's welfare state.

Safer educational options than setting up a controversial school as a single woman in a foreign country were to join an existing establishment or start something quite simple with official blessing. If you were the daughter of a former Resident of Kashmir – as well as the wife of a prominent educationalist – you were not taking a great risk by starting an embroidery school for the ladies of Srinagar. Nor, when your husband was a district officer in Sind, would a restless wife be jeopardizing the family finances by insisting on teaching at a school in Karachi. For women who had decided on an educational career before setting off for India, there were increasing opportunities in institutions like the Women's Christian College in Madras; there were also jobs in some princely states such as Hyderabad, which had the Mahboubia Girls' School, run on the lines of an English public school and staffed by women graduates from Oxford and Cambridge.[122]

As a profession, teaching was inevitably more open to the influence of Indian society and politics than medical careers. In 1928 Margaret Sykes went from Cambridge to work in Madras at the Bentinck High School for Girls, but in a few years, after making friends with Indian teachers, she found herself gravitating towards Gandhian views and eventually leaving conventional teaching altogether to join the educational community of Rabindranath Tagore at Santiniketan in Bengal. Other women might go even further, setting out for India as confirmed Gandhians intent on confronting and subverting the Raj. Margaret Cousins, an Irish suffragette who had spent some time in Holloway Prison, was one of these, a somewhat histrionic figure who in India embraced almost every fad and cause she came across, including those connected with Annie Besant and her Theosophical Society. Cousins saw herself as a martyr as well as a believer and, after dutifully defying the authorities, spent a brief and contented period in the women's prison at Vellore, where she was given a second cell as a sitting room.[123]

Considering the enormous number of servants there were in Britain, it is curious how few of them were ever wanted in India. The paucity was even more pronounced with men than with women. Viceroys and governors might employ the occasional French chef, but the sahibs seldom had a British butler or a valet; nearly all of them were content with Indian bearers and khansamas. Jeeves did not go to India.

Gubernatorial families sometimes brought out a governess for their children, often a German fräulein but sometimes a French mademoiselle. Annette Beveridge insisted that her children should speak German, so a succession of fräuleins trekked out to Bengal to teach them.[124] British nannies, usually Scottish, were sometimes employed, especially by families frightened by exaggerated tales that Indian nannies – or ayahs – gave infants opium to keep them quiet. But again most British families preferred to have an ayah, a much cheaper option. It was expensive to bring out a nanny to India, and when she got there she might not 'fit in' to a job with a problematical social status. She would often feel both awkward and isolated in her position, unable to mix socially with the ayahs and Eurasian women looking after the other children at the station. It was a far cry from prams beside the Round Pond in Kensington Gardens.

Yet a nanny might also fit in so well that she soon gave in her notice in order to get married. Mrs Pack, the widowed matron who came out in 1715, married the Company's master carpenter almost as soon as she landed at Bombay. She set a trend that persisted. Later diaries and memoirs often record that so-and-so's pretty nanny or governess, recently brought out from Bournemouth or Torquay, 'was soon snapped up', especially if she was working for an officer and thus inescapably in sight of his regiment's sergeants. One governess who remained single for longer than most was Naida Tierney, who, after spending the First World War in London working for MI5, wanted to travel abroad. She thus accepted a job with the Dawkins family* in Burma and spent a happy two and a half years travelling in the jungles, swimming in the lakes and looking after three small boys. Like her employers, she did not much like the local clubs, where too much bridge was played, too

---

* See below, pp. 199–202, 428–33.

much whisky was drunk, and the armchairs harboured bugs. Besides, as a single woman, she had to learn how to fend off amorous old men and subalterns who got 'merry'. Eventually she married a captain in the Indian Army, but only at the end of her contract.[125]

In all professions in India except the medical and the missionary, British women worked in comparatively small numbers, far fewer than they would have done in their home country. This was understandable. Why would a girl wish to be a shop assistant in Madras if she could get a similar job in her natal town of Peterborough? There were jobs in shops in India that only women could do: the Army and Navy Stores in Calcutta, for example, needed an assistant manageress to open the shop on Sunday mornings to look after Indian ladies in purdah who could not be served by a man.[126] But they were few. There are sometimes archival references to women who owned a milliner's shop in Kanpur or had opened a dress shop in Srinagar, yet the owners were nearly always widows who had stayed on after their husband's death. They had not set out from Britain with the ambition of becoming shopkeepers in India.

London in the Edwardian era had plenty of openings for girls working in racier professions than shopkeeping. There was not much reason, therefore, for them to go to India. Yet advertisements for barmaids to work in hotels in Calcutta and Rangoon painted a sufficiently alluring picture of the exotic East in the years around 1900 for a number of them to come out and behave in a manner that provoked protests from the Bishop of Rangoon and the Burma Women's Christian Temperance Union: one of them committed suicide while another 'became so degraded as to solicit Corringhi coolies in public houses'. When the Viceroy's Council debated whether the barmaids should be banned and sent home, some members argued that, although 'the idea of English women serving liquor to natives' might be rather 'repugnant', the activity itself was not immoral and should not be prohibited. Others, including the viceroy Curzon, claimed that the girls were being exploited, that they did not realize what they were coming out to, and that they were being used as 'baits behind the counter' to get men to drink. What was the need of them? he asked. 'Why bring them out from home, whether it be to ruin, or to concubinage, or to marriage?'[127]

British men who recorded their visits – either as punters or as wardens – to the red-light districts of Indian cities, often expressed their relief that these places seemed to contain no British women. Most prostitutes were Indian, some were from the Far East, and the few white ones usually came from eastern Europe. In 1891 the Bombay police were thus astonished to receive a letter from a Mr Epstein in Manchester informing them that his daughter might be working in the city and asking them to identify her and send her back to him. Investigations quickly revealed that Fanny Epstein, looking about twenty years of age, had bought and furnished a brothel in Bazar Road. Assuming that she must have been coerced into doing such a thing, the police commissioner interviewed her, told her of her father's anxiety and assured her that her passage home would be paid for. But Fanny laughed at the idea that she was being coerced, expressed no contrition about the job she was doing, insisted she was entirely her own mistress, and stated that she had no intention of returning to her father. Furthermore, she had no need of financial assistance.

The bewildered commissioner noted that Fanny's 'manner of speech and bearing showed [him] that she belonged to a rank superior' to that of most women entering 'that line of life' in Bombay. His bewilderment was shared by a number of other people who felt obliged to get involved and interrogate Fanny: a member of the Methodist Mission, the principal of a 'Home for Women', and the wife of the Rev. Mr Manwaring of the Church Missionary Society. She assured them all that she had come to Bombay of her own volition, that she was not under any restraint, and that she had no need of pecuniary aid. While these good people fretted about what they should do next, Fanny relieved them of the quandary by suddenly settling her debts, selling her furniture and sailing away. The last they heard of her was that she was living in the Rue Mazard in Marseille under the name of Mademoiselle Kahn.[128]

3

Origins and Identities

DOLPHIN FAMILIES

'Certain families,' wrote Rudyard Kipling, 'serve India generation after generation as dolphins follow in line across the open sea.' He was writing a short story, 'The Tomb of His Ancestors', about a fictional family, the Chins, who had been sailing from Devonshire to India since the capture of Seringapatam in 1799. And whatever their abilities, the Chins kept going out generation after generation: 'A clever Chin passes for the Bombay Civil Service . . . A dull Chin enters the Police Department or the Woods and Forests.' But 'according to Chin tradition', the eldest son always became an officer in the Indian Army.

Alongside the Chins, Kipling listed some real families such as the Rivett-Carnacs, who over the generations produced a score of civil servants, policemen and army officers, including a governor of Bombay. Another dolphin family in Kipling's list – the Plowdens or Chichele Plowdens – was even more prolific. From the end of the eighteenth century thirty-nine Plowden males served in India, thirteen in the Indian Army, most of the rest in the civil services. In the same period sixteen Plowden women married men in those same careers.[1]*

Dolphin families often followed a single profession. Four generations of Hancocks served in the Bombay Army. Five Meneaud-Lissenburg brothers joined the military, following their father, grandfather and

---

* One of those who did not was Pamela, the daughter of Sir Trevor Chichele Plowden, the Resident of Hyderabad. She was the first love of Winston Churchill but married Victor Bulwer-Lytton, who succeeded his father (the viceroy) as Earl of Lytton. The Indian connection was revived when he was made governor of Bengal in 1922.

great-grandfather, who had all been officers in the Madras Army. The Salmon family produced five generations of colonels and lieutenant-colonels (one became a general), each of whom survived, unusually, into old age. While these had served variously in the Bombay, Bengal and British armies, officers of the Beyts family were more exclusive, concentrating so much on the 3rd Battalion of the 6th Rajputana Rifles that it became known as the 'family regiment'.[2]

Like the Chins, other families diversified. Between the two world wars, three Happell brothers divided themselves, like the Rivett-Carnacs, between the Indian Army, the Indian Police and the Indian Civil Service, a division of service that the Cox family managed to spread over four generations. Other families worked in India for lengthy durations but ceased to behave like dolphins after choosing to live on the Subcontinent, when those born there became known as 'country-born', a rather disparaging description. Like the Chins, the Dyers were sailing back and forth from Devonshire to India until one of them began to brew beer in the Himalayan foothills, an enterprise so successful that he decided to settle in India and expand his business, eventually setting up breweries in Simla, Rawalpindi and Mandalay.[3] Unfortunately his son Reginald did not follow him into the family firm; instead he became a soldier and eventually the brigadier who ordered his troops to carry out the Amritsar Massacre in 1919.

'Country-born' families might retain such British customs as serving soup, a roast and a pudding for dinner, but they often regarded themselves as 'white natives' of India with little need or incentive to go 'home' to Britain. Lillian Luker Ashby was one of five generations 'to be born under the hot Indian sun'. Her great-grandfather had been a trader in Calcutta, her grandfather was an indigo planter who traded in elephants, and her great-uncle, father, husband and nephew were officers in the Indian Police. The family did not educate its children in England but in schools in the hill stations of Darjeeling and Mussoorie. Nor did its elderly members retire to towns like Eastbourne or Cheltenham; they stayed in their 'native land' in places such as Dinapur, a Bihar garrison town known as 'Dusty-pores' where, it was said, one would swallow a bushel of dust in the course of a lifetime. When Lillian's daughter Hazel went on her honeymoon to Burma at the end of the First World War, she was the first woman of the family to leave

Indian soil for four generations. Lillian herself did not step outside India until as an elderly grandmother she also visited Burma.[4]

Many of the true dolphin families were Scottish, such as the Glasfurds of Inverness or the Wedderburns from Dundee, who described the Indian Civil Service as 'a sort of hereditary calling' in the nineteenth century.* Among the most persistent clans was the Macnabb, which sent four generations of civil servants to India to serve in provinces as disparate as Burma and the Punjab. James Monro Macnabb, the first of the 'Civilians', lost his fortune in the collapse of Alexander's Bank in Calcutta in 1832 and was forced to sell the Perthshire estate his father had bought from the proceeds of a prosperous career as a surgeon in India. Yet his three sons followed him to the Subcontinent, the two eldest as Civilians, the youngest an ensign who was killed in the Rebellion. Donald, the middle son, a linguist who enjoyed disguising himself as a Pathan, became an enthusiast for irrigation and dug at his own expense a canal in the Punjab subsequently known as the Macnabbwah.[5]

Sir Alec Ogilvie, who died in in 1997, was described by his obituarist as 'the seventh generation of his family to serve with distinction in India', ending his career as president of the Bengal Chamber of Commerce and Industry.[6] Yet the family with the longest tradition of administrative service was the Cottons, who followed Indian careers for six generations in a direct male line. Joseph, the progenitor, was a ship's captain who made several voyages to India in the 1770s before he became a director of the East India Company. A son, grandson and great-great-grandson joined the civil service in Madras, a great-grandson became chief commissioner of Assam, and John, the representative of the sixth generation, was a member of the Indian Political Service, a career that involved a brief change of continents in 1936 when he was sent to Addis Ababa to defend the British Legation at the time of Mussolini's invasion of Ethiopia.†

The Cottons and other dolphin families clearly felt a compulsion to follow their ancestors in their careers: a sense of duty, a belief in tradition, a feeling that they would be letting down their family and their

---

* Their hereditary calling in the eighteenth century had been fighting for the Jacobite cause, for which one of them, Sir John Wedderburn, had been executed for treason.
† After Independence he joined the Foreign Office, returned to Africa and ended his career as ambassador to the Congo Republic and Burundi.

country if they did not carry on the custom. No doubt some sense of satisfaction would be experienced by achieving something similar to what your father had achieved and then by watching your son start climbing the same rungs after you. Yet there was nothing cosy and sentimental about the process of succession. It was not like inheriting an estate or entering the family firm when father and son could sit by the fireside with a drink in their hands and chat about planting trees or the next business deal. Dolphins of different generations hardly saw each other: the father was usually about to retire just as the son was beginning his career. In the only period when two generations of Cottons were in India at the same time, they were unable to meet because they were living so far apart, one up in Assam and the other in Madras.

After thirty years' service, Kipling's Colonel Chin retired and sailed for Britain; as his steamer went through the Suez Canal, it 'passed the outward-bound troopship, carrying his son eastward to the family duties'. Even if that generational handover seems a little too poignant, similar transfers were taking place all the time. One Resident in Kashmir, Adelbert Talbot, retired in the same month as his son Addy came out to begin his career in the ICS. John Glasfurd, an engineer from the Highlands, departed from India in 1860, the year his son Fred began his Indian apprenticeship in the same profession. Father Glasfurd had lost two wives and two children in India but does not seem to have considered anything other than an Indian career for his surviving sons. While he was still working on the Subcontinent, these motherless children were being brought up by their aunt and grandmother near Inverness. Charles, the elder, never saw his father after the age of five (although he was thirty-three at the time of John's death). Nor did Fred, the younger, after he had gone out to India in 1861; a few years later, he was drowned while escorting a group of convicts to the penal settlement on the Andaman Islands.[7] Kipling would have had in mind families like the Glasfurds, the Talbots and the Cottons when he portrayed 'the soul of our sad East' as it was carried back and forth between Britain and India in the ships of the P&O Company.

> Bound in the wheel of Empire, one by one,
> The chain-gangs of the East from sire to son,
> The Exiles' Line takes out the exiles' line
> And ships them homeward when their work is done.[8]

Many dolphin families continued their voyages until Independence denied them both a vocation and a destination. Yet one of them, at a certain moment the most influential of all, petered out long before 1947. Four generations of Stracheys went out to India from the time that Henry Strachey had been Clive's secretary, and two brothers so dominated the government of Lord Mayo (1868–72) that the administration was dubbed the 'Strachey Raj'. John was a Civilian who became finance member of the Viceroy's Council and lieutenant-governor of the North-Western Provinces, while his elder brother Richard was an engineer and botanist who became secretary of the Public Works Department, inspector-general of Irrigation and president of the Famine Commission. They had another brother, William, who might have helped to expand their 'Raj' had he not decided to retire early from India and return to England, where he decided to continue living by Calcutta time, thus spending his mornings in the dark for the next fifty-six years.[9]

Richard Strachey's wife, Jane, was the daughter of a lieutenant-governor of Bengal, and her mother was a member of the premier dolphins, the Chichele Plowdens. Determined that her five sons would continue their families' traditions, she lined them up for the ICS and the Indian Army. Each in turn disappointed her. The eldest, Dick, twice failed the entrance examination to the Military Academy at Woolwich, prompting his father to moan that the 'Strachey tendency' would not be carried into the future by his offspring.[10] The second son, Ralph, failed his army medical, and the third, Oliver, gave up his plan to join the ICS because he wished to become a musician. Eventually these three did in fact have Indian careers, Dick going to India in the Rifle Brigade and ending up as a colonel, Ralph becoming chief engineer of the East Indian Railway, and Oliver, after failing to become a composer in Vienna, acquiring a job on his brother's railway.

These modest triumphs did not, however, appease their bossy and disconsolate mother, who could in any case appreciate them only in her old age. She had before then decided to focus her ambitions on her fourth son, Lytton, who had been baptized with the name of his godfather, the viceroy Lord Lytton. She wanted him to go to Balliol, then the most popular college for India's aspiring civil servants, but to his relief he was not offered a place there. Lytton had no wish to go to India, and anyway he preferred Cambridge to Oxford. He was not hostile to the Raj, unlike such friends among the Bloomsbury Group as E. M. Forster and the Woolfs; according to his biographer, he even retained a 'filial affection' for it, and as a young man he spent two and a half years writing a dissertation on Warren Hastings, defending the governor-general against the diatribes of James Mill.[11] Yet neither he nor his younger brother James wanted physically to go near the Subcontinent. To the disappointment of Jane Strachey, all her younger and more talented children – her daughters included – preferred Cambridge and Bloomsbury to India and the empire.

Dolphin families did not have to 'go it alone' in India or in retirement. Like the Rivetts and Carnacs, they often intermarried and thereby set up wider networks of relations and even more powerful dynasties. When Henry Staveley Lawrence married Phyllis Napier in 1899 and, after her death, her sister Rosamond in 1914, he united families that had governed both the Punjab and Madras. Intermarriage might sometimes lead to diversification in the family career. The Lows of Fife were essentially a military family in British India. Captain Robert had two sons and three sons-in-law in the Indian Army, and one of his grandsons became a general. But his son John married into the Shakespears, who were cousins of the Thackerays, and this large extended family, most of it living in India, became more 'Civilian'. When Richmond Thackeray, a civil servant, died in Calcutta in 1816, his five-year-old son, William Makepeace, was sent to England under the guardianship of James Monro Macnabb, who made him learn to read on board ship by ensconcing him in a coil of rope to prevent him escaping his lessons.[12] The boy never returned to India, but he retained an inquisitive interest in the lives of his cousins who remained there, and his portrait of the elderly colonel in *The Newcomes* was inspired by John Low. The less attractive figure of Jos Sedley, the portly nabob figure in *Vanity Fair*, was partly based on his cousin George Shakespear, a sad and discontented Civilian who killed himself in Geneva in 1844.

NEPHEWS AND COMPETITORS

When Napoleon Bonaparte told his brother Lucien that he was thinking of joining the East India Company, he cannot have had much idea of the nature of that institution. If he had been a mercenary fighting for a Maratha prince somewhere near Poona, his prowess might have got him co-opted by its forces in India. But in Europe he could have joined it only if he had been nominated as a cadet by one of its directors in London. Napoleon later espoused the idea of *la carrière ouverte aux talents*, but this was not a policy promoted by the EIC at the time; nor did it become one for another sixty years. The directors tended to favour their young relations, nephews, sons and cousins, and the children of their friends. They would have been extremely unlikely to select a Corsican artillery captain from Revolutionary France who had just helped defeat a British garrison and its royalist allies at the Siege of Toulon.

The EIC's Court of Directors was a self-perpetuating oligarchy which gave its members the privilege of individually choosing an agreed number of young men to become the Company's writers, cadets, surgeons, and chaplains, as well as the officers in the Bombay Marine and the London staffs of East India House and the Company's warehouses. The directors themselves were men with Indian interests and usually with Indian experience, and after they had considered candidates from their own circles, they looked at the current crop of dolphin sons to see what these had to offer. 'If one of them ran to brain,' an apologist of the system nostalgically recalled, 'we got intellectual ability of an order no competitive examination' could produce; and the lad would be duly educated to become a civil servant at the Company's college, Haileybury. But 'those of them who went to muscle' – 'passionate high-spirited' boys who were 'good examples of the English country gentleman' – were trained for the Company's armies at the military college of Addiscombe.[13]

Even beneficiaries of this system did not always condone it. Sir George Campbell, a clever and acerbic Scotsman who rose to become lieutenant-governor of Bengal, declared in his memoirs that, except in rare cases, 'there was of course no pretence that the directors went about looking for the best young men'; nepotism, he averred, was their principal motivation. No doubt it was, but they still tried to choose the best of their nephews and the most capable of their friends' sons. And some of them took the trouble to go back to their old schools and ask the current headmasters whom they should nominate.[14] It was not in a director's interest to select a boy who might embarrass him by failing the entrance exam to Haileybury, damaging the Company's reputation in India, and by incompetent behaviour ultimately jeopardizing his dividend. In any case there was a way out for nominated youths deemed incapable of passing through either of the training colleges: the Indian cavalry, where no training was needed. As the crotchety Campbell put it, 'a young man too idle or too stupid to go through Haileybury' could not be turned adrift.[15] And he could still lead a cavalry charge.

During the first half of the nineteenth century Addiscombe and Haileybury trained many of British India's most distinguished soldiers, engineers and administrators. These may not have been very representative of the British people, though perhaps no less so than Anglican bishops or members of Parliament. There was one cadet born in Montreal and educated in Quebec, and similar cases occasionally occurred. Yet most boys who went to Addiscombe had family or business ties with India and the East India Company. When John Jacob (the founder of Jacobabad in Sind) went to the college in 1826, he was following his elder brother Herbert and would be followed there by his younger one, William; one of his cousins had already studied there and was now serving in the Bombay artillery, while another was in the native infantry. Most of the EIC's officers and Civilians came from the same prosperous middle class as the directors, usually in London and southern England.*

After the dolphin families, the commonest background for the Company's employees was the vicarage. The connection between Church and Empire may now seem a little strange, but at the height of the EIC's powers the prestige, prominence and influence of the Anglican clergy were high. The directors would know vicars in the parishes of their country houses and in the districts where they lived in London, and many of them would have been taught by the dons in holy orders who staffed the colleges at Oxford and Cambridge. Vicars were more learned than most people, and they were likely not only to educate their sons well but also to encourage them to be industrious and conscientious. Besides, as few of them were wealthy enough to support idle children, their offspring had an incentive to seek skilled and remunerative employment.

A few Anglican families allowed themselves to be almost completely

---

* A significant minority came from Scotland, where its class base was slightly different. See below, pp. 99–101.

taken over by India. The Rev. Henry Lushington, vicar of Eastbourne, had three sons in the EIC, one of whom was killed in the Patna Massacre of 1763; another became a director of the Company, an MP and a baronet; and for three further generations his male posterity went into the Bengal Civil Service (and married the daughters of Civilians in Bengal), while his female descendants married men in the same line of work. A similar process took place in the family of his cousin, the Rev. James Lushington, a Cambridgeshire vicar who had five sons in the EIC, one of whom became governor of Madras (though he also spent twenty-five years as an MP, first for Rye and then for Canterbury). They were followed by a further two generations of Lushingtons serving in both the Indian Army and the civil service.[16]

The connections between Anglicanism and Anglo-India are intricately illustrated by the family of Alfred and James Lyall, brothers who reached the top of the ICS as lieutenant-governors respectively of the North-Western Provinces (1882–7) and the Punjab (1887–92). In their father's generation the eldest brother was an MP and a director of the EIC, another was in the Indian Army, a third joined the navy, a fourth was dean of Canterbury, and the fifth (the Lyalls' father) was another clergyman.* The talented Alfred had hesitated whether to accept his uncle's nomination for the EIC; one tempting option had been to try for a scholarship to Cambridge, which he was intelligent enough to have won. A man who could always see two sides of a question and who often wished he was doing something different somewhere else, he spent much of his career in India wondering whether he would have been happier in Cambridge. Sometimes in the heat and solitude of India he even wished he had had a canonry, which would have given him time to write books, for he was among the most literary of civil servants. Yet however attractive that prospect may have seemed, it would have been a disastrous choice for him. A sceptic about human motivations, he read Darwin and Renan and became a sceptic also about religion. In distinguished retirement his agnosticism flourished and

---

* Such a balance was not maintained beyond these siblings. On the Lyalls' mother's side, the Broadwoods (the family of piano-makers), their uncle was a clergyman and so were the husbands of their four maternal aunts. On their father's side five of their first cousins were also clergymen, and so were two of their brothers-in-law.

influenced a number of his younger relations so that he helped de-convert an illustrious Anglican family.[17]

The British government had been extending its control over the workings of the EIC since the 1770s, and in the middle of the nineteenth century it decided that appointments to the Indian Civil Service should be made on merit rather than through patronage. Although such a reform was not yet deemed necessary for either Britain's Home Office or its Foreign Office, Parliament decided in 1853 to recruit men to the ICS through competitive examinations. A committee headed by Lord Macaulay concluded that India should be administered not by young men rather randomly chosen and sent to Haileybury, but by 'gentlemen' educated at Oxford and Cambridge. According to one of its members, Benjamin Jowett, the future master of Balliol College, the ICS would be a splendid career for 'the picked men of the universities'. It would also solve the problem that bedevilled Oxford dons like himself when faced with an undergraduate worrying about his future and confessing that he had 'no calling to take holy orders and no taste for the Bar'.[18]

The new system certainly broadened the class base of potential recruits, opening up the possibility of an Indian career to thousands of young men who had never met a director of the EIC. One group that suffered from the change was the dolphin families, whose sons might retain their fervour for the ancestral profession but who now had to compete with well-educated rivals in exams. Clergymen's sons, by contrast, suffered no such problems and did even better in the competition than they had done under patronage. Between 1860 and 1874 they provided over a quarter of the entrants into the ICS and a high proportion of lieutenant-governors; at the beginning of the twentieth century almost half of the most senior Civilians came from this very small social sub-class in England. After them came the sons of doctors and surgeons, who supplied a tenth of the new recruits, followed by children of lawyers, bankers and industrialists. Over three-quarters of the new ICS came from the Church and the professional middle classes.[19]

The class composition of the service reflected the status of the public schools educating the candidates. As fewer than 10 per cent of Civilians came from the aristocracy or the landed gentry, Eton and Harrow naturally did not figure very highly in the list of entrants' schools. An Etonian education might be regarded as an advantage for viceroys and the governors of Madras and Bombay, but it may even have been a drawback for civil servants: the wife of one of these complained that her British neighbours in India could not forgive the couple because her husband had been to Eton, both of them read books, and neither had been brought up in a suburb.[20]

More popular schools for aspiring imperialists were those where the fees were lower than at Eton and Harrow and where the curriculum concentrated more on subjects likely to be useful in India such as mathematics and languages rather than the traditional Latin and Greek. One such institution was Cheltenham College which in the half-century before 1889 claimed to have educated 65 Indian civil servants and as many as 1,771 officers of the British and Indian armies.[21] The next most favoured 'middle-class' schools were Marlborough College and the Rugby of Dr Arnold's successors.[22] Regional affiliations were also influential in a parent's choice of school for his sons. Candidates for the ICS from Devon were nearly always educated at Blundell's School in Tiverton.

In the twentieth century the number of schools educating entrants to the ICS increased enormously. The *India Office List* of 1938, which published career notes on all Civilians who were then still alive, names 285 schools from Swansea Grammar to Gordon's, Aberdeen, and Clongowes Wood College in County Kildare. Rugby and Marlborough remained popular among the traditional institutions, but Cheltenham had dropped behind St Paul's in London and was now less esteemed than Winchester, a school where the traditional sense of public service had become directed towards India as well as within Britain. Also in the 1938 List are schools that did not appear in earlier lists such as Wintringham Secondary in Grimsby and Washington Secondary in Durham. Such names, together with those of a large number of grammar schools, indicate how the ICS had become more open to families from the working class and the lower middle class. Between 1900 and the Second World War the grammar schools of Bedford, Bradford, Aberdeen and St Olave's each provided more civil servants than such established public schools as Radley, Stowe, Oundle, Sherborne and Tonbridge. With the help of school scholarships, what had been a socially elitist civil service could now include a mill worker's son from Yorkshire, a teacher's son from Wandsworth, a house-furnisher's son from Dundee and a stationmaster's son from Taunton. Bill Cowley was an orphan from Middlesborough who lived with his grandfather, who was a carpenter, and got into the ICS after winning a scholarship to Cambridge.[23]

According to Kipling, clever Chins went into the Civil Service, and dull Chins entered 'the Woods and Forests'. In fact it was not as straightforward as that. Most men joined the Indian Forest Service for reasons of temperament, interest and opportunity rather than because they were not intelligent enough to pass the ICS exams; many of them were attracted by solitude, the outdoor life and the opportunity to shoot game in the jungles. There was actually a degree of overlap between the services, both matrimonially and professionally, and for years a Civilian was conservator of forests in the Punjab. If the department lacked the prestige of the other services, this was chiefly a consequence of British ignorance and lack of interest in the subject. Although local 'conservatorships' had been set up in the 1840s and 1850s, the Indian Forest Service was not established until 1864 and its department did not begin to function properly for several years after then.

At that time Britain itself did not possess public forests managed by trained professionals: its woods, privately owned, were valued as much for their sport and scenic beauty as for their timber; besides, the demands of naval construction had largely exhausted the supply of oak trees. The Indian government's first problem, therefore, was to find men capable of heading its new department. Surprisingly and courageously, it decided that there were no Britons suitable for the post and so appointed a German, Herr Dietrich Brandis, as inspector-general of forests. Even more surprisingly, for another thirty-six years it held on to the belief that only a German expert was fit to run Britain's Indian woodlands. Brandis was succeeded by Wilhelm Schlich, who became a British citizen and was knighted for his achievements, and then by Berthold Ribbentrop, who held the post until the start of the twentieth century.

It was almost as difficult to find suitable subordinates, except for men who had studied at forestry schools in Germany and France. The early British recruits were a medley of army officers who were fond of hunting, medical officers who enjoyed botany, tea and coffee planters who had not been successful, and Allen Thornton Shuttleworth, who, in 1863, after several years in the Indian Naval Service, decided he preferred land to sea and spent the next thirty-six years in the forests of western India.[24] The medley did not end there but included policemen, surveyors, Eurasians, 'country-born' British and at least one Dutchman, a Dr Slym, who had practised medicine on a Dutch ship and in Burma before joining the Forest Service and later writing a *Treatise on the Treatment of Elephants in Health and Disease*. The amateur approach to recruitment gradually became more organized, and applicants soon had to pass exams at special schools before continuing their training in France and, until 1914, in Germany. Yet the service remained more open than others, more receptive to the dreams and fancies of restless boys gazing at the pink areas of the schoolroom map and wondering where they might find a satisfyingly adventurous life. A child of the Hebrides could envisage a career as a forester in India as easily as a veteran of the Great War who had read Kipling in convalescence and yearned to work in the Punjab.[25]

SOLDIERING BY CHANCE

John Norton, a Birmingham lad born in 1801, found himself at the age of sixteen fitting chandeliers to the ceiling of the Crown and Anchor public house in the Strand in London. Since enlisting in the Royal Navy two years earlier, he had already seen something of the world, even sailing down the Atlantic to St Helena, where he had managed to share a plate of biscuits with Napoleon. On his return, his mother had made him promise not to go to sea again, and so now he found himself working for a brass fitter in Holborn. When the work at the Crown and Anchor finished, he was contemplating what to do next when he met a soldier in the EIC who told him that mechanics prospered in India and advised him to go there. John duly visited a recruiting sergeant, enlisted in the Company's artillery and went to India, where some years later he erected the machinery of the Bombay Mint.[26]

John Norton's Indian career may have been the result of a chance encounter in the Strand, but he made a conscious decision to go to India. Other men also enlisted with the intention of getting there, often for the reasons that the Duke of Wellington had given for many of the men who had joined his armies: some 'from having got bastard children – some for minor offences – many more for drink'.[27] If the

British Army in Europe was a convenient refuge for rogues evading the law, the Army in India was an even better place in which to conceal an identity and a doubtful past. We have already met Mauger Monk, who changed his name and enlisted in the EIC artillery probably to escape his debtors, as well as his future father-in-law, Benjamin Levi, who had served in India in the 8th Dragoons 'having got into trouble over a girl' at home. There were many like them who went to India to escape. Yet numerous other soldiers found themselves on the Subcontinent by chance, or at least without having chosen to be there, especially since the introduction of the short service system in 1870, after which men were sent to India in greater numbers than before. When joining their local regiment in Britain, men often had little idea where they would be sent, especially in time of war. They might be dispatched to Dublin or Cairo or the Cape; they might be sent for a brief stint to Malta and a longer one to India and thence unexpectedly find themselves in Kandahar in a war in Afghanistan. Sometimes they might not receive a hint that their destination was India until injections and vaccinations had begun, confirmation coming when they were issued with shorts, topis and angola shirts.

Soldiers' parents might naturally be upset to learn that their sons were going to India. It was 'absolute lunacy', Private John Fraser's mother exclaimed, on hearing that her boy was going there with the Northumberland Fusiliers. In her opinion it was 'such a land of blood-thirsty atrocities' that he 'might as well go and commit suicide straightaway'.[28] Norman Wisdom's parents, by contrast, do not seem to have cared that he was sent to India, certainly not his violent bully of a father, who had kicked and 'walloped' him all through his child-hood. And the boy did not mind where he went as long as he escaped from Paddington and a life of beatings, barefoot walks to school and, later, sleeping on the streets. He tried a spell as a cabin boy on a ship and afterwards joined the 10th Hussars as a band boy. At the age of fifteen the diminutive lad, not quite five feet tall, was learning the clarinet and trumpet in Lucknow. He was soon also playing the xylophone and three other instruments, singing solos in garrison concerts and learning to tap-dance like Fred Astaire, though more comically, arms flailing, in his army boots; at the same time he learned to trip and fall over things in a way that made people laugh. The officers appreciated him in the Mess – 'Cerry orn, Wisdom! Good work, leddie!' – and by the time he returned to England in 1936 he had done the apprenticeship that would take him to the Collins' Music Hall in Islington and later to fame as a great comedian in the cinema. In later life he admitted that he owed 'everything of my good fortune to the army'. [29]

While joining a regiment might not help you find out where you were going, belonging to one did not necessarily reveal from where you had come. Although the regional affiliations of a unit obviously had historical origins, with time these often became inaccurate and sometimes completely misleading. A Welshman who went to India with the Welch Fusiliers early in the twentieth century observed that there were 'not three hundred . . . proper Welshmen' in his battalion of a thousand; the other 700 men were 'Cockneys and Midlanders', and over the next few years the proportions changed further, the Welshmen and Cockneys getting fewer and the Midlanders becoming so numerous that by 1914 the battalion was jokingly known as the Birmingham Fusiliers. In the late 1920s the East Yorkshire Regiment, stationed in Lucknow, was even more of a misnomer: 90 per cent of its men were Geordies from Newcastle and the north-east, a proportion that continued with successive drafts until 1933, when the annual draft consisted entirely of Londoners. [30]

Regional affiliation may have been stronger on the whole in Scotland, recruits to the KOSB (the King's Own Scottish Borderers) usually coming from the counties on the Border. But there the choice of regiments could be influenced by feelings of romanticism, clannishness and historical sentimentality. Men remembered which sides their ancestors had fought on in the civil wars of the 1640s and in the Jacobite rebellions of 1689, 1715 and 1745–6 (which, whatever else they were, were Scottish civil wars as well), and they chose their regiments accordingly. Kipling confessed that he had been taught by his mother (a Macdonald) 'never to like a Campbell' because of that clan's anti-Jacobite history and the massacre carried out by soldiers of a Campbell regiment against the Macdonalds of Glencoe in 1692; even in middle age, while admiring the scenery of 'enemy' territory in Argyllshire, he found himself 'cursing all Campbells'. [31] Other people shared his prejudices. Memories of two or three centuries past could still determine the career of an aspiring soldier in the Highlands. When Donald Currie, who made his name in the Indian Forest Service, wanted to enlist in the First World War, his mother (again a Macdonald) told him to join a 'decent' Scottish regiment and steer clear of the Argyll and Sutherland

Highlanders, which, she said, was full of Campbells. Donald thus dutifully joined the Cameron Highlanders, a regiment originally raised from a clan that, like most of the Macdonalds, had 'come out' for the Stuart cause in the three Jacobite rebellions.[32]

Soldiers who went to India by chance and sometimes with reluctance were usually glad to come home again when their 'time expired' after six or twelve years abroad. Yet a good many of them were reluctant to leave because they had come to like the country or because they had found a nice post-army job or often because they had married a local girl – British, Indian, Eurasian or Burmese – and preferred to remain in India with her family than take her back to Britain. John O'Brien, Billy Connolly's ancestor,* was one of many men who retired to Bangalore with an Indian wife. Soldiers who had left the colours often found jobs in the various forces of the Indian Police, which were also a tempting destination both for demobbed soldiers after the First World War and for former members of the Royal Irish Constabulary, which was disbanded in 1922 after the establishment of the Irish Free State. Philip Banham had worked for a bakery in Paignton, but the war took him to the north-western frontier and to much of western India, and at the end of it he was not tempted to return to baking. So he joined the Bombay Police as a traffic sergeant and by 1936 he was a superintendent. In many cases the deciding factor was human relationships. One reliable police sergeant in Burma at the end of the Raj was a man who had come out with a Scottish regiment, married a Burmese girl and, at the end of his army service, joined the Rangoon Police.[33]

As with police officers, army officers naturally had more control of their destiny than men from the rank and file. Unlike in Britain, there were seldom great social differences in the Indian Army between officers in the cavalry, the infantry and the artillery: one thing that nearly all of them had in common was that they were not rich enough to belong to a smart regiment in the British Army. As with Indian Army officers, police careers might run in families, with sons following their fathers into the same province as well as the same profession. There was also some interchange between the two services, with army officers sometimes employed as policemen when a new territory such as Upper Burma was brought under British control. And it was possible to

---

* See above, pp. 1–2.

buy oneself out of the British Army, as Herman Luker did, and join the Indian Police, a career embraced by several generations of his second wife's family. Herman had left Gloucestershire as a lad to enlist, he had fought in China at Peking and the Taku Forts, and had been transferred to India after the Rebellion. There, at the cantonment station of Barrackpore, he had married the daughter of an army widow and decided to stay in the country, buying himself out of the army and being welcomed as an inspector of police.[34]

As with the other services, careers in the Indian Police were often the result of chance encounters. University students at the end of their courses might be wondering what to do with their lives when they suddenly met someone who said, 'What about the police? Why don't you join me at Hendon Police College?' In 1872 C. E. Coles was given a job in the Bombay Police by the then governor as a reward for 'some small assistance to his sister in the matter of a savage Newfoundland dog'. His unpremeditated rescue action led to a lengthy career in the police both in India and Egypt, where he was known as 'Coles Pasha', the name under which he wrote his memoirs.[35] As with the other services, the career could of course appeal to young men without Indian connections, the very idea of keeping order in a distant imperial domain being a sufficient draw for a certain kind of recruit. Yet one significant difference between the police and the other services, especially the Indian Army, was the attitudes to officers of mixed race. It may not be very relevant that Eric Handyside was half Cornish and half Russian, or that other successful officers had mothers from continental Europe, although possession of a double identity like theirs might make it easier for a man to understand and penetrate a complicated criminal underworld than an all-English one nurtured in the Home Counties and educated at Cheltenham.

It was certainly easier if the officer had Indian blood, like Charles Forjett, who was superintendent of the Bombay Police in the mid-nineteenth century: such a man, with native languages and a dark complexion, and with an innate understanding of the variety of Indian customs, had a good chance of finding out what was happening in the bazaars of his city. Another almost legendary figure was John Paul Warburton, who was certainly half Afghan (through his mother) and may have been wholly so (depending on whether she was already pregnant when she escaped her Afghan husband to fall into the arms of her protector, Ensign Robert Warburton). Regarded as India's greatest detective, he became known as the 'Controller of Devils' and was probably a model for Kipling's fictional character Strickland, who spends his leave disguised as an Indian, 'swallowed up for a while' by the Subcontinent, and who after his marriage hears the sound of the bazaars beseeching him to return and take up his wanderings and his discoveries.[36] British literature loves characters such as Sherlock Holmes and Percy Blakeney who deceive their friends and acquaintances (and in Blakeney's case his own wife) with impossible accents and disguises. Yet Warburton/Strickland was in fact a plausible figure. So was the explorer Richard Burton, perhaps another model for Strickland, who after his years in the Indian Army could pass himself off on his journey to Mecca as a Persian, a dervish and a Pathan. Not many Englishmen could do that, but then not many could speak – as Burton could – twenty-nine languages and twelve dialects.

Few such exotic figures inhabited the Indian Medical Service (IMS). From the mid-nineteenth century it was difficult for doctors in India to belong to anything other than the British middle classes because they had to study for five years at home and be able to afford the fees required to do so. Yet that had not been the case with the earlier medical men in the East India Company. The 'surgeons' sent out in the first EIC ships were ill paid, ill educated and ill considered; their medieval association with apothecaries and barbers still lingered. They were also often extremely young, boys who, it might be hoped, had attended some classes in a hospital but who were not required to pass any exams before they practised. The routines of their careers were naturally not very tempting for later and more educated doctors. Working onboard ship, sometimes spending two years going to India and then on to China or Malaya before coming back, was for most an unpleasant experience: it could be too cold in the Channel, too hot in Bengal, too dangerous everywhere and yet at the same time crushingly monotonous, a life of drudgery and routine punctuated by scurvy and other illnesses. Surgeons often made the journeys just to acquire enough money to set up practices on dry land; sometimes they got off their ships at Madras or Calcutta and carried on their careers in those cities. Others, especially in the eighteenth century, were too discouraged by their experiences onboard to remain in the medical profession indefinitely. A number of future nabobs, such as John Holwell and

Joseph Hume, were surgeons or surgeons' mates before they worked for the Bengal government and in due course amassed their fortunes.

The skills and status of surgeons in India improved towards the end of the eighteenth century, when they were given military rank and attached to regiments in the army. The pay was good enough to tempt the poet John Keats who in 1819, troubled by poverty, illness and bad reviews, contemplated his future and concluded that being a 'surgeon to an India-man' would probably be his fate: his choices in life seemed limited to one of 'two Poisons', either 'leading a feverous life alone with Poetry' or else 'voyaging to and from India for a few years'.[37] As standards advanced, and surgeons were required to pass exams, the prestige of the service rose. By the end of the nineteenth century the class backgrounds of the IMS were not so very different from those of the ICS: entrants tended to come from business, manufacturing and medical families, yet others were the sons of vicars, soldiers and officials in India.[38]

Yet recruitment here, as in the other services, remained unpredictable, even arbitrary; boys could join up by accident or sometimes indeed almost by mistake. Owen Berkeley-Hill's career in the IMS was, as he admitted, the 'outcome of a row' with his widowed mother. He had inherited a little money of his own (providing an income of £150 a year), he enjoyed free board and lodging at home in London, and as a medical student he was spending his time as an unpaid assistant at the London Lock Hospital, 'learning something about anaesthetics and something about venereal disease'. Many mothers might have considered this a reasonable apprenticeship for their son, but Mrs Berkeley-Hill did not. One day she denounced Owen's idleness and lack of ambition with such fervour that, in order 'to placate' her, he promised to apply for the IMS and take its exam as soon as possible. This was, as he recalled in old age, 'the stupidest act' of his entire life, because no one could have been 'less amenable to military discipline' than himself. When the colonel in charge of his training showed him an army regulation that 'forbade an officer to shave his upper lip' (i.e. he was being ordered to grow a moustache), Owen became so angry that he decided to provoke his superior on as many occasions as possible: he even brought his own decanter of port into the communal suppers. Despite this unpromising start, he joined the IMS in 1907, became an expert on 'nervous disorders' and spent fifteen years in charge of the mental hospital in Ranchi.[39]

BOXWALLAHS AND PLANTERS

'Wallah' is a Hindustani suffix denoting a man who is occupied in doing something indicated by the preceding noun. A punkah wallah, for example, was an Indian who pulled the rope of a large and inefficient cloth fan known as a punkah. Yet wallahs were not necessarily Indians. An 'amen wallah' was an army chaplain, a 'lemonade wallah' was a teetotaller, a 'puzzled wallah' was a soldier who had gone insane and was being repatriated to Britain, and a 'competition wallah' was a man who had joined the civil service after passing a competitive set of exams. In most cases there was something slightly pejorative, or at any rate condescending, about the suffix. A jungle wallah suggested not merely a forestry officer but one who had lived so long in the jungles that he had become 'jungly' and uncouth and unfit for 'polite society'.

'Boxwallah' was also a word often used pejoratively. In Hindustani it meant an itinerant pedlar, an Indian seller of small household goods, or, when anglicized, the much lampooned commercial traveller. In English it denoted someone originally dealing with bales and boxes, a merchant or later a businessman, a term spoken with an unflattering stress, as if the man in question was not quite 'proper', perhaps rather 'flash' and maybe even a bit of a bounder, the sort of chap who in the 1930s might wear a white suit and two-tone co-respondent shoes. Whatever else he might be, he could not be considered a 'pukka sahib', a real gentleman. Snobbery about the species was inherent in the word, and it was engraved on the tablets of the social hierarchy. Its members allegedly went to India not for Glory or Ideals but simply to make money; even worse, they did not care about the people of India and their welfare. If officers of the army and the civil service looked down on the boxwallah, their memsahibs would probably sneer even more obviously at his wife. In Calcutta, a city whose prosperity was created by businessmen, this snootiness was prolonged even beyond Indian Independence: in the 1950s a former civil servant's family could disapprove of a daughter's fiancé because he belonged to a company that managed jute mills, coal mines and tea gardens.[40]

The snobbery was bizarre, misplaced and in any case inconsistent. For much of its history the merchants and officers of the East India Company had been the same people. Even after the division had been made, young men recruited to different professions could come from the same backgrounds and sometimes the same educational establishments. King's was one of the Cambridge colleges most proficient at educating probationers of the ICS, but it also had a tradition of sending 'Kingsmen' into the Bombay Burmah Trading Company, which was run by the brother of the senior tutor, W. H. Macaulay.[41] And although many clubs might shun the boxwallah, one of the oldest and most prestigious did not. The rules of the Bengal Club, founded in 1827, stated that at least one hundred of its members must be residents of the city who did not belong to the British Army or to any of the services of the EIC. As a result, many of its founding members were businessmen, managing agents and directors of the Bank of Hindustan.[42]

An anthropology of boxwallahs would at some points resemble one about members of any of the official services. Sons of the gentry, sons of the vicarage, offspring from commercial and professional families, boys from public schools, boys from grammar schools, graduates from the universities – all went to India to work for commercial enterprises. When looking for suitable recruits, businesses often regarded character, sporting prowess and the ability to 'fit in' socially above other considerations. The founder of Parry's, the most famous trading firm in the whole of southern India, was the second son of a Welsh country squire, Edward Parry of Leighton Hall in Montgomeryshire. As with the services, sons followed fathers into their profession as businessmen: a hundred years after the birth of Parry's, its retired directors in Britain were still encouraging their sons to join the company in Madras.[43] Boys went out to join an uncle on a coffee plantation, a very risky business, or in equally hazardous concerns such as a tobacco firm, a stud farm or a coconut plantation (an industry the Indians were more successful at), harvesting the fruit and selling the coir for matting and the copra for oil. When an entrepreneur established a business in India, it was natural for his sons and other relations to join him in the enterprise. John Maxwell, a son of the manse from Aberdeenshire, established a dynasty of indigo planters near Kanpur; the Rev. Henry Baker of the Church Missionary Society founded a line of tea and coffee planters in Travancore.[44]

Patterns of settlement in India occasionally reflected a regional expertise in Britain. Mining for tin may be very different from mining for gold, but perhaps there was some logic in the fact that the mining engineers at the Kolar Gold Field in south India were Cornish except for one man – and he came from Devon. It might also have been understandable for the Tinplate Company to set up a mill manned by eighty-eight Welshmen, though it is not easy to fathom why the mill's joint owners (Tata Iron and Steel) pursued such a different policy of recruitment close by at its steelworks at Jamshedpur, where the skilled workers came from almost every European country except France. Typical of the employment structure of British-owned companies in India were the Buckingham and Carnatic Cotton Mills, which were 'managed by Scots, with Lancashire men in charge of the spinning and weaving departments, and Leeds graduates for dyeing and finishing'.[45] The rest of the workforce was Indian.

The Scots in India, who will be discussed separately in the next section, had a role in business, industry and the plantations out of all proportion to their numbers within the population of Great Britain. They went to India as apprentices seemingly prepared to work in – and eventually run – any business from a managing agency to a flotilla river company. They were prominent in the factories of Bombay and Kanpur, they dominated the tea plantations of the south, and they – specifically, those who came from Dundee – ran the jute industry in Bengal. In Coonor, a hill station of the south, Scottish tea planters built themselves numerous bungalows, many of which still exist, named after remembered places of home such as Strathmore, Blair Gowrie and – more pretentiously or perhaps just more teasingly – Blair Atholl.

The first British planters in India were men who oversaw the production of indigo for export to Europe. Some of the earliest came from the West Indies, where the production of indigo was giving way to sugar, and some were former mercenaries with the Marathas who changed profession at the beginning of the nineteenth century. They lived deep in the country districts of Bihar and Bengal and put down 'roots' more firmly than any other group in British India. In the early decades of their prosperity their lives were redolent of the Middle Ages, revolving around horses and hunting and prodigious bouts of feasting and dancing. The planters were 'squireens' living bucolically in a bungalow that was more like a mansion or a manor house. They did not care much for the authority of the EIC, and many of them came not to care very much for Britain itself. Generations of them stayed put, becoming 'country-born' and in many cases marrying Indian women. Most of them could have afforded to educate their children in England, but they did not see the point: 'Indianized' and tending to regard themselves as 'white natives', they sent them to schools in Darjeeling or to the La Martinière schools in Lucknow and Calcutta.

It is impossible to write generally about the social origins of planters and businessmen because so many of their careers happened by chance. An army sergeant on the eve of retirement might suddenly find an opportunity in the coffee business; a missionary's son stifling in the Plains might yearn for a tea plantation in the hills. Businessmen often had so many different interests that they defy professional categories. The first jute mill in India was set up by a coffee planter from Ceylon. Among the small entrepreneurial community of Kanpur the sheer diversity of business was remarkable. John Maxwell, the progenitor of the indigo dynasty, was also a journalist (editor of the *India Gazette*) who made money from the cotton and rum industries. Other men's combinations in the town were made up of sugar, railways, sawn timber and opium. David Begg, a doctor in Kanpur from the 1830s, combined his medical duties with trading in wine, saltpetre, indigo seed and the hides of animals.[46]

What planters, boxwallahs and other businessmen of British India had in common was not so much social class or regional origin as a temperament open to the appeal of distant opportunity, to the lure of Calcutta or of a hillside with potential, a personality willing to take risks, the talent to see an opening that no one else had yet seen. A business career was usually unpredictable, and it was often lonely. Unlike officers of the army or the civil service, the boxwallah did not enjoy the camaraderie of the Mess or the support of the district officer and his team. Yet also unlike them, he did not have to spend his entire career in India. Working for a British firm, at least in the later years of the Raj, meant that Indian sojourns could often be punctuated by spells in its London offices.

CELTS AND NORTH BRITONS

When a stranger asked, 'Are you a Cork man, sir?' Richardson Evans answered in the affirmative, 'half with pride at being one and half with pride that I had been taken for an Englishman'.[47] Young Evans, an orphan who entered the ICS in 1867, thereby encapsulated the ambivalent feelings of many Irishmen living and working in India. He was simultaneously proud of being Irish, of seeming to be English and of being part of the British imperial enterprise.

The Irish soldier in India was a familiar figure long before Kipling immortalized him in fiction as Private Terence Mulvaney. In the nineteenth century he and his compatriots made up half of the British troops in India, most of them Catholics motivated by pay, food and the prospect of adventure, men largely indifferent to the currents of Anglophobia swirling at home. Ireland also produced some of British India's finest generals, including Fred Roberts, Arthur Wellesley and Eyre Coote, the man who saved Madras from Haidar Ali's forces in the early 1780s. All three of these officers belonged, however, to the Protestant gentry.

Few civil servants in the early nineteenth century came from Ireland – only about one in twenty – and those who did were almost invariably Protestants from the north. The introduction of competition for the ICS briefly increased their numbers in mid-century, Trinity College Dublin proving adept at preparing candidates for the exams, but these soon returned to something like the previous ratio. As in England, applicants usually came from the urban middle classes. John Lawrence's father was the son of a mill owner from Derry, while his mother was the daughter of a clergyman from Donegal; his successor as lieutenant-governor of the Punjab, Robert Montgomery, was the grandson of a wine and spirits merchant from Londonderry. Belonging to a later generation, Richardson Evans had a background that seemed even more unpropitious to imperial adventure: his grandfather had been a cobbler, and his father had been a bookseller whose 'Tract Shop' had been popular with the Evangelical clergy of Cork and its surroundings.[48]

Protestants outnumbered Catholics in the ICS in inverse proportion to their numbers in Ireland: that is by about four to one. Yet a number of Catholics from modest rural backgrounds far from Belfast or Dublin enjoyed illustrious and sometimes controversial Civilian careers. Anthony MacDonnell was brought up in a village in Galway, while Michael O'Dwyer was one of fourteen children raised on a farm near Tipperary. MacDonnell, who at the end of the nineteenth century ruled nearly 48 million Indians as lieutenant-governor of the North-Western

Provinces, found no difficulty in combining his role as a professional imperialist with his support for Irish nationalism and Home Rule. Nor did Charles James O'Donnell, born in Donegal in 1849, who believed in 'the supremacy of the Celt' over 'the Saxon element' in Britain and yet was still proud to belong to a largely English ICS. His real name was actually Macdonald, but he had changed it to assist the political ambitions of his brother, who thought the name sounded too Scottish and who entered the House of Commons in 1874 as an Irish nationalist under the name of Frank Hugh O'Donnell. From their bases in Europe and Asia the brothers promoted Home Rule in both Ireland and India, indeed 'Home Rule All Round, radiating from the centre of a really imperial Parliament' at Westminster.[49]

The Irish fared well at the higher end of the administration in the last decades of the nineteenth century. They produced successive vice-roys (Dufferin and Lansdowne), half the members of the Viceroy's Council in 1886, and in the course of the 1890s rulers of seven of the eight Indian provinces, including Burma. (Only the Bombay governor-ship was unhibernicized.) Not all of them were Protestants. Apart from MacDonnell, who at different times headed four provincial govern-ments, the Catholic community was represented by Dennis Fitzpatrick, who was chief commissioner of both Assam and the Central Provinces as well as lieutenant-governor of the Punjab. Another Catholic, O'Donnell, reached the senior ranks of the ICS despite repeated insub-ordination and criticisms of his superiors that would have had him court-martialled in the army and sacked in any other profession; although he was twice demoted and three times transferred, he suc-ceeded in becoming a collector and retired as a commissioner.

The success of the Irish in the ICS did not mean that they were always admired by their British colleagues. O'Donnell was tolerated, partly because he was a competent official but mainly because the India Office in London and the government in Calcutta did not want him to return home, join forces with his brother Frank and make a nuisance of himself at Westminster.*[50] Even less controversial Irishmen were not always appreciated by the India Office. When Lord Minto, the viceroy,

---

* After his retirement he did go to Westminster, as a Liberal MP from 1906 to 1910, but he greatly disliked his own party in government, especially its leader Asquith, who refused to recommend him for a knighthood.

tried to convince John Morley, the secretary of state, to promote Louis Dane, a Protestant from Wexford, the cabinet minister expressed misgivings because 'Irish gentlemen' were 'not always accurate or sure-footed'.[51]* More justified criticism, though less justifiably expressed, was made of two Irishmen tainted by the Amritsar Massacre of 1919, Brigadier Dyer (who carried it out) and Sir Michael O'Dwyer, the lieutenant-governor of the Punjab who defended the action afterwards. The blunders, observed Harcourt Butler, who was then lieutenant-governor of the neighbouring United Provinces, were committed by a 'countrybred Irishman' (i.e. one born in India) and a 'low-bred' Irish-man from Tipperary. Dyer was an *indigène enragé*; no British man would have behaved like he had done. 'Had we had Englishmen in their places the trouble would not have arisen, or would not have reached anything like the same dimensions.'[52]

The Scots in India were spread across a far wider range of professions than the Irish. Even before the Act of Union of 1707, the East India Company had employed them as merchants and ship's surgeons. Subsequently they went out also as soldiers, administrators and engineers, and later still as planters, businessmen, missionaries and teachers. Scotland enjoyed an advantage in the field of medicine after Edinburgh University opened its medical school in 1726, and it retained a disproportionate influence there until the end of the Raj: three of the first five director-generals of the Indian Medical Service were Scots. Individual stories of young Scotsmen determined to become doctors in India are abundant in each century of British rule: one young Highlander, Duncan Finlayson, even financed his training at Glasgow Medical School by playing professional rugby in Motherwell.[53] The country's teachers showed a comparable dedication from the days of the early Church of Scotland missions in the 1830s. Chakravarti Rajagopalachari, a close colleague of Gandhi who became premier of Madras in the 1930s, was so grateful to his Scottish teacher at Central College in Bangalore that he kept a photograph of him on his bookcase until the end of his life. Although he never visited Scotland nor sampled its whisky, this wise,

* Dane had, very unusually, retired midway through his ICS career, but as his wife had found Ireland 'intolerable after India', he had asked to return. He became Resident in Kashmir and then secretary to the Foreign Department before Minto overcame Morley's objections and gave him the lieutenant-governorship of the Punjab.

teetotal and vegetarian statesman remained a devotee of Walter Scott's novels, and in 1938 he disregarded a Congress taboo by attending a St Andrew's Day dinner in Madras.[54]

Scottish regiments were among the first to be sent to India in the eighteenth century, defending the Company's positions against its French and Indian adversaries, and Scottish generals such as Hector Monro and David Baird were substantial figures in the enlargement of its territories in Bengal and the south. By 1800 Scots in the military were outnumbered by the Irish, but soldiering in India remained a popular career for them. Robbie Burns himself may have been more of a rebel than an imperialist, but two of his sons went to India and became lieutenant-colonels in the Company's forces; and both a daughter-in-law and a grandson of the Ayrshire bard are buried in the cantonment cemetery of Neemuch in Gwalior. Scottish officers in the Indian Army were eager to join the regiments of the Dogras, Hindus from the Himalayan foothills, because they were fellow hillmen who enjoyed playing pipes and dancing reels.[55] Highland regiments such as the Gordons often had a battalion in India, yet there was no question of them dressing for the climate or resembling their English colleagues: out they went with kilt, plaid and hose, plus tartan trews with yellow stripes running through the dark squares of blue, black and green. As in England and Ireland, many of the Scottish rank and file ended up in India because they had failed to find employment at home. A battalion of the Highland Light Infantry stationed in Bangalore in the 1920s may have looked very smart and Highland, wearing trews and glengarries, when it was marching on parade. But its ranks consisted almost entirely of short and stocky Lowlanders, usually Glaswegians from the Gorbals, who could find no work in Scotland. In India they proved to be often violent and difficult to control, especially at Hogmanay, and were sent on long route marches as punishment.[56]

Anyone looking at the lists of EIC employees at the beginning of the nineteenth century would think that Scots must have formed almost half the population of the British Isles. In fact they were about a tenth, some 1,600,000 people from a total of nearly 16 million. Nearly half the Writers and officer cadets appointed to Bengal in the decade after 1774 were Scots; so were more than half the medical recruits and 60 per cent of the 'free merchants' allowed by the Company to reside in Bengal. Traditionally it has been thought that the Scots benefited unfairly from the patronage of Henry Dundas, the powerful Edinburgh politician who was both the younger Pitt's chief ally in the north and in charge of India at Westminster as president of the Board of Control. The truth is that they had done even better under such earlier English patrons as the prime minister Robert Walpole, who was keen to demonstrate the advantages of the Union, and Warren Hastings, the governor-general so beleaguered by English enemies in Calcutta that he relied on advisers whom he called his 'Scotch guardians'.

The advantages of a Scottish education, much extolled then and since by its beneficiaries, should have helped maintain the position of Scots in the ICS after the service was opened to competition. Yet in fact the Scottish candidates performed poorly in the competitive system. 'Scotland failed egregiously,' reported the *Edinburgh Review* after the results of the first examinations revealed that only a single Scot had passed them. The fault, however, lay more with the universities than with their pupils. As Edinburgh's professor of Greek pointed out, several of the subjects examined, including political philosophy and modern history, were not taught at any of the venerable Scottish institutions.[57]

As the results did not improve very much in subsequent years, young Scots turned away from administrative careers and concentrated on business and commercial opportunities in India. In these fields their education probably did assist them because Lowland academies, such as those at Irvine and Kilmarnock, where pupils could learn about surveying, navigation and book-keeping, must have been better places to learn their trades than an English public school with its perennial emphasis on Latin and Greek. By the late nineteenth century there was hardly a commercial or industrial field in India in which Scots were not prominent. They established the oil industry in Burma; they manned the Bengal & North-Western Railway line at Gorakhpur; in the unpublished memoir of a tea planter's daughter in Travancore almost every character is a Scot from Stirling, Paisley, Dundee or the Black Isle.[58] In the 1930s the Irrawaddy Flotilla Company possessed a fleet of 600 vessels, most of them built by Denny's Yard at Dumbarton and nearly all of them skippered by men from there or from Glasgow. The Scottish monopoly was even more complete in the production of jute, a tough natural fibre indigenous to Bengal and used for cordage and the making of sandbags. Large quantities of it were imported to Scotland and processed in Dundee until demand became so strong that Dundonians went out to Calcutta to set up factories in Bengal. By the beginning of the twentieth century there were 450 'jute wallahs' from Dundee, usually pupils of the town's High School, managing jute mills near Calcutta that employed a total of 184,000 Indians.

It is sometimes said that Scots were the eternal deputies, the permanent 'number twos' in British India, gruff, sensible, hard-working men like Kipling's engineer in 'McAndrew's Hymn', people who got things done even if their superior, perhaps a rather idle Englishman, took the credit. In fact too many of the men in control were Scottish for this to have ever been more than partially true. During the years of the Raj most British business in India was in the hands of 'managing agencies', large partnership firms, mostly based in Calcutta, that oversaw a number of disparate businesses such as jute mills, coal mines, cotton mills, paper mills and tea plantations. In 1931 the largest of these agencies was Tata, founded by the Indian Parsi family, but the next four were all Scottish in origin: Andrew Yule, Inchcape, James Finlay and Burn & Co.[59]

Scotland sent to India a good number of its middle classes, sons of the manse, sons of farmers and doctors, children of entrepreneurs in the industrializing Lowlands of the west. The four Muir brothers who went to India in the 1820s and 1830s (two dying young, the other two distinguishing themselves as both scholars and administrators) were grandsons of a grocer in Kilmarnock and sons of a man who went to Glasgow to set up a calico printing works.[60] Yet Scotland also sent out more of its landed classes than England, members of families with great estates and small rent-rolls, their younger sons going to India, as Walter Scott observed, to feed at its cornchest. The names on the gravestones in the Park Street cemetery of Calcutta are of families that have resonated in Scottish history, some of them since Bannockburn or before: Bruce, Dunbar, Lindsay, Gordon, Crawford, Ker, Inglis and Bowes-Lyon. Many of their inscriptions engraved in those pro-Union days follow their home addresses not with the word 'Scotland' but with the initials NB, North Britain.

The Scots, as we have seen earlier, tended to operate more tribally in India even than the English. In Shropshire a brother of a peer or a younger son of a baronet might be persuaded to accept a Company nomination as a Writer or a Cadet. Yet from Scotland entire families often sought to emigrate, not as a group that might go to Canada or New Zealand in order to settle, but as individuals setting off one after the other, spending their working lives in India before coming back to prosperous retirement in Scotland or, as often happened with persons now habituated to a warmer climate, the southern counties of England. The idea of India entered the head, if not perhaps always the heart, of numerous Scottish families who had friends and relations there and who understood how compatriot networks functioned and would assist them.

George Loch of Drylaw died in 1788 before he was forty after being forced to sell his estate near Edinburgh on account of debts his family had incurred through its support for the Jacobite cause. His descendants might have moped, lamenting their bad luck, and entered the annals as yet another example of romantically defunct Scottish lairds. Instead they resurrected themselves, George's sons becoming MPs, an admiral, a civil servant and a director of the EIC, and subsequent generations having extensive careers in India and the armed forces. Thirty of George's male descendants spent their professional lives in the Subcontinent, six in the civil service, more in the Indian Army, and the rest as doctors, tea planters, indigo planters, miners and engineers. Some of his great-granddaughters and great-great-granddaughters went out too: Catherine became one of the first superintendents of the Indian Nursing Service, and Margaret, after marrying an ICS officer, worked for the Bombay government during the plague epidemic of 1897; earlier she had refused the job of governess to Kaiser Wilhelm's children because she preferred to go to India.[61]

The kinship networks that nurtured Scottish careers in India simply did not exist for the population of Wales. As a notable Scottish historian has observed, 'the Welsh failed to make their mark in India . . . Apart from figures like Sir William Jones their presence in the Subcontinent was hardly noticed.'[62] Some individuals might be influential, such as Thomas Parry, the leading entrepreneur of Madras, and certainly no scholar of India was more important and consequential than Jones, the Welshman sent out as a judge of the High Court in Calcutta in 1783. A linguist so brilliant that it was joked he spoke every language except his own (Welsh), he founded the Asiatic Society and did more than anyone – British or Indian – to resuscitate Sanskrit and its remarkable ancient literature. Yet it is true that the Welsh did not

operate very often in packs in India. We have seen that the Welch Fusiliers did not in fact contain many Welshmen. Perhaps the largest Welsh
grouping in India was the missionaries, who from the 1840s usually
operated under the auspices of the Welsh Calvinistic Methodists' Foreign Missionary Society. They tended to gravitate to the north-east, to
places such as the Khasi Hills, apparently attracted by the mists and
hills that reminded them of Wales.[63] In this they resembled certain
Scottish missionaries, who were to be found in remote parts of the
Himalaya, teaching the Bible to Tibetan children.

Scots sometimes claimed that they produced the best missionaries
because they had experienced such a tough training in 'real life' in the
Edinburgh underworld of the old city and Leith. Anyone who could
'tame the savages of Canongate' or survive the city's 'depressing deprav-
ity and ungodliness' could surely handle the gentle heathens of
Hindustan.[64] Like most British people in India, apart from the NCOs
and private soldiers of the British regiments, these and other missionaries came usually from the middle classes, people who, if they were not
already in the ministry, had been students, teachers, doctors and other
professionals. The chief exceptions were 'salvationists', the 'soldiers' of
the Salvation Army who arrived in India in the 1880s. A considerable
number of them, both male and female, came from the working class.
Among those who died in India, according to their 'Promoted to Glory'
files, were former coal miners, clerks, typists, shop assistants and
domestic servants.[65]

ARISTOCRATS

The political reformer John Bright famously claimed that the British
Empire was a 'gigantic system of outdoor relief for the aristocracy of
Great Britain'. The claim was in fact inaccurate by the time he made it,
at a speech in Birmingham in 1858, but two generations earlier it would
have been at least partly true with regard to India. A dozen baronets
figure in the Bengal Civil List during the first two decades of the nineteenth century, a minority certainly but not an insignificant one. Only
one peer appears alongside them, but nineteen children of peers do,
almost invariably 'younger sons'. William Hickey noted a typical case
from the end of the eighteenth century, that of Lord Southampton,

who, 'having a numerous family with a moderate fortune to support them, was glad to accept a writership' for a younger son.[66]

Scotland, as we have already noted, sent to India a higher percentage of its aristocrats than any other part of the British Isles. The Company's lists of the later eighteenth century include sons or brothers of the earls of Strathmore, Dundonald and Bute (the prime minister), and three Lindsays from the family of the earls of Crawford and Balcarres. Several baronets and peers' sons from Scotland also joined the EIC's maritime service although few of them made it their career for life. Hugh Lindsay, the youngest son of Balcarres, left the Royal Navy when his promotion prospects looked dim, transferred to the EIC's ships, made his fortune in India and retired to enjoy a parliamentary seat and a lengthy directorship of the Company. William, a son of Lord Elphinstone, also retired early from sailing to India for the EIC, but in his case he could afford to do so because he had married an heiress.[67]

Few figures such as these appeared in India in the middle of the nineteenth century. One of the rarities who did was Lord Henry Ulick Browne, a son of the second Marquess of Sligo. Joining the ICS in 1851, Browne served the maximum number of years (thirty-five) in the service and, although he did not quite reach the top – Campbell, the lieutenant-governor of Bengal, judging that his 'many excellent qualities' were offset by 'considerable weaknesses and littlenesses'[68] – he enjoyed a distinguished career as a commissioner and member of the Bengal Board of Revenue. Retiring in 1886, he succeeded two childless brothers to become the fifth Marquess of Sligo at the age of seventy-two.

By Bright's day few aristocrats like Browne were prepared to make a career in India or the rest of the Empire, and matters did not change over the following generations. Noblemen might come out for a few years as viceroys or colonial governors, and some of them might serve in British regiments stationed, also for a limited number of years, in India. A few of them went to East Africa to settle and to farm – and often make noisy nuisances of themselves – but their imperial contribution was paltry. 'Of course,' said Lady Maud Cecil, the daughter of the prime minister Lord Salisbury, 'the best class of English don't come out to the colonies and those that do are apt to be bounders'. Raymond Asquith, the son of another prime minister, went further when he told John Buchan that 'empire' was encouraging cads to rule it: 'the day of the clever cad is at hand'.[69] One does not have to agree with either of their judgements or the ways they were expressed to accept the view that imperial administration, at every level except the highest, was not a nobleman's pursuit.

While peers' sons turned against Indian careers in the course of the nineteenth century, the names of baronets still recur in the various service lists; some of them were founding members of the Bengal Club in 1827. Several went into the military or the civil service, but the less fashionable services were not spurned. Sir Henry Farrington, the sixth baronet in his family, joined the Indian Forest Service and became chief conservator of the Central Provinces, while Sir Otway Wheeler-Cuffe from Kilkenny joined the Public Works Department and worked as a superintending engineer in Burma. Another Irishman, Sir Vere Henry Levinge of Westmeath, was a civil servant who developed the southern hill station of Kodaikanal, creating its lake by dredging and damming its streams, and then introducing fish. He is commemorated not only by a Celtic stone cross at the water's edge but also by a village in the vicinity called Levingepuram and by a temple devoted to him at Vellakavi. His popularity was such that, although he died in 1885, Indian boys in the area were still being named Levingedurai in the twenty-first century.[70]

Yet the numbers of baronets in India give a rather misleading impression. These were not landed squires, voluntarily forsaking their pheasants and woodlands to spend thirty-five years in the Punjab; Domesday Book was seldom a part of their ancestral history. Many of them were in fact sons or grandsons of soldiers and politicians who for varying reasons had been rewarded with an hereditary baronetcy rather than the more customary knighthood. They did not have estates or other forms of wealth to provide them with a livelihood. One ICS baronet was William Herschel, the grandson of the astronomer knighted for his discovery of the planet Uranus and son of another astronomer who was created a baronet for his work on stellar paradox and the southern hemisphere. William himself would have deserved a baronetcy in his own right: as a district officer in Bengal, he became the discoverer and pioneer of fingerprinting.[71]

One place in India where you would usually encounter a titled aristocrat was Government House Madras, and you would often find one also occupying Government House Bombay. Apart from the Duke of Buckingham, who governed Madras from 1875 to 1880, these occupants were never peers of the highest rank. Nor were they often men selected to govern large imperial territories because they had shown great talents in other fields. However important the jobs were, they were not very popular: there were no long queues in the House of Lords of peers eager for an Indian governorship. Some men accepted the post because they were almost professional governors doing the rounds of Ceylon, Australia and the Caribbean, but many more were rather minor politicians whose parliamentary careers were stagnating and who hoped they might be revived by a five-year spell in the Raj. As Lord Hardinge, a former viceroy, told Lord Erskine, a junior whip appointed as governor of Madras in 1934, his new job was not only 'the best post in India' after that of viceroy, but on his return it would put him 'in the running for ministerial posts and for governor-generalships'.[72]* Such men, however, were not guaranteed to shine in India. Madras might be considered the easiest province to rule, its inhabitants regarded as pliant, lethargic and unwarlike, but even a clever politician such as Mountstuart Grant Duff, a Liberal intellectual at ease at Westminster and the India Office, could destroy his reputation by an inept performance in an unfamiliar ambience after he became governor in 1881.

All the Indian provinces were headed by members of the ICS except Madras and Bombay.† These two were no larger or more important than Bengal or the United Provinces, but they had been independent of Calcutta before Warren Hastings became governor-general in 1773, and their governors had always been selected by the government in London. The expansion of the empire and the improvements in communications made their status an anomaly, one criticized by almost everyone involved in Indian administration, but the British fondness for tradition and precedent ensured that it was retained. The

---

* In Erskine's case it did not. After his return to England in 1940, he won a by-election for the Conservatives at Brighton and hoped to become part of the wartime government. But for Churchill he was too liberal on Indian matters and too attached to the appeasement policies of Neville Chamberlain. Erskine soon resigned as an MP and died in 1953 before he could succeed his father as the thirteenth earl of Mar and fifteenth earl of Kellie.

† The number of provinces altered over time, as did some of their names and the titles of their chiefs. Of the nine provinces in, for example, 1902, Madras and Bombay were administered by governors, Bengal, Burma, the United Provinces and the Punjab by lieutenant-governors, and the Central Provinces, Assam and the North-West Frontier Province by chief commissioners.

consequence was that, while the other provinces were in the hands of men seasoned by thirty years' service in India, Bombay and Madras were usually administered by men with no experience and often little knowledge of the Subcontinent. When Arthur Hope (later Lord Rankeillour) was appointed to succeed Erskine in Madras in 1939, he wrote to his predecessor, 'I have never been to India and know nothing of its life, so if I ask a lot of foolish questions you must excuse me.'[73]

After 1812 Madras had no civil service governors, though it would have had one, James Thomason, if he had not died on the day Queen Victoria signed his warrant of appointment at Balmoral. The situation at Bombay was less exclusive: four of its eighteen governors after 1812 were distinguished Civilians, including Mountstuart Elphinstone and Bartle Frere.* Yet some of its later appointments were as unsuitable and incomprehensible as Arthur Hope's. In 1894 Lord Sandhurst, a former army officer without experience of India, was preferred to Alfred Lyall, a former lieutenant-governor considered to be the ablest civil servant of his generation, partly because Sandhurst's father had been commander-in-chief in India but mainly because he was the brother-in-law of Earl Spencer, an influential ally of Gladstone and at that moment a member of Lord Rosebery's Liberal cabinet. His brother officers in the Coldstream Guards had apparently regarded him as 'incurably dense', and his officials in India considered him almost illiterate; when he was succeeded by Lord Northcote, one of them pointed out that 'at any rate he can read, which is more than can be said for Lord Sandhurst'.[74] Curzon, who was an old friend of the governor, arrived as viceroy during his tenure, railed against his 'complete administrative incompetence' and told Lord George Hamilton, the secretary of state, that they should 'sweep away these picturesque excrescences on the surface of the most specialized service in the world'.[75] After an early skirmish with Northcote, the viceroy came to realize that Sandhurst's successor was an able administrator; so did the British government, which promoted him to the governor-generalship of Australia after only three years in Bombay. Curzon was then exasperated by the appointment of another 'excrescence', Lord Lamington, an Old Etonian former MP who had happened to be the 'best man' at his wedding. As someone who, to the detriment

---

* These statistics exclude 'acting governors' often appointed for a few months to fill the gap between the death or resignation of an incumbent and the arrival of his successor.

of his future career, placed competence above friendship in political matters, the viceroy argued strenuously against the appointment of another unqualified peer to an Indian governorship. Lamington, he told Hamilton, was one of 'those delightfully irresolute people' who never knew which train to travel on; he did not even know which girl to propose to until Curzon made the choice for him.[76]

Viceroys, like the governors of Bombay and Madras, were appointed by the British government, and with the exception of John Lawrence (1864–9) they were never former members of the ICS. In their case this made sense because so much of their work consisted of persuading the government in London to support their policies that it was an advantage for them to have had political experience at Westminster. The first of the governor-generals (the earlier and statutory title of the viceroys) was a commoner, Warren Hastings, and so, a few years after him, was Sir John Shore, both members of the covenanted civil service. Yet from the tenure of Wellesley (1798–1805) the post was always held by an hereditary or recently ennobled peer except for Lawrence and Sir Henry Hardinge (1844–8). As with the governorships of Bombay and Madras, the governor-general was seldom a grandee: no Norfolks, Devonshires, Somersets or Northumberlands. Scotland may have sent more of its aristocrats to India, but these too did not come from the ducal houses: no Argylls, Atholls, Hamiltons or Buccleuchs. It was two smaller landowning families, the Bruces of Elgin and the Elliots of Minto, which between them produced four viceroys within the span of a century.

Eton College may not have been a great training ground for India's civil servants, but it was a popular nursery for viceroys and governors. Old Etonians naturally felt at ease in large mansions in the cities and in country houses on the Plains and in the Hills, and one of them (Curzon) could boast that his Indian headquarters (Government House Calcutta) was based on the same architectural plans as his ancestral home, Kedleston Hall in Derbyshire. Between 1884 and 1943 eight of the twelve viceroys were Old Etonians (two others went to Winchester and one was at Harrow), and from 1890 exactly half the governors of Bombay were educated at Eton, as were half the governors of Madras. The three Etonian viceroys of the 1890s also went to the same Oxford college, Balliol, though of the three only Curzon seemed born to the purple, a natural proconsul, one destined to rule. His predecessor, Lord Elgin, was bullied into accepting the post by Gladstone and

Rosebery after several more suitable Liberals had refused it; and he was delighted after his term (1894–9) to return to such domestic duties as chairing parliamentary inquiries into the pollution of salmon rivers and adjudicating in property disputes between schismatic sects of the Free Church of Scotland. 'Balliol made me, Balliol fed me . . .' proclaims a verse of Hilaire Belloc, and the college certainly 'made' the 5th Marquess of Lansdowne, Elgin's predecessor as viceroy. After a mediocre result in his Finals, his tutor Benjamin Jowett gently suggested that his pupil had not altogether done justice to his talent. In reply the young peer admitted that he had been 'too fond of the society of jolly dogs' to work very hard, but he quite quickly changed his attitude, putting his jolly dogs in their kennels and embarking on a public life that lasted fifty years and included becoming, besides viceroy of India, governor-general of Canada, secretary of state for war, foreign secretary, and chairman of both the British Red Cross and the Trustees of the National Gallery. Had it not been for Jowett, Lansdowne later recalled, he would have done little with his life.[77]

Like other expatriates, Etonians in India strove to keep past identities alive, writing in school jargon, reminding each other of old 'beaks' and 'fags' and 'm'tutors', and corresponding about the school's annual cricket match against Harrow at Lord's. St John Brodrick, the Etonian secretary of state, informed Curzon that a new member on the viceroy's council 'should be thoroughly agreeable socially' because he had been Alfred Lyttelton's fag at Eton, a recommendation that cannot have impressed a viceroy who was an obsessive believer in promotion by merit. Yet it was a camaraderie rather than a freemasonry that old members of the school enjoyed in India. Men may often have been appointed to posts for wrong and nepotistic reasons but not just because they had been to school at Eton.

The great day in the Etonian calendar, the Fourth of June, was celebrated in India with an expatriate fervour quite foreign to the school's domestic cult of hands-in-the-pocket nonchalance. In 1894 the headmaster, Dr Warre, received a telegram on the Fourth from the viceroy (Elgin) and the governors of Bombay (Lord Harris) and Madras (Lord Wenlock) who had not only been to the same school together but also in Warre's house (before he became headmaster).[78] If the viceroy was an Etonian, he gave a dinner in Simla for fellow OEs in the town and received telegrams from those unable to travel there for the occasion:

'Calcutta Etonians, revelling in jolly boating weather,* drink your Excellency's and Simla Etonians' health. Floreat Etona.'[79] In 1909 Lady Minto, the viceroy's wife, recorded a Fourth of June dinner at Simla of fifteen Etonians at which her husband presided. She and several other ladies dined next door with a small number of Old Harrovians who sang 'Forty Years On', *their* school anthem, to counter the band's rendition of the 'Eton Boating Song'. At the end of the dinner the commanding officer of the 9th Lancers, the Etonian Colonel Nicholls, 'instigated by Minto, precipitated himself through the door, followed by all the Etonians, who completely annihilated the Harrovians. Pandemonium ensued. After this we sang choruses and ended with "Auld Lang Syne". Everyone declared they had not had such a good rag since they left school.'[80]

---

* A reference to the 'Eton Boating Song'.

4

Imperial Apprentices

'RATHER A FARCE . . .'

For the first two hundred years of its existence, the East India Company paid virtually no attention to training its employees for the work they would be doing in India. In every field, from the military to the medical, the principle seemed undeviating: let the chaps learn as they go along. By the end of the eighteenth century it was at last accepted that a little training might be a good thing, but even when the value of apprenticeships was admitted, it was sometimes difficult to find satisfactory masters. When the Indian Forest Department was set up in 1864, there was no place to train recruits in Britain and no one qualified to train them. For a generation they were sent to study in France or Germany, countries with resident experts, and even after forestry schools were established at Cooper's Hill in Surrey and later at Oxford, they still did part of their training on the Continent. As we have noted, the department's heads were Germans until the beginning of the twentieth century.

For two centuries the only educational qualification required of a Company Writer was 'book-keeping', an ability to understand a set of merchants' accounts. Realizing that this was an inadequate preparation for administering India, Lord Wellesley as governor-general (1798–1805) decided to set up the College of Fort William in Calcutta to educate young civil servants in such subjects as the history, languages, law and religions of India. Unfortunately Wellesley had a tendency to irritate the directors of the EIC by acting without their permission, and they had a tendency to react to his insubordination by thwarting him. Although Fort William, inaugurated in 1800, was one of Wellesley's more useful schemes, the college was emasculated, allowed to remain only as a language school until it was closed down in 1854.

The directors did, however, now accept the principle of educating their employees, and in 1806 they established the East India College, initially at Hertford Castle, and three years later at nearby Haileybury. The permanent home was built by William Wilkins, the architect of London's National Gallery, but its 'Cockney Grecian' facade of porticoes and Ionic columns was more successful than the Trafalgar Square building with its meagre dome and pepper-pot cupolas. Behind the facade was a dingy quadrangle of yellow brick, but the surrounding countryside was sufficiently sprinkled with charm and literary allusion to induce nostalgia among old Haileyburians serving in India. There they liked to recall how they used to plunge into the River Lea, 'immortalized by the pen and angle of Isaac Walton', or ride along the high road where Cowper's John Gilpin galloped wildly from Edmonton to Ware.[1]

Haileybury's annual intake of forty to fifty pupils was nominated by the EIC directors, though the boys had to pass some exams at East India House in Leadenhall Street before they were admitted to the college. Starting at the age of seventeen, they then spent two years on a curriculum of mathematics and natural philosophy, classical and other literature, history, law and general economy, and those oriental languages relevant to the Indian province they were destined for. While Fort William concentrated on India's vernaculars, Haileybury followed the usual British reverence for the classical, in this case Sanskrit, Persian and Arabic. A student preparing for the North-Western Provinces in the 1850s was still required to pass exams in Persian because, although it had been replaced as the language of the Company's courts in 1837, a knowledge of Persian was regarded as essential for an understanding of Urdu and Bengali, languages that partly stemmed from it. For similar reasons Arabic was taught because it was the 'repository of the Mahometan faith' and a key to Pashto and Sindi, while Sanskrit was favoured because it was 'the storehouse of the Religious Ceremonies of the Brahmin' and 'the mainspring of the daily avocations'.[2]

John Beames, a caustic and irreverent Civilian who worked mainly in Bengal, recorded in his memoirs that Haileybury had been 'a happy place, though rather a farce as far as learning was concerned'.[3] The obsession with classical languages bedevilled education for India well into the twentieth century: as late as 1913 a knowledge of Latin was considered essential for anyone aspiring to join the Imperial School of Forestry at Oxford. Civil servants educated at Haileybury became aware of the place's limitations after they arrived in India and began their new jobs. Lewis Bowring had won prizes for Persian and Sanskrit but soon realized that for his work on the Subcontinent his proficiency in these languages was 'nearly useless'. George Campbell was even blunter about Sanskrit, which he regarded as 'no more useful' to a Civilian 'than a knowledge of the tongue of the ancient Germans would be to a modern [English] commissioner of police'.[4]

Charles Grant, who was at Haileybury in the 1850s, complained that he was treated there more as a schoolboy than a student, and that the style of work was more like a school's than anything he had experienced in the sixth form at Harrow.[5] According to others, Haileybury managed to combine the defects of both school and university. At eight in the morning, John Beames recalled, the students rushed to chapel, concealing their nightshirts under a gown or an overcoat. Then they returned to their rooms for breakfast, which might include 'tankards of beer and claret', after which they smoked their pipes and dealt with tailors and other tradesmen who had arrived from Hertford to clothe and supply them. At ten o'clock they were summoned to lectures, which lasted two or three hours, after which they drank more beer with their lunch of bread and cheese. They were then free to do more or less what they liked. The oarsmen ran down to the river, the 'athletic men' went to 'their field', a studious minority known as the 'steadies' went for a 'solemn constitutional' along country lanes, and the 'fast men' slipped off by train to London or clattered off in dog carts to play billiards at Hertford or Ware. After dinner in Hall and more chapel at eight, the 'steadies' retired to their rooms and read far into the night, most of the others spent their time smoking, drinking and singing, and at about two in the morning the 'fast men' returned very drunk from Broxbourne Station after catching the last train from Shoreditch.[6]

It does not sound very like Victorian schooling, and no comparable record of college behaviour exists. Besides, as he went there in the 1850s, Beames would have missed Haileybury's more earnest period, in the 1820s and 1830s, when a number of students came from Evangelical backgrounds connected to William Wilberforce and the Clapham Sect. Yet if Beames exaggerated the frivolity of his contemporaries, he did not overstress the inadequacies of Haileybury either as a language school or as an institution designed to educate young imperialists.

The professors might lecture on Indian subjects, but no one at the college ever discussed such topics or talked about India; it was considered 'bad form'. Even teachers with experience of the Subcontinent felt it superfluous to tell their pupils what their lives as officials would be like; they reasoned that they would find out soon enough for themselves.[7]

Most Haileyburians agreed with Beames that they had been poorly educated, learning little about India and only a smattering of its languages. But nearly all – even the unsentimental Beames – believed that the college had fostered an *esprit de corps* that served them well in their careers in India. William Muir, a Scottish Evangelical who reached the top of the service, was always grateful for the 'marked advantage' given by the 'collegiate training' he had received at Haileybury.[8] The camaraderie of the cricket pitch and the rowing boat, and even of the pipe, the claret jug and the billiard tables at Ware, allowed men to get to know each other and measure their merits and deficiencies. As secretary of state for India in the 1870s, Lord Salisbury could recognize that the great advantage of Haileybury (by that time abolished) had been 'the close friendships formed there, which softened the rivalries of after life and secured devoted instead of perfunctory co-operation'.[9] Friendships formed in the yellow-brick quadrangle could later determine the running of an Indian province. When Richard Temple was commissioner of the Central Provinces, his cousin Rivett-Carnac arranged for the most talented Haileyburians of his generation to be stationed at Nagpur and help him direct the administration.

The pupils at Haileybury were selected virtually without regard to merit, the teaching they received was uninspired and of doubtful relevance, and the discipline of the college was lax and easily exploited by idlers and 'ne'er do wells' who were treated leniently by teachers anxious not to offend the boys' patrons and their own employers, the directors of the East India Company. Yet somehow, in spite of all these defects, Haileybury managed, in its half-century of existence, to produce a consistent number of capable administrators.

COMPETITION WALLAHS

Haileybury closed in 1857, its existence deemed incompatible with the new system of selecting civil servants by competitive examination rather than by the patronage of the directors of the East India Company. This new method was undoubtedly fairer, and in due course it produced desirable results. Yet for some years its inadequacies were so obvious that many people, not only reactionaries, felt nostalgia for the old college at Haileybury.

At the Indian Civil Service exams held annually at Burlington House in Piccadilly, some two hundred candidates competed for about forty places. The successful ones returned to London a few weeks later for a medical examination, unfairly timed to take place after students had gone through all the labours and expense of studying for the exams. If a man was disqualified on health grounds, that was the end of his hopes for a career in the ICS: he could neither appeal nor submit himself for a second medical examination later on. E. P. Eardley-Wilmot was rejected on account of a 'slight irregularity of action' in a heart valve caused many years earlier by rheumatic fever. The 'irregularity' had not stopped him from getting into the cricket and football Elevens of his school, not did it prevent him from enjoying cricket and rowing in middle age, but it ended his Indian career before it had begun.[10]

Successful candidates had to jump another hurdle before they reached India, the attainment of a 'minimum proficiency' in 'equestrianism'. In their instructions 'for the guidance of examinees', the civil commissioners announced that, 'as the duties of Civilians in India are such as often require the performance of journeys on horseback', candidates would have to produce 'satisfactory evidence of their ability in this respect'.[11] For the Haileyburians, most of whom had learned to ride as children, this would seldom have been a problem. But the more middle-class and urbanized 'competition wallahs' usually needed tuition in what was – in most of India – the usual form of travel for an official in his district; even towards the end of the Raj it was recognized that on long rides 'men saw the country and could talk with the people', which they could not do while 'rushing along the road in a car at great pace'.[12] Candidates thus had to find a riding school, often run by an ex-cavalryman, or a farmer with a livery stable, and practise the activity before taking the test at the Royal Artillery barracks at Woolwich or later at the Police College at Hendon. One Civilian, the son of a housemaster at Harrow, recalled how he had 'had to suffer the discomforts of learning to ride at a riding school . . . and of hiring a rough nag from the King's Head Hotel to practise along the lanes . . . around

Harrow'.[13] Unlike the medical examination, candidates were allowed a second chance if they failed the riding test first time.

After they had taken their exams, successful candidates were given a choice of Indian province according to their rank in the results table. The highest placed normally went where they wanted, the lowest filled the vacancies spurned by others, usually Madras or Burma, which were regarded as administrative backwaters. Iris Butler, the daughter of a Punjab Civilian, remembered in old age that she had 'rather despised a girl whose father was a Madras Civilian',[14] regarded as a 'mull' (because in the south he would have drunk mulligatawny soup) who may have lacked the brains and ambition to work in the north. The mull's presidency had a spacious capital, some attractive hill stations, and a population that was seldom troublesome. Yet its enervating climate and poor sporting opportunities deterred young civil servants. So did its distance from Calcutta and Bombay, cities which by the second half of the nineteenth century were each more prosperous and important than Madras. From the time of Thomas Munro, governor of Madras (1820–27), Civilians in the south were noticeably more sympathetic to indigenous culture than their counterparts in the north, but this did not help their careers and they were seldom given posts in the central government at Simla and Calcutta.

Candidates near the top of the list almost invariably opted for the Punjab or the United Provinces. The former appealed to men drawn to a frontier life and later to those eager to work among the great irrigation projects of the province; the latter's attractions included sport, especially shooting and pig-sticking, and the cultured cities of Agra and Lucknow. Both also offered the social life provided by British officers and their families quartered in such garrison towns as Meerut, Kanpur, Sialkot and Lahore. The candidates' third choice was often Bengal, which attracted the more sedentary, those hoping to work in the government secretariats in the capital. Yet its allure was largely limited to Calcutta. Much of the rest of the presidency was lonely for a district officer, with little 'society' and a climate of almost unrelenting humidity. Chittagong in the east was regarded as a sort of penal station for difficult Civilians, a place so damp that their books rotted and they thought themselves lucky to escape from it without their health breaking down. In the twentieth century Bengal's popularity dropped further when it became associated with revolutionary nationalism:

three successive district officers of Midnapore were assassinated in the 1930s. As a result, ICS novices who had opted for the Punjab or the United Provinces sometimes found themselves posted against their will to Bengal.[15]

Lord Dalhousie, the governor-general before the Rebellion, observed that while a 'member of the Civil Service in England is a clerk, a member of the Civil Service in India may be a proconsul'.[16] By the 1870s – years after Dalhousie's death – the best graduates from Oxford and Cambridge were apparently preferring to be clerks: the great majority of them were going into the home civil service. Most of Haileybury's pupils had started their work in India at the age of nineteen. Yet the British government's enthusiasm to recruit graduates to the Indian Civil Service had led them to raise the age limit for entry to twenty-three. This meant that successful candidates, who would still have two years' training to do, might not begin their Indian work until they were twenty-five – rather an advanced age to be learning apprentice skills. The age limit, repeatedly tinkered with in subsequent years, was one deterrent to promising graduates. Another was the nature of the examinations.

Although a district officer in India was obliged to lead an active physical life, this was not reflected in the design of the exams, which demanded little beyond a good factual memory and a concentrated study of such subjects as mathematics and natural sciences, moral sciences (logic and moral philosophy) and the history, language and literature of Britain and continental Europe. Furthermore, as few of these subjects formed part of the classical studies favoured at Oxford and Cambridge, candidates soon realized they had a better chance of success if they went to a 'crammer', an establishment in London specializing in preparing them for the examinations. If an undergraduate such as Archibald Macnabb could fail at Balliol but then succeed from Wren and Gurney, the most famous of the crammers, there was clearly little point in his father paying for a university education. Even housemasters at Harrow recommended that candidates should skip university altogether and go straight to Wren's.[17]

Almost everyone who had taken part in devising the competition scheme was appalled by the way it had turned out. The idea, articulated by Balliol's Jowett, that the ICS would consist of 'the picked men of the universities', had been made to look ridiculous: it now seemed to consist of diligent pupils of the Victorian crammer, boys described by the poet Matthew Arnold, who worked for a time as an examiner, 'as crammed men not formed men'; they knew a lot of 'facts' that were relevant to the exam but irrelevant to India. In 1879 Salisbury changed the system, making candidates take the exam at school-leaving age (seventeen to nineteen) and then, if successful, spending two 'probationary' years at a university studying a curriculum that included the languages of their chosen province. Although the age limit was lifted again in 1892, the primacy of Oxford had been established by Salisbury's reforms. In 1884 fifty-five of the current seventy-eight probationers were studying at the university.

Following Salisbury's reforms, the successful candidates became probationers for two years at one of the 'approved' universities: Oxford, Cambridge, Aberdeen, Glasgow, St Andrew's, Edinburgh, Trinity College Dublin, and both King's College and University College in London. They would not obtain a degree while they were there, but they would take two 'periodical' exams and a final one at Burlington House that would determine their seniority in their chosen province. Oxford owed its pre-eminence among the universities largely to the vision and persistence of Benjamin Jowett, a leading advocate of the competition system who became master of Balliol and vice-chancellor of the university. Inspired by the work of two of his brothers who had died in India, one in the army, the other in the medical service, Jowett encouraged young men who wished to do 'great and permanent good' to go to India and take the 'opportunity of benefiting the natives'. He duly wrote to the successful ICS examinees suggesting they spend their university careers at his college. In 1880 Balliol was the home of half of all probationers, twice as many as Cambridge and the other Oxford colleges put together. Jowett also campaigned for the recruitment of Indians to the ICS, a career unlocked for them by a parliamentary act of 1853 opening the service to 'all natural-born subjects of the Crown'. The difficulties for Indian candidates – above all, having to sit an exam with an alien curriculum in a distant country – ensured that their recruitment was slow.* Yet Jowett did his best. Of the first thirty-three Indian undergraduates at Oxford, twenty-two went to Balliol.

---

* Although thirty-four Indians joined the ICS in the 1890s, their proportion in the service remained low until after the First World War: in 1910 only 6 per cent of its officers were Indians.

At the time of Jowett's death in 1893 Oxford remained the principal training ground for civil servants in India: over half of them had been probationers there, and another quarter had gone to Cambridge. The pattern continued into the next century, 47 per cent of entrants studying at Oxford and 29 per cent at Cambridge in the years from 1900 to 1914,[18] and a similar ratio persisted until the Second World War. Of the 1,184 British Civilians recorded in the *India Office List* of 1938 – which included all those still alive even if retired – 568 had gone to Oxford, 334 to Cambridge, and 282 to other universities, principally Edinburgh (52), University College London (51) and Trinity College Dublin (49). The most dramatic change since Jowett's day was the decline of Balliol, by now more of a school for British politicians than a nursery for colonial administrators. Although it still educated more probationers (87) than any other Oxford college (Christ Church came next with 66, followed by New College with 48), the figure was now less than 8 per cent of the total. The leading Cambridge colleges were St John's (39), Emmanuel (37), Trinity (33) and King's (31).

At their universities probationers were taught little about the administrative system of British India except for magisterial duties, of which they needed to have some practical knowledge. They therefore attended court cases and wrote reports of what they had seen; most of them went to the Old Bailey, where they learned the principles of procedure and evidence, and Marylebone and Bow Street, where they observed the duties of a magistrate. The rest of the curriculum was academic, consisting chiefly of Indian history, geography and law, the classical languages (Sanskrit, Arabic or Persian) again and the chief vernaculars of their chosen province. Their linguistic studies did not alas ensure that they would arrive in their first district able to understand the language being spoken in it. Some provinces simply had too many vernaculars to study. In Bombay, for instance, Hindustani was adjudged the principal one, although it was not in fact used in the courts, the revenue administration or in official correspondence. More useful for a civil servant in the province was a knowledge of Marathi and Gujarati, although even these were of little help if he was posted to Sind in the west, where the language had Persian and Arabic roots, a different script and an alphabet of fifty-three letters.

The India Office did at least recognize that its officials could not assume serious responsibilities without absorbing 'living languages' on the spot and passing what were known as 'departmental exams' in these idioms. On arrival in their first post, 'griffins' (as newcomers were known)* were given 'ordinary' or 'third-class powers', which limited them to trying petty cases and passing very light sentences. To qualify for 'second-class' and later 'full powers' (and higher salaries) they had to study for two further sets of exams both in languages and in criminal and revenue law.

The Haileybury griffins usually did their studying in Calcutta, often with disastrous results for their finances. After years of schooling and parental supervision, they arrived in India at the age of nineteen, feeling independent and looking forward to the high salaries they would receive in the future. So they followed the example of the previous year's griffins, enjoying dancing and drinking and going shooting, and borrowing the money needed to hire servants and buy wine, guns and horses. Reluctant to relinquish such a merry existence, many delayed passing the exams required to take up a post in the interior. So they stayed in Calcutta and encumbered themselves with debts that sometimes took them decades to pay off. John Beames, who spent eleven months in the city working just two hours a day on his languages, accumulated a debt that 'clung' to him and 'harassed' him throughout his career. Robert Montgomery (the grandfather of the field marshal) confessed that he went into debt on his first day in Calcutta and remained so until he became lieutenant-governor of the Punjab thirty years later.[20]

Under the competition system griffins were steered away from the temptations of Calcutta and sent immediately to a district to learn their duties and improve their languages under the supervision of the district officer. This custom naturally spared them the dangers of extravagance, but it did not provide many other advantages. At least their predecessors had enjoyed the camaraderie of Haileybury and a social life in Calcutta that had given them the opportunity to make friends over tiffin and evening rides to the Eden Gardens; they had managed to acquire a kind of imperial self-confidence from mixing with their fellows. The new griffins, scattered over remote districts, might not find anyone of their own age to live with or confide in. Nor did they undergo

---

* According to General George Pearse, 'A griffin in India is a person who has not been in the country a year and everyone during that time is anxious to teach him the ropes.'[19]

any proper training apart from a course of practical surveying. As even some of the most successful Civilians later complained, such instruction as they received was haphazard and inadequate. Nobody taught them the principles of administration or how the different services and departments of government functioned. 'We were left to pick up what we could from others and from our mistakes.'[21]

Before they left England, both Haileyburians and competition wallahs had to sign a covenant setting out their duties and requiring them to promise, among 'general fidelity' and other things, 'not to accept corrupt presents or make corrupt bargains'. This made both sets 'covenanted civil servants',* two groups of men who, with historical perspective we can see, with all due allowance made for social and other changes, as players in the same game, just as their employers, even if theoretically distinct (the EIC and the British government), were in practice very similar managers. Yet many of them – especially among the Haileyburians – regarded each other as entirely separate species, distinct in character, class and methods of rule.

Admirers of Haileybury were appalled by their successors from the crammers, whom they regarded as bookworms without practical knowledge of the world. Lepel Griffin, who joined the service through competition just before the heyday of the crammers, grumbled that 'they neither ride, nor shoot, nor dance, nor play cricket, and prefer the companionship of their books to the attractions of Indian society'.[22] Even the graduate recruits who came later seldom enjoyed the approval of their predecessors, who might think it more important for an official to be a cricketer and 'the champion of bullied fags' than to have got a double first at Oxford.[23] To Sir James Fergusson, the governor of Bombay from 1880 to 1885, the new Civilians were milksops who fell sick, lacked stamina and were unable to shoot or even ride properly: one of his officials, he complained, could not have earned a genuine 'certificate of equitation' because he went out riding with servants walking on either side of his horse to catch him if he fell off.[24]

Such criticisms were often laced with snobbery, especially in the case

---

* The Uncovenanted Civil Service consisted of some Britons and many more Indians who were not part of the ICS but members of what was sometimes known as the Provincial Civil Service. The highest posts in this service, which did not require entrance examinations in London, were deputy collector and deputy magistrate.

of Fergusson, who observed that the manners of the new officials were 'not suggestive of the drawing room'. The governor, a Scottish land-owner who in *Who's Who* listed his top three recreations as hunting, shooting and fishing, clearly had some bias in such matters. Yet less traditional figures agreed that there had been a certain change of 'tone', that some of the new men were 'conceited' and 'underbred' and less sympathetic to the people they governed. One of them was William Wedderburn, himself a competition wallah, a supporter of Indian nationalism and later a Liberal MP. For him the Haileybury system had created officials who maintained a 'certain atmosphere of friendly sympathy' with Indians that had been dissipated by the new class of ambitious and academic bureaucrats belonging to families unconnected with India.[25]

In devising the entrance exams to the ICS, the civil service commis-sioners had been at fault in establishing almost exclusively academic criteria for success. District officers spent half their year in a hot and hazardous climate, and the other half riding about their districts, and at any time they might be called upon to direct firefighters or quell a riot or hunt down a 'man-eating' tiger. They needed to be capable and intelligent, especially in their magisterial work, but they also needed to be physically fit, able to ride a horse unaided by servants. In fact most of them *were* fit, or became so, whatever the Bombay governor said, and after thirty years few men apart from Fergusson were advocating the revival of Haileybury. In the end many people concurred with George Hamilton, the secretary of state for India in London, who observed in 1898 that the new ICS had 'fewer bad bargains, and fewer geniuses' – that is, fewer men who had 'gone to the bad' and drunk their brains away, and fewer of those 'legendary figures' who had 'quashed' a mutiny unarmed, killed a tiger with one arm, and crossed a river by stepping on the backs of crocodiles. Even a Haileybury critic of the competition system who complained to the viceroy John Law-rence of the 'low moral tone' of some of the new men, admitted that he had not 'the smallest doubt that as regards the average of ability and efficiency the existing system' was better than the old one. Lawrence, a Haileybury man himself, 'quite agreed' that it was superior'.[26]

Most of the carping came from a senior generation that was being superseded by younger men and a world that was changing quickly and alarmingly. The older Haileybury fellows had gone to India before the invention of steamships and the railway. They had spent six months sailing to their destination and, after they reached it, they travelled on very slow forms of transport, carried by boats and animals and human beings. They often had to make decisions on the spot, without the opportunity of consulting colleagues, and they seldom bothered to go home on leave. The competition wallahs travelled by rail, waited for instructions by telegraph, and took advantage of the Suez Canal (opened in 1869) to make quite frequent visits to Britain. Their predecessors viewed them and their ways with exasperation and some envy; their lives seemed too easy. In Calcutta the two groups even tended to segregate in the city's clubs, the older men going to the Bengal Club and the new recruits joining army officers in the United Services Club. Forty years after Haileybury closed, its Old Boys were still holding their exclusive reunion dinners at the Grand Hotel in Charing Cross.

Examinations remained the usual path to membership of the ICS, except in the years at the end of the First World War when the procedure was waived to allow some vacancies to be filled by the 'special selection' of officers who had served 'with distinction' during the war. Ronald Johnston was one of sixteen Indian Army officers who joined after a friendly interview and a 'purely qualifying' exam that did little more than test the candidates' literacy skills in English. British Army officers could also join the ICS, even if they had no experience of India. L. G. 'Jumbo' Pinnell, a classical scholar, planned to go to Balliol in 1915 with the intention of pursuing an academic career, but he joined the army, was wounded at Salonika, and lost interest in classical studies. Pondering his future, he wrote to the current master of Balliol, A. L. Smith, who suggested he should come to the college to do a shortened honours degree which, 'with a good military record behind' him, should enable him to get a job in the civil service 'by nomination'.[27] It did. Jumbo Pinnell arrived in Bengal in December 1920, became a district officer a dozen years later, and private secretary to the viceroy in 1942.

GENTLEMEN CADETS

Training for officers in the Indian Army was comparable in its early absence and later deficiencies to that for officers in the civil service.

Until the end of the eighteenth century no formal training was required for an officer to be commissioned in the army. A sixteen-year-old lad, with less than a year's service, could suddenly find himself in command of a hundred 'native' grenadiers of the Bengal Army.[28] In 1796 a handful of Company cadetships was created at the Royal Military Academy at Woolwich, and in 1809 the EIC established its military equivalent of Haileybury at Addiscombe near Croydon, where its cadets would take a two-year course. Yet no further qualifications were considered necessary for a commissioned officer, no matter how specialized or difficult his appointment, until the middle of the nineteenth century. And even then, as Philip Mason observed, 'nothing so vulgar as training was required for the Company's cavalry'.[29] As we have noted, there was an unapologetic tradition of placing Haileybury's failures in the Indian regiments of horse.

The East India Company Military Seminary at Addiscombe was built around a mansion in Surrey inhabited until 1808 by Lord Liverpool. Like Haileybury, its pupils were all nominated by directors of the EIC, but unlike the Hertfordshire college the seminary could not train every youth destined for its branches of the Company; the Indian Army required many more officers than the civil service. Addiscombe therefore concentrated on teaching cadets for the company's artillery and engineering units, those most in need of technological education; most officers in other branches went out to India with hardly any training at all.

As the cadet Henry Tyler recalled, the entrance exam 'God knows, was simple enough, being confined to a knowledge of *Caesar's Commentaries*, vulgar fractions and writing of a legible hand . . .' After he had passed, Tyler was 'transferred to the hands of the Drill Sergeant, who marched' him and his fellows off to the storeroom, fitted them out with uniforms, and within half an hour had them out on parade.[30] There was much more parading to be done over the next couple of years, many hours of drill and such activities as sword exercises. There was also a heavy academic programme that included frequent classes of mathematics, lesser quantities of geology, chemistry and surveying, and a perfunctory study of Indian vernaculars. As with Haileybury, pupils arriving in India found that some of the things they had learned had little relevance to the jobs they were required to do there. What use was a close study of Vauban's fortifications in seventeenth-century France to an engineer who was going to construct a barracks in Bengal?

As at the civil service college the course lasted two years, but Addiscombe was on the whole a harder-working and more disciplined place than the Haileybury of John Beames. At the end of their time there the students had to pass an exam before they were declared qualified as artillery cadets. The best of these were then selected as engineers and sent to do a further course at the Royal Engineers Establishment at Chatham in Kent. The Indian Army had priorities rather different from those of the British Army. Its elite units were neither foot guards nor cavalry regiments but engineers.

As part of the winding down of the East India Company, Addiscombe was closed in 1861, a few years after Haileybury, and candidates for the artillery and engineers were thereafter sent to the Royal Military Academy at Woolwich, affectionately known as 'the Shop'. Aspiring officers of the Indian Army were now educated in the same way as their contemporaries aiming for British regiments. As with the ICS, Cheltenham College was probably the most favoured school, but new institutions promoting military enthusiasm included Wellington College, opened in 1859 mainly for the orphans of army officers, and Kipling's school, the United Services College founded at Westward Ho! in Devon in 1874: no fewer than 666 USC Old Boys between its opening and 1922 were officers in the British and Indian armies.[31] The military schooling of the writer John Masters, whose family had been in India for five generations, was typical of a post-Addiscombe cadet: early years at Cheltenham Junior School, where he lodged with an aunt married to a retired engineer from the Indian Public Works Department, and then teenage years at Wellington from where he passed, as a potential infantry officer, into the Royal Military College of Sandhurst at Camberley.[32] Cormell Price, who had been Kipling's headmaster at the USC, was particularly adept at getting his pupils into Sandhurst 'direct from the school ... without the delay and expense of cramming'.[33]

In mid-Victorian Britain it was no longer possible to become an officer in the Indian Army without any kind of professional training. Candidates for the infantry now had to undertake an eighteen-month course at Sandhurst consisting of daily routines of drill followed by riding, PT, musketry and classroom lectures. If they survived the rather lax discipline – one had to 'avoid being seen downtown in uniform with some awful tart'[34] – they ended their time with an exam and the ceremonial passing-out parade. The Indian Army was allocated a variable number of places from the Sandhurst list – usually between thirty-five and forty-five – and competition for them was fervent: as we have seen, Auchinleck squeezed into the army in last place, while Montgomery missed out. After they reached India, subalterns had to spend their first year attached to a British regiment, getting used to the country and learning the relevant language before they were considered ready to join their Indian unit.

Courses for officers proliferated during the last decades of the Raj. The most popular was at the Small Arms School at Pachmarhi, the summer capital of the Central Provinces, where the social life was merry and included a ladies' rifle club. Less appealing was the course at the Royal Indian Army Service Corps depot at Jullundur, where officers learned how to handle mules, the chief means of transport on the north-west frontier. Basil Amies, a future colonel, was sent to most of the courses on offer: cadet training at the Staff College at Quetta in 1915,* signal school at Rawalpindi, musketry and Maxim machine-gun courses near Murree, then musketry again at Mhow near Indore, a Lewis gun course at Pachmarhi, six weeks of 'minor tactics and administration' near Poona, and both a rifle and a 'light automatic' course at Satara. By then regarded as a 'small arms specialist', Amies became an instructor and returned for two years to Quetta. In between courses he was attached to a Sikh company ('big burly men with neatly curled beards' and 'thick bucolic accents' which he could not understand), the 21st Punjabis, the 2/16th Punjabis (as second-in-command) and the 49th Bengalis; he also became military adviser to the state forces in Bikaner and three other native states, worked at Simla in the adjutant-general's office, at Bangalore in military intelligence, and in Rangoon as a staff officer; he was eventually chosen to work on the official history of the Indian Army in the Second World War. The military career of Colonel Amies did not include any fighting until 1942,

---

* In wartime Indian Army cadets were not required to do the eighteen-month course at Sandhurst. After three months with an officer cadet battalion in England, they spent half a year at a cadet college in India, either at Quetta or at Wellington in the Nilgiri Hills.

twenty-seven years after its commencement, when he came under fire in the retreat from Burma.[35]

Quetta was a strange place to establish a staff college, the Indian equivalent of the college at Camberley. It was in the remote tribal lands of Baluchistan, the western rampart of the Indian Empire, occupied by the British in 1876. Rocky, treeless, infertile and insalubrious, it was described by a missionary in that period as a 'howling wilderness' where the sanitation was so bad that Handel's 'Dead March' from *Saul*, habitually played at soldiers' funerals, might be heard five or six times a week.[36] In one of his earliest poems Kipling sent 'Jack Barrett' there, the victim of a conspiracy between his wife and her lover to get him out of the way so that they could enjoy themselves together in Simla. Jack dies in the appalling climate and, like Uriah the Hittite, is briefly 'mourned' by his Bathsheba.[37]

Although Quetta's tombstones and memorials tell a sad tale (long before the earthquake of 1935) of tragic and premature deaths, British residents came to appreciate the town, the labyrinthine bazaars, the approach roads lined by blossoming almond trees. The government provided public gardens, a shady 'Mall' and a fine cantonment, and it irrigated the valley beyond so that its 'verdant outlook' now reminded that same missionary of 'a bright emerald set in the midst of sparkling rubies'.[38] And however barren the hills around it might remain, there was 'the moment of sunset when the dust colour changed magically to the hue of molten copper'. One of Baluchistan's commissioners became so fond of the place that on his return to Teddington on the Thames he named his retirement home 'Quetta'.[39]

Basil Amies was part of the staff college's first intake, studying during the First World War before beginning his service with the 26th Punjabis. Several of Britain's most senior Second World War generals also spent time at Quetta, including Montgomery, Auchinleck and Slim. After having failed to get into the Indian Army in his youth, Colonel Montgomery accepted the post of chief instructor to its cadets in 1934. His Indian experiences did not, however, reconcile him to the force he had not succeeded in joining. While he thought the older officers were 'useless, quite useless', he considered the 'average young officer' to be no better, going 'to India to drink gin, play polo and have a good time'. The only men in the army Montgomery admired were its Indian rank and file, who were 'splendid', 'natural soldiers and as good material as anyone could want'.[40]

SURGEONS ON HORSEBACK

In 1758 the butcher on board a ship of the East India Company was allegedly promoted to the job of ship's surgeon in the middle of a voyage. The tale may be apocryphal, but the Company's early surgeons were no better trained than most of its other employees at the time; only the ships' captains, who had worked their way up from midshipmen and junior mates, had pursued proper apprenticeships. It was even said that 'a man need only sleep under a medicine chest for a single night to become perfectly qualified' to be a surgeon.⁴¹ In 1688 Dr Samuel Browne was appointed second surgeon in Madras, but he soon showed that he was both incompetent and inebriate; he killed a judge by giving him arsenic by mistake, and he drunkenly challenged one of his colleagues to a duel. Neither incident, however, prevented his promotion to the position of 'Surgeon of the West Coast'. One of Browne's contemporaries, Surgeon Thomas Faucet, was as much of a liability. Not only was he understandably mistrusted 'by reason of Moon Frenzy that seldom fails him full or new', he was also 'old, perverse, and ignorant in business', as well as 'intollerably [sic] addicted to drinking'.⁴²

Dr John Maxwell of the factory in Surat must have been regarded as even worse because he was expelled from the EIC in 1704 for his 'lewd debauched life'.⁴³ 'Lewdness' and 'debauchery' continued to be used as nouns in connection with the behaviour of surgeons, but they became less frequent in the second half of the eighteenth century. Before then men without any knowledge of tropical diseases or conditions would have had to be pretty desperate – and without prospects in Britain – to want to go to India, where their place in the social hierarchy would be extremely low. But their status rose after the establishment of medical services for the three presidencies in 1763–4 (subsequently known as the Indian Medical Service, IMS), and later when they were given military rank. Simultaneously their skills improved after it was realized that they needed to train properly and pass examinations; desultory attendance at classes at London's St Bartholomew's Hospital was no longer enough. From 1769 they had to be examined by a physician in the presence of two directors, and twenty years later they needed to have three months' training in a general hospital and spend eighteen months as a hospital mate. By 1822 they were required to be at least twenty-two years of age, to know some Hindustani, and to have a diploma and certificates of attendance from the Royal College of Surgeons in London or its equivalent in Dublin, Glasgow or Edinburgh. From 1855 entry to the IMS was by competitive examination.[44]

Although the new type of medical officer was now well trained and in Calcutta or Madras might match his contemporaries in London or Edinburgh, similar abilities might not often be encountered among the doctors of civil stations in the mofussil (rural districts). John Beames recalled that in the early 1860s 'many of these old fogies had not been home for years, they never read medical books or kept themselves abreast of the progress of medical science, they did their work in a perfunctory, careless manner, and spent most of their time in playing cards and drinking'. An acerbic critic at the best of times, Beames's opinions may have been influenced by the 'stupid, careless, drunken old' doctor who had damaged his son during childbirth, and a week later, when the baby was in great pain, prescribed rhubarb for his 'wind'. The infant died that night.[45]

By the end of the nineteenth century the Indian Medical Service had become more professional, and its aspiring doctors had to do five years of training and pass a more difficult series of exams. Here again was a post-university role for the crammer in advance of an entrance examination. At the end of a three-month course, Dr Campbell's institution in London was able to provide useful inside information about the examiners: Dr 'Y', for example, had 'a fad about manual external support of the uterus in the last stages of labour'; it was 'worth ten marks' if the pupil remembered it on the day. After the exams, which lasted a week and included practical sessions in surgery and anatomy, the successful candidates did a three-month course studying tropical diseases and learning 'the ABC of military manners' at the Royal Army Medical College on the Thames Embankment. Later they did yet another three-month course at the Aldershot Garrison, learning to drill and understand the conduct of courts-martial, and as a 'mounted service' doing an 'equitation course' with a dragoon regiment. Most of their training, however, was done at a teaching hospital. Later, after they reached India, they had to take a further course in hygiene and public health.[46]

All officers of the IMS went to India, and so did many members of the Army Medical Department, which was renamed in 1898 the Royal Army Medical Corps (RAMC). Yet while the latter worked exclusively for British regiments stationed there, the former were attached to Indian Army regiments and civil stations, and they were encouraged to work privately as well. Rivalries between the two services were endemic, mainly because IMS officers had greater opportunities to enrich themselves. Yet some resentments could arise over pettier things. As a 'mounted service', even junior IMS officers were allowed to wear spurs with their 'mess kit' at dinner, but young RAMC officers could not. As in the British Army, they were only allowed to wear them when they attained the rank of major.[47]

5

Voyages and Other Journeys

SAIL

In 1828 John Glasfurd's ship took 147 days to sail to India via the Cape of Good Hope. Twenty years later his son made the British–Indian journey in thirty-eight days, passing through the Mediterranean and the Red Sea in different boats and getting from one to the other by traversing Egypt overland. Eighty years after that his grandson took only fourteen days to reach Bombay from Marseille in a single ship, though it would have taken him six days longer if he had embarked in England and gone through the Straits of Gibraltar.[1]

In the days of sail the dates and lengths of voyages were determined by trade winds, no winds, monsoons and bad weather. Hurricanes in the 'Madras Roads' were so strong in autumn that ships were forbidden to remain off the Coromandel Coast between mid-October and mid-December. Steamships were less affected by such things, but passenger liners and troopships departing from India in March were always overcrowded because everyone was keen to leave India before the hot weather began. Travelling in June across the Indian Ocean was cheaper and much less crowded, but a good deal more uncomfortable in the heat and the turbulence of the monsoon.

John Glasfurd's 147-day journey was actually rather fast compared to earlier voyages, which might take seven months if the ship was damaged in a storm or blown across the Atlantic to Brazil. Robert Clive's first journey to India in 1744 took double that time because his ship ran aground off the Brazilian coast, was immovable for four months and then required repairs that lasted five further months. For the crews the voyages were of course longer than for passengers because many of their members would be making the return journey; and the ships were often going beyond India, heading for Canton, Penang and Bencoolen in Sumatra. The 'log' of the ship *Fame* records an uncomplicated voyage to India and back that began at the Blackwall Docks in January 1804 when a pilot guided it to Gravesend. At Woolwich it took on beef, beer and bread, stopped for a few days at Northfleet for work on its sails, and then headed towards Portsmouth and Plymouth. At the end of March it reached Madeira, always a popular spot because of the islands' climate and their eponymous wine, and then headed off to Madras, where it arrived in late July. After a three-week stay it turned north into the Bay of Bengal, obtaining a pilot to help navigate the River Hooghly and reaching Calcutta in early September. There it remained for three months, avoiding the hurricanes in the Madras Roads, before starting its return voyage, dropping anchor off Madras in February and setting off for England a month later. By late June it was at St Helena and in early September it reached the English Channel, docking at Blackwall once more on the 18th, over 600 days since its departure.[2] Not many voyages were as smooth as these ones. Nor did the *Fame* fare so well on its next. Although it was armed, like other 'Indiamen' (as the larger ships used by the East India Company were known), it was outgunned by a French frigate, the *Piémontaise*, and captured off the Malabar Coast in September 1806.*

The owners of ships used by the EIC appointed the officers and paid their salaries, but the captain and the first four mates were actually Company servants. Indeed the captain was among the Company's most superior officers. His ships were armed, his officers were uniformed and allowed to carry swords, and he himself was allotted servants, including a tailor, and entitled, whenever he landed at a Company settlement, to a thirteen-gun salute. His career at sea, unless truncated by illness, war or shipwreck, lasted some thirty years. Charles Mitchell began his apprenticeship in 1770 as a midshipman, was a fourth mate during his third voyage to India (1774) and a third mate during his fourth (1777), became successively second mate and chief mate (1781–5), and then did his last six voyages (ending in 1800) as commander or captain.[3] The slightly younger Henry Meriton made a record thirteen

---

* The frigate was itself captured by a British ship in 1808 and joined the Royal Navy as HMS *Piedmontaise*.

voyages, usually to China via the Coromandel Coast, and survived a shipwreck and engagements with vessels from Napoleonic France; he captured one of them (the *Médée*) but lost one of his (the *Ceylon*), although he was later able to witness its recapture and return to its moorings on the Thames.[4] Many such captains could make large fortunes, both from their passengers and from private trading at the ports they visited: a two-year round trip via India to China and Bencoolen might net them a return of £10,000 even though their official pay was only ten pounds a month. Although they might not compete with the nabobs in wealth or scurrility, some could afford to buy estates in England for their retirement. Of course, just as not all traders became nabobs, not all commanders made fortunes. Captain John Wordsworth, the brother of the Lakeland poet, lost money on his first two voyages as commander of the *Earl of Abergavenny*, and although he carried a potentially enriching cargo on his third (some of it an investment from his siblings William and Dorothy), he lost it – and his life – when the ship was wrecked in the Channel in February 1805.

At the end of the eighteenth century, 'Indiamen' of 800 tons or more had to have a crew of one hundred men, including a caulker, an armourer, a purser and a sailmaker, a baker, a butcher, a cooper and a poulterer, plus several mates, stewards, gunners and midshipmen. The number would also include fifty experienced sailors or 'able-seamen'. A captain would hope and expect to keep his officers on both the voyage out and the return home; the mates and midshipmen were supposed to be 'gentlemen', as were the surgeon, the purser and the captain's mate. But the ordinary sailors belonged to a more shifting population. For the outward voyage the first mate would hire most of his crew from communities living on the banks of the Thames between Wapping and Rotherhithe. Yet as some European seamen invariably died or deserted along the way, they had to be replaced by 'Lascars', South Asian sailors who congregated among the wharves and along the watersides of the ports in the Indian Ocean. On the return voyage the number of eastern seamen inevitably increased. Any ship reaching Canton almost always recruited Chinese sailors. An early Company ship leaving Japan in 1613 had a crew of forty-six Englishmen, fifteen Japanese and five individuals described as 'swarts', swarthy-looking men who had probably been hired in India. Two hundred years later William Hickey found a 'strange motley crew' on his Indiaman, consisting of nine Americans, eighteen Chinese and 'natives of almost every nation of Europe'; there were apparently 'not more than ten Englishmen on board'.[5]

Ships' logs refer frequently to the floggings carried out to maintain discipline among the seamen; 'the cat o' nine tails was constantly at work,' recorded one soldier on board an Indiaman.[6] Captains rarely lost sailors to mutiny, but men often died from illness, especially dysentery, and sometimes they fell overboard. The most disruptive cause of loss was the 'impressment' at sea of men for the Royal Navy, which was a persistent anxiety for the captain of an Indiaman; the loss of crew members might mean that he no longer had enough men to sail his ship safely or, when confronted by an enemy vessel, to man its guns or repel boarders. On one of his return voyages to England, Hickey witnessed a lieutenant of the navy coming aboard the Company's ship in the Channel, removing three men, including the carpenter's mate and the 'very steady quartermaster', and despite the captain's remonstrances, returning to impress twenty-two other sailors. Similar incidents occurred at the other end of the journey. Arriving in Madras in about 1820, one army officer espied 'a man-of-war's boat pulling for us, which caused a considerable sensation amongst the crew, to whom the prospect of impressment was anything but agreeable'. The boat, 'manned by a stout crew of slashing young fellows, in straw hats, and with tattooed arms', came alongside, and the naval lieutenant, 'with the air of a monarch, mounted the deck' and proceeded to choose which sailors to remove, 'something after the manner in which a Smithfield butcher selects his fat sheep'. Tragedy might of course follow the impressed men. At the beginning of 1807 the captain of the *Perseverance* reported that he had lost forty-one of his best sailors to HMS *Blenheim*, which Admiral Troubridge was using as his flagship to take him across the Indian Ocean to his new command at the Cape. A few weeks later, the *Blenheim* was sucked into a cyclone off Madagascar and was lost, together with several hundred passengers and crew.[7]

Formality played an important role in the routine life of an Indiaman. On the day after weighing anchor, recalled Hickey, each person at the captain's table 'took his seat in the station to be retained during the voyage', the captain himself 'in the middle of the table, fronting the windows that looked to the quarter-deck', with the senior ladies seated on either side of him; on his first voyage Hickey had to pay fifty pounds to secure a seat at it for himself. The water was undrinkable, the first load drawn straight from the Thames, and was really only used for making tea. There was usually enough beer and other alcohol to drink, but the food was variable: Hickey yearned for fresh bread instead of ship's biscuit that was 'uncommonly hard and flinty'.[8] Captains and their passengers could keep livestock on board, including sheep and cows in very cramped conditions, as well as chickens and turkeys living in coops on the poop, upsetting Bishop Heber of Calcutta with their 'vile stench'. The crew consumed quantities of salt beef, salt pork and suet.

Voyages often began badly, with what Hickey described as 'tempestuous weather' and a 'prodigious sea' in the Bay of Biscay. Many passengers had not travelled in a ship before and were duly and frighteningly seasick until the storm blew itself out. Calmer and happier times were to be enjoyed when the ship dropped anchor at Madeira, although Hickey's mistress Charlotte (whom he passed off as his wife) was 'sadly annoyed by lizards', which apparently infested the islands. It was anyway reassuring to watch the captain shipping a large cargo of Madeira's fortified wine, Calcutta society's favourite drink in the late eighteenth century. Fine weather and smooth water were also often found around the Canaries and the Cape Verde islands, the ship perhaps picking up the north-east trade wind as it sailed into the Tropic of Capricorn. On Arthur Wellesley's voyage to India in 1796, his ship encountered a small Portuguese vessel eager to supply it with some excellent oranges.

Next came the equator, which provided a rather unpleasant experience for male novices but entertainment for everyone else. This was a ceremony known as 'crossing the line', an elaborate farce and homage to the god Neptune in which any man who had not previously crossed the equator was shaved with pitch and ducked in water unless he bought a gallon of rum for the ship's crew. The subsequent landmarks were Ascension Island and St Helena, which were usually visited on the return voyage. The chief attraction of Ascension was 'turning' the local turtles, which according to Hickey provided 'rich and esteemed food', though it was difficult to catch them on the beach. St Helena, a Company possession from 1659 to 1834, had wider appeal. It was a great supplier of watercress, which like lime juice was a useful remedy if scurvy appeared among sailors or troops on board, and its climate was so mild that sick people were often left there to recuperate.

One such invalid was George Bellasis, an acquaintance of Arthur

Wellesley in Bombay, who used his long convalescence on the island to learn to draw and depict its landscapes. A dozen years later, when St Helena became famous for its eminent French prisoner, he published his aquatints and dedicated them to the ex-emperor's nemesis.[9] Napoleon in his exile became a tourist attraction, even British children being taken up to his house at Longwood to spy on the 'Corsican ogre'. Before his remains were removed to Les Invalides in Paris his tomb became a focus of Anglo-French bitterness. One local guide in the 1830s used to remove part of the railings and invite Englishmen to 'tread on the corpse of Bonaparte'. A few years later Fanny Parkes saw Longwood's visitors' book, 'many pages . . . filled by the French with lamentations over their Emperor, and execrations upon the English'.[10] St Helena soon lost its appeal to both nations. From 1840 French pilgrims could stay at home and pay their respects on the Seine, and the British found a route to India that did not go within several thousand miles of the island.

Ships were often becalmed for a fortnight or so as they neared the Cape, rolling about on a glassy sea with a heavy swell beneath them. If his vessel was making no progress, a captain might lower the jolly-boat and let the gentlemen row off and shoot albatrosses and Cape pigeons; these 'sportsmen' also entertained themselves on deck blazing away at sharks. The high point of the voyage was a sojourn of a few days at the Cape, which had been occupied by the British in 1795 and became a colony in 1814; a captain would make himself unpopular if he decided the weather conditions were so good that he should sail straight on towards the island of Johanna, off the coast of Madagascar, where he could also stock up on water, fruit and other provisions. After three months in the Atlantic Cape Town was a good place to stretch one's legs and enjoy the fruit and the Constantia wine. 'We remained at the Cape about ten days,' recalled one Addiscombe cadet, 'and spent our time very [happily] devouring quantities of grapes and galloping about the adjacent country'.[11]

Few pleasures were to be found on a long voyage aboard an Indiaman. People became bored, querulous and ill-tempered. Many fell sick with scurvy, dysentery or something else; some died and were buried at sea. And there was never a period entirely free of danger. At different times and in different strengths there were pirates – Arab, African, Indian and European – off the west coast of Africa, in the Mozambique Channel, in the Red Sea and the Persian Gulf, off the Malabar Coast and in the Bay of Bengal. In the early days Company ships fought small engagements with the Portuguese, but a more formidable enemy was the Dutch Republic, whose navy captured or sank six EIC vessels in the Indian Ocean during the First Anglo-Dutch War (1652–4). The Company's chief official enemy until Waterloo was of course France. In 1809, four years after the Battle of Trafalgar, French frigates captured two Indiamen on their way home from Bengal and three more on their way out.[12]

More frightening and dangerous than hostile ships was extreme weather, storms frequently opening bows, splitting sails and shattering masts. The more fortunate vessels might survive a battering, limp to the nearest land and find a place where they could be repaired, but few could endure cyclones or hurricanes. In 1768 a hurricane destroyed the *Chatham*, which had been kept in the Madras Roads beyond the season, and no trace of the ship or its crew was ever found. In 1808 three Indiamen on their way home foundered in a gale off Mauritius, and in the terrible year following (when the French frigates were causing their havoc) four more ships disappeared off the same island, and a fifth was lost in the China Seas. One passenger who died off Mauritius was a Mrs Scott, who had survived the wreck of Captain Wordsworth's ship on her way out in 1805 and had then nearly drowned with her husband when their pinnace sank in a river in Bengal. The Scottish missionary Alexander Duff was luckier with his misadventures. On his journey to India in 1829 he survived when his first ship was wrecked off the Cape and his second was grounded and badly damaged in the mouth of the River Hooghly.[13] No wonder that news of his escapes, which seemed miraculous, impressed the people he was hoping to convert.

Inexperienced passengers might feel that after crossing two oceans and reaching Bengal they were now safe. Yet the River Hooghly, which would lead them to Calcutta, contained so many perilous shoals and sandbanks that a local pilot was required to navigate the passage. Such obstacles shifted, moreover, after storms and during the monsoon, the depths changing so often that many vessels ran aground and were lost. One of the most dangerous of the shallows was the 'James and Mary' shoal, so named because the *Royal James and Mary*, a ship with a cargo of Sumatra pepper, had foundered on it in 1694;[14] in later years 'wreck buoys' around the shoal indicated where other ships had come to grief.

One of the oldest professions of British India was work in the Bengal Pilot Service (BPS), which was founded in the seventeenth century so that the Company was not reliant on foreign pilots. By 1870 the service's establishment had some 130 men, headed by the 'senior branch pilot' and including ordinary branch pilots, master pilots and fifty-four mates of different species. It also had a 'compiler in the Wreck Chart for India Department'. Pilots of the BPS would board vessels off the Sandheads in the Bay of Bengal and then guide them more than 120 miles upriver to Garden Reach at the southern limit of the Port of Calcutta. There they would hand their charge over to the harbour pilot (unofficially known as 'the mud pilot') who would take the ship on its last mile to the docks and moorings of a port that in 1914 was annually handling over 85,000 vessels.[15]

Calcutta also had a special judge in the Small Causes Court to try pilots for their mistakes. In a minority of cases pilot error was to blame for accidents on the Hooghly, just as it for some of the shipwrecks at the other end of the voyage, in the English Channel. Captain Wordsworth was drowned along with more than 200 passengers and crew after a pilot's blunder took his Indiaman on to the Shambles off Portland Bill. Another man-made hazard was fire, which destroyed several Company ships; the *Duke of Atholl* blew up in the Madras Roads in 1783 apparently after a steward dropped a candle into a cask of spirits in a storeroom. According to the historian of the EIC Marine Service, 'between 1700 and 1818 no less than 160 Indiamen were lost by wreck, burning or capture'.[16]

STEAM

Voyages to India became much less dangerous when sail gave way to steam and the Atlantic was exchanged for the Mediterranean. Yet calamities still occurred, and ships bound for India were harried by the German enemy in both world wars and by the Japanese in the second. The initial Mediterranean journey was known as the 'Overland Route', which was pioneered by Thomas Waghorn, who had been a naval lieutenant and a pilot on the Hooghly. Only a fraction of his route in fact went overland. Passengers travelled by sea from England to Alexandria, and from Suez to India likewise. In the 1840s they went to Cairo by canal and river (by the 1850s there was a railway) and then, while their baggage was put on the backs of camels, they crossed the desert in vans or small omnibuses drawn by teams of mules. It was a jolting, uncomfortable journey, but it was much faster than going round by the Cape; it also gave travellers a chance to see Cairo and the Pyramids.

After the opening of the Suez Canal, the Egyptian stage of the journey was amended: Alexandria gave way to Port Said, and Cairo, the omnibuses and the second ship were discarded. You could now travel from England to Bombay in a single vessel in twenty days. Otherwise the route had not changed. If you were on a ship belonging to the Peninsular and Oriental Steam Navigation Company, universally known as P&O, you sailed down the Channel, usually from Tilbury or Southampton, pausing off Portland Bill to let the pilot climb down a rope ladder into a rowing boat sent to fetch him, and after passing Plymouth you reached the Bay of Biscay, where, like your predecessors in sailing ships, you were likely to be seasick. Your steamer stopped to pick up passengers at Gibraltar (where some 'noble and amiable hidalgos' came aboard and proceeded to teach Beames Spanish), Marseille, Malta (where Beames 'witnessed the Carnaval and took part in the fun') and Port Said. You could cut several days from your journey by taking a train through France and joining the ship at Marseille, but if you were a griffin this might be a mistake because friendships and social groups were already being formed in the Bay of Biscay. Not that you could probably have joined any group formed by people in different professions from your own. On his way out to Ceylon, Leonard Woolf witnessed how a concourse of 'isolated atoms' developed into 'a complex community with an elaborate system of castes and classes'. Snobbery on board was as common as inclusiveness was rare. Marjorie Innes sailed to India in 1920 but, as her daughter later remarked, she could not enjoy the voyage because 'various army and Civilian ladies had snubbed her or patronized her for her lowly status as the bride of a tea planter, and for travelling alone'. When E. M. Forster went to India for the first time in 1912, he insisted on playing a game of 'deck shovel' with two commercial travellers because they had been boycotted by the other passengers.[17]

As the ship headed eastwards across the Mediterranean, its clock was advanced by twenty-five minutes each morning before breakfast. Port Said was the most memorable stop, the halfway stage, the cultural frontier and also a climatic one, the 'first real glimpse of the East' for the griffin. Passengers were encouraged by the ship's officers to disembark before 'the grimy business of coaling began', with 'lines of coal-blackened coolies' or 'ebony Sudanese like a moving frieze' filling the bunkers with the contents of their sacks.[18] For a few, Port Said was exciting for what it was and what it heralded, poinsettias and the desert, the sight of 'a camel led by an ancient Arab, both looking as if they had walked thus since the Pharoahs . . .' If you wanted, you could buy real Turkish Delight, and if you were a griffin you were more or less obliged to follow custom and buy a sola topi at Simon Artz's emporium. Yet even Forster was disappointed by the town, which had 'no minarets' and 'only one dome'.[19]

A representative female reaction to Port Said might be that of Norah Rowan Hamilton, a British lady who travelled to India just before the First World War and wrote a book about her experiences, *Through Wonderful India and Beyond*. In this 'sordid eastern port' she was immediately struck by 'the shrill babel of Eastern voices' sounding in her ears and by 'the strange pungent odour of the bazaars' that were 'probably compounded of things strangely unpleasant in the eyes of Westerners!' Things got better when she 'strayed into a garden sweet with clumps of oleanders and pomegranates' and walked 'through the short Eastern twilight' to the Savoy Hotel, a 'quaint little Turko-Egyptian caravanserai that lies on the Quay'. Sadly, however, this was 'a very poor relation of the mighty head of the tribe on the Thames'.[20]

Most masculine reactions were blunter and earthier than Mrs Rowan Hamilton's, focusing on the stench and squalor of this 'haunt of vice', this 'picturesque but abominable refuse of humanity'. Among the descriptions of its inhabitants, 'vendors of dirty postcards' is the politest. Otherwise they were the 'dregs of society', 'a set of the vilest swindlers' and 'the worst blackguards of the world'. Bored and arrogant young Englishmen complained that there was nothing to do in the town except visit 'some of the exceedingly noisome gambling dens' and win a few francs at their roulette tables. Less blasé fellows managed to organize cricket teams and play their sport on pitches made of coir matting spread out on the Egyptian beach.[21]

Between Port Said and Suez the ship slowed its speed to six miles per hour so as not to wash away the banks of the canal. The heat grew, the punkahs were put up, and griffins began to think they had let

THE BRITISH IN INDIA

themselves in for an 'unpleasantly warm job'. When the temperature in their cabins reached the nineties – 'something fearful' – some passengers abandoned them and slept on deck. In the canal the ship's crew changed into tropical uniform, its officers and stewards suddenly appearing in white ducks. A similar transformation took place in the troopships when the officer in command declared 'a state of hot weather': stiff shirts and waistcoats were abandoned and replaced by white drill monkey jackets, white drill slacks and red silk sashes wound around the midriff.[22]

Aden, the next stop, had been acquired by the Company in 1839 to prevent its use as a base by pirates and to establish a coaling station for itself. The arrival of the ship excited the port's residents, and a gun was fired to let them know that their mail had arrived. Some passengers got up early to watch the sun rise over the volcanic range of Jebel Shamsan, but for most of them Aden was a dispiriting place, hot, dusty and treeless, with little to do except swim in the sea within a fence erected to keep out sharks. By now most griffins were feeling 'flabby and cramped', bored of the food, starved of their usual physical activity, and longing to reach Bombay.

Before 1830 most people had travelled to India in a ship hired by the East India Company and officered by its employees. With the ending of the EIC monopoly of trade and the demise of its maritime service in 1834, various choices became available. P&O began sending steamships to India in 1842, at first round the Cape and later via the Overland Route. Although it soon had competitors, its liners were usually the swiftest and were considered to have the best stewards and the best organized games on board; they also provided free deckchairs, a free library, a shop 'conducted by the Army and Navy Stores' and in due course wireless news bulletins printed and circulated each day in the public rooms. Many passengers always travelled by P&O and regarded it as unpatriotic not to 'support the British line'.[23]

Yet the line had its defects. The company was more expensive than its rivals, and it refused to take women 'sufficiently advanced in pregnancy' as likely to give birth during the voyage.[24] It also refused to take pets: Leonard Woolf had to put his dog Charles on a Bibby Line vessel while he himself travelled with the 'patriots'. Unconventional types tended to dislike P&O and its atmosphere of 'overconfident upper-middle-class Britishness'. For the journalist Ian Stephens, his one venture on a P&O vessel was 'too like being back at public school', discouraging him from ever using the Company again.[25] Conditions on board changed of course over the decades, as did the ships themselves. Valentine Chirol, another journalist, went out on a 3,000-ton steamer in the 1880s and on a liner of 20,000 tons forty years later. The larger vessels were naturally less cramped and better ventilated, and they were not lit by oil lamps. Yet the poor quality of the food remained a constant, and the performance of the kitchens was persistently criticized. After Lord Curzon travelled P&O to take up his viceroyalty in 1898, he felt obliged to tell his friend Lord Selborne, a director of the Company, that the food was so appalling that it had made one of his wife's sisters ill. When Selborne disputed the criticism, the viceroy replied with a further eight pages on the subject, and a year later he was still sending his friend evidence from other passengers who had suffered from the cooking.[26]

Towards the end of the nineteenth century, P&O had British competitors – such as the Anchor Line and the City Line – as well as rivals from continental Europe. The Rubatino Line, sailing between Genoa and Bombay, was one cheaper option. Another was Austrian Lloyd, whose ships went from Trieste to Bombay and back via Brindisi. John Morris, the gay Gurkha officer, preferred a later incarnation of this line (renamed Lloyd Triestino after its home port was transferred to Italy in 1919) because he thought P&O was too much 'run on hierarchical lines'.[27] Another challenger was Messageries Maritimes de France, which, when sailing from Calcutta, added French links (Pondicherry and Djibouti) to more normal stops on its way to Marseille. This line, called Messageries Impériales before Napoleon III's overthrow in 1870, had expanded to take advantage of the opening of the Suez Canal (which had after all been built by a Frenchman) to steam beyond India to the Far East and France's colonies in Indochina. One traveller, who found himself on its *paquebot Sindh*, was extremely unimpressed: the vessel, young Winston Churchill complained to his mother in 1898, was 'a filthy tramp – manned by . . . detestable French sailors'.[28]

Boredom and inactivity were perennial problems on the voyages, although they were naturally more difficult to cope with when spending half a year under canvas rather than just three weeks on a steamer. When a ship was becalmed near the Cape in the eighteenth century, gentlemen might do some shooting or fishing, but their routine amusements were liquor, cards and music – as they were for Lieutenant Churchill when he travelled across the Mediterranean on the SS *Britannica* in 1896, though he also managed to improve his chess before reaching India. Some people read books and studied Hindustani, but card-playing was a more widespread diversion. One ensign going out in the 1830s recalled that so much gambling had gone on during the voyage that many passengers were broke by the time they reached Madras. A generation later, an ICS griffin reported that passengers had organized a lottery for nothing more interesting than the precise time the ship would pass the beacon at Alexandria.[29]

Organized games became a speciality of P&O, and those who enjoyed them would never defect, whatever culinary advantages they might find elsewhere, to Lloyd Triestino or Messageries Maritimes. Games on deck were under the supervision of the chief officer, and quartermasters and desk stewards were in attendance, explaining the rules and lighting the cigarettes of the players. 'Deck quoits', requiring little space, was a staple game, yet P&O also organized more ambitious sports, which in other circumstances needed a court or even a field but were now ingeniously amended by the company so that tennis was played not with a racket and ball but with hands and a small circle of rope, while cricket was performed on the upper deck with squashy string balls and very thin bats. More boisterous and less skilful activities included organized pillow-fights, obstacle races and 'Are you there, Moriarty?', a contest in which two blindfolded men tried to hit each other on the head with a rolled-up newspaper. Tugs-o'-war gave men the opportunity to show team spirit and divide into natural rivalries such as 'varsity' struggles between ICS griffins from Oxford and Cambridge. On one voyage in 1917 the 'Passenger' team consistently defeated the 'Navy' at this because, as one passenger pointed out, the 'passengers were much bigger and heavier than the sailors', who needed an extra man to even things out. Lest anyone should think that P&O only bothered with masculine sports, the company produced a postcard of Edwardian ladies charging along the deck in an egg-and-spoon race, hitching up the skirts of their dresses; later evidence suggests that the crucial item in such races was not in fact an egg but a potato.[30]

Enthusiasm for such frivolities does not seem to have been dampened by the presence of chaplains, whom the EIC had long employed to hold Sunday matins and burials at sea during the voyage. If none was on board, the captain or, on a troopship, the colonel of the regiment would conduct the service, reading the lesson and lustily singing the hymns; one of the favourites was 'Eternal Father, Strong to Save' with its apt and crescendoed refrain, 'O hear us when we cry to Thee / For those in peril on the sea'. Even if the official ecclesiastical presence on board was scant, a P&O liner was bound to be carrying an unofficial complement of missionaries and religious tourists who were naturally more enthused by the eastern Mediterranean than their predecessors had been by the Cape. Among the hazards recorded by the griffin Maurice Hayward in 1889 was 'a member of the Plymouth Brethren . . . who gave me a religious lecture as we were passing Mount Sinai on Sunday'. The Red Sea was inevitably a danger zone, an invitation to religious bores to speculate about Moses, the Israelites and their Egyptian pursuers. Madge Green, the sister of an ICS officer, got stuck with one 'padre' who 'talks and talks and talks, chiefly about the Israelites, and the exact spot at which they crossed'. A more realistic assessment of the biblical episode came from Private J. P. Swindlehurst of the Lancashire Fusiliers, who looked at the sea and wondered how the Israelites could have crossed 'with Pharoah hot on their heels'; he also wondered 'how anywhere near here could have been a land of milk and honey'.[31]

Cultural entertainment on board appears to have reached its peak in the very early years of the East India Company. According to entries in the journal of Captain William Keeling, commander of the EIC's Third Voyage to India, his 'company' or companions acted *Hamlet* to a local dignitary off Sierra Leone and *Richard II* at a dinner party on board the *Red Dragon* in September 1607; the following March, when his ship was becalmed on the other side of Africa, Keeling permitted another performance of *Hamlet* to deter his men 'from idleness and unlawful games, or sleep'.[32]

It was downhill after that, despite the efforts of amateur enthusiasts on the P&O liners. 'Some very energetic spirits', complained one officer's wife on her first voyage in 1903, were 'always pestering' her to take part in 'dances or concerts or some such show . . .' The pesterers themselves sometimes got on each other's nerves. Madge Green, who had suffered from the boring padre, reported 'some crisis, and the concert committee has resigned', but she herself was determined to participate in the concert and sing a Gilbert and Sullivan duet with her brother. Harry Lauder songs were very popular at such events, especially if the performer was Glaswegian and also a 'tippler', thus capable of doing an authentic rendition of 'A Wee Deoch an' Doris'.[33]

Songs were even more popular on troopships. 'Auld Lang Syne' was a natural for embarkation and leave-taking, especially when soldiers' wives were being left behind.* There was not much else to do on board except singing, boxing and playing cards and 'housey-housey', later known as bingo. Soldiers in the twentieth century were given a 'slap-up meal' that included rabbit pie before they embarked at Southampton and were allocated their mess decks and the racks that would hold their hammocks. Troopships were slower and more overcrowded than passenger liners, usually containing 2,000 soldiers in a much smaller space. While the hundred or so officers might have a large promenade deck reserved for themselves, the men were only allowed on two smaller decks, fore and aft, so that, in the words of one NCO from the Somerset Light Infantry, they were 'packed in like beasts in Taunton market on a Saturday'.†[34] At Port Said the men were allowed to swim in the sea but, as they had no 'costumes', they had to be out of the water by eight in the morning when 'the ladies on the saloon deck' might appear.[35]

Officers bound for the Indian Army naturally did not sail out with their men, who were already in India in their forts or barracks; they could therefore go by themselves in P&O or in Bibby liners, where alcohol was duty free and a tot of gin cost only a penny ha'penny. Soldiers of the British Army travelled on troopships with their officers, even if they were segregated on different decks. Food was plentiful but monotonous, with too much corned beef and plum jam, but Private Swindlehurst was happy with his kippers for breakfast, custard with prunes for tea, and sausages with a pint of beer for dinner. Most soldiers on board had special duties, and he was made the ship's assistant butcher, a job that came with a special llama coat so that he could work in the refrigerators, using a crowbar to detach the carcasses that had frozen to the deck.[36]

Before the opening of the Suez Canal most people's first view of India was Madras on the Coromandel Coast. From afar the place

---

* See below, p. 294.
† One of the Somerset men on this voyage reported that on his return to Britain at the end of the First World War the troops on his ship were rebellious, refusing to let the officers cordon off a deck for themselves and cutting the ropes with artillery knives.

looked attractive – a line of white buildings amidst a profusion of greenery – but reaching it was hazardous, for there was no harbour and not even a pier until 1861. After the ship had anchored in the Madras Roads, its passengers were lowered into flat-bottomed vessels called masulah boats which then had to navigate a triple line of surf. On reaching the shore atop one of the breakers, the steersman turned the boat broadside to the sea, the crew jumped off with ropes to prevent it being dragged out again, and they waited for the next breaker to drive it high on to dry sand, the accompanying spray soaking all the passengers. Small rafts called catamarans were also employed, following the masulahs to pick up anyone who had fallen out.[37]

Disembarking at Calcutta was not always straightforward either. In the early years passengers often left their ship at Fulta, clambered into boats called budgerows and were then rowed to the so-called 'city of palaces'. As with Madras, first impressions were mostly favourable. John Beames was much impressed by 'the long rows of shipping, the lines of stately white houses . . . and the beautiful villas with their luxuriant gardens . . .'[38] Beames arrived in 1858. By the time he left India in 1893, Calcutta had been greatly altered, its principal street, Chowringee, transformed from a parade of handsome pillared mansions into a restless thoroughfare of mainly red-brick shops, offices and hotels.

First impressions of Bombay were not often appreciative. Old soldiers, like other memoirists, might recall them in romantic and nostalgic tones, the crowds on the waterfront and the colours of the bazaars, the kaleidoscopic confusion of turbans and saris, the scent of sandalwood and the cooking smells of turmeric and other spices. But the immediate unedited version of young soldiers' responses was very different; Bombay's filth and stench usually exploded the notion of a romantic Orient. Private Clemens of the East Yorkshire Regiment was appalled by 'the smell, the flies, the whining of the beggars with their continuous wailing cry of "buckshee, sahib, buckshee"; and to cap it all the sweat was pouring out of me, which made those damn flies stick to you'. As one sergeant-major put it, India seemed to be 'hotter than Hades, and a damned sight less interesting'. First journeys in a troop train seldom led to a revision of such opinions. Just as British troops in the First World War regarded Mesopotamia as 'miles and miles of sweet FA', so were they demoralized by the journey from Karachi to the north-west frontier. Private Swindlehurst had dreamed of rajas and elephants, of temples and mosques and 'waving palm trees', but found himself instead in 'lousy scenery', just 'miles of burnt-up earth . . . and scrub and dusty-looking trees'.[39]

Men who had read and prepared for India might see beyond Bombay's flies and crippled beggars and admire a city where the Post Office was like 'a palace, and the Railway Terminus is a cathedral'. For some, especially those with family connections with India, the moment of docking at Bombay presaged a feeling of 'coming home'. Ian Stephens felt that India was where he 'belonged' as soon as he descended on to a station platform on his first journey from Bombay. Others realized that in their childhoods they had absorbed so much of the Subcontinent through books, pictures and the stories of retired relatives that it all seemed familiar even though they were seeing it for the first time. The 'Persian wheels', the 'wallowing buffaloes', the 'white incandescence of midday over the endless plain as we rattled north' in the Frontier Mail: such sights for one ICS griffin were 'at once a preview of the environment in which we were to live and a glimpse into, as it seemed, a remembered past'.[40]

RIVERS

Slow as the old voyages to India may have been, they were nothing compared to the slowness of travel on the Subcontinent before the railways. The journey from Calcutta to Delhi, which could be accomplished in under three days by rail, took three months by river a generation earlier. Among the difficulties of river transport before steam were, besides sandbanks and other obstacles beneath the surface, an habitual lack of wind and the problem of struggling against water flowing in force from the Himalaya. In the 1830s Fanny Parkes, the most open-minded of travellers, enjoyed life in a pinnace on an Indian river, the views of temples and stone ghats, the picturesque scenes of 'native' life, but it was a bore to get stuck between rocks or go aground on sandbanks or be moving quite so slowly, sometimes at the rate of a quarter of a mile an hour. Even more annoying were the white ants that ate into the masts and beams of the pinnace so that these eventually snapped, and very frightening was the storm that followed, which was so violent that it tore away the moorings of the boat and drove it against the bastions of a ruined city and sank it.[41]

The grandiose schemes of Richard Wellesley extended from conquests and palaces to the governor-general's flotilla, which included skiffs, pinnaces, cook-boats, the state yacht plus a vessel for his band to play on while he was on the water. Painted green and gold to contrast with the scarlet uniforms of their oarsmen, the boats were normally kept at Barrackpore, the governor-general's country residence, but in 1801 the flotilla proceeded, elegant but sluggish, from Calcutta to Allahabad. The frustrations of river travel were much the same in 1836 when the commander-in-chief, General Fane, opted for the same route with the help of steam. His vessel, recorded his daughter, spent much of the journey 'comfortably aground on a sandbank', but sometimes it was stuck in a more 'awkward place, with rocks on one side, a sandbank and a strong current besides'. It was a relief when he and his party reached Allahabad, where they got off the vessel and travelled on elephants or in palanquins* while their luggage went on camels.[42]

Steam never had the impact on river transport that it had on the oceans or on land. In 1852 Lieutenant Fred Roberts (the future field marshal) took nearly a month to travel from Calcutta to Benares on a barge towed by a steamer. Rivers had shallows before the rains, and frequent changes of channel afterwards, both of which required pilots to sound and find them. Steamers on the Ganges and its tributaries were usually designed to draw less than four feet of water, yet despite the problems steamship services did manage to function on the river. The situation was more difficult to the west on the River Indus, which was too low for boats in winter and almost impossible in the summer, when monsoon rains and melted snow from the mountains turned it into a torrent. For forty years from the 1830s British steamboat companies tried to produce a viable and regular service on the river, but in 1870 the last one gave up.[43] British officials continued to use the Indus sporadically for their work: in 1916 the commissioner of Sind was still chugging in a flat-bottomed paddle steamer during his winter inspections. But river transport there could not compete with the railways.

It was a similar story in most of India: there were several quicker ways of traversing the Gangetic plain than in a boat on the Ganges. Yet in some places of the empire river transport remained the best way of travelling even after the arrival of the motor car. In areas of Burma the only

* See below, p. 149.

viable vehicles were boats and elephants. One district officer found his pony useless because one 'could not ride for half a mile without coming upon an impassable stream'; he did his touring in a rice-boat with rowers, carrying no tents and staying in monasteries and police stations.[44]

Eastern Bengal was even more dominated by rivers. In some areas a district officer could perform his duties by combining boats, bicycles and bullock-carts. In others, especially near Dacca, nearly all the touring had to be done by river; at Khulna on the Delta the Civilian visited his district by boat to the sound of tigers roaring in the Sunderbans. From Rangpati in the Chittagong Hill Tracts the official began most of his journeys in a motor launch until the water became so shallow that he had to transfer first to a flat-bottomed country boat, then to a dugout canoe and finally on to an elephant. When W. H. Saumarez Smith was posted to Bengal in 1936, he found most of his district under water and realized that he would have to sell his horse Peter, because the animal was no more useful there than a rocking-horse. Much of his work, done from a small launch, consisted of visiting 'chars' – islands formed by alluvion as a river changed course in a monsoon – and adjudicating to whom this fresh and fertile land should be assigned.[45]

Some officials in the commissionership of Dacca thought it easiest to live in houseboats, though this could be a fraught and dangerous arrangement. In the mid-nineteenth century one inspector of schools built himself an unusually large and sturdy boat that could be rowed against the wind with ten oarsmen; it even contained enough space for his library and his sizeable collection of botanical specimens. Yet one night a tidal wave on the River Megna, rushing along at the speed of a racehorse, tore the boat from its anchorage and destroyed it entirely; no vestige was ever found. The boatmen survived, as did the inspector, who was swept away to a shallow spot where a 'snag' gave him refuge until he was rescued by a passing boat in the morning; he was lucky that a crocodile did not find him first.[46]

MEN AND ANIMALS

The sight of lean and underfed Indian men hauling large westerners in bicycle rickshaws makes us feel uncomfortable today. It would have been even more unsettling in the past to observe still more emaciated 'natives' pulling them by rickshaw (without a bicycle) or carrying them in a sort of box litter called a 'palanquin' or 'palkee'. Yet, before the railways, journey by palanquin was the quickest and most normal method for British men – and even more for British women – to travel very long distances. In 1844 John Strachey was carried on men's shoulders for almost a thousand miles from Calcutta to his posting in the North-Western Provinces. The journey lasted three weeks, but it would have taken much longer by boat.[47]

There were variants of this form of transport such as the 'dandy', a canvas chair looking rather like a washtub, carried by dandy-wallahs in the Himalaya, and the 'jampan', a similar portable chair or sedan favoured by ladies in hill stations and carried by four jampannies wearing a uniform chosen by their employer. The palanquin was heavier and more elaborate, with curtains and sliding doors, room for provisions, and a mattress, pillow and bolster for the reclining passenger. Two poles jutted out at each end near the top and rested on the shoulders of four bearers. If travelling by night, the usual time, the team was led by a torch-bearer carrying a gourd full of coconut or some other oil which he poured at intervals on to a torch made of rags. Travelling in 1852, Lieutenant Roberts found the experience 'tedious in the extreme'. Starting after dinner with eight bearers, divided into reliefs of four and accompanied by coolies carrying his baggage 'who kept up an incessant chatter', he spent each night being jolted along at a maximum speed of three miles an hour. Every ten or twelve miles the team was relieved by another eight men until the sun was up and their passenger headed for shelter in a rest house known as a dak bungalow.[48]

In the 1840s the government constructed and subsequently maintained a network of dak bungalows. Managed by an Indian caretaker, these were useful for officials and other travellers who were able to rest, eat and have a bath inside them. But the level of comfort did not encourage guests to linger. Each bungalow seemed to have its special infestation – bats, mice, snakes, wasps or pigeons in the roof – and the walls were so thin that one could often hear what was going on in the next room. The food was as entirely predictable as the accommodation. No travellers expected anything other than a tough and flavourless chicken – caught, killed and cooked within half an hour of their arrival – followed by boiled custard or a caramel pudding.

As Calcutta's streets improved in the second half of the eighteenth century, palanquins were gradually replaced by horse-drawn vehicles for urban transport. The capital later thronged with varieties of buggies, barouches and carriages. In finding it 'necessary to keep a carriage' for his 'wife', William Hickey 'purchased a neat London-built chariot' plus a phaeton for his own use and 'three excellent draught horses'.[49] If they had had the choice, the British would have travelled everywhere on horseback or in carriages pulled by horses. Equine reverence was as strong in India as in the shires of England. If he could, a district officer toured his territory by horse, even if his tents and other baggage reached his camping grounds in bullock-carts. When roads improved, horses or ponies were also used for journeys to places far from railway stations. And they were of course essential for those sports adored by horsemen, pig-sticking and polo, the latter a sport taken so seriously by its devotees that, as one exasperated (non-playing) Gurkha officer observed, it was treated as 'a religion rather than a game'.[50]

Yet some areas of India were better suited to camels and elephants than to horses. When he became commissioner of Kumaon in the Himalayan foothills in 1913, Percy Wyndham was given a combination of the two, four elephants and a string of camels for his transport. Inspection tours in Assam and in the Chittagong Hill Tracts were best done on elephants even in the 1930s; at deep, unfordable rivers in Burma, where the rapids were too strong for boats, elephants could cross by swimming; and in parts of Bengal during the monsoon the only way a district officer could see how the crops were faring was on the back of an elephant.

Elephants were of course also used for ceremonial purposes. Photographs of the Coronation Durbar of 1903 – a long elephant procession around Delhi's Red Fort with Curzon and his wife on the leading animal, the Duke and Duchess of Connaught on the one behind, followed by maharajas and other princes on their bejewelled beasts – encapsulate for many the pomp and pointless pageantry of the Raj. Curzon was derided at the time by critics who dubbed the event a 'curzonation' rather than a coronation. As an Oxford undergraduate, he had been mocked in rhyme ('My name is George Nathaniel Curzon / I am a most superior person'), and the jibe stuck for the rest of his life, endlessly re-quoted in the press. Apocryphal stories of his love of formality and etiquette – it was alleged that his wife, Mary, had to curtsey to him in the mornings – circulated in India and Britain. Hostile newspapers, eager to stress the oriental ostentatiousness of his life, claimed he was always on top of an elephant; one jealous contemporary from their Eton days believed he even used them like cabs to meet him at railway stations. In fact Curzon was the first viceroy not to possess an elephant, and he needed to borrow one from a maharaja for the durbar. He never otherwise rode the animals except at tiger shoots – where they were essential – and described the experience as 'one of the most horrible forms of locomotion', especially for someone like himself who suffered from almost incessant back pain.[51]

Camels also had ceremonial roles, though not so grand and in any case limited to the north-west. In the early twentieth century the lieutenant-governor of the Punjab led cavalcades in 'a lumbering old landau drawn by four magnificent camels, each with a blue-turbaned rider on its back'. Yet by the time Edwin Lutyens entered it in 1913 this vehicle had grown or been transformed – or perhaps it had been changed altogether – into 'a sort of charabanc drawn by six huge camels – each camel being mounted by a man in red uniform, with twelve red-coated men on the box'.[52] Camels were sometimes used in combination with elephants in northern India, in Kumaon and in forestry operations in Ramnagar and Haldwani, but camel transport was used only in the hot- or cold-weather seasons: it had to be stopped as soon as the rains began, because the animals were unable to walk in the mud, and if they fell down they could only get up again if branches were spread over the ground to give them a footing. They may have been in their element in the harsh and arid landscape of Sind, where they were the essential conveyance, and even a junior district officer would have seven camels for baggage as well as one for riding. Yet they could be difficult there also, especially when getting them on to boats to cross the Indus. Sometimes they were so obstinate that their legs had to be tied under them when they were kneeling so that they could be rolled like casks down the banks and over planks and on to the vessel.[53]

The British never liked the beasts, at least not in India. Even Private Swindlehurst, cheery and positive though he was about most things, found it impossible 'to love a camel as a man could love a horse'. Camels were 'horrible looking animals, slobbering about, making weird groans and squeaks'; they were also, he insisted, 'treacherous'. Others thought their smell was the worst thing about them, even more disagreeable than the noises they made. The wife of the political agent in Bahrain, where a camel was the obvious means of transport, found it preferable to ride to her camp on a donkey rather than on that 'groaning, grunting, snapping brute'.[54]

MACHINES

In 1886 a group of Indian artisans came to London for the Indian and Colonial Exhibition to demonstrate their traditional skills as weavers, potters, coppersmiths and other craftsmen. Although these men were in fact convicts, serving prison sentences in Agra, Queen Victoria was eager to record the appearance of some of 'her more humble Native subjects' (as the press called them) and she commissioned an Austrian painter, Rudolph Swoboda, to paint portraits of five of them. So delighted was she by the results that later in the year she sent the artist to India to paint some more. She knew what the maharajas looked like – a selection of them was always in London for the 'season' – but she wanted to know about the appearance of her 'more humble' subjects.

Swoboda duly went to India and spent some time in Lahore with Lockwood Kipling, who later designed the Durbar Room for the queen-empress at Osborne on the Isle of Wight. Then he went into the Punjab countryside and with strong colours and vibrant brushwork depicted farmers and soldiers, artisans and village girls, young men with dramatic turbans, old men with terrific beards. The emphasis was on the traditional and the picturesque, as his patron desired. But on one canvas he placed a hint of the modern into an apparently timeless rural scene. In the bottom-left-hand corner of 'A Peep at the Train', below a Sikh family gathered to gaze at the miracle, is a section of gleaming rail, a reminder of one of the great gifts – at least they thought of it as a gift – that the Victorians bequeathed their Indian empire.

India had no railways before 1850, and at the time of the Rebellion only 570 miles of track; by 1875 it had 6,541 miles, by 1900, 25,000 miles of trunk and branch lines, and in 1947, 45,000 miles of railways, by far the largest network in Asia. Financed largely by British capital, it was an enormous enterprise, the largest investment made in the Victorian empire. The colossal scale of the undertaking was unlike anything attempted by British contractors and engineers before; laying tracks across the shires or even across the Pennines was simply not comparable to bridging the Punjab rivers or tunnelling through the Western Ghats. When erecting the girders of the Sher Shah bridge across the Chenab in the 1880s, the North Western Railway (NWR) employed some 5,000 Indian labourers; more than 400,000 Indians were being employed in railway construction in the Subcontinent in the year 1898. In the southern province the diggers or 'excavators' usually came from a caste that British engineers called Wudders or Wodders – more accurately, Oddar in Tamil and Vodda in Kannada.[55]

By the 1860s the railways were the biggest employer of British men in India after the military: railway families numbered over 6,000 people in the 1891 census. Most of them were working for the East Indian Railway Company and other firms in such roles as foremen, fitters, firemen, shunters, lamp-makers and plate-layers. But engineers were also employed by maharajas and nawabs who were developing their own state railways. Thomas Craigie Glover, a Scottish engineer who became a contractor, made forty-two working visits to India, dividing his labour and expertise between British companies such as the Bombay, Baroda and Central Indian Railway and the state railways of the Maharaja of Gwalior and the Begum of Bhopal. Most of the British railwaymen lived in bungalows in railway quarters or 'colonies' (as did a similar number of Eurasian employees),* communities with their own churches, clubs, schools and institutes, but superintendents would live on trains while doing their inspections. They had their personal coach, a long one with room for a family compartment, a bathroom, a kitchen and sleeping quarters for their servants. Sometimes they had their coach pulled into a siding so that they could go out to shoot some birds for supper or on Sundays to take their families to the nearest garrison church.[57]

Nowhere in India were differences in wealth and hierarchy more starkly displayed than on the railways, both in the stations and in the four different classes on the trains. Although first-class passengers had 'waiting-rooms', railwaymen referred to areas for third-class travellers

---

* The figures and ratios of the two communities altered in the twentieth century so that by 1939 the number of British employees of the railways had dropped to 2,500 while the Eurasians (by then known as Anglo-Indians) had risen to nearly 13,000.[56]

as 'waiting-sheds'. Notices in first and second class said 'reserved for ladies', but in the class below they read 'women only'. When fourth class was introduced in 1874, it had no seats, not even the hard wooden benches of the class above, although public criticism forced a change a decade later. Fourth class was then renamed third, and third became 'intermediate', so there were still four classes. Not all railway companies were the same, even when nationalized towards the end of the Raj, but as late as 1941 the NWR was the only one that provided latrines in all its third-class coaches.[58]

At the top of the hierarchy on the tracks were the special trains for viceroys and governors when on tour. For the viceregal southern trip of 1900, which lasted eight weeks and covered 6,000 miles, Curzon's special train carried, apart from the viceroy, his wife and their personal servants, his military secretary, private secretary and assistant private secretary, his surgeon and dispensary, four ADCs, several senior officials and a further eighty-five Indian servants. Gubernatorial trains may have been comfortably fitted out, but they were not much more successful than others at dealing with the heat. On his tours in the 1940s the governor of Madras was often working in the afternoons, his carriage in a siding, with the temperature at times reaching 115°F, when fans ceased to be effective: 'they merely blew hot air down one's neck'. Using damp grass screens and building a palm-leaf shelter over the roof did not make a great deal of difference. The viceroy at the time, Lord Linlithgow, also had a train without air-conditioning, but 'blocks of ice would be loaded at intervals into the compartments, and fans playing on the ice made a grateful breeze'. Some railway companies provided their customers with a large zinc tub with ice, and mothers sometimes wrapped their children in Turkish towelling and sat them on the blocks.[59]

The British often expected their compatriots to travel first class even if they were not officials. When E. C. Cox arrived in Calcutta as an aspiring tea planter in the 1870s, it was 'impressed upon' him that he was a 'sahib' and 'a member of the ruling race', and as such he must not 'lower his position by travelling in anything less than second-class'; even a second-class ticket was 'only permissible' when one's 'financial position absolutely prohibits the luxury of a first'.[60] First class was also considered obligatory for globetrotters from Britain, especially those who came out for a few months planning to become experts on India and perhaps even write a book about it. One of these, who disembarked at Bombay shortly before the First World War, was delighted to find that 'the coupé assigned' to her was much larger than on the 'so-called "train de luxe" in Europe, and the berths both wider and longer'. The compartments usually had leather-covered seating that was transformed into two, three or four beds at night, and they possessed their own lavatory and shower. By the end of the nineteenth century some trains had a comfortable dining car but, as they had no corridors, passengers could only reach it at stations and then had to remain in it until the next stop. By the 1920s the situation had changed. Describing a journey with his brigade by rail in 1929, Sergeant Meneaud-Lissenburg noted how the old compartments had been replaced by long corridor carriages with tip-up sleeping bunks. The officers had their own first-class carriage with its restaurant car at the front of the train, while the men were at the back, receiving meals in tiffin-carriers cooked on Calor gas cookers in the troop kitchen.[61]

The issue of provisions needed advance planning for long and sometimes complicated journeys that often ended in the middle of the night. Some passengers liked the bustle of platforms and refreshment rooms – run by Spencer's in the south and Kellner's in the north-east – enjoying iced aerated drinks at station stops. John Masters loved the restaurant at Pathankot Station, where the menu was always the same – chicken curry and caramel custard – the bottles of pickle and Worcestershire sauce were always the same, and the 'decrepit staff' managed to preserve 'the identical egg and grease stains on the fronts of their off-white clothes'.[62] Less adventurous souls insisted on packing food and drink sufficient for the entire journey. Yet when it lasted a couple of days or more and required not only changes of trains but also changes of transport, a combination of prudence and foraging, domestic rations and discoveries en route, was more common.

The great cities of the Plains were linked by rail by the 1880s, but it took a while longer for the tracks to reach the hill stations. Simla, the summer capital of the empire, did not receive a passenger train until 1903, when the line from Kalka, climbing 5,000 feet of gradients through a succession of loops and 103 tunnels, was completed. The trip from Allahabad, the administrative capital of the United Provinces, to Naini Tal, their summer capital, required six different forms of transport, or seven if you went via Kanpur. When Daisy Clay, a Civilian's wife, did the journey in the years before the First World War, she sent her luggage to the station in hand-barrows or buffalo-drawn carts and took her three small daughters in a tum-tum (dog-cart). They spent the rest of the day in the broad-gauge East Indian Railway to Lucknow, where they changed to the narrow-gauge Rohilkund and Kumaon Railway for the night run to Kathgodam, the end of the line. They then went up into the hills in tongas, two-wheeled carriages usually pulled by small sturdy ponies from Tibet that had to be changed every three miles. After ascending several thousand feet in these, they got out and were carried by dandy wallahs along a path to their accommodation.

In the train Daisy heated the family rations on a small methylated-spirit stove that had its own saucepan and kettle, but as she gave her children goat's milk, which was non-tuberculous, she did not need to boil the milk. At dawn at Lalkuan Junction they ate chota hazri, ordered before from the station's restaurant, but 'everything', recalled Daisy's daughter Audrey, including 'the white buffalo butter on the rather soggy toast, tasted strongly of smoke'. Breakfast at Kathgodam was not a great success either, much like chota hazri but with the addition of *dallia*, 'a sloppy sort of wheat porridge' and a 'soft semolina-like mess called *suji*, made from millet and often given to children'. Better things (though not specified in Audrey's memoir) awaited them in the hills at 'a pleasant hotel' called the Old Brewery, where all travellers stopped for tiffin and a rest before embarking on the final stage.[63]

Railway travel was by far the most important form of mechanical transport in British India. Yet there were a few other types. Horse-drawn trams appeared in the 1870s, and electric trams followed at the turn of the century. The city of Kanpur built some tramways, but these were otherwise limited to Madras, Calcutta, Bombay and Delhi; there were no trams in such large towns as Karachi, Lahore, Bangalore or Dacca. Bicycles became popular at about the same time, and were used over a much larger geographical area; canal engineers often adopted them for riding along the banks to inspect their waterways. Many district officers took to cycling to cutchery (their office and magistrate's court), sometimes with their dogs running at their side. Yet bicycling increased the risk of rabies, the sight of ankles tempting street dogs to have a snap. Civil aviation arrived in India rather later and had made little progress before the Second World War. Boxwallahs in Madras did not much relish going up into the skies when it was so difficult to find somewhere to come down again, 'being foiled by telephone wires and goats' and perhaps forced to land in a dried-up reservoir. Yet air travel could be useful to the privileged. Joan Reid was living with her husband, the political agent at Gilgit, a remote spot with few medical facilities in north-western Kashmir, when in 1938 she discovered she was pregnant. As her father was at that time acting governor of Bengal, she could fly to Darjeeling, at the other end of the Himalaya, and have her baby at Government House.[64]

Governors also liked motor cars, which arrived in India in large numbers after the First World War. When touring the province of Madras in the 1920s, Lord Goschen and his party proceeded in six vehicles, two Arrol Johnstons from Dumfries and four American cars – a Nash, an Oakland and two Chevrolets. As in all modern societies, much discussion took place about which makes were best and which were best suited to differing types of Indian conditions. Sir George Stanley, Goschen's successor in Madras, liked to ride in a Sunbeam made in Wolverhampton, a 20hp touring car with a hood, but he had Fords for his entourage and for his visits to the Hills. In 1934 he advised *his* successor, Lord Erskine, to buy a Ford because it would be 'especially useful up at Ooty [Ootacamund, the summer capital of the province] for going out fishing etc as the roads are indifferent and could knock a good car to pieces'. For more official purposes he should line his car with some sort of insulation material 'so that one can motor in it without a topee', and he should also make sure that it was 'fairly high in the roof' because, when he had an ADC in uniform at his side, the fellow had to 'wear a helmet with a spike and sometimes with feathers', which required 'a good deal of headroom'.[65]

Officials also saw the advantages of having a motor car, although possession necessitated the addition of an extra servant to a household that was already pretty large: a car man who was not a chauffeur and was seldom allowed to drive the vehicle; he was hired to keep it clean and *push* it (with help if necessary) up the drive when it was needed. By the late 1920s some district officers were urging their subordinates to buy cars, which meant that obedient junior Civilians had to raise money on their life assurance or find some other way of buying an Austin or a second-hand Morris Oxford. A 'pram', as the Austin Seven was rather disparagingly known, was the usual choice, but some officials decided it was 'too light for rough roads' and bought instead a

Chevrolet, which was also inexpensive. It may be a telling comment on comparative technologies that officials of the British Raj so often preferred American cars to those manufactured in Britain. A Civilian in Sind bought one Chevrolet after another, while a colleague in Bihar concluded that for his district work, even on rocky and unmetalled roads, his horse was less useful than 'a robust Chevrolet with a good clearance'. The brand might have leather seats that became sticky in the heat, but it was bought with loose covers of khaki drill 'to cope with perspiring passengers'.[66]

Yet motoring in India was far from easy. Sometimes it was better to ride a bicycle, and in hill areas the quickest way to travel was often on motorbikes, though these were not so suitable on the Plains, where there was so much dust that it was difficult to see where you were going, even with goggles. All motor cars, even Chevrolets, could break down or have a puncture on Indian roads. Crescent-shaped bullock shoes, discarded by their wearers and strewn across the way, cut so many tyres to shreds that drivers were advised to carry more than one spare wheel. Overtaking bullock-carts on narrow roads was also dangerous, and further hazards, noted one Civilian, included carts coming in the opposite direction pulled by an 'adventurous bullock that would attempt to climb on the bonnet of the oncoming car'.[67]

PART TWO

ENDEAVOURS

6

Working Lives: Insiders

POOH-BAHS ON THE PLAINS

The essential administrative unit of British India was the 'district'. The empire, as Curzon pointed out, 'may be governed from Simla or Calcutta, but it is administered from the plains', that is, from the civil stations.[1] In 1902 there were some 250 districts, containing an average population of nearly a million people. Although they were both divided into subdivisions and multiplied to form divisions under a commissioner, the fundamental unit was the district, just as the key administrative figure was the district officer.

District officer or 'DO' was a generic description, not a post or a job title. Different provinces gave different names to the same official. In Bengal and the United (formerly North-Western) Provinces he was magistrate and collector, in Madras and Bombay he was known as collector and district magistrate, and in the newer provinces (the Punjab, the Central Provinces, Assam, Burma and – from 1901 – the North-West Frontier) he was called deputy commissioner. The administrative development of British India was haphazard and confusing, but for the role of the district officer there are two crucial dates: 1786, when he became responsible for the assessment and collection of land revenue, and 1831, when his powers as a magistrate were strengthened and specified. From then on he possessed a dual persona with separate offices and different sets of clerks who were prone to write to each other in acrimonious and long-winded styles. One district officer 'used to find drafts from myself as magistrate to myself as collector accusing myself of neglect and delay, and some very trenchant replies placed before me for signature'.[2]

THE BRITISH IN INDIA

In 1913 John Maynard compared his role as a district officer to Pooh-Bah, the Gilbert and Sullivan character in *The Mikado* who 'combined in his person all the functions of state with the exception of the post of public executioner'.[3] While Maynard did not run the railways or the telegraph or the military – though he had the power to call out troops in an emergency – he was responsible for almost everything else. Apart from his duties as chief magistrate and revenue officer, the DO was responsible for law and order and the implementation of new laws; he was in charge of the police, the jail and the law courts, as well as the treasury, the excise and the records, and he had overall responsibility for forests, roads, schools, hospitals, fences, canals and agriculture. In more remote places the DO had even more duties. As deputy commissioner in the 1930s of the Chittagong Hill Tracts, John Christie found he was also district judge, district engineer and district agricultural officer, as well as the public health officer and superintendent of police.[4] Being 'in charge' did not of course mean that the DO ran all these things without delegating. In most stations he was supported by a handful of British officials (assistant magistrates in the ICS, a doctor, a chief of police, plus members of the Forest and Public Works departments) and a large number of Indians working with him, including deputy magistrates and deputy collectors (not in the ICS) as well as a huge office staff with, among many clerks, a 'weeder' of documents and a 'bundle-lifter', and numerous officials in the mofussil such as the tahsildar (a revenue officer in charge of a subdivision), and in each village the patel (the headman), the patwari (the accountant and registrar) and the chowkidar (the policeman). A crucial figure in the office, even where the DO was a good linguist, was the 'head vernacular clerk'.

As a collector in Orissa in 1873, John Beames began his working day in cutchery, listening to petitions and looking at the police-charge book containing the murders, burglaries and other criminal cases recently recorded. After deciding which of these to try himself and which to pass on to the joint magistrate, he interviewed the head clerks of his departments, gave appropriate orders and then settled down to his correspondence with the commissioner and other officials. After a quick tiffin with the joint magistrate and the superintendent of police, Beames dealt with his revenue officials before returning to his bungalow to receive rajas and other local dignitaries.[5]

When he was not in cutchery, the DO was usually inspecting things.

In 1903 the collector of Faridpur in Bengal explained the nature of these duties to his uncle, a clergyman in Devon. Apart from the treasury, where he had to count the notes, he had to inspect his district's twenty police stations and registration offices once a year, the subdivisional offices twice a year, the distillery once a month, and the jail once a week.[6] Inspections filled even more of the district officer's routine during his cold-weather tours, when at each village he visited he had to examine the fields, the drains, the roads, the wells, the school and (if it had one) the dispensary.

Although much of the DO's work was slow and bureaucratic, carried out at a pace determined by the secretariat in his province and the bundle-lifter in his office, he was often required to act quickly and decisively, and sometimes in ways that were bound to make him unpopular with people under his care. If he was near a town when a fire broke out, he had to judge what the wind was doing – and likely to do – and then order his engineers to pull down two rows of houses to leeward; if he sacrificed some buildings, the flames might not spread, and the rest could then be saved. Similar decisions had to be made in floodtime, when the water was rising in the canals, and the Civilian had to choose which areas should be saved and which he should allow to be deluged. During floods in Upper Sind in the early 1940s, an assistant collector, Roger Pearce, decided to cut a canal fed from the Indus, an action that would preserve the town of Larkana but condemn his own subdivision and inundate a lot of land belonging to the Bhuttos, a powerful family destined in due course to become even more powerful. When the Bhuttos sent some of their people to repair the breach, the Indian DO, Venguayyar Isvaran, dispatched policemen to guard it, while Pearce went to his subdistrict to help with the evacuation and try to get the foodgrains, mainly wheat and rice, above the water.[7]

After a terrible famine in Orissa in 1865, the viceroy Lawrence declared that district officers had a duty to preserve the lives of every person in their districts. Few Civilians needed such prompting: careers and reputations, as well as consciences, could be wrecked by a badly managed famine. If the rains were meagre or delayed, explained James Sifton in 1903, he and his colleagues went off 'scouring the district looking for any traces of scarcity'; if they heard the slightest whisper that 'the cattle or the children in any part' of it were 'looking thin', the DO and the commissioner flew off to investigate.[8] When famine did occur, their main duties were to provide relief works, such as digging tanks (small reservoirs) and getting food to the afflicted areas, not an easy task far from railway lines because in districts where people were starving there was unlikely to be enough fodder to feed the bullocks needed to pull the necessary carts. A more unusual problem, which John Beames encountered in the 1860s during his early career in the Punjab, was that hungry people sometimes openly committed theft so that they would be sent to prison and get themselves fed.[9]

Civilians also had to deal with bubonic plague – the Black Death of the Middle Ages – which arrived in Bombay in 1896 (brought by rats on ships from Hong Kong). Heading committees of doctors, sanitary commissioners and inspectors of hospitals, they descended on infected towns and villages and sent their populations to emergency camps. Yet desperate and sometimes over-zealous measures often inflamed people upset by compulsory inspections by doctors and restrictions on how and where they should bury their dead. After British troops were used tactlessly to search for hidden plague corpses in Poona, the assistant collector and an army officer were assassinated by Hindu revivalists objecting to the anti-plague precautions. When the plague spread eastwards to the Bihari districts of Bengal, government officials were ordered to be less interfering. If the inhabitants believed that their rulers were attempting to kill them with disinfectants, then they must not be compelled to use them; it was better not to purify water by pouring Condy's fluid down the wells if the prospective drinkers thought that the process was turning it into poisoned blood.[10]

Some of his duties pitted the DO against animals and nature. He might be pleased if villagers asked him to get rid of a herd of black buck that was damaging their crops, because the request would give him some sport as well as a change of diet from scrawny chicken. He would be happy too when a goatherd appealed to him to shoot a crocodile that grabbed his goats when they went to the river to drink; one would feel little compunction about shooting crocodiles after one had opened them up and found anklets and nose-rings inside them, though the reptiles performed a useful service by devouring corpses thrown into rivers by relatives who had economized on fuel during cremation. It was less enjoyable to shoot rabid-looking street dogs or to get rid of colonies of bats and monkeys, and only the most obsessive hunter relished shooting elephants, whether they were 'rogues' or just wild ones entering a village and pulling down its banana trees, looting rice stores or attacking bullock-carts loaded with grain.

A vigorous approach was also required to combat the water hyacinth, a plant which, as so frequently happens, had been imported to ornament a garden, and then became rampant in Bengal in the 1930s, covering reservoirs and choking waterways, killing fish, obstructing boats and creating a breeding ground for malaria. District officers had to mobilize men in each infected village and persuade them to go into the water and pull out every plant.[11] Vigour was also required to combat desert locusts that would infest an area and strip it of its vegetation. In 1931 at Ajmer in Rajputana Edward Wakefield flooded the land (where there was water) and ploughed it (where there was not) in order to destroy their eggs. But many millions survived to become 'hoppers' – creatures growing from the size of an ant to the dimensions of a grasshopper – which had to be destroyed before they grew wings and became indestructible locusts. Wakefield tried poison, on which the hoppers managed to thrive, but he had more success with digging trenches, driving them into them and then covering them up, a campaign that took several weeks but succeeded with the help of the local birds (especially kites and bee-eaters) and villagers, though not from the local Jain community, whose members refused to take the life of any creature.[12]

A DO's duties also extended to religious and communal affairs. As there were only 110,000 Anglicans in the whole of India, half of them in army barracks and half of the rest in the large cities, Church of England chaplains (in India usually known as 'padres') were very thinly spread. Although the ICS did not require any kind of religious affiliation (after 1853 a Civilian could be a Hindu, a Sikh, a Muslim or a Buddhist), most district officers were Anglicans and were expected to perform certain duties when the padre was absent or did not exist, celebrating matins in the Circuit House or even his own drawing room as well as marrying people, christening babies and conducting the burial service. One of them even married himself to a Burmese girl, though this did not impress the government, which claimed it was illegal to perform one's own marriage ceremony. Even in those places where there was a resident clergyman, the parish might be so enormous that he could not get round it all in the same Sunday. A DO nearly always had to officiate in the Sind town of Hyderabad because the rest of the padre's parish lay on the other side of the Indus.[13]

A more difficult task for the district officer was the handling of other people's religions and the communal tensions sometimes arising from them. He would have liked to intervene with Hindu pilgrimages, which often resulted in the spread of disease and consequent deaths of poor pilgrims. Yet he was aware that this would be interpreted as an attempt to subvert their religion and lead to riots, so it was better to run the risk of plague. He could not stand aside, however, if religious celebrations were used to provoke a rival community. When a Hindu festival such as Dussehra coincided with Muharram, the first month of the Islamic year, he had to take precautions. As Harcourt Butler, then a young Civilian in the North-Western Provinces, reported in 1892, 'We have to take severe measures to prevent riots, riding at the head of procession, with warrants ready signed in our pocket. It is sometimes ticklish work.'[14]

Much of the trouble stemmed from the emergence of cow-protection societies, a consequence of a late-nineteenth-century Hindu revival and resurgence of Brahminical emphases on purity and pollution. 'Kine-killing' soon became an intense political issue, Hindu opponents mobilizing against festivals such as Eid al-Adha, the Islamic 'Feast of the Sacrifice'. Riots – and deaths – frequently ensued. Both communities often found it difficult to resist the temptation to provoke. Muslims did not need to sacrifice a cow – a sheep, a goat or even a camel would do – but, as Butler observed, the wealthier ones would sometimes kill two or three cows just to annoy their neighbours. Hindus might then react by diverting their processions so that they passed by a mosque, where they would place a pig's head under the gate and play loud music during the hour of prayer.[15]

Most of the festivals were all-night affairs, parades carrying on day after day with banners, torches, music, drums and a lot of shouting. DOs and their assistants stayed up till morning to stop them from becoming violent. Sometimes they had to limit the numbers in a procession, the hours when it could take place, the routes it could follow, and the time the music must stop. They might draw a chalk line across the road to show Hindus where they must stop playing their instruments and then not resume until their procession had gone beyond a mosque. Usually the sight of a DO with a couple of policemen outside a temple or a mosque was a deterrent to riot, but they could not patrol every potential battlefield. Midnapore in Bengal possessed an open space used for football, with a mosque at one end and a temple at the other. In 1926 rival mobs gathered at their respective ends, cries of 'Allah! Allah!' trying to drown the sound of temple bells, and then attacked each other. The DO and his policemen were too few to prevent them, and troops from the local auxiliary force had to be called in.[16]

District officers hoped that they deserved to be called 'Ma-Bap' ('mother and father'), the traditional appellation with which Indians in their district addressed them when seeking assistance, submitting a grievance or begging release from some penalty. Paternalistic feelings were inherent in their office; these had often been the motivation behind their joining the ICS, and their early experiences in India tended to reinforce them. While they might be prejudiced against the 'babu'* or 'educated native', they seemed preternaturally predisposed in favour of the 'ryot' or peasant or landless labourer. Walter Francis, a young magistrate stationed near Madras, was typical of many of his colleagues. Writing to his former Oxford tutor in 1893, he admitted that he liked

> the illiterate rustic who can't sign his name. He's a staunch fellow, and a good chap, and treats you as you treat him, and his tremendously strong love of his village and his children and his old parents, and the way he works for them all day in the sun with the prospect of only 2 pounds of cold *raggi* porridge in the evening are things to admire. The animal part of him isn't his fault, so much as that of centuries of suffering and oppression. But your snake of an educated native I can't abide. I've never met one that I respected. They're a crawling, round-the-corner sort of lot, and no one ever knows what they're really up to.[17]

The DO considered himself a patron of the villager, not just because he protected him against the landlord, the money-lender and even the alchemist – important though all this was – but also because he was often urging him to improve the health and prosperity of his family. John Maynard, who joined the ICS in 1886, was a socialist (in retirement he stood unsuccessfully as a Labour Party candidate in three different constituencies), but he realized at the beginning of his Indian career that British rule was essential because 'the natives, gentle, simple and dreamy, [were] dependent on Englishmen for everything'.[18] District officers often became obsessed by their work, as Leonard Woolf was in Ceylon, rarely thinking 'of anything else except the District and the

* See below, p. 404.

people, to increase their prosperity, diminish the poverty and disease, start irrigation works, open schools'.[19] The zeal could sometimes be overdone, and encouragement turn into hectoring, as it did with Frank Lugard Brayne, a talented Punjab Civilian of the twentieth century with an evangelical fervour more common a hundred years earlier. In Gurgaon, south-west of Delhi, he pursued a policy known as 'Village Uplift', exhorting inhabitants to carry out agricultural and sanitary improvements with such vigour that villagers became both sceptical and alarmed. It was generally better to be persuasive than hortatory.

The idea of enlightened despotism, so long as it was benevolent, appealed to district officers. They might miss London and Oxford and their families at home, but they usually felt good, at least when they were young, about themselves and the work they were doing. As one Civilian put it in verse, describing a ride of inspection in the 1930s,

> I knew that the world was on my shoulders
> And for just this reason my heart was light.[20]

A contemporary in Bengal voiced a similar feeling when he wrote, 'On the ride to work in the morning one felt ready to reform the world.'[21] When Walter Francis wrote another letter to his Oxford tutor in 1893, he dwelt on the satisfaction of responsibility. At the age of twenty-four he was in charge of 4,000 square miles and more than a million people. The work was 'real and satisfactory', and one couldn't 'complain that one has nothing to devote one's energies to, or that one's wasting one's life'.[22] Yet however much he and his colleagues might like some of their 'subjects', friendships were seldom made, except perhaps with a local raja or zemindar (landowner). Sometimes they justified this failure by claiming that the people themselves wanted fairness from the British rather than their friendship.[23] Many of them also felt that the necessary 'respect' of the governed would be compromised by closeness, so that they needed to be – or appear to be – aloof at the same time that they had to be accessible. As one Victorian Civilian put it, the DO had to combine two apparently 'incompatible things, a maximum of accessibility to the public without losing the dignity of his office', which he would do if he were 'continually allowing himself to be waylaid in the streets'.[24] Yet the lack of friendship did not prevent many from loving their district and sometimes refusing promotion so that they could remain in it. Robert Carstairs spent fourteen years from 1885 in the remote and forested Santal Parganas because, as a later governor of Bengal put it, he was 'one of those unassuming, devoted officers to whom a life spent in the service of the people of a single district was an end in itself'.[25] Others had the Tennysonian fantasy of the perpetual paternalist putting down his roots and never stirring them. If Virginia Stephen had refused to marry him, Leonard Woolf was planning to return to Ceylon, not aspiring to become a governor with a knighthood but simply to run a district, to take a post that would be 'a final withdrawal, a final solitude, in which, married to a Sinhalese', he would make his district 'the most efficient, the most prosperous place in Asia'.[26]

JUDGES IN THE STATION

The most time-consuming of the DO's various jobs was that of district magistrate. His judicial powers may not have been very extensive, being limited to issuing prison sentences of no more than two years and levying fines of no more than 1,000 rupees, but the spread of his responsibilities was too wide – and their dimensions were too many – for him to be properly effective. It was clearly not a satisfactory system to have to combine the functions of detective, magistrate and minor judge, especially when he had to rely for much of his evidence on corrupt Indian policemen. As Herbert Thompson wrote of his role in the 1920s, 'theoretically I could arrest a culprit, try and sentence him and in the end receive him in my jail to serve it'. The situation became almost surreal when the DO was required to be the prisoners' food-taster as well. Stephen Hatch-Barnwell was a curry enthusiast, but tasting the violently hot dishes of the jail of Dinapur in Bihar in the 1930s left him gasping and 'nearly took the top of [his] head off'.[27]

Crimes such as murder that were beyond a magistrate's powers were tried by a sessions judge, an officer of the ICS who also had a second identity; as district judge he dealt with important civil suits. He was of the same seniority as the DO, although he earned a slightly higher salary, and both had begun their careers as griffins in the same posts, as assistant magistrates in the older provinces and as assistant commissioners in the newer ones. The judges were not necessarily less able than the district officers, but they were usually less active and energetic, and in their thirties they had either opted, or been persuaded, to join the judicial line or what was known as the 'judgey' side. Before the 1870s there had been a certain flexibility, allowing men to pass from, say, a commissionership to a judgeship in a high court, but in that decade provincial governments initiated a policy of forcing Civilians of ten or twelve years' service to choose between spending the rest of their careers as administrators or setting up as judges.

The district judge and the district officer lived in the same station in similarly large bungalows, but the rhythms of their lives were very different. The DO finished his day conscious that there were a hundred things still to do. The judge ended his labours with the closing of the courtroom door. Without a proper lawyer's training, it may have been difficult for him to get on top of his work, assimilating the legal codes and learning how to write judgements and draft decisions on appeals. Yet once he had done so, his life was usually more placid and leisurely than his colleague's. He did not go on tour and he did not go on circuit. If he had intellectual interests – and many judges did – he had plenty of time to pursue the study of such subjects as Sanskrit, ancient inscriptions or south Indian palaeography. Charles Kincaid wrote some twenty books on Indian subjects, including a three-volume history of the Marathas, before he retired as a judge in the Bombay presidency in 1926.

Judges were allowed to be somewhat wayward in their tastes, a little eccentric in their habits. They were after all meant to be independent and impartial in their work, not drivers of the imperial programme in the way that district officers were. Yet they needed to return to conformity if they wished to rejoin the administration, even if only in a judicial position. In the 1890s two judges of the Madras High Court, George Arthur Parker and Francis Henry Wilkinson, were being considered for the post of judicial member of the Madras Council, the executive body of the province. The two had enjoyed very similar careers, both joining the ICS in 1862, both becoming district and sessions judges in 1882, and the two of them reaching the Bench in (respectively) 1886 and 1887. Yet a confidential memo to the governor (Lord Wenlock) on their merits showed that they were very different people. Wilkinson's drawbacks began with his wife, who in 'Madras society' was 'looked on as rather too cultivated, and once too intimate, in a literary sense', with the previous governor, the Liberal politician

Mountstuart Grant Duff. As for her husband – and these were clearly considered defects – it 'was whispered that he knows Italian and learns Hebrew'. 'Consequently' – and the memo-writer does not appear to have been using irony – 'I don't think he stands on such firm ground as Parker', who was not only 'imperturbable' but also 'level-headed, well-off and intensely dull and respectable'.* [28]

If the judge's district headquarters was a small station rather than a city or a garrison town, his life was likely to be lonely as well as sedentary. Even if he was a bachelor, he could not share lodgings with his ICS colleagues or with the superintendent of police in case they polluted his judgement with their views on a current trial. He could of course meet them in the Club, play whist or tennis and drink a brandy pawnee, but only in the hot weather. In the winter months the magistrates would be on tour, and he might be the only Englishman left in the station.

As we have seen, the ICS ran the administration at every level from griffin to lieutenant-governor, being excluded only from the viceroyalty, the governorships of Madras and Bombay, and two or three posts on the Viceroy's Council. Yet it ran the judiciary by itself only at district level. The service received merely a third of the appointments to the high courts, those vast monuments to the Victorian rule of law built in extravagant forms of architectural eclecticism, Flemish Gothic (Calcutta), Venetian Gothic (Bombay), Classical and later Edwardian Baroque (Allahabad) and Indo-Saracenic in red sandstone soaring above the Esplanade at Madras. The ICS might complain of the limitations, especially the one that prevented a Civilian from reaching the top post (chief justice), but few of its men, whatever experience they had gained as district and sessions judges, were legally well qualified. A law degree had not been part of their training, and almost the only men who had one were those who had passed through the Inns of Court in London on furlough, usually with a view to practising as lawyers in their retirement.

The East India Company had recognized the need for its territories to have judges and lawyers independent of itself; the Supreme Court (the precursor of the High Court) was beyond its jurisdiction. William Hickey had gone to Calcutta as an attorney and made enough money

---

* In the end the post was left unfilled.

to begin 'seriously to think it possible and probable' that he 'might survive long enough once more to visit the congenial shores of Old England . . .'[29] One of his contemporaries in the Bengal capital was Sir Robert Chambers, a friend of Samuel Johnson, who had relinquished his post as professor of law at Oxford University for a seat in the Supreme Court, where he eventually became chief justice. Later, in the days of the high courts, the benches were divided in thirds among judges from the ICS, barristers and advocates from Britain, and lawyers who had practised in India, usually as 'pleaders' in a high court, many of whom were Indians. Other jobs filled by British 'outsiders' in Calcutta in 1870 included solicitors, attorneys, proctors, articled clerks, officials of the Court of Small Causes and the Court for the Relief of Insolvent Debtors; forty-six members of the Calcutta Bar were British barristers-at-law. By 1877 the Bar at Allahabad had admitted forty advocates, some of whom were Indians trained at the Bar in London. Senior British officials were initially sceptical about the worth of Indians in the ICS as administrators, but they appreciated them as judges. Lord Canning appointed an Indian judge to the Calcutta High Court when it was set up in 1862. Alfred Lyall did the same in Allahabad soon after he became lieutenant-governor of the North-Western Provinces twenty years later. The secretariats were slower to react, but in time they saw the advantages of encouraging Indian Civilians to opt for the 'judgey' side. Such men had the advantage over inexperienced British judges in the district or sessions court; they were less likely to be outwitted by nimble Bengali advocates and later pilloried by the press for their shortcomings.

DESPOTS IN THE HILLS

The government of India, ran a Simla joke of the 1870s, was 'a despotism of office boxes tempered by the occasional loss of a key'.* Almost everyone complained about administrative red tape and bureaucracy, except of course those who were responsible for it: the secretaries, chief secretaries and under-secretaries of government who to outsiders seemed to compete with each other in producing the largest quantities

* See below, p. 449.

of paperwork in the form of notes, minutes, dispatches and reports. In George Aberigh-Mackay's satire, *Twenty-one Days in India* (1881), the government secretary

> inquired into everything; he wrote hundredweights of reports; he proved himself to have the true paralytic ink flux, precisely the kind of wordy discharge, or brain haemorrhage, required of a high official in India. He would write ten pages where a clod-hopping collector would write a sentence. He would say the same thing over and over again in a hundred different ways. The feeble forms of official satire were at his command.[30]

Anyone who has studied the files in the old India Office Library* must react with a combination of exasperation and admiration for both the prodigious paperwork and the time required by the administration to read it all and reach decisions. In the beginning is a report on, say, drainage systems, which manages to be long and verbose yet at the same time logical and well-written by a man invariably educated in both Latin and Greek. Beneath it is the minute of his superior, also eloquent and generally approving although plainly keen to demonstrate a slightly higher degree of knowledge, wisdom and experience. More minutes follow, in different coloured inks, as the file is passed to other departments interested in drainage systems, and it duly receives judgement from men who have sat long at their desks polishing the art of the put-down. One senior figure at the Finance Department is famous for needing to 'prove to his own satisfaction that everyone who [has] noted on it already [is] a born fool'.[31] After several months the file returns to its department of origin, where it goes to the secretary (the senior civil servant) and to *his* superior (the member of the Viceroy's Council) and, if deemed important enough, to the private secretary of the viceroy and thence to the viceroy himself. It is not always easy to identify the signatures and initials on the report, and sometimes it was difficult for the viceroy himself. 'On the whole,' Curzon once minuted, 'I agree with the gentleman whose signature resembles a trombone.'[32]

Although he was a notorious minuter himself, Curzon was appalled by the system which, he complained, resulted in 'a sort of literary

---

* The Library is now part of the Asia, Pacific and Africa Collections at the British Library.

Bedlam'. While attempting to run India, he told a subordinate, he did not require 'the personal impression or the opinion of everyone in the Department on everything that comes up'.[33] District officers were relieved when a Curzonian edict was issued, for the bureaucracy was often the chief bane of their working lives. Before railways and the telegraph, they had had to use their own influence and initiative to govern their districts; now they were constantly receiving orders and instructions from the chief secretary of their provincial government. They also had to submit to the new administrative obsession with gathering information, compiling statistics about the population which had limited value, and writing reports which few people bothered to read. In the 1850s a district officer in the Punjab had famously made his decisions on the back of his horse; by the end of the century he was 'required to have at his elbow some seventeen volumes of laws and rules, including three thick volumes of *Acts and Regulations Applicable to the Punjab*'. As George Hamilton, the secretary of state, lamented in 1899, 'in place of the old-fashioned official constantly in the open air, and constantly coming in contact with the Natives, we have substituted a bureaucratic class, who are seldom able to leave their offices, and who govern India with a code in one hand and a telegraph wire to the Governor in another'.[34]

The secretaries were not of course a different species from the district officers. They too were members of the ICS, and all of them had been assistant magistrates (junior district officers) themselves. In 1901, the year that Queen Victoria died, the ICS consisted of just over a thousand men, of whom about a fifth were at any time either sick or on leave. Some ninety of those on active service worked at desks in the capital and in the provincial capitals of Bombay, Madras, Lahore, Allahabad, Nagpur, Shillong, Rangoon and Calcutta (which was the capital both of a province and of the Indian Empire). Each of the seven departments of state in Calcutta had two or three members of the ICS except the Legislative Department, which had one, and the Military Department, which had its own officers. This was the Indian equivalent of Whitehall, but it was not by any standards a bloated bureaucracy.*

The secretary of a department was responsible to the relevant member of the Viceroy's Council, a sort of cabinet that met once a week in

---

* In 1905 Curzon added an eighth department, Commerce and Industry.

Calcutta or Simla and decided issues by a majority vote. Its members oversaw all the departments of state (Finance, Military, Legal, Home, Public Works and the joint one of Revenue and Agriculture) except the Foreign Office, which was under the direct control of the viceroy. They themselves did not always belong to the ICS: the legal and finance departments were usually headed by men sent from Britain, often with no experience of India, while the military member was a general in the Indian Army. The India Office in London liked to think that a combination of fresh blood from Britain and experience from India would produce an administration that was neither stale nor naive. Yet home-grown inexperience sometimes had its drawbacks. When Sir Edward Law was sent out as finance member in 1900, he designed a new rupee coin with a tiger on the reverse side, prompting Hamilton to question the wisdom of selecting a creature that terrified the 'natives'. Law then responded by choosing a lion for his coin, leading Curzon to observe that, as there were only a handful of these beasts still living in India (in the Gir Forest in Junagadh), it could not be regarded as a suitably symbolic animal.[35]

Provincial governments often left their least effective civil servants in the countryside, trekking from one station to another in the mofussil until they ended their careers as a district officer or a district and sessions judge. Yet their ablest men, those likely to reach the top of their government or even become a lieutenant-governor or a member of the Viceroy's Council, were rotated between the districts and the secretariat so that they gained experience of both. Young Civilians, exhilarated by their experiences in forests or hills or a native state, were sometimes reluctant to exchange them for a desk and the routine of a secretariat in a large town. Yet others realized that a change was important both for their careers and for their personalities. After three years in the Chittagong Hill Tracts, a remote area of east Bengal on the borders of Burma, John Christie feared he 'was beginning to resemble some jungle creature hanging by its tail from a tree'. Living mostly by himself, he 'felt like Caliban' and thought he was gaining 'a reputation of the wild man from the hills'.[36]

Christie duly accepted a transfer to New Delhi, by now the capital, allowing himself to be transformed from 'a jungle-cock crowing in the Hill Tracts' to a 'slave of the file'.[37] Most men accepted new postings even if only to avoid annoying the provincial chief secretary, who was the person in charge of their careers. Calibans coming in from the jungle often had to submit to a brisk course in etiquette. When Maurice Hayward was transferred to Poona as under-secretary of the Bombay government, his superior felt the need to coach him about taking his hat off and addressing the governor as 'sir' and his wife as 'your ladyship'. In a society rigid with formality, griffins were always aware of the dangers of a social faux pas. When dining with the lieutenant-governor on tour in the Punjab, Malcolm Darling only dared nibble his food in case the great man asked him a question and caught him with his mouth full.[38]

From the 1860s and 1870s the secretariats of the central and provincial governments spent half the year working in hill stations. Each province had a summer headquarters in the Hills except Assam, which had no need because its capital (Shillong) was already in the Hills. Bengal went to Darjeeling, Madras to Ootacamund, the North-Western (later United) Provinces to Naini Tal, the Central Provinces to Pachmarhi, and Burma to Maymyo, 3,000 feet up in the Shan Hills above Mandalay, where the climate was like an English summer and in spring the place was a paradise of violets and cherry blossom. Climatic considerations prompted Bombay to share its favours with Poona (until the weather was too hot) and Mahabaleshwar (until the monsoons caused landslides and made the buildings unsafe), and administrative complications persuaded the Punjab to distribute itself between Simla, Murree and Dalhousie.

The oddest and longest of the spring migrations was that of the imperial government, which sent hundreds of clerks and officials (together with their files and dispatch boxes) 1,200 miles from Calcutta to Simla, first by train across the Gangetic Plain and then (before the rail link of 1903) up winding gradients by bullock-cart, mail carriage and tonga, until they reached a small English-looking town of tin-roofed houses perched 7,000 feet up in mountains that cut it off from the rest of India. Responsibility for this bizarre proceeding lies mainly with John Lawrence, who as viceroy (1864–9) decided he could do more work in a day in Simla's invigorating climate than in five days of Calcutta's enervating humidity. Most officials naturally preferred to get away from stifling offices, where they sweated under the punkahs over documents clamped by paperweights to stop them blowing about. In the 1880s Anthony MacDonnell was 'very certain' that legislation would be 'infinitely better' if formulated when the thermometer was at 65°F rather than at 90°F. Sir Charles Dilke, the imperialist Liberal MP, shared his views, claiming that Simla's climate gave 'vigour to the Government, and a hearty English tone to the State papers issued in the hot months'.[39]

After working for seventeen years in the mofussil, Alfred Lyall became secretary of the Home Department in 1873. As someone who found it 'much easier to deal with papers than with men' and 'more simple to draft orders than to carry them out', he was delighted to exchange district work for an office. It gave him 'a throb of pure pleasure' to enter 'a large cool quiet office room, with mountains of papers scientifically filed by a first-rate head clerk on each side of an armchair'. He loved to be at Simla, which reminded him of Baden Baden, and he could work there all day in front of a log fire. Yet he worried that the government was 'almost dangerously cut off from the vast country which lives below us and beyond the hills'. It was 'curious to think of a party of Englishmen settled down here within the Asiatic mountains, and holding easily the whole continent of India down to either sea'.[40]

Critics of the Simla exodus also complained that the town was 'dangerously cut off', though for them the danger came less from hostile forces than from the government's annual insistence on distancing itself from the population it was meant to be governing. The scolds consisted mainly of people who were themselves unable to take advantage of hill stations, businessmen who had to carry on their businesses in the cities, newspaper editors who had less news to report, and an older generation of Civilians who in their day had had no choice but to swelter in the Plains or take a humid boat tour around their districts. Paroxysms of resentment were experienced by one former governor when he thought of the bureaucracy being 'above the reach of human censure, not to say human observation, amid the cloud-clapped mountains and mirth-bearing breezes of Simla'. George Russell Clerk had, unusually, been governor of Bombay twice, in the 1840s and the 1860s,* and in his retirement he fulminated against the 'absurdities and extravagances of Simla' and its 'highly-paid functionaries secluding themselves' and 'shirking their duties' by going there.[41] At the beginning of the following century, Lovat Fraser, a distinguished editor

---

* Between those decades he had been sent to southern Africa to help establish the Orange Free State.

of the *Times of India* in Bombay, made a similar but more measured complaint. A civil servant, he argued, should live all year among the people he was working for, he should accept interruptions and uncomfortable conditions, and he should keep himself accessible because 'personal accessibility is a thing that Asiatics greatly prize, and the institution of hill stations denies it to them'. The custom of going to the Hills for the summer, Fraser concluded, logically and undeniably, was 'largely to blame for the growing detachment of the British from the people of India'.[42]

THE POLITICALS

ICS officers did not have to choose only between judicial and administrative work. They also had the option of joining the government of India's Political Service (IPS), which was in charge of relations with the 680 'native states' that were run, with varying degrees of autonomy, by nawabs, maharajas and other hereditary rulers. In 1900 these states contained some 63 million people spread over an area of 700,000 square miles, about 40 per cent of the Indian landmass. Most of the smaller ones, some no larger than Hyde Park, were in the province of Bombay and were regulated by its government. The two largest, Hyderabad and Kashmir, were each the size of England and Scotland combined. They came within the orbit of the Political Department of the Foreign Office in Calcutta, which was under the direct control of the viceroy himself.

The relationships between Britain, the paramount power, and the Indian states varied in almost every case. Some of them were based on military alliances and treaties made by the East India Company in the early nineteenth century; others were more recent and 'less equal'. The chiefs of tiny states in Kathiawar could not exercise civil or criminal jurisdiction in their territories, but the nizam of Hyderabad, a 'subsidiary' ally since 1798, could coin money and execute his subjects. The status of the maharajas and their fellow rulers was a topic of spirited disagreement among their 'allies'. While some British administrators insisted that they were 'vassals' not 'sovereigns', others believed that they should be allowed to retain the pomp and aura of majesty even if they no longer possessed sovereign power.

However their status was defined, the autonomy of most states was gradually eroded during the course of the nineteenth century. As they were now protected by the British, rulers did not need to have their own armies and could spend their feudal rents on acquiring jewels and building palaces. But in return they had to cede control of foreign policy – they were not allowed one – and also in various internal matters, such as when railroads, cantonments or important roads were built on their territories. Degrees of British authority even extended beyond the borders of India, to Nepal, sometimes to Afghanistan, and increasingly to the Middle East. The East India Company had acquired Aden in 1839, and the government in London later extended the British presence in the region primarily to counter a perceived Russian threat to Persia and the Gulf. It then saddled the government of India with the task of staffing a series of posts from Muscat to Kerman with officers of the Indian Political Service.

'Politicals', as these men were called, aspired to become first political agents in small states, often on the frontiers, and in due course 'Residents' at the great Rajput courts (Jaipur, Jodhpur and so on) or with the Maratha princes (Gwalior, Holkar and Baroda) and, ultimately, at the states of Mysore, Hyderabad and (from 1885) Kashmir, which were at the top of the hierarchy. Yet some of them worked always on the periphery, and even beyond. One of the IPS posts was Political Resident in Turkish Arabia and HM consul-general in Baghdad; another was consul-general at Kashgar in Chinese Turkestan. Tom Hickinbotham became a Political in 1930 and spent almost his entire career outside India, in the Middle East and the Persian Gulf, starting at Aden and becoming political agent consecutively in Muscat, Kuwait and Bahrain. When there was no longer an Indian empire to employ him, the British government made him chairman of the Aden Port Trust, and in 1951 it appointed him Governor of the Colony and Protectorate of Aden.

The IPS encouraged diversity among its employees. 'We want lean and keen men on the frontier,' observed Harcourt Butler, 'and fat and good-natured men in the states.'[43]* Whatever their personality or physique, candidates had to be Civilians with five years' experience or army

* Butler himself was fat and good-natured, but he remained an administrator, rising to be lieutenant-governor of Burma in 1915–17 and 1923–7 (by then the post had been

officers under the age of twenty-six; they were also required to be unmarried at the time of entry and to pass a not very taxing exam. Civilians usually joined the service because they wished to see some of India beyond their particular province, especially when the powers of district officers were starting to contract between the world wars with the advance of provincial self-government. In Madras in the 1920s Herbert Thompson was advised to join the Finance Department, if he knew something about finance, or the Politicals if he was 'fond of dressing up in uniform' (princely courts being extremely formal about apparel). Although he does not appear to have been a very dressy individual, Thompson did join the political service and eventually became Resident for the Punjab States, with Lahore as his base, in charge of some forty states stretching from Sind to the western border of Tibet. Some of the rulers were very grand, such as the Sikh Maharaja of Patiala, but in the smallest of the states that Thompson oversaw the raja 'would share his palace with his cattle which walked through the front door and occupied the ground floor . . .'[44]

The political service also appealed to army officers who were bored by peacetime soldiering, spending season after season in a garrison drilling their troops and taking them on route marches. Although he became a general, the most interesting work in the life of John Low (1788–1880) was done as a Political – among other posts he was Resident in Lucknow and Hyderabad – not as a soldier. Military Politicals were certainly more open to Indian 'life' and culture than their colleagues who stayed with their regiments in the barracks, where they feasted with each other in the Mess and stuck together to play cricket and polo and go hunting. Many Politicals, like judges, combined a strong sense of history with a range of cultural hobbies. In a career that included postings to Bombay, Udaipur, Bhopal, Kashmir and Jaipur (as well as Abyssinia and Zanzibar), Colonel William Prideaux was able to indulge his passions for Indian archaeology and numismatics.

Palpable history was also part of the appeal for Civilian Politicals. Walter Lawrence transferred to the IPS in 1881 and went to Rajputana, where he was delighted to find that there at least 'the age of chivalry was not gone'; it was like 'the Middle Ages in sepia'. Anglo-Indian

renamed governor) and lieutenant-governor (later governor) of the United Provinces from 1918 to 1923.

romanticism was not a widespread affliction, but it did infect many of those who were sent to the Rajput courts and who found themselves in a world of castles, courts, minstrels and dancing girls. Even Alfred Lyall, sceptical and fastidious though he was, enjoyed being in a world where he seemed to be living among the barons of medieval Germany. 'The chief nobles hunt, drink, and fight when they are not prevented; they eat the wild boar and get tipsy in their castles.' Yet he did not wish to reform them, and he regretted that their British rulers were curbing their behaviour. 'I am afraid,' he told his mother, 'that we do not altogether improve the nobles by keeping them from fighting.'[45]

Walter Lawrence was even more spellbound by Kashmir than he had been by Rajputana. How wonderful it was to be in the vale, 'unspoiled by railways and roads, innocent of factories and coal', a place where on his travels as settlement commissioner he was 'sleeping in boats or in tents always pitched on green turf under the shade of plane or walnut trees, and always within sound of running, singing water'.[46] Like others, Lawrence was enchanted to be living in a sort of historical present, where history seemed to be still alive, where people lived in much the same way as their ancestors had lived. Humphrey Trevelyan, who joined the IPS a half-century after Lawrence, relished living in what he called 'Indian India', which was 'full of history and remains of the past', and where he was 'living on natural terms with Indians who had no sense of inferiority nor major political grievances'.[47] Politicals did not have to deal with strikers or rioters or difficult Congressmen.

It was said that the IPS consisted of soldiers with brains and Civilians who could ride and shoot. Politicals might concur with this description, but their high opinion of themselves was not always shared by their colleagues in the other services. Denzil Ibbetson, a very able Civilian who became lieutenant-governor of the Punjab, maintained that it was 'better to rule a district than humbug a Raja'. Others claimed that the Politicals did not do a proper job, that the service consisted of Civilians 'who shirked hard work and soldiers who did not get on with their regiments; and that they spent their time shooting and feasting with maharajas and tribesmen'.[48]

The department sent its ICS applicants to the frontier or a native state for six months, and its military aspirants to a district for eighteen months to learn about revenue and judicial work. After this training they were tested on their knowledge of Indian history, law and languages, but proficiency at exams was not the most important requirement for entrance into the service; the candidates had after all already passed the ICS or Sandhurst exams. Other qualities, usually neglected by the civil service, were deemed important for the diplomatic complexities inherent in life at the court of a native prince. Sporting ability was one. As many rulers were good shots, and as quite a few of them were also fine cricketers, it often made sense to choose men who could shoot and ride and make a few runs in a cricket match. Colonel Edward Bradford would never have passed the ICS exam, but he was a great success in Rajputana because of the respect he had won as a horseman who had fought with a tiger (and lost an arm in the combat) and had led his men in the Rebellion with only a riding crop in his hand.[49]

When Harry Grigg became Resident of Travancore and Cochin in 1892, a friend told him that a Residency was now 'the only appointment in the Service that could be occupied by a gentleman'.[50] The friend did not explain exactly what he meant, but gentlemanly behaviour, which included tact and good manners, was plainly essential. So were social *savoir faire* and a sense of etiquette. A Political had to know about uniforms, whether he should wear spurs with levee dress, and when he should put on a frock coat, his Mameluke sword and his white pith helmet with gold spike and chain. Above all he had to be relied upon not to make such social gaffes as shaking hands with an Indian woman or offering a namaste, closing the palms of his hands, to a Muslim man. Gaffes with his fellow countrymen had also to be avoided. Rupert Kilkelly's career as a Political ended abruptly when, while working for a Resident in Rajputana, he 'sent an official invitation to a Miss Hoare, and spelt the name wrong'. It was, apparently, 'the only kind he knew'.[51]

The 'lean and keen men' on the frontier looked down enviously, and sometimes derisively, at the 'fat and good-natured men' in what they called the Great Sloth Belt, the princely states of Rajputana and Central India. The epitome of the Plains Political was Colonel David Barr, a sedentary figure who weighed eighteen stone and was Resident in Gwalior, Kashmir and Hyderabad. Yet not even the 'lean and keen men' questioned his ability in these posts; he was so diplomatically adroit that he made things easy for his successors. Life as the Resident in a great Rajput or Maratha state could be comfortable when the maharaja was an efficient and reasonably submissive ruler, anxious not to cause trouble with the paramount power. But when the ruler was tyrannical or negligent and liked to spend his time at Ascot or in Paris at the Folies Bergères, the Resident had to blend tact with firmness; and sometimes, acting for the government in Calcutta, he had to depose him.

In the Company years British rulers had seldom refrained from overthrowing a ruler who defied it or annexing a state whose dynasty had died out. Yet as such actions had clearly been among the causes of rebellion in 1857, the new viceregal regime was more circumspect. A ruler would now be dethroned only in exceptional circumstances, not for mere misrule or debauchery. The Nawab of Tonk was deposed in 1867 for complicity in the murder of his uncle and various other people. In 1893 the Khan of Kalat was forced to abdicate after committing various 'deeds of savagery', including the killing of his wazir, the chief minister.

More usual duties of a Political were those of guardian, tutor or private secretary to chiefs who were minors or young men. He had to balance the requirement to educate them and teach them how to run their state with the need to prevent them from losing touch with the religion and customs of their people. Maharajas who played cricket for Cambridge and frequented nightclubs in London were seldom good rulers in India. The Resident's difficulties could start early if the minor was an infant, pampered and coddled in his palace and treated like a king by relatives and courtiers who prostrated themselves before him, spoke in an abject manner and gratified every whim. When in 1869 Colonel George Malleson, the historian, was appointed guardian of the adopted heir of the late maharaja of Mysore, a six-year-old, he came up against the child's mother plus the two widows of the previous ruler who all insisted that the boy could not move out of the palace to meet him unless accompanied by an escort of thirty-six cavalrymen, thirteen running footmen and sixteen personal attendants.[52]

Residents in large states lived in the style of an ambassador to Paris or Vienna, inhabiting vast mansions and dealing with a single government from a position of enormous strength and prestige. Other Politicals led a much more varied and complicated existence. They might have to conduct operations against brigands preying on wedding processions in the Aravali Hills; they might need to persuade an

Anglophile Sikh maharaja (educated at Sandhurst) to let his beard grow for the sake of his state; they might even have to smuggle a baby out of a princely court to a convent in south India in case the ruler discovered that his widowed mother had had an illegitimate child – as Leslie Chauncy did when stationed in the Gujarat states in the late 1930s. The most stressful job for a Political was that of agent in Kathiawar, the peninsula in the Bombay presidency that contained 300 states (nearly half of the total in India); Mohandas Gandhi came from one of them, Porbandar, where his father was the diwan (another term for chief minister) of the maharaja. When William Lee-Warner was offered the post in 1887, his doctor warned he would get an abscess on his liver if he accepted it.[53]

Political officers on the frontiers also had stressful jobs, and their work was anything but sedentary. Those on the north-west frontier spent much of their lives with people who were naturally and potentially hostile, tribesmen in the mountains living with the perennial temptation to descend upon the Punjab plains and carry off people, animals and other kinds of booty. The Political's job was to keep the peace or at least restrict violence to an acceptable level. He thus had to know the tribes, their languages and customs, to be on good terms with local khans and village headmen, to know how and when he could persuade a jirga, a council of elders, to help settle a dispute. Such men often acquired a kind of legendary status: Robert Warburton on the Khyber and Robert Sandeman in Baluchistan in the late nineteenth century, Harold Deane and George Roos-Keppel administering the frontier from Peshawar in the first two decades of the twentieth. In his novel *The Broken Road* (1907) A. E. W. Mason summed up the type in a character who was 'of no assistance at a dinner-party, but when there was trouble upon the Frontier, or beyond it, he was usually found to be the chief agent in the settlement'.

It made no sense to transfer officers like these every four or five years, as provincial governments moved their collectors and district magistrates. Warburton spent eighteen years as political officer of the Khyber, one of the most perilous posts in the British Empire, and he established such close relations with the Afridis, that most unaccommodating of Pathan tribes, that he could camp unarmed among them. Robert Sandeman spent the last fifteen years of his life controlling Baluchistan, where he established a highly effective 'system', making friends with the tribes, dealing with them through their chiefs, observing tribal customs and employing jirgas instead of law courts to settle disputes. Of course this could only be done if backed by a military power that was both ready and visible. Yet it was seldom deployed, and when Sandeman died in 1892, Baluchis disputed among themselves over who would have the honour of burying 'Senamann Sahib'.[54]

Political officers were often more popular with the tribes, whom they tried to dissuade from raiding and other actions likely to bring retribution from the government, than with British army officers, who were longing for a 'scrap' and to 'have a whack' at some foe. A Political was frequently regarded by the military as annoying, as 'the man who stood between the soldier and his medal'.[55] When recalling a frontier expedition of 1897, Winston Churchill remembered that one such man, Harold Deane, 'was much disliked because he always stopped military operations. Just when we were looking forward to having a splendid fight and all the guns were loaded and everyone keyed up, this Major Deane . . . would come along and put a stop to it all. Apparently, all these savage chiefs were his old friends and almost his blood relations.'[56]

Standards of living for Politicals differed very greatly. The Resident in Hyderabad might live in splendour in a palace with a Corinthian portico forty feet high, but many political agents lived in modest bungalows. In the 1880s the Resident in Turkish Arabia (Colonel Tweedie) inhabited a squalid rented building in a lane in Baghdad, spending summer days in the cellar with 'damp, darkness and vermin' and summer nights on the roof with 'publicity and frequent hot winds'. When his wife wanted to go out, she had to ride 'swathed in sheets and veils' on a donkey in case she was mistaken for a prostitute; eventually she renounced her position and departed, leaving her husband to look after himself. The colonel's 'pitiable existence' did not end after 'consigning [his] wife to the monsoon in the Indian Ocean'. Unusually for a Political, he was continually being transferred to new posts to cover for men who were sick or on leave. Between 1879 and 1885 he did three stints in Rajputana, three more in Gwalior, two in Baghdad, one in Jalalabad and another between Peshawar and Kabul as political officer during the invasion of Afghanistan. At the same time he suffered badly from a skin disease known as 'Date Mark' or 'Bouton de Baghdad'. No wonder his letters to his superiors in the Political Department were rather querulous.[57]

Accommodation for IPS officers beyond India's borders improved after Tweedie's time, but it could never compare with the grand Residencies in the states of Rajputana and central India. In 1911 the Political Agent in Bahrain, the former Indian Army officer David Lorimer, was living in what his wife described as 'a fine two-storey building with a big flagstaff . . . and a little rude pier running into the water'. The ground floor contained his office and a kitchen, and the house was surrounded by a verandah with a fine view of the sea. As was usual with such buildings, it was part of a compound, but not so usual were two of the other buildings in it, 'a nice little barracks in one corner' housing a guard of nineteen sepoys, and a small prison whose five or six inmates were employed cleaning the place, pulling the punkahs and levelling some ground for a tennis court.[58]

Great Britain may have been the paramount power in the Persian Gulf, but its aims in the region, apart from a desire to counter Russian influence, were seldom clear. 'We don't want [Kuwait],' Arthur Godley at the India Office told Curzon in 1899, 'but we don't want anyone else to have it.' He conceded that this policy might sound 'rather bad' when 'baldly stated', but it was 'the true explanation of a good deal of our diplomacy'.[59] Oil was not an explanation because Kuwait, like Bahrain, was not yet a producer. Local rulers were certainly often pro-British, mainly because they needed protection both from pirates and from more powerful neighbours. When Curzon toured the Gulf in 1901, he reported that the Sultan of Muscat behaved more like a 'loyal feudatory than . . . an independent sovereign', while the Sheikh of Kuwait declared himself 'a fighting man for England'.[60] If the Sheikh of Bahrain was less enthusiastic, it may have been because the viceroy had lectured him on the financial condition of his island.

As Britain's constitutional positions in the Gulf were imprecise, the Politicals from India were rather vague about what they were meant to be doing there. In Bahrain Mrs Lorimer, a scholar of German who had given up a career at Oxford to marry David, was perennially perplexed. On arrival she realized that the 'first obvious thing' was to 'protect British trade and British shipping', but it also seemed that somehow 'we have gradually adopted a sort of tacit protectorate footing . . . and practically administer justice'. The political agent was supposed to protect all 'foreigners' (African, Asian or European) but not the subjects of the sheikh, although Lorimer was tempted to interfere in cases of punishment by amputation. Bahrain had its own courts for disputes in its pearl fisheries, but any Persian or non-Bahraini Arab who was involved in them or other matters could refer the case to Lorimer. This meant that slaves who escaped from Arabia and reached Bahrain, after hiding in a boat or being picked up by a steamer, could appeal to the political agent: if satisfied by their stories of kidnapping and slavery, he would then release them. This was one of the rare satisfactions of the job. On other issues the British and Indian governments both found the subjects of jurisdiction and constitutional status too complicated and difficult to define – to the exasperation of the Lorimers, who found it 'peculiarly trying to be expected to hold a fort with no instructions save that no shots are to be fired, no one is to be hurt, and – above all – no action of a decisive nature is to be taken'.[61]

DR NESTOR AND THE IMS

The surgeons dispatched by the EIC in the first century and a half of its existence were at best semi-skilled civilians. Yet once the Company began to raise its own armies in India, it sent out better trained medical men to look after them, attaching the surgeons to regiments and giving them military rank (surgeon-major, surgeon-general and so on) and establishing the Indian Medical Service (IMS). In practice, however, British surgeons and doctors – the words were used almost synonymously in British India – combined both military and civilian duties. They staffed the hospitals, ran the medical colleges, became the 'civil surgeons' at the headquarters of a district.

On arriving in India, a young Company surgeon would probably spend a short time in Calcutta (or Madras or Bombay), learning a bit about diets, languages and tropical diseases, before joining his regiment and receiving some basic military training. When the regiment went on campaign, he naturally accompanied it and carried out the usual gruesome battlefield duties, bandaging wounds, applying tourniquets, using laudanum and belladonna as painkillers in the pre-chloroform days. He also performed amputations, though without much hope of success: one Highland officer, recalling his service in India in the 1850s, said he 'never knew or heard of a case when the patient survived the amputation of a leg'.[62] Yet the peacetime duties of a medical officer were not burdensome unless an epidemic of cholera or some other disease broke out. In the early morning he would visit the regimental hospital, seeing the in-patients and anyone reporting sick, usually with dysentery or a fever; if any surgery were required, he carried it out with the assistance of the Indian sub-assistant-surgeon attached to the regiment. After that he did what office work was required, which was little, and his military duties were usually finished before noon. With so much spare time, he might help out at the horse hospital – there were never enough vets – or become secretary of the officers' Mess and do the accounts.[63]

After two years in their regiments, IMS officers were given the chance to transfer to civil work, although they retained their military rank and could be recalled in time of war or some other emergency. Those who chose to remain in the military branch had little opportunity to practise privately and seldom reached the top of the service. Yet they had as much leisure as the combatant officers in their regiment and hence equivalent opportunities for sport. Like their colleagues in the Indian Army, they might be transferred to different regiments in the course of their career, but otherwise the pattern of their lives resembled those of men in the Army Medical Department (later named the Royal Army Medical Corps), who went to India to look after British Army regiments and run their military hospitals.

Those who opted for the civil branch usually became the doctor of the district, the inspector of its dispensaries and a colleague of the magistrate and the judge. His work took longer and was more varied than that of his colleagues who remained with their regiments. Each day he had to visit the district jail, of which he was the superintendent, then the district hospital, which he also ran, and then the police hospital, before going to his office, where he had to deal with his correspondence from the sanitary commissioner and the inspector-general of hospitals. Later he visited his patients, both official and private, though the delimitation between them was often quite hazy. He was obliged to treat army officers and their families without charge, yet while senior non-military officials, British or Indian, could also be seen for free, these had to pay for their wives and children to be treated.

Civil surgeons were forced to be 'all-rounders' because, unless the district was a city, there were unlikely to be specialists of any kind anywhere near. A woman wishing to see a female doctor had no chance unless there was a mission hospital in the vicinity, and if she needed a man more specialized than a general practitioner, she might have to travel several hundred miles before she found one in Calcutta or Bombay. In 1871 there were only ten British dentists in the whole of India, and so few did they remain that people were given leave off work for several days to visit them: when in 1918 Lieutenant Amies was suffering pain from a swollen mouth, he had to travel 350 miles to Bombay from his cantonment at Mhow near Indore 'to seek relief from toothache'.[64] Civil surgeons may have improved after John Beames's day,* and the best of them went on to higher things, but many settled into a comfortable billet and showed little inclination to move. The hill station of Lansdowne, observed one Gurkha officer, was 'ideal for a lazy and unambitious doctor who was fond of sport and social life'.[65]

The ambitious ones did not stay in the station, happy to play snooker in the club with the major and the padre. They went on to become professors at medical colleges, directors of research institutes and surgeons-general, while the top man became the director-general running the IMS and its nearly 700 officers, overseeing the hundreds of hospitals and thousands of dispensaries under the government of India.† Professional lives in the IMS could be as varied as any in India. Men might work on vaccines for rabies in Kasauli and on antidotes to snake bites in Madras; they might administer a lunatic asylum in Ranchi or go on malaria surveys in Persia. Underfunded though their research was, the laboratories of the IMS made some significant contributions to the knowledge and treatment of tropical diseases. It was an officer of the service, Robert Ross, who, despite very parsimonious encouragement from the government, discovered that malaria was spread by mosquitoes.

The IMS enjoyed a number of scientific appointments such as superintendent of the Calcutta Museum and surgeon-naturalist to the Indian Marine Survey, a post which came with a permanent berth on the steamer Investigator. A junior surgeon could aspire to become curator of the Herbarium at the Calcutta Botanical Gardens with the chance of succeeding the superintendent, a senior colleague who was also the government quinologist and professor of Botany at Calcutta Medical

---

* See above, p. 128.
† The Indianization of the IMS began in the 1890s, rather later than in the ICS. One reason for this was the attitude of Indian newspapers such as the Hindoo Patriot, which for religious reasons discouraged Hindus from travelling abroad and taking the exams in London. By 1940 the service had 695 doctors, 460 of them Britons and 235 Indians.

College. Like Civilians and army officers, IMS men could join the Political Service and become 'surgeons to the Residents at Native Courts'. As with other positions in that service, some of these were leisurely and lucrative and situated in agreeable places; others were not. Walter Crichton was the political agent's surgeon in Seistan, a remote part of the Persian–Afghan border, before he was transferred to the agency in Kurram in Waziristan, where, in the Parachinar bazaar in February 1932, he was attacked by an Afghan tribesman with an axe and injured so badly that he could never use his left arm properly again.[66]

Lieutenant-Colonel Crichton CIE (Companion of the Indian Empire) merits a diversion. He actually came from a Catholic family from Malta called Critian that owned the principal bookshop on the island. After going to school at the Jesuit College in Sliema, he had studied medicine at Edinburgh University, passed into the IMS, converted to the Church of England and anglicized (or celticized) his name to Crichton. Following his injury in the Parachinar bazaar, he became medical officer in Simla and then Delhi, and in the Second World War he served with Indian troops in Italy, where his work in combating typhoid and venereal disease in 1943 won him 'the freedom of the city' of Naples. After later gaining the Order of Orange Nassau for his services to liberated Holland, he returned to India as director of public health in Bihar, and after Independence he became chief of the World Health Organization's mission to Korea, a post followed by jobs for WHO in the Middle East. According to his obituary in the *Lancet*, he had been so concerned for poor rickshaw drivers in the 1930s that he invented the 'crickshaw', a light, rubber-tyred rickshaw which he designed to 'alleviate the work of coolies in Indian hill stations'. The viceroy, Lord Willingdon, encouraged the scheme and even bought a small fleet of the vehicles for the use of his staff at Simla.[67]

It is hard to find records of dull careers in the IMS or ones without considerable variety. Even men who would have been happy to stay for decades as civil surgeon at Ooty or Residency surgeon at Jaipur were moved about by superiors who were impervious to their desires. Indeed men in the IMS were transferred more frequently than in any other service. Within the space of five years, beginning in 1897, Surgeon-Lieutenant Leventon, the son of a Dublin vicar, was medical officer of the Queen's Own Bengal Light Infantry in Assam, medical officer in charge of a military police force in an expedition against the Apa Tani hill tribe, officer in charge of a cholera camp, civil surgeon in Manipur and simultaneously medical officer of the 43rd Gurkha Rifles, civil surgeon at Sibsagar and finally medical officer to the Assam Camp at the Coronation Durbar at Delhi.[68]

Ernest Bradfield passed into the IMS in 1903 and soon found himself attached to the 88th Carnatic Infantry in Madras, a city he found agreeable because the 'large merchant community . . . took life fairly easily, so there was never any difficulty in finding a team to go away for two days' cricket'; in Madras 'matches were generally played all day Saturday, Sunday being reserved for shooting and other sport . . .' Yet after a period on special cholera duty he was transferred to the Bombay presidency and seconded for plague duty to Mahabaleshwar, trying to eliminate rats, and thence to plague duty on the coast at Surat. Although he was soon longing to return to Madras, he was instead sent to Peshawar, where, as sanitary officer of an expeditionary force, he had to deal with an outbreak of cholera among soldiers and camp followers. Subsequently he was dispatched to the garrison of Meerut, where he could at least enjoy 'the best polo and pig-sticking in India' and take part in regimental tent-pegging competitions. It was not until after a visit to England, accompanying a mental patient on a cargo boat (such cases were not accepted on passenger liners), that he returned to his old province in 1912 as civil surgeon at Tinnevelly. His brief spell in the south gave this compulsive sportsman a couple of seasons as 'whipper-in' of the Madras Hunt.[69]

A number of IMS officers accompanied the expeditionary force to Mesopotamia in the First World War, working with the Indian Army regiments or in the military hospital in Basra or in some cases being put in charge of escorting Turkish prisoners to India.[70] Bradfield was also sent to the front, working on a hospital ship on the River Tigris before returning to India to administer a leper asylum. In 1924 he became professor of surgery at the Madras Medical College and superintendent of the General Hospital. While working in the province, he found time to specialize in stomach and duodenal ulcers and in compression fracture of the spine, an injury frequently suffered by Nadar toddy tappers after falling on to their buttocks while climbing palm trees.[71]

After his early-morning ride, Bradfield saw one or two private patients and dropped in at the Willingdon Nursing Home before reaching the hospital, where his ward rounds began at ten o'clock. He carried out operations on three mornings a week and spent the afternoons in his office until he thought it time to look for some sport. By now in his mid-forties, he no longer played polo – since the war it had been diffi-cult to find ponies anyway – but he was keen on squash and tennis, and he captained a European Eleven in an annual cricket match against a Hindu team. After an hour whacking a ball somewhere, he might find refreshment in the Madras Club at the Long Bar – which was said to be the longest bar in Asia – before 'collecting [his] wife at the ladies' annexe variously known as the "dovecot" or "hen-run"'.[72]

This agreeable routine lasted only a few years because his wife, Margaret, whom he had married in 1920, decided to take their young daughters to England and live with them there for most of the year, returning to Madras to spend the winter months with her husband. This was an expensive arrangement, forcing Bradfield to keep two houses and pay for school fees, sea passages and a holiday home for the children at Christmas. Presumably for financial reasons, he decided to give up his life in south India and 'choose the less arduous prospect of a few years' military advancement' – earning promotion and hence a higher salary. So in 1930, at the age of fifty, he exiled himself to the north-west frontier, stationed first at Kohat and then at Peshawar, cut-ting all links with the south except for his Madrasi bearer, who loyally accompanied him into the mountains. Promotion came in 1935 when he was appointed surgeon-general (with the rank of major-general) to the Bombay government, and again two years later when he was made director-general of the IMS. The appointment to the second post was announced in a telegram from the departing director-general, Sir Cuth-bert Sprawson, which read, 'Troilus and Cressida, Act Four, Scene Five, Line One' (Agamemnon's 'Here art thou in appointment fresh and fair'). Bradfield replied with a line from Nestor in the same scene: 'Our general doth salute you with a kiss'.[73]*

---

* The exchange was not quite as subtle or cryptic as Curzon's telegraphed appointment of David Barr to the Residency of Hyderabad in 1900. Barr, who happened to be bald, felt the need to remind the viceroy of his existence before a candidate was selected for the post. Therefore, as Humphrey Trevelyan described, he 'telegraphed to Curzon, who was then in Simla: "Psalm 132, verse 1", which, being interpreted, read, "Lord, remember David". Curzon replied with "Psalm 75, verse 6": "For promotion cometh neither from the East, nor from the West, nor from the South." Barr was presumably encouraged, since Curzon was in the north. He telegraphed: "Psalm 121, verse 1", "I will lift up my eyes to the hills from whence cometh my help." Curzon rounded off the series neatly with "II Kings, 2, verse 23", "Go up, thou bald head."'[74]

7

Working Lives: The Open Air

ON TOUR

In Britain in 1900 most people did their work with a roof over their heads. Farmers and fishermen obviously did not – nor did most rural folk – but the great majority worked under shelter in factories, mines, trains, warehouses, shops and offices. In India, by contrast, most of the British worked mostly out of doors, the chief exceptions being judges, bankers, businessmen and the civil servants who manned the secretariats. Almost every other profession demanded an outdoor life. India was crawling with surveyors – fiscal, cadastral, geological, mineralogical, topographical, trigonometrical – always on the move, always measuring things. Even the officials of the Opium Department lived and worked in the open. Richard Blair spent his entire career in the service, making his way up from assistant sub-deputy opium agent, moving from post to post in Bengal and the United Provinces, living much of his life in tents as he surveyed the poppy fields and the methods farmers used to cultivate their crop. Although described by a relative as a 'superbly unadventurous' man, at the age of thirty-nine he married a half-French girl barely half his age who came from a family working in Burma in boat-building and the teak trade. In 1898 the couple had a daughter, Marjorie, and five years later, at Motihari in Bengal, a son called Eric, who became a policeman in Burma; later he resigned from the service to become a writer and publish his books under the name of George Orwell.[1]

As we have seen, the district officer spent his summer as a magistrate sweltering in a court room, but in the autumn, after the monsoons, he put on his topi and became the collector, the man in charge of the revenue, whose job it was to tour his district and to see for himself what was going on, how the people were faring and how their crops were doing. On tour even his desk work was done outside, at a folding table under a tree near his tent, his dog at his feet, his chaprasis (messengers) hovering, and his clerks sitting cross-legged on the ground with ink-horns and bundles of paper. Before setting up this archetypal scene, the DO would have spent the morning riding through villages with Indian officials, inspecting the land and the buildings and talking to the patel, the patwari and local farmers. He would then have returned to his tents, had a bath in his zinc tub and eaten his tiffin while small groups of men congregated at the edge of his camp, litigants and petitioners, policemen (with prisoners) arriving with petty cases for him to try.

In much of India junior Civilians, the assistant magistrates or sub-divisional officers, spent most of their year on tour, setting off in early November and returning to their station, if they got their timing right, just before the monsoon broke some time in June. As late as 1939 Maurice Zinkin was spending 210 days a year touring an area of the Bombay presidency still so remote that 'shooting tigers which had been attacking the village cattle was a public duty', though it was one at which he personally was 'singularly ineffective'.*² Seventy years earlier, Andrew Wingate had enjoyed his seven months a year on tour in the same province, 'never knowing a dull day' although he rarely met an Englishman or even spoke English during that time. Belonging to the intermediate generation in the Bombay service, Evan Maconochie appreciated 'camp life thoroughly, the feeling of always being in the open air, the constant change of scenery and faces, the nature of the work and the feeling that you are doing something for the people about you even if it is in a very small way'. Although he often did 'not see a white face for two or three months together', his 'seven months under canvas' were 'the pleasantest part' of his life.³

The details of touring were amended over the years. By the 1930s much of it was done by motor car in the Plains, while in the Hills, in the tribal areas of Assam and the Central Provinces, officials sometimes took a portable gramophone, entertaining villagers with records

---

* Zinkin was in the presidency by mistake, having chosen it 'under the illusion that Bangalore and Ootacamund were in Bombay'. His mother thought he should not be in India anyway, because she did not consider him 'capable of coping with tigers'.

of Jack Hulbert and Harry Lauder; in return a DO in the Lushai Hills might have to accept the headman's hospitality and drink a lot of *zu*, the alcoholic beverage of the Hill Tracts. Yet the essence of the tour remained the same. It was the Civilian's means of getting to know a district and its people and attempting to gain their confidence, which was always easier if he had some medical knowledge and some supplies for treatment. And it was good for him to leave his station, where he had spent the summer immersed in court cases, and go to the mofussil and encounter what Harcourt Butler termed 'the orderly elements of the population' or 'the permanent and more agreeable side of oriental life'; later in his career, when he was governor of Burma, Butler reflected that 'the world seems full of hope . . . when one is in the jungle'.[4]

A Civilian also got to know a district when he was made a settlement officer, a job that lasted three or four years during which he 'assessed' an area of some two or three thousand villages, surveying fields, computing yields and revenues, endeavouring to settle disputes about leases, tenancies and boundaries, and later writing an enormous report about what he had done. Yet another outdoor post for a Civilian was colonization officer, a man who was in charge of establishing and then regulating the 'canal colonies' of the Punjab created in the 1890s on the millions of acres of land irrigated by the Chenab and Jhelum schemes. He had to plan his colony, lay out the farms, roads and villages, and arrange for its new tenants – preferably solid yeoman types – to live productively and harmoniously with each other. Care was taken to group people coming from the same district into the same village and to keep Sikhs and Muslims apart. The chief task for one young officer in 1930 was to ensure that the tenants built themselves proper houses on the site allotted to them and lived in them instead of becoming absentee landowners staying in their old villages and coming to the colony just to harvest the crops.[5]

Going on tour was not something that was easy, quick or possible to do without a great deal of planning. Even a griffin on his first cold-weather tour would set off with eight or more bullock-carts carrying servants, tents and utensils; a DO or a commissioner might need as many as twenty-four of them, no doubt an impressive sight as they lumbered along in a line, although their maximum speed even on straight flat roads was only two miles an hour. We have seen that some district officers had to do their touring on camels, elephants and river launches, but most used horses for themselves and bullock-carts for their servants and equipment. As the carts were so slow, nearly everything had to be done in duplicate. While a Civilian sat listening to petitions outside his first tent, carts were already on their way to the next camp with his second so that it would be ready for him in the mango grove when he cantered up in the evening.

DOs would sometimes stay in a dak bungalow, where they might enjoy a shelf of old books and some out-of-date copies of *Blackwood's* magazine, but they usually preferred their tents, which were provided by the government. These were not simple affairs that could be erected in a few minutes with a hammer and some tent-pegs. James Sifton, a young SDO, enjoyed his 'gipsy life' but admitted it was of a very 'luxurious sort'. His father, he informed him, was mistaken if he thought his son and his fellow 'tent-dwellers' were in any way 'roughing it'. 'My tent is as big as your drawing room. I have a carpet, and a bathroom attached, and a verandah in front, tables, chairs, bed and everything comfortable'. An SDO would also have a kitchen, with plates, cutlery and lamps, a dog basket for his terrier and, if he had greyhounds, charpoys (string beds) for them to sleep on. As china was even more likely to be broken on tour than in his compound, he would probably eat and drink from enamel (unless he had heeded the memsahibs' view that this was an error. 'Enamel ware,' pronounced Anne Wilson, author of *Hints for the First Years of Residence in India*, 'is not pleasant to look at, nor palatable to drink out of, as the cup becomes too hot.')[6]

Excluding family members and local officials who might join the cavalcade at certain stages, a DO's retinue on tour would consist of some twenty people: clerks, servants and messengers. Even a forest officer would take a dozen men with him when camping in a forest: bearer, groom, cook, cook's mate, sweeper, laundryman and half-a-dozen cartmen. The British were even more dependent on their servants on tour than they were at headquarters. Their cook would forage for vegetables in villages along the way and sometimes buy meat in a bazaar, although a glimpse of the village butcher's, haunted by flies, often encouraged Civilians to bring their own meat supply with them. If they had Hindu servants, this obviously could not include cattle; Hindu coolies sometimes refused to carry even Oxo cubes because of the bull's head on the packet. It was safer to take a small flock of sheep and hire a local Muslim butcher at the appropriate moment. Even in Hindu areas it was possible to bring a cow and her calf for milk, though the supply might be unreliable, and it would be dangerous if not boiled. Some men preferred to have buffaloes, but the best solution, especially for officials with children, was a goat, whose milk was non-tuberculous and safe. Clinton Dawkins, a forest officer who toured Burma with his wife, Enid, accompanied by their small sons slung in Moses baskets, thought goat's milk the healthiest option for his children, but he kept a supply of alternative foods in case a tiger dashed out of the jungle and grabbed the goat.[7]

The tours of a governor or a viceroy were of course very different kinds of expeditions. Yet they had certain similarities, at least in intent, for the British were always trying to demonstrate their power with visits and inspections and displays of highly organized ceremonial. As early as 1866 Emily Eden was lamenting that the 'splendour' of a vice-roy's progress was at an end; she was remembering her years in India when her brother Lord Auckland was governor-general (1836–42), and she believed that the splendour she had known then had been destroyed because India had now 'fallen under the curse of railroads'.[8] Yet later viceroys and governors managed some fairly splendid 'pro-gresses' by rail and, between the world wars, in a combination of trains and motor cars. We have mentioned Lord Goschen's fondness for American vehicles, but a governor's retinue and baggage could not fit into just six cars. For the journey from Madras to his summer capital of Ooty Goschen needed a train called the 'stable special' for his horses, silver and wine cases, although his bandsmen and their families would travel in the ordinary passenger train. A governor of Madras would not require his band or his silver when he was on tour from Ooty, but he would still need a butler, who travelled in a 'lorry in charge of advance baggage', as well as a wine butler, and a pastry cook as well as ordinary cooks. He was often entertained by other people – in a club, a Resi-dency or a raja's palace – but on the Plains he did most of his touring in a special train, which included a dining car and needed a staff.[9]

The governor's military secretary (who was in fact a soldier acting as a social secretary) would arrange and then print the tour programme in advance, with details of visits, timings and uniforms to be worn. In their 1925 tour of the south-west of the province – Cochin, Tinnevelly, Travancore and the Anaimalai Hills – Lord and Lady Goschen divided their duties: while he was at the Hindu College of Tinnevelly, she was at the Women's and Children's Hospital; when he visited the Arts and Science Colleges of Trivandrum, she went off to the Maharaja's College for Women. Together they inspected the Periyar Dam and the new harbour in Cochin, they visited tea estates and planters' associations, they received delegations and listened to lengthy addresses, and on several occasions they were garlanded by 'Indian worthies'. Among the garden parties, state banquets and other social occasions was a meal with the Bishop of Travancore and Cochin, which failed to impress one of Goschen's ADCs, Captain Portal, who described it as 'a sticky lunch (teetotal)'.[10]

Such tours created a great deal of work not only for a governor's entourage but also for the people nervously waiting to greet it and desperately hoping that nothing would go badly wrong. If a governor was 'in his old clothes' because he had not been warned that a large guard of honour was waiting for him somewhere, the resulting crisis might sour a visit.[11] When in 1922 George Lloyd, the governor of Bombay, 'signified his intention' of visiting Karachi and doing some shooting at Christmas in Sind, Civilians at the commissioner's headquarters realized that their holidays would be ruined. One of the governor's ADCs then sent a list of what His Excellency would require in his tents, which included fireplaces, a hatstand and 'superior carpets', demands which, according to Madge Green, who organized the bachelor commissioner's social life, left 'everyone . . . extremely fractious and peeved'. When Lloyd arrived, Madge's social life was 'a perfect whirlwind' of garden party, state dinner and various lunches. Her 'whole time' seemed to be spent in 'tearing wildly from one function to change one's frock for the next, and at that function discussing the weather in all its aspects'. What was the point of such visits? Even Curzon's private secretary, Walter Lawrence, was sceptical of the value of viceregal tours. They were so formally prepared and so rapidly completed; so much time was wasted going shooting and sightseeing; so little was achieved at receptions and state dinners; and officials were so nervous about meeting the viceroy and answering his questions that they were tongue-tied or said silly things.[12] Yet it was good for the viceroy or governor to get away from Government House and look at different parts of India: it may have been good for people to see him and feel that he was taking an interest in their affairs; and it was probably good to keep officials on their toes.

JUNGLE WALLAHS

Forest officers in Burma were teased by their colleagues in other parts of the empire for being 'one tree men', people who had no interest in any timber except teak trees and who had no professional programme except to protect them from fire.[13] In the solitudes of the forests of Upper Burma a man might easily become obsessed by teak, and not only because it was a valuable wood for ships and furniture and contained a useful preservatory oil. He would spend much of his life searching for it, selecting the right specimens, choosing the moment when they were ready to cut, and later trying to ensure that the timber reached its destination without being stolen by river thieves. One retired forest officer, who acted as a steward at the annual show of the Bath and West Society, was almost overcome when a little rain fell on the exhibited furniture, and the aromatic scent of teakwood 'tantalized' his senses and made him remember his first days in the jungles of Asia. Others like him remained haunted by the beauty of the giant trees, their tops often invisible in the morning mists, by the vastness and mystery of the forests, the freshness of the air, the daily marches under bamboos that arched and swayed fifty feet above them.[14]

Clinton Dawkins was rather a 'one tree' person but fortunately he was married to Enid, the daughter and sister of forest officers, and she was also an enthusiast; in retirement they both gave lectures on teak to the Arts Guild and the Women's Institute at Little Baddow in Essex. His uncle was another Clinton Dawkins, a friend of Curzon at Balliol who had served as finance member of the Viceroy's Council before leaving Calcutta to work for Pierpont Morgan's interests in London. The nephew also went to Balliol,* at his uncle's expense, and in 1908, after his training in Germany, he went out to Burma, working his way up from assistant conservator of forests to deputy conservator and finally conservator in Pyinmana. 'Clinton *loves* Burma,' reported Enid to her mother, 'and gets so annoyed with those numerous people who are always grousing at it.' In the dry weather, from November to April, he toured the forests; during the rains he worked as an instructor in a

---

* The Balliol tradition continued with his son John, who became a colonial officer in Nyasaland, and his grandson Richard Dawkins, the biologist and atheist.

forestry school, teaching Burmese students how to make maps, build bridges and lay out cart roads in the hills.[15]

Before he met Enid, Clinton went on tour with a fellow forest officer and a team of 'elephant wallahs', porters and 'dak wallahs', postal runners who ran through the forest with the mail, quite easy targets for tigers and bears even when they carried a spear. After a long morning of inspections, he dealt with his correspondence and then went out on an elephant to try to shoot a deer or a jungle-fowl for the next day's supper; the undergrowth was so thick that it was impossible to see anything at ground level. 'Without any feminine influence,' he informed his mother, he and his colleague 'always put on ties for dinner'; they also regularly brushed their hair and shaved every two or three days (a rare ritual for a jungle wallah). At nights they tied their dogs up inside a tent so that a panther would not steal them, then sat around a large camp fire with the rest of the party before going to sleep on a hard bamboo bed.[16]

Winter and early spring were the seasons for 'girdling' teak. It was 'not a gregarious tree,' noted Dawkins, by which he meant that it did not grow in clumps, where it would have been easy to find and to cut down. A suitable specimen for felling, which had to have a girth of at least seven feet, might be found only once in two or three acres of forest, and then often in precipitous terrain, surrounded by other trees and very dense undergrowth. As it was often hard to find, a forest officer would 'let loose' a 'gang of half wild jungle folk with orders to search' for large teak trees and 'to shout when they had found one'. After he had selected a suitable tree, the officer marked it with a special hammer and then instructed a man to cut a deep girdle all around the trunk, through the bark and the living sapwood to the heartwood, thereby preventing sap rising from the roots. This effectively killed the tree but, as it did not 'season' very well when left lying on the ground, it was left standing until it became light enough to float down a Burmese river.

It was a 'tragic sight', Dawkins admitted, to see a great tree droop and die, and it looked even more tragic when he returned to the site three years later and saw 'the gaunt white skeletons of the giants that had been girdled in readiness for this day ... twig-less, bark-less and bare'. The officer had returned to keep an eye on the timber firms that had undertaken to saw up and remove the dead wood, and to make sure that no ungirdled trees were added to the crop. Bullocks were sometimes used by the firms, but elephants, though more expensive to keep, were much stronger and more effective in dragging the logs down hillsides into a watercourse that would be flooded during the monsoon. Elephants would be used again to sort out the inevitable 'log-jams' blocking streams and ravines and even rivers, the logs jumbled up in their hundreds and at all angles; as Kipling's soldier remembered, 'Elephints a-pilin' teak / In the sludgy, squdgy creak / Where the silence 'ung that 'eavy you was 'arf afraid to speak!' When the logs finally reached the rivers, the Irrawaddy or one of its affluents, they were caught and tied up into rafts, some two hundred together, their rafts-men living on them in little thatched huts as they floated down to a revenue-collecting station, where a forest officer saw them for the last time, assessing and charging the government's royalty before letting them pass on to their destination, the timber firms' depot and sawmills in Rangoon.

In retirement at Little Baddow, Clinton Dawkins was often asked what a forest officer or jungle wallah actually did – 'go around the trees and prune them?' As an official was in charge of a forest block of 1,200 or even 2,000 square miles, personal pruning would have had limited effect. His role was more that of inspector, touring his woods to see how they should be protected, how they could be improved, to plan what roads and bridges might be needed for the coming year; during the rainy season he returned to his desk to scrutinize proposals, pre-pare the estimates and write the inevitable report. Forest officers are often assumed to have exploited and even 'plundered' their areas for the benefit of the Raj, but in fact such plundering took place earlier, the work of speculators and timber merchants, before the establishment of the Forest Service and before Lord Dalhousie wrote his important memorandum on forest management and conservation in 1855. Yet jungle wallahs did of course have to try to balance the duty of conser-vation with both the needs of forest-dwellers and the economy of India. Apart from teak for boats and furniture, and other timber for railway sleepers and building poles, he had to encourage the production of 'minor forest products' such as lac or shellac for making gramophone records, and tendu, whose leaves were used to wrap tobacco and create *bidis*, the poor man's cigarette. He himself would have a small team of Indian clerks and subordinates, but the large workforces in the forest were those of the big timber firms such as MacGregors in Burma, which employed two or three thousand men and 600 elephants for their operations. Elephants were useful too in time of war. Under the supervision of 'Elephant Bill' Williams, a senior forest officer, hundreds of the animals and their riders were taken out of timber work and used to build the bridges and roads needed to get large numbers of Indian refugees across the Chindwin and out of Burma along the Manipur route in the spring of 1942.[17]

The forest officer's early job title of 'superintendent' was changed to 'conservator' of forests to reflect his primary duty. As Dawkins explained, 'his basic principle [was] to allow no more to be taken out' of the forest 'than is replaced by nature, or by himself in replanting'. If it took a hundred years to grow a good tree, explained another jungle wallah, 'then a forester is not justified in cutting more than a hundredth part of the growing stock annually'. The problem was that nature, animals and other human beings often conspired to remove a good deal more than 1 per cent. Natural regeneration could not take place if the dairy cattle of Darjeeling were turned out to graze in the forest; nor did a young plantation stand a chance of surviving if black bear were in the area ready to claw around the bark of each tree. Yet in established woods fire was a much greater danger than bears: each year about 4,500 fires in Indian forests were reported. In the woodlands of the Terai on the Nepalese border the forest officer's Indian workers abandoned their boss in late March or April, after the Holi Festival, when malaria became prevalent in the area. Sainthill Eardley-Wilmot thus spent the dry season almost entirely alone, in the middle of an inflammable forest, alert for a glow at night or a plume of smoke in the day, waiting for reports from district fire-watchers and knowing that there was not much he could do before he found relief with the first burst of the monsoon.[18]

Forest officers recognized that local people needed bamboo and wood to build themselves houses and to use as fuel, but they had little sympathy for ancient woodland practices: they certainly refused to condone the 'immemorial custom' of *kumri*, of tribal hillmen burning patches of forest. In Burma Dawkins saw them sowing rice in the ashes, flooding the area, taking the crop, and then moving on. Up in the Terai Eardley-Wilmot found large tracts felled and burned to clear undergrowth for hunters and give graziers a crop of young grass. In central

India James Best had to contend with the Baiga tribesmen, who had the 'greatest contempt for tillers of the soil' and who descended with their axes in the dry season, cut down and burned numerous trees and then chucked a few handfuls of seed on to the ashes.[19] For such officials, who came from a country of settled agriculture in a temperate zone – and whose jobs were all about managing, improving and exploiting woodland – the practice of 'shifting cultivation' was anathema, and they made little attempt to understand it. Yet this type of agriculture was less haphazard than it appeared and, if practised over a large area by small numbers of people, was in fact an ecologically sustainable system of cultivation.

The experiences of a forest officer on tour were much the same as those of a district officer, except that he went to even more remote places and saw even fewer of his fellow countrymen; he also spent more time on elephants. Jungle wallahs who toured in both India and Burma testified to the relative luxury of the former existence: 'the duplicated outfit of tents and camp-furniture laden on many carts, the horses and traps, the troupes of servants, and the patriarchal herds of cows, sheep and goats', compared to the usual Burmese situation of two servants and three elephants in a primeval forest without roads and often without paths.[20] One jungle wallah who did not care how primitive the conditions were was William Horsley, a Civilian who worked both for his official boss, the collector, and for the conservator of forests in the province of Bombay. Relishing his 'very Bedouin sort of life', he spent his time inspecting jungles, demarcating forest reserves and slipping away with his greyhounds to shoot something for supper. When offered a desk job that would have accelerated his promotion in the service, he rejected it because he preferred 'independence and the healthy out of doors life' that he led as an assistant collector 'in charge of the Khandesh Forests knocking about his jungles in stained brown raiment, rifle in hand, often from early dawn to sunset, eating his breakfasts under a tree by the side of a running stream'.[21]

Most forest officers seem to have been happy in their wilderness, appreciating the charm and mystery of the hill forests, especially when they married and had children with them in camp, playing with pets such as mouse-deer and riding on the backs of elephants. Yet without a family the loneliness could be oppressive and even frightening. James Best did not mind his nickname of 'Jungly', but he realized that it was

'not good for a man to go wholly "jungly" ', having dinner in his pyjamas and not bothering to shave, living on his own with nothing to do
in the hot weather except stalk wild animals and keep a look-out for
fires. Forest officers were encouraged to shoot game because the activity helped them get to know their woods and the people who lived in
them. Before his marriage, Best recalled, it also 'helped to save one's
reason' because at certain seasons of the year it was his 'sole recreation
in a very lonely existence'.[22] Yet even that solace was forbidden to one
senior officer who seems to have spent too much time by himself in the
jungles. He had become a believer in 'transmigration', he announced at
dinners in camp; as a result he had decided to give up shooting for 'fear
of killing his deceased ancestors'.[23]

POLICEMEN

The East India Company never regarded policing as one of its priorities.
For most of its existence it relied on a local militia to keep some sort of
order in the presidency towns. In fact one cannot speak of a police
force organized in any recognizable way until the middle of the nineteenth century when Bombay appointed a superintendent for each
district. Bengal took its policing more seriously after the Rebellion, and
within a few years the Indian provinces had established a senior hierarchy, ascending from assistant district superintendent of police (the
rank at which British men joined the service after passing the exams in
England) to inspector-general. In 1909 there were 670 officers (almost
entirely British) within these ranks. Below them were thousands of sergeants and constables, mainly Indian but including a number of
Tommies who had joined up because they wanted to stay in India.

The salaries of the new police officers allowed them to live reasonably well. A district superintendent might earn about half what a
district officer was paid, yet in the mofussil even an inspector could
afford a large bungalow and a dozen servants. The police service may
have been less prestigious than the ICS, but it was not socially demean-
ing, not like being a tradesman or a planter. A police officer's wife
could even become a 'master' of the Ooty Hunt; Bombay's commissioner of police might even be an Old Etonian and a graduate of Christ
Church. It was hard, of course, to stay solvent as a junior officer, as it

was for a subaltern. And while army officers received free medical care for themselves and their families, policemen (like Civilians) had to pay for their wives and children. As a junior police officer in Delhi in the 1930s, the married Vernon Bayley could only make 'ends meet by reading the six o'clock news on Delhi Radio'.[24]

A district superintendent's routine had much in common with that of a district officer (inspections) and an army officer (inspections and parades), inspecting the stables, the quarter guard and the police hospital, then taking the mounted police out for a cross-country ride. More varied work included hunting down bandit gangs in forests, pursuing tigers and panthers that had acquired a reputation for being 'man-eaters', and keeping an eye on fairs and pilgrimages, which provided fertile opportunities for pickpockets to operate disguised as sadhus and fakirs. These were also occasions for things to go wrong or get badly out of control in the form of stampedes, epidemics or asphyxia in a small and overcrowded temple: during the annual pilgrimage to Pandharpur in the 1880s, one of Superintendent Coles's most important duties was pumping air into the 'Holiest of Holies'.[25] After the First World War the police had to deal increasingly with political and communal problems such as Hindu–Muslim rioting, the Moplah Muslim rebellion in Malabar against Hindu and British targets, and the rise, in defiance of Gandhi's wishes, of violent political nationalism, especially in Bengal. Between 1930 and 1932 several police officers were assassinated in Dacca, Calcutta and Midnapore.

The urban work of a policeman had other, often seamier dimensions, especially in ports inhabited by different grades and species of 'low life'. Traffic control took up much of Peter Hansen's early work in Calcutta at the beginning of the twentieth century, but he was soon transferred to an area that included 'Chinatown', where he had to deal with gambling booths, opium dens and cocaine-smuggling, all of which survived and prospered thanks to the corruption of Indian policemen. All this happened in Bombay too, where until 1888 the police commissioner had the additional burden of running the city's fire brigade. Fortunately the police in that city had some remarkable chiefs. We have already met the Eurasian Charles Forjett, who was brought up in India, spoke the vernaculars of Bombay and was a master of disguise; after a governor of the province, Lord Elphinstone, challenged him to get past all the sentries and staff at Government House, he turned up in the governor's bedroom the following morning in the guise of a sweeper. One of his successors was Hartley Kennedy, who liked to dress up as an Arab, or even as a purdah nashin, a Muslim woman with a veil, and wander about the city at night, checking the behaviour of his officers at their police stations. Another commissioner with an intimate knowledge of Bombay was F. A. M. ('Fatty') Vincent, whose father had been commissioner in the 1890s, and whose knowledge of Marathi had come from his ayah. According to one of his subordinates, his language was colloquial and even indecent in its jests, but it 'was not without a useful effect when dealing with people like the millhands of Bombay'. It also had its uses in dealing with crimes connected with prostitution.[26]

The opening of the Suez Canal in 1869 brought many advantages to Bombay, increasing its trade, wealth and population. It also brought prostitutes from eastern Europe and their attendant pimps or procurers and 'fancy-men'. Once the shipping companies had established their routes via Port Said – 'an asylum for the riff-raff of Europe' in the description of yet another Bombay commissioner – these people had an easy voyage to the city, and they soon established themselves in brothels along Grant Road and its neighbourhood. From time to time the police made efforts to deport the pimps, but they were generally content to let the women stay as a 'necessary evil'. It was better for them to be in Grant Road, where they were controlled by a 'mistress' who housed and fed them and took 50 per cent of their earnings, than to be independent, 'liable to thieve and quarrel', looking for custom in restaurants or on the race course, and walking the streets of the European quarter.[27]

For purposes of protection, pimps and prostitutes naturally turned to policemen whom they thought they might be able to corrupt. In the early twentieth century several of the Bombay women were Jewish Russians, and so were some of the pimps. So also was Inspector Simon Favel, who had been born in Odessa, had become a naturalized British subject, and who liked to boast that he was 'the only Jew in the Police who had won' the King's Police Medal. During the First World War, 'Fatty' Vincent recorded that Favel had been his 'right-hand man' in dealing with enemy aliens. He soon discovered that his inspector was also good at dealing with people for sexual and financial profit. With the help of Indian witnesses, including a tailor known as 'Barny', an hereditary dressmaker to the prostitutes of Bombay, Vincent was able to map out the hierarchy and chronology of the European procurers in the city. One Jewish Russian known as Adolph had been the 'go-between' for the police and the prostitutes, greeting the women from the ships, taking them to the Hotel Balcon, and introducing them to the 'mistresses' of the brothels. After his death he was succeeded by another, called Toster, who soon had a rival, Maurice Finckelstein, who allied himself to Favel, by now (1909) regarded as the unofficial supervisor of the European prostitutes. The two of them managed to force Toster out of Bombay and over to Karachi, but later they quarrelled over their portions of extortion money, and the inspector managed to get Finckelstein deported on the orders of Fatty Vincent.

Favel was now effectively the 'godfather' of the underworld. According to the evidence of brothel managers as well as Barny, he took commissions on everything, even when a bordello changed hands. Deportation, or the threat of deportation, was an especially lucrative business. After he had expelled a Japanese pimp, he received regular payments from Japanese girls and procurers who were anxious to stay in India. He deported Sophie, a German woman, but not Mina, an Austrian subject who gave him enough rupees to be allowed to remain. He also permitted another Austrian woman, Fritza, to stay because she married a British subject called Shalome. He may also have been influenced by the fact that Fritza had once been his mistress, though fidelity and sentimentality were not usually his strong points. According to Barny, he frequently visited 'the brothels for the purpose of enjoying the girls', though 'on these occasions the Mistress of the House herself pays the girl so honoured. Mr Favel pays nothing.'

After surveying the evidence, Vincent summoned Favel, suspended him, and told him that he would be holding a departmental inquiry into the charges. His subordinate made no attempt to deny them. Instead, after begging the commissioner to let him resign, he handed over both a written letter of resignation and the King's Police Medal he had been awarded only the year before. Vincent was lenient. In a letter to the Bombay government he explained that he had abandoned the plan of holding the inquiry because he 'considered it highly impolitic publicly to disgrace, however much he might deserve it', an officer who had so recently been lauded. The government of India was not impressed by this reasoning. Its secretary in the Home Department believed that, while a scandal would have been embarrassing, 'the ruthless exposure of evil doing and heavy punishment of the culprit would inspire confidence in the public that Govt is determined to prevent such abuses'. In the circumstances he felt that Favel had been 'fortunate in escaping a criminal prosecution, and still more fortunate in being allowed to leave the service without the public disgrace of dismissal'. Subsequently the government hoped it might be possible to deport Favel (as he was a naturalized British subject, it was not) or at any rate ensure that he would not receive a pension. The Bombay government assured it that he would not. Probably Favel had made enough money not to need one.[28]

Another city with a multi-ethnic society and the usual goings-on of a large port was Rangoon. An inadequately manned police force tried to control the brothels on the waterfront, the gambling dens across the city, and the lucrative trade in pornography, but its most complicated problem was its opium dens, which were concentrated in 'China Town' though they proliferated beyond the urban limits. In India users of the drug usually chewed a less harmful hemp known as 'ghany', but the addicts in Burma, many of them Chinese, smoked pipes of opium. Bill Tydd, a British police officer, spent much of his time in the 1930s raiding these insalubrious dens. Whenever he did so, he felt 'more sorrow than anger for the emaciated and decrepit smokers lying around on filthy couches or floors, invariably looking years older than their real age'.[29]

The Indian Imperial Police had in Burma two unusual officers who both left the force to become writers. The first was Hector Monro, who was born in Burma in 1870, the son of a British Army officer. When his mother died, soon after his birth, his father took Hector and his older siblings to England, deposited them with their unmarried aunts at the family home in Devonshire, and returned to take up a new post as chief of the Burmese Police. According to the memoirs of Hector's sister, Ethel, the aunts were imperious and bad-tempered, and their regime may have contributed to the streaks of cruelty and cynicism that underlie the witty and light-hearted stories Hector later wrote under his pen-name Saki. Acceding to pressure from his father, the boy followed his brother into the Burmese Police and spent about a year near Mandalay. After half a dozen fevers and a bout of malaria, he was invalided home, never to return.[30]

His Burmese experience appears to have had virtually no effect on Saki's literary output. Very different was the case of Eric Blair, whose years in Burma inspired his novel *Burmese Days* and helped to form his ideas on politics and colonialism. As we have seen, Blair had been born in Bengal, where his father was a government official, but he had come home with his mother and sister and was educated (at reduced fees) at Eton, where he made a reputation as an independent-minded boy at 'College', the boarding house of the school's scholars. Although he did not do enough work to gain a scholarship to Oxford or Cambridge, his subsequent choice of career was odd: there would have been several openings more obviously appealing to an intelligent Old Etonian than life as a colonial policeman. Yet later it was remembered that at school he had often talked about 'the East', and he gave one friend the impression that he longed to go back there.[31] In any event he applied to join the Indian Police and chose Burma as his province because of his mother's relations there.* In 1922 he went to London to take the necessary exams, doing fairly well in the academic subjects but so badly in the riding that he was placed near the bottom of the list of successful candidates. A few weeks later he sailed to Burma to join the ninety British police officers who tried to keep order in that enormous province.

Blair spent five years an an imperial policeman in Burma. After learning his profession at the police training school at Mandalay, he was posted to the Irrawaddy Delta and thence to various other stations, including Moulmein, before he was sent to Katha in the forested hills of Upper Burma. There he got dengue fever, a debilitating disease for which there was no apparent cure. He applied for sick leave, and when this was approved, he sailed for England in July 1927. Like Monro, he never returned to Burma.

Eric Blair was a competent and well-paid policeman who liked the people and the landscapes of Burma. But he did not like the job, or at least the imperial essentials of it. He accepted that the British did some good things in the country: they 'constructed roads and canals', they 'built hospitals, opened schools, and maintained national order and security'. Yet for him the relationship between Burman and Briton was all wrong: it was that of servant to master, and however good that master might be, it was not a relationship that he now wished to be part of. In his years abroad he had become increasingly sensitive about the hostility of the Burmese people, their 'accusing looks', the behaviour of young Buddhist priests who seemed to have nothing 'to do except stand

* See above, p. 193.

on street corners and jeer at Europeans'. During his illness at Katha he realized that he could no longer continue a career as an agent of imperialism. So he went back to England, resigned the service, and told his parents that he wished to be a writer, a profession for which he had hitherto shown little aptitude. Richard Blair, who had spent thirty-five years in his Indian service, living alone for three-quarters of that time, was appalled. His son's plan, he believed, sounded like that of a 'dilettante' – almost the last word one could associate with the character of the future George Orwell.[32]

SAPPERS AND CANALS

Officers in the sappers and engineers were the most highly trained men in the Indian Army. Educated at Addiscombe Military Seminary and Chatham Royal Engineers Establishment, they were elite figures in Victorian India, able to enjoy a range of professional opportunities often only loosely connected with warfare. Lieutenant-General Sir Richard Strachey fought only in a single military campaign, the first Sikh War of 1845–6. The other seventy years of his service in India and work on Indian matters in London were spent digging canals, building railways, inspecting irrigation, investigating famine and administering public works. Completely unqualified though he was for the job, he even became finance member of the Viceroy's Council in the late 1870s, deputizing for his brother John, who had to return to England for an eye operation.

Like Strachey, Jack Shaw Stewart was an engineer who became a general without seeing much combat: his activities in the field were limited to commanding the Madras Sappers in the expeditionary force to China in 1860 and directing various siege operations around Peking. Again like Strachey, he was in India during the Rebellion but did no fighting (he was stationed in unrebellious Madras), and like his colleague he devoted much of his career to railway engineering, famine relief and administration in the Public Works Department (PWD). A more military life was led by Richard Baird Smith, although his first job in the Bengal Engineers was the removal of a shipwreck in the River Hooghly. He spent most of his subsequent career in canal work and was sent to Lombardy to study irrigation (after which he published

Italian Irrigation in two volumes) before he was appointed director of the Ganges Canal. Yet he was several times recalled to do the job he had been trained for, military engineering, and he took part in both Sikh wars, his involvement including ferrying troops with their artillery and baggage trains over the great River Chenab. In the Rebellion he held the crucial post of chief engineer at Delhi, responsible for maintaining and strengthening the defences of the British forces on the Ridge outside the city. During the final and successful assault on Delhi's walls in September 1857 he saved the day by persuading General Wilson, the indecisive British commander who was inclined to withdraw, to remain resilient and press on.

One parallel career much practised by engineers was civil architecture. Those who went to Addiscombe had absorbed the rudiments of the art at the seminary, but their predecessors had been largely self-taught, basing their designs on books and treatises. As governor-general, Richard Wellesley had set a trend by appointing the unknown Captain Wyatt rather than Calcutta's civil architect to build Government House, which he did to a plan based on a Palladian design also used for Robert Adam's scheme for Kedleston in Derbyshire. The building inspired similar designs, even for Indian rulers, such as the nawab of Bengal's palace in Murshidabad, built in 1837 by Duncan McLeod of the Bengal Engineers. The East India Company certainly encouraged its engineers to diversify: after several years of poor health (in India) and injury (while recuperating in Tasmania), Arthur Cotton was given a rest from his irrigation schemes along the River Cauvery and told to build a church in a healthy spot further north in the Godaveri delta.[33] Some engineers managed to become distinguished architects. After a decade working for the PWD in Rajputana and as a field engineer in Aden, Lieutenant Swinton Jacob made a study of Rajput architecture that resulted in the formation of the Indo-Saracenic style he used for a series of remarkable buildings in Jaipur, Bikaner and other towns of the north and north-west; after his retirement as a colonel in the Indian Army in 1896, the Maharaja of Jaipur retained him as an adviser and superintending engineer in his state. Yet more often engineers made competent rather than inspired architects. There was just too much eclecticism in their large rambling buildings: a veneer of Venetian Gothic here, a touch of Swiss chalet there, some stern Scottish baronial somewhere else, and then on top, dominating the medley, an Italianate tower inspired by Prince Albert's designs for Osborne on the Isle of Wight.

The Indian Army's custom of allowing its most talented engineers to spend their careers designing buildings or digging canals was criticized by people who accused them of forgetting that they belonged to a military corps and were essentially soldier-engineers. Even Shaw Stewart, who was one of the elect, railed against a system in which a young officer was sent, as soon as he arrived in India, to a station in the interior, where for years his duties were purely civil, where he was not called on to do a day's military duty or to wear uniform or 'do anything which may in any way remind him that he is by profession a soldier'. Such a man almost invariably regarded 'his military duties as of secondary importance' and, although aware that he might be called upon to perform them, he would sometimes consider himself 'unfortunate in being selected for service in the field'. In any case it was ridiculous for engineer officers to be sent on active service 'without having had any previous knowledge or experience of their men'. Here Shaw Stewart was arguing from an informed position. Until he was sent to China, he 'had never done duty with the sappers', and outside Peking he 'felt very greatly the want of a previous acquaintance with the men under [his] command'.[34]

No doubt he had a point. Yet Baird Smith's career had shown how a good officer could successfully oscillate between civil and military work. And it would have been a great waste to keep educated engineers in barracks when they could be usefully employed in digging canals. Two engineers who each spent over thirty productive years working on large irrigation schemes were Proby Cautley and Arthur Cotton, who both went to Addiscombe in 1818. Like the younger Baird Smith, Cautley interrupted his work to visit northern Italy, where he studied drainage and distribution systems, and then returned to his principal project, the construction of the Ganges Canal, a massive waterway 350 miles long (excluding hundreds of miles of branch canals) that was built without any kind of mechanical assistance. While Cautley seems to have been motivated by a constructor's ambition, to build bigger and better than anyone else, Cotton was inspired by a clear humanitarian vision. After witnessing the effects of a famine in 1833, he saw irrigation as a moral duty, a benefit that India's rulers were obliged to provide for their subjects. His canals, aqueducts and dams along the Cauvery and Godavari rivers – two of the three great river systems flowing east from the Western Ghats – enormously increased the prosperity of the adjacent farmland. In 1987, forty years after Independence, a statue in his honour was erected in the state of Andhra Pradesh.[35]

Like canals, railways could also absorb the life of an engineer officer educated at Addiscombe or later at the Royal Indian Engineering College at Cooper's Hill in Surrey. George Rose of the Public Works Department began his career in 1877 as an assistant engineer of the Indian State Railways and occupied a variety of other railway posts – executive engineer, deputy manager, superintendent of works and engineer-in-chief at Hyderabad – before retiring in 1904 as a consulting engineer to the government of India in Calcutta; while working on the Sind–Pishin Railways between 1884 and 1887 he won, according to his obituary in The Times, the 'confidence of the gangs of wild border men – Afridi, Waziri, and Baluch – upon whose good will and exertions much of his subsequent success depended'.[36]

Railway construction expanded at such a rate after 1860 that the Indian Army could not possibly provide all the engineers needed to build all the lines and tunnels as well as the great cantilevered bridges over the rivers. Technicians, hired by contractors, were thus sent out from Britain to work on specific projects without the obligation of remaining in India after their work was done. Mark Carr worked on the Jubbulpore railway extension in the 1860s but then left India to build a railway in Hungary before becoming general manager of the Rio Tinto Mining Company in Spain. His contemporary Henry Le Mesurier, who had done his apprenticeship building breakwaters in Guernsey, also worked on the Jubbulpore scheme but later left India to work in Egypt and eventually become president of the Board of Administration of Egyptian Railways.[37]

Work as a maintenance engineer on the railways and canals meant a lonely, arduous and often anxious existence. As an assistant engineer on the nizam's railways at Hyderabad, Cyril Lloyd Jones found himself always on the move, touring the lines on his 'trolley', inspecting tracks and bridges and seldom spending more than a day or two a month at the cantonment at Secunderabad, the base where he could relax and play tennis at the club. He had gone to India because he wished 'to widen [his] engineering experience' and because he was 'attracted to an open air life with a spice for adventure'. He certainly found adventure during the monsoons, which brought the danger of floods damaging the line, collapsing the walls of a reservoir and washing away the girders of the piers of a bridge. Yet he loved the life, 'being in the jungle and free of social demands', with comforts limited to oil lamps, a rough cot and a canvas bath, and the day ending with camp fires and 'the odour of burning wood'. When describing his routine in letters to his fiancée, Kathleen, he evidently exaggerated 'the charms of life on line, trundling slowly along on a trolley through the heat of the day or tramping through the jungle with a gun'. As a young wife, Kathleen soon discovered that living alone (Lloyd Jones was always working) in an 'antique rest house with a thatched roof harbouring all kinds of vermin and snakes' was not 'a glamorous alternative to consorting with interesting and amusing people of her own age, interspersed with theatres, concerts and art exhibitions'. In fact, according to their son, she became so 'miserably unhappy' and lonely that she 'seriously thought of leaving her husband and returning to England'.[38]

The routine of a canal engineer was no friendlier to married life than that of a railwayman. He would have his own bungalow, often in an isolated and sometimes malarious spot somewhere along the line of his canal. Yet he was usually not in it, for his was a job that required him to be frequently on the move, staying at resthouses built along the banks as he checked the distributaries in the growing season, ensuring that each village received its share of water for its crops; he also had to see that the water in the canals flowed fast enough to prevent weeds growing on their beds but not so swiftly that it eroded the banks. Other professions gave their workers respite during the monsoon, but not his. He could not take a summer holiday when there was a risk of canals bursting their banks, flooding the countryside and endangering lives.[39]

Many British engineers working in India were not 'covenanted' officers like Cotton and Cautley, Strachey and Shaw Stewart. Without the job security provided by Chatham or Cooper's Hill, they would go out to work for some company, which might sack them or go bust, leaving them to drift about on the Subcontinent, finding one job after another, often in different fields, finishing up in some backwater, cheroot in hand, telling yarns and never thinking of going 'home' to that street in Clacton or that cottage near Lyme Regis. John Beames found one such fellow, George Faulkner, who had ended up running the canal workshops at Cuttack in Orissa.

He looked like an old lion, a grand, jovial, coarse, hard-drinking old Viking, full of songs and jokes and highly improper stories. Utterly reckless and wild about money matters, always in debt, always full of wild schemes, and yet this rough old creature had the most exquisitely delicate taste as a designer, and the greatest skill and fineness of touch as an artisan. He painted, he carved, he moulded; he designed buildings, boats, bridges; he grew the most beautiful flowers, planned and laid out the most lovely gardens . . .

Faulkner and his sons read literature – they 'loved their Ruskin' – and his daughters, who had been sent to France, spoke French 'with a pure Parisian accent'. Yet although he had lived in India for forty years, the father 'could not speak a dozen words of any Indian language'. He was 'thoroughly English in manners and feelings' and spoke of England 'with pride and affection', yet he had no desire to return to a land where, so Beames believed, he would have been unhappy, out of place and misunderstood. For him India had become 'a second mother-country', and he needed to stay there.[40]

INDIGO BLUE AND ASSAMESE TEA

The indigo planter, it was said, lived and dreamed on horseback. 'That noble animal' dominated his life. He used it for work, for sport, for transport and for recreation; he admired it in action and in its stable; and it 'formed the staple of his conversation'.[41] Planters of indigo lived such isolated lives that they were prepared to ride forty or fifty miles for a party. At their 'meets', their occasional 'get-togethers', they would rise from a night's feasting and go careering after polo balls, charging after wild boar and racing across the countryside. They were numerically a very small set, at their maximum size barely 200 of them in India.

Gerald Ritchie was a young magistrate posted in the 1870s to a district in Bengal dominated by the indigo business. Staying one night at a 'palatial indigo bungalow' and listening to stories about the crop and the Rebellion, he realized that the planters were a different type from any he had so far come across in British India. They were 'rough, daring, practical colonists', both cheery and resourceful, 'great heroes in their own eyes', though some had 'an unpleasing note of excessive self-assertion and bravado'. In Ritchie's description, their day at the 'factory' began very early with a long ride 'round the cultivation, varied with a gallop after jackal, till the sun was straight overhead'. These activities were followed by 'a bath and a very heavy breakfast [tiffin] with cool beer and whisky pegs', followed by 'a smoke and a game of billiards' until 'everybody went to bed for a siesta under the flapping punkah'. The sleep was succeeded by a drive or a polo match, which was followed by more pegs, 'another bath, dinner with more beer and whisky, and sitting out in the cool [of the evening] with more pegs'. Observing this routine, Ritchie was not surprised that 'the planters presented a sturdy, red-faced appearance, bubbling over with bucolic health, full of strange oaths, and delighting in practical jokes'.[42]

This narration might have been coloured by the fact that Ritchie was one of those overworked Civilians who believed, probably rightly, that nobody laboured as hard as they did. Other accounts suggest that the morning ride and the 'gallop after jackal' were in fact a fairly thorough inspection of horses, bullocks, ploughmen and cultivated land, which might last five hours, and that, although in the hot weather a siesta was permitted, this was followed by a spell with the office accounts and an evening inspection of the work done since the morning.[43] In any case inspections were concentrated over quite a limited period, in summer when the crops were actually growing. In late June or early July, depending when the rains were expected, the planter had to oversee the cutting of the crop, its loading into carts, its conveyance to the factory and its emptying into a large number of vats. The steeping of the indigo, the beating of the water containing the dye, the subsequent boiling to improve the colour, followed by repeated straining until the grains were large enough to be collected and pressed into cakes, was a long and complicated process. When the violet-blue substance was finally dry, it was cut into cubes, packed into chests and sent by boat to Calcutta, where it was sold at auction and exported, mostly to Europe and America.[44]

Indigo was the earliest of the British plantation crops in India, long before coffee and tea, because an indigenous industry had long existed, although it was by then in decline. Encouraged by the East India Company, planters arrived in the late eighteenth century from Scotland and the West Indies and set up their factories in areas of Bengal that later became part of the state of Bihar. Although capable of engendering large profits, indigo was always an unpredictable business, prone to speculation and to market collapses when production was excessive. The crop was also dependent on the coming of the rains at the right time and in the right quantities; it would be fatal if it was still unripe when the waters came down. Like many other enterprises in the Indian plains, indigo plantations were in perennial danger of flooding. Twelve of the fourteen factories belonging to one indigo planter in Bengal were washed away in a single flood in 1878.[45]

A further problem for indigo farming was poor 'industrial relations', the worst in India, more acrimonious even than in the jute industry. Although the East India Company had encouraged the planters to come to India, it had refused to let them buy land there. Later it eased the restriction, but the system of plantations, as known in the Caribbean and later in East Africa, did not exist in India. The planters built the factory, processed the crop and sold the product in Calcutta. But they seldom owned the land on which it was grown, though they might sometimes lease it from a local zemindar. Nor did they have a relationship with the growers (peasant cultivators or ryots) like those of landowners or industrialists in other places: the ryots were not their serfs or their tenants or their sharecroppers or their factory workers. The usual system was for the planter and the ryots to make an agreement whereby he would advance the money to grow the indigo and would later buy it from them at a fixed price. It was when the ryots believed that the price was too low and chose to grow something more profitable, such as rice, that the problems began. Planters seldom believed in conciliation, or even in negotiation, and they were prone to using 'bludgeon men' to enforce their will upon the ryots. Their intimidatory behaviour was such that only a tough Civilian magistrate could stand up to them.

One of the reasons the ICS was disliked and distrusted by British planters was that it was regarded as inherently pro-peasant and pro-native. In Nadia in Bengal William Herschel was considered to be 'excessively sympathetic' to the ryots; so was John Beames in the same province. When he was posted to Purneah in eastern Bihar in 1862, Beames realized that his 'duty was to see that the ryots were not oppressed' at the same time that he tried to 'keep on good terms with the planters'. In that area, where the indigo growers were usually quite amenable Eurasians, he succeeded. In his next posting, Champaran in north-western Bihar, he did not. Many of the original planters of the region had made enough money to return to England, leaving their estates in the hands of 'rough, uneducated men, hard drinkers, loose livers and destitute of sympathy for the natives'. When Beames discovered that one of the principal managers in Champaran, a man called Baldwin, was using methods of eviction and forced labour to cow recalcitrant ryots, he decided he had no option but to confront him with a summons, impose a 500-rupee fine, and threaten to jail him if he did it again.[46]

Yet even a tough magistrate could not leave a legacy that endured. Planters remained so obdurate and exploitative that they inspired Gandhi to visit Champaran during the First World War and launch his first campaign of *satyagraha* (civil disobedience). At the end of the previous century their industry had in any case received a devastating blow when synthetic indigo was invented in Germany, aniline dyes that could be produced and sold very much more cheaply than real indigo. The business had been in trouble for some time, and some planters had diversified with sugar cane, another unreliable crop in India, but it was now in the long run doomed. Exports to the United States halved in the last four years of the nineteenth century. Gandhi's opponents enjoyed a limited revival during the war, when the German invention was unobtainable, but they could not last, even if a couple of them survived for a while by exporting indigo to China, where carpet-makers preferred it to the synthetic dye.[47]

The chief problem for the planters was that the decline of their industry left them without assets. They did not often own the land, which could still be used for other crops, but they did own the factories, which were now useless. The British managers departed in search of new occupations, but the old planting families which had intermarried tended to stay put, living in crumbling mansions among empty factories and half-empty stables, hemmed in by a jungle that was gradually reclaiming the land that their ancestors had cleared.

Coffee and tea were more attractive crops to invest in than indigo or indeed opium. And for the cultivator it was more pleasant to work in the hills of Assam, in charge of a generally docile workforce, than to be in the Bengal plains dealing with resentful ryots. Yet no crops were immune to risk. Rubber plantations could be wrecked by elephants, cinchona (grown to produce quinine to combat malaria) could be undercut by Dutch rivals, tea seedlings could be destroyed by white ants, red spiders, crickets and 'China blight', and coffee could be damaged by borer insects and leaf rust, especially the Arabica variety brought from Yemen to Ceylon in the seventeenth century and subsequently cultivated by the British in southern India. Furthermore, while it might be cooler and healthier (if often malarious) in the hills, planters there were as isolated as anyone anywhere: they had to live on the estates they managed rather than congregate in towns. When in the 1840s William Knighton gave up coffee planting for journalism, he knew he would not miss 'the leeches and solitude, the coolies and the lonely bungalow'.[48]

Coffee in India, which was produced in the south, in Mysore and the Nilgiris, never enjoyed the success of tea, whose planters, working at a harder and higher altitude, liked to sneer at coffee as 'an orchard crop for idlers to grow'. In the late nineteenth entury it suffered from competition with the produce of Brazil and central America – and from the fact that the British themselves preferred to drink tea – yet it remained the planters' principal crop in south India until the First World War. Tea cultivation, which had no history in India, first appeared in Assam around 1840 and then spread to Kumaon and the Kangra Valley, and later to Darjeeling. Yet the gardens were established with such speed and recklessness that the 'tea rush' ended in a 'collapse' and numerous bankruptcies in 1865. As demand in Britain was still on the increase, the industry picked itself up and expanded again, now also in the south, in the Nilgiris and in the High Ranges of Travancore, an area so effectively colonized by its planters that as late as the 1950s it was regarded by some as 'white man's country', a place where the men grew tea, played rugby and fished for trout.[49]

Planters required patience and stamina and the strength to combat loneliness and ill health. Before a tea garden could be established, an area of jungle had to be cleared, usually with elephants, and a bungalow, a factory and shelter for the coolies all had to be built. One year of preparing the land and putting in the plants was followed by a second of tending and pruning the bushes, and it was only in the third year that plucking could begin, the leaves then going through various processes of rolling and fermenting before they were dried and packed in chests for sale.[50]

In 1881 there were fewer than 800 tea planters in India. As so often, there was a disproportionately high number of Scots, many of them with nicknames such as 'Mac' and 'Wee Jimmy', in this case largely because so many tea gardens in southern India were owned by the Glaswegian firm of James Finlay. 'Glasgow' might order Mac to make a new garden by felling, clearing and planting an area of jungle subsequently known as 'the new clearings'. Or it might put him in charge of an established garden of some 300 acres, which had a factory, an estate office, a doctor and a small bazaar to cater for his Indian assistants, clerks, sirdars (who marshalled the workforce) and some 400 workers of both sexes. Mac began his working day at six in the morning with 'muster', sometimes announced by the blowing of a great conch shell – 'a melancholy penetrating booming noise' – after which he watched the sirdars take their gangs of coolies off to their allotted tasks. Like other planters, Mac would spend much of his day on horseback, supervising the work, perhaps like Mr Tolson, 'a funny old card' in the High Ranges who in the 1920s rode about, led by his 'horsekeeper', with 'a big Trichy cigar in one hand' and a 'large open black umbrella in the other'. Eric Francis, one of Finlay's men, would have preferred to ride a motorbike, but he also did his inspecting by horse because it 'raised him to the ideal height above the fields'. One day of the week, Friday, was known as 'Teaspit Day', when 'the week's crops were subjected to formal group tea-tasting at HQ'.[51]

Mac would probably begin his career, and perhaps also his married life, in a decrepit bungalow with sparse wooden furniture, surrounded by jungle, with his nearest British neighbours five or six miles away along hill paths, and the nearest club even more distant. Most men in Mac's position tended to combat their loneliness by occasional loud and exuberant forays into 'matey' social life, with 'great drunken binges' and 'incredibly rough horseplay', especially after games of rugby.[52] Witnesses from outside the planters' society often described its members as 'raucous' and 'rowdy'. John Beames described those in Bengal as 'rough, rowdy bachelors, hardly fit society for ladies and gentlemen, and all disposed to be hostile or at least unpleasant to officials'. Henry Cotton, who as chief commissioner in Assam had a good view of their habits, noted what vast amounts they drank of Bass beer and 'brandy pawnee'.[53]

Hospitality and heavy drinking were perhaps inherent in the lives of planters of all sorts, an essential antidote to the routine and monotony, a reward for missing out on what people in Britain might take for granted – friendships, a social life, a visit to the pub and the music hall; they seem to have been a way of reassuring themselves that the sacrifices they were making (the loneliness, the bad climate and their frequent ill health) were worthwhile, that in spite of all the hardships they could live like barons on a magnificent scale. In the winter months, after the indigo had been dispatched, its planters liked to throw open the doors of their large two-storeyed 'bungalows', which they had sometimes castellated and usually surrounded by a park with mango groves. Their parties would last for three or four days, riding and hunting in the light, followed by feasting, dancing, billiards, card-playing and of course yarning into the night. One guest at an indigo mansion in Bengal in the 1870s described a 'breakfast' (presumably tiffin) with consecutive courses of 'Nawabee Pillaw' (piled on lamb or chicken), local and 'splendid Biktee and Ruhoo fish', wild duck in a savoury stew, 'plump quail' and 'plumper ortolan' (a bunting) and 'piquant Bombay duck' (a kind of dried fish). Another guest, the writer Emma Roberts, noted forty years earlier the 'air of barbaric grandeur about these feasts' that reminded her of what she had 'read of the old baronial style of living'.[54]

Even the critical John Beames appreciated the 'open-hearted, lordly hospitality', the scale of living, the swarms of servants and animals, the indigo patriarch with his elephants and his horde of children, especially one genial planter with a paunch who would sometimes 'take up a little coffee-coloured imp that was crawling about the veranda and look at it for some time before he was certain it was one of his offspring or not'. That particular patriarch, whom Beames referred to as 'Joe', was British-Indian, like most of the planters in Purneah, people who had been in India for two or three generations, who were seldom tempted to visit England, and who sent their children to schools in Darjeeling, Lucknow and Calcutta. Stubborn and independent though they often were, these men were easier to deal with than British planters and managers whose ancestors had not been in India. The latter too were friendly and generous, offering free meals to strangers, but as Beames soon realized when he was shown around the district of Tirhut, there was a glaring ulterior motive. They hoped to subvert the district officer by gregarious hospitality, but if that was not enough (and it seldom *was* enough), they aimed to cow him with a display of wealth and power to demonstrate that they and not the civil authorities effectively ran their district.

Beames described the tea planters of Bengal as being hostile or unpleasant to officials. Almost all planters seem to have been so. They had acquired the sense of independence of pioneers, of men with a sort of frontier mentality, rugged individuals who were determined to run their lands and businesses without the interference of meddling officials. Many of them, especially the indigo planters, were essentially 'Indianized' – most did not dream of retiring to England – but Indianized in a 'settler' sense, as men confident that they knew the land, knew the people who lived on it, and knew how to run the one with the other. Notions of 'native' rights or social reform or any kind of trade-union bargaining were completely alien to them. They were convinced that the only way to make the ryot or the coolie work was coercion, a policy that all too frequently involved physical force. If a DO tried to defend plantation workers, he could expect animosity and intimidation: one tea planter threatened to shoot any official who even attempted to inspect his tea garden.[55] The lamentable consequence of such behaviour was that, when they were taken to court for maltreatment of their workers, planters often received extremely light sentences, sometimes a fine of a few rupees for a thrashing that had caused terrible injuries.

MISSIONS AND MORAL FIBRE

Before 1813 no British missionaries lived and practised their calling in British India. They might live and work for missions in other parts of India, as the Baptist William Carey did in the Danish settlement of Serampore, where the Protestant Danes were partly funded by the English Society for the Promotion of Christian Knowledge. Yet they were not allowed to work in British India until their allies in the British Parliament forced the East India Company to end its restrictions on missionary activity in its territories.

Until the Charter Act of 1813, Christian ceremonies in the EIC's dominions were performed by the Company's chaplains, men who carried out the duties of an eighteenth-century parson to British congregations without excessive energy or zeal; the Church of England did not have a bishop in India or even an archdeacon. The East India Company had no desire to anglicize India or convert it to Christianity, and it was determined to avoid alarming Hindus and Muslims by giving them the impression that it did. Yet by the early nineteenth century there were enough Evangelicals at Westminster to insist that Indians should hear their message, however alarmed they might become. Their most powerful advocate was William Wilberforce, the politician and orator who claimed that, after the slave trade, 'the foulest blot on the moral character' of Britain was its irresponsibility in allowing its Indian subjects 'to remain . . . under the grossest, the darkest and most degrading system of idolatrous superstition that almost ever existed upon earth'.[56] One of his closest allies was Charles Grant, a former civil servant in India who had become an Evangelical Christian after two baby daughters had died there of smallpox. On his return to England, where he became both an MP and a senior director of the EIC, he argued that Hindus were so 'exceedingly depraved', so mired in superstition and vice, that Britain had a moral duty to introduce them to Christianity.[57] This became the core Evangelical position on Hinduism: the religion was cruel and obscene, its scriptures (the Vedas) were also obscene, and so it was no wonder that its practitioners were cruel and lascivious, burners of widows and killers of female babies.

The 1813 act heralded two significant changes in the status of Western Christianity on the Subcontinent. The Church of England was now given a structure with a bishopric created for Calcutta and later two more for Bombay and Madras; the metropolitan see of Calcutta eventually became so enormous that in 1877 a new diocese was made at either end, in Lahore and Rangoon. More influential for the inhabitants of India was the arrival of the missionaries. When the British ones were finally allowed in, they faced a good deal of competition. Theirs was in fact the only occupation in the Subcontinent in which Britons were outnumbered by rivals from other parts of Europe and the United States.* The first Protestant missionaries were the Danes, but Catholics had long preceded them; Jesuits were working from the sixteenth century in Goa, where the Portuguese authorities used them and the Inquisition to make forced conversions of thousands of Hindus. During

---

* With the exception of prostitution, though the numbers in this profession were very much lower. See below, pp. 330–32.

the nineteenth century a bewildering variety of European missions descended on India, such as Swedish Seventh Day Adventists and the Berlin Women's Association for the Education of Females in the Orient. Yet the country that provided the greatest number of missionaries was the United States, whose Baptists, Presbyterians, Congregationalists and others spread out to the three corners of the Subcontinent, to Assam and Burma, to the Tamil country in the south, and to the Punjab soon after the area was annexed by the British. Some observers were surprised that citizens of a country where slavery still flourished should be preaching the Christian message so far from home. Yet American missionaries were extremely persistent and fairly effective, especially Baptists working among the Nagas from their mission at Kohima in the north-east. Less effectual was a branch of the Assemblies of God at Basti, east of Lucknow, where the missionary, an elderly lady called Miss Gager, toured the area playing evangelistic records on her gramophone.[58]

The Church of Scotland sent several talented preachers to set up missions in India in the 1820s, but the Kirk's impact was blunted by the Disruption or schism of 1843, when its adherents split between those who remained within it and those who entered the new Free Church. In Bengal all its missionaries immediately joined the Free Church, which possessed no place where they could work or worship, while the established Kirk kept the colleges and mission buildings although it had nobody to live in them except three chaplains of the East India Company. The Disruption did not, however, deter Presbyterian enthusiasts from training at the established universities or, if Congregationalists, at the Glasgow Theological Academy, and then setting out for India. In England the largest training colleges for early-nineteenth-century missionaries were the Church Missionary Society's Institution in Islington and the London Missionary Society's Seminary at Gosport. Other prominent suppliers were the Bristol Baptist College, the Newport Pagnell Evangelical Institution and the Wesleyan Theological Institution for Methodists.[59]

The activities of Christian missionaries in India took the form of proselytizing, educating and looking after the health of the people they had chosen to live among. Yet until 1830 the proclamation of the gospel, by preaching or by reading the Bible, was almost the only activity of missionaries in India. Their work later expanded to include education and, a generation later, medical care. The Rebellion convinced many people, in the administration and elsewhere, that proselytism had been a mistake, that 'tampering with native religions' had been one of the main causes of the terrible war. Yet many missionaries remained unconvinced: now was the time, some of them insisted, to redouble their efforts. Two years after the fighting had ended, the newly married Beatrice Batty set off for India, under the auspices of the Church Missionary Society, to promote 'the kingdom of our blessed Lord among the nations still in heathen darkness or in ignorance of the gospel of Christ'.[60] Fifty years later, there were still missionaries who believed that Hinduism could be overcome, that its 'simple' adherents could not indefinitely 'bow in worship' before the 'bloodthirsty' Kali, the destructive Siva, the sensuous Krishna and 'the gross, elephant-headed god' Ganesh.[61] Even so clever a man as J. E. C. Welldon, bishop of Calcutta from 1898 to 1902, believed that a 'native prince' might become a 'Constantine or Clovis' and 'by his personal influence or example convert' India to Christianity. The prelate had been better suited to his previous job as headmaster of Harrow. He was so out of touch with India that he could not understand why Queen Victoria, their ruling sovereign, should be more popular with its inhabitants than Jesus Christ.[62]

Missionaries were seldom very popular with their compatriots. Queen Victoria herself, who felt maternal about her Indian subjects, especially the Muslims, said towards the end of her life that she 'wished the Mohammedans could be let alone by missionaries'.[63] Officials in India usually found them a nuisance and their activities dangerous; most of them shared the views of George Clerk, the two-time governor of Bombay, who believed that British rule could only be 'securely maintained' if it was administered 'in a spirit of tolerant and reasonable respect for the usages and the religions of the different nations and tribes there'.[64] In an article on 'India and Christianity' in the *Theological Review* in 1869, the Civilian Henry Beveridge admitted that missionaries might be 'honest and god-fearing men' who were good linguists and who came to India 'for other purposes than to make a fortune'. But he did not wish for any more preachers and proselytizers, who were quite 'mistaken when they imagine that they will ever convert the Hindoos'.[65]

Some missionary work was unobjectionable, even in Civilian eyes. If the London Missionary Society wished to subsidize Benjamin Rice's two decades of revising a Kannada translation of the Bible in the mid-nineteenth century, the activity was no doubt harmless, if also rather futile (it had to be re-revised twice more by other scholars before the century was out).[66] At the end of the eighteenth century William Carey had established a mission at Danish Serampore where with two assistants he embarked on the astonishing task of translating the whole Bible into Bengali, Hindi, Marathi and Sanskrit, as well as long portions of it into other Indian languages and dialects, including Kashmiri and Assamese. Impressive though the endeavour was, this one also turned out to be fairly futile. By the end of the nineteenth century not one of these volumes was still in use; the entire works, noted one missionary scholar, were 'obsolete' and 'unserviceable', 'inaccurate in language', 'imperfect in idiom' and 'so faulty that they had to be replaced by completely new versions'.[67]

Another single-minded figure was George Shirt, who decided in his twenties that the translation of 'the sacred scriptures' into Sindhi was to be the main objective of his life. First, however, he had to learn Sindhi and its complicated script, then he had to produce a grammar of the language (which had not been done before) as well as compile a dictionary (which also did not exist). He then, according to his biographer, began 'to elaborate the Sindhi Bible', though he diverted himself along the way with translations of the Book of Common Prayer and Bunyan's Pilgrim's Progress, always a favourite with Protestant missionaries.[68] He died aged forty-four in 1887, a year after he had opened a new mission at Quetta.

Other aspects of Shirt's missionary work were more controversial. In the hot weather (for some unknown reason) and with the Indus in flood, he and his 'little band of evangelists' would tie their boat up 'at some convenient point' and then 'wend their way on foot to the nearest village' or 'enter the gates of some ill-savoured, insanitary city' and start preaching in the bazaars, where they were hoping (but failing) to emulate the success of 'that prince of itinerant preachers, St Paul'.[69] According to an American tract of 1850, a missionary's duties included 'arguing with Brahmins, mingling with the thousands [of Hindus] who were congregating at annual festivals, and warning them of their sin and danger'.[70] As we have noted, the young Gandhi found such behaviour at Hindu fairs unendurable, but few missionaries thought they were being provocative or wondered whether they themselves would tolerate 'little bands' of mullahs or Brahmin priests preaching at Canterbury or along the pilgrims' road to Compostela. They did not seem to consider that they, belonging to a race that ate beef and drank alcohol, were bound to be regarded as innate enemies of the Hindus.[71]

The British might find missionaries annoying when they objected to badminton on Sundays or attempted to impose fines on men who used swear words in a club.[72] Those involved were certainly angry – and embarrassed – when in the 1890s members of the 'Bombay Midnight Mission', led by American missionaries, began patrolling the red-light district of Bombay, parading up and down its main street, knocking on doors, singing hymns outside brothels, even accosting any 'gentlemen' found in the area and publishing their names in a journal which they then sent to the men's clubs.[73] Such busybodies also interfered, tactlessly and self-righteously, in Indian life, especially when sex or alcohol might be involved. In 1935 Lutheran missionaries in an area of Bihar sabotaged the silver-jubilee celebrations of King George V when their campaigns against dancing and drinking rice beer dissuaded villagers from taking part. A few years later, in a tribal area of Assam, American missionaries convinced a village of unhappy Miris that their converts there would go to hell if they contined to drink rice wine.[74]

Soon after their arrival in India in the nineteenth century, many missionaries became obsessed by connections between sex and religion. Temple girls dancing before idols were especially repellent to them; so were 'nautch' girls hired by wealthy Brahmins to perform in front of British guests. In the 1830s missionaries in Calcutta campaigned successfully to curtail such 'disgraceful exhibitions' by putting pressure on the Brahmins. What seems to have upset them more than anything was the sight of a lingam, the phallic symbol of Siva worship, an emblem 'with all its disgusting and bestial rites' that in the opinion of one woman writer 'scarcely dispose[d] one to belief in the spirituality of Hindus as a nation'.[75] 'Lingamism,' opined Macaulay in the House of Commons in 1843, 'was 'not merely idolatry, but idolatry in its most pernicious form'.[76] Phallic symbols were not of course displayed as public sculpture in Britain, and the sight of a lingam was to some devout Christians unbearable. In southern India in the 1830s two Dissenter missionaries were 'living completely among the natives' and running a successful school until a missionary from outside arrived, 'got hold of a man's *lingam*, or badge of caste, and took it away'.* Although he was forced eventually to return it, the town was 'in ferment at the insult', most of the children left the school, and those who remained insisted on returning to 'their own Heathen books'.[77]

The most controversial aspect of missionary activity was proselytism, especially when it was practised in provocative places, outside mosques or at Hindu fairs or pilgrimages. Although this clearly infuriated some Indian listeners, others seem to have been bemused by the spectacle of strange-looking people attempting to deliver a religious message in a language they could barely speak. In any case, in its primary aim – the conversion of caste Hindus and Muslims – proselytism was an almost total failure. Missionaries were naturally successful in converting many orphans, and often the children of orphans, and they were also able to convert thousands of illiterate non-Hindu tribal peoples as well as low-caste 'untouchables', who had little to lose by abandoning Hinduism. No doubt a good number of these people were genuine converts who accepted the faith and were grateful for the education and employment that Christian missions might offer them. Complexity of motive is a natural and perennial human condition.

Yet for the missionaries it was not very satisfying to convert so many others plainly more interested in the prospect of Christian charity – as directed towards themselves – than in doctrines of salvation. In the areas where missionary success might have had an influence on wider Indian society, the histories of missions are invariably similar: one or two converts in thirty years of preaching – and sometimes not even that. The Rev. A. F. Lacroix of the London Missionary Society, who led the offensive against the Calcutta nautches in the 1830s, was 'reputed to have been the greatest vernacular preacher' in Bengal. According to Julius Richter, a missionary historian writing in the early twentieth century,

> he had command of Bengali such as was possessed by no other European. By his attractive delivery, his sympathetic expression, and the felicitous use of really idiomatic Bengali, he everywhere drew together vast crowds

---

* The chronicler of this scene, Julia Charlotte Maitland, probably meant a *'lingait'*, a badge with a figure of the lingam.

of listeners, and his convincing eloquence and his speech so rich in Oriental allusion charmed and fascinated the Hindus.

Another great itinerant preacher was McComby, a Baptist missionary who for forty-five years was indefatigable in the prosecution of long preaching tours, but who, like Lacroix, died without leaving a single convert, each furnishing a striking example of the relative fruitlessness of purely itinerant preaching.[78]

George Shirt's admiring biographer had a similar tale to relate. His subject had spent years in Baluchistan, teaching as well as translating, and 'it must have been a constant disappointment for him to find that he made few or no converts'. Nevertheless, he consoled himself with the thought that he was 'the voice of one crying in the wilderness'; he had done his duty to God.[79] That was also the attitude of other dispirited missionaries. In 1883 James Monro retired from the ICS in Bengal, where he had been inspector-general of police, went home to London to become commissioner of the Metropolitan Police, but then returned to India to start a medical mission at Ranaghat in Bengal. Yet as his friend Henry Beveridge observed, he was 'under no delusion as to the prospect of Christianising the people'. Monro's view was that he and his fellow Christians were 'commanded to deliver their message'. It was the responsibility of his listeners to accept or reject it.[80]

A recurring theme of missionary endeavour was the desire to 'break fresh ground', the need to go somewhere really difficult and to target and try to convert very unpromising people. It was what inspired George Shirt to go to Quetta and Miss Annie Taylor to convert Tibetans (with similar lack of success); it was what drove the CMS to work among the Sikhs in Amritsar, the Methodists to tackle Shia Muslims in Bangalore, the Church of Scotland to establish a mission in the Himalaya among the ancient temples of Chamba. And it was what sent David Morling of the Strict Baptist Mission from High Wycombe to the Kolli Hills in south India, which he regarded as 'one of the dark places of the earth, for no Protestant missionary or Christian teacher has ever been there, and we learn that the people are rude, unlettered, strange in their customs, and wholly given over to demonolatry'.[81]

While prospecting territory for a Baptist mission in 1906, the intrepid and naive Morling could 'not help contrasting the poor, wretched, tumble-down houses, mere hovels' of the inhabitants, with 'the spacious, stone-built, gold-pinnacled temples that confront us at every turn' – as if the Gothic cathedrals of Europe had not been surrounded by the squalor of the Middle Ages and later. As he continued his progress, Morling passed 'oily shrines, gory altars' and hundreds of 'horses and elephants of baked clay, painted in the gaudiest of colours, for the nightly delectation of the gods and godlings as they scour the countryside'. Worst of all was that 'incredible monstrosity – streets devoted *by religion* to commercialized vice'. Sometimes he and his companions were so overcome by what they saw that they had to read a passage from the Bible and then kneel on the floor of their cart to 'place our burden upon the Lord, and beseech His guidance'. To Morling it was tragic that there had hitherto been 'no Christian worker to sound forth the message of salvation from sin, shame and sorrow; not a single light to lead these poor deluded ones from the darkness of heathendom to the glory of God's Kingdom'. Yet at least he had now 'discovered the most needy part of the whole vast Tamil country'.[82]

Setting up a mission in a south Indian town was, as Morling soon discovered, a fraught and complicated business. 'Our seasons are hot, hotter and hottest', and he and his colleagues realized that they could not live in 'native quarters' because this would lead to 'the ruin of health and the hindering of work'. Obtaining a lease of land for building the mission was difficult, because the landowners quarrelled among themselves, and it then took four years of blasting through granite rock before they could obtain a water supply. There were also difficulties in constructing their chapel because Hindu villagers intimidated and even physically attacked Morling's team of builders. If the missionaries employed indigenous Christians* to help them, these were often ostracized, their houses stoned, and they themselves 'refused the services of the barber and the village washerman'. Sometimes when Morling, his wife and child arrived in a village 'highly redolent of cows and goats', the inhabitants would refuse to sell them any supplies: 'no water, no milk for the baby, no foodstuffs, cut off from the world as though marooned on a mudbank!'[83]

---

* The 1891 census counted just over two million Indian Christians, about three-quarters of them living in the Madras presidency. Although there had been a Christian presence in India since the second century, most of them were people whose ancestors had been converted – usually forcibly – by the Portuguese in the sixteenth century.

Preaching tours could sometimes be dispiriting. When Morling and his band approached a village, the 'simple rustics' often saw them coming and ran away, leaving the missionaries with an 'entrapped audience' of one crippled old woman and two thatchers who had not managed to get down in time from the roof of the house they were working on. Even when the villagers had not managed to escape, it was difficult to make much of an impact in a brief visit to a place 'where Christ had not been heard of', especially when the missionaries had problems in speaking Tamil and the people were illiterate and could not read the Bible. Morling and his followers had had great hopes of the town where they had gained their 'first and most earnest enquirers' and received their 'first laurels in the shape of rejected idols and forsaken Hindu *shastras* [sacred writings]'. But years later – 'oh, the disappointment of it all! . . . we have yet to win here the first trophy of a baptised convert from Hinduism'. In a life of repeated disappointment and tribulation, Morling remained convinced that it had all been worthwhile, that his decades in India had had a noble aim – 'the glory of Christ in the salvation of souls'. It did not matter that so few Hindus had been able 'to cross the Rubicon of baptism, to make the great and final break with the monster of caste'. God's work among men could not be measured 'with any rod of calculation, least of all in India'.[84]

At the time Morling began his mission he was already something of an anachronism. By 1906 a missionary in India was less likely to be a wandering preacher in a pith helmet than a teacher, a doctor or an administrator in a school or hospital. And by then most missionaries were females.[85]

When opening Wilson College's new building at Bombay University in 1889, the local governor, the Scottish Lord Reay, told students that the new institution's professors wished to 'ennoble your hearts by imparting to you . . . that moral fibre which is the mainspring of the Scotch character'.[86] Few men possessed as much moral fibre as Alexander Duff, one of the first Church of Scotland missionaries, who had arrived in India, following his brace of shipwrecks, in 1830.* A fine scholar and debater, this redoubtable product of St Andrews was the father of missionary education in India, and in his school in Calcutta the pupils

* See above, p. 136

were soon learning – and apparently enjoying – the poetry of Robbie Burns and Walter Scott. Duff's heroes were the Scottish Covenanters of the seventeenth century, and he appealed to his contemporary Scots to show a similar spirit, not to worship fame and wealth and 'perishable renown' but to allow their children to go forth with 'the army of the great Immanuel' and to 'win crowns of glory' in his service by working among the heathens of India.[87]

Yet missionary education was a controversial issue, especially for those who believed it was not evangelical enough. Supporters of the missions in Britain usually preferred to convert the 'heathen' rather than educate them, and in 1892 the General Assembly of the Church of Scotland even prohibited the expansion of education in its missions. Not only was it much cheaper to send out a preacher than to fund a school; it seemed to many people more in keeping with their fundamental aim, which was to 'win souls'. The fact that many Indian children seemed to appreciate a British education without showing any interest in changing their religion appeared to prove their argument.[88]

Missionary schools continued, however, to convey an overt Christian message. Even as late as 1935, by which time proselytizing zeal had long been in decline, the Women's Christian College in Madras declared that its 'first aim' was 'to extend the Kingdom of God in the land in which' it is planted and to present God's truth 'so clearly that it will have an irresistible attraction for those who hear it'.[89] Such statements of intent inevitably provoked suspicion among the parents of potential pupils who had to weigh the advantages of education against the possibility that their children might be made to eat meat and kick a (leather) football or otherwise be turned against their Hindu or Muslim faith. In the 1890s the first girls' school in Srinagar had to close down after it was rumoured that British guests at the first prize-giving ceremony had come there to kidnap the girls.[90]

It was in fact safer and more productive to start mission schools in hilly tribal areas where most of the inhabitants were neither Hindus nor Muslims but animists. Nagaland and neighbouring areas were especially congenial territory, where Welsh Calvinists and Methodists, English and American Baptists and continental Catholics managed to compete with apparent harmony for the souls of people who rated 'headhunting' in their neighbours' villages as the primary masculine virtue. Most British visitors to the area had appreciative things to say about the activities of the Welsh missions. One IMS officer noted that in those villages of the Garos that were under the influence of European Catholics, the women used opium and 'went about bare-breasted', whereas in the villages near the Welsh Mission Hospital they refrained from opium and 'were more or less clothed'.[91]

Writing at the end of the Victorian era, the Rev. A. R. Macduff described Kashmir as a beautiful land yet one that was 'morally a stagnant cesspool . . . the land of eternal snows and of everlasting dunghills'. It was, he declared, 'the despair of all social reformers, Government officials, and others charged with bearing "the White Man's burden" '.[92] One man who did not despair was Cecil Earle Tyndale-Biscoe, who went to Kashmir in 1890 and was principal of the Church Missionary Society's boys' school in Srinagar for half a century. He agreed with Macduff about the cesspool – Srinagar's 'moral filth was even greater than' its physical stench – but he was determined to try to cleanse it. Unhindered by feelings of self-doubt, he moulded an institution that was not a typical missionary school (conversion was not on the agenda), but its ethos was that of the 'muscular Christianity' then in vogue in British schools with their emphasis on character building and the physical exercise that allegedly helped boys to develop it. His pupils, most of them high-caste Hindus, offered different and more complicated challenges than the boys of schools such as Rugby and Loreto, but Tyndale-Biscoe was energetic, self-confident (and self-righteous), and he assembled a staff of Oxford and Cambridge graduates, most of them ordained, to assist him.

He soon learned not to offend Brahmin pupils by squashing an insect (taking life) or patting them on the back (defiling them) when they had done well. More difficult to deal with was the defilement caused by sport, kicking a football (that 'unholy piece of leather'), catching a cricket ball (ditto) and boxing with leather gloves. In time all these issues were settled, in the case of boxing by substituting cloth gloves. In his overbearing way Tyndale-Biscoe encouraged Pathan youths to regard fists not knives as the schoolboys' best weapons, and he personally gave boxing lessons for purposes of self-defence. As a schoolboy at Bradfield, he had nearly been raped, and he was determined to protect his pupils from the Kashmiri pederasts of the Srinagar Sodomy Club, whose leaders he eventually managed to catch and hand over to the police.[93]

The parents, who had sent their sons to the school to pass exams and thence obtain jobs, were 'quite against what they call waste of time in sports'. So were the boys, who thought them beneath the dignity of a Brahmin: only a low-caste person would handle an oar or row a boat, and anyway the boys had no wish to develop muscles. When a pupil was ordered to have a swimming lesson, he refused, explaining that he was a gentleman 'not a coolie'. Yet Tyndale-Biscoe was adamant, arguing that, apart from the intrinsic merit of swimming, the boy might need to rescue his mother if she accidentally fell into a river. Despite the boy's reply that he would order a coolie to pull her out, the tenacious schoolmaster overcame Brahmin opposition by increasing the school fees in annual increments for those who had not passed a swimming test by the age of thirteen. He subsequently claimed that his aquatic pupils, who regularly swam the Dal Lake, annually saved up to twenty of their fellow Kashmiris from drowning in the water.[94]

The least controversial and most appreciated of the Christian vocations in India was the work of the medical missions. Two generations of proselytizers had gone to India before the Free Church of Scotland sent out a doctor to work as a medical missionary in 1856. Before then itinerant preachers had of course often found themselves in places where potential converts had begged them for medical help. If, as was usually the case, the missionary possessed no medical training, then his aid was, as he sometimes confessed, 'quack work'. Every missionary, admitted F. Colyer Sackett, who spent decades as one in Hyderabad, 'became a quack doctor'. His remedies were 'perhaps a bit risky', but fortunately the 'results were never tabulated', and in any case they must have been 'a trifle better than the work of the village barber! Alas,' reflected the honest missionary, 'that was not saying much.'[95]

Scottish missionary societies may sometimes have admitted an ulterior aim – 'The work of the doctor is to open the door, that the evangelist may enter in' – though this was an objective that was probably not often attained. As one Brahmin put it, 'the doctrine of the Christians is bad but their medicine is good'. Yet whatever their aims, the missionary societies that set up hospitals and sanatoria insisted that their medical missionaries were properly qualified. The Bombay Missionary Conference of 1892–3 emphasized this position, passing a resolution that all medical missionaries in India should possess a medical degree or diploma that would qualify them to practise in the West.[96]

'Clinical Christianity', as it was sometimes called, had an impressive record. By 1936 its missions in India maintained nearly two hundred hospitals, more than one hundred dispensaries, and a large number of leper asylums and sanatoria; in these places they employed several hundred European and American doctors, rather more Indian doctors, and over 2,000 nurses.[97] As in so many fields of British India, medical missions sometimes became dynastic. Ronald Holland was born in 1914 in Quetta, where his father Henry had founded the Church Missionary Society Hospital and pioneered the idea of eye-camps.* After studying at Edinburgh University, he joined his father and elder brother at the mission hospital, and together the family was soon running a mobile eye-camp covering 2,000 miles from Kashmir to Baluchistan; the three men were credited with saving the eyesight of 150,000 Indians.† Missionaries might annoy people in their daily work and yet provoke admiration for their self-sacrifice and energy in a crisis. One forestry officer admitted that he had 'not always been pro-missionary' himself and had sometimes 'found them a great nuisance', but when the influenza plague hit the villages in his area after the First World War, the 'Quaker missionaries were splendid in their work of relief'. They organized the pupils who, 'led by their teachers, gave the finest example of real Christian work'.[98]

In 1900 there were a similar number of male and female British missionary doctors in India, yet from then on the proportion of women increased. Many of them were graduates of the London School of Medicine for Women and of the new women's colleges at Oxford and Cambridge. Women began medical work in India in the 1860s, often opening and running dispensaries, but they came in greater numbers from the late 1880s, after Lady Dufferin set up the National Association for Supplying Female Medical Aid to the Women of India. Like some of their male counterparts, women sometimes wished to be itinerant preachers, wandering from place to place or even setting up home in an Indian village, where their very presence was bound to excite interest in a patriarchal society. But most of them preferred more

---

* These were later run in India and elsewhere by the Royal Commonwealth Society for the Blind.
† According to the *DNB*, this was the figure in the citation when Sir Henry and Ronald received the international Ramon Magsaysay Award in Manila in 1960.

practical occupations, working as teachers in schools or doctors in hospitals. One of their most popular destinations was a zenana mission such as the Church of England Zenana Missionary Society, which built a string of hospitals in the Punjab and later opened others both in Bangalore and at Krishnagar in Bengal. In the zenana, where Indian women in purdah led lives of almost unimaginable restrictions, they felt they could help not only with medical problems but also with human sympathy for their situation and perhaps even with friendship. As one woman noted in 1903, 'I think one gets a kind of passion for one's own sex out here; it is so downtrodden, and so much nicer than the other, in spite of everything.'[99]

8

The Military Life

THE ARMY IN INDIA

The empire's soldiery in India consisted of British regiments sent out for a variable number of years and the Indian Army (an amalgamation of the armies of Bengal, Bombay and Madras), a force of Indian regiments with British officers stationed permanently on the Subcontinent. From the end of the nineteenth century they were together known as the 'Army in India' and had the same commander-in-chief, who was normally a general in the British Army, though two of the ablest men to hold this post (Roberts, 1885–93, and Auchinleck, 1941 and 1943–7) were Indian Army officers. Before the Rebellion Indian soldiers had outnumbered British troops in a ratio of about six to one, but afterwards the Indian contingent was reduced and the size of the British Army (which had absorbed the EIC's own European regiments) was increased. Except in the two world wars, the 'Army in India' consisted of some 62,000–75,000 British troops and roughly 140,000–150,000 Indians.

From 1863 the number of British officers in Indian regiments was also reduced. An infantry battalion of 600 sepoys and a cavalry regiment of 420 sowars (troopers) would now have only six British officers, including the CO and the adjutant. There were no British non-commissioned officers in these units. The ranks were both managed and led by men originally known as 'native officers' and later renamed VCOs – Viceroy's Commissioned Officers; the most senior of these figures in the infantry was the subedar-major and in the cavalry the rissaldar-major. The 'Indianization' of the officer corps turned out to be a slower process than in the ICS or the Indian Medical Service. At the beginning of the twentieth century Curzon had badgered the British government into letting him set up an Indian cadet corps, whose well-born apprentices would in time become officers of the Indian Army, but the project languished under his successor, Lord Minto, who was fond of reversing Curzonian schemes.

Not until the end of the First World War were young Indian men admitted to Sandhurst and subsequently given combatant commissions. In 1923 some infantry battalions and cavalry regiments were chosen as 'Indianizing' units that would be taking no more British subalterns. In 1916 Maurice Henry had joined a regiment of Mahratta Light Infantry as a second lieutenant; after postings in other units to Iraq, Quetta, Delhi and Aden, he was recalled to command his battalion in 1940 to discover that he and his second-in-command were its only officers who were British; the others were Indians trained at Dehra Dun, the Indian Military Academy that had been opened in 1932 and was run very like a public school. By the outbreak of the Second World War there were nearly 400 Indian officers, yet they still formed only a tenth of the total figure in the Indian Army. From 1940 necessity dictated an increase. In the summer of 1945 there were 8,340 Indian officers, yet so greatly had the army expanded in the meantime that British officers still outnumbered them by a ratio of four to one.[1]

The writer and journalist Edmund Candler identified sixteen different types of sepoy, all of whom he had met in Mesopotamia during the First World War. They included Gurkhas, Sikhs, Jats, Dogras, Punjabi 'Mussulmans' and Garhwalis; if Candler had counted groups such as Gujars and Meos as separate types (instead of bracketing them with, respectively, Jats and Merats), there would have been even more.[2] The striking feature of the list is that all except one* came from the north or north-west of the Subcontinent. A hundred years earlier, the East India Company armies had been recruited mainly from the south and the north-east, but the Madrasis had fallen out of favour, and most of the Bengali regiments had mutinied in 1857. Madrasi troops had fought at Arcot with Clive and at Assaye with Wellesley, but they had done little fighting since, and by the 1840s, as one of their officers lamented, they were regarded as a 'mere civil police', kept more for gathering the revenue and keeping 'the peasantry ... in check, than for actual

---

* The Jharwas from Assam.

service'.³ By the end of the nineteenth century the eight cavalry regiments from Madras had been reduced to three. And when southern troops did go into action, their performance might not always be impressive. On an expedition against Burmese dacoits in 1885, a British officer reported, they were so frightened that they 'ran every time they saw an armed Burman', throwing away their arms and ammunition belts and begging to be taken back to Madras.⁴

Since the middle of the nineteenth century, the Indian Army had relied on what the British liked to call the 'martial races' from the north. Large numbers of defeated Sikh soldiers had been incorporated into the Company's forces after the conquest of the Punjab, a province that was soon supplying half the soldiers of the Indian Army. When recruiting in the Punjab, officers did not have to rely on Wellington's 'scum of the earth' or their Indian equivalents in the bazaars or among the unemployed; they went to rural areas and had the pick of the men who worked the land. The 'different types of sepoy' were usually kept apart at company level, but their units were often placed together in a regimental battalion. The 28th Punjab Infantry, for example, had separate companies of Sikhs, Hindu Jats and Punjabi Muslims, and one that was half Pathan and half Dogra. A young British officer soon learned to avoid pork and alcohol when he was with the Muslims, but the etiquette with the Sikhs was more complicated. 'One had to remember never to offer' them tobacco yet not forget that they did like their alcohol. 'The Patiala peg' was 'measured with two fingers – the first and the last'. 'Stalky' Dunsterville was delighted to come across a retired Sikh officer who told him that brandy and soda (brandy pawnee, the officers' favourite drink) would be improved by doubling the quantity of brandy and replacing the soda with champagne.⁵

The most popular regiments for British subalterns were the Gurkha Rifles, which had formed part of British India's armed forces since 1815. Unlike other units, their battalions were homogeneous – consisting only of Gurkhas – and they were also unusual in having permanent homes, up in the hills where the climate suited them and where they could train for mountain warfare. In a station such as Lansdowne, in the Himalayan foothills, they would quarry the stone, saw the timber and build their own barracks among the rhododendrons and the ilex trees. Life with the Gurkhas might have certain drawbacks. Their food, observed one officer, required 'an asbestos throat' and 'the digestion of an ox', and at the festival of Dussehra normal work had to be suspended because the men were drunk for nearly ten days.[6] The Gurkhas were also 'proverbially bad marchers along a road' though they were 'excellent' in the jungle. Yet these and any other defects were forgiven by British officers who longed to command these hardy soldiers, 'short in stature, strongly built, with semi-Mongolian features', men of 'cheerful obedience' who were 'quick to smile and laugh' and who were above all reliable.[7] Competition for commissions to their battalions was stronger than anywhere else in the Indian Army. John Masters, who won one, learned the songs or *jaunris* that the Gurkhas sang when marching, and discovered that the words varied 'from obscenity to nostalgia with every sort of weirdly pointless little fable in between'.[8] Officers who had served in Gurkha battalions invariably missed their 'grand little men' and often annoyed colleagues from other units by talking so much about them. 'Not one of them,' complained a cavalry officer, 'can talk five minutes without starting to tell you about "my little men".' Such talk could deter a cadet from choosing them. When Ronald Johnston was asked at Quetta in 1915 which regiment he would like to join, he felt he 'had heard so much of the little Gurkha this and the little Gurkha that' that he applied for the Punjab infantry.[9]

With a couple of regimental exceptions, the cavalry of the Indian Army did not enjoy a great reputation apart from certain 'irregular' units such as Gardner's Horse and Skinner's 'Yellowboys'. Its officers, who had sometimes been rejects from Haileybury, were untrained and were often out of touch with their troops: all their regiments in the Bengal cavalry joined the Rebellion in 1857 and were subsequently disbanded. Even before then nobody could claim that their exploits on the battlefield had resembled those of the Scots Greys at Waterloo or the Light Brigade at Balaclava. Probyn's Horse, one of the regimental exceptions, performed well in China in 1860, charging thousands of Tartar horsemen at the Battle of the Taku Forts; its commander, Dighton Probyn, who had won the Victoria Cross in the Rebellion, led them on his renowned steed Clear-the-Line. Several cavalry regiments took part in the Second Afghan War (1878–1880) and did some useful work, as they also did, occasionally, on the north-west frontier. Yet unless his main ambitions were to play polo and go pig-sticking, it was frustrating to be a cavalryman in India. There was never enough to do.

Two cavalry divisions went to France in the First World War, and General Haig, who had served in India as inspector-general of cavalry, retained the illusion that, after a successful assault by his infantry, he could 'pour them into the gap' and thereby rout the German enemy. In the real world of trenches and barbed wire the cavalry was unable to operate, and some of the Indian regiments were eventually dismounted and turned into infantry.[10]

Except in Madras the Indian Army cavalry usually operated a system known as 'silladari' whereby the sowars brought their own horses to the regiments. The result was that they were seldom very dashingly mounted. Until late in the nineteenth century most of the animals were bought at country fairs, local beasts from Kathiawar or Baluchistan or the Persian Gulf; they may not have been very swift, but they were probably easier to train to swim across the great Punjab rivers than sleeker and more temperamental foreign horses. Country steeds were, however, gradually replaced by 'walers' (horses from New South Wales) brought from Australia to Calcutta or Bombay, where they were inspected and selected by officers of the Remount Depot. These men, who mainly supplied horses to the British regiments, belonged to an unglamorous branch of the army and had a reputation for being tough, hard-drinking men. Philip Mason encountered a group of them who played polo extremely slowly, partly because they liked to drink whisky between chukkas.[11]

If one regiment exchanged stations with another far away, the two might find it easier to take over each other's horses rather than transport them thousands of miles, though the deal could require some retraining of the equines: when in the 1930s the 8th Cavalry (who were lancers) replaced a sabre regiment, the animals, frightened by 'the unaccustomed flurry of lance pennants', simply bolted.[12] Probyn's Horse was, however, determined to retain its own animals. Investing the 'batta' it received from the China War in a stud farm at Probynabad, it soon ensured that it was the best-mounted regiment in India. Probyn himself retired early to spend nearly forty years as a senior courtier to both Queen Victoria and King Edward VII, and his regiment, which in consequence was renamed the 11th King Edward's Own Lancers (Probyn being its honorary colonel and the king its colonel-in-chief), came to be regarded as the most fashionable in the Indian Army. It was certainly nattily clad, with blue turban and scarlet cummerbund. Yet such regiments became glamorous – as well as more numerous – only shortly before they became redundant on the battlefield. First their uniforms were turned into khaki, which officers at the time called 'snuff-coloured', though the word in Hindi means 'dust-coloured'; then the cavalrymen were told they could only use their lances for ceremonies; and finally, as their regiments became mechanized, their horses were taken away to be replaced by light tanks and armoured cars. One or two units managed to keep going in their traditional style until the Second World War: the Grand Trunk Road heard the hooves of Gardner's Horse for the last time in November 1939, as it marched from Jullundur to Sialkot; a year later, the 19th Hussars held the last cavalry parade on horseback. After that, as one officer lamented, one could hear 'no more that most familiar and beautiful of trumpet-calls – "Stables" '.[13]

The horse artillery, originally known as 'the galloper guns', saw the end of their horses at the same time. After the scare of the Rebellion, it had been decided that the gunners of the Royal Artillery should be British rather than Indian, though this precaution was made pointless by the retention of Indian drivers who in another rebellion could take the horses with them and thus immobilize the guns. The great division among the 'Gunners' was between the Royal Horse (RH) and Royal Field Artillery (RFA) and the less prestigious Royal Garrison Artillery (RGA), which, as its name suggests, was usually stuck in one place, on a hill top, in a fort or defending a coastal town. The RH and RFA were wont to disdain the garrison gunners for being dismounted 'robots within a concrete fort', but the RGA men, whose mountain batteries *did* contain Indian gunners, hit back at their snooty colleagues. There *they* were, defending the frontier, doing something useful, working in khaki shorts and short-sleeved shirts and engaged in sporadic warfare, while those fellows in the horse and field branches were doing nothing but spear pigs and play polo in the Sloth Belt, 'popinjays' careering about on horses, 'trailing toy guns' and strutting 'about in tight over-alls and jingling spurs'. A real man's work was on the frontier, where it also had pecuniary advantages, allowing RGA subalterns (almost uniquely) to live on their pay. Not only were their living expenses lower than in the Sloth Belt – there was not much to spend one's money on in a fort near the Khyber – but they also received an extra two shillings a day known as 'armament pay'.[14]

TOMMY ATKINS

Kipling regarded 'Tommy Atkins'* as a most maligned man. Tommy could of course be rather rowdy, he often drank too much, and he should have been 'supplied with a new adjective to help him express his opinions'. Yet as the writer explained in his poem 'Tommy', 'single men in barracks don't grow into plaster saints'. Kipling accepted that every regiment would have a few 'blackguards', yet most of the soldiers he knew in India were decent fellows, bewildered to hear themselves described by the public as 'brutal and licentious soldiery' except in times of national danger – 'when the drums begin to roll' – when they were quickly transformed into a 'thin red line of 'eroes'. For the poet they were certainly better men than the aesthetes and 'long-haired literati' whom he had come to know in London after his return from India and whom he despised for 'makin' mock o' uniforms that guard you while you sleep'.[15]

We last saw Tommy Atkins – in the guise of Private Clemens of the East Yorkshire Regiment – while disembarking at Bombay (although most earlier incarnations would have arrived at Calcutta or Madras) in 1929. After warding off the flies and beggars in the port, he (Clemens) is now experiencing his first Indian parade, a ceremony at which (to his surprise) he is handed two packets of cigarettes. Later, after 'a real good smoke', he is put on a train – 'very uncomfortable as the seats were wooden' – that eventually arrives at Lucknow Station. There he and his mates are greeted by the Band and Drums of the 1st Battalion which 'play' them to the Barracks Square, where the commanding officer is ready to give them a short speech of welcome. Afterwards they are paraded outside the regimental stores and issued with two sheets, three blankets, two pillow cases (though only one pillow), plus a mosquito net with rods and three coir-filled mattresses known as 'biscuits'.[16]

The next morning they are woken by a bugle sounding reveille. They wash and put on shorts and open-necked shirts – the hot weather is

---

* 'Tommy Atkins' was a generic name chosen by the War Office in 1815 for sample forms for infantrymen, as in 'I, Private Thomas Atkins, of His Majesty's 33rd Regiment of Foot & etc . . .'

beginning – before enjoying a 'pretty good breakfast' of cornflakes followed by 'sausage, egg and bacon, with bread and butter and marmalade to finish'. They are then issued with rifle, bayonet and web equipment, plus a blue durrie to carry their blankets, ground sheet and mosquito net while marching or going on exercises. In the hot weather they are made to wear spine pads, a sort of waistcoat supposed to protect the spine when on guard duty, but these are soon recognized as useless and are abolished. More beneficial is a light pith helmet as a substitute for their topis, which will now be used only for guard duties and ceremonial purposes when a 'puggaree' or light turban will be wound around them. This particular puggaree carries a XV on its right side and a black band on its top edge to commemorate the death of General Wolfe at Quebec 170 years earlier; the 15th Foot, the regiment that later became the East Yorkshires, had been under Wolfe's command in North America.

Soon after Private Clemens arrives in Lucknow, the drum major visits his company looking for recruits to the Corps of Drums. After the officer has announced that volunteers would need to be 'proficient' in two instruments, Clemens steps forward and chooses the bugle and the flute. Although he finds the flute hard to play, he is soon marching with the 'drum boys' and 'beating the retreat' on ceremonial parades. Boys of fifteen could join the army as drummer boys, as Norman Wisdom did, with the option of going into the ranks at eighteen. A generation before Wisdom and Clemens, Dudley Meneaud-Lissenburg signed on as a boy as a potential bugler and trumpeter in the artillery. Bands used to practise some distance from the barracks: Clemens played in a 'little wood', while Meneaud-Lissenburg trumpeted in a mango tope. Buglers and trumpeters were also required to perform independently, blowing their 'calls' at various hours during the day. After returning from reveille duty at 6.30 a.m., Wisdom was pursued by regular cries of 'Piss orf' from men he had just woken up. Other 'calls' included 'Letters', sounded on Sunday morning after the mail had been sorted out following its arrival the previous evening, 'Cook House' for the three daily meals, 'Parade' and 'Fall-in' for mustering troops, 'Guard' when the guard was being changed, 'Action' and 'Cease-fire' (when in a fort during gun practice) and 'Last Post' for Lights Out.[17]

The diet of British soldiers in India revolved around meat, a pound a day (including fat and gristle), which even some of them thought was 'perhaps too heavy a ration in such a climate'. In the 1760s soldiers of the Madras garrison ate beef, pork or mutton six days a week, and in the field their daily ration was increased to a pound and a half. The problem was not the quantity of meat but its quality and the way it was prepared; on the Plains it was bound to be tough because meat could not be 'hung' in that climate without going bad. In 1900 part of the meat ration was small steaks at breakfast known as 'khaki patches' which, according to Private Richards of the Welch Fusiliers, were so tough that 'a man's jaws would ache for hours after he had masticated one of them'. In the nineteenth century soldiers had been given a curry dish for breakfast, but this custom had been dropped in favour of porridge, sausages, eggs and 'khaki patches'. Meat later in the day was almost invariably boiled with vegetables and presented as an 'all-in-stew'.[18]

Poor Meneaud-Lissenburg, who had never been to England, could not cope with it all. He had been born in Ooty in 1894 into a family that had served in the Madras Army for three generations. Educated intermittently at Bangalore, Coimbatore and Coonor, he had spent much of his boyhood roaming the Nilgiri Hills among the Todas and other tribal peoples. After joining the artillery at the age of sixteen, he was sent to the large cantonment of Secunderabad, next to Hyderabad, where he was shocked by the regimental brothel, an 'offensive adjunct', and appalled by the flavourless English-style food. After his morning bugle practice, he had to sit down to a breakfast consisting of bread and butter, 'a hard, dried piece of meat floating in a black gravy', which he 'washed down with a basin of lukewarm tea, coloured by a lot of buffalo milk'. After 'dinner' at one – 'a monotonous diet of khaki steak and boiled potatoes, varied twice a week by stew, plugged a hole for a few hours' – the basin reappeared at tea-time, though at this occasion the tea was black and sweet and accompanied by 'a soup-plate of salted porridge'. That was Meneaud-Lissenburg's last meal of the day unless he was in training for the garrison boxing tournaments, when he was given another plate of porridge at half-past six. No wonder he saved up his pay to reward himself with an occasional meal outside the barracks. When, at the age of eighteen, he was posted to Bombay as his company's trumpeter, he gave himself dinner once a week at Green's Hotel, near the Apollo Bunder, where he ate 'a succulent porterhouse steak', drank a small glass of 'concentrated ginger wine' and smoked a Flor de

Dindigul cigar from Madras. The treat cost him one rupee and four annas, a quarter of his weekly salary.[19]

Other soldiers avoided the monotony of barracks rations by pooling their pay and employing an Indian cook. In the cantonment outside Lahore Private Swindlehurst and five of his mates in the Lancashire Fusiliers each paid a man eight annas a week to go to the vegetable and poultry markets and prepare some decent meals. Around every barracks lurked various 'wallahs' ready to cater for the needs of the troops. Although Private Clemens had enjoyed a 'pretty good' breakfast when he arrived in Lucknow, the quality of that meal evidently soon declined. 'Some mornings', when it 'wasn't very palatable', he would go out on to the verandah of his shared bungalow 'where the egg wallah was cooking large eggs' that were 'tasty and really enjoyable'. He could also get fresh milk and butter from a 'dudh wallah', he could purchase tea and sandwiches from a 'char wallah', who was always nearby and who would be ready with his 'tea-urn' at every halt on a march, and, when he went fishing (as he often did), he could find another wallah to cook his catch for him. At Meerut the 'wallahs' congregated under a tree called 'the Ration Stand' to sell cheap eggs, meat and vegetables to the men of the Royal Welch Fusiliers. Private Richards even found a 'shrivelled old chap' known as the 'bacon wallah', a rare bird in India, who was about ninety years old and might have been British, Indian or Eurasian. In fact, as Richards eventually discovered, he was an Englishman who had joined the army some seventy years earlier, had stayed in India on a pension of a shilling a day and had then married a Eurasian girl half his age.[20]

Like their compatriots in other careers, British soldiers quickly found it normal and natural to have Indian servants, people who shopped for them, cooked for them, and washed their clothes. On his first morning in Lahore, Private Swindlehurst woke up to find a turbanned Indian saying, 'Sahib, you want shave?' Many soldiers gladly accepted the offer of being shaved in bed just before reveille, and some were such heavy sleepers that a good barber, working with a hurricane lamp, could apparently conduct the operation without waking them up. Once they had succumbed to this luxury, soldiers soon became accustomed to other 'natives' working for them, such as bishti wallahs who brought them water in goatskins and punkah wallahs who tried to keep them cool between March and October by flapping the punkah and creating a breeze.

Accommodation for soldiers varied according to time and place. In 1919 troops at Mir Ali in Waziristan were living in tents lit by hurricane lamps, but by 1943 they were housed there in barracks with electric light and electric fans. Soldiers' quarters in the nineteenth century usually consisted of long gloomy dormitories with two rows of beds spaced very closely together. Later they were often housed in large bungalows, which had their own well and latrines, and which were divided in two by a dining room. Each half, Clemens noted appreciatively, had its own char wallah, sitting on the verandah from early morning until late in the evening, always ready with his tea-urn and his box full of sandwiches, cakes and cigarettes. He even gave his customers credit until pay day.[21]

The barracks routine was boring and monotonous for both officers and men. Thomas Dowdall, a subaltern in the Yorkshire Light Infantry, summarized it for his mother in the winter of 1889: '7.30 go up to barracks ... 8–9 parade ... 9–9.30 back here ... 9.30 breakfast ... 10.00 go up to barracks ... 10.30 parade ... 12–1.30 orderly room ... 1.30–2.00 come back here ... 2 lunch ... 3.30 back to barracks ... 4 parade till 5 ... 5.30 down here ... 8 dress for dinner.' This pattern was varied one or two days a week when he was on duty as 'subaltern of the day', which meant that he had to spend his hours checking things, the food and other rations, the cookhouses and the workshops, the NCOs' Mess, the billiard room, the stores and the guard room, as well as all the dormitories, making sure the men's charpoys were 'quite tidy'. After dinner the NCOs paraded to tell him who was ill or absent, and at some stage during the night he had to turn out the guard and check that the sentries were alert.[22]

Fifty years earlier, Albert Hervey, a subaltern in a Madras regiment, had complained that his men were 'worn out and dispirited ... by paltry, nonsensical parades and drill' and endless 'going on guard over places which require no guarding'.[23] Parades took up an enormous amount of time, although in the Punjab they were often cancelled as a result of dust storms. Dowdall's letters from the barracks at Quetta mention CO's parade, Brigade parade, Adjutant's parade and Church parade, when, although the garrison town did not yet have a church, the battalion was marched on Sundays to a patch of ground where a pulpit had been erected. There were many other time-wasting duties, ranging from large full dress parades for a general to less formal early-morning ones: John Morris could parade his Gurkhas in shorts, khaki stockings and an open-necked bush shirt, but he had to be properly attired in service uniform before attending the CO's daily meeting at half-past eleven.[24]

Besides parades, a soldier's life was regularly punctuated by saluting ('smartly' not 'slovenly'), mounting guard and marching at attention. There were also endless inspections to endure: a general's desire to visit a barracks meant a 'spit and polish' day for the men, but at least, observed Private Swindlehurst, it gave bored 'troops something to do'. In the cold weather the men were more usefully employed, going on musketry courses, route marches, 'camps of exercise' and 'winter manoeuvres', which officers in the Indian Army took very seriously. Another diversion was sport, increasingly promoted by the military authorities from around the middle of the nineteenth century. Boxing became of paramount importance – 'Front rank, about turn! Box!' – even for undersized teenagers. To his growing reputation as the 'camp jester' in Lucknow, Norman Wisdom added the accolade of flyweight champion of the British Army in India. Cricket was encouraged, the pitches usually made of matting rather than grass, as were hockey and to a lesser extent basketball.[25]

The most popular sport of the early twentieth century was football, which was played not just between mates in the barracks on their day off but in organized competitions such as the Murree Cup (the championship of the Punjab), the Durand Cup (initiated by Mortimer Durand, the foreign secretary)* and the India Football Association Shield with its final in Calcutta. Private Clemens and his Drums team in the East Yorkshires sometimes played a 'native team', whose players kicked the ball harder with their bare feet than he did with his boots, though they were not so keen on tackling.[26] Britons and Indians were permitted to play sports together, as individuals, in mixed teams or in any combination except one: teams from British Army regiments were not allowed to play in competitions against teams from Indian Army units.[27] No doubt it was feared that such contests would become 'nationalist'.

Some regiments of the British Army had their own special holidays.

---

* He was also responsible for drawing the 'Durand Line', running through the tribal areas of the north-west, which later became the international frontier between Pakistan and Afghanistan.

On 1 August Private Swindlehurst and the rest of the Lancashire Fusiliers had a banquet with a lot of beer to celebrate their regiment's performance at the Battle of Minden in 1759, when it had helped the Duke of Brunswick to defeat a French army in the Seven Years War. All regiments in India had a holiday on Thursday, known as 'All Soldiers Day', when no reveille was blown and men could lie in bed as long as they wished (except the guard and the officer who was 'subaltern of the day'). Although officers encouraged their men to play sport on this day – and many did so – the soldiers were not obliged to stay in barracks. A good many would slope off to a town's bazaar, have a few drinks, buy some cheap cigars, have a look at the local women. His first visit left Private Swindlehurst appalled: it was 'very embarrassing to be mauled by women' who certainly 'wanted some shaking off'. It was also unpleasant to be ordered to picket the brothels in Lahore to deter soldiers from visiting them at a time when the regiment was suffering a very high rate of venereal disease.* Yet Swindlehurst could enjoy more innocent excursions to the Punjabi capital, and his return to barracks at Mian Mir was enlivened by a race in tongas, or small chariots, with his pals – seven miles from the Bank of Bengal to the gate of the cantonment.

Sporting images of the Raj, in pictures or in photographs, usually concentrate on the higher end of the social scale, cavalry officers going pig-sticking (also known as hog-hunting), viceroys aiming at tigers from the backs of elephants, aristocratic guests of the Maharaja of Bikaner (including the future King George V) shooting sandgrouse by the thousand on the Gajner Lake in Rajputana. Yet in India, unlike in Britain, working-class men could also go shooting, private soldiers roaming the countryside with shotguns. From the second half of the nineteenth century, India had shooting seasons and game regulations, but the land was not divided into large estates in which poachers and gamekeepers tried to outwit each other. All the soldiers had to do, recalled Private Fraser of the Northumberland Fusiliers, was to ask their colonel for 'sports leave', which was 'readily granted', to promise not to shoot monkeys and peacocks, 'for they were held sacred by the natives', and to go about in groups of at least three people. If there was no interpreter among them, one of the three had to be able to speak the

* See below, pp. 332–3.

local language, and one had to know how 'to dress any injuries which might be sustained'.[28]

Such precautions were not always taken and were in any case often inadequate. While Curzon was viceroy, four or five Indians were annually killed by soldiers in brawls or shooting incidents, not a high number for so large an area but high enough to infuriate the viceroy, who said that 'such gross outrages' ate into his 'very soul', especially when the perpetrators were not properly punished. In one incident, he reported to the secretary of state, four soldiers had gone out shooting, 'as usual without passes [and] without an interpreter'. They had then 'shot, as usual, a peacock, had the usual row with the villagers, in the course of which their guns went off, as usual by accident, and as usual killed two natives'. At the subsequent trial 'the prisoners were, as usual, acquitted and released' in a conspiracy 'to screen the guilty' that was, for Curzon, 'a black and permanent blot upon the British name'.[29]

In his early career in the 1870s, long before he invented the Boy Scouts and the Girl Guides, Robert Baden-Powell was a subaltern of hussars in India where he 'worked hard, almost desperately, at theatricals and the like' to fight the 'ennui' that he believed to be 'the breeding ground of sickness' for British soldiers.[30] If these were stationed in a large garrison town, they might occasionally be visited by a travelling theatre company, performing light musical comedies in the evenings. In the 1920s films arrived, requiring a room in the barracks to be transformed into a cinema, usually with a rather dodgy projector. Yet a regiment's external diversions were inevitably intermittent, and its entertainment was largely, as it always had been, 'home-made'.

Band concerts continued to be the most popular form of entertainment until the end of the Raj, even if they came to resemble a music-hall or variety show, with jokes and comic sketches as well as traditional songs. Private Richards recalled that the twice-weekly concerts in his regiment on the barracks lawn 'meant a lot to . . . even the most hard-bitten of us' because 'the tunes revived memories of happy days and nights in England'. Concerts also took place on the march, especially on Saturday evenings in camp, around the fire, with officers sitting in deck-chairs and the 'other ranks' squatting on the ground, an arrangement which in late-Victorian years was said to be 'very jolly and convivial' and 'calculated to improve the relations between officers and men'. Bands naturally played all the regimental marches, and did so even on active service, which struck Lieutenant Dowdall as 'extraordinary', but it was done, so he was told, 'to impress the natives'. Yet a band's repertoire was not limited to simple marches and tunes by Gilbert and Sullivan. At a grand military tattoo in Delhi in 1925, massed bands played, apart from some obligatory Elgar, overtures by Tchaikovsky (*1812*) and Wagner (*Tannhäuser*), and *Finlandia* by Sibelius.[31]

The British had well over a hundred cantonments or military stations in India, most of them with similar grid streets, bungalows and barracks, cemeteries and churches and, in the middle, Flagstaff House, the residence of the commanding officer. The complexes were spread out over a large area next to the 'civil lines' and a few miles upwind of the neighbouring Indian town. Some military stations were regarded as decent, others as tolerable, and a few as appalling. In the 1840s Lieutenant Hervey described Arni in the Madras presidency as 'an abominable hot oven', where Europeans regularly died of cholera or fever, but Cuddalore nearby was a 'delightful spot' with 'plenty of fresh air and sea bathing' for the troops, and Bangalore (with 'English fruit and vegetables thriving') was healthy, social and fun, 'one of the best stations in the whole country'.[32] Kipling made his army friends among the Tommy Atkinses of the Northumberland Fusiliers in the barracks of Mian Mir outside Lahore, but this was regarded as an unhealthy cantonment and was sometimes dubbed 'the graveyard of India'. Other places in the Punjab had a better reputation, Ambala partly because it was good for sport (its maidan could accommodate a dozen polo matches), and Rawalpindi, which was regarded as the Indian equivalent of Aldershot and was close to plains suitable for winter manoeuvres. Another popular station for private soldiers was Rangoon, not because they liked the climate but because at the time of the First World War it provided cheap and tasty food, boating on the royal lakes, plus four cinemas and a playhouse where 'Burmese girls would come and dance, stark naked'. British soldiers usually liked the Burmese people, and not just the girls in the bazaars who tried to entice them to their beds with Kipling's line, 'Come you back, you British soldier; come you back to Mandalay!'[33]

Units of the British and Indian armies were regularly moved, on purpose, in an effort to combat boredom and feelings of stagnation. They had to take their turn in healthy and unhealthy stations, and would regret a transfer from the north-west frontier, where the work and climate were invigorating, to some enervating spot in the Central Provinces in the Sloth Belt, where it was difficult to keep men fit, healthy and alert.[34] The one insoluble problem was the hot weather, because the entire army in India could not be sent up to the Hills for six months to cool off. By early March the thermometer on the northern plains would be in the nineties – with higher to go in the coming months – and summer regulations came into force on the 15th: rations were issued at seven in the morning instead of the evening before, in case they went bad overnight. 'Roll on the day when we go to the hills' was a common sentiment.

Companies rotated in the Hills, half the battalion moving up in April and returning to the furnace of June, when the other half replaced it. They rarely went to the smart hill stations, such as Simla or Ooty, that would be full of officials and generals and 'grass widows', the wives of senior Civilians still at work in the Plains. If stationed at Lucknow, in the United Provinces, they did not stay at Naini Tal, the summer capital of the province, but at obscure villages such as Kailana, which was as difficult to reach as the fashionable resorts, requiring a train journey to Dehra Dun followed by three or four days' marching uphill to the station. If troops were garrisoned at Peshawar, they might have to march to Upper Tota, but they found consolation on the way, after two days on the road, when they reached Trett, where the Murree Brewery sent complementary barrels of beer down the mountainside to soldiers passing by. Once they had arrived at their destination, the only real changes in their lives were the scenery and the climate. The hill station would still have a canteen, a bazaar, a football field and a tattoo shop, a 'popular haunt' for Private Clemens where he 'used to have drawings done regularly with the needle'.[35] There were still drills and parades and training exercises. The troops were not meant to be on holiday.

A soldier's life in a barracks in the hot weather was boring and demoralizing. As the early morning was the only part of the day when anything worthwhile could be accomplished, as much as possible was crammed into that period. At Shwebo, a rice-growing station north of Mandalay, troops got out of bed at five and paraded: over the next three hours they did PT, rifle drill, some marching and 'a bit of musketry drill' before the heat became so 'hellish' that they were 'dismissed for the day at 8 or 9'. At Multan in the Punjab, Lieutenant Ian

Hamilton of the Gordons got up at 4.40, 'chucked' on some clothes and rode to the barracks, taking care to keep his arms away from his body 'or else the perspiration spoils your white jacket'. After parade he returned at 6.30 to his bungalow, where, following a sleepless and sweltering night, he now felt so exhausted that he had to have either a brandy and soda or (less often, one suspects) a cup of tea.[36]

The problem, both for officers and men, was what to do for the next dozen hours or so until the evening when, as Hamilton put it, 'one begins to brighten up and feel fit again'. In the twentieth century regiments had their own swimming baths, but these were seldom large, and they were always over-crowded; they also had washrooms with cold showers. The men spent most of their time sitting on their charpoys, reading, eating, playing cards and trying to sleep, and the officers whiled away the hours in the Mess, also reading, eating, playing cards and trying to sleep. Yet at least the latter had the freedom to move about (if they wished) and have a drink, whereas private soldiers were often confined to barracks in case they were 'smitten by heatstroke', and their canteen was frequently closed until the evening in case they were tempted to counter the heat with a gallon of beer. No soldiers felt well in the hot weather. Officers invariably complained of feeling 'seedy' or at least 'languid and peevish'. The 'other ranks' usually suffered more extensively. Those on guard duty might 'dress down' in the hot weather, wearing only shirts and shorts, but the garb, however cooling, made them still more attractive to mosquitoes. Most soldiers had to endure prickly heat, which 'tortured' or 'itched intolerably', and a good many also had to put up with boils and water blisters. Private Richards recalled that thirty men in his battalion were 'in hospital at the same time with water-blisters on their privates'.[37]

The British soldier in India was not poor in comparison with working men in Britain or with British soldiers in other parts of the empire. With the cost of living in India so cheap, even a short-service man could afford reasonable amounts of beer, food and tobacco – as well as occasional visits to a brothel; and if he passed various 'proficiency' tests – in drumming, say, or marksmanship – he would add to his pay. After six years he would become a 'time-expired man', congregating with his fellows at Deolali transit camp ('Doolaly'), or later at an embarkation port, to wait for his troopship home. But if he decided to stay in India and sign on for another twelve years, he would probably become a staff-sergeant or sergeant-major and get an increase in salary that would allow him to keep a horse and two servants. A further stint would give him another rise plus a pension and lengthy holidays on full pay.[38]

Yet reasonable pay could not make Tommy Atkins feel comfortable and contented in the hot weather. Indeed in 1830 Fanny Parkes had wondered whether any existence could be 'more wretched than the life of a private soldier in the East?' With his profession occupying so 'little of his time', he was forced to spend the 'heat of the day' within 'intensely hot barrack-rooms', where he became thirsty and idle, the first condition encouraging him to drink arrack 'like a fish', the second making him so bored and discontented that he soon found 'life a burden, almost insupportable'.[39] Conditions fifty or a hundred years later were certainly better. Soldiers did not now have to spend the whole of the hot weather in the Plains. Nor did they have to go to war in an Indian summer, unlike their predecessors who had fought the battles of Plassey in June, Assaye in September, Seringapatam in May, and the most vicious conflicts of the Rebellion between June and September 1857. Yet a soldier's life in the last ninety years of the Raj was usually dull and often desperate. The sepoys of the Indian Army were living in their own country, in familiar surroundings, often with relatives close by. British officers of both armies had the support and camaraderie of the station's club and their regimental Mess; many had family traditions in India, some of them had wives, and even the younger, unmarried ones could take part in the station's social life and flirt with the daughters of the colonel and the district officer. Yet young Tommies, without wives, without traditions and often without family connections, boys who hardly ever spoke to a woman except the sergeant's wife or occasionally a woman from the bazaar (whom they were sometimes too scared to touch in case they got VD), youths who were too shy or innocent to be comfortable with the fellowship of the dormitory and the canteen, and who might there be the victims of a bullying NCO or a loud-mouthed veteran – for them life could be, as Fanny Parkes knew, 'insupportable'. Some of them felt that they had to leave the army as soon as possible, that they could not bear to wait until their time was up. The licit means of achieving this was to buy one's way out, but few men could afford to do so: it cost about half a year's salary. Other methods included desertion, which was of course risky, and shamming sickness, which was difficult to do successfully in front of the regimental surgeon. Some men went to great lengths to pretend that they had become deaf – dropping a rupee behind them was one way of sorting out that deception – or had suddenly gone mad, acting out the state by grinning inanely and sticking straws in their hair. Yet some alas went even further, as so many graveyard inscriptions do *not* say. 'When an officer committed suicide,' John Masters observed, 'some reason was usually found, but scores of British soldiers killed themselves without any cause ever becoming apparent.'[40]

Most British soldiers combatted boredom with alcohol. They had enough money and enough opportunity to get very drunk quite often, especially after a short campaign during which the troops had had no occasion to spend their wages. 'It is needless to say,' a lieutenant reported after a frontier expedition in 1890, 'that being greatly in credit the whole regiment has been drunk' for four days.[41] More regular opportunities were provided by 'pay day and the few following days', when, recalled Private Fraser of the Northumberland Fusiliers, 'the canteen would be crowded, and a good many men would be completely drunk'. The next day the guardroom would be 'full of drunks for the CO to dispose of', 'though a man put under arrest for being drunk had to "cool his coppers" for at least twenty-four hours before being brought up on the charge'. Writing of the 1880s, Fraser did not blame them, for 'what was there else for the soldier to do but drink? He had no sorrows to drown, but he had a great deal of spare time and practically nothing to do with it.' The fault lay with 'the authorities who provided no alternative recreation for the Tommy in those days'.[42] A generation later, stationed at Jubbulpore in the Central Provinces, Sergeant Menaud-Lissenburg observed similar scenes and came to a similar conclusion. 'Despite the unceasing efforts of the Army Temperance Association . . . a majority of the troops sought solace, and often oblivion, in the wet-canteen where beer was consumed in great quantities. There was not much else for them to do in their leisure hours.'[43]

In the eighteenth century the soldiers' drink was arrack, a spirit usually made from 'toddy', the fermented sap of palm trees, though rice and dates could also provide the essential ingredient for distilling. Rum appeared at the beginning of the next century, produced from the distillery at Kanpur, and this or arrack was given to the troops, one dram daily in barracks and two on the march or in the rainy season. Further drams could be purchased in the canteen or the bazaar, and the quantity bought, combined with the poor quality of some of the 'native fire-water', resulted in so much liver disease and so many deaths that in the 1850s the governor-general, Lord Dalhousie, ordered the rum ration to be diluted by water; he also encouraged the introduction of porter and beer. A later governor-general, Lord Northbrook, put his faith in the temperance movement, optimistically assuring Queen Victoria in 1875 that it was making great strides in India, where 'bad native spirits' were 'one of the worst temptations to which the British soldier was exposed'.[44]

The temperance movement burgeoned with the support of General Roberts, the commander-in-chief from 1885 to 1893, and a large military station might have competing societies: Bangalore in the 1920s had the Royal Temperance Association, the Gospel Temperance Association, the Church of England Temperance Society and the Soldiers' Gospel Temperance League.[45] But theirs was always going to be a losing battle. The best answer was Dalhousie's, the substitution of beer for spirits, because even though it did not do much to reduce drunkenness, it greatly lowered the casualty figures. The East India Company had also favoured ale, once sending some bags of hops to Bombay in a half-hearted attempt to encourage brewing, but imported beer from Britain, such as Hodgson's or the Burton ales, was naturally much more expensive than the often lethal spirits distilled in the bazaars. Imported beer became cheaper, however, after the opening of the Suez Canal, and the building of British breweries in India soon made ale the preferred beverage of the troops. Among its nicknames were 'purge' and 'neck-oil', and its consumers were known, among other things, as 'beer wallahs' and 'purge-shifters'. To have 'a damned good wet together' was one of the few pleasures of military life. According to Private Richards, soldiers formed 'boozing schools', three or four men pooling their resources to ensure a regular supply of beer, tobacco and a monthly visit to a brothel; but beer was the chief item of expenditure.[46]

Army officers drank a good deal in the Mess, where it was permitted and expected, but it was considered bad form for them to be drunk on duty or in public, because their behaviour might embarrass the reputations of the regiment and the ruling race. The worst and most persistent offenders would be discharged. But greater leniency was usually shown, in this respect at least, to private soldiers who were roaring drunk and singing bawdy songs in the street. It was as if Tommy Atkins was expected to be like this, to be 'goin' large a bit' (in Kipling's phrase) as compensation for his exceedingly boring routine. Gunner William Carter arrived in India in March 1842 and in that same month got into trouble for going absent without leave. Over the following two years he went AWOL on other occasions, sometimes for several nights at a time; he was also found guilty of fighting in the Agra barracks and for being drunk both on guard duty and when he was meant to be at instruction drill. Yet the punishments for his misdemeanours were consistently light. For being drunk when on guard – and this was not a first offence – Gunner Carter merely suffered a week's privation with no liquor and with food limited to 'congee', a sort of rice porridge which he had to consume in solitary confinement in a cell known as 'Congee House'.[47]

ON THE MARCH AND ALONG
THE FRONTIER

'Capital preparations' for an early-morning march, recalled Captain Hervey of the Madras Native Infantry, consisted of a hot cup of tea or coffee 'with a spoonful of good brandy in it', plus 'a bit of dry toast . . . after which the warmth of a good Manilla cigar [was] really very comforting to the inner man'. These preparations took place in the middle of the night. As the winters in the south were much warmer than in the north, marching began in the dark, long before dawn, the tents being dismantled at about three in the morning, and Hervey, suitably comforted, setting off with the column soon afterwards. Marching by torchlight was inevitably rather slow, especially as the roads were already crowded with people, carts and bullocks, but with daylight the 'men jerked up their packs' and increased their pace. The aim was to reach the next camp 'as soon as possible after sunrise'; 11 a.m. was far too late, because by then the sun was *'precious* hot'.[48]

Hervey was marching in the 1830s with a regiment of a thousand men. At the head of the column was the band, the drums and fifes, followed by the colonel, riding 'in stately grandeur' in front of his retinue of orderlies and his 'horsekeeper'. Then came the troops, succeeded by the adjutant and the 'medico', and behind them were the 'sick doolies', litters carrying sick or wounded men. On the flanks and at the back about 5,000 camp-followers shuffled along – soldiers' wives, grooms, grass-cutters, bullock-drivers and a large number of officers' servants. As they neared their camp, the band struck up 'a merry tune' and the troops did a quick march, though if they were arriving at a new station, they would pause a mile or so outside and 'brush up a bit' before marching into the cantonment to the music of 'Rule Britannia'. On reaching their destination, the British officers would 'run off to the mess-tent' and shout for 'the eatables and drinkables'. Meanwhile the latrines were dug and the camp was laid out according to a pattern, the CO's pavilion flanked by the tents of the adjutant and the quartermaster, the key figures in the peacetime functioning of a regiment, with the Mess tent and the hospital and the Union Jack (on a pole) close by; beyond them were the tents of the captains, subalterns and men, all in lines. Farther out, the 'poor tents' of the camp-followers were pitched 'more haphazardly'. In that period and that climate, dinner would take place in the afternoon, when the band would be drawn up outside the Mess, 'enlivening' Hervey and his colleagues with music. In the evening, if the ground was 'even and grassy', they had a dance although, given the ratio of men to women, this cannot have been very satisfactory.[49]

Marching essentials did not change very much over the following hundred years. Railways could transport troops great distances on the Plains, but there were not many of them on the northern frontiers or in the hills, and after it had reached the railhead, a battalion might have to march for three or four days to its destination. Besides, marching was not simply a means of travel: it was important for fitness, discipline and team spirit. John Masters and his Gurkhas annually marched about 1,500 miles 'under load', taking in some 80,000 feet in altitude. In the 1930s, as in the 1830s, troops kept up their spiritis by singing as they marched, songs that were often bawdy and usually repetitive. Men of the Lancashire Fusiliers set to music Kipling's poem 'Route Marchin' – '. . . you've 'eard the bugle blowed,/ There's a regiment a comin' down the Grand Trunk Road' – each company singing a verse in turn and all joining in with the chorus.[50] It can't have taken their minds off the daily slog much better than the same poet's 'Boots – boots – boots – boots – movin' up an' down again!' The Royal Welch Fusiliers had a more homely and comforting lyric: as soon as they were near a halt for coffee and a short rest, the band struck up with 'Polly put the kettle on'.[51]

In the north during winter the day's march did not need to start at three in the morning. Reveille would sound at five-thirty or six, the column would move off at seven, and between one and two in the afternoon it would reach its destination and find – as the Lancashire Fusiliers liked to sing – 'An' every bloomin' campin'-ground exactly like the last'. The north may have been cooler than the south, but it was also dustier. In the Punjab thick clouds of dust would hang over a column, and the men would march with handkerchiefs tied across their mouths and noses. The army's systems of marching aggravated the problems caused by dust. Infantrymen were supposed to march ahead of the long train of baggage camels, which went at two and a half miles an hour, slightly slower than the regiments. After every fifty minutes, however, the men would halt for a ten-minute rest, and the camels, which did not halt, lurched past them, forcing the soldiers to struggle through fresh clouds of dust to overtake the 'swaying, padding monsters' after their stop.[52] The Royal Corps of Signals had a similar problem on the northwest frontier in the 1920s. Its men were supposed to lead the column but at every rest halt they had to communicate with Base HQ. This meant that they needed to unload their equipment from the backs of mules, erect a wireless station and aerial, establish contact with 'Base' and clear any messages to and from the column. By the time they had done this and packed up again, their comrades had already left, and they had to push their way through them and the dust to get back in front.[53]

Movements such as these, by single battalions or cavalry regiments, were the usual type of marches undertaken in India. Of course there were some tremendous processions, with elephants and artillery trains and tens of thousands of bullocks, huge advances against such enemies as the sultans of Mysore, the chiefs of the Marathas and, fatally, the Afghans. Yet there were not very many of them. A glance at the military history of the East India Company might suggest that its forces were constantly fighting, not only in the cases just mentioned but in the eighteenth century against the French and the Bengalis, and later in Sind, the Punjab and of course the Rebellion. All these campaigns naturally contained battles – though again not many – including those which British schoolchildren used to learn about, such as Clive's victory at Plassey and Arthur Wellesley's at Assaye. At these and other actions British soldiers fought bravely and well, overcoming the heat and alien conditions to defeat much larger enemy armies; the victories were said to show 'the spirit of Agincourt', and no doubt they did. But the soldiers took part in other fighting in India which the children did not read about, combat which displayed the spirit not of Agincourt but of the sack in 1812 of the Spanish city of Badajoz, an atrocity which its inhabitants have apparently not forgotten.[54] During the Rebellion of 1857 British troops (and their officers) displayed a sickening bloodlust and brutality, often against unarmed Indians. The columns marching to relieve Lucknow executed Indians in their hundreds on the way, while the army that captured Delhi sacked the city and massacred large numbers of civilians as well as rebels. Afterwards excuses were made for the avenging forces: that they knew about the massacre of British women and children at Kanpur, that some of them had lost relations murdered at the outbreak of the Rebellion, that the troops at Delhi had spent all summer and the monsoon on the Ridge outside the city, where they had been subjected to almost daily attacks and where many of their comrades had died of wounds or disease. These may have been reasons but they were not excuses for revenge on such a scale. The retribution was a terrible crime, the worst thing the British did in India.

The Company's wars in India were in fact sporadic and never required the whole of its forces on the Subcontinent. In the 1780s and 1790s a cadet joining the army in Madras could look forward to military action and consequently medals, enrichment and promotion. But after the defeat of Tipu Sultan at Seringapatam in 1799 the prospects for these became small and extremely slow. Young officers in Madras soon realized that their military lives would consist of little more than attending parades, mounting guard and practising with guns they were unlikely ever to use on campaign. Some quit, but most stayed on, resigned to a life without active service unless they were selected for an expedition overseas. 'Alas,' wrote Hervey on leaving India in 1843 after ten years in the Madras army, 'mine has not been a service of hard-fought battles; of lengthened sieges; or of dangers dire by flood and field.'[55] Both Alexander Cannan and Jack Shaw Stewart retired from the Madras Army with the rank of major-general, although neither of them had seen active service more than once – in campaigns far from Madras, Shaw Stewart in China, Cannan in an expedition against a petty raja in Orissa which involved virtually no fighting.

After 1858 this frustration extended to northern India. Between the Rebellion and the First World War, there were plenty of military expeditions, among others to Abyssinia, to China, to Cyprus and to Tibet; there was the Second Afghan War and the Third Burmese War, and also the South African War, although from India only British regiments took part in this conflict. Yet none of these campaigns involved a tenth (and usually far less) of the fighting forces of the Raj. The service records of senior officers, men who had spent some thirty years in India, reveal that they seldom participated in more than two campaigns during their entire careers. Some fought even less often. Major-General Edward Beale fought only in the Persian Expedition of 1856, while Lieutenant-Colonel Henry Beale seems to have done no fighting at all.

Even when an officer went on campaign, there was a good chance that he would see no combat. In 1885, while he was still in a British regiment, Lieutenant 'Stalky' Dunsterville joined the Nile Expedition to rescue General Gordon at Khartoum, but he and his battalion were ordered to remain at Cairo, where they did 'all the dull work of duty at the Base and never heard a shot fired'. In India two years later he was thrilled to be sent on an expedition against the Hazaras in the Black Mountain country until, to his 'horror', the CO sent for him and gave him 'the command of the depot'. In 1893, after nine years of expensive Indian living without experiencing any active service, he decided to quit the army and start a new life in South America. Only a chat with a friendly bank manager, who offered to square his debts and arrange very gradual repayment, persuaded him to stay in India.[56]

Later in his career Dunsterville did see a fair amount of action, and he ended the First World War as a major-general in charge of an Allied unit known as 'Dunsterforce' fighting a Turkish army at Baku in the Caucasus. Yet there were no further campaigns for him (he retired in 1920) – or indeed for much of the Indian Army for another twenty years. In the interwar decades the chief role for the army – and for the British regiments in India – was participation in what was known as Internal Security. In the past troops had been called out to deal with internal disorder, but not very often, perhaps two or three times a year in the 1860s and 1870s. Such call-outs increased during the next half-century, and between February and May 1922 soldiers were summoned on sixty-two occasions to help the civil administration and the police deal with such problems as nationalist agitation, communal violence and trade-union protests. Their intervention was called 'Aid to the Civil Power'.[57]

In his memoirs General Slim described how as a junior officer he would be called upon by a district officer to support the police in a situation they were unable to control. It was 'the usual hot weather communal trouble', he recalled of one occasion when a town's Hindus had congregated in the main square to confront local Muslims over the building of a meat market too close to their quarter. Rushing to the place with his troops, who were 'cheered up at the prospect of action . . . as is the way of British soldiers', Slim took up position on the top of a bus with a view of the antagonistic crowds yelling and throwing stones at each other, separated by a thin line of policemen. Only when the crowds surged forward, and the police seemed about to be overwhelmed, did he station some soldiers on the bus beside him and warn the crowd that they would open fire. When this had no effect (most people could not have heard him in the uproar), and three of the policemen had been knocked to the ground, he ordered two of his men each to fire a single bullet at the Muslim crowd and two others each to fire one round at the Hindu crowd – 'and for God's sake don't hit the police'. The order had to be repeated and obeyed before 'the mob broke' and ran for it. Slim then marched his men across the square, where they did what they could for the wounded policemen and the injured rioters. For the next four days they patrolled the town and made house-to-house searches for the ringleaders.[58] The crucial thing to remember in such situations was the doctrine of 'minimum necessary force', a doctrine usually followed by British officers except at Amritsar in 1919, when it was notoriously ignored by Brigadier Dyer.*

Before the First World War adventurous officers hoping for action used to volunteer for wars outside India. Europe itself was no good because British troops did no fighting there between 1815 and 1914, except in the Crimea, but Africa offered opportunities for those prepared to be persistent. Captain Ian Hamilton of the 92nd (the Gordons)

---

* 'Aid to the Civil Power' acquired new dimensions in the violence of Partition in 1947, but that is a subject beyond the scope of this book. The Eastern Command of the army managed to limit the violence in Calcutta in March 1947, but later in the Punjab, with the police and the administration collapsing, there was little that Northern Command could do to prevent the massacres.

managed to 'wangle' himself on to the Gordon Relief Expedition by pretending to go on leave to Britain, getting off the ship at Suez and dashing to Cairo, where he implored senior officers to take him with them. 'Bursting with joy', he eventually succeeded, but 'shortlived was [his] joy', because, like Dunsterville, he was ordered to 'do garrison duty in a dull frontier station'. Joy returned when the order was rescinded, allowing him and his company to tackle five cataracts of the Nile before finding and defeating 'the Dervish host' at the Battle of Kirbekan.[59]

Another officer refusing to accept refusals was William Birdwood of the 11th Bengal Lancers (a future commander-in-chief in India), who was allowed to serve in the South African War only because the British Army had suffered so many casualties in Natal. Yet the prize for successful importunity must go to Lieutenant Winston Spencer-Churchill, who had the advantage of an almost equally importunate mother campaigning on his behalf in London. At Sandhurst in 1893 he had been intending to join a rifle unit, but he then decided that he would prefer to be in a cavalry regiment, the 4th Hussars, which was scheduled to go to India in 1896. Yet soon after he had achieved the transfer he regretted it and wished he was going to Africa with the 9th Lancers instead. An Indian adventure suddenly seemed to be 'utterly unattractive', a 'useless and unprofitable exile' in a 'tedious land' where he would 'be equally out of the pleasures of peace and the chances of war'. He did, however, sail with the regiment and – despite frequent absences – remained with it until 1899, when he sent in his papers and resigned his commission.[60]

Churchill's commanding officer in the Hussars was a colonel who in nearly thirty years in the army had never seen a day of active service. His new subaltern was determined not to emulate him. Although he loved playing polo at Bangalore, Churchill realized that the 'chances of war' were very slim down there, and within a few months he was plotting to go as a special correspondent to a conflict that had suddenly broken out between Greece and Turkey. This project did not materialize because, as he was sailing across the Indian Ocean, the Greeks sued for peace, and the war came to a rapid end. Returning to England, he went to Goodwood Races and there learned that General Sir Bindon Blood was forming a field force to lead against Pathan tribesmen on the north-west frontier. Pausing only to telegraph Blood and request inclusion in the expedition, Churchill dashed back to Bangalore, sending more 'wires' on the way, which the general did not answer. Finally Blood, who had other matters to worry about, did reply, suggesting that the young subaltern (whom he had met socially in England the year before) should accompany his troops as a 'press correspondent' and be 'put on the strength' (i.e. in a military capacity) when a vacancy occurred. Obtaining leave from his regiment in Bangalore (which for him was seldom difficult), Churchill rushed up to the frontier to join what became known as the Malakand Field Force. As its casualty rate was quite high, he soon became a temporary officer of the 31st Punjab Infantry and did enough fighting to win a medal and gather enough information to write a short book about the expedition.

On his return to the Hussars in Bangalore, Churchill renewed his passion for polo, participating in the Inter-regimental Polo Tournament in Meerut, but once again the sport had to give way to his desire for military action. His new aim was to join the Tirah Expedition, also on the north-west frontier, and as his son later wrote, he was 'constantly . . . devising means of joining it', principally by visiting or telegraphing the senior officers connected with the project. Although his subsequent experience in Tirah was less active and fulfilling than his time with the Malakand Field Force, he was afterwards, as he wrote ironically, 'entitled to a medal and two clasps' for his 'gallantry' amid the 'hardships & dangers' he had encountered. Yet all the time he had been scheming to get himself sent to the frontier, he had also been plotting, with the help of his mother, to get himself attached to another expedition up the Nile, this one General Kitchener's extremely slow reconquest of the Sudan. As usual he was successful: he reached Kitchener before Omdurman, he took part in a cavalry charge during the battle, and he experienced enough of the campaign to write another book. Soon afterwards he went home to England, returned to India to play again in the Inter-regimental Polo Tournament in Meerut (this time with a dislocated shoulder), and left the Subcontinent for good in March 1899, intending to begin a parliamentary career, though he did not become an MP until after he had participated in yet another conflict, the South African War. He had been stationed in India for two and a half years, during which time he had taken part in three campaigns (none of them with his regiment), had spent several weeks in

England on leave and, when he was with the Hussars in Bangalore, had devoted most of his time to playing polo and writing his books.[61]*

Sergeants, corporals and private soldiers might be as keen to fight as their officers, but they did not have the option to abandon their regiments and volunteer overseas. The best they could hope for – unless the whole battalion was sent abroad – was an expedition to the frontier, usually against the tribes of Waziristan. When the Yorkshire Light Infantry was chosen for the Tirah Force, 'every single man', Lieutenant Dowdall told his mother, was 'as keen as blazes, and we are all in tearing spirits'. The only worry was that they might not see any fighting.

That was often the worry. Seven years earlier, in 1890, Dowdall and his battalion had been 'all in the wildest state of excitement' because they were under orders to form part of an expedition against the Shirani Pashtun tribe in the Zhob Valley in Baluchistan. Although the men 'simply loathed marching', everyone was 'keen as ginger' to go and so 'bucked up' that two colour-sergeants, whose time was up and who were about to go home, had 're-engaged simply on the chance of fighting', although for them this meant five more years of privations in a country that they both disliked. Again the fear was that the tribal enemy might 'give in without fighting, in which case of course we shall be terribly disappointed'. As he marched slowly up the valley, Dowdall reflected that the drudgery would be worthwhile if they could have 'a whack at the Shiranis', but if not it would be just a tedious waste of effort. Things began to go wrong for the expedition when the tribesmen 'bolted' as soon as they saw it coming, and they got worse for Dowdall when he was ordered to take a baggage train to Apozai; he felt 'utterly sick' at being detached from the expedition and having to spend his time 'loading and unloading camels and marching at two miles an hour' with these 'terribly obstinate brutes'.[62]

Morale improved when he was allowed to return to the main force, although he remained anxious that the Shiranis might avoid a proper fight and thus deprive him of a medal; they might prefer just to hide behind rocks on the hillsides and take potshots at the column below.

---

* He never returned to India, but in the 1930s he became the most prominent Tory opponent of the British government's efforts to pass legislation granting Indians a substantial measure of internal self-government. Stanley Baldwin, whose administration passed the Government of India Act (1935), believed that Churchill had returned to the feelings of his youth to become once again 'the subaltern of Hussars of '96'.

His battalion's 'excitement was intense' when the force was split into two columns and sent to surprise the Shiranis, but, after a night's march intended to achieve this objective, the columns bumped into each other at daybreak without having seen any sign of the enemy. A couple of days later, the force did manage to encircle the Shiranis, who, seeing that they were surrounded, 'all came out and gave themselves up', an 'admirable' outcome for the generals but 'a knock out blow for us'. The men had gone out that morning 'in the highest spirits' and returned 'silent and depressed' and 'terribly disappointed'; it was 'too annoying' that it had turned out to be 'such a hollow affair'. On their return to their barracks at Quetta on a Thursday, the regiment immediately got drunk and was still drinking on Monday.[63]

'Punitive expeditions' also took place on the greener north-east frontier, usually against tribes which had raided a tea plantation or attacked a neighbouring tribe living under the protection of the Indian government. In Burma in November 1905 a small column of Sikhs and Gurkhas was sent to 'exact satisfaction' from the people of Wellaung for 'a wanton outrage' (which included murder and theft) on the people of Lungno. The Wellaungs had intimated that they would fight, but in the end they opted to pay a fine and return the stolen property, perhaps because their crops were then just ready to harvest.[64]

Such expeditions might take place without pitched battles, but they rarely ended without violence. Even a surveying expedition risked stirring things up among aboriginal tribes which had no experience of such missions and were naturally wary of intruders. When a survey team with an escort of riflemen camped with a 'friendly' tribe in the Aka Hills of Assam, it would provoke hostility and perhaps an attack from a less friendly one in the next valley; men armed with bows and arrows and wearing 'arrow-proof leather or wickerwork jackets' would suddenly approach the camp, a scuffle would break out, and casualties would result. Even if there were few deaths among the soldiers, there was invariably a high mortality rate among the baggage carriers and the pack animals. In 1871 Fred Roberts was the assistant quartermaster-general on an expedition against the Lushais (well-known raiders of tea plantations) in which 251 of the Nepalese coolies died of cholera, an equivalent number deserted or became incapacitated, and 124 of the column's 157 elephants turned out to be useless.[65] Whatever purposes they might serve, punitive expeditions were extremely expensive.

In any case, as British soldiers acknowledged, real men's fighting was to be found on the north-west frontier, not the north-east. One found proper fighters there, not 'puny savages' with bows and arrows but tough Pathan warriors with long-barrelled jezails (Afghan muskets) and a lengthy tradition of merciless warfare. They might be 'a truculent set of turbulent scoundrels', but they knew how to fight among the jagged rocks of their terrain: as one British officer put it, the tribesmen 'on their own wicket' were 'hard to dislodge'.[66] An expeditionary force could not just march up a valley because it would be an easy target for a hidden enemy firing down at it. Therefore an advance guard had to be sent scrambling up the slopes on either side to clear and 'picket' the hilltops as the column and the baggage train moved slowly down below. These manoeuvres had to be repeated over every stretch of hilly country, and even when a suitable camping ground was reached, its surroundings too had to be picketed before a 'colour party' with marking flags laid out the ground for the various units, and the troops arrived to build a perimeter. Men who might have eaten nothing all day except unleavened bread and a raw onion then had their dinner, told jokes and afterwards slept in hollowed-out holes in the ground, their rifles at their side. It was not difficult to remain alert on the frontier. All through the day troops had been expecting and trying to anticipate an ambush. Their scout patrols had a signaller with two carrier pigeons in a wicker basket for when they came under attack and needed to send for reinforcements. They always took two birds to hilly country in case a falcon swooped down and got the messenger, a sensible precaution, although it carried the danger that the pigeons would become friends and, instead of delivering their messages, would settle on a rock and coo at each other.[67]

Large expeditionary forces might include units such as Dowdall's Yorkshire Light Infantry, but the routine defence of the frontier was in the hands of the Punjab Regular Force, whose men were known as 'Piffers', which consisted of mortar batteries, infantry battalions and five regiments of cavalry; among them were some of the most famous units in India, including Harry Lumsden's 'Guides' and 'Sam Browne's Cavalry', regiments raised in the 1840s. Besides the 'Piffers' there were the Frontier Scouts, which consisted almost entirely of Pathan tribesmen and a very small number of British officers. Organized into units such as the Tochi Scouts, the Khyber Rifles and the Khurram Militia, their job was to patrol their own tribes, a curious arrangement that worked reasonably well from the end of the nineteenth century until the Third Afghan War in 1919. Curzon, who was largely responsible for the policy, described his way of managing the Pathan tribesman: 'to pay him and humour him when he behaves, but to lay him out flat when he does not'.[68]

The Tochi Scouts wore loose khaki shirts over baggy trousers and heavily nailed sandals instead of army boots for gripping steep slopes. Their British officers wore the same uniform, which included a small turban, so as not to attract the attention of hostile marksmen, although these, apparently, were seldom fooled by the disguise. Scouts officers, usually seconded from the Piffer regiments, were invariably men who liked activity and the frontier life and who accepted the risks in return for the higher pay and longer holidays that they received as reward and compensation for the hardships. Some of them, such as Lieutenant John Prendergast, joined the Scouts so that they could save up enough money to get married at the end of their three-year stint. Life was so dangerous with the Scouts that only bachelors were selected as officers; anyone who disregarded this condition on their first tour of duty would be dismissed and returned to a regular unit. The army did not wish to pay pensions to nineteen-year-old widows.[69]

Some officers might find 'Beau Geste romance' on the frontier, but all found vivid danger as well. It was dangerous enough in the north-east, where five political agents in Manipur and in the Naga Hills were killed between 1876 and 1891, but the perils were more persistent in the north-west, where, as one frontier officer put it, 'the price of a man's life was considerably less than that of a Government rifle'. Political agents and officers of the Scouts were sometimes kidnapped or murdered, the assassin invariably described afterwards as 'a Muslim fanatic'. Major 'Barney' Barnes survived two murder attempts in Waziristan in the early 1930s but later succumbed to one in Zhob, the third political agent to be assassinated there in thirty years.[70]

Soldiers on the frontier spent a lot of time in forts and blockhouses. In the Punjab you might be sent to Dera Ghazi Khan, which was extremely hot, or to its even more remote neighbour, Dera Ismail Khan, the two known to British soldiery as 'Dreary Ghastly Khan' and 'Dreary Dismal Khan'. There was nothing much to do in either place unless you liked hawking and could acquire a peregrine to hunt a local type of bustard in the desert. Duties on the frontier consisted mainly of guarding and watching, making sure you were ready if the Mohands or Afridis or some other tribe made a sudden foray. One soldier at Landi Kotal, headquarters of the brigade responsible for the defence of the Khyber, summed up his duties as 'to keep the tribes quiet, to allow the caravans peaceful transit through the pass and to keep an eye on the Afghan frontier'.[71]

Most officers hoped to be stationed at Peshawar, the town that became the provincial capital when the North-West Frontier was set up in 1901. It is true that the cantonment was a very dangerous place, that it was surrounded by a perimeter of dense barbed wire, and that the British were robbed there more frequently than in any other part of India.[72] But it had avenues of trees, and a club with gardens and grass tennis courts, and in spring the sound of doves and the scent of orange blossom made it a place which officers loved to recall and hoped to revisit. Above all, it was a place where they could live with their wives. Much of the frontier was out of bounds to women even before the raid on Colonel Ellis's bungalow in Kohat in 1923, when his wife was killed and his daughter was abducted (though later rescued).

'Relations with the other sex,' an officer understated, 'did not play a large part in our Frontier life.' In fact they played no part at all in most of the north-west except by letter. Razmak, deep in Waziristan, was one of several 'non-family stations'. Sometimes described as 'the world's largest monastery', it was 6,500 feet above sea level and surrounded by arc lights and a triple circle of barbed wire. Inside lived some 5,000 soldiers, British and Indian, an equivalent number of camp-followers, and 3,000 mules that drove men half crazy with their braying. British women were not allowed to come within ninety miles of the place. To the south, in Baluchistan, they could live at Quetta, see their husbands and have a social life in one of the largest garrison stations in the empire. Yet in Waziristan officers' wives were holed up in Bannu in what was known as 'the cats' home', hoping that their husbands would come down for the odd weekend but in the meantime living together in bungalows around a communal dining area and, according to the Gurkha officer John Morris, carrying 'on their internecine feuds in conditions so cramped that after a few weeks they were hardly on speaking terms with one another'.[73]

Razmak and the other forts were only bearable for men who liked the landscape and enjoyed sport even in fairly restricted conditions. Not everyone enjoyed shooting when there was a good chance of being shot at yourself. Nor was it much fun to play football on a stony wasteland, aware that you were being protected by armed pickets. It may have been relaxing to play golf at Simla or Gulmarg in Kashmir or at the Tollygunge Club in Calcutta, but it was not so on the frontier, where the 'greens' were in fact 'browns', the fairways were 'scrubs', and it was advisable to send an advance guard in case an ambush was being prepared in one of the bunkers.[74] One sport that seems to have been followed more or less without restrictions was hunting jackals, an exception ascribed by admirers of the Pathans to the tribesmen's sense of honour and their innate love of sport. Political officers apparently managed to convince local chieftains that British riders galloping with packs of hounds did not present a military threat, even when their quarry led them into tribal territory. Members of the Wana Drag Hunt were consequently unmolested. So were officers at Landi Kotal, who used to drive in the dark through thirty miles of the Khyber to get to the early-morning meets of the Peshawar Vale Hunt.[75]

The frontier was, as John Masters observed, 'a betwixt-and-between place, part India, part Central Asia'. Its landscape was craggy, arid and inhospitable, yet it appealed to most of the soldiers who were stationed there. So did its inhabitants. Richard Hilton, who was stationed there with the Royal Garrison Artillery, recalled that 'nearly all British officers (and men) who really came to know the Pathans . . . grew to like and respect them . . . [and] the feeling was certainly reciprocated'. If the tribesmen had their 'thieving ways' and were sometimes treacherous, they were also chivalrous, brave, sporting and hospitable. They were good foes to fight and good friends to feast with. Olaf Caroe, the penultimate British governor of the North-West Frontier Province, was not the only Englishman who thought that 'living among the Pathans' was the central experience of his life.[76]

Not everyone suffered from what one army cynic called 'Pathanitis'. Certainly John Morris, the Gurkha officer, was unaffected. He had wanted to be stationed in Sikkim, Nepal, or somewhere in the northeast but was sent instead to the 'brigand lands' of the north-west. When stationed at Dardoni in Waziristan, he 'acquired a passionate hatred' for the 'barbarian tribesmen' as well as contempt for the British officers in the Scouts who were such 'unqualified admirers of the virile but untrustworthy hooligans under their command'.[77] Sidney and Beatrice Webb held similar views. When that judgemental Fabian couple visited India in 1912, they were much surprised by the 'universal praise of the wild Pathans', who were said to be 'fine fellows, far superior to the Hindoos'. The Webbs soon ascertained that this was not true, that they were in fact 'cruel and treacherous, shockingly addicted to unnatural vice and habitually given to stealing each other's wives'. How anyone could admire a people who broke 'nearly every Commandment' and were 'apparently of no earthly use in the universe' was a question that defeated them.[78]

OFFICERS AND THE MESS

Captain Hervey of the Madras Native Infantry was not fond of officers from British regiments in India. They 'fancied themselves superior to those of the Indian Army', he complained in the mid-nineteenth century, 'and consequently gave themselves many foolish airs'.[79] This was no doubt a 'mistaken notion', as Hervey contended, which was bolstered by a sense of superior wealth and class background: few officers of the Indian Army enjoyed paternal allowances or private incomes. And it persisted for a long time, though often in the form of light-hearted mockery. An Indian Army colonel was assumed to be a peppery old fellow with leathery skin and a fondness for hot curries and long Trichy cheroots. When 'Stalky' Dunsterville revisited Aldershot as a colonel in 1914, the resident officers expressed surprise that he did not have a red face and white whiskers; they offered him brandy pawnee instead of iced claret-cup, apologized for the absence of curry at his meals and, if they met him in the afternoon, wondered why he was not enjoying a siesta.[80]

The ideal Indian Army officer was a paternalist who spoke Urdu and the language of his regiment (Punjabi, Gurkhali or whatever) and who knew not only every man in the unit but also his background. In the words of John Morris, an officer who was usually sceptical and critical of his colleagues, 'this feature of the old Indian Army largely accounted for the unique relationship between officers and men. The company commander was looked upon as the father of a family and so must be ready to give advice and help on any problem, however trivial.'[81] No doubt many officers were model paternalists in this fashion. According to General Tuker, who was in India at the time of Partition, 'some of them knew the true India [of peasants and other country folk] better than many of those Indians [i.e. middle-class urban Congressmen] who spoke for her',[82] and although this may not often have been true, many did know and love the country well.

Yet quite a few did not. The surprise caused by the outbreak of the Rebellion in 1857, and those moments of denial, that strange refusal to believe that their own regiments could rebel, revealed how complacent and out-of-touch many officers of the Bengal Army were at that time. And although many officers were good linguists – Dunsterville passed exams in Punjabi, Pushtu and Persian (as well as Urdu) within two years of joining the Indian Army – quite a few were not. Passing the compulsory lower standard exam in Urdu, the language of the army, did not mean that officers could read the great poets of the language. Some of them could not do much more than bark ungrammatical orders. When making his farewell speech after twenty-seven years in India, one commanding officer is said to have prefaced it 'by saying that he had not been long enough in the country to learn the language'.[83] But perhaps he was making a joke which the reporter did not understand.

Although the Indian Army produced some of Britain's best generals, its officers were bound to be rather parochial, living in cantonments with little military excitement and not much incentive to keep abreast of the latest techniques of warfare. Theirs was a profession for life, and many of them were content to trundle along, very slowly ascending the promotion list until eventually they became a colonel. In the Indian Army, thought John Morris, it was considered rather peculiar, not quite right, to want to reach the top and become a general: 'a good officer should be content to devote himself to furthering the interests of his regiment, and to look beyond this was rather like feeling ashamed of one's family and wanting to get away from it'.[84]

Attitudes like these did not, however, make such men very different from officers of British regiments. It was not as if captains of the Somersets or majors of the West Kents were sitting in their barracks swotting up on Clausewitz or trying to invent a new rifle. Officers of the Gordons never – as one of them admitted – volunteered for 'anything; not for the Staff College; not for Active Service, still less for . . . an exam in an oriental language'.[85] They too were wary of a life outside the regiment. British Army officers in India had even less work to do than their compatriots in the Indian Army, and they usually knew how to take good advantage of their leisure. Horace Smith-Dorrien, an Old Harrovian in the Derby Regiment, was in 1892 posted to Lucknow, the heart of the racing world for 'gentleman riders', and two years later to Ambala, a centre of the polo world. Although he was by then a fairly senior officer, assistant adjutant-general, his diary does not suggest that his duties took up very much of his time.

> An ordinary day at Umballa would begin at dawn, galloping ponies on the racecourse; then attendance on the General at inspection of a regiment; afternoon the polo ground; an hour of whist at the club; a big dinner followed by a dance or theatre; supper; another hour at the club chatting with 'Kitty' Apthorp (of the Royal Irish) or 'Jinks' Jenkinson of the Derbyshires.[86]

Among the many things that officers of both armies had in common was the Officers' Mess. This was very much a phenomenon of the nineteenth and twentieth centuries; before then officers tended to make their own dining arrangements, inviting their colleagues to enjoy their hospitality. The institution of the 'Mess' had three 'scales': a mobile column Mess providing a kind of picnic, eaten on the ground on enamelware unloaded from mules; a camp Mess that added tents and folding furniture to the picnic; and the real thing, the 'peacetime Mess' with all the comforts of a permanent home at the barracks. This domestic Mess was a place to be revered, a 'sanctuary', according to Morris, 'a sort of holy place' that could not on any 'account be made the subject of a joke'. Veneration was certainly accorded it by Shahid Hamid, an Indian Army officer who graduated at Sandhurst, fought in Burma and became a major-general in Pakistan. For him the Mess was the officers' 'real "Home"', where he absorbed the regimental customs and traditions and learned a correct 'code of behaviour'. 'In the Mess the officer is . . . moulded and rounded till he has no corners left and becomes a happy member of a happy family. He gradually learns to take a pride in his unit and to uphold the honour of the regiment.'[87]

The sanctuary was a place of moral and emotional force rather than a shrine of beauty and craftsmanship. The concept was nobler than its physical embodiment. The Mess was in fact more or less 'jerry-built', designed by officers and constructed by soldiers with whatever materials were available locally. The regimental silver might be quite grand, but the furniture very seldom was. In Dunsterville's Mess it was 'scanty and dilapidated' and 'local', while coconut matting took the place of carpets. A Mess would usually have a sort of anteroom where officers could read books and journals and drink tea from a pot embellished with the regimental crest. Here, decorating the walls, were fading photographs of former officers and, in the last decades, among the bookcases, a gramophone and a wireless set. Other important spaces were the card room, a place for bridge enthusiasts and a refuge for senior officers when guest nights became rowdy, and the billiard room, usually a temple to shooting and the chase, with stuffed animals' heads on the walls. These were often mangy and moth-eaten, but Lieutenant Henry Haughton from the 36th Sikhs was much impressed by the Mess of the Munsters, who had got 'some very fine African heads', among them 'two rhinos shot by Major Williams'.[88] Other mural decorations in a Mess might include spears, flags and other trophies of war, but the most important, lining the walls on either side of the long dining table, were the portraits, occasionally in oil, more often photographs, of the current commanding officer and his predecessors.

Initiation into a Mess was rather a forbidding rite for a young subaltern. There were so many unwritten rules about what you should do and not do, about what you were permitted to talk about and what you were never allowed to mention. There were also various arcane customs, such as 'taking wine' with someone, which took time and practice to assimilate. Lieutenant George Godfrey Pearse, who joined the Madras artillery in 1844, was appalled by a gaffe he made by asking a senior officer to 'take sherry' with him after curry when the 'correct' tipple in the circumstances would have been beer.[89]

A more persistent anxiety for the novice was the expense of belonging to a Mess on a subaltern's salary. He would have to subscribe to various funds, contribute to the upkeep of the band, pay his share for newspapers and stationery, and on arrival he was expected to give some item of silver to the regiment, although he would often be allowed to club together with other junior officers and make a joint donation of salt cellars. Yet by far his heaviest expenditure was on food and drink. John Prendergast complained that a third of his pay went on 'a restrained Mess bill', but many subalterns, not only those with 'a tropical thirst', had to devote a much higher proportion.[90] As Ian Hamilton of the Gordons pointed out, 'one of the drawbacks of belonging to a crack regiment' like his own was the vast Mess bills. He himself tried to economize by drinking commissariat rum instead of brandy and commissariat tea instead of 'best Souchong'. Yet this did not help much because he still had to contribute to the hospitality the Gordons famously gave their guests, 'champagne always flowing'. In the 1870s Hamilton was spending more than three-quarters of his pay on his Mess bills.[91] In situations like this, many young subalterns had to resort to Hindu money-lenders, as did Lieutenant Winston Churchill, who found them 'fat', 'urbane', 'agreeable' and 'rapacious'.[92] In 1931, 'in response to the international recession', the commander-in-chief in India, General Chetwode, appealed to officers (whose pay was being cut as a result of the economic crisis) to make economies in their way of life, to desist from hosting expensive dinners and serving champagne on guest nights, and when in the Club to discontinue 'the custom for officers to stand drinks to circles of fellow-members whom they happen to meet', especially because impoverished young officers found 'a difficulty in refusing to conform to this custom'.[93]

Each generation of army officers claimed to drink less than the one before. In Madras in the 1840s Lieutenant Hervey witnessed scenes of dissipation that continued until daybreak unless servants carried their inebriated masters home. When Lieutenant Pearse joined the army in 1844, 'it was simply the very devil': 'wheelbarrows' were still 'an institution and part of the Mess', and officers in a 'not sober state' were put in them after dinner and 'rolled home'. It was 'simply not at all the same thing' now, when he was writing, as a general, in 1877. In his recollection of the 1870s, Ian Hamilton claimed that he and his fellow officers in the Gordons 'drank far less than the old Maori War warriors of the Suffolks' despite the fact that the champagne was 'always flowing' in the Mess. Yet when Colonel Western, a cavalry officer, wrote his memoirs in 1922, he recalled that in the 1870s 'the consumption of wine or spirits in a mess was treble and quadruple what it is now'.[94]

Whatever reduction in consumption had been achieved over the decades, it was certainly not enough for Bernard Montgomery, who, as a subaltern in Peshawar before the First World War, was appalled to find that in every Mess there was 'a strict rule against non-alcoholic beverages'. The experience left him with 'a lifelong aversion to alcoholic excess' and to the Indian Army as well.[95]

In 1918 Basil Amies joined a regiment where the colonel drank gin before breakfast, but that was not a normal occurrence. Breakfast was not an occasion for drinking or jollity, at least not in that age. In John Morris's Mess it was 'by common consent . . . a silent meal', emphasized by the fact that each place at table had a wire newspaper rest, though this was not often used because the papers did not arrive until the afternoon.[96]

The noise levels of the Mess did not rise noticeably until the evening. Married officers usually dined in their bungalows with their wives, leaving the battalion's bachelors, perhaps six or seven of them, to eat at the Mess table, though on guest nights the number might quadruple, all the officers would come, and the silver would be laid out on display. 'Mess dress' was obligatory on these occasions, and as scarlet was the dominant colour of the Indian and British regiments, there was a lot of red about. Even in the hot weather, remembered James Fairweather, a young IMS officer in the 1850s, it was 'considered de rigueur' to arrive at a Mess dinner wearing a heavy red cloth jacket and wait until one's host invited one to change into the light white garment that one's servant had brought for this purpose. Red was not worn, however, by the artillery or the Gurkhas or the 'native' cavalry. In his Gurkha regiment in the 1920s John Morris had to wear a starched shirt, a stiff collar (with 'a special kind of black satin bow-tie') above 'skin-tight braided black trousers strapped down under patent-leather Wellington boots'. Covering the stiffened garments was a 'heavily braided and embroidered bottle-green cloth waistcoat' and then a short Eton jacket, 'frogged, like a Hussar's jacket', and with some additional rigidity, 'a high, stiffened collar'. When he was being fitted for this costume in London, Morris was told by the tailor, 'You may not be aware, sir, that mess dress is not meant to be sat down in'.[97]

Elegantly but uncomfortably attired, the officers and guests assembled in the anteroom for an aperitif that was customarily a choice between sherry and Madeira. In honour of these beverages, smoking was banned for half an hour before dinner so that they could be savoured uncontaminated by tobacco fumes. Most European drinks went through varying stages of popularity in India, but Madeira always remained fashionable, bolstered by the bizarre belief that its long voyage round the Cape and the later one through the Red Sea had an 'improving effect' on its flavour. Morris thought the reverse was true of his battalion's sherry, that its quality had in fact been so impaired by its journey over the seas and across the hot plains of India that 'a few whiffs of smoke could hardly have affected it'.[98]

While the guests were arriving and the aperitifs were being savoured in the smokeless air, the regimental band, brass or pipes, was in full swing, pounding out its tunes either on the verandah or on the lawn outside the Mess. As the commanding officer led the procession into dinner (in order of rank), it would strike up 'The Roast Beef of Old England'. Like the building itself, the dinner was more glorious in concept than in reality. The food was elaborately and even pretentiously presented, but it was seldom very good. The six courses consisted of *hors d'œuvres* or 'first toast' – either a sardine or half a boiled egg on usually soggy toast – followed by some flavourless soup, some kind of fish (tinned 'if we were lucky'), a roast joint of some sort (with Yorkshire pudding if it was beef), pudding (the usual prep-school favourites – steamed, sago or bread-and-butter – or perhaps trifle or pink blancmange) and then a 'second toast' or savoury, which was more or less the same as the first toast.[99]

As they advanced through the menu, officers drank claret and tried to avoid discussing the subjects that seem to have been forbidden in every regimental Mess. As Morris recalled, 'it was not permissible to discuss religion, politics or anything to do with our profession', while the 'inadvertent mention of a lady's name was punished by a round of drinks at the culprit's expense'. This was the quintessential officers' punishment, whether for some infringement in the Mess or on the hunting field: buying drinks for one's fellows. On three occasions Dunsterville 'had to stand the whole Mess Port-wine': when he 'spoke of some religious matter', when he 'opened a political discussion', and when he 'mentioned a lady's name'. He also had to give port to a brother officer whom he had accidentally sprayed with shotgun pellets when shooting duck together. At a rate of one glass for each pellet extracted by a doctor from under the man's skin, this proved 'an expensive affair' for young Dunsterville.[100]

The restrictions on conversational topics were an invitation to the bore to remind junior officers of his exploits as a sportsman. This could go on for a long time, for such a man inevitably had a well-stocked repertoire of hunting stories. Although they might listen politely, Morris and his fellow officers were naturally 'bored by the nightly small-talk about missed pheasants, fish caught, and how the latest recruit to the football team was coming along at inside-right'.[101] Yet relief came, at least temporarily, when the feeding was finished, the tablecloth was removed, and the decanters were brought in. The staple liquids in these vessels were port and Madeira, though there might also be sherry, Marsala and, in the twentieth century, whisky. The commanding officer would remove the stoppers and sniff the wines to make sure they had not 'gone off', and then push them towards his neighbour on his left. They would then circulate slowly around the table in a clockwise direction; in regiments where people still took it, snuff would go the other way.

Conversation was halted on guest nights when the toasts were made, and the sovereign's health was drunk. By the end of the nineteenth century this part of the evening was a very meagre affair compared to what it had been a hundred years earlier, when the ceremony was quite Russian in its scale. Then toasts were made accompanied by appropriate music from the band, the national anthem when it was the king, 'Rule Britannia' when the 'toastees' were the Duke of Clarence and the navy. In 1797 William Hickey dined in Calcutta with Arthur Wellesley's regiment (the 33rd) and, after the usual liquid dinner, was forced to down twenty-two formal toasts, 'bumpers in glasses of considerable magnitude'. Heavy drinker though he was, Hickey had an 'excruciating headache' the next day and was 'incapable' of getting out of bed; it was the most 'severe debauch' he had ever experienced'.[102]

A hundred years later, the toasts were little more than 'the Queen-Empress' or, from 1901, 'the King-Emperor'. The only vestige left of the eighteenth century was the custom, in some regiments, of orderlies removing the water glasses before the toast so that officers would not pass their port over them and thus toast 'the king over the water' – i.e. the Jacobite Pretender.[103] * During dinner the band had been playing intermittently somewhere outside the dining room, and the colonel now invited the bandmaster or pipe-major to come in and take a glass of port with him. By this time officers were smoking and enjoying the second circuit of the decanters, and were thus in good humour to

---

* There was of course no recognized Pretender at that time. The last one, who called himself King Henry IX after the death of his brother Bonnie Prince Charlie, died in 1807. He had been a cardinal and bishop of Frascati.

welcome the pipe band (if there was one) attached not only to Scottish regiments but also to several Indian Army units (including the Gurkhas, who were coached by the Seaforth Highlanders). Pipers duly arrived and marched around the table, behind the chairs of the diners, playing a slow march, a quick march, a strathspey and a reel before marching out again. When they did this on the king's birthday in the Banqueting Hall in Madras, an enormous building, this might have been bearable and even impressive. In the confines of a regimental Mess the performance was deafening. For John Morris it was one of the worst things about being a Gurkha officer: he was 'never at any time' of his life 'able to appreciate the mournful squeals of the bagpipe'. The amir of Afghanistan, Habibullah Khan, may have been a fellow sufferer. In 1907 Sir Harold Deane, the chief commissioner of the North-West Frontier, entertained him at Peshawar and brought in sixteen pipers of the Black Watch to march around the table and then, as a special compliment, to play behind the royal chair. When Deane afterwards asked his royal guest how he had liked the pipers, the amir replied, 'Splendid, magnificent! But *one* would have been sufficient.'[104]

No one could leave the table before the commanding officer, and if that august personage chose to stay, drinking port and telling stories, everyone else had to stay too. Even when he had gone, there might be a major who wished to reminisce, in which case the lieutenants took it in turns to stay with him and listen. And even those subalterns who escaped the major might then be caught by another senior officer and be forced, as Winston Churchill was, 'to play a tiresome game then in vogue called "whist"'.[105]

What most well-fuelled subalterns wished to do at this stage of a guest night was to take part in some vigorous and very puerile 'horseplay'. One favourite jape was to smuggle a mongoose into the Mess and see what havoc the little animal could create. A more ambitious idiocy was the introduction of a bullock, unyoked from a cart outside, which gave subalterns an opportunity to demonstrate their matador skills, flapping their coats and shouting '*Olé! Olé!*' at the poor passive creature. Most 'high jinks', however, involved only themselves. If a lieutenant at Kohat was sufficiently well 'oiled', he would ride a bicycle at great speed down the Mess steps and over several hedges, 'hopefully to land on the Mall some 75 feet below'. Other more communal activities seem to have been designed to injure people's backs. 'Piggy-back scrimmages' in one Mess led to such bad concussion that they had to be forbidden. Dunsterville recalled that even Ring a Ring o' Roses became 'a fairly dangerous game when played by a lot of grown men, and casualties – sometimes serious ones – were pretty frequent'. One of the most dangerous games was a bewildering one called 'Bounding Brothers of the Bosphorus' which required participants to do somersaults over a desk and then land on their backs on top of a pile of upturned furniture.[106]

At the end of an evening like this, some officers attempted 'a sort of insurance against the morning hangover' by drinking a 'prairie oyster' – raw egg, Worcestershire sauce, cayenne pepper and olive oil – 'to rally an already assaulted liver'. Others, at least in the 1930s, could fill in printed apology cards to their hosts, ticking the boxes where they could admit they had been guilty of 'inebriation', 'singing ribald songs', 'breaking china and glassware' and 'insisting on telling naughty stories'. Whatever they had done, and at whatever hour they had gone to bed, they knew – and they were proud of the fact – that they would have to be on parade at six in the morning, looking spruce, efficient and 'impeccably turned out', as well as showing no 'sign of having been the worse for wear a few hours earlier'.[107]

PART THREE
EXPERIENCES

9
Intimacies

THE RISE AND FALL OF THE BIBI

Until the last decades of the East India Company, most British men in India spent at least part of their careers living with at least one Indian or Eurasian woman – usually more than one, and often for most of their time in India. It was not a matter of class, temperament, availability or an excessively licentious manner of living. In the eighteenth century it was what happened. A member of council was as likely to have a 'bibi' or native mistress as a tradesman in Calcutta. John Shore was a pious official in the Company who had an Indian bibi and two half-Indian children; he returned to England and married an English girl (who produced nine children), went back to India as governor-general (1793–8) and in retirement became president of the British and Foreign Bible Society.

The bibi was very much more than a concubine. Richard Burton, who spent seven years as an officer in India in the 1840s, lauded his first mistress as a nurse, a housekeeper and a teacher 'not only [of] Hindostani grammar, but the syntaxes of native life' too; furthermore she knew how to keep 'the servants in order'. In later years he recalled that the erotic skills of Indian women were so superior to those of English men that no bibi had ever been able to love her lover, a deduction which, whether true or not, was – as one of his biographers has pointed out – 'a melancholy admission on his own part'.[1] As he later demonstrated with his translations of the *Kama Sutra* and *The Perfumed Garden*, Burton was an expert on sex, a prototype sexologist, but he may not have been an expert 'practitioner'. One of his theories was that British soldiers were too rough and rapid when copulating – which may well have been the case – while Hindu women, 'whose natural cold-ness' was increased by their 'vegetable diet and unuse of stimulants', could not 'be satisfied ... with less than twenty minutes'. The men would have performed better, he believed, if they had learned the Hindu 'retaining art', delaying their ejaculation by drinking sherbert, chewing betel-nut or even smoking.[2]

There are many romantic stories, at least in the telling, of love affairs between British men and Indian women. When Job Charnock, tradi-tionally regarded as the founder of Calcutta, came across a young Hindu widow about to be immolated on her husband's funeral pyre, he was so struck by her beauty that he carried her off and married her. When William Linnaeus Gardner, a British officer and former merce-nary, was negotiating a treaty in Surat, he suddenly glimpsed behind a curtain 'the most beautiful black eyes in the world'. They belonged to the fourteen-year-old daughter of a nawab who, despite initial parental disapproval, was allowed to marry Gardner the following year: the marriage was so successful that, as he put it some decades later, he had never wished to take 'another wife', which surprised 'the Musselmans very much'.[3] Other marriages of this kind were equally enduring. In 1810, at the early age of twenty-two, the Company official Thomas Cobbe married 'Nuzzeer Begum', a Muslim from Bengal, with whom he had ten children. Their relationship lasted until 1836, when, on the voyage to England, he died after suffering a paralytic stroke while play-ing chess and was buried at sea.[4]

Several marriages between senior Company officials and upper-class Indian women took place at the end of the eighteenth century. Both James Dalrymple, commander of the British forces at Hyderabad, and James Kirpatrick, Resident at the nizam's court at Hyderabad, married aristocratic Muslims. David Ochterlony, the Resident in Delhi early in the nineteenth century, is reported to have had thirteen wives who each had her own elephant in order to accompany him on his evening ride around the city walls.

Yet marriages at all levels of society were less frequent than relation-ships with a bibi. A native mistress might require a couple of servants and an allowance for betel, clothes and ornaments, but she would be less expensive to maintain than a wife (and safer, of course, to have sex with than prostitutes). One army officer believed that it was cheaper for him to keep a 'harem' of sixteen Indian mistresses than to look after a single English wife.[5] Another pattern, common before about 1830, was for British men to have a bibi when young and then in middle age to marry an Englishwoman, often with the consequence, as in the case of John Shore, of having two sets of children. The artist Tilly Kettle arrived in India in 1769 and earned his living by painting portraits of Indian aristocrats in the style of Reynolds; while on the Subcontinent he had two children with an Indian woman, and on his return he had some more with an English wife.[6] Sometimes it is difficult to tell from the records how many of such and such a general's children were 'natural' and how many were legitimate. In the eighteenth century General Sir Robert Sloper, a commander-in-chief in India, certainly had six legitimate sons (two in British regiments, another in the Madras Army) and seems to have had at least half a dozen 'natural' children, including one son in the Dragoon Guards and another in the Light Dragoons, as well as a daughter whose husband was a Writer in the Company and a future postmaster-general in Bengal.[7]

William Hickey found it difficult to make the transition from one ethnic type to another. After his English mistress, Charlotte Barry, had died in Calcutta in 1783, Hickey remained chaste for some time but, being 'of an amorous disposition', he 'one night sent for a native woman'. When one arrived, however, he lost all desire. Impotence recurred on two further occasions as he felt 'the horror' of the thought of 'a connection with black women'. The horror receded when he realized that some Indian ladies were in fact 'very lovely' and that it was not 'correct to call them black'; those from the Upper Provinces were actually 'very fair'. Soon his wealthy friend Robert Pott, the Resident at Murshidabad, sent him 'a very pretty little native girl' called Kiraum 'whom he recommended for my private use'. After cohabiting together for a year, she produced a boy whom Hickey considered to be 'suspiciously dark', and his suspicions about the paternity were confirmed when he found Kiraum in bed with another servant. Matters improved for Hickey when he met a 'lovely Hindostanee girl' called Jemdanee, whom he invited to 'become an intimate . . . which she consented to do'. By his own account, the relationship was a great success. Unlike other women, 'she never secluded herself from the sight of strangers' and she took part in his extremely boozy 'male parties, cordially joining in the mirth which prevailed, though she never touched wine or spirits of any kind'. They went to live in Chinsura, the old Dutch settlement on the Hooghly which was slightly cooler than Calcutta, and Jemdanee became pregnant. She hoped for a 'chota William sahib' and did indeed have a boy, this one 'remarkably fair', but alas she died in childbirth, and the baby died not long afterwards.[8] Burra William sahib was deeply upset by their deaths.

Hickey's love life in Calcutta was not unusual, and it was certainly less chaotic than those of some of his contemporaries. Richard Blechynden began his career as a midshipman but soon realized he preferred dry land to sea, and by 1784, at the age of twenty-four, he was working as an assistant to the Company's civil architect in Calcutta. He never married, but he had mistresses who were Indian, Eurasian, Armenian and 'country-born' English. His favourite bibi was a Muslim lady with whom he lived openly in Calcutta, much as Hickey did with Jemdanee, though she did not visit his married friends. When she died in his arms, he wrote in his diary: 'Thus have I lost one who had slept in them for near 7 years and an half and by whom I have had 5 children, 3 of whom survive her, and have lost an affectionate and too indulgent a mother.'[9] Yet he had not been faithful to her and within a few weeks he had a new mistress, followed 'to my sorrow' by 'plenty' since. He usually kept them, one at a time, in a 'garden house' outside Calcutta.

None of Blechynden's other lovers was in the same league as the Muslim lady. They did, however, belong to a different league of very heavy drinkers. An Armenian girl was a 'drunken baggage', but at least she was good-tempered, while 'country-born' Charlotte had tantrums after drinking beer, Madeira or bazaar arrack – it does not seem to have mattered what, as long as there was enough of it; she once drank nine bottles of Madeira in two days. In the mornings she would wake up in such a temper that she would pour water over her lover and tear his clothes. Even more violent was Isabella (probably Eurasian), who was prone to smashing things, drinking a couple of decanters of Madeira and then tearing the curtains and sweeping all the plates off the table and the sideboard. Even when she was sober she annoyed Blechynden by doing little all day except lounge about on a charpoy entertaining a 'whole gang of Mousaalmannys singing and tom-toming'.[10]

One might conclude that Blechynden was a poor picker, but he did not really pick the girls. They effectively chose him and were either introduced by his servants or else they arrived at his gate as supplicants looking winsome and attractive. Although experienced, Blechynden was quite naive, and he would quickly convince himself that he had met the perfect girl with whom to enjoy 'all the comforts of marriage without its plagues'. Only later would he realize that he had formed 'one of the most unfortunate connections' of his life.[11]

Blechynden's diaries tell us a good deal about how a moderately prosperous Englishman might arrange his life in Calcutta in the decades either side of 1800. They also tell us a fair amount about masculine attitudes towards bibis and other women: one man called Doncaster was supposed to be looking after the bibi of his friend Collier, who was away, but as she was three months 'gone with child', he felt he could 'strum' her without risking a pregnancy. Blechynden's pages are informative too about British women in Bengal who did not belong to the class that married colonels and civil servants. According to a scornful letter of Surgeon John Stewart, most of the women in Kanpur at that time were apparently 'mere adventuresses from the milliners' shops on Ludgate Hill and some even from Covent Garden and Old Drury'.[12] At least some of the women in Calcutta belonged to a similar class. Blechynden's Charlotte, who was now twenty, had been married at the age of thirteen to a sergeant-major in a Madras regiment; when she was too ill to accompany him to some place, she allowed herself to be seduced and kept by a lieutenant. Numerous acquaintances come to life in descriptions from Blechynden's pen or his editor's: a Mrs Rees who found her husband (a journalist) in bed with a Miss Rawlinson and so went to live with an army medical officer called Frushard; a Mrs Mulder who left her husband to live with a pilot called Collins: a Mrs Tucker who kept a brothel, a Mrs Macnamara who procured mistresses, and a Mrs Wade, whose husband found 'a black fellow in bed with her', after which she 'moved in with the blacksmith Myers'.[13]

It is not always clear whether these and other women mentioned were British, Eurasian, 'country-born' or sometimes Indian. To Blechynden and his friends it did not seem to make much difference. We are still in an age when class mattered more than race as, at a different level of society, the marriages of Gardner and the British officers in Hyderabad have already shown. Blechynden treated his mistresses in much the same way, regardless of race, though the Muslim lady who died in his arms seems to have had certain advantages – in terms of respect, so-cial life and household expenses – over the others.

Nobody could claim that relationships between British men and their Indian bibis were fair or balanced, yet many of them were endur-ingly affectionate; often they ended only in death. Hickey gave a number of examples of mutual concern and attachment: one 'beautiful Hindostanee woman' tried to wean her mate (Colonel Cooper) 'from the destructive and baneful practice of drinking brandy or other spirits profusely ... even in the morning', while Dr Wilson, who had been ordered home for health reasons, was 'so miserable at the idea of for-ever quitting a Hindostanee woman who had lived with him many years and borne him several children, that he could not prevail on him-self to leave her'. He died soon afterwards, still in India.[14]

Bibis also received more concrete proofs of affection, including ser-vants and allowances, and, after their lovers' deaths, legacies to themselves and their children. When Major Charles Hay Elliot drew up his will in 1817, he left specific sums to three illegitimate daughters, and a further 35,000 rupees were set aside for the unborn baby which his bibi was carrying; a codicil later in the year revealed that the 'expected child has now arrived'. If a man died unmarried, his bibi might receive the entire fortune, houses and animals as well as money and jewels. Even if he also had a wife and legitimate children, he would often attempt a reasonable distribution of his wealth. Captain James Nicholson wanted his estate to be divided equally among his ten chil-dren, two of whom he had had with his British wife, and the others with several Indian women. The legacy of Major Charles Campbell was to be shared more simply between just two sets of progeny, three children born to an Indian woman between 1820 and 1822, and five born to his British wife between 1825 and 1831. The wife was given custody of the three half-Indian children.[15]

By the time of Major Campbell's Indian romance, the era of the bibi was already in decline. Analysis of the wills of the period has shown how after 1800 she became gradually less often a beneficiary.[16] The custom did not of course end abruptly. Nobody was going to force old Colonel Chutney to give up his hookah, his bibi and his mulligatawny soup. At Gwalior in 1840 Emily Eden and her party dined with 'Col-onel J', who lived 'quite in the native style, with a few black Mrs Js gracing his domestic circle when we are not here'. A few years later,

Colonel Meadows Taylor, an administrator and novelist, was found living at Sholapur like 'a Turkish pasha in the midst of a well-filled harem' that included one girl whose only duty was to 'mull' the colonel's eyebrows.[17] But young officers and Civilians were no longer openly keeping Indian mistresses. They did not keep British ones either, and very few had wives before they were thirty. Celibacy in their most sexually potent decade was for many British men now unavoidable.

The eclipse of the Indian mistress has traditionally been blamed on the arrival – in large numbers – of British women, who could travel to India much quicker than before and who, when they got there, were not prepared to tolerate someone who was both a competitor and a moral affront. Yet customs and morals had changed in Britain, and among men too. The kind of society that the Prince Regent had relished would have been abhorrent to the Prince Consort. Evangelicals may have been enthusiasts for the abolition of slavery, but they were not enthusiasts for cohabiting with other races or even sympathizing with their cultures. Utilitarian ideas were often accompanied by contempt for beliefs that were not Christian – and often for the holders of those beliefs themselves. As an obvious consequence, the British came to know and understand India very much less well. The old Company officers with their bibis had lived at least partly in another culture, imbibing, even passively, the scents and sounds of other peoples and other religions; they were bound to learn not only the grammar of their lovers' language but also some of its nuances, just as they were bound to understand something about Diwali or Mohurrum if they were attached to someone who celebrated such festivals.

The disappearance of the bibi from British lives was followed by an attempt to efface her from British history. When Captain Williamson wrote *The East India Vade Mecum* in 1810, his book contained interesting information about bibis; when the second edition appeared in 1825, this had all been removed.[18] When in 1854 John Kaye published his life of Sir Charles Metcalfe, he suppressed the fact that his subject had had an Indian wife and three half-Indian sons, one of them a distinguished soldier who was awarded the Order of the Bath and an entry in the *Oxford Dictionary of National Biography*.* It seemed that the

---

* Metcalfe (1785–1846) was the most distinguished Civilian of his time in northern India, his posts including Resident at Delhi and lieutenant-governor of the North–Western

whole idea of interracial physical relationships was so appalling that people had to pretend not just that they had stopped but that they had not even happened. Henceforth only the inquisitive or the antiquarian would understand the significance of that little ruined building in a corner of a compound, concealed behind palms and smothered by convolvulus, that once had been the *bibi khana*, the residence of the bibi.

For the British the loss was much greater than what Sudipta Sen has called 'the decline of intimacy',[19] much more drastic than the deprivation of erotic and domestic pleasure. The loss meant above all a forfeiture of understanding, of connection and even of knowledge. By disconnecting themselves from this area of human experience, the British were cutting an important link with the people they ruled and whose tacit consent to that rule they needed. The Resident at Hyderabad who had a Muslim wife and Muslim friends learned far more about what was happening in the nizam's court than his Victorian successors were ever able to know.

The disappearance of the bibi did not put an end to British–Indian sexual relationships. British men still married Indian women,* they still used Indian prostitutes,† and some of them still had Indian concubines, though usually in remote places, in the hills or on the periphery, far from the sight of disapproving memsahibs at the Club. In the tea-growing highlands of Travancore, noted Monica Francis, planters often took a 'beautiful plucking-girl' to their beds. So did they in the hills of Assam. As in the stories of Kipling or Somerset Maugham in Malaya, most men had the local girlfriend before they found the English wife, but Maurice Lewis, a tea planter in Assam born in 1901, did it the other way round. After the failure of his conventional marriage, he took up with a 'garden girl' (as they were known in the north-east), with whom he had three daughters. William Sinclair Thom, a retired policemen in Burma, also went maritally from west to east. In 1930, when he was already in his sixties, he divorced his British wife and soon afterwards married a Burmese woman, Ma Tin, with whom he

---

Provinces. He ended his career as governor of British North America. In his will he left £50,000 to his illegitimate son James, an officer in the Bengal Infantry.
* See below, p. 309–14.
† See below, p. 328–33.

had several children; he also took a mistress from the country, with whom he had two more.[20]

The one place in the Indian Empire where something like the bibi system survived for another couple of generations was the part that was least Indian: Burma. British men had admired Burmese women since the eighteenth century, when officers from ships trading at Rangoon found them beautiful, charming and remarkably independent.[21] Such views were retained. Comparing Moulmein in 1850 with what he had seen in India, Lord Dalhousie found 'most singular' the employment of 'Burmese maidens in the shops, the prominence and freedom of the women generally, and their marriage at the mature age of eighteen to husbands of their own choice'.[22] The men too were generally liked. Writing in the 1930s, one ICS officer recalled that he had 'seldom met an English official who did not speak up for the Burmese. It was one of our commonplaces to call them the most engaging people in the Empire.'[23] Orwell's characters in *Burmese Days* may not have agreed with him, but real people did. Besides their charm, their allure and their independence, Burmese women were free of both caste and purdah.

In the last decades of Queen Victoria's reign, the British authorities in Burma concurred that the climate was so bad in so many places that it was unsuitable for British women to live there. Charles Crosthwaite, the chief commissioner in the late 1880s, advised his officials not to marry because he considered the mortality risk to be unacceptably high. Memsahibs from later generations were able to demonstrate that the chief commissioner had been overcautious, but at the time the evidence seemed to prove him right. Alexander Mackenzie, his successor, lost his first wife in Burma in 1892 and nearly lost his second one there three years later. Not surprisingly, he suggested that all British wives in Burma should be advised to leave.

Timber firms working in Burma disapproved of British wives for another reason: they wanted their young recruits to be mobile and unburdened by a family. Such restrictions inevitably led to relationships between British men and Burmese women long after similar liaisons in India had faded away: in the early twentieth century, according to an investigator who lived there, 90 per cent of the British in Burma had local mistresses. Many of them were leading lonely lives in faraway places as Civilians, forest officers, timber agents or frontier policemen; they often did not see another European face for months at a time. Burma was the largest province of the Indian Empire and in 1901 contained just 8,537 British subjects, soldiers and civilians, most of them living in Rangoon or Mandalay. Outside those cities a few hundred British men and a much smaller number of British women were living spread over an area about the size of Spain. A young man in his twenties obviously needed someone to look after him, and if he could not have a British wife – because of his current income and her future health – it was natural for him to find a Burmese girl. So thought the benign George Hamilton, the secretary of state for India at the end of the nineteenth century. Burmese women, so he had 'always understood', made 'most admirable housekeepers' and were, besides, 'busy engaging females, with a natural aptitude for the society of men'.[24]

Burma's chief commissioners tended to be less sympathetic to the plight of their juniors, fearing that the practice of keeping a mistress would encourage corruption (the woman taking bribes from people who thought she had influence), would damage imperial prestige, and would lead to a class of Anglo-Burmans who would not belong to one community or the other. Yet Crosthwaite also felt that it was not the duty of the government 'to enforce morality', Mackenzie thought it was not his business 'to pry into private life', and his successor, Frederick Fryer, agreed that it was 'out of the question' to 'stamp out concubinage in Burma, human nature being what it is'.[25] There was a proviso, however, to all these viewpoints: that there should be no scandals and that nobody would make a fuss.

Unfortunately, these were impossible to prevent. Complaints about the immorality of officials in Burma had been made before; a bishop of Calcutta had been making them since 1870. But in 1900 two new purity-crusaders approached the viceroy (Curzon), Mrs Ada Castle and her husband Reginald, a police officer in Burma whom Fryer had had to remove from his post at Pegu because the couple insisted on criticizing the district officer, a man who, though now middle-aged and married to an Englishwoman, had in his younger days possessed a Burmese mistress. Mrs Castle's new target was a junior district officer, Walter Minns, who, she alleged, lived openly with two Burmese women and even took one of them on official tours. Curzon disliked the idea of Mrs Castle and her 'morbid puritanism', but he was always tetchy if he thought imperial prestige was at stake. When he asked for explanations, Minns claimed that he had been ill on a tour and that the woman had come with him 'not as a mistress but as a nurse'. The viceroy found this explanation 'profoundly unsatisfactory' and suggested that the errant official should be denied promotion for a time. Yet Minns was a good officer and a good linguist (doubtless he had good teachers), and before long he was deputy commissioner of Rangoon.[26]

Fryer's solution to the general problem was to tell his officials to lead 'a clean life' or else forfeit promotion. The response of many was to marry their mistresses, which may have pleased the bishop of Calcutta and the purity-mongers, but it was not what Fryer himself wanted. By 1903 twenty-five British officials in Burma were married to Burmese women, nearly all of whom had previously been their mistresses. Fryer could now envisage lines of supplicants coming to the DO's door, handing a present to the Burmese wife and expecting favours from the deputy commissioner. Curzon too was sufficiently alarmed to ask the India Office in London to issue rules discouraging the practice of marrying Burmese women. Hamilton could not make such decisions himself but had to rely on the judgement of the Council of India, a body of elderly men, most of whom were retired Civilians. Temperamentally inclined to block change – on the grounds that it had not been necessary 'in their day' – the councillors could not become enthusiastic about this issue. Alfred Lyall failed to see why a man should be penalized for marrying his mistress, while Crosthwaite, who knew as much about the problem as anyone, thought the government had no 'right to dictate to its officers whom they shall or shall not marry'. The amiable Hamilton was relieved that he did not have to issue any rules. He admitted that he had 'always been disposed to make very great allowance' for British officers 'shut off from contact with women of their own race and nationality'.[27]

BRITISH MARRIAGES

All British careers in the Indian Empire discouraged early marriage. Some explicitly forbade it. You could not join the Political Department if you were married at the time of your application. Nor could you join the Frontier Scouts unless you were a bachelor who undertook to remain unmarried for at least three years. Other employers might not be so specific yet make it clear that they wished to hire young men who were single and mobile. No tea planter wanted an apprentice encumbered by a young family. When Robin Drummond asked a fellow member of the Forest Service to be the 'best man' at his wedding, the friend refused, insisting that marriage was a 'bad thing for a forester'.[28] India was a country for outdoor work, for young men ready to jump on a horse and gallop across the desert or into the jungle.

Mobility was certainly essential for a cornet or a subaltern, and many young officers would have agreed with Kipling's lines in *The Story of the Gadsbys*:

> Down to Gehenna or up to the Throne,
> He travels the fastest who travels alone.

Early marriage would be a disaster – and fatal to ambition. As Captain Gadsby's friend Mafflin sings,

> You may carve it on his tombstone, you may cut it on his card,
> That a young man married is a young man marred!

Even if a soldier was inclined to marry young, the military made it almost impossible for him to do so. In the late nineteenth century, noted Private Fraser of the Northumberland Fusiliers, only twenty-five or thirty women – known as 'officers' ladies and wives of other ranks' – would be attached to each battalion.[29] When a regiment sailed for India, it usually had a quota of twelve places for women for every hundred for men; if more than 12 per cent of the soldiers were married, some of their wives would thus be left behind – unless, as sometimes happened, they managed to get themselves smuggled on board. In India there was a married quarters 'roll' on which sergeants were given priority, followed by corporals. Although restrictions on the number of women brought obvious financial advantages – the military did not have to spend more money on allowances and married quarters – such a stark gender imbalance in so confined a space as a barracks inevitably encouraged resentments, jealousies, infidelities and, occasionally, murder.

With officers the chief obstacles to marriage were more hierarchical and financial than numerical. One would be a fool, thought an ensign, to 'shackle' oneself to a 'doll' and have to bring up children on a junior officer's salary. An unwritten rule declared that 'subalterns must not marry; captains may marry; majors should marry; and colonels must marry'.[30] A corollary of the rule, as one colonel's wife pointed out, was that subalterns should not waste the time of unmarried girls by dancing with them; they should leave them to waltz with the older men who were in a position to marry them, 'the majors and captains or the very charming deputy commissioner'.[31] Lieutenant Amies, whom we have already encountered, fell in love with Margaret Douglas on his first home leave in 1921 but did not feel he had enough money even to 'declare' himself then or during his next leave; fortunately Margaret was still available in 1926 when he proposed by post.[32] By the time they married, at the end of that year in Bombay Cathedral, Amies was nearly thirty, the age when most officers were captains and when all were entitled to the marriage allowance. Yet their eligibility lasted only for a few years because, as one sharp-eyed memsahib noted, many men became increasingly 'Mess-bound' in their thirties, pampered by their servants and spoilt by the Mess and thus reluctant to exchange so comfortable a life for the uncertain pleasures of matrimony and domesticity.[33] Hesitant suitors might also be put off by the prospect of asking the colonel's permission, even though this was usually a formality,* and of introducing their fiancée to the Mess to make sure she was socially acceptable to senior colleagues and their wives.[34]

Early marriage for civil servants was discouraged almost as fervently as it was for soldiers. 'Don't marry till you have five years' service,' a senior civilian warned a Punjab griffin in 1890; it would be 'ruin, utter ruin to your prospects'. Griffins tended to agree with him, imparting the 'dreadful news' when a colleague became engaged and warning each other of a dismal matrimonial future. Young Civilians were 'generally totally spoilt by marriage', wrote one of them, J. W. Hose, in 1887. From being fairly well off and able to participate in most areas of Indian life, work or sport, they became frugal and reclusive, going nowhere without their wives; instead of riding a horse, they sat on a seat in a dog-cart; instead of playing serious sports such as cricket or tennis, they played badminton; and they went to church with depressing regularity.[35] ICS officers were fairly well paid, but they also had standards to keep up. When his fiancée, Geraldine, tried to hasten the date of their marriage in 1891, Lucas King, who was then thirty-four, pleaded his 'impecuniosity'. Not only would she have to bring from

* Such permission is still required in the Indian Army today.

England her trousseau, plate and crockery, together with a saddle and a piano, but he would need to provide a dog-cart, at least three horses plus a dining-room table and some other furniture for their house.[36]

In spite of the impediments, early marriages in the ICS did sometimes occur, and not always to the 'utter ruin' of the husband's prospects. Henry Cotton rose to become chief commissioner of Assam in 1896 even though at the age of twenty-one he had married a teenage Irish girl whom the photographer Julia Margaret Cameron had found begging with her mother on Putney Heath. It was more common for civil service probationers to become engaged while still in England and then to wait a few years before they married. Sometimes the delay might be enforced by parental disapproval: hoping that his son would find a more suitable bride in Calcutta, John Beames's father extracted a promise from him that he and his fiancée, Ellen, would wait two years without seeing each other before they married. (His ploy failed.) Others delayed their marriages until they had earned some promotion and saved enough money – or until they received financial support from one of their relations. Maurice Hayward could afford to marry in his mid-twenties only because his future mother-in-law, a widow, gave him the money. And Lucas King did not really have to fret about the cost of his wedding and his future domesticity: Geraldine's brother was Alfred Harmsworth (the future founder of the *Daily Mail*), who paid for her trousseau and the piano, and later gave her an extremely generous allowance.[37]

For those without financial assistance, there was nothing to be done except wait in India, write letters and hope for the best. Engagements often lasted four or five years – sometimes without a single leave during that time when the pair could meet – and towards the end they would become fraught with anxieties, about the wedding day, about the couple's feelings for each other, about how the girl would adapt to the realities of India and her husband's commitment to his work. 'I quite dread your being depressed by the monotony of India', wrote Walter Ritchie to his fiancée, Augusta, in 1845, three years after he had last seen her, a monotony 'which I, being interested in my labours, have never found disagreeable'.[38]

Even in Britain young people in the eighteenth and nineteenth centuries got engaged without knowing very much about their future partner. In India the situation was exacerbated by distance and by the extreme slowness of communications: a man writing to his fiancée from Calcutta at Christmas 1795 might not receive a loving reply before 1797. Even in the twentieth century men working in India sometimes felt that they did not know a girl well enough to propose face to face and decided it would be less awkward to do so later on by airmail or by telegram. Philip Martyn ICS met his future wife, Margaret, in Manchester in 1936, saw her twice more that summer before he returned to Bengal, proposed to her by letter six months later and, two and a half years after that, announced his intention to marry her in England and return with her to India.[39]

Perhaps the oddest engagement in a pretty rum catalogue was that of Maurice Zinkin, one of the last and cleverest members of the ICS (he got a triple first at Cambridge). At his university in 1936 he had a single meeting with his future wife, Taya, who corresponded with him over the following nine years under the impression that he was 'the handsome six-footer' she had met on the River Cam rather than his 'shy companion'. For people who had only met once, their letters were certainly intimate: in 1942 he told her that he was 'a snob' about whom he went to bed with because it was 'very sordid to sleep with somebody one can neither talk to the following morning nor introduce to one's friends the next evening'. Perhaps this put her off. At any rate they both became engaged to other people and then got simultaneously disengaged from them. As if it were the most logical thing in the world, Maurice then proposed by post from India and Taya accepted by post from America even though 'ten thousand miles and nine years separated us'.[40]

As far as one can judge, most of the long and hazardous engagements had an appropriately happy ending. Yet some inevitably went wrong. The betrothed of Henry Middleton Rogers decided in the end to stay in England to become in 1874 the second wife of the 10th Duke of St Albans. Such an act of decisiveness at least spared the girl the trauma of the voyage to India, the danger of falling for someone attractive on board ship, and the risk of an unhappy meeting on the quayside when, after so many years apart, the couple realized that they no longer found each other appealing. In the 1780s a Major Burn proposed by letter to a Miss Kearman, whom he had known many years earlier in Ireland, and on her acceptance sent her money for the journey. She duly arrived to find that the major, away on campaign, had asked his friend

Colonel Watson to look after her in his absence. The colonel duly did so but, according to Hickey, 'became so deeply enamoured of the Major's intended as to render him quite miserable'. As Miss Kearman returned 'the Colonel's passion', he felt obliged to confess all to the major, who, instead of following the custom of the time and challenging his friend to a duel, said that no 'consideration upon earth [would] unite himself to so errant a jilt' and that the colonel was 'heartily welcome to the capricious lady'.[41]

A fortunate minority of British men found British wives in India, often daughters of senior officers and officials. Given the gender imbalance, there was inevitably a lot of competition for the daughter of a general or a lieutenant-governor but, unless the father rebuffed all suitors, somebody had to win. ADCs, lounging about Government House with nothing much to do except organize parties, were especially well placed. When Lord Minto was viceroy (1905–10), his daughter Lady Eileen Elliot was keen to marry one of her father's ADCs, but for snobbish reasons her mother disapproved of the match – the man was a subaltern in the Deccan Horse – and she eventually married another ADC who was in the Grenadier Guards and more socially acceptable: Lord Francis Scott, a younger son of the Duke of Buccleuch, who was a neighbour of the Mintos in the Borders.[42] Junior Civilians in the secretariats had a similar advantage because they were bound to mix socially with the families of lieutenant-governors and other senior officials, meeting them at dances and picnics and tennis matches. They certainly had the upper hand over jungle wallahs or colleagues working as subdivisional officers in the mofussil. William Mackworth Young was one of several Civilians who married the daughter of a lieutenant-governor and who, twenty or thirty years later, occupied the same post (or a comparable one) – in this case the Punjab.

It was common to marry within one's service. Several officers in the Royal Engineers married the daughters of older officers in the Royal Engineers.[43] Frederick Currie, a Civilian and the last chairman of the East India Company, had twelve children from three wives, all of them daughters of civil servants. Yet such marriages were more the result of opportunity and circumstance than of snobbery and superior feelings of exclusivity. Several Civilians found wives in the business community of Kanpur: Philip Hutchins married a girl whose father owned a sugar factory.[44] Business families may in fact have been more exclusive than

Captain Wordsworth's ill-fated ship, the *Earl of Abergavenny*, sank on its way to India in 1805.

The hazards of landing at Madras, early nineteenth century.

Steaming to India through the Suez Canal.

CALCUTTA.
THE ESPLANADE.

Calcutta:
Government House
and the Esplanade,
early nineteenth
century.

Calcutta: Old Court House Street, with
St Andrew's Church at its end.

The Residency,
Bangalore, as it
was in 1922.

The Mall at Simla: social centre of the summer Raj.

Christ Church, Lucknow, built in 1860 as a memorial to the victims of 1857–8.

Bombay's Victoria Terminus (1878–87), which looked to some people more like a cathedral than a railway station.

James Skinner (1778–1841),
British-Indian cavalryman and
founder of Skinner's Horse.

Richard Wellesley, expansionist
and governor-general from
1798 to 1805.

Charles Trevelyan as governor of
Madras (1859–60).

James Rivett-Carnac as governor of
Bombay (1838–41).

Lockwood Kipling, sculptor and
craftsman, with his son Rudyard
in Lahore in 1883.

John Beames ICS as an irreverent
griffin in Calcutta, 1858.

Alfred Lyall, lieutenant-governor
of the North-Western Provinces
(1882–7).

Harcourt Butler, governor
of both Burma and the
United Provinces (1915–27).

THE MILITARY LIFE

19th Lancers: officers and men, 1874.

General Roberts (commander-in-chief, India, 1885–93) with his staff.

Sitting down to tiffin: officers of the 40th Pathans near Quetta, 1894.

Horns on the wall, silver on the sideboard, spears on the mantelpiece: a regimental Mess in Ambala, 1909.

'Daily Means of Occupation and Amusement' (1863): barracks life and the attempt to combat boredom.

Emily Eden (1797–1869), traveller, writer and sister of the governor-general, Lord Auckland.

Begum Johnson (*c.* 1726–1812, *née* Frances Croke), the much-married matriarch of Calcutta.

Viceregal wives: Charlotte Canning (1817–61), painter and botanist (*left*), and Hariot Dufferin (1843–1936), pioneer of medical care for Indian women.

The district officer on tour: J. J. Cotton in Madras, early twentieth century.

'Farewell to Waltair' (Madras): the district officer and his family pose
with British and Indian subordinates, 1920s.

RAILWAYS

The railway engineer and his staff at Guntakal Station (Madras), early twentieth century.

An inspection carriage on the Madras and Southern Mahratta Railway, early twentieth century.

Bridge-building on the Godaveri, *c.* 1900.

BURMA

The conservator of forests on tour, early twentieth century.

Jungle wallah with his elephants.

'The way we learn Burmese'.

The elegant west front, *c.* 1930.

Servant and
hunting trophies
in the hall.

Lady Stokes
having tea on
the verandah.

The Residency at Rajkot (Kathiawar) in the 1920s.

British women and Indian servants on a houseboat in Kashmir.

A jungle wallah's Burmese home.

Baba with
dandy-wallahs,
c. 1900.

Bathtime with ayah.

(*Above*) Chota sahib with syces; (*below*) chota sahibs with their dogs.

GETTING MARRIED

The wedding of Charles
Watson ICS and Phyllis
Field, Government House,
Bombay, 1912.

Pamela Edith Condon's
marriage to Roy Urquhart
in 1939, after a shipboard
romance on the way out to
India. Five years later,
Urquhart led the parachute
drop on Arnhem.

The Mughal emperor Shah Alam II granting revenue collection rights in Bengal to Robert Clive and the East India Company, 1765.

Major William Palmer and his Indian family (1785), by Johann Zoffany.

PICNICS AND OUTINGS

Wesleyan
missionaries with
bicycles at a picnic
near Bangalore,
c. 1900.

Off for the
evening drive,
1906.

Lounging around,
al fresco.

A tea party in
Calcutta, 1890.

British and Indian
members of the Nilgiri
Ladies Club, c. 1930.

A purdah picnic of the
Nilgiri Ladies Club.
Hugo the spaniel is the
only male present.

Games weeks at
Naini Tal, summer
capital of the
United Provinces:
(*top*) a regatta
(1907) and
(*below*) a cricket
match (1890).

Colonel
Cotterell
putting.

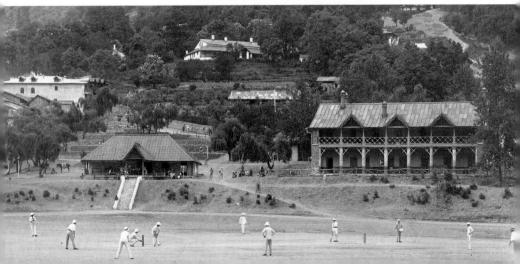

Charles Watson ICS
with servants, dogs and
polo ponies, *c.* 1908.

Polo players in Burma,
early 1920s.

Officers gathered for the
Inter-regimental Polo
Tournament at Meerut
in 1899. Winston
Churchill of the 4th
Hussars is standing
second from right.

Lepidopterists in
Burma, with
elephants and
butterfly nets, late
nineteenth century.

Fishing party on
the River Cubbany
(Madras), *c.* 1900.

Shooting snipe
in Burma, late
nineteenth
century.

The Ooty Hunt meets before going hunting for jackals, *c*. 1930.

Pig-stickers (or hog-hunters) and their boar, early twentieth century.

A lady hunter and her blackbuck, early twentieth century.

Monuments of the eighteenth-century British, South Park
Street Cemetery, Calcutta.

Remains of the Raj: a bungalow in Barrackpore in 2016.

those higher up in the social rankings. They were after all rooted to a certain place, to Kanpur say, or Calcutta, in a way that Civilians and army officers obviously were not. Many girls from these backgrounds understandably preferred to remain near their families rather than follow husbands from one station or cantonment to another. Rumer Godden, the novelist, was one of four sisters brought up in Bengal who all married businessmen in Calcutta. Rumer's own marriage, unlike her sisters', was a disaster, her husband Laurence being a 'cheerful Philistine' who fell asleep in concerts and thought Omar Khayyam was a curry. According to one of their friends, Laurence was also 'completely sports-mad' while Rumer 'didn't know a golf ball from a tennis ball'. He was also financially idiotic. They got divorced in 1948.[45]

Some British men met their future wives on board ship. In 1938 Roy Urquhart, an army officer aged thirty-six, was on his way to the north-west frontier to rejoin his regiment, the Highland Light Infantry, when he found himself playing deck games with the twenty-year-old Pamela Edith Condon.[46] They married the following year in India, a few years before Urquhart, by now a major-general, led the parachute drop on Arnhem, an exploit that earned him further fame when he was played by Sean Connery in the film *A Bridge Too Far*. Other men were lucky enough to meet in India and later marry the relative of a friend, a girl who had come out to visit a brother or to chaperone a sister about to marry a planter or a forestry official.

Yet these people were always in a minority. Most officers and officials had to wait until their first furlough, their first return to Britain, before they had a good chance of finding a wife. By that time they were thirty years of age and often feeling what one IMS officer called 'the pangs of sexual starvation'. After years in a remote station, some were so desperate that, as Emily Eden noted, they proposed to 'the very first girl' they met. On his voyage west the Civilian John Maynard encountered his future wife in Egypt and proposed to her in Venice, behind a pillar in St Mark's, before he had even got home. The policeman Bill Tydd waited till he had got to Edinburgh and then proposed to a girl under an arch of the Forth Bridge.[47]

Yet most courtships, at least in the Victorian era, were more methodical and less romantic than these. For many men, sex and love were lower priorities than 'suitability' and 'character' and whether a woman could be considered 'well fitted to adorn an Indian home'. George

Campbell, a future lieutenant-governor of Bengal, thought that on the whole it would be advantageous to 'provide' himself with a mate, though on furlough he spent less time looking for one than writing books and reading for the Bar. John Lawrence, the only Civilian ever to become viceroy, embarked on his furlough with the intention of finding a woman of good health, good temper and good sense. He had no ambitions for a romantic attachment – he referred to his still-imaginary future wife as 'the calamity' – and diligently sought 'good sense' first in Bath and then, having failed to find her there, in Donegal, where he succeeded. When George Partridge, a Madras Civilian born in Devon in 1865, started looking for a wife in his forties, he set off on the quest not because he wanted a companion in India but because he required a chatelaine for the small estate he had bought for his retirement in Devonshire. At Ooty one year he had been so taken by the charms of two married sisters that on his next furlough he went to their family home in northern Ireland and persuaded one of their siblings to marry him.[48]

Sometimes a wedding could be arranged quickly and celebrated on home ground. More often, even when engagements were made face to face in Britain, preparations were done intercontinentally. The man went back to his work in India, and his fiancée followed him, generally with a chaperone, months – or often years – later. Some parents opposed to the marriage took advantage of this interval to attempt to persuade their daughters to change their minds. The mother of Gwendolyn Prideaux tried to put her daughter off by telling her about all the unpleasant insects she would find in India; Gwendolyn disregarded the warnings and, after a two-year engagement, sailed to India in 1909 to marry Reginald Gadsby in Bombay Cathedral.[49] Even with maternal co-operation, there was a lot to organize for a girl about to undertake three very big adventures: marriage to a man she hardly knew, life on a continent she may never have visited, and the beginning, in difficult conditions, of many years of motherhood. Geraldine Harmsworth did her best to prepare herself by taking riding lessons and reading Kipling: her bossy fiancé, Lucas King, had told her that she would have to ride well if she was going to be a 'burra memsahib', and he had recommended *Plain Tales from the Hills* because it was 'delicious reading' and would give her 'a capital idea of Indian life'. Geraldine was more independent with her choice of items for her trousseau. The figure '36' must have had some fascination for her because she bought thirty-six camisoles, thirty-six nightdresses and thirty-six 'combinations' (an all-in-one vest and knickers).[50]

Weddings could take place anywhere from Karachi to Rangoon, but after 1869 the most common venue was Bombay, which possessed two cathedrals and almost all the relevant chapels, kirks and churches. Every Friday, recalled one local businessman, 'The voice that breathed o'er Eden' could be heard 'from morn to evening as the newest batch of brides was wedded' at the Anglican Cathedral.[51] Bombay was the favoured spot because, even if the groom lived in Kanpur or Madras, it was considered preferable for the girl to get married as soon as she reached India, and after Bombay to enjoy a brief honeymoon – sometimes in Agra, visiting the Taj Mahal – before travelling to her husband's station. Like many other women, Phyllis Field was married straight 'off the ship' in Bombay. She had met Charles Watson ICS in 1910 at St Moritz, where her mother took her for winter sports and where she became part of a bobsleigh team driven down the snow run by the German crown prince, known as 'Little Willy'. She was at the time twenty-three; Watson was thirty-five and on leave from his post as political and judicial secretary of the Bombay government. In London a few weeks later, he put on a silk top hat, took her to Chelsea to see Wren's chapel in the Royal Hospital and proposed to her in a hansom cab afterwards. For reasons unknown, they then had to wait two years before Phyllis sailed to Bombay; she was married the day of her arrival at All Saints Church and, thanks to her husband's position, had the wedding reception at Government House on Malabar Point.[52]

The pattern for Bombay weddings was followed over four generations. In 1929 Laurence Fleming's mother was also married 'off the ship' in the city. She arrived on the morning of her wedding day on a Lloyd Triestino boat from Genoa and was met on board ship by her fiancé, who worked for the Assam and Burmah Oil Companies; he had reached the city after 2,000 miles of train journeys. After disembarking, the bride spent the morning at the hairdresser's and a shoe shop – her silver kid shoes had been ruined during the voyage – before lunching with a few friends at the Yacht Club. The wedding took place in the afternoon at the Church of Scotland in Waudby Road, following which the newly married couple moved to the Taj Hotel, where they gave a dinner for their wedding guests and danced to the music of Cherpino's

Broadway Follies, who were in town at the time. The next day they set off for their honeymoon in Pachmarhi, the chief hill station of the Central Provinces.[53]

Few people left records of wedding nights and honeymoons. Some of those who did left no doubt – even implicitly – how difficult and sometimes disastrous these could be. Fanny Maxwell's Indian honeymoon consisted of accompanying her husband, an ICS officer, on a working tour of his district at the beginning of the hot weather. Her diary does not describe the couple's physical relationship, but curt references to 'cross husband' and entries no more romantic than 'usual number of meals, nothing else worth chronicling' or 'I have not room to describe my feelings' do not suggest that it was an idyll.[54] Mary Collyer had a Scottish honeymoon with her much older husband, the engineer Jack Shaw Stewart, but it was clearly such a failure that she refused afterwards to go with him to India, where her mother had died of cholera when she was a baby. She remained in Britain for six months and only joined her husband because her father took her to Marseille and forcibly put her on the steamer, 'accompanied by her maid Knowles'.[55] One man who bravely recorded in Stendhalian terms the 'fiasco' of his wedding night was Roger Pearce, who belonged to the last batch of British ICS officers in Sind. After a year's separation on different continents, his bride, Joan, arrived in Karachi, met a lot of strangers, got married the same day and spent her wedding night at a hotel where at breakfast next morning the other guests 'were doubtless imagining a night passed full of bliss and passion'. Alas it had not happened. As her husband sadly recalled, 'Two virgins meeting on their wedding night' had been 'very tired, overwrought, unsure' – and 'unskilled too'. Luckily things improved the next day when they moved to a cabin on a bay north of Karachi, a place where they could sleep, swim, lie in the sun and make love.[56]

We cannot know how often impotence was a wedding-night problem, though we might guess it was unusual for the husband also to be virginal. Yet even if the sexual dimension worked from the start, there were many other sides of the relationship that were unknown, untested and potential marriage-wreckers. Rumer Godden was not the only intellectual to marry the sort of man who disliked concerts and had never heard of Omar Khayyam. Edyth Gubbins was a passionate Wagnerian and lover of Mughal architecture who discovered she had married an army captain who thought the Taj Mahal was 'a hideous monstrosity' and whose chief interest was shooting and recording the numbers and species of birds he had killed.[57] One problem was the fact that most couples had hardly had any time to get to know each other before they were married. Another snag was the ignorance of older husbands, set in their ways after years in the Mess or the jungle or the civil station, who had had no tutoring in understanding their young wives' needs. 'Stalky' Dunsterville, who married on his thirty-second birthday, was engagingly frank about his shortcomings in this respect. After referring to his wedding in Bishopsteignton, his brief honeymoon in Devonshire, and the long voyage to Bombay, he recognized that this had been 'rather a rough start in life for my wife', which had perhaps been 'made rougher by the fact that I was not at all cut out for the rôle of the kind, thoughtful, protecting husband'. Matters did not improve after they reached the port. During the train journey from Bombay to Peshawar, 'my wife was rather wishing she had never come to India'.[58]

A third drawback, common to most professions in India but especially true of the military, was the custom of transferring employees, often every couple of years, so that wives could seldom feel they had settled down in a place long enough to have a family home and plan a garden. Dunsterville and his wife had to set up house five times in the first two years of their marriage, a process of upheaval that prompted Mrs Dunsterville to write 'Disillusionment', a newspaper article contrasting the expectations of a bride in India with the reality of her life there. The military was invariably unsentimental about the movements of married couples. After his honeymoon Captain John Prendergast went back to his fort on the Khyber, while his wife, Peggy, began married life by herself in a flat in Peshawar. The Gurkha officer Robert Bristow had a similar experience, returning after his wedding to his battalion at 'monastic' Razmak and leaving his wife in a hotel in Murree. In his twenty-nine years in India Bristow lived in fifteen 'peacetime' stations, not counting army courses and summer leaves in hill stations.[59]

In addition to the other shocks – marriage, sex, sea voyage, strange land and usually pregnancy – a new wife had to begin married life in a home which very seldom possessed the amenities she had known in Britain. Towards the end of her time in India, Alice Hayward may have lived rather grandly in Bombay, where her husband was a High Court judge, but at the beginning (1892) the future Lady Hayward had to live in a bungalow where the floors were made of cow dung (covered in date matting) and where, on first arrival, she found a cobra lying outside the door.[60] Other wives might find nicer bungalows but in unpleasant and dangerous places. Jacobabad in Sind had one of the worst climates in India, a place which in the nineteenth century took a terrible toll on the lives of wives and children. Even though the risks were reduced in the following century, the Civilian Roger Pearce (who liked it) knew that he 'would have courted marital disaster' if he had extended his term there.[61]

In his story 'By Word of Mouth' Kipling described India as 'a delightful country for married folk who are wrapped up in one another. They can live absolutely alone and without interruption.' This was doubtless very true, though one wonders how many couples Kipling saw – apart from his parents – where the folk really were 'wrapped up in one another'. And for those who were not, India must have been a terrible place. In the mofussil, in jungles or canal homes or remote stations, a husband and wife would be more dependent on each other than they would ever need to be in the cities or in Britain. And unless one of them died, they were probably stuck with one another for a very long time in an extremely difficult environment.

The alternative was divorce, which could not take place just because spouses got bored of each other, or separation, which could be done gradually and quite discreetly, especially if the children were at schools in Britain and needing the presence of their mother. Yet separations could be handled, in India as anywhere else, quite brutally. In 1890 Alexandra Campbell, the daughter of an army officer, married Reginald Warneford, a railway engineer who had rescued her when the ponies of her trap had bolted. Yet after a few years she clearly felt she could have 'done better' for herself. Although she stayed with him long enough to produce a son and four daughters, she resented his profession, his attachment to the railways, and his fondness for his Indian employees. Eventually she left him, without a note or an explanation, and took their daughters to live with her parents in Darjeeling. After waiting a few months for Reginald to drink himself to death in the Plains, she married an army officer and sent her son Rex to live with her former father-in-law in England.*[62]

* Rex later joined the RAF and won the VC in 1915 before he was killed in an air accident over France.

Most couples, however, did not separate. They felt it would be too difficult to do so, too embarrassing, too unsettling for their children, their relations and their professions in India. It was easier, really, just to keep plugging on. Alfred Lyall was one of numerous Civilians who realized he had made a mistake on his first furlough, in his case when in 1863 he married a Dutch girl called Cora Cloete. 'The way to get on with a male Lyall,' he reminded one of his sisters, was 'to leave him a good deal alone'. Yet this was obviously not a policy poor Cora could pursue: she was forced to follow him around, with their growing family, as Alfred was promoted from the North-Western Provinces to the Central Provinces, to Calcutta and Simla, to Rajputana, to Calcutta and Simla again, and finally back to where he started, in the NWP as lieutenant-governor. Soon after the birth of his elder son, Lyall said that he did not want to be 'hampered' by any more children, partly because he wished to concentrate on his work but also because he was 'generally averse to babies and their appurtenances'. Even though he was presumably at least partly to blame for soon accumulating four children, he resented them and sometimes wished they did not exist, especially his daughter Sophy, whom he suspected of having 'very strong sexual instincts' and who embarrassed him by her blatant infatuation with his private secretary.

Yet his resentment was chiefly directed at his wife, whom he described in letters to his sisters as his 'misfortune'. Half his life, he moaned, had 'been wasted by one mistake': Cora was no help with his work and gave him no counsel or rest at times when a man needed them. He realized with bitterness but also with resignation that he would never have 'a pleasant home' with her in India or afterwards. After fifteen years of marriage he was wishing she would go to England and look after the children there, but the more he tried to persaude her, 'the more she [was] disposed to hold tight'. Cora did indeed stick it out till the end, enjoying 'her rank and dignities' as a lieutenant-governor's wife in Naini Tal and Allahabad, leaving India with him for good in 1887, and living with him in South Kensington until his death in 1911.[63]

Alfred Lyall was one of several lieutenant-governors of the North-Western (later known as United) Provinces who were very unhappily married. When John Hewett was appointed to the post in 1907, his separated wife insisted on returning to him to enjoy being 'her ladyship', though they lived in different wings of Naini Tal's Government

House and seldom spoke to each other. They were succeeded by James Meston, who had a sick wife unable to control her jealousy, and then by Harcourt Butler, whose wife, Florence, apparently abandoned him – at least temporarily – as they came out of church on their wedding day; she had rejected his first wedding proposal and was clearly regretting that she had changed her mind. Many years later, she gave an order to her husband's under-secretary: 'Mr Lupton, never leave me in the room with Harcourt.' Poor Butler, a highly sexed man with a salacious sense of humour, confessed to the same subordinate that, although he and his wife had been married for many years, they had not lived together for more than eight days. One of the cleverest and most erudite of British officials, he drank himself slowly to a premature death in 1938. Florence did not attend his memorial service.[64]

Few British marriages in India ended in divorce, but many ended early in death, which led to a good deal of rapid remarrying. In the army second and further marriages were partly a consequence of age gaps – a teenage girl from an orphanage having married a much older sergeant – but also a result of financial imperatives. Such considerations did not greatly affect the widows of ICS officers, who received a good pension whatever age or rank their husbands had attained, or widows of other officials, who were likewise looked after. But the widows of private soldiers enjoyed no such security. Within three months of the deaths of their husbands, they were struck 'off the strength' of the regiment and needed to find somewhere to live and something to live on. The mortality rate among soldiers was so high – from disease and drink more than from death in battle – that anxiety was almost a constant. Fortunately, the gender imbalance being what it was, a widow could usually – unless she had made herself obnoxious to everyone – find herself a replacement before the three months were over. Marianne Postans, the wife of a captain in Bombay, recorded in the 1830s an incident when, within an hour of a gunner's death from fever in a hospital, his widow had received three offers of marriage, and within a week she remarried. The process was repeated twice more, after similar intervals, and might presumably have continued indefinitely if the woman herself had not died, still at a young age.[65]

In 1846 a British army ended the First Sikh War with a victory at Sobraon on the banks of the River Sutlej. Yet the casualty rate was high, creating fourteen or fifteen widows in one dragoon regiment.

Several of these women, according to Sergeant Pearman, had been married three or four times already, and most of them were able to re-marry within a month, almost immediately after their 'return to quarters'; when one of them married Sergeant Gooderson of H Troop, she was embarking on her sixth marriage.[66] Mrs Postans criticized the 'heartless indifference' of the way such women talked 'of the probable fate of their husbands', but she also understood the 'temptations, restraints and miseries' to which they were subjected in their daily lives.[67] If, as was alleged, some of them had lined up potential replace-ments before their husbands were in any obvious danger, this might be regarded as sensible rather than heartless, especially if the age gap was such that even in the normal course of events their spouses would pre-decease them by two or three decades. In any case such things did not only happen in their particular class. William Hickey was unusually and unfairly censorious when he criticized Sir Arthur Heselrige's second wife – 'a wild and giddy girl of fifteen' whom he had married in his forties – for being a 'wanton widow' when, after Heselrige had died from 'bilious fever', she 'consoled herself in the arms of a handsome young lieutenant of infantry . . . who became her second husband'.[68]

Soldiers' wives may have been the most needy, but they were not of course the only widows who wanted to remarry and stay in India. If a woman had been away for many years and had got used to large houses, lots of servants and summers in the Hills, then she might find it more convenient and less disruptive to seek a bachelor or a widower still at work on the Subcontinent than to go home alone and live by herself (at least to start with) in Eastbourne or Cheltenham. Maurice Hayward observed how one widow, the sister of a Colonel Grantham, targeted the district judge of Poona, William Henry Crowe, ingratiated herself by pruning the creepers on his bungalow and, 'in spite of wearing bloomers to the scandal of Poona', succeeded in becoming Mrs Crowe.[69]

The eighteenth century witnessed rather more colourful and 'scan-dalous' examples of remarriage. In 1709 Katherine Cooke, 'a most beautiful lady not exceeding thirteen or fourteen years of age', was obliged by her parents to marry the chief of the factory at Karwar, south of Bombay, a Company official 'in years' and apparently 'deformed'. Within two years her husband died, and she married a younger, more suitable factor. Before another year was over he had been killed at sea by a cannonball fired by Maratha 'pirates', who then boarded her ship and captured this twice-widowed and heavily pregnant teenager. After she had been rescued, she married yet another Company official, who was also killed in a fight with 'natives', this time in southern India, after which – by now in her mid-twenties – she became the mistress of the commodore of a British squadron who took her home to England.[70]

The most famous remarried widow in British Indian history was Frances Croke, who was born in the south at Fort St David in 1728. The daughter of a civil servant of the EIC, she became Mrs Templer at the age of fifteen, Mrs Altham at the age of twenty, and Mrs Watts also at the age of twenty (James Altham having died of smallpox twelve days after their wedding). Now living in Bengal, she had four children with William Watts and retired with him to England, but after his death in 1764 she realized that India was where she wanted to be. On returning to Calcutta she made the worst mistake of her life when, at the age of forty-six, she married the Rev. William Johnson, a smug and greedy chaplain sixteen years her junior. As death this time did not remove her husband, she had to do so herself, giving him a sizeable pension on condition that he went to England and did not return. Now known as Begum Johnson, Frances remained in Calcutta for another quarter of a century, a well-known hostess and much-loved figure. She died in her eighties in 1812, the year that her grandson, the second Lord Liverpool, became prime minister of Great Britain.[71]

British men might have been as keen to remarry as British women, but the ratio of the sexes gave them fewer opportunities to do so, certainly among the rank and file of the army. In Britain it was generally accepted that a man should wait at least a year after his wife's death before he remarried, but such restrictions were rarely observed in India. Three months or so seem to have been a reasonable time limit, even for senior officials and army officers. A shorter period managed to outrage William Hickey, himself no slouch when it came to promiscuous and indecorous behaviour. After Mary Keighley's death in the 1780s, her husband, who was head of the Company's factory at Cossimbazaar, 'seemed inconsolable', yet 'at the end of a fortnight took unto himself another spouse, marrying a Miss Peach'. Bizarrely Hickey chiefly blamed the second wife, declaring that he could not conceive how any 'female possessing a particle of feeling could have consented to unite herself to a man who had been only a widower a few days'.[72]

Hickey did not live long enough to witness the marital career of George Jenkin Waters, a judge in the south who became known as 'the Bluebeard of the civil service' after burying four wives in the decade from 1823, the first two honoured by a large mausoleum in Chittoor. Later he slowed down. He did not bury his fifth wife until 1857 and then delayed until 1871 before marrying his sixth. He himself died at Brighton in 1882 at the age of ninety.[73]

MIXED MARRIAGES

Whatever criticism the custom provoked, British men continued to marry Indian, Burmese and Eurasian women until the end of the Raj and beyond. In smaller numbers British women also married Indian men. As we have noted, a few senior Company officials married aristocratic Indian girls, in Hyderabad and elsewhere, at the end of the eighteenth century, and a hundred years later officials in Burma were marrying their mistresses. Yet a good deal of intermarriage took place at other times and in other places.

Few sites in British India were more 'establishment' – to use a later word – than the Bengal Club in Calcutta, which was founded in 1827 at about the same time that the Garrick, the Reform and the Athenaeum clubs were set up in London. Yet a glance at the list of founder members suggests neither the snobbery – it includes bankers, boxwallahs and managing agents – nor the racial exclusivity normally associated with the place and the period. The mother of Colonel Taylor (born in 1790) was 'the daughter of an Indian rajah', and her son was married first to 'an East Indian lady' and then to two Englishwomen. General Richards, who died in 1861 at the age of eighty-three, may have been English by birth (though he never in his life returned to England), but he was married first to 'an Indian lady' (in fact she was Eurasian) and then to a woman described by the *Bengal Herald* as 'a native lady of the Jat tribe'.[74] A generation later, Judge Kemp, who joined the ICS in 1831, married an Indian woman, as did a number of other judges, especially in Burma, until Independence. Sir Henry Sheldon Pratt, who was chief justice in Rangoon, married Ma Win from Bassein in 1902, and together they produced five children. After his wife's death, near Maymyo in 1935, Pratt had her tomb inscribed with the words 'Far above Rubies'.[75]

Planters, policemen, missionaries and members of every other profession also married Indian and Burmese women. Often they chose tribal brides from the hills, girls unhampered by the inhibitions of caste or purdah. When Ernest Bradfield, the head of the Indian Medical Service, visited the Kulu Valley in 1937, he found that most of the British settlers in that part of the Himalayan foothills had married hill women. At Darjeeling in the same period, the Scottish manager of a tea garden, a widower in his sixties, married Jeti, a teenage girl from a local tribe who had worked for him as a tea-picker. Another admirer of tribal women was the remarkable Verrier Elwin, once described as 'the anthropologist who married his fieldwork'. In fact he did so twice, first with a Gond girl called Kosi and later with a Pardhan girl called Kachari; while living with them and their tribes he became recognized as an academic expert on tribal sexual behaviour.[76]

Such unions were not of course easily accepted. The tea manager was not permitted to take Jeti to lunch in the Planters' Club at Darjeeling. Verrier Elwin's mother told her son that with his 'brains and powers' he really couldn't 'go on as a cave man'.[77] The surgeon Owen Berkeley-Hill had had problems with his mother all his life and only went into the IMS to stop her nagging him. When stationed at the Secunderabad cantonment before the First World War he had an affair with a (female) punkah wallah, and he later married Karimbil Kunhimanny, a Tiyyan girl by caste, an event that 'incurred the displeasure' of many of his friends and family. It could not, however, incur the displeasure of his mother because he did not dare tell her until a few years before her death that he had an Indian wife and four children.[78]

British–Indian marriages might not ultimately affect a Civilian's career, but they remained frowned upon in the ICS until the closing years of the Raj. In the 1930s Michael Carritt was advised by his superiors 'in the most friendly and avuncular way' that it would do his career 'no good' if he married a girl from the Armenian community of the Bengali town of Asansol. In Agra in the same decade W. H. Pridmore received a less friendly warning from his very unsympathetic collector: he would be banished to a difficult and unpleasant district in the UP if he married a girl called Sybil who had a half-Indian mother and a father who was an Irish soldier.[79] Yet such disapproval seems to have melted away in the Second World War. Robert Dutch ICS had a comparatively easy ride when in 1946 he married a Bengali widow with three children.

British–Indian marriages naturally led to a great many children variously described as 'half-caste', Eurasian and (in the twentieth century) Anglo-Indian. In their turn the daughters of these unions often married British men, especially soldiers. At the beginning of the nineteenth century General James Innes in Madras had six Eurasian daughters, most of whom married British Army officers.[80] Such situations became less common over the years, but a few survived well into the era of mid-Victorian disapproval. In Calcutta on the eve of the Rebellion John Beames met General Birch's wife, whom he described as 'an aged half-caste of vast rotundity'.[81] One of her contemporaries was Frances Marsden, the daughter of an Irish major and his Indian bibi: she lost her first husband, Colonel Thomas Oliver, in Afghanistan in 1841, but by then she already had eight children by another British officer, Hugh Massy Wheeler, and a ninth one was on the way. As a Eurasian and an adulteress, she was obviously a scandalous figure in British society, but she and Wheeler married three months after Oliver's death. Hugh Wheeler later became a knight, a general and commander of the garrison at Kanpur, the town where he, Frances and the two daughters then with them were murdered in the Rebellion in June 1857.

It had been a 'common occurrence', wrote Captain Albert Hervey in the 1840s, for officers and Civilians to marry what he called 'Vepery Brahmins', 'half-caste' inhabitants of the Vepery district of Madras. 'Time was when officers of the Madras Army used to mix promiscuously with them.' Yet while he had known a few 'young care-for-nothing lads' who had been 'entrapped' by Eurasian girls, 'such things seldom happen now-a-days'. A few years after Hervey wrote, Alfred Lyall sensed potential entrapment when he arrived as a griffin in Calcutta in 1856. He was invited to a dance given by 'a young ladies' school', where the 'avowed purpose' was to get the girls married off with the inducement of a dowry of £200. Lyall was proud to be considered 'an eligible party' but relieved that he was not tempted by the girls (all 'more or less [with] a shade of colour') and that after passing 'the ordeal safely', he emerged 'as a free man'.[82]

Eurasian girls were seldom aimed at Old Etonian Haileyburians like Lyall. Many of them were brought up in military orphanages – either as orphans or as girls whose fathers had left India – from which they might emerge as soldiers' wives, nannies or governesses, and later on as nurses, midwives or typists. The marital success rate of these places was high. Between 1800 and 1818, 380 girls from the Lower Orphan School in Calcutta – mostly Eurasian, though probably a few of them were 'poor white' – married British men.[83] Some institutions continued to aim for the elite, but not usually with much success. In the 1870s the Kidderpore Orphanage in Calcutta invited all the new medical officers to an annual dance but, according to one of the guests, none of 'the dusky beauties' found a mate among the IMS.[84] The most promising territories were those places, such as Lucknow and Dinapur, that contained both a cantonment and a Eurasian/Anglo-Indian railway community. In 1945 Brigadier Packard noted how British soldiers stationed in them would be 'invited to dances and other social occasions' and that, 'despite official discouragement', some then 'married locally'. Older soldiers nearing the end of their service in India also married into the community. Private Richards recalled several men of his battalion who stayed on after doing a course of railway training and married Eurasian girls.[85]

It was widely agreed that the British-Indian 'mix' tended to produce attractive girls, but men and women from the British middle classes looked down on them for both snobbish and racial reasons, mocking their provincialism, their 'chee-chee' accents and the way (they said) that they smelled of garlic and cheap scent. The barrier between 'true caste' and 'half-caste' had become so rigid since the days of General Innes that Eurasian/Anglo-Indian girls went to desperate lengths to pretend that they were not at all Indian and that, if their skin was slightly darker than was normal in England, it was because they had a Spanish grandmother. Yet they seldom fooled a class of people well attuned to the nuances of class deception; apart from the problem with their voices, they were often over made-up, and sometimes they put on so much powder that, instead of becoming white, their faces went slightly mauve, especially in the shadows under their eyes.[86]

Occasionally the deception worked. Jimmie Simon, an English dancing teacher in Calcutta, recalled how British girls refused to perform in the same class as a pretty Anglo-Indian girl called Queenie Thomson, who 'used to whitewash herself from the waist up'. All her life 'Queenie' pretended that she was a native of Tasmania, though in fact she had been born in Bombay, the daughter of a Eurasian woman and a man said to have been a railway engineer from Darlington. It made no difference in the long run because she ended up as a celebrated actress in Hollywood with the name Merle Oberon. Nor did the 'half-caste' stigma affect the career of her Eurasian contemporary, Vivien Hartley, whose mother seems to have been partly Parsi. She also went to Hollywood and became famous as the actress Vivien Leigh.[87]

When King Edward VII requested the presence of Indian soldiers at his coronation in London in 1902, the viceroy Curzon was worried because, 'strange as it may seem, English women of the housemaid class, and even higher', were so attracted by Indian uniforms and physiques that they might offer themselves to these men.[88] Many other Britons believed – or affected to believe – that it was 'stranger' for English women to fall for Indian men than for Englishmen to be attracted by Indian women. M. M. Kaye, a novelist who spent much of her life in India, declared that, although she knew 'several very happy and successful marriages between Western men and Asian women – who make marvellous wives!', she had never come across 'one, the other way round, that [had] lasted'.[89] Probably this view reflects the society she lived in and a social life in the 'Roaring Twenties' that evolved around 'hilarious parties' and 'screamingly' funny japes in Simla, Delhi and Kashmir. A wider look at British–Indian unions suggests that those involving Indian men were at least as successful as the others.

There existed a long tradition of nawabs, rajas and maharajas having – or wishing to have – European women as wives or mistresses. In 1903 Curzon had felt the need to urge the Raja of Jind 'to resume conjugal relations' with his two Sikh wives, whom he had ignored since his marriage to the daughter of a European aeronaut, because it was his duty to produce a son and heir for his state.[90] Yet there was also a tradition of middle-class Indian–British marriages which did not have to contend with this type of problem. In 1892 Henry Beveridge visited an English woman in Bengal, 'alone in Murshidabad among the Mahomedans', contentedly married with ten children. She was 'very big and blonde', he noted, while her husband was 'insignificant looking' although 'well disposed' and 'an excellent billiard player'.[91]

Some such unions were of course unsuccessful. Memoirs of the last decades of the Raj tell tales of a Kutchi who had lured an English-woman into marriage with false promises, or a 'rascally Powindah money-lender' who had abducted a British woman and then refused to marry her.[92] Yet in his recollections of the period, the policeman Leslie Robins blamed the failures of unions he had witnessed on impossible English women who had got bored of their decent and honourable Indian husbands.[93] More memoirs, however, mention marriages that were both successful and 'socially acceptable' in a way that many unions 'the other way round' were not. The marriage between an Indian judge or doctor or Kashmiri pandit to an educated English girl was obviously a very different thing from a union between a Scottish planter and a plucking girl from his tea garden.

It created a very different future for the children too. Whereas the progeny of the tea garden would probably be consigned to an orphanage in the Hills and might with luck get a job on the railways, the children of the other marriages could aspire – at least in the twentieth century – to the same positions as their parents had gained. Born in 1891, Vivian Bose was Indian on his father's side – his grandfather was a High Court judge – and English on his mother's. He himself studied in England, at Dulwich and Cambridge, was called to the Bar in London and then returned to practise in India, where he married Irene, the daughter of John R. Mott, an American Christian leader and winner of the Nobel Peace Prize. After Independence Bose became a much-admired judge of the Indian Supreme Court. A generation later, Keith Roy, who had a Bengali father and an English mother, was educated in Leicester and London, joined the ICS in 1935, was a government under-secretary by 1947, worked for the States' Department in independent India, and subsequently became the managing director of an American pharmaceutical firm linked to Tata.[94] Mixed parentage was at last no longer a stigma.

ADULTERIES

In the spring of 1885 Lieutenant Hubert Du Cane, stationed at Rawalpindi with the Royal Artillery, informed his father that he had applied for three months' leave at Simla. The prospect did not enthuse him, however, because he had heard that the town's 'main occupations' were 'gambling, drinking and breaking the 7th Commandment ["Thou Shalt not Commit Adultery"], none of which presents any great attraction to me'.[95] Perhaps Du Cane was rather a prig, or perhaps he was trying to reassure his father, because in British India Simla was known as 'Capua', the Italian town famous for its perfumes and loose living in the early Roman Empire. Otherwise, how could a subaltern, sweltering in the Punjab in the hot weather, *not* want to go to Simla?

The hill station's reputation has traditionally been blamed on Kipling, but Du Cane's disapproval – and the Capuan comparison – preceded the publication of any of the writer's stories. The artillery officer blamed Simla's notoriety on the regime of Lord Lytton, a flirtatious viceroy of the 1870s who was suspected of having affairs with the wives of two of his ICS subordinates. In fact these women were not his lovers but those of two of his ADCs. One of them, Mabel Batten, was an unusual memsahib. After a childhood in India, she had studied music in Dresden and Italian in Florence and had then returned to India, where, at the age of nineteen, she had married George Batten, a forty-three-year-old Civilian. Within months of her marriage she was flirting with Edward, Prince of Wales, on his visit to Agra in 1876, but while the attraction was strong and mutual, a recent biographer of the future king thinks 'it was probably no more than a flirtation'.[96] At Simla the following year, the beautiful Mabel met one of Lytton's visiting friends, Wilfrid Scawen Blunt, a Tory radical who modelled himself on his wife's grandfather (Byron), but whose principal triumphs were philanderous rather than political or poetical. She confided in him at their first meeting, apparently telling him about her own love affairs and those of 'all Simla'. Whether or not the two of them were lovers in India, they certainly became so in the summer of 1880 when, on a trip to Goodwood Races, she stayed at his house in Sussex and left her door ajar at midnight. The next morning he felt like 'a god' and later believed he had been the only person to satisfy Mabel's 'nameless cravings'.[97] In fact he was not. In London, years after her husband's retirement, she enjoyed the most important relationship of her life, a very passionate love affair with the young lesbian writer Radclyffe Hall.

If Simla's reputation for amorous immorality was first suggested by the ambience of Lytton's court, it endured afterwards thanks to the writings of Rudyard Kipling, who spent parts of five summers there in the 1880s as a reporter for the *Civil & Military Gazette* in Lahore. The young writer was quite blatant about his search for characters and 'copy' for his stories, using one of his first afternoons in the town to lope alongside his mother's rickshaw, 'learning most of the scandal'.

Then he would spend his time talking – and above all listening – to anyone from whom he could acquire 'curious yarns' or 'goodish material'. From Isabella Burton, the effervescent lady who inspired his fictional Mrs Hauksbee, he gained 'half a hundred ideas and some stories'. Sometimes he did not need to listen but merely to observe, as in the case of Lady Edge, the wife of the chief justice of the Allahabad High Court, who 'was inclined to be naughty though much over forty'. According to Kipling, she gave 'herself away in double handfuls'.[98]

In his first book, *Departmental Ditties and Other Verses*, published when Kipling was twenty, half the verses in the 'Ditties' section have adultery as their main subject. In *Plain Tales from the Hills*, which came out two years later, marital infidelity is a recurring topic in the stories set in Simla, as it was subsequently in *The Story of the Gadsbys* and *Under the Deodars*. For someone who appears never to have committed adultery himself – or indeed to have had a love affair with anyone other than his wife – this is an interesting fixation. It certainly interested numerous critics who thought it reprehensible and irresponsible for someone to write about such 'flagrant immorality' in the summer capital of Queen Victoria's Indian Empire. Kipling seldom made concessions to his critics but he did deny that he thought all Simla life was frivolous or improper. In his preface to *Under the Deodars* (1888) he attempted 'to assure the ill-informed' that British India was 'not entirely inhabited by men and women playing tennis and breaking the Seventh Commandment' – an assurance that may have puzzled the ill-informed when they discovered that most of the stories in the book were precisely about such people (minus the tennis).[99]

In *Don Juan* Byron had quipped that 'adultery' was 'much more common when the climate's sultry'. Yet he had been contrasting the south of Europe with the north. In India the situation was reversed, at any rate for the British. The climate in Madras, observed one sardonic Civilian, 'runs to getting into the billiard room and taking off one's coat and calling for a succession of long drinks, but it emphatically does not run to Plain Tales from the Hills'. You could not have 'a Plain Tale' in so 'enervating' an atmosphere.[100] But 7,000 feet up in the Himalaya, surrounded by forests of pine and cedar, 'Plain Tales' behaviour was more appealing. Simla and other hill stations were romantic and hedonistic places, where the parties went on day after day, where the summer nights were warm enough for moonlit picnics, and where officials and their families from remote stations could relax in the company of their fellow countrymen. Bishop Welldon suggested that the men and women who went to Simla for their holidays were like 'people dancing under the shadow of a volcanic mountain'.[101] Perhaps they were. Perhaps that explains the frivolity of so much of their behaviour when they were there.

Most people who recorded their memories of Simla insisted that Kipling exaggerated and that a good majority of 'those little liaisons in the Hills were as harmless as you can think of'. When a young man in jodhpurs went 'doe-hacking' at Simla, it meant he was taking a girl for an innocent ride, not planning to do anything improper with the doe.[102] In 1909 Maud Diver published her book, *The Englishwoman in India*, with the purpose of refuting the idea that British women habitually misbehaved on the Subcontinent. Those who agreed with her liked to emphasize the practical difficulties of committing adultery in a country where privacy scarcely existed. It was sometimes said that the only safe place to do it was on a night train. Harcourt Butler thought that British society was so 'moral in act' because it lived in rooms with six doors, usually open, and servants padding about at all hours in bare feet. 'Illicit loves' were thus an impossibility, and the British reputation for having them was quite 'undeserved'.[103] Amorous governors and viceroys had the additional problems of ADCs who never left them alone. Lord Carmichael, the governor of Bengal during the First World War, tried to dodge them so that he could flirt with 'a very pretty maharani' in the garden of Government House, but even if he had succeeded he could not have achieved anything other than a tête-à-tête.[104]

Yet from Simla and other hill stations there is much evidence, not just from Kipling's sources and Mrs Batten's remarks to Blunt, that 'illicit loves' were common though perhaps not compulsory. In Simla's early days, recalled General Godfrey Pearse, who was born in 1827, 'there had been a few frisky young dames, and a few young fellows full of mischief', who used to have 'tender meetings' in jampans along 'those dark umbrageous pine-lined roads'.[105] Later the idea of the predatory 'grass widow' – a middle-aged woman spending the summer in a hill station while her husband was working in the Plains – became a widespread reality, even a sort of institution. The most notorious of such ladies acquired nicknames, widely circulated and laughed about, such as 'the Passionate Haystack' ('pretty doll-like girl . . . china blue eyes'), 'the Charpoy Cobra' ('languorous dark-eyed brunette . . . finger-nails as scarlet as her lips'), 'Bed-and-Breakfast', 'the Lilo', 'the Subaltern's Guide to Knowledge' and 'the Vice Queen', a woman who 'collected other ladies' husbands and cut a notch in her bedstead for every conquest. No one knew why the bedstead was still standing.' As in other places, sexual promiscuity in British India increased in war-time, and the Passionate Haystack was especially active in Karachi at the time of VE Day. M. M. Kaye blamed 'the pressures of war' for her affair with an officer who could not divorce his wife and marry her until 1945, when she was pregnant with their second child. Wartime India also seems to have had its share of officers 'missing, presumed dead', who returned to find their 'widows' consoling themselves in the arms of other men.[106]

John Masters, the Gurkha officer who became a novelist, was like Kipling a perceptive observer of society in hill stations. Grass widows, he maintained, were competing with each other and measuring their success not by comparative wit or beauty or intelligence but by their 'ability to annexe the most desirable man and hold on to him in the face of all competition'. What Masters found strange was that people behaved in a fashion which they might have got away with in a large city but could not possibly do so – unnoticed – in a hill station.

> Captain A. comes up to join his wife in Mussoorie for his month's leave. The station forms a wordless conspiracy never to let him know of the existence of Mr B., a resident official who has, they all know, spent most of his days and nights with Mrs A. for some weeks past, and will resume this practice as soon as Captain A. has returned to Sweattypore. And around Mrs C. there are wonderfully public manoeuvrings for po-sition; she has really given up any pretence of being monogamous. Her husband eventually cites sixteen co-respondents in his divorce suit.[107]

In his unpublished autobiography Harcourt Butler may have claimed that British society in India conducted itself with an almost unequalled sense of morality. Yet in his private correspondence as a governor he relished the details of scandals. Writing to an old friend in 1920, he salivated over a 'full-blooded scandal' in Simla that was heading for the divorce courts. A Mr and Mrs King were staying at Corstorphine's Hotel with their friend, a cavalry officer called Vikhary. As Mr King could not dance, he encouraged his friend to take his wife to balls, but he soon became suspicious at the lateness of their return from these parties. He therefore 'filled himself up with drink one night, went up to V's rooms and found his wife in bed with him. Laid out V with a poker (not seriously), woke the hotel up to call witnesses . . .' After such a noisy melodrama, the three of them quickly fled Simla. Butler was chortling with delight. 'As soon as I got the news, I wired back, "the poker pokered".' He was chortling again when he heard that Vikhary had been sent to the Remount Department: the appointment suggested that the army had a sense of humour.[108]

Neither Kipling nor Masters suggested that adultery only took place in hill stations. Intrigues, passions and tragedies could happen anywhere, even in enervating Madras. Men and women agonized over the same dilemmas, faced the same kinds of choices, and made the same sorts of mistakes all over India – and beyond. One district officer, a man with nine children, was seduced by a predatory 'Becky Sharp' while his wife and family were in England; the novelist Flora Annie Steel, a very forceful lady, realized that he was having a nervous breakdown and so marched into his bungalow, took up residence inside it, and eventually forced poor 'Becky' to retire and give birth to her lover's baby in a place specially prepared for her.[109] Another mature DO, a collector of Kanpur in the late nineteenth century, was not so lucky. He married a sergeant-major's daughter and, in the hope of turning her into a burra memsahib, sent her to England to learn manners. The scheme did not work. On her return she was still, apparently, 'coarse and rude', 'behaved very badly' and had an affair with a manager of the Elgin Mills; the DO then took to drink and died of alcoholism, and his wife died in the same week, probably from a mismanaged abortion.[110] Similar tragedies might also happen in the army, especially if a middle-aged officer married a much younger woman who refused to take part in station life. In 1905 Major Cooper of a Punjabi regiment shot himself because he was unable to control a young wife whose behaviour with 'a bad lot' was so 'unseemly' that she had been thrown out of hotels in Mussoorie. A few years later, when serving in Africa, Captain Manners killed himself after learning of his wife's infidelity in India.[111]

Romantic disappointment very nearly claimed the life of Frederick Lugard too, encouraging the army officer to undertake desperate adventures in a quest, according to his biographer, 'for excitement and danger and, if possible, death in some distant place'. In the 1880s he had made a good start to his career in India, serving in the Afghan and Burmese campaigns, but then he fell in love with a remarried divorcée, a veteran femme fatale, who jilted him. On hearing that she had been badly injured in a coach accident in Lucknow, he dashed from Burma to see her, only to discover that she had sailed for England; rushing after her again, he arrived home only to find that she had quite recovered and was 'bestowing her affections elsewhere'. Thinking he would go mad, the highly strung Lugard then fled to Africa, risking his life in reckless attacks against Arab slavers before he was badly wounded near Lake Nyasa.[112] He recovered to become one of the great 'empire-builders' and in due course the founder, for good or ill, of a united Nigeria.

Such cases are not of course representative of the behaviour of British women in India. Few of these were femmes fatales, Becky Sharps or Passionate Haystacks. Many were unhappy with their marriages – and the strains that India put on their relationships – but very few subjected themselves to the stress and publicity of a nineteenth-century divorce. Many more gradually and discreetly achieved a sort of de facto separation, the wife spending increasing amounts of time in Britain with the children, the husband visiting them (if they were still on friendly terms) when he was on leave. When Sir John Grant retired as lieutenant-governor of Bengal in 1862, he did not wish to go on living with a wife who had produced, among her eight children, two who were not his. Not divorce or cohabitation but lives led separately – it seemed a reasonable solution. Yet Grant's wife and his eldest daughter, Jane Strachey, begged him to change his mind, which he eventually did: the resulting 'reconciliation' alas led to a further three decades of married misery.[113]

Discretion was impossible, however, if a husband sued for divorce, as George Hilario Barlow did when, after a controversial period as governor of Madras (1807–13), he discovered that his wife's fifteenth child had been fathered by his cousin and ADC, Captain George Pratt Barlow. Angry husbands like Barlow tended to go straight to their lawyers, as Lieutenant-Colonel Johnston Napier of the 40th Native Infantry also did in January 1838 on discovering that his wife, Isabella, had left their home in Madras to move in with Edward Elliot, the city's superintendent of police. He immediately filed two suits, one against his wife for divorce, the other against Elliot for 'trespass' and 'adulterous and criminal conversation'. A trial quickly took place at which Napier's lawyer called Isabella a woman of 'lewd and vicious temper' and Elliot a man 'of loose morals and profligate habits'. In February the police superintendent was ordered to pay Napier a large sum in damages, in April a divorce was granted, and in November this was ratified by an act of Parliament in London. In the course of that year Isabella had a child by Elliot, and two more later on, after the couple had married in 1839.[114]

Matters took longer in Britain than in India. When Captain Cautley, the engineer on the Ganges canal, found out that he was not the father of his wife's twin babies, he also immediately began divorce proceedings. As he was then (1846) in England on leave, this meant that first he had to go to the civil court to claim damages, then to the ecclesiastical court, which dealt with the matrimonial offence, and ultimately to the House of Lords, where the matter was very publicly settled.[115] The Matrimonial Causes Act of 1857 made the divorce process simpler, cheaper, quicker and sometimes less embarrassing, but it was still very public and stressful. And the act failed to make things fairer for the wife. Jane Strachey may have prevented her father from divorcing her mother but she could not prevent her son Oliver in India from divorcing his wife, Ruby, for adultery, gaining custody of their child (whom he subsequently ignored) and presenting himself as the wronged party even though he had infected his wife with VD, had consistently been the more unfaithful of the two, and had long been pursuing his programme of getting 'on copulating terms' with as many women as possible.[116]

Patterns of separation and reconciliation were much the same in India as in Britain, even if the process was sometimes longer and spread over two continents. The parents of the film director Lindsay Anderson separated in India in 1926 following an affair between his mother, Estelle, and Major Cuthbert Sleigh. Estelle then took her small sons to England but returned to Bangalore in 1932 to attempt a reconciliation with her husband. This lasted long enough for her to become pregnant but was otherwise a failure; the couple was divorced, and in 1936 Estelle married the major, who had by now been invalided out of the army.[117]

Adultery in Victorian Britain was regarded as so scandalous a matter that it could ruin political lives, as it did in the cases of Charles Dilke and Charles Stewart Parnell. Yet in Victorian India it did not destroy administrative careers or even delay promotions very much.

Perhaps a spectacular break-up in Simla or at a Government House might have had repercussions, but this did not happen even with unhappy lieutenant-governors like Lyall, Hewett and Harcourt Butler. And below their level the officials in charge of promotion did not seem to care. His long and noisy divorce did not prevent Probyn Cautley from becoming the director of Canals in the north, a member of the Council of India in retirement, and a knight commander of the Bath. Even citation as co-respondent did not usually wreck careers. Elliot remained superintendent of police and also became the chief magistrate of Madras until his retirement in 1856. During a stay at the Cape in 1850, assistant surgeon Lestock Wilson Stewart began an affair with Mrs Martha Bell. He was cited by her husband, Charles Bell, the surveyor-general of Cape Colony, and it was well known that he was the father of Mrs Bell's fourth child, but none of this obstructed his rise in the Indian Medical Service; when he died at the age of fifty-two, he was already deputy surgeon-general. His contemporary in the ICS, Charles Moore, made similar progress: his role as co-respondent, after running off with an army officer's wife, did not impede his advancement to the post of district judge. He duly married the officer's wife, Margaret Emma, and had four children with her, but she later seems to have disappeared from the records. Moore took early retirement and in the 1890s was living in London's Cavendish Square with another spouse; he was also visiting someone else's wife, whom he kept as his mistress, in Chelsea.[118]

The ICS was a difficult institution to join because the exams were hard and the competition was vigorous. Yet once you were in, it was hard to get rid of you unless you committed the greatest sin of Victorian (and post-Victorian) India: peculation or some other form of corruption. Arthur Travers Crawford, a Bombay Civilian born in 1835, led a far more rackety life than his contemporary Moore but managed to rise higher in the service. In his fifties he was described by a younger colleague, A. R. Bonus, as a man who had already 'run away with two women, has been separated from his own wife, and during one Poona season lived with two actresses whom he imported from America'. Yet afterwards 'he was received back into social circles as if nothing had happened'.[119] What ruined Crawford's career was not his sexually promiscuous style of living but the ways in which he funded it, which included taking bribes and accepting advances from certain rajas.

When news of some of these appeared in the press, his own government placed Crawford under house arrest, but he escaped from Poona and was apprehended in Bombay wearing a false beard. He did not go to jail, but he was dismissed from the ICS without a pension.[120]

When explaining Crawford's earlier social rehabilitation, Bonus had suggested that it was the climate that encouraged British ladies to say things that had 'almost petrified' him 'with surprise' and which 'would create the wildest scandal in England'.[121] Men like Bonus, in that first generation of readers of Plain Tales from the Hills, often experienced such conversations, were amazed by 'the malicious scandal talked', and concluded that Kipling was 'much more true to the life in his women-kind than most Anglo-Indians would allow'.[122] Such an ambience might explain the survival of a figure such as Lepel Griffin, a Civilian who in the 1880s filled the senior post of Resident of Indore and Agent to the Governor-General in Central India. Griffin was 'a flashy and not very reputable person' in the view of the viceroy, Lord Dufferin, who was repelled by his subordinate's 'pleasure in passing himself off as a destroyer of female virtue' and by his 'habit of ostentatiously main-taining intimate relations with some vulgar second-rate woman'.[123] Although Dufferin became unusually obsessive on the subject of Grif-fin, his views were shared by some of the Civilian's contemporaries. When Alfred Lyall saw his colleague flirting in Simla with Kipling's friend Mrs Burton, he compared him to an 'unblushing rake' and on another occasion to Louis XIV for always having 'somebody else's wife living with him in state, a reigning favourite to whom everyone else must bow down'.[124] When the Duke of Connaught, the son of Queen Victoria and commander-in-chief in Bombay (1886–90), arrived to stay in Indore, his wife hinted that the current mistress, a divorced lady, might absent herself when she lunched at the Residency. Sir Lepel noticed the hint but refused to take it, informing Her Highness that if she felt unable to meet ladies staying in his house, then he would have to forgo the pleasure of entertaining her.[125]

In spite of alienating the royal family, the viceroy, his colleagues and several of the princes of central India (notably the Begum of Bhopal and the Maharaja of Holkar), Griffin reached the top of the service because he was very able, even though he was clearly deficient in both tact and good sense. Dufferin may have refused to give him the post he wanted, the lieutenant-governorship of the Punjab (where he had been an excellent chief secretary), because of his 'vanity and egotism' and scandalous private life, but he did offer him the top job in another province, Burma, where he would have been 'less *en évidence* from a social point of view'. Shattered by the Punjab rebuff, Griffin showed no interest in Rangoon. Accusing the viceroy of treating him 'with a complete absence of consideration',[126] he retired early to England, married at the age of fifty-one and tried unsuccessfully to begin a political career.

Adultery in British India had to be a mainly middle-class pastime because few British working-class women lived there. Even for those who did, the cramped married quarters of a barracks were not an ideal location. Private Richards recalled that most of the married women with the Welch Fusiliers were 'very respectable'. Only two of them had 'regular fancy-men'; one of the husbands gave his wife 'two lovely black eyes' (while she cracked his head open with a jug), but the other was either complaisant or else 'too thick to find her out'. Whenever there was a 'serious squabble between a married couple', Mrs Bertie, the colonel's wife, would step in: 'nobody could continue cursing and throwing things at each other in her presence'.[127] Yet sometimes matters were resolved before a colonel's wife was able to reach the scene. At Sialkot in 1854 the soldier Thomas Pacey was sentenced to transportation for life for murdering Sergeant Robert French, who, he had just discovered, was having an affair with his wife.[128] In 'Love o' Women' (1893), one of his most moving stories, Kipling wrote of a similar incident, and after it 'there remained only on the barrack square the blood of man calling from the ground . . . while inside a woman shrieked and raved with wicked filthy words'.

Adulterous officers had wider choices, better locations and greater opportunities than NCOs and private soldiers. Yet there is little written evidence of their activities, and what exists is often unreliable. A Captain Charles Devereux, plainly a pseudonym, wrote a 'memoir', *Venus in India*, that belongs to the genre of classic Victorian erotica. Much of the tale is obvious fantasy. The 'captain', who has left his young wife in Britain, rescues an English girl, who is being anally raped by an Afghan, and later seduces her and her two teenage sisters; meanwhile the girls' father, the colonel, is galloping off to Peshawar to try out the regiment's new prostitutes – at the rate of four a night – before they are brought to the cantonment.[129] Captain Edward Sellon's *The*

Ups and Downs of Life is a more credible memoir, and the author was at least a real person, who in 1866, at the age of forty-eight, shot himself in Piccadilly. Although the author's exploits with British wives are rather formulaic, his narrative displays more individuality after he had 'commenced a regular course of fucking with native women'. His knowledge of prices and habits, and his appreciation of the art of the courtesan, indicate that he was writing from experience. In his life after India Sellon admitted that no European woman bore 'comparison with those salacious, succulent houris of the East'.[130]

Richard Burton wrote of his fellow officers and their bibis when he was with his regiment in Baroda in the 1840s. He also noted how some young ensigns seduced their superior officers' wives and took them to rented rooms in the Indian quarter of the cantonment.[131] Later generations of senior officers frowned on 'poodle-fakers', subalterns or other young men who went on leave to the Hills to play, party and – with luck – have an affair with one of the grass widows in residence. Young men, recalled John Masters, were supposed to 'pursue animals, not girls'.[132] Greater allowance may have been made for older officers, even if they were married. Owen Berkeley-Hill, whose own tastes were for Indian women, could not disguise his admiration for his superior officer, Lieutenant-Colonel Sutherland, 'an enthusiastic sexualist' who, despite his German wife, was 'never without at least one mistress' and, when his junior knew him (before the First World War), had two, the wife of a government official and a midwife at the Saugor Hospital in the Central Provinces.[133]

The problem for officers with adulterous ambitions was that the obvious candidates for their attentions, the women they saw most of, were their brother officers' wives. And they were the great taboo. Whatever else happened, among the havoc and heartbreak that an affair entailed, an officer who disregarded it had to resign from his regiment. Inter-regimental liaisons might be tolerable, but intra-regimental relationships were not. In 1936 Miles Smeeton had to leave the Green Howards for an Indian Army regiment when he fell for the wife of his CO, an adventurous lady called Beryl, who had once walked across China to Burma. When warned about the hazards of the journey, the bandits and the risk of being raped on the way, she replied, 'Oh, I shan't worry about that. I'd far prefer dishonour to death.'[134]

NECESSITIES

There was once a belief that British 'empire-builders' did not enjoy normal sex lives because they were concentrating too hard on building the empire to dissipate their energies in frivolous pursuits. It is true that some unmarried imperial figures, such as Gordon and Kitchener, do not appear to have had sex lives, and that others, while married, may not have had very active ones. Yet this was because they were more or less asexual or, in some cases, because they might have indulged in a kind of sex that was illegal in Britain. They were not sublimating their desires for the glory of the empire.

Young middle-class men who went to India during the last century of the British presence knew they were unlikely to enjoy extensive sex lives unless they were prepared to defy the conventions of the time on mistresses, adultery, homosexuality and Indian women. Some decided that the gender imbalance with British women was so bad and the competition for them so strong that it was pointless to try. Why bother to compete with cavalry officers on leave? If uncommercial sex was unobtainable, why not settle for something that was almost as 'delicious' such as 'strawberries-and-cream'?[135] Long after Independence, Lieutenant-Colonel Paddy Massey summed up the position he had faced in India as a subaltern:

> Sex was a subject which, possibly because it was so difficult to get, did not occupy one's mind and was certainly not the universal topic it has become today. Marriage on a subaltern's pay was out of the question; the pill had not been invented; one parent families were not acceptable; brothels only for the very foolish, and all that was left was lots of exercise.[136]

Exercise was indeed regarded as the panacea, as it was in so many British public schools. 'Sweat the sex out of you' was the rationale behind all those football games for Tommy Atkins and all those polo matches for the captains and the subalterns. 'Pig-sticking' or 'hog-hunting', the most dangerous and exhausting of sports, was considered the most effective and 'pleasurable' of antidotes. Yet you had to take it seriously, insisted its fraternity, and renounce other pleasures. 'You must give up all attendance on "the Mall",' commanded Frank Simson, a senior Civilian in Dacca; 'the pleasant morning and evening drives with the charming ladies of the station must be forgone.' A serious pig-sticker should ask to be posted to a district with no society and no racecourse but plenty of tigers and wild boar.[137] Major Alexander Wardrop agreed. In his book *Modern Pig-sticking*, a classic of a rather restricted genre, he admitted that in India he had spent all his leave and all his money on 'spear and rifle' and that he had ridden down and speared over 700 wild boar. In his opinion the man who married was a fool: he would get 'far more pleasure by keeping good animals' and going hunting.[138]*

The misogyny of the pig-stickers and hog-hunters was frankly expressed in their verse. Captain Morris of the 9th Bombay Native Infantry, who was apparently regarded as 'the poet-laureate of Indian sport', was the author of a poem called 'The Boar', which was inappropriately sung to the tune of 'My luve is like a red, red rose'. Another of his offerings was 'Saddle, Spur, and Spear', which included the lines:

> Let others boast and proudly toast
> The light of ladies' eyes . . .
> But since for me no charms I see
> In all the sex can show . . .
> I'll change my theme and fondly dream,
> True sportsmen pledge me here,
> And fill my cup and drain it up
> To Saddle, Spur and Spear![139]

In case the message was not strong enough, a bard known as 'C' spelt it out again in 'The Hunter's Song':

> We value not false woman's kiss,
> We value not the miser's bliss . . .
> Let fools with women while away
> The precious hours of youthful day . . .
> A boar to us is comelier far
> Than Venus in her dove-drawn car . . .

It was better for men to go pig-sticking than to 'pass their lives . . . with snarling wives'.[140]

Few British men in India accepted the notion that sport was an adequate substitute for sex. Most would have agreed with the view of

---

* A few years after publishing his book in 1914, Wardrop himself got married. He also became a senior general, retiring as GOC the Northern Command in India in 1937.

Francis Yeats-Brown, the cavalry officer who wrote *Bengal Lancer*, that a regular sex life was 'more necessary in a hot than a cold country'.[141] Britain's greatest empire-builder – in terms of territory acquired for the empire – was in complete agreement. When Richard Wellesley was sent to Calcutta as governor-general in 1798, his wife, Hyacinthe, refused to go with him. Although their relationship in Europe had been tempestuous, it had also been very amorous, and he needed her in India. 'This climate,' he told her, 'excites one sexually most terribly.' In a long and accusatory correspondence – it took at least ten months to receive a reply to a complaint that one of them had made in the previous letter – he pleaded, cajoled and threatened. 'As for sex,' he told her, 'one must have it in this climate.' Hyacinthe told him to live without it as she had to do herself, but this eventually proved impossible.[142] A mistress was found.

Whatever its injustices and its inequalities, the bibi system had some merits, certainly for British men and certainly to the advantage of relations between the races. Its demise encouraged the expansion of another system, prostitution, which had very few. Unmarried Civilians do not appear to have visited brothels, at least not in their own districts where the threat of exposure and blackmail was too great. Unmarried officers in the army and police did go to such places, though we do not know what proportion of them stuck to pig-sticking or stayed away for reasons of fear, aversion or morality. Customers were naturally more likely to look for the red-light areas of a large city, where they had a greater choice and a smaller risk of being seen, than to seek gratification in a cantonment. The bungalows of Karaya Road in Ballygunge, set back in secluded gardens, were a discreet venue for officers in Calcutta. In Delhi in the 1920s junior officers frequented a brothel known as the Turkish Baths.[143]

In his *Studies in the Psychology of Sex*, the pioneering sexologist Havelock Ellis published his case history of 'GR', a British officer keen to sample different forms of sex with different kinds of sexual partner. He confessed to Ellis that he 'used to have horrible orgies' with his brother-officers: on his birthday one year he 'ordered' six women to his bungalow and 'made a present of them' to five of his friends after dinner. On another occasion, accompanied by two fellow officers, he had an 'orgy in Bombay which lasted three nights. I started on a Greek and a Pole and finished up with a Japanese . . .'[144]

GR became emotionally involved with women who were not

prostitutes and with comrades in the army,* and he also enjoyed physical experiments with animals and fruit. Remembering the Pathan proverb – 'women for breeding, boys for pleasure, and melons for delight' – he one day grabbed a melon 'to try whether the proverb was in any way true'. It was. But a papaya was even better than a melon, 'being the nearest approach to the human vagina'. GR might have become over-attached to his papayas had it not been for 'the opportune arrival of a fairly good-looking punkah woman [who] put an end to this form of enjoyment by providing' him with what he 'wanted'. As it was clearly important for him to work out what he really did want, he gave Havelock Ellis a list of his preferences, beginning with 'a woman, a friend and lady of [his] own class', but if she was not available he would descend to a lady for whom he did not 'care', and thence to 'prostitutes of all classes and colours', followed by 'men, boys, animals, melons and masturbation'.[145]

Tommy Atkins would never have had the chance to compile such a list as this. Apart from prostitutes, he seldom spoke to a woman except in the married quarters of the barracks, perhaps the wife of the bandmaster or the sergeant-major. Yet he would have heard a great deal about sex from the time of his recruitment, both from medical officers who warned him of 'temptations' and the risks of venereal disease, and from veterans in the barracks dormitories reminiscing after 'lights out' about women they had known and brothels they had visited: they could 'keep an audience of fellows . . . attentive for hours on end', complained Private Swindlehurst of the Lancashire Fusiliers. The private's real complaint, however, was not the lack of sleep this caused, but the 'constant repetition' of their exploits that broke the 'natural repugnance' of young lads and encouraged them to 'become patrons on pay nights', pick fights in Lahore's brothels, and end up in hospital with VD.[146]

Tommy would quickly learn the lingo of sex talk. If he was in India between the world wars, he would soon identify women as 'a bit of skirt', 'a bit of fluff', 'a bit of crumpet', 'a bit of all right' and, if Anglo-Indian, a 'chilliecracker'. He would learn the meaning of 'gobbling', 'jig-jig' and 'dipping your wick', and might be in a position to ask a comrade, 'Will she drop 'em?' He would probably be made to understand what was meant by 'the gunge' (VD), 'a dose' (VD) and 'copping

* See below, p. 335.

a packet' (catching VD). Yet whatever his linguistic expertise, the phrase most applicable to his own activities would have been 'bashing the bishop' – masturbating.[147]

In the nineteenth century the prostitutes that Tommy would most often see were the girls from the 'lal bazaar', a special area of the regimental bazaar, where they would be superintended (by an elderly lady) and inspected by doctors. In Agra they were housed in the Suddar Bazaar in a brothel known as 'the Rag', which was reserved for British soldiers. Some of the 'barracks tarts' followed the troops on the march and up into the Hills, spending the summer in the mountains and earning their livelihood in a cooler climate than in Agra.[148]

When he was in transit or stationed near a large city, Tommy could, if he chose, broaden his experience. Trumpeter Meneaud-Lissenburg did not realize how broad this potentially might be until, shortly before the First World War, he took a wrong turning after visiting the Botanical Gardens in Bombay and found himself in Grant Road, 'a veritable den of iniquity and vice, where morphinists, sodomists and prostitutes ply their evil trades with the utmost vigour and semi-naked exposure'. Turning off the road, he entered Sutlej Street, where he was shocked to see 'amidst the glittering lights hordes of sailors, soldiers and civilians [who] were literally falling out of taxis and gharries and forming groups . . .' The street consisted of one-storeyed terraced houses with illuminated forecourts. On one side the trumpeter found 'European women of every nationality, except British, displaying themselves seated on low chairs and clad only in semi-transparent chemises and stockings, loudly proclaiming their charms'. On the other, in contrast, 'Japanese women [were] demurely seated on the forecourt patiently sewing or knitting and seemingly content to rely on their charming attire to attract customers'.[149]

The young Meneaud-Lissenburg had already been shocked by the regimental brothel at his first posting at Secunderabad. The red-light district of Bombay offended him far more. After crossing the first intersection on Sutlej Street, he was confronted by 'an even more revolting spectacle' than before: Indian, Eurasian and other Asian women, dressed in white cotton chemises, were 'shamelessly lifting the garment, exposing a blancoed torso . . .' Yet worse was still to come – 'the ultimate in degradation' – after the next intersection: 'native women of the coolie class seated behind bars like animals in a zoo were greedily gaped at by lascars, sepoys and coolies bargaining a price for admission'. As a commissioner of the Bombay Police admitted, the bars looked very bad, making the girls seem like 'caged animals', but they were put there to 'save the women from being overwhelmed by a low-class male rabble, ready for violence on the smallest provocation'. The bars obliged the 'low-class clientele to form a queue outside' and enabled the 'women to admit one customer at a time'.[150]

The vast majority of prostitutes in India were Indian, and so were a large majority of clients. Tommy Atkins spent more time with Indian women than with others because they were more available, but he was quite catholic in his tastes. As official reports from the 1870s noted, he was 'not very particular in the distribution of his amorous patronage', and sometimes he was too drunk to remember what nationality he had 'cohabited' with.[151] When he was able to tell the difference, he particularly liked Japanese women, who were clean and seldom had VD; there was 'a colony' of them at Lucknow where they 'obtained their living by the soldier'. The officer 'GR' also rated the Japanese the best because, apart from their cleanliness, their 'charming manners and beautiful bodies', they took an 'intelligent interest in the proceedings'. His runners-up were Kashmiris and Chinese, but the 'white women in the East were insupportable . . . the dregs of the European and American markets'.[152]

European prostitutes were usually found in Calcutta, Bombay, Madras, Rangoon and Karachi – all port cities, a fact which suggests that their clientele consisted mainly of sailors unaccustomed to Indian women. Not that there were very many of them even on the waterfronts. Calcutta had sixty-five in 1880, less than 1 per cent of the number of women working in the trade in that city. A few years earlier the capital had nine registered Englishwomen, but most places had fewer or none at all. In Rangoon in 1913 the European prostitutes consisted of one Spaniard, one Romanian, two Italians plus sixteen Jewish women, three from the Middle East and thirteen from Russia. Arriving in the Burmese capital in the same period, Private Richards was relieved to find there was not an English girl among them. In fact, according to a report of the Home Department of the government of India in 1913, there were 'no British women openly plying this trade' among India's 234 European prostitutes, half of whom were in Bombay. Gratified though the authorities may have been that no British girls were there to damage the prestige of the imperial power, they were worried that the 'natives' might mistake the Russians and Italians for Englishwomen. A town-dweller, suggested a police superintendent in Rangoon, would know that the prostitutes were 'not of the same class or race' as a burra memsahib, but it was 'doubtful whether the ignorant villager who pays a visit to Rangoon is equally aware of the difference'.[153]

In his quest for sexual gratification the chief problem for Tommy Atkins was the risk of venereal infection. This had been a hazard since soon after his arrival in India in the eighteenth century: by the first years of the following century a quarter of the British troops in Madras were diseased. The military authorities recognized their men's need for sexual activity and, holding the belief that buggery and masturbation had harmful effects, both moral and physical, they thought they had no alternative but to permit prostitution and try to reduce the rate of venereal infection. 'Lock hospitals', where infected girls from the 'lal bazaar' in the barracks were detained, examined and treated, were thus set up. They did not bring the numbers down very greatly, mainly because soldiers continued to use girls from outside their bazaar, but, repressive and degrading though they were for the women, they were better than nothing for the troops.

After VD the next obstacle for Tommy Atkins and his quest was the 'purity lobby' that was outraged, in Britain and India, by the India Contagious Diseases Act of 1868, which led to the compulsory registration of brothels and the compulsory treatment of prostitutes available to soldiers. The lobby was appalled to discover the existence of sanctioned cantonment brothels, even though their purpose was to meliorate the health of British soldiers and allow them to do the job they had been sent out to do rather than lie in agony on a hospital bed, subjected to mercury and other treatments with excruciating side-effects. In the 1880s the Anglican bishops of India and Ceylon denounced all measures to help the troops because for them 'the discouragement and repression of vice' were 'of far higher importance than the diminution of suffering or of other evils resulting from vice ...' They received plenty of support from outside the Church, among 'purity-mongers' in civil life and in Parliament. Under pressure from them, the lock hospitals and cantonment brothels were closed, which led to an immediate and inevitable surge in venereal disease: in some areas of Bengal in the late 1880s almost half the British troops were being treated; in parts of

Bombay the proportion was even higher. The closures also led, according to the viceroy Elgin, 'to even more deplorable evils . . . an increase in unnatural crimes'. When an Indian Government Act of 1895 reflected the victory of the purity lobby in Britain, officers were incandescent that such a measure so detrimental to the health of soldiers had been passed at the behest of 'morbid married faddists and sexless unprofessional sisters'.[154] Yet George Hamilton, who became secretary of state in that year, soon realized that the unregulated system of recent years was impractical and unworkable, and the brothels were discreetly reopened. Disapproval, however, remained the official attitude. General Kitchener, who became commander-in-chief of India in 1902, exhorted his men to use self-control and urged them to imagine what their mothers would think if they did not. He also warned them that, if they became infected, they would not only suffer 'cantankerous and stinking ulcerations'; their noses would rot and fall off as well.[155]

SODOM AND ADVENTURE

A career in the empire might survive adultery, divorce and kept mistresses, but it could not survive a homosexual scandal. Even a hint of an inclination could badly damage a reputation.

In 1845 General Napier, the recent conqueror of Sind, asked Richard Burton to investigate a rumour that some British troops might be using homosexual brothels in Karachi. As an incipient explorer and sexologist, Burton relished the commission, disguising himself as a merchant from Persia and observing very closely what went on in three of these establishments. Although he found no evidence of British involvement, he still wrote a report for Napier containing detailed descriptions of what services were on offer in these places and at what price they could be obtained. While the general had assured Burton that he would not forward it to his superiors in the Bombay government, the document was discovered after Napier's resignation two years later. Its readers, enemies of Napier and his subordinate from within the army and the Bombay secretariat, believed – or affected to believe – that only a homosexual could have written such a report, and so they attempted to get Burton cashiered. Although in the end he was not dismissed – he had after all only been following the general's orders – it was made clear that he would not be promoted and that his army career was at an end. In 1849 Burton left India to begin a new career as a writer and explorer.[156]

When it heard the revelations at the Oscar Wilde trials, the British public was horrified. It would have been even more appalled had it learned the details in the case of Hector Macdonald, the commander-in-chief in Ceylon. Macdonald was an authentic imperial hero, the son of a crofter who had risen from the ranks, beginning his career in India and serving in the Second Afghan War, the First South African War, the Nile Expedition, the Sudan Expedition and the Second South African War. In 1902 he was appointed commander-in-chief in Ceylon, where his military duties were undemanding and left him plenty of spare time, which he spent – allegedly – with dancing boys, temple catamites and waiters at the Grand Oriental Hotel. When he was caught misbehaving in a train with four Sinhalese boys, charges were laid before the governor, Sir Joseph West Ridgeway, a former officer of the Indian Army who had also served in the Second Afghan War. Macdonald's behaviour had for some time been so reckless (with British boys as well, so it was said) that other charges were soon made, and apparently some seventy witnesses could have been called. Desperate to avoid a scandal, Ridgeway sent Macdonald on leave to England with the suggestion that he should ponder his future. In London the general met Roberts, then commander-in-chief in Britain, who told him he could only remain in the army if he returned to Ceylon to face a court-martial. In Paris on his way back, Macdonald wrote to tell him that he could not face a court-martial, which led the field marshal to hope that he would disappear, find some distant part of the world and be forgotten. The current c-in-c in India, General Kitchener, who may have been a repressed homosexual himself, hoped for a more dramatic finale: he wanted his colleague to be court-martialled and shot. In the end Macdonald shot himself in his Parisian hotel.[157]

Kitchener's attitude may have been caused by resentment that Macdonald had broken a rule of celibacy that he and some of his bachelor entourage seem to have observed. For fear of exposure, many British homosexuals decided to lead chaste lives in India. The ICS had no scandals of this kind although, by the law of averages, a couple of gay men would have entered its ranks every year. On joining the service in 1930, Michael Carritt came across two examples, one known as 'Oscar' because he was a friend of 'Bosie' Douglas, Wilde's most notorious boyfriend: he was clever, charming and ebullient and, as he caused no scandal, he rose high. The other, also an aesthete, was the district judge in Midnapore. 'Welcome, dear boy . . . welcome indeed. I am Jameson,' he told Carritt with a slightly affected lisp, 'but call me Jimmie, dear boy,' he added as he offered 'a limp hand to shake'. Jimmie had won a Military Cross in Flanders, and he was brave in India too, refusing to carry a revolver in violent Midnapore and making himself a target for assassination by volunteering to sit on a tribunal to try cases of terrorism. He had a wife and child, but they lived in England, and he was a lonely unhappy man, wishing he was in Oxford or London rather than doing a job in a place where there was no outlet for his culture or his sexuality. Apparently he vented his frustrations on Indians by passing 'notoriously severe' judicial sentences.[158]

Homosexual relationships did exist in the army, though not in the numbers one would expect in a more tolerant society. Brigadier Packard, who commanded a battalion in the Indian Army in 1945, observed that his sepoys 'often had homosexual relationships with fellow sepoys and any trouble within the platoon was usually connected with this'.[159] Not a great deal seems to have gone on in British regiments although enough for the creation of a special vocabulary: 'budlee-budlee' for buggery in a barracks between 'hammock-chums' or, if they were bivouacking on a march, 'bivvy-chums'; and enough rhyming slang was adopted for 'arse' to become Khyber Pass, though this could be used with sexual neutrality as in 'Up your Khyber, mate!'[160]

Homosexual relationships among army officers were rare, but they too did happen. GR, the bisexual patient of Havelock Ellis, had an affair with a brother officer, who told him that he had 'had connection' with three other officers in their regiment; he did not mention them by name, but GR could guess who they were.[161] Army men involved in homosexual activities were usually discreet, though an exception was Kenneth Searight, a young officer of the West Kent Regiment who befriended E. M. Forster on a voyage to Bombay in 1912 and confessed to a life that astonished the sexually inexperienced writer by its fullness and variety.[162]

With all their risks, homosexual adventures were probably easier to pursue in India than in Britain. As John Masters recalled, 'a few homosexuals followed their secret star with comparative comfort in that large and easy-going country'.[163] Lieutenant Searight certainly did. Although he had left England at the age of twenty-six as pretty much a sexual novice, he enjoyed a rampant sex life in India, especially with Pathan boys when he was stationed in Peshawar. Recording his exploits in 2,706 lines of rhyming couplets ('Each boy of certain age will let on hire / His charms to indiscriminate desire' is one of the more restrained ones) in a manuscript he called 'Paedikion', the officer added an appendix giving the names and ages of his partners with details of dates, places and the number of orgasms he achieved.[164]

Soon after his arrival in India, Forster went to Peshawar with two travelling companions to visit Searight, who invited them to guest night at his regimental Mess. Although Forster lost a collar-stud, arrived late and kept the band waiting before it could play 'The Roast Beef of Old England', the dinner was a success. Afterwards Searight made Forster dance with him and gave piggy-back rides to one of his friends. According to the historian Ronald Hyam, Forster's encounters with Searight made him more open to the possibility of sexual adventure and also to writing about it in his fiction; he started to work on his novel *Maurice*, unpublished in his lifetime, soon after his return to England.[165]

Searight's exploits did not, however, inspire Forster to become similarly adventurous when he returned to India in 1921 as secretary to the maharaja of Dewas, a state near Indore. He sat about the palace in the hot weather, lonely, idle and sexually frustrated. Bored with masturbation, he finally made a botched attempt to seduce a Hindu workman, and afterwards, fearing that the maharaja had been informed of the episode, confessed it to his employer. Although the prince was sympathetic, he suggested it was more natural to want a woman, to which Forster replied that it was not in his case, because he had 'no feeling for women'. The maharaja remained sympathetic, exclaiming that, as God had made Forster the way he was, he (the prince) must provide his secretary with a catamite. After much thought he suggested 'K', a palace barber, whose payment he would see to, though he begged the writer not to assume the passive role in the relationship. We do not know what role Forster did assume, but we do know that the two were lovers for a time, meeting (with the maharaja's connivance) in a disused suite of the palace.[166]

10

Domesticities

HOMES

The first British inhabitants of India lived in the East India Company 'factories' or in the forts which they constructed in their principal settlements. Until early in the eighteenth century the population of Madras lived in Fort St George for protection from the Company's real or potential enemies. There the merchants built themselves airy residences above their storerooms, fine white-stuccoed houses with broad verandahs but one principal flaw: flat roofs that cracked in the hot weather and let the rain in during the monsoon.

When the British felt more secure, many of them moved out of the fort (rather prematurely in view of the upcoming Mysore wars) and into 'garden houses' which they built in the Choultry Plain outside the town, much in the manner of their compatriots constructing villas along the Thames to the south-west of London, at Richmond, Petersham and Twickenham. By 1780 there were 200 of these dwellings, and by 1800, a year regarded as the zenith of the fortunes of Madras, even more. According to Maria Graham, who arrived in the city soon afterwards, 'everybody lived in the country' despite the fact that all the offices and counting-houses were in the town or in the fort. Even the governor, who lived in magnificent Government House, with its two storeys of deep verandahs, felt the need for a large country house surrounded by a deer park the size of the Bois de Boulogne, although this building at Guindy was only seven miles from his normal residence. In the 1830s Julia Maitland observed that the British had 'tried to make Madras as English as they could' – 'England in a perspiration' – and she did not like it. Lord Irwin, the viceroy a hundred years later, had a

337

different view. The house at Guindy, he declared, was 'the most delicious place' as well as 'the most English place' that he had seen in all
India.[1]

The owners of garden houses, which were also known as 'flat-tops',
loved to give parties on their roofs, where their guests, shaded by an
awning, were better protected from the nuisance of frogs and snakes
than in the garden.[2] The buildings were of classical, often Palladian,
inspiration, as they were in Calcutta and in much of the rest of the
Indian Empire. Although Gothic in varying forms was the style of the
later and most spectacular buildings in Bombay, it was often disliked
and mistrusted by imperialists, especially by those who regarded themselves as the heirs of Rome and classical civilization. 'A Gothic building
in India,' said Curzon rather foolishly, 'would be like putting the Taj in
Hyde Park.'[3]

The British in Calcutta, like the denizens of Madras, also acquired
houses outside the town after the Company had secured control of the surrounding province. The most fashionable area was Garden Reach, on
the shores of the Hooghly, where in the late eighteenth century Robert
Lindsay went into ecstasy at the sight of the 'banks, everywhere stud-
ded with country villas, covered with beautiful verdure'. William
Hickey, a contemporary of Lindsay, was also ecstatic, exclaiming about
the view from his house at Garden Reach – the river, the fort, the palaces, the 'immense forest' of ships' masts. As in Madras, the Calcutta
style was predominantly Palladian, though later it was challenged by
Greek Revival, but unlike the southern city, where 'everybody' lived in
the country, British people still lived and built themselves houses in the
city. These homes, however, were not terraced buildings as in London,
lining a street or a square, but more like villas, detached and surrounded by their gardens.[4]

Madras and Calcutta were not like other residential areas in the
early nineteenth century. Most British people in India did not inhabit
Palladian garden houses on the banks of a river surrounded by 'verdure'. Outside the cities most of them lived – and continued to live until
Independence – in a 'bungalow', a word that originally signified a peasant's hut in Bengal. In the late eighteenth century the British-Indian
bungalow was a single-storeyed building made of sun-dried bricks with
a thatched roof, high ceilings and a verandah with wooden posts. It
soon became grander, a white pukka house with tiled roofs, classical

features and very large gardens. Balustrades now lined the roof, Doric columns replaced the wooden posts, and the verandah often stretched in a colonnade along the whole length of the bungalow. Another addition was the pillared portico, a porte-cochère that allowed carriages to drive up and unload their passengers untouched by sun or rain. In very grand houses it was made high enough for elephants to pass under.

Bungalows were often constructed along the roads of cantonments for officers and in the 'civil lines' for DOs, judges, and other officials to live in. Sometimes they overrode their definition and added a storey, and sometimes they expanded (while remaining on one floor) to become a Residency or a Government House, as in the thatched, half-timbered building at Manipur and the low, rambling summer residence at Pachmarhi. They could also be quirky, especially in the hill stations where they were not subject to street grids and the pressure of uniformity. Simla, which was not developed until the second half of the nineteenth century, after British India's classical phase had ended, possessed an amalgam of styles that included mock Tudor and Swiss-Bavarian and even the occasional hint that the town might be in Asia. As a cantonment Bangalore went through its classical stage with balustrades and colonnades but then veered off in the 1880s towards a vaguely Gothic and Romantic style with steep roofs and decorated gables: its most distinctive feature was the 'monkey-top', a pointed hood over the top half of the window, painted green in contrast with the white walls of the bungalow, that was supposed to give protection from the sun and the rain but which was essentially decorative.[5]

The interiors consisted of large rooms leading from one to another and on to the verandah without corridors or staircases and with as few doors and walls as possible; the aim was to minimize obstacles to the circulation of the air. Interiors of the bungalows were conditioned by the climate and the local fauna. There was no point having wooden floorboards if these were going to warp or be eaten by white ants. It was cheaper and more effective to make a floor with a brick base, coat it with a mixture of mud and cow dung and then cover it with palm-leaf matting. Furniture also needed precautions against the ants. Beds, tables and wardrobes were all made less vulnerable if the feet of their legs were wrapped in strips of cloth wrung out in paraffin and then stood in old tins containing an inch of water.[6]

Some people defied the hazards and spent time and money buying fine furniture, chairs of ebony and rosewood in the eighteenth century, sideboards and large cupboards in Victorian times, which were heavy and dark, often made from stained or painted teak. Others got hold of catalogues from the top London stores and then persuaded local crafts-men to copy the designs of Heal's or Maples.[7] Yet many, especially the itinerant ones, did not bother. If you were living in a climate like India's, and being moved from one post to another every two years, what was the point of carting about valuable things for hundreds of miles when they were bound to be damaged in transit and gnawed by insects? It was better to sell your stuff locally, though invariably at a loss, and buy new things in your next district, or rent them from the Public Works Department. The furniture you would find was seldom very comfort-able. Inside the humbler bungalows you might have folding Roorkee chairs, made of canvas stretched over wood, and outside some veran-dah chairs, known as the 'planter's long-sleever', which had open cane-work that allowed air to circulate around sweaty bodies. These were fine for men to lounge about on, especially as they contained 'pockets' to put their drinks in, yet, as one tea planter's new wife com-plained (on finding that her husband's bungalow contained almost no other furniture), 'no lady could ever sit at ease' in them.[8]

Simplicity was thought desirable in the private rooms. A bathroom did not need much furniture except for a zinc tub and a moveable lav-atory known as a 'thunderbox' that was emptied by the sweeper. All a bedroom required, according to M. M. Kaye, was an iron bedstead (with a mosquito net), a cupboard called an almirah, a stool, a cheval-glass, two cane chairs and a marble-topped dressing table.[9] Yet middle-aged and middle-class Victorians, in India as in England, could not see a sitting room without cluttering it with superfluous objects: in the Subcontinent with little teak tables and decorated screens, brass trays and bowls, rugs made of panther skins and hunting trophies fixed to the wall, where they might mingle with depictions of the Trossachs or watercolours of Venice, but not with paintings by any Indians. Among the more unusual wall decorations of British India were the nude pictures that Betty Montgomery painted for the bedroom walls of her bungalow in Quetta. When asked where she had found her models, the wife of the future field marshal replied, 'I have a mirror.'[10]

Hunting trophies had the potential to cause early marital rifts. A girl fresh out of England, upset by the journey, nervous of married life and frightened by India, might feel it was the last straw to find her new home decorated with dead animals, their heads on the wall and their skins on the floor. Some insisted on their removal. Marjorie Francis was married to a tea planter near Travancore who did not himself like 'shikar' (hunting), so she was 'spared the stuffed heads with glazed eyes . . . and the worse horror of a fully stuffed bearcub with paw outstretched holding a brass salver for the reception of . . . visiting cards'. Yet she had opportunities to see how hunting men furnished their bungalows with heads of deer and bison 'stuffed and mounted' on the wall, amidst 'the lost lords of the jungle' – tiger, leopard and black panther – 'snarling between their gentler prey'. Ashtrays were made of hooves, photograph frames were made of turtle shells, while the 'wastepaper bin was an elephant's hollowed foot, and the doorstop its huge tooth'.[11] Marjorie may have been spared another – and fortunately rare – obscenity: a bag for golf clubs made out of an elephant's penis.

The most important piece of furniture in a bungalow was the device used to ameliorate the effects of the hot weather. Punkahs were introduced in the eighteenth century and later became a household staple. They consisted of a piece of cloth with a frill on a wooden pole or frame suspended from the ceiling and attached to a rope pulled by a punkah wallah to create a breeze. Hanging up the punkahs, like putting up the mosquito curtains, was part of the memsahib's spring routine. Another part of life's routine, usually administered by men, was chastisement of the punkah wallah, who was often to be found lying on his back on the verandah with the rope attached to his big toe. The most important part of his stupefyingly boring job was to stay awake, especially at night, which was when he, like other people, most wanted to sleep; he was often woken up by a flying boot. 'You can have no idea,' H. M. Kisch wrote to his family in England, 'of the irritation caused in a tropical climate by a sleepy punkah wallah at night.' After a hard day's work in rural Bengal in the 1860s, the young Civilian would go to bed under a punkah but 'just before you are asleep, the punkah wallah himself sleeps, and your punkah stops. Then you become food for mosquitoes on your face and sandflies on your feet, while the heat of the climate and wrath at the punkah wallah irritate you beyond endurance.' You had to get up to rouse your servant, which would make you thoroughly awake yourself, and then the process would be repeated once more so that you might 'not get an hour's sleep all night'.[12]

A more complicated contraption was the 'thermantidote', a huge machine with four fans rotated by hand that forced air into a room cooled on the way by khus-khus tatties, mats of khus-khus grass upon which water was constantly poured. A less labour-intensive method was to have the khus-khus tatties without the machine, hanging them across an open door to catch any breeze, but you still needed servants to keep them wet. These may not have been very effective, but the grass had aromatic roots that perfumed and (slightly) cooled the air. They were made redundant – as were the punkahs and the thermantidote – by the invention of the electric ceiling fan, which became widely used after the First World War.

Most bungalows were surrounded by large compounds which also contained stables, servants' quarters and the kitchen – built outside the house to reduce the heat and the risk of fire in the bungalow. They also had a garden which, like all the buildings in the compound (except the stables), formed part of the memsahib's domain, a place to be inspected in the cool of the mornings and evenings. The work that British women put into their Indian gardens (though in an administrative way, seldom by hand), was remarkable, considering how often they had to abandon them in order to accompany their husbands to their next posting. Margaret Hannay, the wife of a major in the Indian Army, noted sadly in her diary in 1829 that she had felt attached to 'every tree and shrub' that she had 'planted and arranged' by herself, but it had not been her 'fate to see them come to perfection', and they would now 'in all probability go to ruin'.[13]

Even if a couple stayed in one place long enough to create a garden, there were perennial obstacles to its success such as garden pests, the scarcity of local horticultural skills and above all the relentlessness of the hot weather in the Plains. The monsoons brought relief, yet it was impossible to cut grass or keep weeds under control when they sprang up within hours of being cut down. Soil and climate often made it foolhardy to try to grow anything except indigenous plants, which limited the political agent in Bahrain to little more than date palms, tamarisks and a few salt-tolerant shrubs. Even when the growing conditions were good, gardeners had to face the hazards of wild life. One kitchen garden in the hills of Travancore was regularly raided by porcupine, which ravaged the root crops; jackals, which had a craving for the pineapples; flying squirrels, which dropped out of trees to feed on the runner beans;

and langurs, which stripped the peas and broke the sprouts and had to be chased away by servants banging saucepans and screaming abuse.[14]

British women have been much mocked for attempting to create English gardens in unsuitable places. It was indeed rather futile to try to grow tulips or geraniums in the Plains, and lawns were often a disappointment, however much they were nurtured and needed for garden parties and games of croquet. Yet for women who felt they were in a sort of exile – unlike their husbands who were in India for a reason – it was reassuring to be able to grow petunias and chrysanthemums, just as it was reassuring to be ordering seeds from Carter and Sutton in Calcutta or 'doing the flowers' in the house, arranging them in vases and placing them on tables, even in remote bungalows where no one was likely to see them. And even if the higher hill stations were the easiest places to garden – and grow roses – you could be successful at lower altitudes. You could grow hollyhocks in Bangalore, or sweet peas in Sholapur, and most kinds of British flowers and vegetables in Burmese Maymyo. A successful botanical garden was established by the East India Company in the low Himalayan foothills at Saharanpur, about a thousand feet above the sea.

In the Plains it was sensible to put plants in pots – to regulate the sun, shade and watering – and to keep them close to the house, on the verandahs and by the entrance. For creepers up the walls and flowers in the borders, it was obviously best to have things that enjoyed the climate: cascades of bougainvillea and clusters of marigolds, lines of canna lilies and clumps of oleanders and poinsettias. All of them looked strongly colourful and suitably tropical in their setting, but none is in fact indigenously Indian. Nor are many of the favoured trees such as the jacaranda, the papaya, the tamarind and the tulip tree.

A number of British women became enthusiasts for native plants, notably the wives of two governor-generals, Lady Amherst and Lady Canning. Sarah Amherst was a serious botanist who loved Indian flowers and derided the fashion for growing English ones in a 'climate nature never intended them for'. She went plant-collecting in the Himalaya, and her name endures with *Amherstia nobilis*, a strikingly beautiful species otherwise known as the Pride of Burma or Orchid Tree.[15] Charlotte Canning was an imaginative gardener and a talented painter of plants and landscapes. She too relished the 'jungly lanes' and tropical fauna of the viceregal garden at Barrackpore on the Hooghly.

She also went plant-collecting in the mountains, and it was on a visit to Darjeeling that she caught the malaria which killed her, at the end of 1861, a few weeks before she and her husband were due to return to England.

Amateur botanists, fascinated by local flora, abounded in British India. James Kirkpatrick planted mango orchards in Hyderabad; Warren Hastings tried to grow lychees and custard-apples in retirement in Gloucestershire. In 1835 the Duke of Devonshire sent out a young gardener from Chatsworth to collect orchideous plants from southern Burma, and brought back two specimens of Lady Amherst's tree, one of which died on the voyage home.[16] Yet the most successful botanical work was done by professionals – often 'surgeon-botanists' – employed by the East India Company to collect, study and classify the many thousands of different plants in the Subcontinent, in the Himalaya and the Nilgiris as well as on the Plains. The EIC also set up a number of botanical gardens, the first in Calcutta, and employed a skilled and enthusiastic line of superintendents and directors to look after them.

Many of these horticulturalists were sent out from Kew Gardens, but Sydney Percy-Lancaster was 'home-grown'. Born in Meerut in 1886, he spent much of his life collecting and hybridizing the Alipore Canna Collection, which had been begun by his father in Calcutta. He also established a nursery that provided the trees for the roads and avenues of New Delhi, and at Independence he was the government of India's superintendent of horticultural operations. Deciding not to go 'home' in 1947, he joined the Botanic Garden at Lucknow and worked there until 1959, when his son persuaded him to join his family in southern Rhodesia. Two years later, following the unexpected deaths of both his wife and his son, he returned to Lucknow and remained there for the rest of his life.

SERVANTS AND SHOPPING

On the eve of his departure from Calcutta in 1807, William Hickey wrote a list of the servants he would need to pay off with three months' wages. The number came to sixty-three, which included eight men who waited at table and another eight who looked after his horses: a coachman, three grass-cutters and four grooms.[17] By the standards of the time it was not an enormous number. Hickey was a fairly prosperous lawyer, but he was not a nabob, and governors as well as Residents and judges of the Supreme Court would have had more. When Sir Harry Fane was commander-in-chief in India in the 1830s, he had six 'waiting servants' behind his chair at dinner, and his daughter had three.

The nineteenth and twentieth centuries saw a general reduction in the numbers partly because British employers became comparatively poorer and partly because some of the servants' roles were made redundant by fashion or 'progress'. Wig-barbers, hookah-burdars and palanquin bearers all left the scene, along with wigs, hookahs and palanquins. So did the 'shootman', who in the 1830s was sent by Julia Maitland 'into the jungle every day to catch us half our dinner', mainly wild ducks and pigeons.[18] Staff numbers remained high, however, because religion and caste imposed restrictions on what duties a person could perform. Writing of these factors in Calcutta in 1768, Mrs Kindersley described them as 'the cause of great inconveniences and expense to the English, as it obliges them to hire three times the number of servants which would otherwise be necessary'. Even in 'the greatest emergency', she went on, servants would not 'perform the most trifling office which does not belong to their particular caste'. Such complaints persisted until the end of the Raj. When in the 1920s Marjorie Cashmore asked for a dead bird to be removed from her compound at Ranchi, not one of the servants would touch it; she had to get a sweeper from the bazaar to take it away.[19]

In 1882 Henry Beveridge had thirty-nine servants at his house in the Bengal station of Bankipore. This still seems a huge figure for the household of an unostentatious judge who was an early supporter of Indian nationalism. Yet as his son William* later pointed out, many of these servants provided services that in Britain would have been supplied by shops or local government. The water-carrier and the sweeper were substitutes for a water supply and sanitation; the gardeners and the fowlman were employed to provide essential food; and the grooms and grass-cutters were needed because there were no trams or buses in Bankipur. The Beveridges were not living as Hickey had done in the eighteenth century.[20]

---

* The future Lord Beveridge, author of the wartime report outlining the future welfare state.

Servants were selected according to their caste and religion as well as to abilities attested in recommendations from former employers. It was better to have a Muslim rather than a Hindu as cook, khansama or anyone waiting at table, because these would have to touch beef; in the age of the motor car it might also be preferable to have a Muslim as a driver, because high-caste Hindus did not wish to clean animal dung from the tyres.[21] Most of the outdoor jobs could be done by Hindus – gardeners, laundrymen, grooms, grass-cutters and nightwatchmen – but only an 'untouchable' would be a sweeper. In some places, of course, one had little choice. Ethel Grimwood, wife of the political agent at Manipur in the early 1890s, might have wished for Hindu gardeners, clad in dhotis, but she had to put up with Naga tribesmen, who did their gardening in the nude. When she gave them bathing-drawers in an attempt to 'inculcate decency', they preferred to use the garments as turbans.[22]

Among themselves the British argued about where the best servants might be found. The 'bearer' or valet, the crucial figure for the man of the house, could be from anywhere, but some employers 'swore' that the 'finest' in all India were from a small group of villages in Orissa. Opinions differed on the merits of chefs. Many were Muslims, and it was claimed that some of the best of them came from the Arakan–Chittagong area on the Burmese–Bengal border. Other chefs in demand were Christians from Portuguese Goa, who brought 'no caste or food complications with them', and who were often ranked at the top of the servants' hierarchy. Yet although they were generally 'excellent', they were 'apt' to get drunk 'at critical times'.[23] Goan Christians were also employed as ayahs (nannies or nurse-maids), a role for which their chief competitors were women educated by Christian missions in Madras. Like a bearer, however, an ayah could come from anywhere, even the hill tribes. When Raleigh Trevelyan was born in 1923, his father was in charge of the garrison at Port Blair, a penal settlement in the Andaman Islands: in consequence, the child's 'first ayah was a Burmese murderess called Mimi'. Two other murderers had carried his mother to the hospital where she gave birth.[24]

Alert to the dangers of inadvertent poisoning, memsahibs were diligent in their supervision of what went on in the kitchen. The British were impressed by the ingenuity of Indian cooks, by the way they could rustle up meals with rudimentary utensils – and often basic ingredients – in camp in the jungle. They were less impressed by the standard of hygiene in the kitchen, not just because they liked clean pots and pans but because they knew how quickly one could catch a disease and die after drinking water or milk that was contaminated. In the 1940s Anne Henry remembered her mother in Kashmir 'always watching the servants boil the drinking water, washing lettuce in *"pinky pani"* – permanganate of potash'.[25] Mothers could also be stern about less life-threatening issues, forbidding the cook to sleep in the kitchen or smoke his pipe there, and checking the accounts to make sure he was not making more than the traditional – and acceptable – profit from his visits to the bazaar.

Master–servant relationships in British India doubtless had the affections and abuses, the loyalties and resentments, and the kind-nesses and exploitations of such connections in other times and in other places. Knowing that their masters and mistresses would be firm, the servants hoped that they would also be fair, that although they might shout at them, they would not hit them or make them do things that were 'beneath them' or contrary to their religion. Probationers in the ICS were told never to 'hit a native', and a man could be dismissed from the service if he used violence. Yet at lower levels of society, rude-ness and violence were endemic and seldom received the punishment they deserved. Throwing a boot at a sleeping punkah wallah was a comparatively mild offence.

Richard Blechynden in Calcutta found his servants in about 1800 to be idle, dishonest, sometimes drunk and often quarrelsome. Yet, as was the case with his mistresses, he seems to have been inept with his selec-tions and in his dealings with them. Quarrels and drunkenness are seldom listed in the complaints of later employers, and dishonesty was usually limited to excessive 'commissions' on the shopping expeditions. When Georgina McRobert in Kanpur discovered that the sweeper was stealing her hens' eggs and then selling them to the cook, who after-wards sold them to his mistress as eggs from the bazaar, she decided to 'grin and bear it' because the servants 'have some good qualities after all'. Small things were often the most annoying, like finding the night-watchman asleep and snoring or hearing servants spitting and gargling, making 'the most excruciating noises by filling their mouths with water and then clearing their throats with a stick'.[26]

Servants, wrote one young Civilian in 1890, might be 'occasionally irritating beyond measure, but the way they stick to you covers a multitude of sins'. This was a widespread sentiment. Violet Haig, whose husband ended his career in 1939 as governor of the United Provinces, recalled that, although they had often been 'done' by servants in 'the milder forms of corruption in small money matters, there were many qualities of real affection and loyalty to level the scales'.[27] After a long furlough in Britain – and feelings of depression at going back to work – it was heartening to return to Bombay and find your old bearer on the Apollo Bunder with garlands of flowers to welcome you. Even the most unsentimental of Civilians admitted that returning to find 'the usual crowd of servants' at his bungalow was 'not without its charm'.[28]

Richard Blechynden may have found his servants annoying, but he and many of his compatriots would often support them before the law and in disputes with other Britons. Wealth and status made it easy for employers to be benevolent and paternalistic. They might reward their servants with dowries for their daughters or help them out when they got into debt. When Britons left India and said goodbye to their retainers, their renowned reticence might make these farewells seem less emotional than they were. After Alfred Lyall retired as lieutenant-governor in 1887, he sailed to England on the same ship as Mortimer Durand (his colleague and future biographer), who was going home on furlough. Durand watched him say goodbye to his old bearer on deck where 'the two men stood looking at one another in a silent life-long farewell that was very pathetic'. Lyall then patted his servant on the shoulder 'with something very like a caress' before he turned and went below. It was his farewell to India.[29]

Retiring Civilians usually tried to ensure that their bearers had another employer to take their place when they had gone. Some relationships were strong enough for master and servant to stay in touch even though they both knew they would never see each other again. Bill Cowley retired in 1947 but continued to correspond with his Punjabi bearer until the man died in 1974, even though the poor Indian could not write and had to employ a letter-writer to fulfil his part of the correspondence.[30] Other servants received more practical help from departing employers, whose assistance might sometimes last for decades. Matthew Calvocoressi was an English businessman of Greek origin who retired as a director of Ralli Brothers in 1923 and returned from Calcutta to England. Following his departure he continued to pay monthly allowances to his family's four closest household servants – including the bearer, the driver and the ayah – until his death in 1939. After that his widow, Hermione Melville, carried on the payments until the servants died in the mid-1950s. On the deaths of Lizzie (the ayah) and Ratan (the bearer), she sent money to their daughters to pay for their funerals.[31]

In 1928 the Labour politician Clement Attlee went to India as a member of the Simon Commission and acquired a bearer called Aseervatham whom he too kept in touch with. Many years later, in the 1950s, after Attlee had been prime minister and responsible for the belated independence of India, he helped the bearer obtain a licence to open a bar in Bangalore. The former prime minister died in 1967, but in the 1980s Mr Aseervatham was still paying for an annual requiem mass to be said on Attlee's birthday at the St Francis Xavier Cathedral at Bangalore.[32]*

British women in India usually relied on servants to do the household shopping. In a typical urban household in Bombay or Calcutta the cook and his assistant would set out before dawn, buy the day's provisions at the market, and return in time to prepare breakfast. In the mofussil they would use the nearest bazaars, but if these were considered inadequate or dangerously unhygienic, families often preferred to produce some of their supplies themselves. In Bankipore the Beveridges had cows and a 'cowman' so that they could have fresh milk and butter, and hens and a 'fowlman' so that they could eat their own eggs and chickens.[34]

One way of shopping for the memsahib was to sit on the verandah inspecting the wares that tradesmen unwrapped in her presence. Certain families, such as the Beveridges, employed their own darzi (tailor) or shared one with a neighbour in the station. For those who did not, a local darzi would arrive on the verandah with his sewing machine and take measurements. The memsahib would show him a pattern and give him some material, which the darzi would rapidly and dexterously, sitting cross-legged on the verandah, turn into a garment. Even

---

* British relationships with their bearers did not have to begin or end during the time of the Raj. When Donald Milner, the BBC's radio correspondent in Delhi, retired to rural Oxfordshire in the 1980s, he took his bearer with him and installed him in a large room above his garage.[33]

middle-class women in towns such as Madras and Bangalore often pre-ferred to have clothes made by a *darzi* than to buy them ready-made in a store. Tailors or other clothes-makers also penetrated the canton-ments. At the barracks in Mhow, recalled Mrs Davidson, a soldier's wife, the 'silk-wallah' would come to your verandah and measure you for a dress; 'you choose your pattern, he goes back to the bazaar and a short time after comes along with your garment beautifully made and dirt cheap'.[35]

Another form of shopping, important in distant places, was ordering goods by mail from the catalogues sent out by the large department stores, such as the Army & Navy Stores, which opened in Bombay in 1891 and Calcutta in 1901. Daisy Clay, the DO's wife in Garhwal, a remote and mountainous region in the north, made large orders twice a year that arrived after forty-eight hours on a train followed by three or four days on the backs of coolies. They contained everything Mrs Clay regarded as essential for the next six months for herself, her husband and her daughters, including Pears soap and Vaseline, Anadin and shoe polish, and Huntley & Palmer's 'Superior Reading Biscuits'.[36]

Enjoyable shopping excursions were rare events in most of India. You might find an excellent shop in an unexpected place, such as Hig-ginbotham's Bookshop in Ooty or the carpet store that Major Hadow established in Srinagar, yet for an 'all-round' shopping experience you had to be in one of the big cities. Calcutta had always considered itself to be sophisticated, a city where even in the middle of the nineteenth century you could get York and Westphalia hams and, allegedly, 'all the stock to be found at Fortnum & Mason's'.[37] Madras believed it could compete, and not only because it had Spencers, a store dubbed 'the Harrods of the Carnatic'. If you walked along the city's Mount Street in the 1930s, you would certainly find some useful and varied establishments. Just before you reached the New Elphin-stone, a Parsi-owned cinema, you could visit Maclure's, a pharmacy that made well-regarded soda water, and E. C. Barnes, a leading opti-cian. After the cinema you would find more pharmacies and the photographers, Klein and Weile, followed by the Hotel d'Angelis, set up by a confectioner from Corsica, where the English cricket team stayed in 1934 when led by the notorious advocate of 'bodyline' bowl-ing, Douglas Jardine. Further along you encountered some of the leading commercial names of British India, Whiteway Laidlaw's ('General Drapers'), Longman and Greens (publishers) and Wrenn Bennett's (general goods but especially toys). After them you could visit the high-steepled Christ Church, built in 1852, the showroom of W. E. Smith ('dealers in surgical instruments and makers of aerated waters'), the Madras headquarters of Higginbotham's, the showroom of Addison's (dealers in automobiles and motorcycles) and finally the Harrods of the Carnatic, which at its Dindigul factory made what it claimed to be Winston Churchill's favourite cigar, the 'Light of Asia'.[38] It was a far cry from Garhwal.

EDIBLES

In 1689 John Ovington, the chaplain on an Indiaman, recorded his experiences of dining with the Company's merchants at their factory in Surat. Three cooks – English, Indian and Portuguese – 'dressed' the meat 'in different ways for the gratification of every Stomach', producing among other things 'the most common *Indian* dish' (a 'palau' with boiled rice, boiled fowl and 'Spices intermixt') and an 'Indian Savory Dish' ('Cabob' – or kebab – roasted with herbs and garlic). On Sundays and holidays these 'entertainments' were 'made more large and splendid' with the addition of such meats as peacock and antelope plus '*Persian* fruits' such as 'Pistachoes, Plumbs [and] Apricocks'. Although English beer and European wine were normally drunk at the factory, 'upon high Festivals' Persian as well as European wines were 'drunk with Temperance and Alacrity', a phrase the chaplain evidently did not regard as a contradiction.[39]

The interesting 'fusion' menu of the Surat factory did not endure long into the eighteenth century. While the taste for such preserves as guava jelly and mango pickle survived and were imported to Britain, the carnivorous tastes of the English squirearchy commandeered the main course in India and – combined with squirearchical fondness for ostentation and abundance – was displayed on tables heaving with turkeys and huge joints of mutton and beef. Before she went to India in 1779, Eliza Fay was often told that 'the heat in Bengal destroyed the appetite'. On arriving, she found no evidence for this assertion and indeed, despite dining 'at two o'clock, in the very heat of the day', she thought she had never seen 'an equal quantity of victuals consumed'. Sometimes she might eat a Burdwan Stew in which everything was thrown into the pot – 'fish, flesh and fowl' – but more often she went to dinner parties and sat at tables (that 'groaned with the weight of the feast') containing (apart from hams, tongues, fowls and turkeys) 'nearly half a Bengal sheep' and 'every joint of a calf on the table at once'.[40] Not much seemed to have changed by the 1830s, when Julia Maitland, who was living in southern India, found four times as much food on the table as you would have at a dinner party in England – 'with goose and turkeys and joints of mutton for side-dishes'.[41]

Yet at that time the cuisine was in fact beginning to change, gradually becoming less blatantly 'meaty' and more French. As Marianne Postans observed in Bombay in 1838, 'hecatombs of slaughtered animals' had given place to 'lighter delicacies' such as Périgord pies, preserved meats and a local fish known as pomfret.[42] Dishes were no longer plonked on the table all at once but served as courses à la russe, their details described in menus written in French. According to Colonel Kenney-Herbert, the author of Culinary Jottings for Madras (1885), 'a taste for light wines' and a 'more moderate indulgence' in alcoholic beverages had stimulated 'a desire for delicate and artistic cookery'. Yet as joints of meat were withdrawn from the menu, so too were curry and rice; the Victorians in India preferred dishes that were European and, in their eyes, more sophisticated. 'Quality,' claimed Kenney-Herbert, had 'superseded quantity, and the molten curries and florid oriental compositions of the olden time' had been 'gradually banished from our dinner tables'.[43]

They had not, however, been banished altogether. The British always relished the three great hybrids of British-Indian cooking: spicy mulligatawny soup (originally known as 'pepper water' – milagu tanni in Tamil – and later, more pretentiously, as potage de Madras); kedgeree (the smoked fish and hard-boiled egg were British amendments to khichri, an Indian concoction made of lentils, rice and spices); and the spicy dishes in a thick sauce which the British called curry – and to which they tended to add too much curry powder.[44] Even Kenney-Herbert quite liked these comestibles. Mulligatawny or a 'well-considered curry' were 'capital things in their way' and fine to have for breakfast or tiffin or in camp. But they could 'no longer occupy' positions on dinner menus of 'the new regime' of 'dainty fare'.[45]

Whatever French or Indian influences the food might have gained or retained, at its core it was British. A dish might have a French name but it must not resemble what Curzon called 'greasy French cooking'. Major Somerset of the IMS was typical of many of his compatriots when he said he 'liked very simple English cooking and disliked good food being mucked about with fancy sauces so that you could not taste what sort of meat you were eating'.[46] Good plain cooking, good wholesome fare – it was a sort of mantra with the British. There is something rather forbidding and unappetizing about the word 'wholesome' when applied to food and drink; even the sherry at the Bengal Club was described as 'wholesome'.[47] In the 1860s the Madras Club established a farm and built 'sheep fattening sheds' in its compound with the stated object of supplying its membership 'with good and wholesome food'. The experiment was not a success and was soon abandoned.[48]

Few English people were more open to India and its landscapes than Edward Lear, the painter and writer of 'nonsense' verse who spent fourteen months travelling in the Subcontinent in the 1870s as a guest of the viceroy, his friend Lord Northbrook. He loved the scenery, he loved the vegetation, the palms and the mangoes, he even loved the Hindu holy city of Benares, which many Victorians loathed – and he disliked *English* India, Calcutta, which he called Hustlefussabad, and Ooty, which reminded him of Leatherhead. Yet his meals, carefully noted in his journal when on painting tours, consisted entirely of 'wholesome' English food, a constant repetition of a very basic diet: 'breakfast: eggs and beefsteak', 'breakfast: beefsteak and claret', 'breakfast: cold beefsteak and fowl', and then one extravaganza, 'capital breakfast: cutlets, stewed rabbit and grilled fowl, bread and butter, a bottle of claret . . .' And he wasn't keeping plain wholesome fare just for breakfast. Representative meals at other times of the day were a 'trivial supper of beer and mutton', a lunch of 'divine boiled mutton, potatoes and half a bottle of beer', and at some stage 'a roly-poly jam pudding'.[49]

For those who wished to stick closely to a British diet, the invention of tinned food was a great blessing. The initial drawback was that in the nineteenth century the tins gave the food a metallic taste and carried the risk of tin poisoning, especially if they had fish inside them. Tinned margarine, cheaper than tinned butter, was considered vile even if it wasn't metallic and poisonous.[50] By the interwar period, tin technology had improved, and almost everything that could be tinned – sardines, sausages, asparagus, smoked sprats and so on – was exported to India, often from Harrods in Knightsbridge. His order book for Mazda's, 'the premier wine and provision store' of Calcutta, reveals that in September 1936 W. H. Saumarez Smith, a subdivisional officer, received tins of (among other things) Polson's Butter, Cadbury's Chocolate, Pascal's Crême de Menthe, Cooper's Oxford Marmalade, Nestlé's Thick Cream, Liptons Pure Empire Coffee, Del Monte's large white asparagus, and McVitie and Price's Round Scottish Shortbread.[51] Even in the riverine flatlands of east Bengal he must have felt at home.

Chota hazri or little breakfast, which consisted of little more than a cup of tea and slice of toast soon after dawn, and proper breakfast, eaten at about nine o'clock (preferably after a nice morning ride), were routines that remained fairly constant in British India. So too, for those who had it, was tea-time. Like breakfast, this was ideally taken on the verandah, with sandwiches and cakes, but it was usually a private, familial meal; tea parties for women were quite popular in Victorian times, but by the twentieth century they had become 'a rare form of entertainment' in India. As in Britain, the cup of tea, whenever taken, was usually drunk with milk and sugar.

The other meals were more moveable. When Hickey was in India in the mid-1770s, 'the dining hour' was one o'clock, although a few years later Mrs Fay put it at two. As governor-general, Lord Cornwallis sensibly advanced it to more Spanish hours – three o'clock in the winter, four in the hot weather – and by the end of the century his successor Lord Wellesley had taken it to five. The hour progressed through the following century until eventually it reached eight or eight-thirty in the evening. Such a transformation clearly required the addition of an extra meal earlier, a light (or light-ish) lunch called tiffin, often of curry. In most households this took place between one and two, though officials on tour, who had missed out on breakfast, usually had their tiffin between eleven and twelve.

However anglicized the food in India was intended to be, intentions were bound to be compromised by the quality of the ingredients available. For a man like Philip Martyn, who joined the ICS in 1927, breakfast doubtless seemed a very English meal, as it would to one who insisted on having eggs and bacon seven days a week.[52] Yet the milk he drank did not resemble the produce of any cow he had seen in Britain;

it probably came from a buffalo. The butter too was probably buffalo, dyed to stop it looking too white, and the cream tasted like the milk. As for bread, anything similar to the loaves he had eaten in Europe was unachievable – at least outside the main cities – because of the primitive ovens and the poor quality of flour and yeast; it was best to stick to chapattis. The idea of 'rumble-tumble' (scrambled eggs) was an appealing one, but the reality – flavourless eggs from scrawny chickens – made this too a disappointment. Bacon would have been recognizable only if tinned and imported.

Climatic considerations combined with defective ingredients caused frustration and problems for carnivores, although diners in the eighteenth century hardly seem to have noticed them. In Britain you hung meat to make it tender and tasty, but if you hung it on the Indian Plains after February, it quickly went bad. You had to eat it within a day of the killing, which made it tough and tasteless.

Apart from mutton, red meat was often unavailable. As pork was unclean for Muslims and abhorrent to many Hindus, the British who required it had to find their own supplies, usually from a few piggeries in the hills. Yet home-grown pork was never a regular part of the British Indian diet; as with cheese and wine, hams were nearly always imported – at great expense. Although beef was forbidden to Hindus, there was a larger supply of this meat because it was a part of the Muslim diet. Its chief problem was the quality. The small brahmin cattle had not been bred for its beef and did not taste anything like a Galloway or an Aberdeen Angus. As Colonel Kenney-Herbert explained, it needed a lot of horseradish sauce to make it palatable, though Lear's diaries do not inform us whether he used this condiment when eating his customary lunches of boiled beef, cold beef, roast beef and salt beef. As we have noted, the British regiments needed huge quantitites of some beef-type substance to make the daily diet of stews and 'khaki patches'. The main ingredient of these, however, was often not beef. As the soldier's wife Mrs Davidson quickly noticed in the cantonment at Secunderabad in the 1930s, 'we ate buffalo for beef, and goat for mutton [and] it was very tough'.[53]

Even outside the barracks goat masquerading as mutton was often what you found yourself eating. Real mutton was in fact the only red meat appreciated in the later Raj, even if, like other kinds, it was tough because it could not be hung. Eliza Fay found Bengal mutton 'excellent', and others praised breeds of sheep raised around Patna and in the Deccan. But not everyone agreed on the merits of the Plains mutton. Up on the north-west frontier Captain Prendergast thought the Pathans' fat-tailed sheep was 'the finest' and perhaps the 'only edible meat in the Indian subcontinent'; eaten with Pathan soldiers, a 'feast of mutton pilau and thick fat wholemeal bread' was the 'finest food in the world'.[54]

One sure way of avoiding goat meat was to the join 'the Mutton Club', one of the quintessential institutions of Victorian India. In up-country stations men and women would band together in groups of five or multiples of five and buy a small flock of sheep. Periodically the animals would be slaughtered, cut up into fifths – the forequarters, the hind legs and the saddle – and their parts distributed in rotation among the club members. When it was the turn of a senior figure, the judge or the district officer, to receive the saddle, he often felt it incumbent on him to 'dine the station', a rather grim occasion at which members and their wives dressed up and sat down in rigid order of precedence. One junior magistrate recalled that at his first station he had to sit next to the wife of the district engineer every time he went to a dinner.[55]

The Mutton Club was at least a relief from the monotony of chicken, the one ubiquitous meat in India. 'You can hardly imagine how tired people in India get of fowls,' H. M. Kisch wrote in 1876 to his family in England. At his station in the Bengal mofussil, he ate five chicken dishes a day: hot and cold ones for breakfast, then chicken soup, roast chicken and a 'side dish of fowl' for dinner.[56] Considering that India had produced the world's ancestral chicken (the red jungle fowl), it seemed strange that it had not developed something larger and more tasty. Indian chickens were so scraggy and flavourless that many people found them inedible without splashing Worcestershire Sauce all over them. Numerous attempts were made to diversify feathered diets, including breeding turkeys, though these rarely flourished in an Indian climate, and shooting peafowl, yet although a roast peacock, redolent of medieval banquets, looked handsome on the Christmas table, its meat was dry and fairly tasteless; and its killing was an affront to Hindus. The most succulent farmed birds in India were quail, raised in 'quaileries', in pits or dark sheds.

Diversification was more successfully achieved by hunting than by breeding. 'Shooting for the pot', going out with a gun after work, is a familiar phrase in the letters and diaries of officials on tour. A good way of relaxing after a day of inspections, it was also a means of varying one's diet. On one of his hunting expeditions, J. Moray Brown of the Cameron Highlanders, a famous 'sportsman', enjoyed a dinner consisting of 'hare soup, salmi of green pigeons, roast jungle-fowl, deer's brain curry, cheetal [spotted deer] kidneys on toast and stewed fruit of the bher [Indian jujube]'. Doubtless it was, as the officer claimed, 'a dinner not to be despised'.[57] Yet satisfying as it must have been to hunt (and gather) one's own meals, the excitement of the achievement may have often been greater than the enjoyment of Indian game as food. Sand-grouse, the bird shot in the greatest numbers, was virtually inedible, and so were most species of wild duck. In 'the country of the Carnatic,' wrote Albert Hervey of the 1840s, the game was 'particularly insipid, dry eating and rather tough to boot'. Roast hare was 'dry and tasteless', not 'palatable' even with jelly or tamarind sauce, and nor was 'it nice in a stew'; it was only 'eatable' when potted. Similarly, the best way to deal with feathered game, such as snipe or duck, was 'to put it into pickle'. In the north, in the same period, Miss Fane took very much the same view. On one winter's day the gentlemen of her party had shot some black partridges, which were 'reckoned great delicacies', but in her opinion they were 'upon a par with all Indian game and are perfectly tasteless'.[58]

Fish in India was not tasteless, not at any rate the saltwater species off the Malabar coast or in the Bay of Bengal. In the hot weather fish would go bad even quicker than meat, which is why it was so frequently eaten at breakfast (often in kedgeree) soon after it was caught and why people living inland were limited to the less interesting freshwater fish, notably the mahseer, which anglers found as exciting to tackle as salmon but, being boney and rather flavourless, was much less exciting to eat. On the coasts shellfish were plentiful, one of the few local luxuries that the political agent in Bahrain was able to enjoy, but prawns and shrimps gathered too near a harbour carried a health risk. One Bombay speciality was the sweet-flavoured pomfret, served with an anchovy-butter sauce; another, rather strangely cherished by the British, was a salty dried fish curiously called 'Bombay duck'. Some of the best Indian fish, such as the becktie and the hilsa, were found on the other side of the country, in the estuaries of the Bay of Bengal. According to connoisseurs, the most delicious of all was the mango-fish, especially if smoked for breakfast. Captain Bellew considered it 'the whitebait of India', which the 'Calcutta bon vivant' should eat by the River Hooghly at 'the white tavern of Fultah'.[59]

For the British who loved their arboreal fruits – apples, pears and plums – the Plains were as bleak an environment as they were for those who loved their roses and rhododendrons. In India the trees grew best in the hills at altitudes of about 7,000 feet, very much higher than Scotland's Ben Nevis. Vegetables, most of which were native to Europe and America, were more successful in the Plains. If the seeds were sown at the end of the rainy season, they would ripen in time for Christmas. Spinach could be grown in the hot weather, and so, fortunately, could lettuce; salads (when carefully washed) came into their own in the summer.

A refreshing hot-weather dessert was mango fool (sugar, cream and mangoes). 'Everyone has it here,' reported a Civilian's sister in Sind, served in a wine glass. Yet the memsahibs' cakes and puddings were usually as British as anything else they confected or supervised; even if they gave a cake an Indian name such as Tirhoot Tea Cake, it might not contain an authentically Indian ingredient. The British never came to appreciate sticky Indian desserts except perhaps for halva, though they adopted rice and coconut for their own concoctions. Puddings are often the part of childhood that adults feel least nostalgic about, especially when consumed at school, and 'Malabar pudding' at Hebron School in the Nilgiris was remembered with horror: cold tapioca pudding ('frog spawn') 'stuck together like a blancmange with thick brown molasses over the top'. At home, however, the pudding could be amended, and fondly remembered, if served with black treacle and coconut milk.[60]

DRINKABLES

In the last decades of the Raj the most comforting moment of the day for many Britons was six o'clock in the evening, the hour of the sundowner, the first alcoholic drink of the day. In the cities some of them might drink a glass of beer at lunch, but most would stick to refreshing glasses of lime juice, ginger ale and soda water; in all his years in India Robert Bristow, the man responsible for the construction of the deep-water port at Cochin, knew only one European who drank whisky during the day.[61] And in the mofussil people were even more abstemious, awaiting the moment, some doubtless with impatience, like naval officers waiting for the sun to go over the yardarm, though in their case the phrase was referring to late morning. It had been a long day – most officials had been up since six o'clock – and they felt they deserved a strong drink, a chota or burra peg (a measure the width of two or three fingers of brandy or whisky) with plenty of soda water and ice. The second favourite drink of the twentieth century, one also enjoyed by women, was the gimlet, a cocktail made of gin and lime juice and again a lot of ice.

How different it had been in the days of their ancestors. Punch had been the chief drink of the seventeenth century, a bowl consisting of arrack (preferably from Goa), water, spices or rose water, lime or lemon juice, and a good deal of sugar. It retained its popularity into the following century but was then challenged by various drinks that had been made far away and further north and could not in any way be regarded as thirst-quenchers: Madeira (which replaced wine previously imported from Persia), cherry brandy (much enjoyed by the ladies) and mulled wine known as 'burnt wine' (warmed and mixed with cloves and cinnamon). In Calcutta William Hickey and his friends even drank 'burnt champagne': as president of the Catch Club, he established a rule that members must drink 'kettles of burnt champagne' from two in the morning till sunrise.[62]

On arriving in Calcutta in 1777, Hickey admitted that he lived a very 'dissipated' life, drinking 'superabundant potations of champagne and claret' every day.[63] Later he became a generous host, proud of the quality of his claret, hock and Madeira. Fortified wines travelled better than claret and, as we have seen, Madeira remained popular in India partly because of 'the improving effect' the voyage from the Atlantic was supposed to have on its taste.[64] It was enjoyed by all classes, from Blechynden's mistresses in the 1790s (who were two-bottle girls) to the guests of the governor of Madras in the 1940s; Leonard Woolf knew a civil servant in Ceylon who thought 'a gentleman should drink [Madeira] for lunch in whatever climate he might live'.[65]* Its rival

---

* Woolf himself considered it an 'uninteresting wine' in any climate and thought it should not be drunk by anyone, gentleman or not, in a place as warm as northern Ceylon.

sherry was almost as ubiquitous. During the fourteen months of his painting tours in India Edward Lear managed to find it almost everywhere he went and drank it, with soda when he was 'athirst', at breakfast, lunch and supper. A few years earlier, a 'sherry cobbler' (an American cocktail of sherry and lime with sugar and crushed ice), had been briefly fashionable in Calcutta, where its popularity may have been boosted by Charles Dickens, whose Martin Chuzzlewit had taken a sip and 'cast up his eyes . . . in ecstasy'.

As a colonel in India, Arthur Wellesley was considered 'very abstemious with wine', but the man who described him thus recorded in the same sentence that the officer 'drank four or five glasses with people at dinner, and about a pint of claret after'. Although we don't know the alcoholic content of the claret at that time, a recent biographer of Wellington has argued that these bottles must have been naturally weak or else diluted by servants.[66] The popularity of wine in India declined shortly after Wellesley returned to Europe, soon to combat Napoleon's marshals in Iberia. A vintner in the Calcutta of Hickey's time might extol his 'highly flavoured' claret and 'rich and old' hock, but it was difficult to pretend that European wine tasted as good in Asia as it did in Europe.[67] It might be all right to import communion wine from Tarragona, but not even the French in Pondicherry thought their burgundy was comparable to the Chambertin Napoleon drank at Malmaison. Conscious of this, the Jesuit College of St Joseph's in Trichinopoly imported wine from Australia in the belief that it stood the sea voyage better than European products.[68] Wine continued to be drunk, especially in the regimental Mess, but it must have been disheartening to be a wine merchant in India. When a twentieth-century griffin, Malcolm Darling, entered Mr Phipston's Bombay wineshop in 1907 to make his first nervous order, the proprietor felt obliged to warn him that, as 'wine will not stand the climate', his customer would be 'wise' to buy it 'in small quantities'. Such frankness earned him thirty-three years of loyalty from Darling.[69]

Soon after 1820 wine lost much of its popularity to beer, which was more reliable in transit and a more appropriate drink in an Indian climate. From the end of the eighteenth century the British in India were drinking 'country beer', which apparently went well with curry but was in fact a sort of beer cocktail: to a fifth of a bottle of imported beer or porter were added a wine glass of toddy or palm wine, some sugar and ginger, and perhaps the dried peel of limes or oranges. Early attempts at brewing beer in India were unsuccessful, partly because the Indian timber used to make the casks tainted the beer unpleasantly. Yet by the 1880s there were a number of breweries in the Hills, several of them run by the family of Brigadier Dyer. In the twentieth century Dyer Meakin was advertising its 'Luncheon Ale' as 'equal to the best Pilsener yet manufactured . . . produced from the choicest of English Hops and best of Malts . . . an ideal drink for athletes and strongly recommended by Physicians to invalids owing to its purity and wholesomeness'.[70]

Yet the bulk of beer in India was always imported. Realizing that stout and porter were unsuited to India, British breweries concentrated on ale and bitter, Hodgson's leading the way with its Pale Ale, a formula that was later more or less copied by the Burton breweries, Bass and Allsopp's, with their India Pale Ale or IPA. By 1870, according to Henry Cotton, 'Bass's bottle beer reigned supreme', while Hodgson's, whose firm had misjudged its pricing, 'had had its day'.[71]

Beer of course saved Tommy Atkins from the often lethal effects of bazaar rum and arrack. Yet imported 'purge' or 'neck-oil' was not only drunk by the 'beer-wallahs' and 'purge-shifters' in the army canteen. It was now fashionable in society. In Calcutta in the 1830s, noted Thomas Babington Macaulay, even his sister Hannah and his brother-in-law (Charles Trevelyan) 'generally indulged in ale' although he 'more aristocratically confined' himself to 'sherry or hock and soda water'. When Philip Hutchins began his ICS career in Madras in 1858, 'nearly everyone drank beer . . . Almost the only alternatives were light claret from Pondicherry or Brandy-and-Soda'; whisky was 'hardly known except, perhaps, among some Scotsmen'. In the Central Provinces in the same period, 'beer was the drink even of those who had acquired high rank'. Everyone, recalled J. H. Rivett-Carnac, had his beer 'after the sun had gone down' and also took a 'bottle at luncheon on high days and holidays, and at a Sunday "tiffin"'. In the following century Lieutenant Prendergast had a commanding officer who could not function without a bottle of Allsopp's beer close at hand.[72]

The next favoured drink of the Raj was brandy, which could compete with beer as a thirst-quencher because it could be drunk 'long', with fizzy water and ice. For decades a 'peg' meant brandy not whisky, and its attractions were enhanced by the medical belief that it was good for people with fever. In India it was not swirled about in bulbous glasses but drunk with soda water, first manufactured by the British in a factory in Farrukhabad in the 1830s, and regarded as much better and fizzier in bottles than the 'flat aerated water' made from 'sparklets'. The other essential ingredient was ice. Since their arrival in India, the British had been desperately searching for ways to cool their drinks, wrapping bottles in khus-khus, putting them in wells or immersing pewter flasks in a vessel containing water and saltpetre. The problem was partially solved in 1833 with the first arrival of ice from the United States in a ship belonging to the American Tudor Ice Company (named after its founder Frederic Tudor). Yet the supply remained sufficiently erratic for Calcutta society to wait in a state of anxiety for announcements that a boat with a cargo of Lake Wenham ice was approaching.[73] Enterprising though Mr Tudor was – and grateful to him that the British certainly were – it was not an ideal system. After four months at sea, much of the cargo had unsurprisingly thawed by the time it arrived, and more of it thawed when it was transported to the mofussil. The situation improved again with the establishment of ice factories in 1878, but the problem of distribution remained. Labouring in the heat of the Punjab, Malcolm Darling thought there was no 'music sweeter to the ear than the sound of clinking ice', but by the time his daily consignment reached him after the train journey from Multan, there was only enough for a single drink.[74] Another useful development was the invention of the ice-box, which meant one could take bottles of cold soda water to tennis parties.

Brandy pawnee lost its pre-eminence through no fault of its own, through no change of taste, or sudden aversion, or even a realization that, like port, it was unwise to drink too much of it in a tropical climate. It lost because the phylloxera louse came to Europe from North America and devastated the vines that produced it. Brandy's replacement was Scotch whisky, its popularity enhanced by dubious claims that it helped combat insomnia, that it helped protect the imbiber from bubonic plague and that, according to the Islay distilleries' advertisements in India, 'the most eminent physicians of the day prescribe it where a stimulant is required'.[75] Yet not everyone admired brandy's successor. Winston Churchill 'disliked the flavour intensely' and observed that his father, Lord Randolph, 'could never have drunk whisky except when shooting on a moor or in some very dull chilly place'. Winston only overcame his 'repulsion' when he was with the Malakand Field Force and found there was nothing else to drink except tea or lime juice. Following his initiation, however, he 'never shrunk when occasion warranted it from the main basic standing refreshment of the white officer of the East'.[76]

Many women were also repelled by the flavour of whisky, although the Dawkins family governess found an exception in a club in Burma where British women drank 'a terrific lot of it'.[77] Those who did not like it had an alternative in gin, which was now respectable in the empire because it improved the taste of tonic water, which was recommended by doctors because its quinine was a prophylactic against malaria. A more doubtful additive was Rose's lime juice, which the manufacturers claimed should be taken at night to avoid hangovers, but its combination with gin earlier in the evening (in the popular gimlet) might perhaps have been the origin of that putative hangover. One advantage that gin had over whisky was that it could be made in India without tasting disgusting, and it was available in both world wars. In the second global conflict Parry's of Madras invented Parry's Navy Gin, a liquor soon so sought after that it was used as a sort of currency: large consignments were flown to Singapore (before 1942) and even by American Boeings into China.[78]

CHILDREN

Most British women who went to India gave birth to their first child on the Subcontinent. If they had married in Britain and become pregnant soon afterwards, they were likely to have an uncomfortable journey and 'an awful time in the Bay of Biscay'. In the days of the long Company voyages around the Cape births quite often took place on board the 'Indiamen', and they continued to do so on troopships on the Mediterranean route. In January 1868 two soldiers' wives gave birth off the coast of Portugal only a few days after their ship, HMS *Crocodile*, had left Ireland for India.[79] Such births were not necessarily the result of careless planning. Soldiers and their wives were often not told where they would be in nine months' time.

Rough seas in the Bay of Biscay might cause a miscarriage, and so might rough roads and long journeys across India. Births themselves were often both difficult and dangerous. An established memsahib, the wife of a colonel or a commissioner, might arrange to have her baby in a nursing home in the Hills, but this was rarely an option for the young wife of a soldier or a forestry official. In April 1918 Florence Milligan, the wife of a gunner from Sligo, had to travel by bullock-cart to reach a hospital in Ahmednagar where she could give birth to her son Terence Alan, the boy who grew up to become the comedian Spike Milligan.[80] Yet at least Terence was born in a hospital. Many women gave birth in places without any medical facilities. In the 1890s Jenny Partridge, the wife of a district officer, had one baby in a dak bungalow on the way to a new posting at Garhwal, and another the day before her husband disappeared on tour, leaving her for a month in remote mountains with no Europeans anywhere near except the nanny she had brought out from Devon.* [81] Women often had to resign themselves to giving birth at inconvenient times and places to fit in with their husbands' career movements. When travelling by boat down the Ganges in the winter of 1867, John Beames recalled that he had been 'obliged to stop for a time as my wife was about to be confined'. After Ellen had given birth to their first daughter in the old fort at Monghyr, the voyage was resumed.[82]

Middle-class children born in India in the last decades of the Raj were almost unanimous in their memories of a 'golden' infancy. They might have forgotten that they hated fancy-dress parties, they might have been unaware of the snobbery that prevented them playing with a child like the young Spike Milligan (who was a sergeant's son),† but they invariably remembered the colours and the warmth, their ponies and other pets, the scents of the bazaars, the crowd of adoring Indian servants. Many of them contrasted the behaviour of their parents, frequently so busy and aloof, with the apparently limitless capacity of the Indians of the household to humour them, play with them, and even do such things as build them a wendy house in a large neem tree. As the Civilian Walter Lawrence recalled, the servants would croon incomparable lullabies, invent endless games and play 'patiently for hours

* The second Partridge child was called Rex. As an adult he became a friend of Lytton Strachey and the Bloomsbury Group, who persuaded him to change his name to the less regal-sounding Ralph.
† Spike was allowed to play with Indian children, but in their 'warfare' games it was tacitly accepted by both sides (and their parents) that the Indians would never win them.[83]

with the *baba log* [the child folk], never reproaching them for their desultory, changing moods'.[84]

For most of the sahibs' *baba log*, the most important and beloved of the servants was the ayah, often a small woman in a white sari with a beatific smile, a nanny who gave them affection and attention but very little discipline. As adults, many remembered her as a second mother, perhaps more loveable than their real mother, an always reassuring figure who had represented warmth and security in the years of their early childhood. The ayah looked after the children, took them on outings, taught them her own language so that many in the north spoke Hindustani before they could speak English. The Kiplings' ayah in Bombay took Rudyard to market and for walks by the sea under the palm trees, and on their return to the family's home she would remind him to speak English to his parents.

Parents were less enchanted by the ayah and were anxious that the endless indulging of her charges – the perpetual deference to the wishes of 'missy baba' or the 'chota sahib' – would spoil them and turn them into little tyrants requiring firm discipline. A further worry was that so much exposure to servants might encourage children to pick up bad habits, dodgy accents and perhaps even some sympathy for Indian culture and religion. Yet another fear – though the risk was exaggerated – was that infants would be given a little opium to stop them crying and make them sleep. This did happen, but extremely rarely.[85]

Rudyard Kipling recalled his Indian infancy as a paradise and ascribed his expulsion (to England) to the British feeling that it was 'inexpedient and dangerous for a white child to be reared' in India throughout his youth.[86] Of course there were dangers. The Indian climate and hygiene killed a lot of people, adults as well as children; those who survived and retired in their fifties often looked like septuagenarians when they arrived home. British children were likely to be healthier in a British climate and, although they might die of illness or disease in Britain, they also did so in India, often from dysentery or cholera. Children who lived in the Plains in the hot weather became 'slight, weedy and delicate' – in the words of the IMS doctor Joseph Frayer[87] – but from the 1860s there were schools for them in the Hills. None of them needed to go home for climatic reasons alone.

Sir Bamphylde Fuller, a former lieutenant-governor, was articulating a strange but popular belief when he claimed, just before the First

World War, that the Indian climate was 'injurious to the European temperament' as well as to the body, and that British children who stayed in India after the age of seven would not only 'lose their energy of mind and body' but also 'experience sexual feelings earlier than is habitual with their race'.[88] Here we enter a new dimension, perhaps hinted at by Kipling's use of the word 'inexpedient', that is moralistic and pseudo-scientific rather than climatic. It is what Dr Frayer regarded as the moral deterioration caused by the Indian environment, an ambience which tended to make British children 'deceitful and vain' and 'indisposed to study'.[89] When in 1939 Sheila Fraser suggested that their children might be educated in India, her husband Sir Denholm replied, 'Certainly not.' As Resident in Kashmir (a post his father had filled at the start of the previous world war), he would have had access to good tutors and good schools, but he wouldn't 'hear' of the suggestion allegedly because the children would 'end up speaking chee-chee'.[90] Yet behind the anxiety about accents was the fear that children would be indoctrinated, even if passively and unintentionally, and influenced by 'native' ways of thought. A hundred years previously, in Madras in the 1830s, Julia Maitland had voiced this anxiety when she said she would try to prevent her children learning Indian languages because otherwise they would learn 'all sorts of mischief with them, and grow like little Hindoos'.[91]

There were of course *good* reasons to send children to Britain just as there were for a Roman governor of Cilicia to have his sons educated in Rome or a Spanish viceroy to Mexico to place his children in Seville or Madrid. And it was not a specifically Victorian or imperialist habit to exile one's children to a place several thousand miles from where one was living. In the 1780s Major William Palmer proudly sent his eldest half-Indian son (also called William) to be educated in Britain; a generation later, James Kirkpatrick, the Resident at Hyderabad, sent his infants (aged three and five) to England, despite the protests and despair of their Muslim mother, Khair un-Nissa.[92] From Calcutta in the same period, Richard Blechynden sent the progeny of his various bibis and mistresses to England for their education so as to 'enlarge' their ideas and make them more culturally English, a process that would help them find good careers and suitable marriages.[93]

In subsequent eras parents also recognized that a boy who was sent to school in Britain and shared the training and discipline of his schoolfellows would enjoy later benefits; and through acquaintances and the 'old boy network', he would have advantages on going to university or starting a career that a boy who stayed in India, even if he did not acquire a chee-chee accent, would never have. Apart from 'country-born' people, planting families who had settled in India, almost everyone who could afford to send their children to school in England did so, even those who were not part of the imperial enterprise. From the 1820s to the 1840s the Rev. Henry Baker, a missionary in south India, sent at least ten of his children to England to be educated at the expense of the Church Missionary Society.[94] Even William and Mildred Archer, a Civilian and his wife who were pro-Congress and longing for the Raj to end, had no hesitation about their children's schooling in 1945. Their little son Michael had already had an English governess and had then gone to an American school in Mussoorie, but he was now 'eight years old', his mother pointed out, and 'it was clear that he must go to school and start a European education' – at the Dragon School in Oxford for him and at a boarding school in the Lake District for his five-year-old sister Margaret.[95]

The misery caused by separation was often unbearable, especially for those Indian women such as Khair un-Nissa who feared (rightly in her case) that they would never see their children again. When the missionary Alexander Duff returned to India in 1839, he and his wife left their four children in Scotland, including a baby whom they did not see again until he was eleven years old.[96] In the same year the Civilian James Thomason took his sick wife and their seven children to England, left them all there and returned to India. When he reached Bombay he learned that his wife had died, but the 'call of duty' was such – he was an Evangelical as well as an administrator – that he did not consider returning to look after his children (all of them under the age of ten), who were left in the care of his sister. He returned to his post at Agra and over the years tried to persuade his children that duty and the 'providence of God' were more important things than the cult of the family.[97] Yet even men less driven and zealous than Duff and Thomason felt that it was part of their duty, part of their imperial obligations, to abandon their children when necessary. 'When we returned to India after furlough in 1880,' wrote the Civilian G. R. Elsmie, 'we left our ten children at home.' As it turned out, they were luckier than most parents. Over the following decade all the children, in dribs and drabs, went out to India, some as wives, others as subalterns, and in 1890 the entire family (including grandchildren and sons-in-law) was able to celebrate Christmas Day in Lahore Cathedral.[98] Such family reunions were extremely rare – and the Elsmies never enjoyed another one.

Hazel Squire, a Civilian's daughter, confessed that it had taken all her 'adult life to unravel and resolve' the 'trauma of separation' from her parents in the 1930s.[99] Many children failed to resolve it at all. Gillon Aitken, the son of a manager of Finlay's, was born in Calcutta in 1939 and sent to his first boarding school at Darjeeling at the age of three; at Independence he was removed and sent to his second in Britain in 1947. 'I lost my parents when I was seven,' he recalled, 'I thought they were dead.'[100] From the eighteenth to the twentieth century six was considered the normal age for a boy to go 'home', preferably with his parents, who would arrange to be on furlough at the time and who would then leave him behind, probably at a preparatory school in southern England, when they returned to India. In 1782 Eliza Fay noted that a boy who was 'nearly seven years of age' was still living in Calcutta, though it was 'rather late'. One hundred and thirty years later, 'popular opinion' held that a boy should be 'sent home' at 'five or six' to prevent him being spoilt and 'becoming overbearing and backward as a result of missing the early training, education and discipline provided by British preparatory schools'.[101]

As girls were not required to reach the same levels of training and education, there was less rigidity about the timing of their departure. They often went 'home' later and came back earlier. But they might also have to go away sooner in order to accompany a brother who had reached the age of five or six. Such was the fate of poor Trix Kipling, who was only three when her parents took her to England with five-year-old Rudyard. After a few months spent all together, Lockwood and Alice Kipling took their children to a boarding house at Southsea, deposited them there and, without explaining what they were doing, returned to India. Even if Mrs Holloway, the owner of the boarding house, had turned out to be a kind woman instead of an Evangelical tyrant who beat him, the young Rudyard would have struggled to understand why his parents had betrayed and abandoned him and why he was left in Southsea for five and a half years before Alice learned of his misery (from one of her sisters) and came home and removed him.

At the age of twenty-two Kipling described his experiences, only slightly fictionalized, in 'Baa, Baa, Black Sheep', a harrowing story that understandably – and perhaps justly – upset his parents.

Men and women tried to be philosophical about separations from their children, assuring themselves that they were having to pay the 'price of empire'. Children trying to recall those partings as adults remained confused by their mothers' apparent composure and lack of feelings. Yet perhaps they never realized how much effort had gone into *not* crying, into not showing emotion in case a display of feelings made it even harder for the children. Anne Wilson, who married a Scottish Civilian in 1888, understood 'the anguish of a thousand mothers, who pay for India with their babies, like birds dropped from the parent nest before their wings have learnt to fly . . .'[102] She knew that memsahibs, who might be regarded as shallow and frivolous, were often women trying not to break down when they heard baby voices, women whose most intimate moments were spent opening letters from England and reading tear-smudged descriptions of experiences that they were unable to share.

After the first separation, women might wonder how many more of them they would be able to endure. Matters were quite straightforward when travel between Britain and India was via the Cape: you couldn't visit the children for Christmas or the summer holidays. You either stayed with your husband in India or you remained with your children in Britain. When Robert Clive's son Edward was offered the governorship of Madras in 1797, his wife Henrietta went with him on an adventure she compared to the 'Arabian Nights', even though it meant leaving her sons in the care of her brother (Lord Powis) and the bishop of Bristol.[103] Yet her contemporary Hyacinthe Wellesley made the other choice, staying with her children in England and leaving her husband to go half crazy with sexual frustration in Calcutta.

Women's responses to the dilemma altered over the period of the British presence in India. Until the middle of the nineteenth century wives usually felt that their first duty was with their husband. When in the 1840s Fanny Pratt decided to go with hers, a lieutenant-colonel who had been offered a place on the staff of the governor of Madras, she left their four children in England. As her chief worry seems to have been that their religious education would be neglected, she sent them 'devout outpourings' by post, but the children, perhaps more concerned about motherly neglect, proved unresponsive.[104] In subsequent years more women came to feel that maternal care in Britain was as important as support for a husband in India. Some thought it more so. Henry Cotton's wife, Mary, took her two sons home before her husband was thirty, had a third child in England, and never returned to India; for the next twenty-eight years the boys saw their father only when he was on leave.

Like other people explaining such arrangements, Cotton ascribed his to the climate and his wife's delicate health after six consecutive hot weathers in the Plains.[105] Here, as elsewhere, there may have been other reasons, including a deterioration in the relationship. Yet except in cases of total separation or divorce, most couples looked for solutions less drastic than Mary Cotton's. As we have seen in the case of the surgeon Ernest Bradfield, a wife might spend the winter months with her husband in Madras and the rest of the year with their children in England. The advent of air travel made other compromises possible. In the 1930s Richard Hilton and his wife decided that the best thing for their sons would be to send them to England with their mother so that they could live with her parents in a rectory on the Isle of Wight; as an artillery officer on the north-west frontier, Hilton would then volunteer for 'non-family' hardship stations that would give him three months' annual leave that, after three days of air flights, allowed him to spend the summer holidays with his family in Yarmouth.[106]

In earlier periods of the Raj fathers had to wait much longer before they could see children whom they had sent or taken to England for their education. Lockwood Kipling did not see his for nearly seven years after he had exiled them to Southsea. Some children never saw their father after their early years even if he was still alive when they became adults: Charles Glasfurd was sent to Scotland in 1837 at the age of six and never met his parent again although they were both soldiers in India in the 1850s.[107] The saddest fathers were those unable to enjoy even their children's infancy because their wives had died young, in childbirth or from disease, and as widowers they had had to take their offspring back to Britain and leave them with grandparents when they returned to their jobs. This meant not only the loss of their company but also the loss of influence on how they were brought up. Hopetoun Stokes, a Madras Civilian, was resigned to becoming a stranger to his children after he had taken them home to live with their grandmother following his young wife's death. 'They must all grow up,' he wrote from his post in Madras, 'without knowing or caring much for me.'[108]

It was common for 'children of the Raj' to recall in later life that they had never been able 'to get to know' their father. Sometimes it was because, as in Hugh Gaitskell's case, the father died abroad when the child was at school in Britain. More often it was because the parent had been able to see his children only intermittently – between the ages of five or six until their late teens or adulthood. A relationship of goodwill might be established, a sort of distant affection, but not much more than that, and often a good deal less. Children might resent the long absence of a father and then resent even more his presence as a virtual stranger returned to live with them on his retirement. Peter Pears, the future singer and partner of Benjamin Britten, admitted that he 'never forgave' his father, an engineer on the Burmese railways, for coming home when Peter was thirteen and taking his place as (in his biographer's words) 'the man of the house and his mother's protector'.[109]

Children arriving in England were almost invariably bewildered and then depressed by the sight of 'home'. Tilbury or Southampton on a February morning was a depressing start, especially if the dockers were on strike: bleak, wet and uninviting. 'Terrible noise, and everything so cold and grey,' was the first impression of Spike Milligan; although his Indian childhood had been far from gilded, he was soon longing to return to Rangoon.[110] Indian towns may have been squalid and chaotic – not that many British children lived in them – but English towns were grimy, dingy, permeated by soot and above all colourless. Matters did not improve when children went to school, got chilblains and lived on a diet of stews, suet puddings and over-boiled vegetables. Most of them soon yearned for India, not just for their parents, pets and servants – and the sense of security these gave them – but also for the colours and the sun and the spicy smells. Having been born in India, they felt that they belonged there. They found it difficult to make friends with children who had never smelt sandalwood or ridden an elephant or heard the screech of the brainfever bird. One of the few things they liked about Britain was that its houses had staircases with banisters to slide down.

Lucky children had a family base in England, as the Hilton boys did at their grandparents' house on the Isle of Wight, a place of reassurance to return to at the end of the school term. Yet the hospitality of relatives was not always reassuring or even forthcoming. Raleigh Trevelyan, the son of an Indian Army officer, felt that his life between the ages of eight and fourteen was summed up by a remark he overheard one relative telling another: 'it's your turn to have Raleigh for Christmas'.[111] Evidently Alice Kipling feared that her sisters and sisters-in-law – of whom she had eight – would be equally grudging; she was in any case unwilling to impose upon them a son who, on his previous visit to England at the age of two and a half, had been noisy, aggressive and prone to tantrums. Yet at least the little Kiplings were able to stay with one aunt and uncle – Georgy Burne-Jones and her pre-Raphaelite husband – for the Christmas holidays, and at least they were able to live together in Southsea during the rest of the year. Many siblings were separated from the beginning, living with different sets of aunts and uncles in the holidays and going to different schools in the term, the boys frequently to boarding schools on the south coast, the girls often to a day school or some kind of 'establishment' for 'young ladies' near their relations.

Educational agencies existed to advise parents in India which schools in Britain would be appropriate for their children. In 1913 John Christie went to St Cyprian's on the Sussex coast because his father had been informed that it included 'other boys with an Indian background', among them a Rivett-Carnac and Eric Blair, who at the time was busy hating the place and who later (when he was George Orwell) attacked it with vehemence in his essay 'Such, Such were the Joys'.[112]* Yet most parents had their own ideas about where they wanted to send their children. Alan Ross, the future poet and editor, found himself in a small unknown prep school in Cornwall because his mother 'had the idea that the Cornish climate was suited to an Indian-born child'. His father, however, was disappointed; he would have preferred to send young Alan to his own homeland, Scotland, and educate him in Edinburgh, at Cargilfield and Fettes.[114]

Most parents went for less obscure choices, to the places they or their brothers had gone to, or to schools (like St Cyprian's) on the south

---

* Christie followed Blair as a scholar at Eton, went on to Cambridge, joined the ICS and was the viceroy's private secretary at the time of Independence. In old age he wrote an essay refuting Orwell's views on the horrors of St Cyprian's and the brutality of its headmaster.[113]

coast where other children born in India were educated. Schools around Eastbourne were especially attractive because many Civilians and other officials retired to the town and its surroundings and could thus hold reunions with younger colleagues visiting their children on leave. When Emily Boon and her siblings (children of a Civilian) went to live in Sussex, they conformed to a familiar pattern: the brother was a boarder at Lancing College near Worthing, while the sisters lived with their mother and were day pupils at a school in Eastbourne.[115] From prep school, boys advanced naturally to public school, often the one their father had been at, or else to one of the newer establishments intended to be – and later known as – 'nurseries of empire', schools such as Bedford, Clifton, Westward Ho! and Marlborough. Cheltenham may have lost its place as the premier kindergarten for the ICS, but it still sent a lot of boys to other services in the Subcontinent. When one distinguished Old Cheltonian, the Civilian Walter Lawrence, visited the college and gave a speech there, he told the boys that India was the 'tied house' of Cheltenham and that it was their duty to serve it.[116]

A few ICS couples resisted pressure from friends, family and colleagues to send their six-year-olds to Britain, though it was easier to remain firm if the children were girls and the current posting was in the Hills. In the years before the First World War Joseph Clay's daughters managed to have a long and fairly idyllic Indian childhood, much of it spent camping in the hills of Garhwal, and in the same period Evan Maconochie took advantage of the benign climate of Bangalore to keep his children with him for four years longer than was normal. Among the most devoted Britrish parents was William Horsley, once a surveyor of jungles and from the 1880s a judge in the province of Bombay. He and his wife so longed to 'hang on' to their children that he waited sixteen years for his first furlough in case he felt obliged to leave his eldest girls behind when he returned to India. When finally he did go to England, he could not face a separation and so returned from furlough with all his four daughters plus a governess. Knowing how criticized he would be if any of them fell ill and died, he felt worried and guilty when they had a fever and relieved when he saw them 'well and jolly' in their garden in Sind. When eventually the elder ones did go to England, he had arranged matters so that there would be little more than a year before he could take early retirement and join them.[117]

Most British children born in India did *not* go to school In Britain, only those whose parents could afford the school fees, the boat tickets and often some kind of payment to guardians or relatives for the holidays. The Clays and the Horsleys had the choice, but most parents did not. Nor of course did the thousands of orphans who were a natural consequence of keeping British soldiers in India.

In the eighteenth century the civil and military authorities provided schools and orphanages in Calcutta and Madras, mainly for the children of soldiers and officers. Many of these were not in fact 'full orphans': they might be children whose fathers had died of disease or on campaign, or motherless Eurasian children whose fathers' regiments were returning to Britain and who preferred to stay in the country of their birth and upbringing. When in 1863 Private Patrick Carroll gave his children the choice of going 'home' with him or remaining in India, they chose to stay at the Catholic orphanage in Agra.[118]

Orphanages in cities or attached to a barracks in the Plains were not healthy places for small British children, especially in the hot weather, and in the 1840s Henry Lawrence suggested that new ones should be built in the Hills. 'Barracks children', he lamented, lived rotten lives, both morally and physically, and would only thrive in the atmosphere of a hill school and orphanage. By cajoling his fellow officers and making a generous donation himself, he raised enough money for the first Lawrence Military Asylum to be opened, at Sanawar near Simla, in 1847. Another one was built at Mount Abu in Rajputana, followed by two more after Lawrence's death in the Rebellion, Lovedale at Ootacamund and Ghora Gali at Murree. Herbert Edwardes, one of Lawrence's lieutenants and a devout Evangelical, extolled the vision of 'hundreds of little boys and girls playing upon a green mountainside', running about 'without hats and bonnets' and catching 'butterflies instead of deadly fevers', children who, once they had been removed from the barracks, would no longer be 'pale and sickly' but 'hale, hearty [and] useful', living in a place where they would 'see no drunkenness and hear no oaths, and where all the impressions of their childhood should be those of religion and not those of vice'. When in 1857 he visited the asylum, Edwardes could see what a 'real blessing' it had become: 'the Boys and Girls are real English Children – well grown, well filled-out, rosy-cheeked and high-spirited'. By 1864, 419 'real English Children' were enjoying the amenities of Sanawar.[119]

The motto of the asylum-schools was 'Never Give In' – allegedly the dying words of Henry Lawrence at the Siege of Lucknow – and the institutions retained their sturdy military ethos. Senior boys were summoned to their activities by bugle calls, although their juniors and also the girls assembled to the sound of bells. Priority was given to soldiers' children, whether of British or mixed parentage, but the children of officials and employees of the railways were also accepted, and so later on were those of boxwallahs and Indians. The schools gave the children plenty of food – the daily diet included eight ounces of meat and sixteen ounces of bread – and were obviously a boon to bereaved families. When Staff Sergeant Howie died suddenly at Quetta in 1920, the school at Sanawar accepted all four of his children as free boarders and helped his widow to do a teacher-training course so that in time she could earn a salary.[120]

As the hill stations developed after the middle of the nineteenth century, private schools proliferated among them. The first, subsequently known as Maddock's, had been established even earlier, in 1835, when its headmaster brought his boys' school up from the cauldron of Meerut to the slopes of Mussoorie. Later schools dotted the slopes of the Himalaya from Darjeeling to Murree and on to Kashmir; in fewer numbers they were also set up in the south, in the Nilgiri Hills. These institutions were mainly boarding schools, and the most expensive of them hoped to have only British pupils, which would then increase their appeal to parents afraid that their offspring would acquire chee-chee accents if they mixed with Anglo-Indians. When Molly Kaye's mother heard her daughters lilting in chee-chee, she took them away from their school (Auckland House in Simla) and had them taught by a friend's governess. Such snobbery was quite common. Ann Burkinshaw was not allowed to attend school in Calcutta, where her family lived, and was sent a thousand miles away to a Simla school so tiny that no chee-chee accents would be heard. In his memoirs Alan Ross (the child who had been sent to Cornwall) recalled that hills schools 'were not regarded as quite the thing'.[121]

Whatever the origins of their pupils, most schools aspired to be as British as possible in character. They were organized along the lines of similar places at 'home', captained by prefects, divided into 'houses' and imbued with the spirit of organized sports. Many of them occupied buildings inspired by Victorian architecture, with gabled exteriors, austere interiors and long stone corridors. They bore no resemblance to any Indian style, and their cultural associations were almost exclusively British. Even in a girls' school run by American Methodists (Mount Hermon in Darjeeling) the pupils' houses were named Tudor, York and Windsor. And like all schools in such places, the girls were made to wear black woollen stockings.

The top schools had headmasters who were graduates of Oxford or Cambridge and as many assistant masters from those universities whom they could attract. Schoolmistresses seem to have been drawn from a slightly wider geographical range: in the the 1930s most of those at Hebron School in the Nilgiris came from Australia or New Zealand. In its prospectus the Boys' School at Panchgani in the Bombay presidency announced that its teachers would be 'recruited, under normal conditions, entirely from England'. Founded in 1903 by the Colonial and Continental Church Society, it promised to 'provide a thorough English education on the lines of an English public school' and to pay 'special attention' to sports, which it 'regarded as a means of developing body and character and not as as end in themselves'. The boys there would enjoy 'a plentiful supply of wholesome food' and an equable climate (4,300 feet above sea level), and their uniform would be khaki-coloured cotton suits, except on Sundays when they would wear blue suits if they were five feet seven or taller; if shorter, they would have to wear Eton jackets (or 'bum-freezers'). In the school magazine the founders (and owners) made the improbable and (for a church society) surprising claim that theirs was 'the only society in existence which devotes its energies exclusively to help the White Man scattered all over the Empire'.[122]

Long before the Hills became fashionable, there had been large schools in the Plains, such as the La Martinière colleges at Lucknow and Calcutta. Yet most of them were unable to compete with the attractions of the Himalaya. In 1864 George Cotton, the bishop of Calcutta, removed St Paul's School from the capital city and took it to Darjeeling, where it remained. Apart from Lawrence, Cotton was the most important figure in the establishment of hill schools in India. A disciple of Dr Arnold at Rugby, and later headmaster of Marlborough, the new bishop's aim was to establish a school in the central section of the Himalaya that catered not for the 'richer residents', who were 'fully impressed with the value of home education', but for what he called 'the middle class in point of wealth', officials and other government employees who could not afford to send their children to Britain. He convinced the viceroy, Lord Canning, to back the scheme, and Simla Public School was duly opened in 1863. After the bishop died three years later, drowned in the Gorai River in east Bengal, it was renamed Bishop Cotton's School, subsequently known as BCS.[123] Close by a girls' school, Auckland House, was set up, inspired by Mrs Cotton. After several teachers from Cheltenham Ladies' College came out to work there, it was dubbed 'the Cheltenham of India', but for Mrs Kaye the dangers of chee-chee accents outweighed the advantages of its education.

The classes Bishop Cotton had aimed at duly provided the pupils for these and other hill schools: the children of engineers and superintendents of police, of station masters and shopkeepers, of accountants and captains of river steamers, of 'uncovenanted' civil servants below the level of the ICS, of people with enough money to give their children an education in India but not enough to send them to schools in England. Another category of parent was the 'country-born' planters, of tea or indigo, who sent their sons and daughters to St Paul's in Darjeeling or to the Mussoorie schools of York House and Hampton Court College; they were delighted to witness their children's transformation from being 'wan, shy and retiring' to becoming 'robust and rosy-cheeked from healthful months in the hills'.[124]

One reason Bishop Cotton gave for the establishment of Protestant schools was the growth of rival Jesuit and other Catholic colleges. These were often set up close to Anglican schools, the Convent of Jesus and Mary in Mussoorie in 1845, the Jesuit St Joseph's College at Darjeeling, where the Loreto Convent had already been founded by an Irish nun in 1846; a Church of the Immaculate Conception, with Bavarian statues, followed in the 1890s. Several Irish orders had an extensive presence in India, including the Brothers of St Patrick and the Irish Christian Brothers, which ran a number of schools, including St Edward's in Simla 'under the patronage' of the Catholic archibishop of the diocese. In the 1930s the Sisters of the Congregation of Jesus and Mary had entire pages of advertisements in the *Simla Times* (a Catholic newspaper) extolling the attractions of the twenty-three schools it ran stretching from Lahore to Dehra Dun and south to Bombay and Poona. These were not all intended for British and Anglo-Indian children: they included an 'orphanage and creche' for Indian girls in Sardhana and St Joseph's Orphanage for Indian Girls at Agra.

For reasons of pride and advertisement, all schools liked to publicize the achievements of their pupils. They needed to show prospective parents that their sons could emulate recent leavers and also get into the Survey Department or the Engineering College at Roorkee, or even gain a place at Sandhurst. They would also glorify Old Boys such as the pupil from Ghora Gali who became a brigadier of the Gurkhas, or the Willcocks brothers at Mussoorie who had won prizes at school and been successful in later life: one of them commanded the Indian Army Corps in France in the First World War. In 1933 the *Simla Times* proclaimed that Old Boys of St Joseph's College at Naini Tal, run by the Irish Christian Brothers, included the 'present head of the Nizam's Railway, the Commissioner of Opium in India, the present Deputy Commissioner in Bara Banki and a Governor in West Africa'.[125]

Some 5,000 children, British and Eurasian/Anglo-Indian, were pupils of the Hill schools at any one time, far more than the number of British children from India at schools in England. Some of the pupils were only transient, especially in wartime. Tom Stoppard, the future playwright, went to Mount Hermon at Darjeeling after his father's death (his widowed mother married an officer in the Indian Army); the actress Felicity Kendal spent brief periods in several Loreto convents when in the 1950s her father's acting troupe was touring India. The ethnic origins of pupils fluctuated over the years, with fewer poor British (whose parents could not afford the fees) and fewer well-off British (whose parents could pay English bills) and more Anglo-Indians and Indians. In the twenty years before Independence Bishop Cotton's School had four Indian school captains, who were being 'groomed for leadership of Indian affairs'. Yet the Second World War caused a resurgence of British pupils, children who were stranded in India because their parents would not risk sending them to Britain by boat. In 1941 the admissions to BCS jumped from 200 to 400.[126] Another change caused by war was the composition of the teaching staff. As male members left to join the armed forces, their places were usually taken by women, the wives of army officers, government officials and boxwallahs. One of the more unusual schools set up at this time was in Karachi, Miss Hickey's War School, run by an eccentric lady who, according to one of her pupils, 'waged a one-woman war against the mistreatment of the local donkeys'. If alerted that a donkey-cart was passing by the school, Miss Hickey would rush out of the classroom, berate the surprised driver, remove the 'bit' from the animal's mouth and confiscate it.[127]

The defeat of Germany and the coming of Independence ended the existence of the Hill schools as British institutions, although British teachers continued to work in them. Yet as Indian schools they continued to function and to flourish. Most of them still do. The three Lawrence colleges – two in India, one in Pakistan – are still there, retaining their motto 'Never Give In'. St Paul's and Mount Hermon are still in Darjeeling, Hebron is still near Ooty, and the Boys' School (later called St Peter's) is still at Panchgani.* Bishop Cotton's School and Auckland House remain in the Himalaya in what is now Shimla. At BCS the boys are still divided into four houses, one (Lefroy) named after a bishop of Lahore, two (Rivaz and Ibbetson) named after lieutenant-governors of the Punjab – and the fourth, which needs no explanation, Curzon.

PETS

Ethel St Clair Grimwood, the wife of the political agent in Manipur, concentrated her affections on her large variety of pets. Each morning she and her husband fed all their animals, from the horses down to 'the two little otters which were so tame that they followed us about like dogs'. She had no children and no profession, except that of running the agent's household, and she lived in a remote and dangerous place, a small Hindu state surrounded by hills inhabited by Naga and Kuki tribesmen; in the garden of the Residency the graves of former agents were a permanent reminder of her isolation and vulnerability.† She

---

* The most famous Old Boy of St Peter's was a Parsi lad called Farrokh Bulsara, who as an adult became Freddie Mercury of the rock band Queen.

† For the Grimwoods, the danger turned out to come not from the tribesmen but from the Manipuri royal family. In 1890, after a palace revolution overthrew the maharaja and installed a brother in his place, the chief commissioner of Assam (James Quinton) marched into the state with a small force of Gurkhas to restore order. Everything from the plan itself to the way it was implemented was a blunder. After fighting broke out, Grimwood, Quinton and three army officers went to the palace to negotiate with the new 'regime', but there they were kidnapped and executed, forcing Ethel and the Gurkhas, outnumbered by the state forces, to abandon the Residency and flee the state.

needed to look after pets. 'What would life in India be without one's animals?' she wondered.[128]

Ethel liked collecting animals and, as 'the natives got to know it', they brought her everything they caught: deer, bears, monkeys and other creatures. The number of species treated as pets by the British in India could have filled an entire zoo. Even children might possess – apart from ponies, cats, rabbits and tortoises – gibbons, porcupines and different types of squirrel. Men often reared the cubs of tigers and panthers which they found in the jungle, or which they were given by villagers, though they could not keep them for ever: eventually the animals had to be sent to a zoo or returned to the wild. When Courtenay Ilbert retired as law member of the Viceroy's Council in 1886, his family could not bear to leave all its pets behind: the panther thus went home and was given to London Zoo, and the parakeet accompanied his daughter to Somerville College, Oxford.[129]

Pets were at least as important to the British in India as they were in Britain itself. They were needed when their owners were single and lonely, when those owners had children to entertain and, perhaps especially, when those children had gone away to school. And they were usually treated even more indulgently and eccentrically than they were at home. Lady Hailey's donkey joined her for breakfast on the verandah of Government House in Lucknow; the future founder of the Boy Scouts (Baden-Powell) had ponies that followed him about like dogs as well as a pet pig called Algernon, and Eric Blair had, as one astonished visitor recalled, 'goats, geese and ducks and all sort of things' living *inside* his house in the Burmese town of Insein. In his various stations in Bengal H. M. Kisch, an assistant magistrate, also preferred to keep his menagerie inside his bungalow, including a young panther and a young elephant until they grew too large. He also had a hog deer, an otter, a very large lizard and four mongooses. Although these last were not pretty or cuddly pets, they were popular in British India because, like Rikki-Tikki-Tavi in Kipling's *Jungle Book*, they killed snakes in the compound and they also rid the bungalows of 'vermin'. If caught young, they could become tame and affectionate. Kisch had one of them sleeping in his fireplace and another in his bathroom. The only worry was that they might try to eat his bird collection, which included eight lorikeets; he thus had to hang his cages under the ceiling.

Senior officials could maintain more extensive and professional menageries than a junior Civilian in Bengal. At their retreat at Barrack-pore the governor-generals had at times an aviary as well as a menagerie and an elephant stud. In Calcutta the chief justice, Sir Elijah Impey, assembled such a collection of birds and animals that it took three Indian artists five years from 1777 to paint them all.[130] Collectors usually assembled their fauna according to the regions they lived in. If they were in Burma it made sense to collect gibbons and monkeys; if in the Himalaya, they would go for bears, lynx, snow leopards and local ibex. They could assemble aviaries and parrot cages in most places, and it was easy to catch parrots, mynahs and parakeets. The Civilian Godfrey Davis possessed an enormous collection of birds, from Java sparrows to Bengalese finches, which he kept in a vast number of cages. Each morning in his house in Karachi he, his daughter and two servants took all the cages out on to the lawn, where he sprayed the birds with his watering-can and removed the trays so that they could play about on the grass for a while. Then he took all the cages inside again, said goodbye to the birds and went off to the magistrate's court.[131]

The pre-eminent pet was of course the dog, epitomized by the wire-haired fox terrier with its rough white coat and brown V-shaped ears. There were many other breeds – spaniels, Airedales, greyhounds among them – and of course mongrels, but terriers (Scotch and bull as well as fox) were the favourites; and these, moreover, earned their keep by killing rats. Like all pets, however, dogs had specific Indian vulnerabilities. They could be bitten by snakes. They could get prickly heat, scratch themselves raw and, if on the coast, make things worse by charging into the sea. A greater danger was the panther. James Best, a jungle wallah, knew that panthers would be prowling around his compound hoping to get at his sheep, but that was a nuisance to be expected. Harder to deal with was their appetite for well-fed English dogs and their effrontery in hunting them; they were even known to raid verandahs and carry off a bull terrier. When going for walks at Naini Tal, Ann Mitchell 'talked and sang loudly, hoping to keep the panthers away from our own dogs, which we kept on a short lead between us'.[132]

Panthers were one deterrent to keeping dogs, but a bigger one was rabies, transmitted by jackals as well as by other canines. In some places such as Sind it was endemic; Roger Pearce lost one of his dogs to rabies and the other to distemper. Pet dogs often died, and so sometimes did people, even after the establishment in 1900 of the Pasteur

Institute at Kasauli, situated in the Punjab 180 miles north of Delhi. Unfortunately Kasauli was so far away from most of India that victims in a suspected case of rabies could not wait to find out if the dog that bit them really was rabid: they would be bundled into a bullock-cart, taken to the nearest railway station, and then carried by train to the Punjab, a journey that might take four days in all.

The Godden family's experience of Kasauli was particularly traumatic. Arthur Godden had been asked by his wife, Katherine, not to have dogs in their house in Assam because she had two small daughters and was frightened of rabies. Yet he disregarded her wishes and acquired three spaniels which duly caught rabies and bit both him and their little girl Rumer. While Arthur and his daughter set off across northern India for their course of injections in the stomach, Katherine went to stay in a tea garden, where unluckily her host's dog also became rabid and bit her other child on the lip. Although it was July and she was seven months' pregnant, Katherine had no alternative but to follow the other half of her family up the Ganges Plain by rail to Kasauli; so traumatized was she by the events that on arrival she gave birth to her third daughter. Everyone survived the drama but, according to Rumer, Arthur was never quite forgiven by his wife.[133]

I I

Formalities

'THE ETIQUETTE OF PRECEDENCE'

Social distinctions in British India were arranged in two separate categories. One of the snobberies was essentially racial. As the Civilian Edward Wakefield put it, 'Those born in Britain looked down on those who were "country-bred". The country-bred families scorned those of mixed blood; and those of mixed blood seemed to think that, by disparaging everything Indian, they were somehow purging themselves of an impurity.'[1] The second snobbery was professional and in some ways resembled the caste systems of the Hindus, with the ICS as the Brahmins in the hierarchy, and the boxwallahs (like the Hindu Vaishyas) fairly low down the order. As the civil servants of the East India Company had once been merchants themselves, this was a rather ridiculous situation, but there it was.

Army officers considered themselves to be socially on a par with Civilians, but in fact, mainly because they were less well paid and less influential, they were implicitly ranked just below them. Next were doctors from the IMS, lawyers from Britain, and engineers from the Public Works Department, and after them came officials from the Education Department, the Posts and Telegraphs, and the Railways. Beneath the hierarchy of officials were boxwallahs and planters and other people 'in trade'. Naturally there were variations according to the time and the place. Social distinctions were more marked in 1870 than they were in 1910; lawyers had greater social clout in Calcutta than in the Punjab, and the opposite was true of the military. Yet at all times men, and even more their wives, tended to congregate in the circles – or occasionally adjacent circles – of their professions.

Even in those professions there were gradations and subdivisions. Within the cavalry the social standing of the officers in the remounts department was inferior to that of the Lancers. Among businessmen there was a clear hierarchy, with a top layer consisting of leading figures from the main banks, the managing agencies, P&O and the railways. Below them was a jostling of managers and engineers, then a drop to salesmen and shopkeepers.[2] Even the manager of a large store was regarded as a 'counter-jumper' and ranked low, and one particular individual who had 'come out in retail' apparently retained 'a chip on his shoulder' even after he had become a successful businessman: according to William Tully of Gillanders agency, he tried to overcome 'his great inferiority complex' by adopting a 'pompous manner'.[3]

Similar hierarchies seemed to exist in every profession, even the railways, where one stationmaster's wife felt she should go into dinner before another because her rival's husband was *not on the main line*.[4] Only rarely could people escape from the circle in which their class-conscious compatriots (usually female ones) had placed them. It was easier if you were Scottish, noted a perceptive Indian from the Punjab, and had retained your native accent, because you would then be more difficult to classify and, like the padre and the doctor, you acquired at the Club 'a certain social neutralness and a fairly high minimum level of acceptance'.[5] Another means of escape was to be female and pretty and good at tennis. Dora Johnston was the daughter of a railway engineer at Rawalpindi, but she was such a good tennis player that she was 'invited everywhere and picked as a partner by swains in crack regiments that were the cream of "Pindi" society'.[6] In the end she married not an officer in the Lancers but the Civilian Harry St John Philby (later known – after leaving the ICS – as 'Philby of Arabia') and gave birth to their eldest child, the future spy Kim, on New Year's Day 1912 at Ambala in the Punjab.*[7]

Such a hierarchical society as the British built in India needed to be regulated in a formal way and, as one young Civilian complained on arriving in the Punjab, with a 'slavish regard for etiquette'.[8] The most obsessive manifestation of this was the system of calling cards. A

---

* Kim Philby's Christian name was also Harold, but when his father heard the small boy talking to the servants in Punjabi, he was reminded of Kipling's book and said, 'He's a real little Kim.' The name stuck.

newcomer to the station was expected to visit every British home and in a little tin or wooden box outside each bungalow leave a card (not printed but engraved) giving his name, rank (if in the army) and club (but not his address). Even in a small hill station, with houses at different altitudes, it would take several days to do the rounds, but trying to cover Madras in a buggy (and wearing a morning coat) would take weeks. On the initial visit the inhabitants of a bungalow were officially 'not at home', and when the newcomers and the established residents finally did pay formal calls upon each other, wearing their respective uniforms, it was in the heat of the day, between noon and two in the afternoon. It was an eccentric system, and admitted to be insane by one Bombay memsahib, yet it had to be followed because, as she herself explained, from seven to ten in the morning 'one is riding or hunting', and 'the hours between four and six [were] sacred to the club and polo teas, where one [was] sure to meet everyone', so midday was 'really the only time to pay formal calls'.[9]

Almost everyone admitted that the system and its hours were daft, designed, as a correspondent of the *Pioneer* pointed out, to cause 'the maximum of discomfort to a large class of well-intentioned bipeds . . .'[10] Yet nobody attempted to change it. Lieutenant Winston Churchill might choose *not* to 'call' – 'the absurd custom of the country' – but he was grand enough not to worry about local 'society', and in any case he did not plan to stay long in a place where he regarded British 'life' as 'stupid, dull and uninteresting'.[11] Assistant magistrates or Indian Army subalterns who did not leave their calling cards found themselves ostracized. Residents became huffy and refused to acknowledge them, let alone invite them to any gathering. When David Johnson, the bank manager at Lyallpur in the late 1920s, received an invitation to dinner from the district officer, he declined it, stating that as the new junior Civilian (who would be present) had 'not had the courtesy to call on us we would prefer not to meet him'.[12]

Calling cards were not required at the grander homes, the Residency or Government House. Visitors or newcomers simply needed to go to the building and write their names in the visitors' book, after which they would be invited to at least one event. In the 1930s the personal assistant of the Resident in Kashmir typed out the names under diverse headings, 'Cocktails or Buffet Lunch' for the less important, 'Luncheon or Dinner' for the higher ranks; 'Tea and Tennis/Croquet' invitations were presumably allocated to a younger set. Writing one's name in the viceroy's book was a duty important enough to be put into print. In 1923 the temporary Viceregal Lodge in Delhi printed a list sixty-five pages long of all those who had called in the months leading up to February of that year.[13]

Seating plans at dinner in British India were not arranged according to who might get on with whom or which guests might have interests in common; from Government House to a judge's bungalow, placements were regulated entirely by seniority. If the hostess or the ADC did not know whether a brigadier was senior to a commissioner, they could consult a government publication called the *Warrant of Precedence* and discover that he did indeed rank one place higher. Bishop Welldon could not understand why 'the etiquette of precedence' should be taken so much more seriously in India than in Britain and thought its rigidity cast 'a rather depressing shadow' over British-Indian society. People got 'pretty well bored to death' by always sitting next to the same people 'during the season' (the winter months) in Calcutta. At state balls Mary Curzon had to dance first with the lieutenant-governor of Bengal (who in his own province ranked after the viceroy and his wife) and then with the commander-in-chief (who came next). If these two gentlemen were present at dinners, she had to sit between them; if not, the next in line were the chief justice of Bengal and the bishop of Calcutta (Welldon). There was even less variety when a viceroy or governor was on tour. When the viceroy (Lord Chelmsford) visited Sind in 1917, he always sat next to the commissioner's wife (Rosamond Lawrence), who found it 'difficult to be intelligent, attractive and tactful for sixteen consecutive meals'.[14]

Printed protocol covered far more than the placements and menus of a governor and his entourage on tour. Little booklets were produced with details of the travel arrangements, which ADCs would go in what car, who would be in charge of the luggage, whether the surgeon and the private secretary would be sharing a bearer, at what time and in what order the cars would set off to reach their destinations – a school, a hospital, a municipal office, the garden party of a raja or a zemindar – and how long all these visits and meetings would take. When a governor arrived at an important function, the drill was most meticulously followed. As one Civilian, James Halliday, described it, His Excellency's motor car came gracefully to a halt at a red carpet where some important 'personage' was waiting to greet him and his wife; a footman next to the chauffeur jumped out and opened the door; the ADC on duty got out more slowly, followed by the private secretary; the guard of honour then 'sloped arms preparatory to the present' and the band-sergeant 'raised his baton'; at that moment 'H.E. descended followed by Her Excellency, the ADC saluted, the private secretary took off his hat, the personage bowed and shook hands, the guard of honour presented arms, the band-sergeant dipped his baton, and everyone stood still while the band played "God Save the King".'[15]

The social entertainments of British India were mostly imported from Britain. There were dinner parties, tennis parties, fancy-dress parties, morning coffee parties, cocktail parties (from the 1920s), picnics, dances, Sunday lunches, regimental balls (at which officers were allowed to remove their spurs while dancing for fear of tearing the ladies' dresses) and governors' garden parties (at which no one was supposed to leave until 'God Save the King' had been played and the host himself had left). The governors had to entertain people constantly in large numbers, not just Britons who had signed their visitors' book but also Indian notables and 'distinguished' tourists from continental Europe. In his years as Resident in Hyderabad early in the twentieth century, Charles Bayley was obliged to entertain one viceroy, two governors of Madras and the prince and princess of Wales, plus two Bavarian princes, the German crown prince, the titular landgrave of Hesse, and four Bourbon princes from republican France.[16]

Programmes on state occasions were formidably organized and strictly carried out. As vicereine, Lady Reading might be able to organize a 'moonlight fête' at Simla in 'Fancy Dress or Powder or Domino', but at Delhi she had to stick to precedent, starting off a ball with the 'state lancers', followed by a 'valse', a 'fox trot' and a 'one step', the 'valse' and its successors each repeated three times.[17] With their invitations guests received a printed programme with a little pencil so that they could fill in the names of their dancing partners. Correct dress was of course required at all such functions. Inside the porch of Government House ADCs used to keep a box of long white kid gloves (with sixteen buttons) for ladies who had forgotten to bring their own. Those who had also forgotten to put on stockings were not, however, furnished with a new pair; their husbands or fathers were telephoned in the morning and told to issue a reprimand.[18] More importantly, ADCs and secretaries had to ensure that all the appropriate people were invited and that at dinners they were seated in the right places. Occasionally a situation might be too personal and complicated for them to work out even with the help of the *Warrant of Precedence*. If a ball was being given at Simla for both the viceroy and the commander-in-chief, did one invite the woman reputed to be the c-in-c's mistress even though the viceroy had excluded her from his official residence? (The dilemma caused some formidable rows before the ball was for unconnected reasons cancelled.) A different conundrum faced Alfred Lyall when, as lieutenant-governor of the North-Western Provinces, he had to decide whether to invite to a dinner a woman who had run 'away from her husband, was divorced, and then married her husband again'. Although he had doubts about asking her, in the end he did so, concluding 'that her husband knew best'.[19]

Monarchical celebrations – jubilees, coronations and the more frequent royal birthdays – were occasions for formal investitures, the awarding of honours to both British and Indian subjects. Before the state dinner, with all the guests in full uniform, recipients of a knighthood would advance to a dais where the governor with his bodyguard was awaiting them with the letters patent placed upon a cushion. During the reign of George III the governor-general in Calcutta gave a 'public dinner' and a ball and supper in the evening of the king's birthday in June, unless the heat was 'unusually severe', in which case it was postponed until December.[20] The custom continued, and expanded to include military parades across the whole country, from Karachi to Bangalore. The southern city's birthday parades for George V, also in June, were occasions that one family of Greek residents always insisted on attending: if they had not done so, it would have seemed to them a 'blasphemy like missing church on Christmas Day'. Large crowds stood bareheaded as the national anthem was played, and the troops marched across the maidan, the British infantry followed by the Mysore Lancers, the horse artillery and the new armoured cars.[21] Less formal celebrations were the drinking of toasts to the king's health or, as William Hickey put it, 'filling some bumpers to George III and being very merry'. A hundred years later, less merrily, Violet Jacob recorded a party of three celebrating Queen Victoria's birthday in the jungle, drinking 'her health, standing, quite solemnly'.[22]

The almost unchanging formality of social life was supported by a plethora of ceremonial uniform. When Lieutenant Stevenson-Hamilton became an ADC to the governor of the Punjab in 1935, he was required to have 'normal suits' for everyday use when 'there was nothing much on', a formal pinstripe suit for luncheon parties, a light formal suit for tea parties, a morning coat with striped trousers and top hat for garden parties, and several sets of uniform: a staff coat (blue and primrose-coloured tails worn as evening dress), Regimental Full Dress (with a bunch of red swan's feathers fixed as a plume on his helmet) and 'Undress Blue' (which was in fact 'formal in the extreme'), a full-length frock coat worn with boots, spurs, sword and a helmet with a long gilt spike.[23] Seniority of rank did not bring any relaxation of the dress code. In 1939 Lord Erskine advised his successor as governor of Madras that he would need a tailcoat, a frock coat, a levee dress coat (blue with gold collar and cuffs) and a full dress coat (gold all over). His personal concession to India was to wear Mess wellingtons in the evenings in Madras to 'keep off the mosquitoes which [were] apt to go for "fresh blood" out from Europe'. He did not, however, need to take them to Ooty because his summer capital was 'well above the mosquito line'.[24]

The British authorities were usually insistent that certain rituals which took place in London must be copied in Calcutta even though the inhabitants of the Indian city would not know what had taken place in the imperial capital until about five months later. Although the court in London went into mourning on the death of Princess Charlotte, the daughter of the Prince Regent, in early November 1817, the citizens of Calcutta had to wait until 19 April the following year before they too went into black. With mourning dress and other uniform, the authorities were generally impervious to the argument that different climates might require different costumes. On official occasions officers and officials had to 'adhere to London codes of dress' as closely as possible. According to 'General Orders' issued in March 1823, they might be 'allowed during the hot months to wear white cotton, or linen trousers' instead of 'tight pantaloons', but with the exception of this one 'indulgence', officers were 'to be dressed exactly according to the King's Regulations' in London.[25] Arguments between 'sticklers' and 'relaxers' continued for another hundred years. In 1919 the captain of the governor's bodyguard in Bombay was still trying to insist that all officers should wear heavy cloth Mess dress in the hottest weather, even though the viceroy himself was happy for them to dine with him in the lighter 'white Mess kit'. In his viceregal tour of the south in early 1939 Linlithgow compromised: 'Full Dress White' in the daytime but morning coat at garden parties and evening dress at state banquets.[26]

The British in Calcutta were more rigid with their social etiquette than they were elsewhere, perhaps because they had been longer in Bengal than anywhere else (except Madras) and were more addicted to precedent. When John Beames was in the Punjab in the early 1860s, a colleague would say, 'Come and dine tonight', but in Bengal his hosts always sent him written invitations requesting the pleasure of his company.[27] In Bombay half a century later, a boxwallah could lunch in his shirtsleeves, but if transferred to the office in Calcutta he would have to put on a coat and tie for tiffin. Not that Bombay was casual about dress later on in the day. If that boxwallah went sailing in the afternoon, he had to change out of his yachting clothes and into a stiff collar and tie before he could have tea at the Royal Bombay Yacht Club and sit on the lawn listening to the band; and if he stayed for dinner he would have to put on white tie and tails unless he was going to wear the club's own uniform of blue coat with buff facings, white waistcoat and numerous 'anchor and cable' gilt buttons.[28]

Changing into smart clothes for dinner was not of course a habit unique to the Raj. Yet dressing up for dinner in the jungle is an image that invariably provokes a snigger. It might seem rather absurd to pack a starched shirt and a cummerbund for one's evenings in camp, but one had to change into something after sweating all day, inspecting the village drains or hacking one's way through a forest. Indians themselves would do so. When 'old hands' were mocked years later for the custom, they would be bewildered: it seemed 'no more out of the ordinary than brushing one's teeth or shaving'.[29] It was also, as Kipling understood, an important ritual for lonely people struggling not to 'crack up' or 'go to seed'. In his story 'In the Rukh' a forestry official who lives by himself puts on a white shirt each night to 'preserve his self-respect in his isolation'. At his family's home in Lahore Kipling did the same – even when his parents were away – because 'one knew if one broke the ritual of dressing for the last meal one was parting with a sheet-anchor'.[30]

If formality could prevail in the jungle, it would certainly do so in small stations in the mofussil, even if hostesses had to borrow their neighbours' crockery and cutlery because they seldom had enough of their own. The custom of borrowing their servants – in the 1830s Julia Maitland remembered 'a turbaned sultan-like creature behind every chair'[31] – also continued, though in a less grand fashion. When in the 1920s Madge Green and her Civilian brother Arnold went out to dinner at their station in Sind, they were preceded down the lane by a 'patiwallah' (the messenger at Arnold's office), who swung a lantern (to look for snakes) and carried a cloth (to dust their shoes on arrival), and were followed by a boy, 'who always comes to help wait when you go out to dinner'.[32]

Another custom that lasted a long time was writing the menus in French. Madge would not have bothered to do this when she and Arnold entertained in their bungalow in the mofussil, but she did have to do so (and make sure she made no mistakes) when she was working in Karachi as the social secretary of the commissioner of Sind. This ritual, initiated in the middle of the nineteenth century, persisted into the 1920s but then, at least at modest official functions, it declined. At a farewell dinner for a Civilian at Bankipore in 1924, all nine courses – from the *Hors d'Oeuvre* and the *Poisson à la Florentine* to the *Bombe à la Pêche Glacée* and *Café* – were in French, but at equivalent dinners in the following years the menus were all in English, though they included the words (presumably by now regarded as anglicized) 'Hors d'Oeuvre' and 'Entree' (no longer with an acute accent).[33] Grander places than Bankipore resisted the change. Viceregal Lodge in Delhi printed its menus in French (*Dinde Strasbourgeoise*) for the banquet given on the investiture of the Maharaja of Jodhpur, and Indian princes returned the compliment. At a state dinner held at Bhopal in 1923 the ruling begum's menu was in French, although it was not very accurate and several of the dishes (*Concombre Danoise [sic], Asperges Milanaises, Croûtes Norvegiennes [sic]* and *Glace Tutti Frutti*) acknowledged the existence of other countries in Europe besides France.[34] The smart establishments also stuck to French. Formal dinners at Peliti's (one of the best restaurants in Calcutta) and the Taj (the best hotel in Bombay) and even the Willingdon Club still had menus in French in 1938.[35]

The formality of British life in India accentuated what was one of its most obvious features: its essential sameness, its virtual uniformity. The British in a civil station must have formed one of the most unvariegated societies on the planet. As John Perronet Thompson noted on arriving in India as an ICS griffin in 1897, it was bound to be limited because no one was rich, no one was poor, no one was old and no one was young – except a few infants under the age of six. It was a society, as another Civilian put it, 'uninspired by the imagination of youth nor softened by the sentiment of old age'.[36]

Another limiting factor, at least outside the main cities, was that it was an 'official society' – consisting largely of officials – and, as we have seen, an intensely hierarchical one at that. In Thompson's day most of the Civilians had been educated at Oxford and Cambridge – and many other officials had been to university – yet in India they seldom mentioned the intellectual subjects that had interested them during their education. As Bishop Welldon complained, they talked about work, sport, gossip, furlough, life in the Hills and the prospects of promotion, but they seldom discussed art or literature. Of course, as Thompson acknowledged, they had chosen to be 'men of action' leading outdoor lives rather than literary critics in London or classics dons at Balliol. And even if you liked opera, you could not really talk about how it was being transformed by Wagner if you never had a chance to see *Rheingold* or *Parsifal*. One could also make excuses for people not reading much literature – because they worked too hard, because their books fell to pieces in the climate, because bookshops were rare (and so were people who wished to talk about books) – yet these do not quite explain why British society in India was in general so anti-intellectual, why, as the griffin Herbert Gee lamented, 'we almost entirely lose sight of the aesthetic and fine arts side of existence'.[37] People interested in painting might not have been able to follow the fashions and developments of European art, but they could have bought pictures by Indian painters. Few of them became sufficiently interested in Indian art to wish to do so.*

The sameness of British society in India owed much to the fact that most British people there came from similar class backgrounds. As members of the upper classes rarely went to India except for a few years as a governor or an officer in a British regiment, and as the working class was mainly confined to barracks or the rail tracks, society

* Some of the many exceptions to statements made in this paragraph are discussed in the next chapter.

consisted largely of the many different and confusing gradations of the middle classes. This did not stop its men and women being aware of class distinctions among them – or of adding a few more for an Indian environment – but from the outside they might not look very different. Senior Civilians and their wives – often known as 'high-ups' – might seem very grand and superior to an engineer or a stationmaster, but to a general from the gentry stationed in India they were like those 'wretched people who put up little bungalows round my place in Hampshire'.[38]

British women in India have had a bad press, especially from male aesthetes, who were inclined to lump them together. E. M. Forster thought them 'pretty rotten, and vile on the native question' as soon as he heard them talking on his first boat out to India in 1912; later he fictionalized – and caricatured – them as Mrs Turton and Mrs Callander in *A Passage to India*. His friend Goldsworthy Lowes Dickinson, who was also on the boat, was even more savage, mocking them as women 'with empty minds and hearts, trying to fill them by despising the natives'. Another literary friend, J. R. Ackerley, described how British women in India talked 'very loudly in an easy, smart manner' and how one warned him not to try to 'understand the dark and tortuous minds of the natives'. Criticisms such as these were all too frequent. John Morris, the Gurkha captain, described his fellow officers' wives as 'peevish termagants', while Josie Darling, herself the wife of a young Civilian, was enraged by the way that women 'who would be *nobodies* at home' would become very grand and overbearing in India.[39]

Some of the many women who did not conform to this 'type' will be discussed in the next chapter. A type, nevertheless, existed. What antagonized its critics was the way that certain women behaved as if they had moved up a class because in India they could afford servants, horses and a large house. Women who, according to Josie Darling, would belong to 'the "Edinboro ladies'" class or even lower', would in India shake themselves free of 'the Morningside set' and put 'on the airs of a *grande dame*'. Similar transformations had taken place ever since the arrival of women in any numbers at the end of the eighteenth century. According to one observer at that time, officers' wives who, before they came to India, could not have boasted 'a change of dickies twice a month', were now 'attempting the airs of gentlewomen'. Yet they remained, the traveller Maria Graham insisted at the beginning of the nineteenth century, 'under-bred and over-dressed'. When Lady Falkland arrived in Bombay as the governor's wife in 1848, she noticed that the local ladies were 'more tenacious of their rank' than they would be in England. Half a century later, another governor's wife seemed to make the point in person. On their visit to Bombay in 1912 Sidney and Beatrice Webb were scathing about the way Lady Clarke, who had once 'lived in a cottage', had put on ridiculous 'regal airs' after marrying her third husband, the governor Sir George.[40]

If much of this disdain was snobbish, it also contained some truth. The surgeon Owen Berkeley-Hill observed that women who were 'not ladies' by birth – but who in India found themselves in socially superior positions – were 'frequently overbearing and inconsiderate towards persons whom they deem[ed] to be their inferiors'; they were 'a fecund source of several sorts of trouble'.[41] Even Forster would not have claimed that they were all like this, but enough of them were to cohere, to form a sort of wide, informal association, to establish a social and cultural primacy – and to pass their values on to the next generation. British men were forced to get to know Indians other than servants or shopkeepers; through his work an ICS officer would have to meet men of every class from the ryot to the raja. Yet many British women, at least those with no professional motive to meet Indians, often stuck to their own kind. No doubt they felt outnumbered, and sometimes beleaguered, and they reacted to their situation by urging solidarity, by trying to form a united front not only against India and its dangers but also against subversives, potential and real, within their own ranks. That is why senior ladies often took young wives 'in hand', enticed them to the Club and the bridge table, lectured them on etiquette and the need to inspect the kitchen, told them how to treat servants and warned them – if they were showing worrying inclinations – not to mix too much with Indians.

If they had known Leonard Woolf, they would have regarded him as subversive, even though he was less so than Eric Blair and only became mildly mutinous when he was on active duty as an imperialist (like the future author of *Nineteen Eighty-four*). Although Woolf did many of the right things – he played bridge and tennis, he drank whisky at the Club, he kept a dog (a wire-haired fox terrier) – he was too clever, too 'Cambridge' (he had with him the ninety volumes of the 1784 edition of Voltaire) and too fond of going to remote places and experiencing 'the life and transport of the most ancient pastoral civilizations' of Ceylon. He was also, though the ladies might only suspect it, an acute observer of British society on the Subcontinent, its pretensions and its limitations. 'As you can see in Kipling's stories', he wrote, that society – whether in India or Ceylon – was essentially suburban, not so different from that of Putney or Peckham, with 'the circumambient air of a tropical suburbia'. The difference was that people behaved more grandly in the tropics. Their conversation might generally be trivial – gossip, sport and 'shop' (work) – but they themselves were 'grand because we were a ruling caste in a strange Asiatic country'.

Although he was living in Ceylon in the Edwardian years, Woolf always felt he was living in Kipling's India in the 1880s. He would meet a Tamil in a turban and think that 'he might have been a character in a Kipling story', and then he would meet some 'white people' and think that they too were 'in many ways astonishingly like characters in a Kipling story'. And sometimes he would wonder whether he was a real person, a civil servant about to witness a hanging in Bogambra Jail, or whether he was 'living a story by Kipling' in *Under the Deodars*. 'I could never make up my mind,' he wrote, 'whether Kipling had moulded his characters accurately in the image of Anglo-Indian society or whether we were moulding our characters accurately in the image of a Kipling story.'[42]

THE CLUB

For many people, nothing is more emblematic of British India than images of 'the Club'. It might be Forster's fictional club, as filmed by David Lean in *A Passage to India*, with men and women at a meeting becoming strident and irrational, reacting to an obscure incident in a cave as if it had been a murder, and making foolish suggestions about calling out the troops, 'clearing the bazaars' and sending the women and children to the Hills. Yet Forster himself had never witnessed such a scene; nor had anyone else; such meetings would not take place at a club. A truer alternative image – one much photographed and described – would be more leisured and more serene. Men and women are sitting in cane chairs on a verandah, while servants in turbans and cummerbunds are serving them iced drinks; they might be watching fellow members playing croquet, and they can hear the sounds of other members hitting tennis balls; soon the band will begin to play. Inside the clubhouse men are sitting in armchairs reading newspapers and magazines; from across the passage the sound of billiard balls can be heard.

The Club was the social centre of the civil station and the cantonment, more important for officials than for army officers because they had no Mess in which to congregate. It was a place you went for leisure, exercise and conversation, where you could be serious or frivolous as you wished. It was a place where, as one Civilian recalled, 'the annoyances of work' were 'removed'. If the judge and the magistrate had disagreed over a case in court, they could have a cigar and a peg afterwards and remain friends. Yet the Club was not an ancient institution, a legacy of the East India Company's rule. In the great cities a few very grand clubs were founded before the Rebellion, but not in the mofussil until around 1870. Before that year the only meeting places in a station were the church and the coffee-shop (if they had them); after that date clubs proliferated so fast that almost every station had one within a decade.

What the newspaper editor Stanley Reed called 'the aristocracy of the clubs of India' – the Bengal, the Madras and the Byculla of Bombay – were established in, respectively, 1827, 1831 and 1833, in the same period as the principal clubs of Pall Mall in London.* The Bengal Club was needed, according to its first president, Colonel Finch, because 'nothing like a respectable hotel or coffee-house . . . existed' in Calcutta.[43] It began its existence at premises in Tank Square (subsequently Dalhousie Square) before moving to Macaulay's old home on Chowringee and later to another address on the same street, where its grandest incarnation was opened in 1911. This clubhouse was both monumental and impractical. What its historians referred to as its ' "add-a-bit" method of construction' led to 'a number of curious eccentricities', and it was only when 'the building was nearing completion that it was discovered there was no stairway to the first floor' from the ground floor. Although the situation was saved by the addition – as an 'after-thought' – of a 'magnificent marble staircase at the back of the Hall', the maintenance costs of this strange

---

* Reed added a fourth 'aristocrat', the Sind in Karachi, but as the port did not become part of the empire until 1843, this belonged to a later vintage (1871).

and enormous building were always high. As for membership, the club favoured seniority – whether of officials or businessmen – to an extent that, according to its historians, 'imposed a somewhat stately and ponderous if not pompous atmosphere'. One American who visited it during the Second World War described it as 'a Dook's Palace and the Dook's lying dead upstairs', while another, who saw members asleep in the reading room after lunch, remarked 'won'erful, just won'erful, but in the States we bury our dead'.[44]

Perhaps these observations reached the ears of the club's president, who in 1947 recommended the building's demolition on the grounds that it was an 'anachronism . . . ill-conceived and constructed for modern conditions of Club life'.[45] The vast Chowringee block was not in fact knocked down until 1970, when most of the site was sold and the club re-established itself in a smaller building on a parcel of its property on Russell Street. In 2018, with of course an Indian membership, it was still there.

If the Bengal Club was one of the most absurd buildings of British India, its fellow 'aristocrat', the Madras Club, nicknamed the 'Ace of Clubs', was one of the most beautiful, porticoed and Palladianized and so large, a Civilian joked, that 'you can lose yourself in it three or four times running . . . parts of it are still believed to be unexplored'.[46] It was reputed to have the hottest of curries, the most elegant of servants and the longest bar in Asia. One member's terrible verse eulogized 'India's longest bar that links / Spicy yarn with icy drinks'.[47] However jolly the club was, it was also intensely hierarchical. Junior members were expected to congregate at one end of the bar and not to move up unless invited to drink with a senior. Women were not allowed in the bar at all – they had to remain in the ladies' annexe known as the *moorghikhana* ('hen run') – except on Armistice Day in 1918 when they were kidnapped from the annexe and made to serve celebratory drinks.[48]

The Madras Club's refusal to admit women prompted the founding in 1890 of an almost equally beautiful club, the Adyar, with an octagonal cupola and riverine gardens, which people were encouraged to join 'to escape the austerities of the Madras Club'. Long after Independence, the two clubs were forced to merge and base themselves in the Adyar buildings. As the younger one had very belatedly accepted Indian members in 1960, the stalwarts of the Madras too had to make this concession.[49]

397

The clubs in the civil stations were not of course like those in the 'aristocracy'. Some of them were very small indeed. At the subdivisional headquarters of Sirajganj in Bengal the Club was – as the SDO there lamented – 'a tin shed of two rooms, one for bridge and one for billiards'. At Sargodha in the Punjab it was, as a griffin enthused in 1927, 'a very nice little' place with bridge, billiards and grass tennis courts; yet the membership was so small, he soon realized, that it was sometimes impossible to rustle up a four for bridge or tennis.[50] In large stations there were naturally more amenities, including a swimming pool and often a golf course. Such places might also have gymkhana clubs, even more oriented towards sports, and more friendly too to wives and children. Many clubs might limit themselves to the basics (tennis – drinks – bridge – dinner – billiards), but others developed and diversified. At Maymyo, the main hill station of Burma, the Club had not only a large lounge for ladies but also a lawn with seesaws and sandpits.

In the cities a wealthy man with the right connections might join several clubs. In Rangoon he might have the Pegu as his social club and join the gymkhana for sport, the Country Club for riding and the Boat Club for rowing or drinking on the verandah overlooking the Royal Lakes. Even greater variety would be found in Calcutta. A senior Civilian such as Walter Gurner might be a member of the two main 'gentlemen's clubs' (the Bengal and the United Services Club) and also the Saturday Club (where he could take his family to swim, dance and have dinner) and the Tollygunge Club a few miles away, which was popular for Sunday breakfasts and possessed one of the most attractive golf courses in India.[51]

Yet the point of establishing so many clubs was not to enable privileged individuals to enjoy the variety but to encourage people from a particular social or ethnic group to stick together and not try to join other groups. Railway men should be content with their railway club; Anglo-Indians should stay in the establishments meant for them. In 1941 at Digboi, the town where the Assam Oil Company had a refinery, there were four clubs for the company's employees: the Digboi Club for the British, the India Club for the Indians, the Assam Valley Light Horse Club for the Anglo-Indians, and the Sports Club, where they could all meet (as long as they liked sport). Elsewhere the demarcations were usually more blurred, which led to complication and contention.

Watching the goings-on from the sidelines, an Indian judge in the ICS observed that people put in a lot of effort trying to get into a different 'club from the one to which their state of life has called them', while the people of that particular club laboured very hard 'to keep them out'.[52]

Election to a club was a divisive issue. Candidates had to have a proposer and a seconder, they had to be vetted by the club committee, and, to be successful, they had to avoid being blackballed by existing members. Civilians, surgeons and army officers could not easily be blackballed; nor could churchmen. It was 'below' their level that the trouble began. One senior political officer resigned from his club in the 1880s when, according to his grandson, 'he heard of a proposal to admit engineers and forest officers'.[53] People and their clubs prided themselves on becoming less stuffy in the following century, but sometimes the change was merely apparent. The Saturday Club in Calcutta made much of its appeal to the young, with its informality and its dancing, yet on the question of membership it was as rigid and intolerant as anywhere. In the 1930s it was sufficiently 'progressive' to elect a (British) member of the Bengal Pilot Service, but when the man resigned and reapplied – a compulsory procedure for members when they married – he was blackballed. No reason was given, but a friend inside the club surmised that some of the members must have believed his new wife to be either Anglo-Indian or 'country-bred' or perhaps just English and rather 'common'.[54]* Membership of the Saturday Club remained confined to Europeans until the 1950s.[55]

The British who wanted their club to be a preserve of their own based their case on a principle, a practical objection and a prejudice. Freedom of association was a fundamental right that meant the freedom to associate with whom you wished and to exclude others. This particular form of association was, moreover, democratic: it belonged to its members, who could make and change rules by a vote. The practical objection was more difficult to explain, especially to Indians. Its premise was that the British were a tiny minority in the land, many of their men worked long hours with the people of the country, and at the end of the day they needed a place where they could relax, 'let their hair

* Ernest Hartley, the father of Vivien Leigh, had to resign from both the Bengal Club and the Saturday Club when, just before the First World War, he married a woman who was probably half Parsi.

down' and say whatever they wished to people of their own kind without worrying that they might be overheard. After a day in court a judge needed the freedom to rant about a pleader or a false witness without fearing that his remarks might be reported to a journalist or a Congress wallah. The third argument in the case was more of a tit-for-tat debating point: if an Indian gentleman refused to allow his wife to meet British people (because she was in purdah), why should he enjoy the privilege of meeting British ladies?

Clubs rarely had Indian members before the First World War, but they did not usually feel the need to proclaim their exclusivity. In *Thacker's Indian Directory* of 1912 only two were open about it: the Tirhoot Planters Club, for which only 'European men residing' in Bihar were 'eligible for election', and the Coonor Club in the Nilgiris, which was reserved for 'European gentlemen and ladies moving in general society'. This was a short-sighted policy of the Coonor Club, which had so few members that a group of Civilians had to play whist as 'a trio' because it was 'so difficult to get people to make up a rubber'.[56] But far-sightedness was seldom a quality for which club committees were famous. The Bengal Club might have survived without having to knock itself down if, with membership dwindling, it had accepted Indians as members after Independence; by the time it did allow them in (1959), most Indians who might have wished to join were members of other clubs.[57]

Many places relaxed their membership rules between the world wars, partly because of the increasing numbers of Indians in the ICS and other services. Yet redoubts of exclusivity survived, especially in places where boxwallahs and planters could outvote more liberal-minded officials. The Peshawar Club, however, retained its restrictions not through its boxwallahs (of whom there were few on the frontier) but because it allowed its retired members in Britain to vote on club issues. Although Indian officers were finally allowed to drink at its famous horseshoe bar in 1939, the atmosphere apparently did not change. Nor did it change very much after it became part of Pakistan. When one former frontier officer revisited it in 1970, he found himself listening to 'the same noises in the club, the plonk of tennis balls and shouts of "Good shot, old boy!" "Well played Bunty" – all in 1930s English ... Pakistanis still using out-dated English slang and giving their children anglicized nicknames'.[58]

British officials had been urging the admission of Indians to clubs long before 1939. As a junior magistrate in 1914, St John Philby had threatened to resign from the club at Lyallpur if the Indian he had proposed was blackballed; in the end he got his way.[59] Men like Philby realized that the racial exclusivity of clubs was not only unfair and hurtful but also damaging to British rule. As the Bombay journalist Stanley Reed pointed out, it 'isolated' the British 'from warm contacts with the intelligentsia of the land' and caused a natural resentment among 'educated Indians'. Young men who had embraced British culture and could quote Shakespeare in support of any argument were bewildered to find themselves unwelcome in clubs. As a young subdivisional officer in 1891, Harcourt Butler had to deal with a dejected Brahmin who, after four years in his 'dear London', had acquired 'a really considerable knowledge of English literature' and was now 'more English than the English'. In London he had met two former viceroys, Northbrook and Ripon, and had even been elected to the Reform Club in Pall Mall, but he now learned that his candidacy for the club at Allahabad would be blackballed by the military. So 'dreadfully hurt' was he by this news that he 'seriously contemplated becoming a bitter enemy of the British power'. Butler managed to soothe him and remained optimistic about his future candidacy if he would listen to some advice. What his Brahmin needed to learn was the difference between the art of conversation, which he lacked, and the style of public declamation. The British did not want bores of whatever race in their clubs.[60]

In 1873 the Cosmopolitan Club was founded in Madras with the object of introducing Europeans to the city's 'principal residents and thereby' giving them 'some insight into Indian society'. Certain other clubs, such as the one at Indore, were obliged to admit Indians if these had made contributions to its construction. At Balasore in Orissa the club had to have a few Indian members because the local maharaja had provided the building rent free and offered to pay for all its repairs; it was he and not the British who insisted that the Indian membership should be limited to himself and the local rajas of Mowbanj (Mayurbhanj) and Nilgiri.[61]

Schemes for creating clubs for British and Indian members needed the support of viceroys and governors if they were to succeed. As governor of Bombay (1913–18), Lord Willingdon was a zealous and effective promoter of the policy. After Stanley Reed told him that he could not force existing clubs such as the Byculla and the Yacht Club to alter their rules, he decided to set up a new one. Funded by donations from British residents and Indian princes, the Willingdon Sports Club opened its doors to British and Indian membership in November 1917. Thereafter viceroys and governors made a point of patronizing 'mixed' clubs: on his visit to Cochin in 1939 Lord Linlithgow insisted on playing tennis with Indian members of the Lotus Club at Ernakulum, a club opened for Britons and Indians of both sexes, and for all castes and creeds. If the smart clubs in Bombay and Calcutta refused to take the hint, country clubs in the mofussil were different: by 1936 half the members of the club at Vellore, west of Madras, were Indian.[62] And it was easy to make twentieth-century clubs such as the Willingdon and the Gymkhana in Delhi colour-blind in the regulations. As latecomers to this world, women's clubs also enjoyed that advantage. The Ladies' Recreation Club in Madras was set up in 1911 with a double aim, not only 'to promote social and friendly intercourse between European and Indian ladies' but also between 'Indian ladies of all classes and creeds'. Women's clubs were careful to keep a balance between their office holders. At the Nilgiri Ladies' Club in the 1930s the patroness of this establishment was a local rani, the president was the Madras governor's wife, the vice-presidents included Mrs Brackenbury and the Rani of Bobbili, and among the life members was the senior Maharani of Travancore.[63]

RACIAL RELATIONS

It would be too facile to claim that the issue of club membership encapsulated the essence of British–Indian relations, though it did reflect the fairly universal reality that members of clubs tend to admit people who are like them, who share their tastes and values, who are – at least to them – 'clubbable'. And the truth is that the great majority of British and Indians did not find each other clubbable. Even so, relationships between them, fluctuating over centuries, were too complex and variable to reduce to a simplification.

At a personal level they were generally at their best towards the end of the eighteenth century, when men of the Enlightenment ruled and studied in Calcutta, when upper-class Indians and Europeans entertained each other at nautches and dinners, when British men married

Indian wives, learned their languages and respected their religions. Not in great numbers, of course, but enough to create a sense of cultural exchange even at a time when Indians were being defeated on the battlefield and excluded from political power. Parsi gentlemen would feast with the British in Bombay; nawabs and other Muslim noblemen would try European drink and food, even ham if it was labelled 'heron' or 'English venison'.[64]

The idea of cultural exchange went into decline, especially on the British side, as the nineteenth century got into its stride. Racial relations reached their lowest point, for understandable reasons, in the decade after the Rebellion, but cultural separateness, promoted by Evangelical intolerance and Victorian rectitude, was well advanced by 1857. In the early 1850s the British in Delhi and the Indians of the Mughal court may have been inhabitants of the same city, but they were living, as William Dalrymple has put it, 'not only in different mental worlds, but almost in different time zones'.[65] When the Indian feasts began, the British went to bed; when the dancing ended and the courtesans retired, the British woke up and the ladies set off for their morning ride before the sun could damage their complexions.

The British had long inhabited the European quarters of the large cities, but they were now also living in civil lines and cantonments, and they were about to move into yet another segregated type of settlement, the hill station; there was unlikely to be much chance of cultural exchange in Simla or Darjeeling. When Henry Cunningham's novel *Chronicles of Dustypore* was published in 1875, the reviewer in the London *Spectator* marvelled at how the British in India managed to live in a 'world of their own, separated by an invisible but impassable wall from' the rest of India, a world that was 'absolutely exclusive'.[66]

British officials might live in Dustypores with their families and colleagues, but most of them naturally did not lead isolated lives. A subdivisional officer or a canal engineer worked all day with Indian subordinates, as did a forestry official or an officer in the Indian Army. Such men arriving in India at the end of the Victorian era did not attempt to cut themselves off from 'Indian life', though they soon realized which bits of it they liked and which they did not. Those sent out to the mofussil almost invariably liked the people they found there, peasants and ryots toiling on the land to support their families. Those who came out to an Indian regiment nearly always appreciated the sepoys they would be commanding, Sikh, Jats, Dogras or whomever. And those who came across members of the landed classes – a raja or a zemindar or the brother of a nawab; someone who might come to the Club to play tennis and even invite them out shooting – they liked them too, just as later, if they became Politicals, they would like the princely states, the courtly life and the ambience of ancient chivalry.

The one class of person that British newcomers disliked at first sight was the so-called 'babu', a Hindu who often worked as a clerk in a British office, a man who was essentially urban, usually sedentary, and likely to be long-winded in his speech. The type managed to stir every prejudice and preconception in the minds of the arrivals, who were soon writing home to describe babus as 'soapy', 'fat', 'oily', 'smooth-talking', 'devious', 'dishonest', 'servile', 'cowardly' and 'cringing villains';[67] if they were also Bengali, that only made things worse. It is not easy to understand how young British men reacted so strongly to these perceived defects of character when they would surely have been aware of worse failings among their often drunken, violent and foul-mouthed fellow countrymen. Much of their prejudice must have been prepared, at least subconsciously, in Britain, from what they had heard and read, from what they knew of the exploits of small British forces under Clive, Monro and Wellesley defeating large Indian armies. Many of them would have read Macaulay's denunciations of the Bengali, his 'effeminacy', his 'chicanery', and his principal characteristic, his 'deceit'.[68] Despite such propaganda, Civilians in Bengal often came to like the people, appreciating them for their tolerance and amiability and quick wits. Yet even Henry Beveridge, who certainly liked them, could become exasperated by their garrulity. 'The besetting sin of Bengalees', he informed his future second wife, was that they would 'think and talk and talk and think for ever but . . . will not act'.[69]

Rudyard Kipling observed that British men usually became admirers of the religious community that was dominant in the area where they began their work in India. Yet in areas that were mixed, as in most of the United Provinces, they tended to lean, as Kipling himself leaned, towards the Muslims. Like the British, the Muslims were a conquering people; like the Christians, they had a comprehensible monotheistic religion. As a griffin in Allahabad, capital of what later became the United Provinces, Harcourt Butler 'on the whole' preferred 'Mohamedans to Hindus', even though the former were 'more turbulent', gave 'more trouble' and made 'less secret of their desire to get rid of us'. Their religion, he believed, was 'infinitely purer and more elevating' than Hinduism.[70] To other Britons, their habits also seemed more appealing. When working in Bombay in the 1920s, the social worker Maisie Wright found it 'easier to make friends with Muslims than with Hindus, as their habits and way of life are akin to ours'. Her contemporary, the journalist Ian Stephens, agreed. Although he belonged to a fourth-generation 'dolphin' family, the Glasfurds,* he 'adopted Muslim ways' in what he called the 'minor details of life, personal hygiene and so on', and was tempted to go the whole way, swapping his British nationality for Pakistani citizenship after Independence. Although he was an agnostic, he 'felt intellectually nearer to Islam than Christianity' because it made fewer 'demands on one's credulity'.[71]

Stephens may have been tempted to apply for a Pakistani passport, but confusingly, 'as an agnostic', he actually found Hinduism even more attractive: Islam was 'full of sharp, clear rules and definitions', and it treated its women worse.[72] A British pro-Hindu intellectual tradition had existed since the early days of the East India Company. John Ovington, the chaplain who in 1689 had described the feasts at Surat, enthused about the way of life of the Hindus, their vegetarianism and their treatment of animals. So, many years later, did Percy Bysshe Shelley, who considered going to India and working at the court of a maharaja.[73] The East India Company regarded the protection of Hindu religious sites as one of its duties, and its civil servants included a number of distinguished scholars of Sanskrit; John Muir from Kilmarnock was happier working as principal of the Sanskrit College at Benares than as the civil and sessions judge at Fatehpur. In the pre-Evangelical days Britons might collect statues of Hindu gods as an artistic hobby, as Edward and Henrietta Clive did during his governorship of Madras (1798–1803).

Nirad Chaudhuri, the brilliant and eccentric Bengali writer (1897–1999), argued that, 'as soon as the English mind came in contact' with the Hindu mind, 'it completely lost its temper, and so became incapable of dispassionate analysis'.[74] It may have been the environment and conditioning of the different minds that made them unable to appreciate one another, but it needed the addition of Christian intolerance to

* See above, pp. 75, 130.

make it a question of temper. After all the Evangelicals based their case for interference in Hindu customs not just on the claim that those customs – such as *sati* or child marriage – were wrong, but that the religion that produced them was an abomination incapable of reform. The Victorian 'mind' did not so much lose its temper with Hinduism as react with repulsion, turn away with disgust from the fakirs and the beggars, the grotesque idols, the lingam, the erotic sculpture, the whole nightmare band of unintelligible deities. The antipathy became so general that even the more open-minded Victorians might not be bothered to find out what it was all about. In 1893, as a young assistant magistrate, Harcourt Butler decided that 'Hinduism as practised' was 'foolish or foul or both', and consequently he did 'not feel drawn to a study of its tenets'.[75] Even E. M. Forster found the 'Hindu character . . . almost incomprehensible'.[76]

Men like Harcourt Butler were very conscious of antipathy on the Indian side, among both Hindus and Muslims. He himself would have been aware how strange his pink and portly figure would have seemed to the browner and leaner inhabitants of the regions he later governed, Burma and the United Provinces. Orthodox Hindus might be repelled by the British habits of eating beef and drinking alcohol, they might be shocked by the sight of women appearing in public without a veil, and they would be appalled by the idea of sending their own children to school thousands of miles away. Yet the Hindu reaction – unlike the Victorian British – seems to have been generally one of incomprehension rather than horror or censure. When the Maharaja of Jaipur went to England for the coronation of King Edward VII, he visited Kedleston in Derbyshire, the home of the current viceroy (Curzon), and, as he watched the rabbits on the lawn 'gambolling in the sun', he 'wondered how English sahibs could ever go to India'; why did they not stay at home and play the flute?[77] That was certainly one puzzle. Another, for Indians who knew them in both places, was how the British in India could be so different from the British in Britain. When Prakash Tandon, a Punjabi Hindu, sailed to England in 1929 to learn chartered accountancy, he found the British cold and stand-offish until the ship reached Port Said, when they became 'friendly and attractive', qualities they retained during his eight-year residence in Britain. As a result, he 'developed a liking for beer, fish and chips, hot-pot and parkin' and felt he 'got as close to the heart of Lancashire as one could'.[78]

Chaudhuri explained the transformation in his own way. The British, he believed, were essentially 'a brave and kindly people', who in Britain had a sense of proportion and a habit of understatement. Yet in India they became offensive, partly because their numerical inferiority made them always nervous of revolt, and partly because the climate drove them to extremes of thought, habit and behaviour. 'When the Englishman drank in India he drank in hogsheads.'[79] A more diplomatic explanation of Indian feelings about the British came from Salar Jung, the prime minister of Hyderabad, to Richard Temple, Resident at the court in the late 1860s. India had had worse and more violent foreign rulers, the statesman remarked, citing the Mughal Aurangzeb, but 'with all their faults' they had 'settled among and amalgamated themselves with the people'. None of them had been 'so utterly foreign to the country' as the British, 'with all [their] virtues'.[80]

Salar Jung may have complained about the aloofness of the British, but he was well aware of the exclusivity inherent in Indian society as well. Hindus of different castes did not mix or marry or eat together. 'Untouchables' were not even allowed into temples of the religion they supposedly belonged to. When Palwankar Baloo, a brilliant young spin bowler, was selected to play for the Poona Hindus, he was not permitted to enter the club pavilion during the interval; while his team mates sipped their tea from porcelain cups inside, he had to drink his from a disposable clay *matka* outside the building.[81] Mohandas Gandhi, for whom the cause of the Untouchables was as important as any other in his life, even blamed his fellow Hindus for encouraging the British to behave as they did in India: 'It is ourselves who have taught them untouchability.' After the British came to India, he told an education conference at Ahmedabad in 1924, 'they saw that here people followed a queer religion, that one man touching another got polluted and so avoided even standing in the shadow of that person. They thought they too should behave in the same way, else they would expose themselves to danger . . .'[82]

'Untouchability' often extended, in a literal sense, to Hindu behaviour towards the British. The writer J. R. Ackerley, who in the 1920s went to work for the Maharaja of Chhatarpur, excused the reluctance of a Hindu gentleman to shake hands with him on the grounds that it was 'not a natural Hindoo salute and therefore awkward', and anyway it could not be 'pleasant for him to have to touch the hand of a meat-eater'. The maharaja himself had a rule about not eating with Europeans, and although he occasionally broke it by having a cup of tea with his guests, that itself was a gesture of condescension unlikely to appeal to people administering the country.[83] Even British officials who spent their careers trying to improve relations with Indians might find themselves rebuffed if their efforts neglected the correct etiquette. Malcolm Darling, the most pro-Indian of Punjabi Civilians, was reproved by a Muslim husband for not salaaming his wife, and 'ticked off' by a Hindu husband for breaking the 'taboo' of touch – shaking hands with his spouse instead of saluting her with both hands raised palm to palm.[84]

Ackerley and Darling reacted to reproofs with a tolerance unusual among the British. A more typical reaction was surprise followed by annoyance. Shortly before the First World War Mrs Rowan Hamilton was astonished when a Brahmin in Jaipur threw away the food he was cooking because, it was explained by her Indian guide, her 'shadow [had] passed over it'.[85] The young Harcourt Butler was also shocked when a Brahmin visitor shook hands with him and then disappeared to wash the polluted hand in a basin of water which his servant had brought with him.[86] However much a young Civilian might wish to become friends with Hindus in their district, he did not see how this was possible if his touch defiled a man and his shadow polluted his food.

The greatest obstacle to social intercourse between Britons and Indians was the differing attitudes towards the social status of their wives. As Butler put it, 'they want to meet our ladies, and they keep their ladies secluded behind the purdah'.[87] For British memsahibs, endlessly criticized for their failure to 'integrate', this was indeed an impossible issue: one Civilian's wife in the late nineteenth century complained that, not only could she not meet Indian women, she was not allowed even to mention them if she happened to meet their husbands.[88] There was a range of Indian customs – from the age of consent to restrictions on the remarriage of widows – that irked the British, but none that exasperated them more than purdah, keeping women in seclusion, out of sight of men who were not of their family. Purdah was not the same all over India. In Bombay it was more relaxed than in the United Provinces; in the south a raja's daughters could dance in front of the governor of Madras.[89] Yet in most places it was a massive barrier in the way of closer British–Indian relations. It was common for British people to make friends as a couple, for a husband and wife to play tennis with another couple and have dinner together afterwards; that custom was not possible with Indians. Even a viceroy could not meet the wife of a comparatively enlightened maharaja: the closest Minto could get to one in Gwalior was when Scindia's wife sang 'Coming through the Rye' to him from behind the purdah. After Walter Lawrence ended his Indian career in 1903, his principal regret was that he 'had never had the pleasure of meeting the women of India and of understanding their life'. He knew that they could see him from their latticed windows, but he could 'never speak to them nor share their thoughts'. It was a 'crippling convention', he thought, one that had cut the British off 'from the real India' and made it impossible for them to 'come near her heart and mind and soul'.[90]

British reactions to the purdah system were often more basic. As wife of the governor of Madras in the 1870s, Lady Hobart refused to invite Indians to balls unless they brought their wives with them, though she did invite those women to 'ladies only' parties. Yet the common British attitude – 'as you don't let me call on your wife, you shall not call on mine' – was, as Harcourt Butler put it, 'absurd', because it threw away 'the argument of superior education and habits'.[91]

There were in any case other reasons, personal and also official, why numbers of Britons might not wish for very close social relations with the native inhabitants. Many British women did not want to be in India and were only there because their husbands had Indian careers. Some reacted badly from the start, against the dangers and the loneliness and the alien environment; they were not like young women on holiday in Italy, enjoying the sights and sampling the pasta for a few weeks. They knew they would be in India for decades and, for many of them, the only way to survive was to stick together and avoid the crowds. 'Fraternizing' with Indians was in any case sometimes officially discouraged, especially in the years after the Rebellion when new Civilians were taught to be arrogant and to insist on deference from Indians.[92] For many years British officials were encouraged to be 'aloof' and to exhibit their superior status by their dress and their demeanour and by travelling first class on trains.

The British had always invited prominent Indians to the Residency or Government House, but towards the end of the nineteenth century efforts were made to revive the idea of 'mixed parties' given by individuals. As the commissioner of the police in Bombay in the 1880s, Frank Souter liked to host such events but, although the intention may have been laudable, they were, according to Wilfrid Blunt, rather colourless and strained occasions. In the same decade in Bankipore the Beveridges gave what they called 'international parties', erecting separate tents in their compound for Hindus and Muslims to eat in and hoping that all the guests would mingle afterwards, wandering about the house and listening to the musicians but avoiding the bandsmen eating their ham in a separate enclosure. Indian gentlemen also gave 'mixed parties', but there was seldom much mingling at them. James Sifton described how at 'an entertainment with fireworks' at Bhagalpur he shook hands with his host on arrival and departure but did not see him again; the young Civilian had to spend most of the evening in seats reserved for the European guests.[93]

A more promising environment for mingling seemed to be provided by freemasonry, at least in those lodges which admitted Indian members. Kipling's lodge in Lahore contained Muslims, Sikhs, Jews and Christians, and the poet appreciated the sense of intercommunal brotherhood where 'there ain't such things as infidels' among the 'Brethren black an' brown'.* Yet masonic lodges had their drawbacks as meeting places for men of different communities. One was the Hindu reluctance to join them. Another, presumably universal, was the temptation to ask favours of fellow masons. John Beames felt obliged to retire as 'master' of the Lodge Star of Orissa because so many 'loafing ne'er do wells' and 'half-caste clerks' begged him for appointments, 'pleading the sacred tie of masonic brotherhood'.[94]

One group of high-caste Hindus which was open to the idea of British–Indian friendship, or at any rate of cultural fusion, were Bengali anglophiles known as 'Ingabanga' (English-Bengali), who flourished in Calcutta at the end of the nineteenth century. In his book on the Bengal capital the novelist Amit Chaudhuri records how they spoke like late Victorians, saying 'thet' instead of 'that' and 'beck' rather than 'back', and they always knew 'which knife and fork to use at the various stages of a dinner'. For him the Ingabanga was slightly 'fatuous', a member of 'a disliked minority in Bengal that had surrendered to the British way'.[95]

---

* From 'The Mother Lodge'.

Yet it was surely understandable that Indians reading for the Bar in London or studying as ICS probationers at Balliol should become rather anglicized, adopting English habits and admiring Shakespeare and Tennyson. They could still be patriotic Indians even if they worked for the empire and received knighthoods from the king-emperor. Behari Lal Gupta was one of the first Indian members of the ICS, yet he remained a scholar of Persian and Sanskrit, and his argument that Indian judges should be allowed to try British citizens was accepted at least in principle by Lord Ripon's government in 1883. His daughter Dihima was certainly an Ingabanga, as depicted in a delightful essay by her grandson, the journalist Sunanda Datta-Ray. She spoke 'crisp Engish', she ate beef, and Gray's 'Elegy' was her favourite poem, yet she remained 'firmly rooted' in India's nineteenth-century renaissance that was 'leavened by the yeast of England's influence'. Alas such attempts at cultural synthesis did not usually lead to close friendship. As Datta-Ray recalled, Britons and Bengalis paid each other calls, left their cards and sometimes sat down to dinner, but their relationships were 'stiffly formal'.[96]

In Lahore in 1912 E. M. Forster was delighted to meet so many Indians at Malcolm Darling's dinner table, but he was depressed to discover that his friend and his wife, Josie, were an unusual couple in this respect in much of British India. Yet the First World War, which overturned a number of social barriers in Britain, had a similar effect in India. Stiff collars and calling cards went into decline, and people who enjoyed jazz and cocktails were unlikely to kowtow to the *Warrant of Precedence*. Bridge parties, tennis parties, lawn parties, even dances, became occasions where mingling could take place. The coming of the Charleston did not have much of an effect on the practice of purdah, but British women now made more of an effort to give 'purdah-nashin' parties. Their previous visits behind the purdah had often been excruciating affairs, with the veiled ladies of the zenana, unable verbally to communicate with their foreign visitors, taking a pathetic pride in showing them their jewels and their saris. More enjoyable for everyone was the new 'Purdah Club' of Simla, where the wives of British officials and Indian women, both those who were westernized and those who were still 'strictly secluded', met regularly – 'all male servants were excluded' – for evenings of plays, music and 'country dancing'. Another new factor in purdah relations was sport. Barbara Donaldson, a judge's daughter, recalled how in the later 1920s purdah women in 'gorgeous saris' were 'experts at badminton and volley-ball'. When Humphrey Trevelyan became Resident at Udaipur in 1941, he and his wife made 'one social innovation': purdah tennis parties for 'ladies of the court' and the government. Screens would be erected, and 'all males [would] be banished for the afternoon'.[97] Doubtless such events did their bit for racial relations, but they seldom created friendships. As we have seen, social contacts between British and Indians occasionally resulted in marriage, but it was a rare occurrence. And rare too, at least until the last years of the Raj, were genuine interracial friendships. The obstacles of power and prejudice, race and religion, were too forbidding.

On the last page of A Passage to India Mr Fielding, the English teacher, asks the Indian Aziz, 'Why can't we be friends now? ... It's what I want. It's what you want.' But Aziz, who has been tried in court for a crime he did not commit (and which in fact was non-existent), is in a rage and says it will not be possible until he and his fellow Indians have driven 'every blasted Englishman into the sea'. In the final sentence E. M. Forster, who finished his novel in 1924, seems to concur with Aziz that friendship is indeed not possible now – 'no, not yet'.

Forster went to India, like his friend J. R. Ackerley, with no impedimenta from the Raj; they were not officials, and they did not have British employers. Both men wished to make Indian friends, and both of them enjoyed amorous relationships with male servants of the maharajas who employed them. Yet such friendships as they had were not lasting, and even before he finished his novel Forster had decided he didn't like Indians as much as he thought; he was no longer interested in 'whether they [and "English people"] sympathise with one another or not'.[98]

A third novelist who tried to make Indian friendships was Paul Scott, though in one case he was socially too ambitious and – as other friends (both Indian and British) warned – certain to fail. In 1944 he had arrived in Bengal as a lieutenant for No. 1 Air Supply Company and was told to select a new sergeant or havildar. He chose a southerner called Narayan Dass, with whom he stayed in touch after the war. Twenty years later, when he began research for what would become The Raj Quartet, he accepted an invitation from Dass to spend three weeks with him in his home in Andhra Pradesh, where his former subordinate was now the village headman. Scott was excited by the prospect. He envisaged lazy days among the palm trees and paddy fields, inhaling jasmine and nocturnal scents, reminiscing with Dass under a peepul tree. Yet the naive novelist's visit turned out to be a disaster. Instead of behaving like two old comrades swapping war stories, Dass called him 'Sir', treated him like a sahib and put him on display to the villagers – at the same time as insisting that Scott conformed to Hindu sanitary custom, taking a pot of water with him into the fields each morning. Appalled by the squalor of the village, the behaviour of Dass and the Hindu hygienic requirements, Scott felt trapped and desperate. Treated like a sahib, he found himself becoming defensive and even arrogant, allowing a 'sahib's face' – what he called a 'mask of superiority' – to impose itself on his 'mild and liberal one'. More practically he wrote to an Indian publisher imploring him to send a telegram saying that he had to go to Madras to give some lectures. For years afterwards, Scott felt guilty about the subterfuge.[99]

12

Singularities

UNSOUND CIVILIANS

Malcolm Darling never went anywhere without a book. As a junior magistrate in the Punjab, he took his volume of Keats to court to read in his lunch hour, but one day it was seen by a subaltern who picked it up and exclaimed, 'Poetry, by Gosh!' 'Alas,' Darling wrote, when humorously describing the incident, 'my reputation is gone.'[1] Since the days of the Lawrence brothers in the 1850s, officials in the Punjab were meant to be men of action, governing from the saddle, not chaps who read poetry or possessed artistic tendencies. When as chief commissioner John Lawrence discovered that a young Civilian had arrived in the Punjab with a piano, he vowed to 'smash' it for him and moved the official to five different posts over the following two years.[2]

A number of officials like Darling preferred remote postings with little British society to the attractions and greater prestige of a job in a provincial capital. Some, like Sidney Dunlop in Madras, yearned for 'walks in the jungles', for 'the quiet and peace and stillness of the night'; others, such as Leonard Woolf in Ceylon, wished to absorb themselves in 'the slow-pulsing life of the most ancient type of civilization' and experience 'the profound happiness of complete solitude'.[3] Darling too liked to work in, and write about, a slow-moving civilization – in his case village life in the Punjab – and at dinner he wanted to sit in a tennis shirt without wearing 'barbarous' socks and read some Homer or Turgenev.[4] The problem for literary Civilians was that there seldom seems to have been more than one of them in a province at any time. Alfred Lyall and Charles Elliott were Haileybury contemporaries who both became lieutenant-governors and who both retained their literary interests until the end of their careers. Yet as they hardly ever saw each other in India, their cultural friendship could only be epistolary and occasional. Lyall, the talented poet of a thin single-volume *œuvre*, considered Elliott as 'almost too much a "littéraire" for India', but the latter managed to sustain enthusiasms for Indian and European culture in an unpromising ambience. He displayed a very rare interest in local music, and as a magistrate he assembled a group of minstrels to recite a lengthy tale of Rajput chivalry called the 'Lay of Alha'. In his last spring as lieutenant-governor of Bengal, Elliott went in pursuit of Dante, reaching Darjeeling ahead of his files, which enabled him to read a canto each day with a commentary.[5]

Dante was also a solace to Joseph Goudge, a Civilian in the United Provinces whose first wife had died of cholera. He had little interest in the art or literature of India, but after meeting Phyllis (his future second wife) on furlough in Britain – and talking to her about Dante – he became obsessed by the culture of Italy, a country he had never visited. On returning to India without his fiancée, he immersed himself in the poems of Carducci and in Ariosto's *Orlando furioso*. A typical day, as described to Phyllis, began with a little Latin, Tacitus with chota hazri, followed – if feeling 'lazy' – by reading 'a book of Italian lyrics under the sandalwood trees'. He then worked on files and petitions, and received visitors, until tea-time, when he read a novel by Antonio Fogazzaro; further official work followed until dinner and another bout of Italian reading. Yet it was an unsatisfactory life because, much as he cared about literature, books themselves were 'not enough unless' he could 'talk to some congenial soul about them'. According to his granddaughter, the writer Anne Chisholm, poor Goudge may never have visited Italy even in retirement, although as an old man in Sandwich he translated *Orlando furioso* into Spenserian stanzas.[6]

As Civilians were often criticized for keeping aloof from British society, ICS manuals urged them to go regularly to the Club, even if they found its society 'uninteresting'. By virtue of their position, officials had a duty 'to amuse and entertain the other residents, who may not have your resources of culture and interests'.[7] Darling did his best to ignore this directive, preferring to remain sockless with his book than to struggle at the Club to be 'cheery', a word beloved by compatriots in India. Philip Mason was at his happiest in remote Garhwal – he without a tie, his wife without a skirt (i.e. in trousers) – but at Saharanpur he felt that he had to go to the Club to avoid 'being thought stand-offish and superior'. Bahrain might not be a popular posting for an Indian Political, but Emily Lorimer was delighted when her husband was sent there because they would be 'free from the eternal club, the rival dinner parties, the calls and the social claims of an ordinary station'.[8]

In 1934 Mildred Archer went to Bihar as an unusual, intellectual, Oxford-educated wife of an unusual, intellectual, Cambridge-educated Civilian. She was sceptical about everyone connected with the Raj, and when she went to the Club at Ranchi and met the commissioner, John Merriman, she dismissed him as 'an urbane, hard-drinking social charmer'. Later she discovered his library, listened to him talking about the province and its history, and realized how 'British social life in India forced many scholarly people to hide their knowledge and true interests behind a conventional facade'. One officer thought the only way to remain sane in the intense atmosphere of diligent officialdom was 'to take up ... an abstruse subject ... that took some tackling but ... could never be any possible use to you in your profession'.[9] Joseph Goudge certainly took this advice when he embarked on his study of Italian literature from Dante to Fogazzaro. So did two earlier officials at the Hyderabad Residency in the 1860s, one of whom spent his spare time translating Homer from the Greek while the other rendered Hafiz from the Persian.[10]

Yet it was more usual to accept the suggestion of William Hunter, a Civilian chiefly employed by the government as a statistician, to choose an Indian subject as one's hobby, something historical, cultural, linguistic or perhaps scientific. Walter Francis accepted this advice 'so as to try to prevent' himself 'growing into an Anglo-Indian bore with no knowledge of anything outside his own shop'.[11] Most Civilians, however, were more positive in their approach. Douglas Dewar seems to have found no difficulty in choosing his congenial subject: he wrote half a dozen books about Indian birds. Bill Archer, the husband of Mildred, wrote a work on the songs and poetry of the Uraons, an aboriginal tribe of central India, which he followed with a study of primitive Indian sculpture, while Mildred opened her own career as an art historian with a book on painting in Patna.

While some literary efforts, even when published, were superficial and ephemeral, others made useful and original contributions to scholarship. If the books on Islam and 'Mahomet' (1858 and 1883) by

William Muir, who became lieutenant-governor of the North-Western Provinces, can be regarded as just targets for 'orientalist' criticism, those on Sanskrit texts by his elder brother John, who retired more modestly as a district judge, cannot; there was no imperialist agenda in the studies of this unambitious scholar from Kilmarnock.[12] Nor was there in the work of A. C. Burnell, also a judge and also a Sanskritist, who won an international reputation, including an honorary doctorate from Strasbourg University, for his catalogues of the Sanskrit manuscripts in the palace of Tanjore.[13]* As the historian Anil Seal has pointed out, Civilians have been 'accused of contempt for Indians', but it was they who 'worked to establish much of the ancient history and the ethnology of India'.[14]

Linguistics was a favourite 'hobby' of Civilians. Even a man as busy as John Beames liked to refresh his 'weary soul' with a daily 'plunge into Sanskrit and Prakrit' – and in due course he completed a *Comparative Grammar of the Modern Aryan Languages of India*. Anthropology was almost as popular a subject, producing a number of scholars who taught the subject as university dons in retirement. George Grierson embraced both interests, writing, among many other things, *Bihar Peasant Life*, as well as compiling the eight volumes of *Seven Grammars of the Dialects and Subdialects of the Bihari Language*.

An especially fertile terrain for anthropologists was Assam. Although political agents to the Naga Hills in the late nineteenth century were likely to be killed by tribesmen† or, if they survived, to catch malaria, the region remained attractive to several potential anthropologists in the ICS. Among them was John Hutton, who spent almost his entire career as a Civilian (1909–35) in the Naga Hills, where he made wax-cylinder recordings of the tribal people and wrote several studies of Naga tribes; after his retirement he became professor of social anthropology at Cambridge. Another was the slightly younger James

---

* Burnell was also the co-author (with Colonel Henry Yule of the Bengal Engineers) of that most remarkable literary product of British India, *Hobson-Jobson: A Glossary of Anglo-Indian Words and Phrases*, published in 1886 and revised by William Crooke (another Civilian scholar) in 1903. Its thousand pages remain a delight for anyone interested in the etymology of such words as 'punkah', 'bungalow' and 'kedgeree'.

† Between 1876 and 1878 three successive agents met violent deaths: Captain Butler was killed in a fight with the Lhota Nagas, P. J. Carnegy was shot by his sentry, and Guybon Damant was killed in a revolt of the Angami Nagas when he tried to enter one of their villages.

Mills, who also spent his Civilian career in Assam, writing three books on Naga tribes and becoming the governor's adviser on the tribal areas of the north-east; in 1947 he reluctantly left his 'beloved Naga Hills', worked at the School of Oriental and African Studies (SOAS) in London, and later became president of the Royal Anthropological Institute. Like Hutton, Mills was more interested in the tribes of Assam than in the preservation of the British Empire in India. As Jonathan Glancey has written, both men were 'very brave' and 'challenged what they knew and how they had been taught to see the world as Victorian schoolboys'; both of them developed 'a keen sense of justice, as well as a love for landscape' and a 'fascination and care for everything and everyone they met'.[15]

In the second half of the nineteenth century the politics of the British in India – of the military, of officials, of boxwallahs, of planters – were very largely Conservative. The Tories at home seemed to know what they were doing in India and why they were there. Disraeli had made Queen Victoria empress of India, and his chosen viceroy, Lord Mayo, was a paternalist who thought that Britain should hold India 'as long as the sun shines in heaven'. The Liberals had much hazier ideas. Gladstone, so clear about what should happen in Ireland or Italy, did not have an answer or even an aim for India beyond sending *his* viceroys (Northbrook, Ripon and Dufferin) with vague instructions to 'promote the political training of our native fellow-subjects' and to associate more Indians with the administration.[16]

The British in India especially disliked Liberal members of Parliament who came to the Subcontinent, decided during a brief visit what was wrong with it, and then returned to Britain and pressed for reform and enfranchisement. As Walter Francis, a young Civilian, put it in 1893, 'Out here one feels that one lives on the crust of a volcano, and regards with distrust anyone who pours water through the cracks, even if it's only for fun, to see what will happen.'[17] This feeling of anxiety may sometimes have bordered on paranoia, yet it reflected the reality, recognized by the perceptive, that Britain's Indian Empire was more vulnerable to internal tensions than to external threats from Russia or other international rivals. The feelings of insecurity led officials to worry about unconventional colleagues and even about themselves. In 1936 W. H. Saumarez Smith in Bengal asked his parents to stop sending him their copy of the *New Statesman* because it was 'really impossible and undesirable' for a Civilian 'to be an enthusiastic and regular reader' of a left-wing weekly. Realizing that this was rather a feeble attitude to take, he soon asked them to resume sending it, even though he recognized that its political views were 'very unhealthy' for a young ICS officer.[18] The *New Statesman* also appeared in the Officers' Mess of John Morris's Gurkha regiment and was picked up one day by the colonel. Flicking through its pages, he found it subversive and 'bloody red' and asked 'how the hell did it come to be' in the Mess? Nobody knew, but all the officers now eagerly read the issue, opinion being divided between those who thought 'the filthy rag should be banished' from the Mess, and those who considered its 'political ideas so ludicrous that they amounted to humour'. It *was* banished, but Morris, who was not interested in politics, had so enjoyed the arts pages of the Mess copy that he took out a subscription of his own.[19]

Tories may have been in a majority among the officers and officials of British India, but there was a long minority tradition in the civil service of men who did not agree with Lord Mayo, men who believed that, even if the British were *now* necessary for India, their presence should not be permanent and their mission should be a moral one. Such administrators as Thomas Munro, governor of Madras (1820–27), and Mountstuart Elphinstone, governor of Bombay (1819–27), both of them Scots, believed that Britain's aim in India should be more than just the provision of enlightened and efficient government: it should be to try to educate its Indian subjects so that one day they would be capable of governing themselves. 'You are not here,' Munro told the directors of the East India Company,

> to turn India into England or Scotland. Work through, not in spite of, native systems and native ways, with a prejudice in their favour rather than against them; and when in the fulness of time your subjects can frame and maintain a worthy Government for themselves, get out and take the glory of the achievement and the sense of having done your duty as the chief reward for your exertions.[20]

Munro and Elphinstone were governors in an age unsympathetic to their ideas. Cornwallis had already excluded Indians from senior posts in the administration, and now Evangelicals and Utilitarians were intent on undermining 'native systems and native ways'. Yet later in the century, after the trauma and disruption of the Rebellion, the tradition was revived in the civil service, often by Scotsmen. When the Indian National Congress was founded at the end of 1885, its pioneering president was not an Indian but a retired Aberdonian Civilian and celebrated ornithologist, Allan Octavian Hume. Clever, fractious and egotistical, Hume worked as the Congress general secretary for nine years, writing pamphlets, organizing committees and turning himself into an agitator so outspoken that even his Indian colleagues sometimes felt obliged to rebuke him. Another Scottish president of Congress was Hume's biographer, William Wedderburn, who as a Civilian in Bombay had annoyed his superiors by never losing 'an opportunity of associating himself with native political movements'. The views of the pro-Congress officials were best expressed by an English Civilian, Henry Cotton, who pointed out that the administration 'of a great country by a small number of foreign visitors', who were isolated by 'religion, ideas and manners ... from all intimate communion with the people', could 'never exist as a permanent state of things'.[21] Unlike Hume and Wedderburn, Cotton almost reached the top of the ICS, as chief commissioner of Assam, but his vociferous enthusiasm for the nationalist idea probably cost him the most senior job open to him, the lieutenant-governorship of Bengal. Like Wedderburn, he became a Liberal MP after retirement, and like him he made little impact in the House of Commons. Yet he retained his interest in the people of India. In 1906, at the behest of Mohandas Gandhi, then a lawyer based in South Africa, he asked the junior minister at the Colonial Office (at the time Winston Churchill) a series of parliamentary questions about the harassment of Indians in the Transvaal.[22]

The ICS produced a small number of mavericks whose views went beyond those of the British friends – and presidents – of Congress. In the 1930s Michael Carritt, a junior magistrate in Bengal, began working for the Communist Party of Britain, acting as a go-between with comrades in Bombay and delivering bundles of Comintern literature; in 1938, at the age of thirty-three, he felt unable to combine his work with his beliefs and resigned from the service.[23] Yet most 'progressive' Civilians preferred a gradualist approach. In the late nineteenth century Henry Beveridge had advocated Indian self-government – but not just yet: if Britain were to abandon India at that stage, he thought, it would be acting 'like a man-stealer who should kidnap a child, and then in a fit of repentance abandon him in a tiger-jungle'.[24] Later generations of liberals in the ICS were less worried about the tigers. Early in the twentieth century Malcolm Darling realized that 'self-government' had to come in his lifetime – and in consequence he was regarded as 'a red-hot Radical' by his commissioner. When Bill Archer joined the ICS in 1930, after being an active member of the Cambridge Labour Party, he 'felt it almost a moral duty', according to his future wife, 'to test his Labour principles and work actively towards Indian independence through humane administration'. For Darling and Archer, 1947 did not come too soon.[25]

OTHER MEMSAHIBS

In Edward Thompson's novel *An Indian Day* Hilda in Darjeeling wonders if there is 'any country in the world where it was so useless to be a woman – at any rate an English woman' – as India. Many English women would have agreed with her that there was not. Most of the activities that made them 'useful' and effective at home were carried out in India by servants: the cooking, the cleaning, the shopping, the gardening, even the care of their children, were in the hands of others. Nor was there much to take their place when their husbands were at work, especially at remote stations: as one Civilian pointed out, there they were denied 'the ordinary feminine diversions of shopping, visiting friends, and making dainty a permanent home'.[26] And in busier places, how often could one go to the maidan to watch one's husband galloping across the polo field? How much time could one spend playing bridge and mah-jong, or flicking through catalogues and magazines at the Club? Boredom and loneliness, a combination that might have nurtured revolutionary thoughts in other circumstances, were among the chief vexations of British women in India.

These pages are not about the women who suffered and succumbed to inactivity. Nor are they about those who went to India for a specific purpose, like Annie Besant, who went there to promote theosophy, or Madeline Slade (later known as Mira Behn), who was determined to become a disciple of Gandhi.* Nor are they about women who engaged

* For other women who went to India to have careers, see above, pp. 65–71.

negatively or disapprovingly – for whatever reason – with India, like those who were fond of berating Indians for their treatment of animals and inundating the district officer with complaints on the subject. When Richard Burton returned to India in 1876, after an absence of twenty-seven years, his wife, Isabel, had a man arrested for pulling a bullock's tail to make it go faster.* Doubtless such women often had a point, as they would have had if they had visited a slaughterhouse in Britain. This is not to denigrate women such as Mrs Gradidge, who set up an animal hospital in Quetta, although Indians might have been puzzled that someone so concerned with the welfare of donkeys and camels should be such an enthusiast for hunting and pig-sticking.[28]

Some women made a point of distancing themselves from the Raj while remaining linked to it for the sake of their husbands' careers. They might refuse to ride or play bridge or drink gin and tonic at the Club, but they did not cut themselves off completely. Hermione Nethersole, the wife of a Civilian, was one of these, though she took her unconformity further than most, going through stages of Buddhism and vegetarianism and reading D. H. Lawrence.[29] More typically unorthodox was Joan Pearce, a Cambridge graduate and a member (like her Civilian husband, Roger) of the Left Book Club. Soon after her marriage Joan decided that other memsahibs were 'awful', and she alienated them by refusing to play bridge, by having her baby in a Parsi nursing home instead of the civil hospital, and by insisting – very unusually for a Civilian's wife – on working, as a teacher at a convent school in Karachi; presumably the memsahibs did not know that she had also breastfed a Hindu baby whose mother could not produce sufficient milk. Perhaps the teaching job dampened her rebelliousness for later she changed her mind about bridge and became a competent player; she even came to enjoy the Karachi Yacht Club.[30]

These pages are about another type of memsahib, the 'enthusiast' for India who neither embraced the Raj nor rebelled against it. She might not be talented or out of the ordinary, but she was intent on making the best of it, determined to enjoy and appreciate her time on the Subcontinent. One of the early enthusiasts was Fanny Parkes, who *was* talented and out of the ordinary, and for whom 'the pleasure of vagabondizing

* After the arrest she became worried that she might have identified the wrong man; he was therefore released without charge 'if he would promise to pull no more cows' tails'.[27]

over India' was immense. 'Roaming about with a good tent and a good Arab [horse],' she wrote in the 1830s, 'one might be happy for ever in India.' The landscape of Bengal excited her so much that she could barely describe it, even when viewing it from an extremely slow boat on a river: the Hindu temples, the ruined ghats, the twisted roots of an old peepul tree, the women bathing or carrying water on their heads, the 'infinity of beauty' there was in 'all the native boats'.[31]

Two women in the mould of Fanny Parkes were Anne Wilson, the wife of a Civilian in the Punjab, and Rosamond Lawrence, married to a Civilian stationed in Bombay and Sind. Anne, who was from Glasgow, went to India in 1889, having already written a short biography of Savonarola, the radical republican friar of fifteenth-century Florence. Keen to understand how Hindus thought, she studied Hindustani, visited Benares and read the *Vedas* and the *Upanishads*, though this experience turned out to be frustrating, 'a mixed pleasure'. Unmixed, however, was her delight in the Indian countryside, especially at twilight, the cattle returning 'in the gloaming from the wells' and 'the smell of the village smoke' bringing 'with it the sense of elemental things'.[32] Rosamond Lawrence, who went to India in 1914 after marrying her dead's sister's husband, was impressed by the 'majesty' of the scenery, especially in the mountains around Mahabaleshwar, where she found scenes that reminded her of Wagner's 'Ring' cycle. She also loved the landscape of Sind, where her husband was appointed commissioner, and the early-morning rides across the 'coldly blue' sand, the sun rising from the mist, the 'groaning of the Persian [water] wheels' and the 'green parrots flashing from tree to tree'.[33]

Women who liked camping were much more likely to enjoy India than those who did not. On tour they could collect plants and shells and butterflies; they could appreciate dawns and sunsets, the wind bending palm trees and casuarinas, the quality of light on vast expanses of water in Bengal. They would become familiar with the scents of the countryside, not just the bazaar smells, the spices and the scent of jasmine and sandalwood, but also rural smells from the village, the smoke of cow-dung fires or the wafts from fields of yellow mustard. Edward Lear had complained, half jokingly, that 'few birds in India know how to sing', and it was a myth widely held in British India that birds could not sing properly just as flowers did not have the right scent.[34] Many people found them either monotonous – like the unceasing *tonk-tonk-tonk* of the coppersmith – or else 'shrieky' and discordant, like the ascending crescendo of the brainfever bird, a notorious cause of insomnia. Yet those who complained, as Emily Ritchie did, of the 'absence of sweet bird notes', evidently never heard what one Civilian described as 'the lovely liquid notes of that queen of warblers, the fan-tailed fly-catcher'.[35]

A fondness for Indian night sounds was another taste often unacquired by the British. 'Infernal' nocturnal noises included dogs barking, tom-toms beating (accompanied by other Indian instruments) and the howling of jackals, screeching as if in pain. Yet some people loved the sounds of cicadas at night and of Persian water wheels when they awoke in the morning. A good test of people's feelings for India was their reaction to the sound of frogs. If, like Mrs Davidson, a soldier's wife, you loved the 'croaking' of the 'big monsoon frogs' in Madras, you probably liked India. In Karachi Madge Green loved the time when the frogs 'began to chant every evening', and from a paddy field in western India Rosamond Lawrence adored the 'fluty music of millions of frogs', an 'unbroken chorus' of 'brekekekex koax koax' (as the frogs sing in the play by Aristophanes). Yet it was not only a feminine joy. For the Civilian Walter Lawrence (no relation of Rosamond), 'the sound of the frogs' was even 'more soothing than the song of birds'.[36]

The most popular way of recording a liking for the landscape was to paint it. There were of course many male sketchers, especially among the engineers who had been taught to draw at Addiscombe. Captain Hervey of the Madras Infantry thought sketching 'an excellent pastime in India' because there were 'such beautiful subjects for the pencil'; Lord Northbrook, the viceroy, unpacked his sketchbooks directly he began his long autumn tours; and at Hyderabad Richard Temple insisted that his banquets should culminate in a viewing of the watercolours he had most recently painted. Yet sketching in India in the later Raj was very much a female occupation. Katharine Read, a painter successful enough to merit an entry in the *DNB*, set off for Madras in 1777 at the age of fifty-four; and Kay Nixon started the Indian stage of her artistic career in 1927.* But almost all the women in the 150 years in between were amateurs, excellent though many of them were. They were also enthusiasts, as they needed to be, because sketching in the

* See above, p. 63.

open air in India was not like painting olive groves in Tuscany or the lakes in Cumberland. The heat ruled out much of the day, as did the glare, which Madge Green in Karachi found so 'eye-tiring' that she had to learn to paint from memory. When in 1848 Lady Falkland, the Bombay governor's wife, sat down to paint a picturesque scene in Poona, she was nearly trodden on by an elephant and a buffalo; then some children came to see what she was doing, followed by their mothers and some local fakirs; and eventually a herd of cows and goats was driven past, kicking up dust that obscured the view and covered her paper and the inside of her paint box.[37]

Violet Kennedy-Erskine was a Scottish woman who accompanied her Irish husband, Lieutenant Arthur Jacob, when his Hussar regiment was posted to India in 1895. She was a talented person who wrote some stories about India and later some poems praised and published by Hugh MacDiarmid, the Scottish nationalist and communist, who was not always an admirer of his fellow poets. Yet her great passion became the Indian landscape, which she painted incessantly, revelling in the views and the vegetation, studying the roots of the banyan tree, painting exquisite pictures of temples and flowers, especially poppies. She enjoyed visiting the princely states, which she found more interesting than British India, and she loved being in camp, with which there was 'no life to compare', especially if she was in a place where she could sketch 'great domes and tombs' in the twilight. The British-Indian life 'made up of clubs and what passes for society' never touched her. Had it done so, she said, she would have 'died of boredom'.[38]

Emily Overend was born in 1881 and educated in Dublin, where she gained a first-class degree in Modern Languages at Trinity College. From there she went to Oxford, got another first in German and afterwards taught German philology at Somerville College. Yet in 1910 she gave up Oxford and her job to marry a Scottish official in the Indian Political Service, David Lockhart Robinson Lorimer, known as 'Lock'. Both Lock and his elder brother John were members of the IPS, though while the first had joined it from the Indian Army, the other had entered the service from the opposite direction, the ICS. Soon after his marriage, Lock was appointed political agent in Bahrain, a post under the government of India, a place where Emily found the landscape desolate and featureless, consisting mainly of large rough stones, 'without a single bush or leaf' except for a 'date-garden' next to the village well. Her accommodation was not something to get excited about either. As the plaster of their modest house had been made with saltwater, it was always peeling, and the roofs were in constant need of repair; saltwater, combined with an extremely stony soil, also made it virtually impossible to grow anything in the garden. Emily managed to survive the hot weather by cutting out the collars and necks of her muslin dresses and sleeping on the verandah, which was better than indoors, although the moon, so 'nice and romantic at home', was as strong and bright as daylight in the Persian Gulf.

Yet she embraced her life in Bahrain. She relished the local seafood, the prawns and the crabs, and though vegetables and fruit were 'not very plentiful', she could get lemons and bananas from passing ships; lemon juice with soda water became her primary thirst-quencher. There was almost nobody to talk to anywhere near except members of a European mission, which had been there for 'twenty years without making a single convert', but it did the Lorimers and any European visitors 'an immense service . . . by merely being there'. Missionaries might have a rather limited view of the world, admitted Emily, but it was one of people who had 'work to do in life' and thus 'more stimulating than the gossip of people who only kill time'. Later their company began to pall – 'missionaries, however nice, are after all only *half* human' – and for a change she gave a dinner for 'two of the French pearl merchants'.

Luckily society did not matter to her, and she was relieved not to have to live in an Indian station and be expected to attend the Club. She was absorbed in Lock's work, which included such subjects as the manumission of slaves, the operations of the pearl fisheries, and relations with the local sheikhs. Yet her husband's chief interest – like hers – was languages. Having served on the north-west frontier, Lock had learned Pashtu and was now busy compiling a grammar of the language before he forgot it;* at the same time he was learning Arabic and also, Bahrain being where it is, having to conduct much of his work in Persian.

---

* His *Pashtu* was published in 1915, thirteen years after his brother John had written a book on a similar subject, *Grammar and Vocabulary of Waziri Pashto*. Lock later published several books on Persian, including *The Phonology of the Bakhtiari, Badakhshani, and Madaglashti Dialects of Modern Persian* (1922).

As a newcomer to the East, Emily felt she had to start with Hindustani so that she could at least communicate with their Indian cook. Then she went on to Arabic, reading the Koran for two hours each day, though she found it a discouraging language on account of the variations in vocabulary from place to place.

As European languages had been her profession, she was determined to keep them 'fresh', especially 'Gothic' and 'Old English'. She was equally keen to read Gibbon and other 'treats' she had 'long promised' herself but which her work at Oxford had forced her to postpone. With money given to them as wedding presents, the Lorimers bought the new edition of the *Encyclopaedia Britannica*, and they read Trollope to each other in the evenings. She dreaded the day, she told her parents, when they reached the final volume of his works.

At the end of 1912 Lock was appointed consul for Kerman and Persian Baluchistan, another posting for a Political; it was a move welcomed by Emily because she was now studying Persian, which she liked to speak and read – it had 'a decent literature' – much more than Hindustani, which was 'only a sort of servants' esperanto and [seemed] never to be anyone's real tongue'. After two years in Kerman and a brief assignment back inside the Indian Empire to Chitral, in 1915 Lock was summoned for the campaign against the Turks and placed on special duty with the Mesopotamian Expeditionary Force, which consisted largely of Indian Army units and was under the command of the c-in-c at Simla. While he was in Amara as civil governor, Emily spent a short time in Egypt as director of the Red Cross Missing and Wounded Enquiries Department. Later she went to Basra, where Percy Cox, the chief political officer of the expeditionary force, noticed how capable and efficient she was and appointed her editor and manager of the *Basrah Times*, a newsletter published by the force's Political Department and issued daily in English, Arabic and Persian. She enjoyed the routine of the work, the checking of proofs, even the office politics when clerks and translators tried to get each other sacked. She also seems to have enjoyed imposing discipline. Her first reform was to 'insist on shoes coming off before anyone entered the office'; the next was 'to prevent anyone within earshot of [her] desk from making filthy noises in his throat and spitting'; and the third was to 'get hold of the sweeper and insist on something being sometimes cleaned and swept'.

After Lock came back from the Tigris, they returned to Kerman until 1920, when he was sent back to India in the high Himalaya, this time as political agent at Gilgit. On reaching their mountain destination, they found the nine local rajas with their heirs and retinues assembled to meet them, lined up in seniority, the Mir of Hunza first, the Mir of Nagir next, and then the lesser seven. As usual, Emily made the best of the bleak and lonely place that was to be her new home. The mountains might be 'rugged and bare', but Gilgit itself was 'a wonderful little oasis', and the agent's house was 'most attractive' and had 'a jolly garden'.[39]

Enid Smythies was a few years younger than Emily Lorimer and had a British-Indian background; both her father and her brother were officials in the Forest Service. She was a sporty girl whose presents on her twenty-first birthday at Naini Tal included roller skates ('the great rage now'), a silver-tipped riding switch, and a golf club called a niblick ('an absolutely necessary club on these links'). As a guest at Government House, she was given a dance there on the evening of her birthday: it was a 'ripping night', and the moonlight was so bright that she was 'able to go out between dances, which always refreshes one so'. On most days that summer she practised her roller skating on 'the Rink' and coxed a four in preparation for the Naini Tal regatta.

Yet Enid also enjoyed going on tour with her brother Evelyn, in the Himalayan forests and in the inhabited landscapes, among the 'grubby, stuffy, dilapidated old temples'. 'I love the bazaars' smell and all,' she wrote to her mother; 'they *are* India, aren't they?' In 1913 she married Evelyn's friend Clinton Dawkins,* also a forestry official, and went to live with him in the jungles of Burma. She took to her new home immediately. From 'the first glimpse', her husband told his mother, Enid was simply 'revelling in Burma' and its people, whom she found clean and sympathetic. She even liked the weather, although the rain and damp had 'a demoralizing effect' on her piano: 'the top two octaves refused to sound'. She was proud that she was not one of those women who always talked of 'going to the Hills for the hot weather'; she loved the jungles in that season, the leafless trees, some of them in flower, the sun shining through the upper branches, and 'the dead crackly leaves to walk on'. Officials had once warned their juniors not to marry because

* See above, pp. 199–202.

the Burmese climate was dangerous for British women,* but Enid believed their advice was nonsense. She regarded the climate at their headquarters, Pyinmana, as 'ideal', better than at Naini Tal or even in England, and she was delighted when the chief medical officer agreed that there was 'absolutely no need for anyone in any part of Burma to go to the Hills to escape the hot weather'. She could not understand why so many officials chose to spend their careers in the Punjab or the United Provinces when they could have opted for Burma.

Enid found Pyinmana 'one of the prettiest places . . . in the East', a jumble of pagodas, minarets and 'quaint old Burmese houses' with palms and mango trees scattered among them. Seen in the golden light of early morning, it looked 'perfectly beautiful', as did its surroundings, the 'hazy paddy fields and blue hills, and the sun rising in a blaze of orange behind it all'. There and at their next station, Katha on the west bank of the Irrawaddy, she could grow almost every type of English vegetable and soft fruit. Yet unfortunately the station contained 'society' and the Club and card games. Enid soon stopped playing bridge because there was 'always so much unpleasant feeling about it', and she hated 'being embroiled'. She and her husband also stopped going to the Club in the evening because it was 'such a waste of time'.

'Our enjoyment,' wrote Clinton to his mother in the spring of 1914, 'consists of disappearing in the jungle rather than entering the vortex of society.' Enid appreciated the jungles of whatever kind, the deciduous woods around Pyinmana or the mangroves and evergreen forests around the port of Bassein. She also loved having her three sons on tour, taking the babies in Moses baskets or carrying them like the local Karen women did, tied to her back by a shawl; she refused to employ an ayah in case the boys learned to boss her about and had an English nanny instead. Almost the only things she did not like about Burma were leeches, bamboo ticks (whose bites irritated for a month) and bird's-nest soup, which local 'Chinamen' thought a 'great delicacy' and paid high prices for. Enid found it very dull and disappointing – 'just like vermicelli but with no taste at all'.

The couple's letters home suggest they felt their lives to be blessed, as were those of their sons, who – until they were sent 'home' to school – led the sort of existence that Arthur Ransome might have invented.

---

* See above, p. 291.

After Clinton finished his day's 'girdling',* and they had had their tea, he and Enid would go to the nearest river and sit on a rock, he with a gun and a book, she with her 'painting things', sitting affectionately in silence because the noise of the water made speech impossible. She painted regularly in the hot weather, when her fingers did not get cold, and was much stimulated by the scenery, though she found it difficult to paint river rapids with watercolours. By 1915 she was good enough to have her work shown at the art exhibition in Rangoon, where she sold sketches of hills and lakes; she also won a prize. Soon she began to write as well, publishing articles on the Burmese landscape – forests, coasts, pagodas and the Irrawaddy – and a short story in the Christmas number of the *Rangoon Times*. She also reviewed books for the *Rangoon Gazette* and continued to write pieces over the next fifty years.[40]

Madge Green went to India in 1921, at the age of thirty-four, accompanying her younger brother Arnold, who had been a Civilian in Sind for six years and was now returning from furlough. She entered into the spirit of the enterprise on the voyage out. Unlike a fellow first-timer on board, who collapsed in her berth and wept incessantly – which must have been, as Arnold said, a rather 'blighting experience for her husband' – Madge enjoyed everything. She ran potato races, played cricket (with squashy balls) and sang Gilbert and Sullivan duets with her brother at the ship's concerts. The only thing she did not like was the way some British passengers talked about the Indians, which disgusted her and made her feel that such people had 'absolutely no business to have anything to do with India'. But later in Karachi, when she saw ICS officers talking to the inhabitants, she felt 'quite different'. After playing tennis with Indians, it was 'awfully difficult not to feel different when you' spoke to them; 'many people become sort of extra pleasant'. Yet Arnold was completely natural, talking to them in 'exactly the same' way as he talked to British people.

Unlike Enid Dawkins and Emily Lorimer, Madge did not try to avoid social life, and when she became social secretary of the commissioner, it would have been impossible to do so. She enthusiastically played tennis, went sailing, joined a book club (reading Wilde and Ibsen), and had musical evenings with neighbours (Gilbert and Sullivan again). Yet she recognized the 'amusing absurdities' of social life, of

* See above, p. 200.

endlessly changing one's frock, of playing cards so often, of the 'ever-lasting billiard game'. Like Enid she preferred to be on tour, chugging in a launch up the Indus or riding across the desert on borrowed camels, 'decked in silk and silver, and altogether most beautiful to behold'. She had a sensuous relish of places and surroundings, of 'the scent of wet earth' in the monsoon, of the sound of water scattered over dust and the consequent smell, of the chant of frogs and the taste of mangoes (though she needed to wear a bathing dress to eat them), of sudden sights like the time their car got a puncture beside a village pond with a 'bending palm darkly outlined against the sunset sky'; it seemed 'the essence of the East, and we sat and rejoiced'. Britons were often annoyed by the noise and slowness of Indian trains, but Madge revelled in them. Travelling at night was 'delightful', the train just 'lolloping along' until it reached a station, where she enjoyed hearing the voices 'when the sweetmeat sellers cry their wares and everybody argues with everybody about everything'. Like other British women, Madge showed her appreciation of the Indian landscape by depicting it on paper and on canvas: street scenes and palm trees, the creeks and harbour of Karachi, the 'gaily coloured boats with their long bendy masts'.

Madge Green was not a linguist like Emily Lorimer, but she employed a munshi to teach her Hindustani, and read Tagore, though presumably in English. And she played her part, in a limited and very English way, in advancing British–Indian relations, organizing a jumble sale for the Zenana Mission, receiving visits from noblemen's daughters in purdah, and working for the Girl Guides, which contained Muslims, Parsis and Hindus, as well as British and Anglo-Indian girls.* She taught them how to tie knots and make beds and how to bandage wounds; she showed them how to pitch a tent, to make a stretcher with poles and to treat someone with a sprained ankle. She also taught them how to dance a Scottish reel and how to drill and march for a rally on Empire Day. In 1922 her Guides company won a cup and a shield for its efficiency.

After more than five years with Arnold, Madge went back to

---

* Junior Girl Guides in Britain were known as 'Brownies', but for obvious reasons the term was not used in India, and the girls there were instead known as 'Bluebirds'. When Lady Baden-Powell, the wife of their founder, went to India, she was reminded several times to use the appropriate term in her speeches, but apparently the matter 'so preyed on her mind' that she became confused and addressed the girls as 'my little blackbirds'.[41]

England in 1927 but returned to be with her brother again in 1930. As their parents were now dead, there are no letters describing their life in Sind during her second period in India. The only evidence from this time in Madge's papers is a collection of her sketches and some photographs showing the two of them often garlanded, on tour or at cricket matches or in rows at official functions. Arnold, who was now the district officer at Larkana in Upper Sind, is in the middle of the seated figures, and Madge as the senior (often the only) memsahib is also in the centre. The photographs of 1933 show Arnold looking fit and well, but at the end of that year he died at the age of forty-two. The following year's *India Office List* recorded the event but did not reveal the cause. Nor of course did it reveal what happened to Madge, by now forty-six, unmarried and with no immediate family. She lived into her eighties and in 1970 donated her letters and thirteen of her paintings of Sind to the India Office Library.[42]

Their husbands' retirements did not mean the severance of Enid's and Emily's connections with Burma and India. Clinton Dawkins retired in 1936, and he and Enid went to live at Little Baddow in Essex, where she continued to write articles about the East and where they both gave occasional talks about Burmese forests. Their three sons, all born in Burma, each went into the colonial service in Africa, to Nyasaland (now Malawi), Uganda and Sierra Leone.

After her husband's retirement in 1927, Emily Lorimer resumed her life of scholarship, translating several books from the German, including Ernst Kantorowicz's biography of Frederick II, king of Sicily and Holy Roman Emperor. Yet she kept up her interests in India by writing articles on such subjects as 'peasant life in Hunza' for the *Listener* and the *Geographical Magazine*. In 1934 she and Lock returned to the Subcontinent for an anthropological and linguistic expedition to the Karakoram Range, a jaunt that gave her the chance to act as the *Times* correspondent in Kashmir and to write a book about it, *Language Hunting in the Karakoram*. Yet by the late 1930s her fear that Hitler intended to implement the programme in *Mein Kampf* persuaded her to divert her attention to Nazism. In 1939 she published *What Hitler Wants* and, three years later, *What the German Needs* – in effect a drastic re-education to prevent 'him' from starting a third world war. She died in 1949, decades before Madge and Enid.

The three women described here were not very similar. Emily was a scholar who might not have found much to say to Madge, who might have been unnerved by the former Oxford tutor and become rather gushing in her company. Enid might not have seen the point of one woman who could work as a social secretary or of another who would rather translate a book than live in a jungle. Yet they had a number of things in common, above all a sensibility towards their surroundings. All three were in the Indian Empire to be with a relation who was working there; each of them embraced the geographical extremities she found herself in – Burma, Sind, the Persian Gulf and the Himalaya – enjoying it, finding out about it, studying its languages, painting its scenery, writing about it in articles and correspondence. All three, in the vast numbers of letters they sent to their parents in England, wrote year after year with enthusiasm and scarcely a complaint about heat or dirt or noise or inhabitants (except when Emily banned her clerks from spitting near her desk at Basra). Their three sets of papers ended up in the India Office Library (now in the British Library), which is a great thing for historians, although they have not perhaps excited the scholarly interest they merit. In the case of this book, they were not consulted because they might offer an alternative view of the stereotypical memsahib; they were read because they were interesting and well written and seemed to deserve the time required to go through them. Anyone who reads the letters is bound to be struck by the spirit in which they were written – by the enthusiasm, the curiosity, the sympathy for the people and their surroundings – and might be tempted to wonder whether, if E. M. Forster had met Enid or Emily (Madge went out too late for him), Mrs Turton might have been a different character and *A Passage to India* a different book.

GOING NATIVE

'Going native' was not a phrase used to imply approval, to praise a man who had absorbed India's culture and spoke its languages 'like a native'. Rather it was spoken disparagingly of someone who was slightly suspect and 'unsound', who sympathized too much with the native peoples, who had certainly 'gone too far' and might even be potentially disloyal. As a young Civilian in Bihar in the 1930s, Bill Archer was regarded as 'somewhat suspect' and some of his activities 'undesirable'

THE BRITISH IN INDIA

because he wore Indian clothes in his bungalow and took lessons in ragas.[43] Even administrators who were enlightened and understanding usually thought it better to demonstrate these characteristics in a British manner. Humphrey Trevelyan had 'little use for Englishmen who ceased to be English' and tried 'to become Indian in outlook and habits'. He believed that he and his colleagues 'could best serve our country and India by remaining ourselves'.[44]

In 1579 Thomas Stephens, from New College, Oxford, travelled to Goa via Rome, where he became a Jesuit priest. Subsequently he spent the three remaining decades of his life in India and wrote an epic poem in Marathi to explain the lessons of the Bible: he may have 'gone oriental' primarily to convey an occidental message. Thomas Coryate, a generation younger, seems to have had no such agenda. Travelling to India overland, via Persia, he reached Lahore in 1615 and was soon describing himself as a 'fakir dervish, a wandering Sufi ascetic who begs for alms'. He spoke the right languages, wore the right clothes and assumed the right gestures, so that even the Mughal emperor Jehangir was moved to give him a financial reward.[45] Yet he managed to alternate periods of 'going native' with extended stays with the English ambassador to the emperor, Sir Thomas Roe. More genuine perhaps was the example of John Oswald, an aggressive young officer of the Black Watch who arrived in Bombay in 1782. Yet after a few months in India he became disgusted by his job, resigned his commission and went to live with 'some Brahmins', who, according to a contemporary, 'turned his head' so completely that he never ate meat again. After setting off for home via Persia and central Asia, he reappeared in Britain no longer a fierce young soldier but a man with 'the mild philanthropic manners of the Hindoo' Brahmin who, if he saw a butcher's market, 'would go any distance' to avoid it. Only his innate atheism prevented Oswald from becoming a 'Hindoo'.[46]

The heyday of 'going native', or at least of assuming 'native' ways and characteristics, was the last decade or so of the eighteenth century. This was the era when certain officers of the East India Company sported beards or moustaches in the 'Rajput manner', when they dyed their fingers with henna, when they smoked hookahs and gave up eating pork and beef, when they kept bibis and sometimes even harems, when they entertained their friends with dances by troupes of nautch girls, when they wore 'musulmani' clothes and allowed their children to become Muslims, when men such as William Gardner and David Ochterlony adopted India as their home, lived there more than half a century and never thought of returning to Britain. Charles Stuart, an eccentric Irish officer understandably known as 'Hindoo Stuart', performed puja, bathed in the Ganges and campaigned to persuade British women to abandon their traditional garments and adopt flowing Indian robes. Yet he and the others kept a foot on either side of the line. James Kirkpatrick may have adopted Hyderabadi Muslim customs – and married a Muslim wife – but he remained Resident of Hyderabad, one of the most powerful posts in Britain's emerging Indian Empire. Few Englishmen put themselves beyond the pale of their fellow countrymen's emotional frontiers. One who did so, perhaps unintentionally, was David Hare, a watchmaker who used the profits of his business to set up the Hindu College in Calcutta; his affinity with Hinduism was regarded as too intimate to permit his body a Christian burial in the European cemetery after his death from cholera in 1842.[47]

Another man who went too far, also unwittingly, was Richard Burton, whose research into the homosexual brothels of Karachi had been deemed too diligent for an officer of the Indian Army.* No one could ever match Burton's skills at impersonating a 'native'. On his expedition to Mecca in 1853 he resumed his Karachi persona of Mirza Abdullah, a Persian merchant who swore by his beard, but on the way he changed his identity to that of a wandering dervish, and he penetrated the forbidden city as Abdullah Khan, a swaggering Pathan born in India and educated in Rangoon. Yet for Burton 'playing native' was more fun than 'going native'; he wanted the game, not the life change. His chief interests may have been in Asia and Africa, but if he had needed to live among those interests, he would have found some way of doing so and would not have spent the last eighteen years of his life as the British consul in Trieste.

As the nineteenth century advanced, fewer Britons adopted Indian customs and habits, a trend that continued into the last decades of British rule. Some of those who resisted it were 'fakir missionaries', men like the Rev. Rowland Bateman, who abandoned his family to preach in the 'wilderness', wearing a turban, riding a camel and living 'like an Indian'; there were even examples of women 'fakirs', acting their part

---

* See above, pp. 333–4.

in saris and sandals.[48] Those officials who resisted the trend tended to be rather obscure people living in fairly remote places; they were not Residents such as Ochterlony in Delhi or Kirkpatrick in Hyderabad. By the 1870s few officials were like Captain Thomas Lewin, superintendent of the Lushai Hills, who, according to a colleague, roamed 'the wilds . . . in native clothes and lived with the tribesmen'. Nor did many officials imitate Surgeon-Major Brown, the political agent to the Naga Hills, who, as a contemporary recorded, 'lapsed' so entirely into 'what were called "native ways"' that he 'registered the birth of two of his children by separate women on the same day'.[49] By the twentieth century men who had 'gone native' were divided between those who had made a deliberate choice and those who had drifted into it, probably as a result of something going wrong, as part of a process of going downhill, often in the company of alcohol. An example of the first sort was an officer of the Leicestershire Regiment encountered by Leonard Woolf who, as soon as he was made a captain, converted to Islam, resigned his commission and made the pilgrimage to Mecca. Of the second type was Captain Robinson, whom we have already met, who became a Buddhist beggar in Burma as a result of an addiction, though in his case of opium rather than alcohol.[50]

Paul Norris, an anglicized Greek from Bangalore, came across both kinds in the course of the Second World War: an intelligence officer who spent his leaves in his orderly's village in eastern Bengal and who planned to marry the orderly's sister and settle there, and a homeless cashiered former officer who told Norris that he was disillusioned by Western materialism and had 'found peace in Hindu metaphysics and meditation'.[51] Another type, much rarer and far more difficult to track down, was the British woman who 'went native', a mysterious phenomenon seldom seen but occasionally reported to be living in a bazaar, veiled and unrecognizable, or somewhere very remote, in the mountains or on the edge of a desert. When Walter Lawrence was touring the Punjab in the 1880s, a woman came to his tent and, from behind a screen erected by her servants, told the Civilian that after her parents were killed in the Rebellion, a Muslim gentleman had carried her off, had treated her well and – when she was grown up – had married her. Twenty years later, Lawrence heard of another example: an English police officer informed him that a 'white woman [was] living with the Jogis in the caverns of sacred Jumnotri, thirteen thousand feet above sea level'.[52]

Some people who 'went native' might have done so not by accident or force of circumstance but because they needed to find another homeland, a second identity, an adopted country where they could do different things, wear different clothes, speak and even think in a language other than their own. They might not previously have known this, or set out to achieve it; they might only have realized their need at a sudden and unexpected moment. Ursula Graham Bower seems to have been one of these. A schoolgirl at Roedean, and later a debutante in London, she went to India in 1937 to stay with friends in the small station of Imphal in Assam. There she did what young English women usually did – she 'idled comfortably', playing golf at the club and tennis at the Residency – until she went on an excursion into the Naga country with the civil surgeon and his wife. There, suddenly, she became mesmerized by the jungle hills and the people who lived in them. It was, as she recalled later, as if she had discovered the world to which she had 'belonged the whole time' and from which she had accidentally been 'estranged'; on returning to Imphal a few days later, she already felt a little 'divorced' from her 'own race' and longed to go back to that 'wild reality of mountain and jungle'.

The following year she returned to India and received permission from the local political agent to go back to the Naga country, take anthropological photographs and later make a study of the Zemi Nagas. After a long and difficult journey into the North Cachar hills, she reached the village of Laisong and soon afterwards set up a dispensary there. In that malarial country the people accepted her quinine – and her first aid – but 'in all other illnesses they preferred their magico-religious ceremonies'. Ursula Bower was entranced by her new circumstances, and remained so. In due course she realized she had become a Zemi, and so did the villagers, who adopted her and treated her as the reincarnation of a former goddess.[53] For almost seven years she lived alone among them, learning their language and rituals, seeing the world through their eyes, and earning herself the nickname 'the Naga Queen' from her compatriots in the Plains.

Ursula's life among her beloved Zemis was transformed by the Second World War when Nagaland became part of the front line against the Japanese. In March 1942 she went down to Lumding Junction to run a canteen for refugee trains coming from Burma, and she joined a guerrilla organization called V Force (a unit of General Slim's

14th Army), which asked her to persuade Zemis and other Nagas to act as 'native scouts'. She duly recruited 150 of them but, as they were armed with obsolete, long-barrelled muzzle-loaders, it was fortunate that they were used more for intelligence work than as troops to fight General Mutaguchi's invading divisions.

At the end of the war Ursula was visited in her camp by 'a very long, lean, dampish Colonel', who said he wanted to collect butterflies in her area. This was in fact a pretext because Tim Betts had for some time been intrigued by the story of the 'Naga Queen' and, now that the war was over, he was determined to meet her and – so long as she wasn't a 'harpy' or a 'horse-toothed Amazon' – perhaps even try to marry her. As they did not know each other – and she had never heard of him – marriage was clearly a long shot, but in fact it happened, very quickly, though spread over two ceremonies. The first took place at Shillong in British fashion, with wine, a cake and a wedding dress, and the second after Tim, a pipe-smoking Wykehamist, had received the tribe's approval, in Ursula's village, the ritual followed by celebrations of sing-ing, dancing and drinking from vats of rice beer that continued until the middle of the following morning.[54]

After a few months with the Civil Affairs Service in Burma, Colonel Betts was demobilized and, to the delight of his wife, appointed polit-ical officer of the remote Subansiri region in the Himalaya. For another three years Ursula could live in the tribal north-east but, when Inde-pendence left her husband without a job, they decided to return to Britain in 1948. She was depressed from the moment they got 'home'. The English hills were 'too close', she felt as she looked out of a train window; she wanted to 'push them back', to 'have forty and fifty miles of clean air between me and untrodden mountains'. On leaving Assam she felt as if she had 'been torn up by the roots' and 'the wound ached unceasingly'. When people asked why she was not happy, she found it impossible to explain that 'home was no longer home, that it was utterly foreign, that home was in the Assam hills and that there would never be any other . . .'[55] She did try to find another one, in Kenya, where she and Tim and two daughters lived and grew coffee until the Mau Mau Uprising. They then settled on the Isle of Mull, where at least the rain-fall would have reminded them of Assam. At her funeral in 1988 three Naga tribesmen were among the pallbearers.

The best way to avoid withdrawal symptoms was to stay native and remain in India, as Verrier Elwin did, dying in 1964 as an Indian citizen. The son of the British bishop of Sierra Leone, Elwin had got a double First in Oxford (in theology, then in English) before he went to India in 1927 to work at the Christa Seva Sangh, a Christian mission at Poona inspired by the Hindu idea of the ashram. Within a short time of his arrival, however, he was finding it difficult to combine his Christian work with his admiration for the teaching of Mohandas Gandhi, especially the tenet that all religions were equally true or equally false. A week spent in Gandhi's ashram at Sabarmati turned him into both a supporter of the Indian national movement and a disciple of the man he regarded as the 'most sublime and Christ-like figure now living on the planet'.[56] In 1930, when Gandhi defied the government by marching to the sea to make salt, Elwin openly supported him. The following year he left the mission and, in due course, the priesthood and the Church as well.

Elwin's adherence to Gandhi was both personal and political, and with his master's support he set up an ashram for the tribal Gonds of central India. Yet he was soon questioning the applicability of Gandhi's social teaching to tribal people among the hills. How relevant was cotton-spinning to the inhabitants of the forests? Why was it important to preach abstinence and celibacy to people who derived much harmless pleasure from mahua liquor and an uninhibited sex life? After the rigours of his own religious upbringing, Elwin revelled in life among the tribes, among women who, as an Indian friend at the ashram put it, 'used to change husbands as we change socks and forget about it'.[57] Once a follower of St Francis as well as Gandhi, he himself now became sexually promiscuous, marrying two tribal women and enjoying many other liaisons. Sex, he decided, was something everyone should enjoy, a view that led to disparagement from British and (later) Indian officials who considered him 'a sex maniac' who had 'gone tribal'.

Yet Elwin also produced an intellectual defence of India's 25 million aboriginals, arguing that their simple, attractive society required protection from an encroaching Indian world of urban traders and money-lenders as well as from the 'vegetarians and teetotallers' of Congress who aimed to 'force their own bourgeois and Puritan doctrines on the free wild people of the forests'.[58] His early work among the Gonds was as a provider of education and medical aid. Later he saw his duty as that of an anthropologist, explaining tribal life to ignorant and sceptical outsiders, and subsequently as a defender of these people and their way of life. While living with the hill tribes for twenty-five years, he argued their case in a succession of eloquent books. His mother might regard him as a 'caveman', his British contemporaries might mock him as a kind of St Augustine in reverse – travelling from priestly austerity to exuberant promiscuity – but he did receive some recognition in independent India. He was perhaps the first foreigner to be given Indian nationality, and he was appointed by the prime minister Jawaharlal Nehru (who told his officials to 'absorb' Elwin's philosophy) to the post of adviser on tribal affairs to the North-East Frontier Agency. After his death an editorial in an Indian newspaper described him as India's 'most eminent anthropologist' and added that he was 'perhaps the last ... of those liberal-minded Englishmen who had made this country their home and completely identified themselves with its people'.[59]

LOAFERS

When the Civilian Walter Lawrence was stationed at Peshawar in the late 1870s, 'two quaint loafers' came across the Afghan border and told him their story. One was a deserter from the army, the other a sailor who had left his ship at Calcutta, and they had lately been expelled from Kabul by Abdur Rahman, the amir of Afghanistan, who had given them food and blankets and then tried unsuccessfully to convert them to Islam. Earlier they had gone up the Kurram Valley, the soldier dancing and the sailor playing the fiddle, and they had reached Kabul unhurt apparently because the Afghans regarded them as insane – and for them a mad person's life was sacred.[60]

In 1884 Lawrence was posted to Lahore, where he became a friend of Rudyard Kipling, then a young journalist on the *Civil and Military Gazette*. Four years later, Kipling published a tremendous story about two 'loafers' who crossed the same border and then struggled through the snows to make themselves a kingdom in the mountains of 'Kafiristan'. His fictitious pair, Daniel Dravot and Peachey Carnehan, were more swashbuckling figures than the men seen by Lawrence, as were Sean Connery and Michael Caine when they acted them in John Huston's film *The Man Who Would be King*. Kipling may have been inspired by other tales, including the experiences of two American-born adventurers, Josiah Harlan, who a half-century earlier had briefly been a prince in the Hindu Kush, and Alexander Gardner, a freebooter who had fought for the Sikh Empire and who married an Afghan princess. Yet it is unlikely that, as they dined together in the Punjab Club in Lahore, Lawrence failed to tell his friend his story of the loafers. And it is even more unlikely that Kipling, always on the alert for 'copy', would have failed to make some notes afterwards.*

Lawrence came across a number of loafers in his work, but he never knew one 'who made good'. He described the pair expelled from Kabul as 'feckless, hopeless folk', and so was an Englishman he met in a corner room of a serai, 'a well-educated man of good family, who had gone downhill'; fond of books, he 'used to sleep by day and drink at night'. Yet others, like Kipling's duo, were more aggressive and blustering, trying to swindle their way around India, sometimes by pretending to be journalists and blackmailing a raja. Lawrence encountered one who remained in a dak bungalow, terrifying the khansama and running up a bill he would never pay; another who worked as 'a temporary and wholly inefficient servant of some ostentatious Indian magnate who preferred a white coachman to safety'; and a third who even sought his 'advice as to the city or Raja he should next exploit'. Yet Lawrence took a tolerant view of the breed in general. The loafer may have been a cynic but he was 'often a philosopher', and he knew 'much that is hidden from us'.[62]

In the eighteenth century loafers were classified as 'Low Europeans' or, at the bottom of the scale, 'European vagabonds'. They tended to be former sailors or servants or time-expired soldiers, who drank and brawled and got into debt.[63] Yet as the East India Company scrutinized the Europeans who wished to enter its territories, there could not have

---

* Four decades later, when they were both living in Sussex, Kipling persuaded Lawrence to write his memoirs – among the best by an 'old India hand' – which were published as *The India We Served* in 1928. A few years earlier, Kipling had encouraged a more famous Lawrence (T. E.) also to write a book based on his experiences. An almost illegible draft letter at Harvard in the desert hero's handwriting reveals that the two men met in 1918, sat up for a couple of nights while T. E. 'talked very much' until Kipling, 'wanting perhaps to go to bed, told [him] to go and write a book. Well,' Lawrence wrote four years later (after the first draft had been stolen on a train), 'I did'. Kipling agreed to read the typescript of *Seven Pillars of Wisdom* on condition that Lawrence never revealed that he had done so.[61]

been very many of them before the 1850s. New jobs in industry and the railways increased their numbers, but the principal source of 'Low Europeans' or 'vagabonds' – now known as 'vagrants' – remained deserters from British regiments and sailors who had jumped ship or lost their job. It was difficult for Europeans to hide in India, and those unable to do so kept moving, trudging from town to town, sleeping in the open or on an empty verandah, begging and finding temporary jobs with planters and other employers unlikely to enquire too closely into their history.[64] Many no doubt had been unlucky, made redundant when a business or a tea garden went bankrupt, but others had been dismissed for drunkenness or incompetence or even criminal behaviour. Some were like the down-and-out Paul Norris found living in the 1930s 'as a non-paying guest' in the second-class waiting room at Delhi Station. Others were swindlers and charlatans like Corporal Gerald of the Welch Fusiliers, a public-school man who enjoyed a picaresque life masquerading under different identities and 'borrowing' large amounts of cash from money-lenders in Shanghai and Bombay.[65]

The Victorians in India were nervous about anything that might damage the prestige of the 'ruling race'. Vagrancy, asserted one commander-in-chief, was a case in point, a 'serious stigma' on the government that damaged it 'in Native eyes'.[66] After visiting India in the late 1860s, Charles Dilke, the Liberal politician, said it was 'impossible to over-estimate the harm done to the English name by the conduct of drunken soldiers and "European loafers"' – men with 'brutal natures' who became 'ruffianly beyond description' when 'trailing across India' and dealing with 'trembling natives'.[67] If arrested, some of them were sent to workhouses in the provincial capitals, but sailors often went to the 'sailors' homes' established in the main ports, and army deserters were dealt with by the military authorities.[68] Women vagrants usually received quite lenient treatment. Instead of being sent to workhouses, they were often shipped home – in case they became prostitutes in India – or taken in by a charitable institution. The Friends Need Society, which could accommodate sixty women ('aged, infirm or destitute'), was set up in Poonamallee High Road in Madras 'to relieve the deserving poor and suppress mendicity amongst Europeans and Anglo-Indians'.[69]

In districts where there were no workhouses or a military presence, the junior magistrate was expected to meet the tramps, listen to their hard-luck stories and decide what sort of assistance they deserved. James Sifton's habit at Bhagalpur in Bihar was to give them a square meal and then get his chaprasi to escort them to the railway junction and put them on the train going in whichever direction they chose, Calcutta or Bombay.[70] On the other side of India Walter Lawrence pursued a similar policy, but it did not always meet with gratitude. One 'visitor' to his camp in the Punjab became 'indignant and abusive when offered food without drink, and a pass to Bombay instead of a gift of money'.[71] Kipling's Dravot and Carnehan had vowed not to touch alcohol while they pursued their ambitions. Most loafers, whose ambitions were survival and the avoidance of jail, did not see the point of self-denial.

13

At Ease

ARTISTS AND AMATEURS

British society in India was often accused of being philistine, and on the whole it was. It is difficult to see how it could have been otherwise. Most British men had gone there to pursue outdoor careers, and many of them led isolated lives in remote places. Even those living in the larger cities were too few in number to sustain a European cultural life comparable to that in a medium-sized European town. Small Italian cities such as Parma or Bologna might in the nineteenth century support their own opera houses, but their populations were very much greater than the largest concentrations of British inhabitants in India. There were little more than 11,000 of these in either Calcutta or Bombay and fewer than half that number in Madras.

Actors and musicians seldom tried to make a career in India because they realized they could not attract sufficient audiences; a further deterrent to musicians was the climate, which was ruinous to their instruments. Writers suffered a similar problem, an exiguous potential readership. No novelists remained in India except those few who had to stay for other reasons: Henry Cunningham because he earned his living as a government lawyer; Flora Annie Steel because she was married to a Civilian; and Edward Thompson because he was a teacher at a Wesleyan College in Bengal. Kipling was the only writer who sold books in any quantity while still living in India, and he left the Subcontinent at the age of twenty-three. Apart from his *Kim*, the most enduring novels about India until recent times were written by E. M. Forster, who went as a tourist, and Paul Scott, who went there by chance, posted to India in the Second World War. Even authors of Indian novels who lived for long periods on the Subcontinent, writers such as John Masters and Rumer Godden, produced most – sometimes all – of their best work after they had left.

The only people in the arts who had a successful time in India, and who stayed there for long periods, were painters. They had several advantages over artists in other fields: they had Indian customers, who sat for them and paid well for their portraits; they had subjects beyond the British community – buildings, landscapes and the indigenous peoples – which interested and sometimes captivated them; and they were not dependent on their compatriots in India for appreciation of their skills and remuneration for their work. If a governor or a chief justice wished to buy their pictures at a decent price, that was fine; if not, the paintings could be packed up and taken home. After Thomas Daniell arrived in Calcutta in 1786, he and his nephew William produced a series of aquatints of the city which they sold there to finance a long journey up the Ganges; following their return from Delhi, Lucknow and the Himalayan foothills, they sold pictures they had painted along the way to fund another journey to the south; in Madras they sold yet more to get themselves to Bombay and then home via China; and when they reached London nine years after they had left it they still possessed an enormous portfolio, including hundreds of drawings of landscapes and monuments from which they produced the 144 aquatints of their great work, *Oriental Scenery*.

The uncle and nephew were the most famous and successful of the British artists of Indian topography and architecture. Yet there were several others of comparable ability, including William Hodges (a pupil of the great Richard Wilson), who had preceded the Daniells up the Ganges and on to Agra. Many of those who depicted the buildings and landscapes of India were employees of the East India Company, surveyors and engineers such as Thomas Fraser of the Madras Engineers, who specialized in drawing forts and fortresses. Yet it was difficult for even the most talented officers to break into the world of professionals competing for eminence at the Royal Academy in London. When Lieutenant Francis Swain Ward resigned his commission in the Madras Army in 1764, he tried to make a living as a painter in Britain. Nine years later, on recognizing that he had failed, he asked the EIC to reinstate him in the army with the rank of captain, which it did. So delighted was Ward by this development that he gave the Company ten oil paintings, and so pleased with these gifts was his renewed employer that it gave the officer 200 guineas and a further sum when he reached Madras.[1]

British portrait painters who had gone to India via the Cape tended to stay for long periods. The best of them received lucrative patronage, both British and Indian, and some even found posts at Indian courts. Johann Zoffany spent five years in India, and Tilly Kettle stayed for seven, time for them to become fathers of several half-Indian children. George Chinnery sailed to India in 1802, apparently to escape his wife, and never returned to Britain. He earned his living painting portraits of grand people in Madras and Calcutta, but he much preferred to sketch the countryside and its inhabitants. For four years he lived in Dacca in the house of the collector, Sir Charles D'Oyly, whom he taught to paint, and he improved the skills of many British amateurs in Bengal. Yet Chinnery was someone who, however much he earned, always got into debt, and in 1825, after nearly a quarter of a century in India, he escaped his creditors and fled to Macao, where he spent another quarter of a century painting a similar mixture of subjects, the portraits (like those of the Scottish opium dealers, William Jardine and James Matheson) that earned him money, and the rural scenes that were his real passion, in this case the people and landscape of the Pearl River Delta. He has been judged, perhaps rightly, 'the most talented and the most prolific of all the European artists who went to the East in the 19th century'.[2] He died in 1852.

At the time of Chinnery's death a new form of pictorial art was challenging the watercolourists of Victorian India. Photography was actually promoted by the East India Company, which in 1855 sent Captain Linnaeus Tripe as the official photographer on an expedition to the Burmese court at Ava: the captain returned with photographs of landscapes and pagodas so beautiful that in 2007 and 2008 many of them were displayed in an exhibition organized by the National Gallery of Art in Washington and the Metropolitan Museum of Art in New York. The EIC also put photography on the curriculum for its cadets at Addiscombe, and those chosen to become engineers could study it further at the Royal Engineers Establishment at Chatham. Yet the pioneering photographers of the Subcontinent also included individuals working on their own. One of the most remarkable was Samuel Bourne, who gave up his job as a bank clerk in Nottingham to become a photographer in India.

After arriving in Calcutta in 1863, Bourne soon realized he wanted to work in the Hills rather than on the Plains. He therefore embarked on three photographic expeditions to the Himalaya and Kashmir: to Simla, which disappointed him – it had no lakes, 'no rustic bridges, and no ivy-clad ruins'; to Kashmir, which did have some picturesque features, including an entrancing lake; and to the Kulu Valley, where he climbed through high passes and searched for the source of the Ganges. Bourne's work in India was not, as he was keen to point out, like that of a photographer in England, sitting 'on the grassy banks of a stream . . .[or] in the shady avenues of some noble park . . . with every comfort and convenience at hand'. His expeditions, which might last nine months, were like those of an explorer, clambering great heights over mountain ranges with some eighty servants and porters carrying equipment of cameras, tripods, glass plates (which frequently broke), a portable darkroom and 'a good supply of Hennessy's brandy'. And often, when he had reached the chosen place, 'shivering in cold and mist, on the top of that bleak pass', when he had prepared his plate and was waiting for a break in the weather – the clouds would suddenly descend, and he would have to pack up and come back the next day.[3]

People who viewed the portraits and landscapes of British artists in Calcutta might feel that they were seeing work comparable to what was being produced in Britain in that era. They could not possibly have felt the same about any music they heard or any theatre they attended. How could they, when the artists were professionals and the musicians and actors were almost invariably local amateurs? In the 1780s concerts in Calcutta were held at the Harmonic, an establishment in the Lal Bazaar which was a tavern and a 'dancing house' as well as a concert hall. Once a fortnight 'a select number of gentlemen', chosen in 'alphabetic rotation', sponsored an evening consisting of a concert, a ball and supper. Such occasions were enthusiastically applauded by the *Calcutta Gazette*, which reported in May 1786 that a performance of Handel's *Messiah* was an 'astonishing success', a 'delicious treat to the lovers of musick'.[4] In the privacy of its letters and diaries the audience was unlikely to be so charitable. After seeing an unspecified Italian opera in January 1836, Isabella Fane, the commander-in-chief's daughter, vowed never to go again because it was 'so bad' and she was 'so bored'. A fortnight later she did go again and was once more 'horribly bored'. Musical performances may by then have graduated from the Harmonic to a theatre with boxes, as in London, but the operatic performance was 'beyond endurance', and in any case Miss Fane was 'not fond of Italian squalling even when well done'. Concerts at Government House turned out to be no better: the singers and orchestra were 'quite intolerable', and the music was 'so bad' that 'one never thinks of listening to it'; the only thing to do was to treat the evening as a social occasion.[5]

Musical performances were still unsatisfactory a century later in Bombay. Italian opera companies now occasionally toured India, choosing works such as *Carmen*, which they thought the British would like, and causing social and linguistic problems for governors who felt obliged to invite the singers to tea.[6] According to a Bombay reviewer in 1935, *La Traviata* was well sung by the Gonzalez Italian Grand Opera Company, but a 'thoroughly good performance' was marred by the 'very inadequate orchestral pit' which made it impossible for 'Maestro Gonzalez' to 'have a large enough orchestra under his baton'. The consequent 'absence of cellos had the inevitable effect of making the music sound thin and insubstantial', and a further blight on the evening was the 'scene shifting, which was distressingly slow and noisy'. In another article of the period the reviewer mocked Bombay for the difficulty such an enormous city had in 'maintaining one orchestra and supporting one chamber music society', and in a splenetic mood he suggested it was 'the most barren . . . and unspiritual of towns since the days of Sodom and Gomorrah'.[7]

The smaller cities and towns were unlikely to be an improvement. Lucknow's musical diet of the 1890s consisted of fortnightly concerts featuring piano solos, songs and a 'recitation'. In the mofussil musical evenings depended on the enthusiasm of amateurs, on the willingness of men and (more usually) women to sing around an upright piano, sometimes, if they were lucky, accompanied by a fiddle or a cello. Being a piano player himself, Harcourt Butler deplored the fact that so few memsahibs also played. Yet keeping a piano fit for use was a difficult task in India. If it was damaged in transit (as it often was in a bullock-cart) or by the dampness of the climate, one probably had to rely on the local blacksmith to repair the keys and the strings. Sometimes the easier option was to hire a pianola from Bombay or Calcutta and sing along to that.

Church organs caused similar problems on a grander scale. St Stephen's at Ootacamund survived for decades with a barrel organ that possessed two barrels, each of them playing ten tunes, which meant a rather limited repertoire of hymns and psalms for the morning and evening services on Sundays. In 1877 the principal church of the summer capital of Madras finally received an organ. Yet by then Ooty had grown to such an extent that it required a second church, St Thomas's, which was less fortunate. It began its existence with a rather basic harmonium and, although it was later given two second-hand organs, these were judged as 'beyond repair' and 'perfectly useless'; until well into the twentieth century its congregation had to content itself with the harmonium.[8]

Amateurishness in the theatre had a higher standing in British India than it had in the music room. In fact amateur theatricals were among the quintessential activities of the Raj, combining society and jollity with a frisson of daring and sometimes of danger. In her book *The Englishwoman in India* (1909) Maud Diver claimed that 'the two most insidious' pitfalls for grass widows in the Hills 'were amateur theatricals and the military man on leave'. One or other of them was 'accountable for half the domestic tragedies in India'.[9]

Amateur dramatic societies sprang up in hill stations and elsewhere, but the most famous one, often patronized by the viceroy, was in Simla. As early as 1839, long before the place had become the summer capital of the Raj, Emily Eden recorded a theatrical dinner there with the entourage of her brother (Lord Auckland, the governor-general) rehearsing 'tableaux'. Later both Lytton and Lansdowne encouraged theatricals at Simla, and Minto's daughter Eileen once acted so movingly that, according to her mother, the Maharaja of Gwalior 'rushed away, sank on a sofa, tossed off his headgear and brushed away his tears ...'[10] At the Gaiety Theatre the Simla Amateur Dramatic Club usually put on drawing-room comedies imported from England, though the club's '*pièce de résistance*' was apparently Lepel Griffin's 'famous farce on women's rights', which contained the Civilian's well-known aphorism about the government of India: 'a despotism of office boxes, tempered by the occasional loss of a key'.[11]

Simla was the preserve of amateurs, acting without competition from professionals, but this did not deter some 'leading ladies' from behaving like prima donnas, quarrelling over who should play the heroine and stirring up a good deal of 'bad blood'. Amateurs also dominated theatre in the Plains, in the capital with the Calcutta Amateur Theatrical Society, where female roles for much of the nineteenth century were played by boys. The journalist J. H. Stocqueler started off his amateur career in the 1820s playing women's roles in Bombay, but when he reached Bengal in the following decade he was allowed to play Iago, Cassius and Falstaff.[12] Isabella Fane's diaries of those years often record that in Calcutta she 'ended the day with a play', sometimes performed at the town hall, but her experience of the theatre was scarcely more pleasurable than her attendance at concerts. On one occasion the play was tedious, the mosquitoes were 'intolerable', and the house was hot and 'smelt bad of perspirationary people'.[13]

Professional actors did sometimes go to India, after the opening of the Suez Canal, though seldom as individuals. They went as members of a theatrical company, starting off in Bombay and rapidly touring other parts of the country. They would stop off one week in a town, and the next in a cantonment, and put on a different musical comedy each night. During the Second World War ENSA (the Entertainments National Service Association) recruited singers and actors to go abroad and entertain the troops – as Vera Lynn did. Among those sent out to India were Geoffrey Kendal and his 'Gaslight' unit, which went on a tour from Bombay to Calcutta via Darjeeling and Shillong, travelling by train and living on a diet of 'brown Windsor soup, fish and chips, mutton and vegetables, and jelly'. After going up to Peshawar and the frontier, and then down to Karachi, Kendal went to London to 'add *Arms and the Man* to our repertoire' and then returned to India to complete eighty-six shows in six months. He loved the Subcontinent – the heat, the light and the climate – and after the war he toured India with his own troupe, the Shakespearana Company, relishing the Indian appetite for *Othello*, *Macbeth* and *Julius Caesar*. His younger daughter made her debut as Macduff's son, graduated at the age of eleven to Puck, and when she was eighteen she upset her father by telling him she wished to leave the company to start a professional career in England. She duly did so, as Felicity Kendal.[14]

FURLOUGH

The early British inhabitants of India had few options for their holidays. Living within the walls of their forts and factories, they could not escape to hill stations, which did not then exist, or go hunting in jungles, which belonged to powerful neighbours, and they could not of course go back to Britain. Even when, more than a century after the first arrivals, the East India Company acquired territory and elbow room, there was not much to do except go riding and shooting. Sir William Dunkin, an eighteenth-century judge in Bengal, enjoyed excursions on the rivers, but even these must have afforded limited pleasure in the hot weather.

Before the opening of the canal route to India, many Britons never saw their homeland again until they retired – in some cases not even then. When Bartle Frere gave up his job as governor of Bombay in 1867, he returned to a country he had last seen as a teenager thirty-two years before. A generation earlier, John Low, who had recently been the Resident at Lucknow, revisited his family home after an absence of thirty-eight years to find his mother on her deathbed and his sisters preaching the doctrines of the Free Church at her bedside.[15] Even after the canal's opening, some of the 'old hands' failed to take much advantage of it. John Beames, one of the last of the Haileybury men, took home leave only twice in thirty-five years of service (1858–93).

Yet for younger generations the reduction of travel time to three weeks from 1869 was an understandable incentive to go home more often. Officials could now visit Britain on privilege leave (if they saved up their annual month's allocation for three years), special leave for 'urgent private affairs' (often after the death of a parent but sometimes to arrange a marriage), leave on medical certificate, and furlough (from the Dutch word *verlof*, meaning leave of absence), which they could take after they had been eight years in India and which could last for periods of up to two years thereafter. This development naturally made them less 'Indianized' or at any rate less eager to spend their leisure in India and more inclined to return to England, where their children now often went to school. This added another strand to the pattern of racial and cultural segregation and helped negate tentative attempts to improve British–Indian social relations. After an 'old Rajput' told John Perronet Thompson that the 'present sahibs' (in 1900) were not 'equal to those of an older generation', the Civilian realized there was 'a good deal in what' he said. Thompson's predecessors 'were not perpetually going home on leave, they knew the languages better and got more saturated with native ways and ideas . . .'[16]

Although the timing of furlough was dependent on the plans and health of other men in one's province or one's department, most people tried to go to Britain in March so that they could enjoy spring and summer at 'home' after a winter in India. Almost the only men who desired the reverse – the hot weather in India followed by a winter in Britain – were fox-hunters. Michael O'Dwyer, the Punjab Civilian, claimed that a winter in Tipperary (1908–9), with three days' hunting a week, cured him of malaria. A generation later, the Irish cavalry officer William Magan agreed when on leave to a request to become master of the South Westmeath Hunt for a season. But Major 'Branny' Branfoot of the Indian Cavalry refused to leave the matter to chance or ill health. He took home leave only in the winter when, according to Magan, he 'bought two or three hunters, settled down at a favourite pub, and hunted with the Blackmoor Vale'.[17]

Homesickness seems to have affected the later British in India much more than their predecessors. Perhaps the latter realized they had no chance of returning home at any predictable moment and so decided to make the best of it. By contrast, Victorian griffins admitted that they were sometimes overcome by feelings of nostalgia and loneliness. Within weeks of his arrival in Bombay at the end of 1886, John Maynard discarded all notions of fortitude and stoicism and informed his mother that he was in the wrong job, that he was 'pining for a London fog or an Oxford Scotch mist' and that he would be home before the next Christmas.[18]* His contemporaries might not have considered giving up their jobs but they could admit to feelings of yearning, especially for the universities they had recently attended. Oxford griffins of the 1880s repeatedly told their old tutor at Oriel how much they hankered after their panelled rooms, their boats on the Cherwell and the 'congenial surroundings' of the college. A. R. Bonus confessed that he longed to be back in his 'old rooms with a blazer, a pipe, a good fire and a book in my best armchair'.[19]

Such feelings may have been dulled by the work and experience of India, but they would usually remain latent and be rekindled by the prospect of furlough after eight years away. That first voyage contained the liberating ritual of throwing your sola topi into the sea either in Bombay Harbour or when you reached Port Said, the popular dividing

---

* In fact he remained in India for another thirty years, receiving a knighthood after serving as financial commissioner of the Punjab.

line between East and West. At Marseille you found yourself speaking
Hindustani to French porters, but you did not linger in '*la belle France*'
because you were in too much of a hurry to reach the Channel and see
the White Cliffs. And then the 'joy', as one returning police officer put
it, of 'Piccadilly and Pall Mall, of the lovely English country lanes and
fields, after the horrors of Shikarpur' in Upper Sind. For someone
accustomed to trudging across the desert, it was exhilarating to be able
to throw snowballs in Hyde Park.[20]

George Otto Trevelyan, who spent a year in India in the early 1860s,
listed some of the pleasures of return in his book *Competition Wallah*:
'the first sight of turnip fields and broad-backed sheep; the first debauch
on home-made bread and bright yellow butter, and bacon which is
above suspicion; the first picnic; the first visit to the Haymarket Theatre . . .'[21] Much as he enjoyed his polo and hunting in India, the cavalryman Hilary Hook also liked to 'debauch' at home on English things,
the roast beef, the Devonshire cream, the farmhouse cider.[22] The differences of light and landscape struck people more than they had expected,
the gentler rays of England making it no longer necessary to screw up
one's eyes 'against the glare of India'. For Fred Roberts, the future
field marshal, 'the greenness and freshness' were 'a delicious rest to the
eye, wearied' by 'the sameness of dried-up sandy plains'. The 'intense
delight' of that first furlough, thought the young officer, was impossible to exaggerate.[23] So also was the sadness of the first return to India,
the farewells to home, to family, to aged relatives one would not expect
to see again.

Furlough did not of course consist merely of the pleasures described
by Trevelyan. The arrival might very quickly be blighted by bad
weather, striking dockers and unreasonable behaviour from Customs
officials. Intending to spend his leave on scientific study, Captain Shortt
of the Indian Medical Service had brought back two jars of Persian
lizards preserved in alcohol, which were seized by the officials, who
insisted he paid duty on them; when Shortt explained that they were
zoological specimens, the Customs men argued that 'the liquid could
easily be redistilled minus the lizards' and then drunk.[24] A more usual
complaint of the returning official was neglect and indifference. He
often found that people did not remember who he was or – if they did –
cared nothing about his work or about India in general. Even the India
Office showed little interest in him, its haughty employees reacting to a

visit from one Civilian with 'surprise and mild distaste ... that any rough fellow from India should invade their privacy'. Evan Maconochie's grumble was with politicians, who came out to India 'in the cold weather and, having shot our game, drunk our wine and generally done well unto themselves at our expense, abuse us to [the British public] when they get home and cut us when we meet them in Piccadilly'.[25]

Officers and officials made elaborate schemes for their furlough. As few of them had been anywhere except Britain and India, travel in Europe was often included. Lieutenant Dowdall of the Yorkshire Light Infantry planned to go to France and learn French, and then walk to Italy. In addition to those two countries, the Civilian Lewis Bowring toured much of central Europe, visited sixteen British cathedrals and went to China, where his father was governor of Hong Kong.[26] Other projects for the first furlough included finding a wife* and studying. Charles Lawson, who in the 1860s edited first the *Madras Daily News*, then the *Madras Times*, and finally the *Madras Mail*, described the first year of furlough as like a 'mental shower bath'. After years spent in a cantonment or a civil station, one's mind was desperate for self-improvement. The political officer Francis Younghusband was determined to make up for his lack of university education by taking lessons in chemistry, physics, geography, botany, biology, agriculture, photography and social sciences; he would also look at good paintings and listen to good music, and above all he would study what became the dominant subject of his life: religions and great religious men.[27]

Ambitious and far-sighted officials used some of their furlough to assist careers in India and prepare for employment in retirement. Reading for the Bar in the London Inns of Court was popular because, as one Civilian correctly calculated, 'the status of an English barrister would lead to advancement in the judicial line in India'.[28] Another course was to move in literary circles and write a book, as Henry Cotton did, although his particular work, a plea for radical reforms called *New India, or India in Transition*, may not have assisted his career very much. In the early 1850s George Campbell, who did not see the point of leisure (or, apparently, of pleasure), went down both routes, reading for the Bar, writing two long books (*Modern India* and *India*

* See above, pp. 299–300.

as It May Be) and also – as he put it – 'providing' himself 'with a mate'. During a subsequent furlough he tried to become a Liberal MP first for Dumbartonshire and then for St Andrews (which, if successful, would have required his resignation from the ICS), and in between these attempts he wrote another book, this time on Ireland, which advocated 'security of tenure and a thrifty peasantry' as the 'best hope' for the island. After retiring from India he finally realized his parliamentary ambitions, representing Kirkaldy for seventeen years, but even his admirers wished he had chosen some different hobby for his retirement. Henry Cotton, who had been an under-secretary in Bengal when Campbell was lieutenant-governor, reported that at Westminster his old chief 'fell into the category of parliamentary bores': he was 'deficient in tact and deference', his harsh Scottish voice sounded 'like a file', and he had 'the unwise habit of addressing the House on any and every subject'.[29]

HOLIDAYS IN INDIA

The fashion for seaside holidays in Britain, which began in Margate in the middle of the eighteenth century, was not replicated in India. It was too hot to be on the coast in the summer unless one was actually immersed in the water. Before the development of the hill stations, sea voyages were used as a means of escaping the heat, especially for people who were sick, but one had to go a long way before one got much cooler. Penang was regarded as a good destination for health – a reputation it may not have deserved – and so was Malacca. Yet China, though further away, was considered a better bet, especially Canton. In 1863 the Scottish missionary Alexander Duff was sent to China to cure his dysentery, although Darjeeling, which by then had a sanatorium, would have been more convenient. An even more distant option was Australia, where the Beveridge family went for health reasons, accompanied by their Indian servants, in the summer of 1882.

Before the opening of the Suez Canal ill health more usually encouraged people to go south-west, occasionally to Mauritius but more often to the Cape or even beyond it to St Helena. Sea voyages, like river cruises, were regarded as 'last resort cures', and they were often left so late that the patients died on board the boat. Yet if they survived the journey, the climate at the Cape was good for convalescence. Over a career lasting from 1818 to 1840 William Mackenzie of the Bengal Army contrived to spend nearly half of it on sick certificate at the Cape, usually for two years at a time; perhaps it kept him alive when he was in India, but he died soon after retirement, as a lieutenant-colonel, at the age of fifty-seven. Irrespective of health and climate, leave at the Cape – likewise in Australia and Ceylon – had advantages for civil servants of the East India Company. Until the anomaly was abolished in the early 1840s, they could retain their Indian appointments while they were in those places, but they had to give them up – at least temporarily – if they went to Britain.

Swimming in rivers and the sea had a number of devotees among the British in India. Soldiers liked being stationed at Cuddalore in the south because, as Captain Hervey observed, they could have 'plenty of fresh air and sea-bathing, with cheap and wholesome living'.[30] Yet swimming did not catch on as a group activity for holidays. An attempt in the 1860s to create a resort near Balasore in Orissa failed because the place had no shops or drinking water, and it was difficult to reach it from Calcutta. Further south along the Orissan coast, nice hotels were later built at Puri and Gopalpur 'on-sea'. These were attractive places to visit at Christmas, when the temperature was reasonable, but the waves in the Bay of Bengal were far too big for sedate swimming. British children at Gopalpur were each assigned an Indian lifeguard.[31]

The most passionate swimmers of British India were Civilians in southern districts with a littoral. John Thorne, a Madras DO who rose to the top of the ICS, made a point of swimming off all the best coasts in his charge and of encouraging his juniors to do likewise. His assistant S. K. Chettur (who also reached the top of the ICS), became an obsessive swimmer, an enthusiast of the Cauvery and Godaveri rivers, and was later president of the Madras Bathers' Association.[32] The sea is calmer on India's west coast than in the Bay of Bengal, and district officers of the Bombay presidency liked to swim at Ratnagiri, a district north of Goa with sandy beaches and excellent mangoes. Further north, in Kathiawar, the judicial assistant to the Bombay governor was allowed to take his court to the coast for the hottest months. Yet tragedies took place in Malabar as well as on the other side of India. Dennis Kincaid, a young Civilian who had written three novels, was drowned in 1937 at Karwar, sometimes known as 'the Cornwall of India'; he had been unable to sleep on a sweltering night in June and had plunged into a rough, pre-monsoon sea. In the same year Judge Herschel Christian and his wife, Queenie, were drowned in Orissa.[33]

Britons destined for the Hills were yearning for them by April, desperate to escape the 'dog days' of the pre-rain months in the Plains. The monsoons hit the Hills too, of course, but without the same awful build-up or the same intense humidity later on. There were climatic differences between the eighty or so hill stations, between those of the Himalaya and those of the centre and the south, but usually the best seasons in them were spring and the very end of summer.

Holidays in the Hills, which had become pretty general by the 1870s, were regarded as a rest, a health cure and time to spend with friends. The anticipation and excitement began with the journey and continued through changing landscapes and environments. If you started in Calcutta, you went north through the countryside of Bengal, past paddy-fields and plantations of banana and palm, then up into the hills into new vegetation zones until eventually you found yourself looking at Kanchenjunga from the pines and rhododendrons of Darjeeling. Or you could, if you preferred, choose to go to Shillong, with its red earth, its blue hydrangeas and its milder climate; its devotees regarded it as 'Elysium'. The Himalayan hill stations all had wonderful views, of snowy peaks and wooded mountainsides.

Families would rent a cottage, a bungalow or a wooden chalet, or they would stay in a hotel or a boarding house perhaps run by an officer's widow whose guests returned year after year. The changes of air, temperature and scenery were all important. After dusty, sweltering plains, it was a relief to live among ferns and cedar trees, to be above the mosquito line, to wear a straw hat instead of a topi, to sit in front of a log fire in the evenings. Above all, the hill stations provided a mental and physical tonic. Writing in the 1830s about the 'renovating' climate of Mahabaleshwar, Marianne Postans, an officer's wife, claimed that it 're-strings the failing nerves, and plants fresh roses on the pallid cheek'. Twenty years later, Lady Falkland agreed with her. At Mahabaleshwar, wrote the Bombay governor's wife, 'you get up refreshed' and 'think you have received a new set of bones'.[34]

The hill stations often started as sanatoria and were planned as sanctuaries of Britishness. The architecture was British, the gardens were full of British flowers, and the houses usually had names like Willowdale and Meadowbank; Dalhousie in the Punjab possessed, among other inappropriate names, Kelso Cottage, Snowdon Lodge and Lauderdale. The British in India had a propensity for seeing things that reminded them of 'home', even places that frankly bore little resemblance to anywhere in Britain; perhaps they needed to reassure themselves that they were still living on the same planet as the one they had grown up on. Ootacamund, often considered the most British place in all India, provoked a bizarre quantity of contradictory comparisons. Enthusiastic Britons claimed that its landscape resembled the scenery of Windsor Forest, the Malvern Hills, the Sussex Downs, Hertfordshire, Killiecrankie, Devonshire, Westmorland and Braid's Hill in Edinburgh. Lord Erskine, whose summer capital it was in the 1930s, thought it 'a cross between the South Downs and the Morayshire Hills round Cawdor'.[35] In fact Ooty did not look very much like any of these places. After much of its native woodland area had been replanted with eucalyptus and wattle – both a scenic and an environmental disaster – it looked more like Australia. Parts of it of course also looked – and sounded – like the rest of India. As with all hill stations, Ooty needed and attracted a bazaar plus an Indian population that far outnumbered the British inhabitants.

The favourite holiday place for the British between the world wars was Kashmir, though its beauty had been recognized long before then: in the 1880s Walter Lawrence had decided that the Dal Lake was the 'most exquisite corner of the world' and noted that the 'wise' and discerning among his fellow-countrymen avoided the hill stations and made for Kashmir.[36] Lawrence appreciated tranquillity, but in the 1920s and 1930s the British there were not tranquil. The most distinguished among them, a visiting governor perhaps, might dine with the maharaja in the Shalimar Gardens, lit by thousands of lights, sitting on cushions and eating an Indian dinner with their fingers. But many British holidaymakers, staying on houseboats on Srinagar's lakes, were noisy partygoers who played games and danced only with each other. John Masters remembered the sound of gramophones throughout the day playing Noël Coward songs on the water. 'Lunch parties under the awnings began with cocktails at eleven and ended in a drowsy repletion of brandy and ice soufflé at four'.[37]

In the evenings the younger Britons were taken to their dinners and dances in shikaras, boats like gondolas paddled by Kashmiri boatmen. These craft had names such as *Love Nest* and *Kiss Me Quick*, presumably because the gondoliers had realized that their city had become a venue for foreign romance. John de Chazal, a police officer from Madras, noticed how in Kashmir 'British reserve melted', friendships were easily made, and army officers on leave 'made overtures' to grass widows 'which were not always repelled'.[38] In her memoirs M. M. Kaye recalled how a husband returned early from a fishing expedition, surprised his wife with her lover and aroused the houseboat population by firing his pistol at the Lothario as he dived into the lake and swam to safety. One of the duties of the Resident in Kashmir was to make sure that the British on holiday behaved themselves and to arrange for the disorderly ones to leave.[39]

In the hill stations the British might rent houses from Indian landlords but they could build and own their own property. As Kashmir was a native state, however, they had to rent their accommodation. At Srinagar they usually hired a houseboat for a month or so in the summer rather than have one as a permanent home, although a Mr Kennard rented three – one for living, another for entertaining, and a third for his servants and kitchen.[40] Up in Gulmarg, a resort where golf was taken more seriously than social life – it even had a course for children – there were plenty of log huts or chalets to hire. The only snag about Kashmir was that the maharaja was a strict Hindu, and customs searches at the border were rigorous. British families had to remember to pack Marmite rather than Bovril among their provisions. Oxo cubes were also forbidden, children's sweets called 'bulls-eyes' were regarded with suspicion, and a political agent from an earlier period was taken to court for ordering beef extract from England for his invalid wife. Even as late as 1939 the British did not allow their officials to drive a car in Kashmir in case they ran over a cow and got arrested and locked up.[41]

The scenery and architecture of Simla were less appealing than in many of its rivals. The homes were mostly gimcrack, with monkeys clattering over their corrugated iron roofs, and the official buildings were ponderous and unattractive; in 1885 the civil secretariat and the army headquarters moved into offices that reminded people of warehouses in Liverpool. The town, strung out along a narrow ridge, did not sit well in its surroundings, as Ooty and Naini Tal did, and it had only one proper walk, around a mountain called Jakko. Yet as the summer capital of the viceroy, the commander-in-chief and the lieutenant-governor of the Punjab, it was for careerists and the socially ambitious a good place to be. And it was fun too, as we have seen, even if the more adventurous ladies migrated to Kashmir between the wars. There were, as Anne Wilson remembered early in the twentieth century, 'the dances by torchlight under the pines, the musical fêtes on moonlit lawns [and] the pageants of Viceregal Lodge'.[42] Inevitably there was also sport, usually played on pitches in a valley known as Annandale, the nearest piece of flat land. In the 1870s 'rinking' or roller skating became a fashionable hobby, especially for women, and those who went to Simla out of season could indulge in its winter cousins, skating and playing ice hockey on tennis courts that had been flooded and allowed to freeze.[43]

Simla might have sport for most of the year, except when the monsoon turned Annandale into a swamp, but lesser hill stations would hold special 'weeks' that everyone in the vicinity could attend and take part in. In one of his stories Kipling described the British congregating for a Christmas Week, men and women coming in from the mofussil 'with racquets, with bundles of polo-sticks, with dear and bruised cricket bats, with fox-terriers and saddles'. Apart from the normal station 'weeks', the police had 'weeks', the army had 'weeks', the planters had 'weeks', all consisting chiefly of sport and feasting, although the 'saturnalia' of the planters tended to be rowdier than the others. Each 'week' had, besides the cricket, tennis and other matches, its own variations: Kohat had a Canine Grand National, Sialkot a bullock-cart race with women 'at the helm'.[44] The important thing for small stations was to make the programme attractive enough for women to come long distances to attend it. In order to 'induce the girls of Quetta, two hundred miles away, to accept our invitations', John Masters and his committee at the cantonment of Loralai devised a schedule that included a fancy-dress ball, three other dances, a dog show, a treasure hunt and a 'ladies-versus-gentlemen cricket match'[45] – at such events the men would bat left-handed or with umbrellas.

Most stations could provide amenities for most sporting activities except for rowing, a popular sport for young officers and officials who had been to schools and universities with a river and a boat club. Among the best of India's few navigable rivers was the Mula at Poona, where the All-India Regatta was held; other places, such as Madras and Calcutta, which had rivers where oarsmen could train, sent teams there to compete. The only hill stations that could hold regattas were those with large lakes, particularly Naini Tal and Ooty (in its case artificial).

Naini Tal was unusual in having both a large natural lake and an unnatural area of level ground, a consequence of a landslip in 1880 that filled up one end of the lake, greatly increasing the size of the existing 'flats'. The summer capital of the United Provinces became a very sporty place, holding one 'week' at the end of May and an 'autumn week' that included the regatta. It also had a September 'week' for women in which the teams were selected according to marital status. In 1900 the married women did quite well, but the following year they were defeated by the 'spinsters' in the hockey, in the boat race and in the cricket by an innings.[46] As usual in British India, intense sporting activity was accompanied by a frenetic social calendar. As governor of the province in 1920, Harcourt Butler had to host in a single day of Naini Tal's 'autumn week' a lunch at the Yacht Club (as ex-officio commodore), a *thé dansant* and a garden party at Government House, and a dinner at the Club in the evening.

CRICKET AND OTHER GAMES

Before he became bishop of Calcutta in 1898, J. E. C. Welldon was headmaster of Harrow, where he developed his theory that sporting endeavour and imperial achievement went together. It was the lessons that British boys learned on the cricket pitch and the football field, lessons which instilled pluck, perseverance, energy, fortitude, team spirit and discipline, that would later win them 'the day in peace and war'. In a paper delivered to the Royal Colonial Institute in 1895, Welldon declared that 'in the history of the British Empire it is written that England has owed her sovereignty to her sports'.[47]

Welldon was preaching in the era of 'muscular Christianity', and many people sympathized with his creed. Few poems of the age found more resonance than 'Vitaï Lampada' in which Henry Newbolt's hero brings the courage and sense of duty learned on the school cricket pitch to a desert battlefield where, with the Gatling 'jammed and the colonel dead', he rallies the ranks of 'a square that broke' with the call, 'Play up! play up! and play the game!' No doubt team spirit and self-control were good qualities to promote in the army. So were sportsmanship and good manners – and not only for officers. In its handbook of 1933 the Army Sports Control Board in India defined a good sportsman as a man 'who plays for his side and not for himself', who is 'a good winner and a good loser i.e. modest in victory and generous in defeat', who is 'unselfish' and 'chivalrous towards a defeated opponent' and who 'never interferes with referees or judges, no matter what the decision'.[48]

Welldon's contemporaries in India took exercise seriously, not just for the reasons the headmaster gave but also because they felt flaccid and frustrated without it. It was part of the spirit of the age. Previous generations had not cared very much about team games, and it is difficult to imagine a man like William Hickey running between the wickets. The early games and sports in India were usually played by individuals rather than by teams. In 1832 Fanny Parkes was enjoying archery, which she practised with a bow made with strips of buffalo horn, and it remained a common diversion for men and women in the early-Victorian period. Its popularity faded in the 1860s, the pastime eclipsed by croquet, badminton and to a lesser extent bowls, though the activities were hardly incompatible. The viceroy John Lawrence made croquet fashionable at Simla, hitting heavy balls with heavy mallets through very wide hoops, and its popularity spread; it was the ideal game in the hot weather in a small station.

Croquet's chief rival in the last decades of the nineteenth century was badminton, another bisexual, rather gentle game, appealing particularly to middle-aged people who did not wish to put on special sporting clothes. At Chittagong in the 1870s H. M. Kisch gave badminton parties where he handed his guests pegs of brandy and soda. Younger and more energetic men might play badminton on a cow-dung floor at the local gymkhana, but usually they preferred rackets, another non-team sport that had become a favourite among army officers by the 1850s; almost every club and cantonment had rackets courts. The game retained its popularity until the turn of the century, when its support bifurcated, one stem going to squash, the other to lawn tennis.

Squash became popular, especially in the army, because, as one officer explained, it was 'a splendidly concentrated way of getting exercise';

a regimental Mess sometimes had its own court, and even in remote frontier posts a court could often be crammed into a fort's perimeter.* Yet at the beginning of the twentieth century lawn tennis emerged as the enduring racket-and-ball game of British India, one which was played by both sexes. It did have, however, certain specific Indian problems. In spite of its name, the game was usually played on beaten earth or on courts of cement and concrete, which in a place like Sind might become too hot to stand on until 7 p.m., when the light was already fading. The Lorimers' court in Bahrain was better sited, going into the shade at about 5 p.m. and allowing the couple nearly two hours' play before sunset. In Karachi Madge Green played happily on the pink cement courts at Government House, where 'three gentlemen in white with red turbans . . . field the balls', but the damp climate was lethal for the rackets, which had to be constantly restrung. Tennis was a good game for officials and other busy folk because, as an Indian Civilian put it, 'one got all the exercise one needed at the end of a day spent on inspections and files'.[49] And it was agreeable socially too, a game for four people that allowed them to play without the animosities created by the bridge table and then sit together on the verandah, sipping a drink and watching the light fade.

Golf became popular at about the same time as tennis and was provided by most stations. Its courses, however, were more varied than the tennis courts. Many were terrible, with little or no grass on the greens and with rocks and cactus on the fairways. Others, in the Hills or the mofussil, were very small. At his first station in eastern Bengal, Stephen Hatch-Barnwell joined a 'very sporting' seven-hole golf club which had four other members. In large places different sports had to compete for the same space: at the old course at Abbottabad one could not have a round without 'being forced to play one's second [shot] from the middle of a game of football'.[50] Some were not like this: Calcutta had two fine courses, the Tollygunge and the Royal Calcutta Golf Club, founded in 1829, the oldest club in the world outside the British Isles. Yet for Lowell

* The best squash players of the Raj were not British but members of the Khan family from the north-west frontier. The most successful one was Hashim, who worked as a ball boy at an officers' club in Peshawar and was allowed to use the courts with his friends after the members had ended play for the day. In his thirties he won the All-India Championship in Bombay (1944), and in the 1950s he won the British Open seven times in eight years. In his unsuccessful year (1957) he lost to his cousin Roshan.

Thomas, the American journalist who toured India in the 1920s, the only really good courses were those at Ooty and Gulmarg. The 'gaiety of Gulmarg', he observed, was 'something staggering', its short season (July to September) consisting of dances at night and rounds of golf during the day with an occasional break for a picnic and 'gin and bitters'.[51]

The team games that had become so popular in Britain were hindered in India by limitations imposed by numbers, climate and topography. As a station in the mofussil would never have twenty-two men of comparable age and ability to make up the teams, they were confined to large towns, cantonments and hill stations, although few of the latter had the space or level ground for extensive playing fields. For much of the year the weather was too hot to play sports, and in other periods the ground was dangerously hard for such games as hockey and rugby. Rugby was an especially dangerous game on ground like concrete, and there were plenty of injuries at the Adyar Club in Madras even after the local fire brigade had watered the pitch before a match. Enthusiasts enjoyed playing in the monsoon, when, with so much mud around, it became 'largely a mud-lark for the scrum'.[52] The most distinguished rugby player of British India was George Cunningham, who ended his career as governor of the North-West Frontier Province;* before joining the ICS he had been captain of the Scottish rugby team in the Five Nations Championship of 1910.

Football was the most popular sport in British regiments, as hockey was in Indian ones. The army tried to deter aggression by insisting that an officer be present at every game of either sport, and it suggested punishments that might profitably have been adopted by more recent generations: suspension for three months for striking or kicking an opponent, and a ban of six weeks for abusing the referee.[53] Football and hockey were the two games played most often between British and Indian teams, especially in Bengal, whose inhabitants became enthusiasts for both sports in the 1920s and 1930s. Contests between units of the British and Indian armies remained forbidden,† but matches between British soldiers and local Indian teams were encouraged. Footballing soldiers were rather bemused to line up against opponents such

---

* In 1947 he was brought out of retirement to become Pakistan's first governor of the province. See below, p. 510.
† See above, p. 248.

as the 'Bangalore Muslims', who played in bare feet, but it was disconcerting when the game acquired a political edge. Eric Blair was annoyed in Burma when a 'nimble Burman tripped' him up, the Burmese referee 'looked the other way', and 'the crowd yelled with hideous laughter'. This happened more than once. Blair's former schoolfellow, the Civilian John Christie, had similar experiences playing football with young Bengalis: whenever he was left lying in the mud, the crowd was 'overjoyed'; he 'found it uncomfortable to be an instrument for the release of racial tensions'.[54]

The game most associated with British India is cricket, perhaps partly because it later became an absorbing and well-contested sport between England and independent India. Some comforting myths have grown up about the British in the context of colonial sport, how they established an 'empire of cricket' and taught their subject peoples how to play the game. In fact there was not a great deal of teaching, and most of those peoples learned to play by watching and imitating their masters. Lord Harris, who had captained England in four Test matches against Australia, was in 1890 appointed governor of Bombay, where he acquired a reputation as the 'father of Indian cricket'. As the historian Ramachandra Guha has shown, however, this accolade was entirely unmerited. Believing that 'the phlegmatic Anglo-Saxon' was better suited to the game than 'the excitable Asiatic' – 'the best of them were liable to throw away their wickets by some rash stroke' – he did virtually nothing for Indian cricket and was reluctant even to play against Indian teams. In Bombay itself he prolonged an embarrassing injustice, preserving the immaculate turf of the Gymkhana for the sole use of British players while allowing polo-playing army officers to churn up those areas of the maidan where Indians could play their cricket.[55]

Not all British cricketers were like Harris. Doubtless many of them would have preferred to play in conditions that reminded them of earlier days, batting at Fenner's at Cambridge or the Parks at Oxford or perhaps on the village green at home. The highlight of their year may have been their selection for an ICS team against 'the Rest' in an all-British affair during a 'week' at Naini Tal. Yet the sport saw a good deal of racial intermingling – certainly at a local level – during the last century of British rule. In the 1830s the adjutant of Captain Hervey's Madras regiment taught the sepoys how to play, and 'in a very short space of time [they] became perfect adepts in the art of batting, bowling and fielding'. They used to play every evening, recalled Hervey, 'and have capital fun'; no newcomers could have entered 'into the spirit of this noble game as did our fellows'.[56] A generation later, in western India, Major Oliver Probyn captained an Eleven of Bheel militiamen living in his district, and in the same era, at the Mardan cantonment on the frontier, Wigram Battye of the Guides laid a pitch near the well (so it could be watered) and coached the Indian ranks in the techniques of the game.[57] In many cases there was no doubt a practical reason for playing with Indians – the British officers could not make up the numbers by themselves – but before the end of the century contests were regularly taking place between British and Indian teams. At the Mhow cantonment in 1897 Violet Jacob watched a game between the garrison and 'the Indore Mohammedans'.[58]

Matches against communal teams soon became common. In Karachi in the 1920s the king-emperor's birthday was celebrated by a parade followed by a game between a British Eleven and the town's Parsis. Simultaneously officials had taken to playing cricket with nearby schools: St John Philby was doing so at his first posting in the Punjab in 1908. At Malda in eastern Bengal the regular rivalry was between the civil station and the local high school, although, as both found difficulty in recruiting eleven players with adequate skills, talent scouts were sent on match days to meet the train from Calcutta and try to entice 'guest stars'.[59] Cricket in British India did not have to be grand. It was played by soldiers in forts and barracks on matted wickets, and at depots rival majors might pick scratch teams of Britons and Indians whose selection depended not on race but on ability.[60] Sometimes esoteric local rules would be genially introduced. When in the 1930s British officials in Bengal played the railway colony at Lalmanirhat, any of their bowlers who took a wicket was forced to drink a pint of beer on the spot, a handicap that certainly evened up the contest.[61]

After the British created colleges – based on their own 'public school' system – for the sons of Indian princes and noblemen, they guaranteed themselves a new kind of cricketing opponent. At Mayo College at Ajmer, set up in 1875 and often referred to as 'the Indian Eton', the pupils played cricket almost every day of the week, including Sundays. At Rajkumar College in Kathiawar future chieftains enjoyed playing with British officials, and later, when they had come into their inheritance, some of them maintained teams of their own.[62] The princes were in fact largely responsible for the spread of the game in India. Some of them were great players – such as the nawabs of Pataudi, and the maharajas of Patiala and Nawanagar (Ranji) – and some such as 'Vizzy', the Maharaja of Vizianagaram, were embarrassingly poor. Before a match in England Vizzy bribed a county captain with a gold watch so that he would bowl him bad balls that he could hit. The Englishman obliged with 'a full toss and a couple of long hops', but, he added, 'you can't go on bowling like that all day, not in England'.[63]

In India cricket developed in certain ways differently from England. Its heart was urban not rural, partly because, as Guha has pointed out, it would have been impossible to 'select a village eleven satisfactory to Brahmin and Untouchable alike'.[64] Its teams were selected and supported on a communal basis, not a regional one. Instead of rivalries between Lancastrians and Yorkshiremen, India had competitions between Hindus, Muslims, Parsis and Europeans (as the British sides were always described). Between 1907 and 1945 Bombay held tournaments that were originally called Triangular (Hindus, Parsis and Europeans), then Quadrangular (with the addition of a Muslim team) and eventually Pentangular (a team called 'the Rest' consisting of Indian Christians, Jews and Buddhists). Yet these competitions predictably became politicized. British officials were nervous that defeats of their teams would damage imperial prestige, which was of course an incentive for Hindu sides to beat them. Hindu–Muslim contests came to have an even sharper edge, and by the end of the Second World War they were exacerbating communal antagonisms to such an extent that the Bombay tournament was abolished.

In 1933 the MCC made a long winter tour of India.* Its skipper was Douglas Jardine, a cricketer who had recently become notorious for using 'bodyline' tactics against Donald Bradman and his teammates in Australia. Jardine came to the Subcontinent with a reputation for ruthless, unsporting play and for displaying a very unEnglish attitude (he was in fact Scottish), playing not for the sake of the game but ready to injure opposing players for the sake of winning. Yet in India he seemed almost a different person, perhaps because he was returning to the land of his birth. Born in Bombay in 1900, he had quite a Raj inheritance:

---

* Until 1977 the English cricket team went on its overseas tours under the name of the MCC (Marylebone Cricket Club).

his grandfather had been a High Court judge before he died of cholera, an uncle had been in the ICS, and his father was advocate-general for the Bombay presidency. After playing several matches around India, the MCC arrived in Bombay for the first Test in December. Yet instead of spending the day before the match with his fellow players, Jardine sought out his father's former khansama, who wished to visit the Sewrie cemetery to lay wreathes on some family graves. The two men had climbed the hill and walked around the cemetery when the butler complained of pains around his heart. Jardine rushed him to the KEM, the King Edward Memorial Hospital, but the old man was soon dead.

The MCC won the series, but the Indian players had impressed Jardine. When he left the Subcontinent he predicted that 'in ten years India will be one of the top cricketing countries of the world'.[65]

SHIKAR

In his old age James Moore recalled how in the Edwardian era, when he arrived in India as an ICS griffin, men used to say, 'It's a fine day, let's go and kill something . . .'[66] It became less common in subsequent decades, though the appetite for shooting and hunting would have been much the same in Victorian times as it was in 1908. Shooting offered greater opportunities in India than in Britain – certainly in size and variety of targets – with more free time and fewer restrictions on when and where the sport could be practised. Most British men who possessed or could borrow a gun enjoyed shikar in India.*

Field sports were encouraged by the military and other services, though for differing reasons. Shooting was regarded as good training for gunners and infantrymen, just as pig-sticking and jackal-hunting were expected to improve the skills of the cavalry. The Gurkha officer R. C. B. Bristow bought himself a shotgun and a rifle when he realized that the subaltern who did not go shooting was considered to lack 'some military virtue'.[67] Evidence of that virtue was displayed very visibly in British homes in India, with animal trophies on the walls and on the floor and records of achievement pasted into albums, often photographs of the sportsman with gun in hand and carcass at his feet.

---

* Shikar is a word of Persian origin denoting *la chasse* or the pursuit of game.

The ICS and the Forestry Service promoted shooting as a way for officials to help the people in their districts and to gain familiarity with the territory under their control. Tigers and panthers preyed on goats and cattle; herds of black buck and wild boar ravaged the farmers' crops. In the view of the Civilian Edward Blunt, men who got rid of these pests were 'doing the villager a good turn'. Shooting and pig-sticking were in his eyes 'not merely forms of sport' but 'works of agricultural improvement' as well. Blunt advised his fellow Civilians to get to know their district by strolling about, guns over their shoulder, chatting to villagers about sport. Evan Maconochie agreed with him. 'Many a clue to what the villager is thinking,' he claimed, 'is gained over a chat between beats or while watching one's float by some quiet pool.' Forest officers were encouraged to shoot for similar reasons: to get to know the forests, to understand their inhabitants and, as the men responsible for administering the game laws, to be familiar with the wildlife. 'Shooting for the pot' thus had an objective beyond the simple phrase, though the original meaning was still valid. When Maurice Hayward was stalking a 'roving herd of black buck', he might have been helping to rid the Nasik farmers of a nuisance, but he knew he was also providing himself with a fresh source of protein.[68]

Shooting could be fitted in, for an hour or so, at the end of a working day, when the inspections were over and the camp dinner was being prepared, or it could be done on holidays – and there were a great many of these in India. The civil courts in Lahore, for example, did not sit for twenty-five Hindu days (including four for Dussehra and two for Diwali), fifteen Muslim days (including eight for Muharram and two for Eid-al-Fitr), three Christian days (Ash Wednesday, Good Friday and Christmas Day) plus the short vacation (Boxing Day to New Year's Eve), the long vacation (September) and the last Saturday in each month.[69] Obsessive hunters, however, usually preferred longer periods for their sport. When army officers were given two months' leave, they often spent the entire time on a shooting or hunting expedition. After John Jacob was made a first lieutenant in 1835, he celebrated his promotion by going on a two-month hog-hunting* tour in Cutch, pursuing his quarry up to the border with Sind.

In the 1840s Captain Hervey was pleased that there were no game

---

* The term used in western India for pig-sticking. See below, pp. 479–83.

laws in India. Their absence meant that he could have 'capital sport, bagging partridge' and anything else within range of his gun. Forty years later, there *were* game laws and numerous restrictions on the seasons in which the sport could be pursued and the varieties of birds and animals that could be hunted. Among the birds that became immune were orioles, bee-eaters, hoopoes, herons, egrets, warblers and kingfishers. Yet an enormous number of species remained legitimate targets and were shot in great numbers. The Maharaja of Bikaner provided his guests – often viceroys, governors or visiting royalty – with game in quantities unimaginable in Britain. In a two-day shoot for Lord Minto in 1906, the guns bagged 4,914 sand grouse (an almost inedible bird) in an event that cannot have been very sporting: the birds fly in clouds so close together that one can hardly miss them. The Bikaner duck shoots on the Gajner Lake were also strong on quantity. In 1935 Lord Erskine and his fellow guns were within a few birds of a record daily bag (990) when casualties prevented them from achieving it: one of the sportsmen developed 'gun headache', while the maharaja's son put his hand on a hot gun barrel and developed 'an enormous blister'.[70] Standing around a lake and aiming at the birds as they flew over one's head was the easiest way of shooting duck, but many sportsmen preferred going out in boats up rivers or in dug-out canoes on lakes, sitting in the prow, looking for duck among the reeds. Experts advised their readers to concentrate on edible species such as teal (which also tended to fly in 'clouds') and not 'waste a charge of shot' on a Brahminy duck which, despite its 'handsome plumage', was 'worthless for the table'.[71]

India had twelve different types of quail and fourteen varieties of partridge, all of which could be shot, but one sporting authority, Mr W. S. Burke, complained that the Burmese quail 'afforded poor sport' because it was 'difficult to flush' and flew only a short distance. There were six varieties of snipe, and here again one species was dismissed by Burke, the editor of the *Indian Field*: the painted snipe was a 'miserable flyer' which seemed 'more intent on displaying its plumage than on getting away'.[72] The other types, however, 'afforded good sport' with their swerving, jinking flight. Yet they could only be pursued in fairly testing conditions, the shooters standing in the sun and at the same time knee-deep in swamps or flooded rice fields, with leeches forming a ring around their stockings and feasting on their blood. One enthusiast for this sport advised wearing 'light rubber hockey boots' which, while 'no guard against snakes, leeches or mosquitoes', did at least enable him to draw his 'feet out of the mud of the snipe jheels'.[73]

The governors of Madras and Bombay were required (like the viceroy) to write regularly to their sovereign. It was difficult sometimes to find subjects to write about, but those serving in the reigns of George V and George VI hit on a way of filling up the pages by entertaining the monarchs with tales of their shooting experiences.[74] The Madras governors regarded the snipe shooting in their presidency as some of the best sport they had ever known, and Lord Erskine correctly anticipated the king's interest in his stories, how the birds spent the night in wet rice fields and then moved to dry scrub jungle, from which noisy beaters flushed them towards the guns. Replying through his private secretary, King George found the account 'very amusing' and thought the snipe must be 'very difficult to shoot when flying rapidly downhill'. Alas there had been 'quite a dearth of both snipe and woodcock' at Sandringham that year (1938), but in compensation His Majesty had done a lot of 'duck-flighting'.[75]

Keen shooters in India seldom limited themselves to game birds. There were after all a lot of different animals to pursue, and these were easier to kill after the introduction of the .450 Express rifle in the 1880s. Among other beasts the quarry included lynx, panther, tiger and snow leopard, black bear, bison and buffalo, and many varieties of wild goat and deer. Lions were shot in Junagadh until Lord Curzon discovered how few were left in the Gir Forest and consequently banned the sport. Elephant-hunting had been prohibited much earlier, except in the case of 'rogues', those who had gone on the rampage, destroying crops and houses and killing people. That obsessive hunter, Robert Baden-Powell, said he would not have shot elephants anyway because he had 'too much respect for them'. But no one had too much respect for crocodiles, especially if they were 'man-eaters' suspected of killing women at the washing pool. In India, where alligators did not exist, there were two main sorts, the enormous 'mugger', which chiefly inhabited the rivers of Bengal, and the 'gharial', which lived in them too but was also found on the Indus. At Dera Ismail Khan on the frontier, a station which provided few other entertainments, holidaymakers at Christmas sometimes went down the Indus in boats, firing at crocodiles on the river's edge. Similar expeditions were launched up the

Brahmaputra in Bengal.[76] As the victims were usually basking on the sandbanks, it was not a very sporting kind of hunt, but though easy to hit they were difficult to kill unless a bullet penetrated their very small brains.

An enduring image of the Raj is of the tiger shoot, men up trees on little platforms hoping to entice the beast near them with a tethered goat, or else in big hunts on elephants, viceroys and governors firing down on the animal as it emerges from the undergrowth and makes a dash for safety. A sight of skins on the walls at Hopetoun, Lord Linlithgow's house outside Edinburgh, might make one think that tiger-shooting was one of the principal occupations of the viceroys. It was not. Some of them, such as Northbrook, thought it a waste of time, while others did it chiefly to oblige a maharaja they were visiting. Many Britons in India, especially visitors, were desperate to 'bag' at least one tiger, and there were some dedicated tiger-slayers such as George Yule, a Civilian said to have killed hundreds of these animals. But he stalked them on foot, which narrowed the odds. Most of his fellow civil servants did not hunt tigers except when they found one molesting a village.

A more popular form of sport was stalking types of deer and goat in the mountains or in the jungle. Stalking was shikar at its most arduous; it was also, in one enthusiast's eyes, 'the poetry of sport'.[77] It *could* be done in splendour, as at Bikaner when the Mintos stalked gazelles and black buck by galloping over the desert in 'a barouche and six' with the maharaja's shikaris (hunting guides) riding camels to indicate where the herds were.[78] Many stalkers would have considered this a form of cheating. They thought that to honour the sport properly you had to climb thousands of feet, crawl around crags in a blizzard, risk falling off a precipice and then hit a Tibetan gazelle, an Himalayan ibex or a long-bearded markhor with horns fifty-eight inches in length. Yet you did not always have to go to the mountains to be valiant. According to the man who rhapsodized about 'the poetry of sport', stalking antelope 'on the arid and burning plains of India' was 'a greater test of a sportsman's capabilities' than pursuing the 'noble red-deer among the heathery braes and rocky corries of bonnie Scotland'.*[79] Devotees would go to immense lengths to avoid detection in their stalk, crawling

* He was an officer of the Cameron Highlanders, J. Moray Brown.

for miles over 'frightfully thorny' ground in pursuit of antelope or, if 'in the rainy season when the grass was up and green', dyeing their khaki clothing 'a brilliant olive' so that the black buck might not notice them.[80]

Shooting expeditions in India were more strenuous and more dangerous than they were in Britain. They also required more planning and preparation. Provisions for the camp did not just mean accessories for the evening meal – brandy and claret, Worcestershire sauce and anchovy paste – but also cases of pharmaceuticals that included chloroform, quinine, Holloway's ointment, Warburgh's fever drops, vinegar for scorpion stings, onion juice for hornet stings, Fitzsimmons' serum for snake bites and Scrubbs' ammonia. 'Never go into camp,' commanded Mr Burke, 'without a supply of Keating's or Kemp's Insect Powder.'[81] All the experts agreed that 'temperance in the use of liquor' was 'absolutely necessary' when out with a gun. Beer was 'the very worst possible beverage . . . in a hot sun, both in its effect on the shooting and on the liver'; when in the field 'youngsters [should] content themselves with cold weak tea'.[82] After the day's sport Captain Newall and his friends 'invigorated' themselves with a draught of 'mug', a mixture of beer, sherry, sugar, spice and borage, 'the whole rendered brisk and less heavy by the addition of soda water'. Others recommended 'a tot of some spirit' in the evening with brandy as a 'medical comfort'.[83] But one comfort the sportsman in India was denied was the company of his dog, which in most places would be at risk from hungry panthers. Not that a man needed, as one famous hunter put it, a 'canine auxiliary in the field'; when out shooting snipe or quail, he would find that 'native attendants' were 'hardier than dogs'.[84]

Sportsmen sometimes liked to claim that it was not the killing that gave them pleasure but the sense of achievement at outwitting a cunning animal. Yet there is too much evidence of the pleasure experienced by the 'thud' of a bullet striking home to make the claim convincing.[85] When a man shoots two bison, cuts off their heads, measures their size, eats their tongues and then has them stuffed as trophies, there are more motives involved than outwitting a not particularly cunning animal.[86] Such exploits suggest, among other things, a fair degree of vanity and a need to demonstrate virility. So did the obsessive 'collecting' of species. When Guy Fleetwood Wilson, a civil servant from London, was sent to India in 1908 as financial member of the Viceroy's Council, he made up his 'mind to shoot at least one of every kind of the dangerous wild-beast family in India'. Within two and a half years he had killed 'at least one and in some cases three or four specimens', yet, agonizingly, the rhinoceros still eluded him. Not for long. What pleasure he had, how 'elated' he felt, when finally he 'put [his] bullet into the withers'.[87]

Not all the British were like the ineffable Wilson. Even among the Victorians there were those who did not shoot, men such as Richard Temple, who went painting instead, or Edmund Cox, a police officer whose 'shikar was robbers and murderers', or Henry Cotton, who was so haunted by killing a street dog that he never shot anything again except for a crocodile with a bellyful of women's bangles. James Moore observed that among his young Edwardian generation 'a reaction against all this slaughter was starting', at any rate against killing animals, though he admitted that 'for some utterly illogical reason' people like himself went on killing birds and fish. Down in Ceylon his contemporary Leonard Woolf was moving in a similar direction: excitement at first about adventure in the jungle, followed by revulsion at killing, so that in the end he preferred to sit up at night and watch animals at the waterholes. The First World War made others feel the same. After serving in the trenches, John Morris had no desire to kill anything. As an army officer he paid lip service to shikar by owning a shotgun and a rifle, but he never fired either of them.[88]

Shikar, although a word of broad meaning, would not have encompassed cock-fighting, a 'blood sport' of a kind enjoyed by both Britons and Indians, much gambled on in the seventeenth century in Madras, celebrated in the eighteenth century in a great painting by Zoffany,* and continued into the nineteenth century (before it became illegal) by Richard Burton and his fellow officers in Sind. Nor probably could the word be extended to include butterfly-collecting, a hobby mocked as effeminate but one enjoyed by Linlithgow as viceroy and by Winston Churchill in Bangalore until a 'malevolent' rat got into his cabinet and 'devoured all the specimens'.[89] A more authentic shikari sport was hare-coursing with dogs, although, as there were not many hares, jackals and small foxes had to become substitute victims. Hawking or falconry also counted, though it was only rarely practised. Like cock-fighting, it was more popular in the seventeenth century than in

---

* *Colonel Mordaunt's Cock Match* (Tate Gallery), a picture which captures the cosmopolitan ambience of late-eighteenth–century Lucknow.

subsequent eras, and it was mainly confined to the north-west frontier. One could hunt mynahs anywhere with a small sparrowhawk, but it was more challenging to pursue bustards on horseback and, when spying one, to unhood one's falcon and gallop after it as it flew towards its prey; the chase might last a distance of five miles.

Among the squires in Britain, hunting, shooting and fishing enjoyed a rough parity, the three in combination filling up the year and leaving very few gaps. In India fishing was very much the poor relation. Neither the fish nor the rivers could compare with those at 'home', and the sun was usually too bright for the fish to rise. The staple quarry was the mahseer, which was abundant and difficult to catch, but there was not much to be said for other freshwater species; nor was it great fun fishing for them in tiny coracles in a river. The best solution, though not perhaps a very sporting one, was to import trout from Britain and rear them in hatcheries. Although brown trout were successfully introduced into the rivers of Kashmir, they could not breed in the Nilgiris, where the streams were not cold enough, but rainbow trout were brought to the south and soon became the natural piscine prey for the governors of Madras. Their pursuit certainly provided decent sport for Lord Goschen, who liked to relax at Ooty by catching trout in 'scenery like Scotland'.[90]

IN THE SADDLE

It is possible to link the decline of the British Raj to the decline of riding, and certainly to see them as going downhill in tandem. The 'well-mounted man', declared an official in the 1930s, always excited 'respect': in the bazaars he got 'his salaam and the bold glance from the ladies'. Even earlier, when the empire seemed unthreatened, riding was judged to be essential to a man's position. When he 'gives up riding', said a Victorian political officer, 'he ceases to be useful in India. An Englishman on foot is no good in a crowd.'[91]

Regardless of its usefulness, many Britons regarded riding as vital to their daily routine, both for women – whether riding astride or, more decorously and dangerously, side-saddle (a real back-wrecker) – and for men, whether for travel, duty or leisure. Yet whereas all the ball-games they played in India on foot were originally British – or at any rate imported from Europe – all the sports they enjoyed on horseback had either their genesis or their parallel histories in India.

Racecourses were set up in India wherever and whenever the British felt they had acquired enough space and security. In the Hills, of course, there was very rarely enough space; at Darjeeling, where horses would not have had enough room to stretch themselves into a gallop – and at that altitude would have become breathless if they had – the racing was done on hill ponies. The Plains had a number of fine courses, in provincial capitals such as Lucknow and Rangoon as well as in the presidency cities. Enthusiasts in Bombay could indulge their passion nearly all the year round because the Royal Western India Turf Club held twenty-two meetings in the city between November and March and then twelve more in Poona between June and October. The southern presidency had two seasons as well, the winter races in Madras starting in the early morning to escape the heat, the Ooty meetings in the summer taking place in the afternoon. In the 1930s the racing club at Madras used to bring out horses from Britain and then sell them to the governors – and others – for about £240 each.[92]

The Calcutta Turf Club also had early starts, the first race beginning at sunrise or 7 a.m. to avoid great heat and allow 'all classes', as Stocqueler put it in the 1830s, 'to attend and enjoy the sport without trenching upon their daily avocations'.[93] The Club ran (and still runs) its versions of the Epsom and Newmarket Classics and, as at Ascot, the monarch (or in this case the viceroy) would drive up the course in a carriage at the most important meeting of the year. In 1860 the Bengal Club presented one of the victors with an extraordinary cup: a wine-cooler intended to hold champagne and burgundy in the shape of a galley, with Victoria in the prow holding out a crown, and Neptune in the stern.[94] The pomp and ostentation of such events was justified as a way of improving racial relations: the Indian upper classes loved the sport, and they also enjoyed a good show; besides, there were no caste or religious problems with horses. At Mysore Lord Goschen could be pleased that the maharaja's 'royal box and enclosure were worthy of Ascot' and that at Ooty the Governor's Cup was won by the raja of Kohlapur.[95]

One sport adopted from the Subcontinent was 'tent-pegging', which involved riders galloping towards a peg and trying to lift it out of the ground with their lance. Yet although anyone with a horse could take part – and a woman, Maggie Jones of Kanpur, won a cup for her 'tilting' in 1888 – it was largely confined to the cavalry and used as a means of training. Another sport of Indian origin, which again rarely had female participants, was polo, introduced from Manipur soon after the middle of the nineteenth century. Known in its early British years as 'hockey on horseback', it was – as played by the Manipuris – a game pursued skilfully on ponies but without set teams, goal posts or very clear rules. A related contest, also an apparently unruly scramble, was played up at Hunza and elsewhere in the north-west, but it was the Manipuris who influenced the British and who played an exhibition game on the Calcutta racecourse in 1862. The 11th Bengal Lancers then took the sport up, followed by British regiments of lancers and hussars, and it soon became widespread. As the district officer in Dacca, Gerald Gordon was able to enjoy expert tuition from a number of Manipuri chiefs whom he was obliged to keep as hostages after one of their 'little wars'.[96]

Early polo among the British was not the sport it later became, a smart game for rich people. At Aden you could borrow a horse from the cavalry regiment and play on the same stretch of rolled sand that was used as the golf course; in Mandalay 'even the poorest' junior police officers could hire a pony (one rupee each) and 'afford to participate'; elsewhere you could find games organized between bachelors and married men, referred to, with some chortling, as the Desolate versus the Oppressed.[97] Yet when players started to take it seriously, it became a very serious game indeed. According to William Magan, an officer in the Indian Cavalry, three or four of the regiments 'made polo so much their principal recreation that they had spare time, and spare resources, for little else'.[98] In the 1890s at the Ambala cantonment, where half a dozen games could be played simultaneously on the Maidan, the 18th Hussars turned out four or five teams and kept nearly a hundred top-class polo ponies in their stables. It must have been quite galling for the cavalry of both armies that in this particular decade the best British team was the Durham Light Infantry.

When he was not on the north-west frontier – or intriguing to be sent on some other campaign – Lieutenant Winston Churchill concentrated on his polo at Bangalore: the game was his 'serious purpose of life', and he played every chukka he could get into. Even when he had decided to give up his commission, he returned to India at the end of

1898 to take part in the Inter-regimental tournament at Meerut. Just before the competition opened, he fell down some stairs, spraining his ankles and dislocating a shoulder, but he still managed to play matches, and he scored three of the Hussars' four goals in their victory in the final against the 4th Dragoon Guards. As Churchill recognized, however, Indians from the princely states had also learned from the Manipuris and were often equally skilful. The Golconda Brigade, the bodyguard of the nizam of Hyderabad, was 'incomparably the best team' in southern India, while in the north the sportsmen from Jodhpur and Patiala were superb players.[99]

Hunting on horseback with hounds was another Asiatic tradition, but in this case the British were not prepared to learn from their subjects. They insisted on bringing out British foxhounds even though India did not contain the type of fox that these liked to hunt. Cattle were among the imported British animals that failed to acclimatize to India, and so were foxhounds. In the 1840s, recalled Captain Hervey, they would start dying as soon as a pack reached Madras. Until the First World War a fresh supply had to be brought out every year to the south to fill the gaps caused by such tropical diseases as 'Indian tick fever'.[100] The Bombay foxhounds, drawn from different hunts in England, seem to have been healthier, perhaps because they had a more varied season. After a winter hunting on the island of Salsette, they were brought eighty miles inland, where they metamorphosed into the Kirkee and Poona hounds.[101]

The Indian fox (*vulpes bengalensis*) was not like the British version. It was smaller and greyer, its scent was much weaker, and when frightened it quickly disappeared down one of its numerous burrows; in short it was an unsatisfactory quarry. Better sport was to be had from chasing jackals, at least in open country, especially in the northwest. Near Madras these animals made things difficult for horses and hounds by running through rice fields and villages with cactus hedges. Yet up at Ooty, where the opening meet took place at 'Fernhill', the maharaja of Mysore's holiday home, there was plenty of scope for long gallops across the Downs. 'Hounds met' at half-past six, with mist in the valleys and the hills glowing pink, and the sport was fast and short (and usually bloodless), over in time for officials to be at their desks by ten o'clock. Sometimes, when the sun was too hot, the hounds might not be able to scent the jackal, and sometimes they might be diverted by wild boars and charge after them. Lord Goschen was meticulous in recording the joys and vicissitudes of his Ooty hunting in his diaries, but a later governor was unable to share them. As Lord Erskine admitted, he was a 'heretic' who refused to hunt because he regarded the horse as 'a dangerous animal that bites at one end and kicks at the other, and is uncomfortable in the middle'.[102]

The most exhilarating hunting was in the north-west, where the 'field' consisted mainly of officers and their wives from the garrisons of Quetta, Mian Mir and Peshawar. Votaries of the Peshawar Vale Hunt claimed it was comparable to anything outside the best of the English shires, though the country itself could hardly have been less similar. Instead of 'drawing' a covert, finding a fox and pursuing it across fields and over hedges, the huntsmen 'drew' a patch of sugar cane, flushed out a jackal and then galloped after it across stony soil and irrigation ditches. Unlike the British fox, the animal did not live in 'earths' and 'go to ground', yet it was not usually caught, and there was no pretence that the sport was about getting rid of 'vermin'. If officials of the Peshawar were worried there might not be enough jackals about, they would tempt them with a dead mule placed in 'fair hunting country' a couple of days before the meet.[103]

Jackal-hunting was plainly a suitable activity for cavalry officers, but some of their commanders rated another sport even higher. Pig-sticking, declared Colonel Vaughan of the 10th Hussars, was the 'finest training for both horse and man', and he liked to use troop horses for the sport. A man and a horse must also learn to fall, averred Major Wardrop, a colleague of Vaughan, 'six legs in the air'. There was nothing 'so good for a man's nerve as a fall without damage'.[104]

Pig-sticking or hog-hunting had medieval traditions in England and even more ancient origins in India. Under the Raj, wild boar – or 'pig', as hunters always called them – were pursued wherever they lived, which was almost everywhere except Madras, the western Punjab and parts of central India. The sportsmen originally used their spears as javelins, throwing them at the beast when they got near enough, but later they wielded them as lances, holding long ones 'underhand' like a picador, except in Bengal, where shorter ones were carried 'overarm' (perhaps more like a banderillero) and thus hit the boar at a different angle. Whether using the long or the short one – and riding an 'Arab' or a 'waler' – there was little, recalled Robert Baden-Powell, to compare with the thrill of chasing a boar for half a mile, 'twisting and turning as the pig "jinks" to the right or left to evade the pursuer'. Similarly, for the soldier William Birdwood, there were 'few delights to be compared with that of meeting a great, strong, heavy fighting boar coming at you for all he is worth'. It was 'a rough, wild sport', admitted Baden-Powell, 'with perhaps a taint of barbarism about it'. Yet it was not so 'cruel' or 'one-sided' as one might think: 'the horse without a doubt enjoys it almost as much as his rider', and the pig himself, 'endowed with a fighting and blood-thirsty nature as well as a particularly tough and unfeeling nervous system, seems to revel in the fight up to the bitter end'.[105] Aficionados of bull-fighting used to make a similar defence.

One of the 'delights', of course, was that it was extremely dangerous. 'Pig' lived in rough country and 'jinked' about through long grass that disguised holes and hollows, as well as 'blind' or disused wells. Galloping to keep up with the quarry, horses frequently trod in them and turned somersaults, satisfying Wardrop's enthusiasm for 'six legs in the air'. In cultivated areas, melon beds, three feet deep and refilled with soft soil, invariably caused a fall; and the sight of his pursuers on the ground often encouraged the boar to turn round to attack them with his tusks; a rider's leather boots were not much use to him then. Falls frequently resulted in damaged shoulders and broken collar-bones but only occasionally in a fractured skull and death.[106] Horses had a higher mortality rate, usually from broken necks, and those that survived were often badly cut up, unless they wore leather gaiters from knee to fetlock. While pursuing a boar across a river and into some tamarisk scrub, Francis Yeats-Brown, the author of *Bengal Lancer*, managed to spear his horse and his quarry at the same moment, killing them both. He had his horse cremated and its ashes scattered in the Ganges, though he kept one hoof as a souvenir to use as an inkwell.[107]

A passion for pig-sticking could dominate a man's life and the pattern of his career. The Civilian Frank Simson always preferred to be posted to remote stations so that he could ignore 'society' and concentrate on hunting pig and tiger. He chose to stay six years as district officer in Noakhali, a station in eastern Bengal disliked by everyone else, because the pig-sticking there was 'second only to fox-hunting with the best packs' in Leicestershire; in a single day in March 1857 he speared sixteen boar.[108] Like most sports, pig-sticking developed into something larger, smarter and more organized. Simson might have gone out with a couple of friends to rummage about in the scrub, but soon it became a sport of 'meets' with cups and competitions organized by 'tent clubs'. Here now was a recreation that Indian noblemen could be encouraged to take part in, and rulers of states such as Patiala, Kolhapur and Dholpur duly became enthusiasts. As political agent at Bhopawar in the 1880s, Colonel Wylie stressed the advantage of persuading one young maharaja, mollycoddled in his palace and 'prey to flattery', to participate in hunts where he would have to 'compete with Dholpur etc and where he [would] meet pleasant manly English gentlemen'.[109]

The 'blue ribbon of pig-sticking', the Derby of the sport, was the Kadir Cup, which took place over three days in March. It was named after the Hindi word for river-bed, and it was over the dried-up beds of the Jumna and the Ganges that the best hunting was to be had. The competitors assembled on a Sunday evening, sat down for a large dinner and slept in tents pitched away from their horses to avoid the flies. Sixty or seventy officers, each allowed to have two mounts, entered the competition, and the heats – three horses in each, the winner (the man who speared the pig) going into the next round – took place throughout Monday and Tuesday. Riders waited while beaters and elephants (some forty of them) flushed out a boar, and then they rushed after it, their chase umpired by men who, as Major Wardrop put it, had 'an intimate acquaintance with the rules, and a thorough knowledge of pig-craft'.[110] On Wednesday came the semi-finals and finals, followed by the 'Hog-Hunters'' Cup, a race as long as the Grand National at Aintree but over smaller fences and much rougher ground. As inspector-general of cavalry in India, Douglas Haig took part in the 1905 meeting of the Kadir Cup and was much impressed by its organization, the programme and menus that were printed each day, the cut flowers that came from Meerut, and the ice that was brought in from Agra.[111]

At the end of an ordinary day's hunting, the sportsmen would hack back to their camp, white tents under the mango trees, and sip their first alcoholic drink of the day. Lady Erskine-Crum, who in the 1930s wrote articles about the sport for the *Queen* and the *Field*, recommended hot tea 'laced with whisky', and most participants agreed with her: it was, said one, a 'drink for the gods'. The men would then stroll about, patting the horses, inspecting the bag and chatting to the shikaris. What Major Wardrop called 'the aching void till dinner' was filled by sitting inside a hot tub with soap and then beside a camp fire with a glass of whisky 'laced' with ginger wine. At the end of one very typical feast the boar's health was drunk, other toasts were made, and the singing began, 'Fuzzy Graham' leading off with the pig-stickers' anthem accompanied by Captain Holden on the banjo.[112]

> Over the valley, over the level,
> Through the dâk jungle, ride like the devil.
> Hark! forard a boar, away we go!
> Sit down in your saddle and ride Tally Ho.

The sport was controlled by 'tent clubs', which each had its own 'country', and was run by the honorary secretaries, who organized the hunting and thus needed to know, as Wardrop pointed out, the local 'language well enough to talk with the villagers and the coolies on line'. Tent clubs made the hunt rules and imposed the penalties for their transgression. Some of the regulations were analagous to recondite fox-hunting principles in Britain. Just as it was regarded as outrageous to shoot foxes in hunting counties – but all right to do so in, say, the Highlands – so was it 'unpardonable', asserted Captain Newall, to shoot pig 'in the vicinity of ground where they [could] be speared from horseback'. Another taboo was to kill a sow (even with a spear) because these were required to produce future quarry. Such sins were invariably punished with a fine. Rule 8 of the Calcutta Tent Club stated that anyone 'spearing a sow, except in self-defence', would have to pay 'a penalty of one dozen Champagne . . . for the use of those attending the next meet'.[113]

Military members of the tent clubs were used to this kind of penalty because it was the sort of fine they had to pay for mentioning women or politics in the Mess. They took it in good heart, for the Tent club was, like the Mess and the local Club, a bastion of their lives; 'half the joy' of it, thought Wardrop, was that you could there form friendships with men in services other than your own. Another part of the joy was the chief social event in its calendar. At the annual dinner of the Bareilly Tent Club in 1910, the young Yeats-Brown was relieved to find there were no 'grousers' – 'a species from which the Tent Club is happily free' – but only 'good sorts', lustily singing such songs as 'Over the Valley' and 'The Mighty Boar', and making at least ten speeches: 'As an antidote to hot weather dullness there [was] nothing to compare to a pigsticking dinner'. A quarter of a century later, long after he had retired from the Indian Army, Yeats-Brown was still 'haunted by the idea of pig-sticking once more'. How he longed to 'feel the balance of a good Bareilly spear' in his hand and 'the spring of a good horse between [his] knees'.[114]

14

Last Posts

DEATH IN INDIA

'Everything is sudden in India,' recalled an English woman about the early twentieth century, 'the sudden twilights, the sudden death. A man can be talking to you at breakfast and be dead in the afternoon.' It had always been so. In 1805 one visitor reported that he had twice lunched with men whose burials he had been invited to attend before supper that same day.[1] When an epidemic arrived at a station, people began measuring their lives in hours: they went to the Club 'each evening apprehensive to know who was missing from the night before'.[2] Death was so familiar to the British in India, so quick and so frequent, that there hardly seemed room for prolonged grief. If an officer died on campaign, his belongings were auctioned as soon as the funeral was over: horses, clothes, revolver, even his cooking-pot and his water-bottle.

The early mortality rates were extraordinarily high. According to the chaplain Thomas Ovington, the British in Bombay at the end of the seventeenth century had a saying, 'Two monsoons are the age of man.' Many young men did not get beyond one. The British population of Bombay in that era remained static and even decreased in years such as 1692, when the number of deaths far outweighed the combined total of births and new arrivals. As P. J. Marshall has shown, well over half the Company's servants in the eighteenth century died in India; in the decades before Plassey (1757) a full two-thirds of those who went out as Writers eager to make their fortune never saw Britain again.[3] Corresponding from Calcutta in the 1760s, Mrs Nathaniel Kindersley claimed that women died from 'violent fevers' less often than men because they lived 'more temperately' and exposed themselves 'less in the heat of the day'.[4] Yet they still died in large numbers; the few who arrived for the first time in middle age were very likely to die within a year. Perhaps half the Britons who went to India in the eighteenth century survived for fewer than five years. Fourteen of the thirty ensigns who joined the Company's armies in 1775 were dead before they could become lieutenants in 1780: none of them had died in battle.[5]

The statistics took a long time to improve. Between 1796 and 1820, 1,243 officers of the Bengal Army were killed or died on service in India; only 203 – one seventh of the total – retired on a pension.[6] In the other ranks, the mortality rate for British soldiers in India in the first half of the nineteenth century was again very high: an annual average of sixty-nine per thousand, though by 1882 it had been reduced to a quarter of this ratio.[7] But the overall statistics do not have the same impact as burial registers and cemeteries revealing evidence in more human terms. According to those at Dinapur, where the South Wales Borderers were stationed, in the years 1817–18 the regiment lost one officer, six NCOs, ninety-six private soldiers and more than sixty women and children.[8]

British soldiers in India died more often from disease than from enemy action, but they were of course killed and wounded in their hundreds at Assaye and Seringapatam, in the invasions of Afghanistan and the campaign in Mesopotamia, and in the Sikh wars at Ferozeshah, Sobraon and Chillianwallah. Many soldiers also died fighting in the Rebellion of 1857–8 and, in fewer numbers, on the frontiers, on expeditions into the tribal areas and sometimes in camp, attacked in the dark when on sentry duty. British civilians were also victims of violence, dozens of them killed in the 'Black Hole of Calcutta' in 1756 and in the Patna Massacre of 1763, and in larger numbers at the beginning of the Rebellion in 1857, at Delhi, Meerut, Jhansi, Lucknow and above all Kanpur, where several hundred men, women and children were massacred. Some families were virtually wiped out. The Greenways of Kanpur lost nineteen of their members.[9]

Thirty-four members of the ICS were killed during the Rebellion, and eight more died of illnesses incurred during the fighting. In subsequent decades civil servants were only occasional targets. As Harcourt Butler told his father in 1891, Indians 'don't often go for magistrates fortunately'.[10] Political shootings, carried out by revolutionary Bengali nationalists, became more common between the world wars. In 1928 a magistrate was stabbed to death in Chittagong by a bogus petitioner who had intrigued the official by putting the words 'Lord Byron' on his calling card.[11] In the early 1930s three consecutive district officers of Midnapore were assassinated, one when inspecting an exhibition of local crafts, another through a window at a meeting of the district board, and the third as he walked on to the pitch to play football. Civilians were not the only targets of the revolutionaries in Bengal: the victims of 1930 included the inspector-general of police (F. J. Lowman), who was murdered in a Dacca hospital, a police inspector (mistaken for Lowman's successor) and the inspector-general of prisons, who was shot dead in the Writers Building in Calcutta, the heart of the Bengal government. A few months later, the magistrate of Tipperah was shot on his verandah by two teenage girls pretending to hand him a petition. Retirement to Britain did not necessarily give a man immunity. In 1940, two decades after he had retired as lieutenant-governor of the Punjab, Michael O'Dwyer was assassinated in London.

Life was generally more dangerous, for both Politicals and army officers, on the frontiers. As we have seen, officials were quite often killed in the north-east in disputes with various tribes and on one occasion with the Manipuri royal family. In the north-west, when they were not victims of 'raiders' or tribal attacks, officers were often assassinated by individuals for motives that seemed incomprehensible unless ascribed to Islam. The easiest way to explain such deaths, at least on a gravestone, was to state that the victims had been struck down by a ghazi or religious 'fanatic'. A commissioner of Peshawar was killed by a 'religious fanatic' when hearing a petition; a Resident at Tonk was murdered in his sleep by a Mahsud sentry apparently incited by a tribal mullah.

British men in India devised various self-inflicted means of getting themselves killed. Perhaps the most absurd was duelling, a mainly eighteenth-century way – often ending in death – of satisfying a man's honour after an insult, a gambling debt or the discovery that someone had taken 'unwarrantable liberties' with his wife. Although the East India Company tried to prohibit the practice, it could hardly succeed when even the governor-general (Warren Hastings) felt obliged to fight his impossible colleague Philip Francis (whom he wounded) in 1780.

One problem was that sensible men felt that they would be ostracized if they refused a challenge even when they were clearly in the right. When governor of Madras (1781–5), Lord Macartney was wounded in a duel with one of his councillors, who demanded satisfaction for an alleged 'offensive expression', and on his return to England he was again wounded after being forced to fight a general he had dismissed and sent home.

Other activities with steady casualty rates were sports. The most lethal, because the most indulged, was the apparently harmless pastime of riding. Murray's *Handbook to the Punjab* warned travellers that before 1875 'at least 22 ladies and gentlemen [had been] killed by falling over precipices at Simla' with their ponies or horses. Riders died in the same way at Dalhousie, Landour and other hill stations; Rudyard Kipling's horse Joe broke out of his stable one night at Dalhousie and fell to his death down a precipice. All the equestrian sports claimed their fatalities: racing, polo, pig-sticking (though not as many as one might have expected) and jackal-hunting: the master of the Peshawar, a colonel in the IMS, was drowned in 1919 while taking hounds over the River Nagoman. Sometimes, as with 'pig', the hunted turned on their pursuer. Men were killed by tigers, panthers and bears, often after they had wounded them. A man would shoot a tiger and follow it into the jungle or long grass, where the injured beast would jump out at him. In 1865 Lord Edward St Maur died near Mysore after his leg was amputated following a hand-to-hand struggle with a bear he had wounded.[12]

In India people drank themselves to death and killed themselves in other ways, as they did in Britain, and for many of the same reasons: for professional worries or debt or because their business had gone under; because of depression or 'mental aberration'; because they could not cope with bereavement or marital infidelity. But heat coupled with loneliness added an extra category in India. Suicides tended to take place in the hot weather, often in remote areas, and they were more common in the military, among young officers and young soldiers in the ranks, than in most civilian professions.* Yet they also occurred in the mountains. Army suicides at the small Senchal cantonment near Darjeeling were so frequent in the mid-nineteenth century that the

* See above, pp. 254–5.

burial ground was known as 'suicide cemetery'. In the belief that the soldiers' depression was caused by cold winters and damp mists, the cantonment was moved.[13]

The Himalaya may have been regarded as the healthiest regions of India, but they still contained dangers to human lives. Darjeeling was prone to landslips brought on by heavy rain: one in 1899 engulfed the Methodist school, killing ten pupils and taking the lives of dozens of other people in the town. Naini Tal was even more prone, and a landslip in 1880 (coinciding with a small earthquake) took the Victoria Hotel and its residents plus several other buildings down the hill and into the lake: 151 people were killed, including forty-three Britons. Earthquakes were even more widespread and often more damaging. Two of the worst seismic disasters – in which Britons died in their scores and Indians in their tens of thousands – happened at Dharamsala in 1905 and Quetta in 1935.

Captain Hervey of the Madras Infantry was apt to be censorious, often with reason, of British habits on the Subcontinent. When a man died in India, he reported, the 'melancholy circumstance' was always attributed to 'the baneful effects of the climate', whereas, 'if the truth be known', he had often been 'carried off by his own indiscretion'.[14] Hervey was writing of the 1840s, when his fellow-countrymen were slowly starting to be more sensible about their health. In the 1680s Thomas Ovington noted how fevers often came 'after a strong Debauch'. Others also made the connection without having much influence on eating and drinking habits before the nineteenth century. After Rose Aylmer arrived in Calcutta in 1798, William Hickey cautioned this 'very charming and lovely girl' not to eat too much of 'that pernicious and dangerous fruit, the pineapple', but apparently she ignored his advice, was consequently 'attacked with a most severe bowel complaint', and died.[15] We do not know if the poor girl really succumbed to 'a surfeit' of pineapples – more likely she died of cholera – but we do know that the self-indulgent Hickey was lucky not to succumb to heart failure or disease of the liver.

In India the British died of course of diseases that might have killed them in Britain, including tuberculosis, smallpox, cancer, tetanus and hepatitis. In 1942, just after he had been appointed governor of Assam, Edmond Blandy was diagnosed with lung cancer, but he had become ill not as a result of living in India but as a consequence of smoking British cigarettes.* Yet there were also illnesses and diseases in India that would seldom or never have killed people in Britain. There were also circumstances in which death might have been avoided if the victim had not been struck down in a place without a doctor, if a man with appendicitis could have been taken to a hospital by car instead of travelling thirty miles in a bullock-cart and dying of a burst appendix on the way.[17] In his poem 'The Land of Regrets' Alfred Lyall described the sick Englishman in the mofussil. He was addressing India.

> Thou hast racked him with duns and diseases,
> And he lies, as thy scorching winds blow,
> Recollecting old England's sea breezes
> On his back in a lone bungalow.

In India many Britons died alone, in the jungle or in remote stations, without anyone to comfort them or listen to what they were trying to say in their final moments.

The most common disease for the British was malaria (sometimes known as 'jungle fever'), but it was not the most fatal. Numerous people died of it when they were in India or after being invalided home to Britain, but most victims survived despite recurring and debilitating attacks. A less common but more avoidable malady was heatstroke (sometimes known as sunstroke), when the body overheats but is unable to sweat. Not that it was always caused by men heedlessly exposing themselves to the sun. In 1872 the magistrate at Roorkee got it after spending too much time on his elephant, which had got stuck in the sand; he left a widow of thirty-four with nine children.[18] In the summer of 1916, in the worst disaster of its kind, nineteen British soldiers packed into third-class coaches died of it in a train running from Karachi across the Sind desert.

There were a number of killer scourges in India, including dysentery, beriberi and blackwater fever. But the most fatal ones were typhoid (then known as enteric fever), which killed off its victims with a relentless regularity, and cholera, which could swoop on a cantonment and wipe out half a battalion. Cholera was an erratic, almost capricious

---

* A medical examination prevented Blandy from taking up the post. Instead he was given a sinecure, a knighthood and a house in Calcutta, where he read Gibbon and the whole of the Bible before he died a few months later.[16]

disease, seeming sometimes to choose men lying in alternate beds in a barracks dormitory. In an epidemic at Meerut in 1867, the 3rd Regiment of Foot (the 'Buffs') lost 129 soldiers and 59 women and children; and there were many harsher statistics.[19] When cholera hit a camp or a cantonment, soldiers and camp followers woke up each morning wondering if it would be their last. Battalions pursued a policy known as 'cholera dodging' – continuously moving camp, if possible to higher ground – but it was not an effective measure because (unbeknown to them) they were not combating an airborne disease.

Cholera was no respecter of military rank. During the Rebellion of 1857 it killed the commander-in-chief, General Anson, as he marched to Delhi, and his successor, General Barnard, when he was besieging the city. Nor did illnesses and diseases discriminate on the basis of class or affluence. In the nineteenth century cholera killed two governors of Madras (Thomas Munro and George Ward), and typhoid carried off a third (Lord Hobart). Cholera also killed a Bombay governor's wife, Lady Fergusson, whose husband outlived her for twenty-five years before he died in an earthquake in Jamaica in 1907. Three successive governor-generals (Dalhousie, Canning and the first of the Elgins) died not from disease but from ill health and the stress of the job (the first two soon after their return to Britain); Lady Dalhousie died at sea, while Lady Canning died in India of malaria. Anglican bishops in India may have been relatively immune to disease, but they tended to die prematurely, quite often in watery circumstances. The great Bishop Heber of Calcutta (author of such resounding hymns as 'Brightest and Best of the Sons of the Morning') died in his bath, one of his successors, Bishop Cotton (founder of the hill schools), was drowned in a river, while another (Bishop James) died during a voyage and was buried at sea. Among other early bishops of Calcutta, one (Thomas Middleton) died of heat-stroke, and another (John Turner) succumbed to an unspecified fever.[20]

Funerals at sea could be even more harrowing than they were on land, perhaps because passengers and crew could not avoid being present – or close by – when the coffin was 'consigned to the deep'. And there were disproportionately more of them, chiefly because so many people in poor health were advised to go home – or were sent on sick certificate – when it was already too late. Sometimes it was their own fault: they could not bear to be parted, even on doctor's orders, from a husband, a wife, a mistress or their children; or they wanted to finish a project or make one more lakh of rupees for their retirement. Some stayed so long that they did not even reach the ship, dying on the way to Calcutta or Bombay. Between 1892 and 1896 three successive Agents to the Governor-General in Baluchistan (the most senior official there) died in office, on the very eve of demission. Like many men in India, they had not realized when it had become too dangerous to stay.

William Hickey, that colourful chronicler of the good, the bad and the tragic in Calcutta, noted the deaths of acquaintances who had left it too late, dying in the capital, or two days out of Madras, or three weeks later on the ocean. Among the many who were ordered home for health reasons and who died at sea were three contemporaries: General Sleeman, famous for his operations against 'Thuggee' in the 1830s, who died off Ceylon; General Cubbon, the commissioner and virtual ruler of Mysore for a quarter of a century, who died at Suez; and General Fane, the commander-in-chief, who perished off the Azores. The bodies of most people who died on board ship were buried at sea, but sometimes they were preserved in a cask or puncheon of rum for burial at St Helena or even taken all the way back to England for interment there.

There were more than a thousand British burial grounds in the Indian Empire. The most elaborate, and perhaps the most beautiful, is the South Park Street Cemetery, the last resting place of many of Calcutta's grandest inhabitants in the late eighteenth and early nineteenth centuries: few sites are more evocative of the history of British India than the mausoleums between the trees and their medley of architectural motifs, the cupolas, the pyramids, the obelisks and the classical pillars. Later the taste for such tombs died out, a trend assisted by the arrival of so many more Britons in India and the consequent need for many more graves. An officer who in 1770 might have had a mausoleum would be buried a century later in the ground with a headstone and perhaps a commemorative plaque in a church put up by his fellow officers. After the rains came, grave diggers in a cantonment cemetery took the opportunity of digging a dozen or so extra graves in preparation for future deaths when the ground would be hard again. As funerals usually took place on the same day as the death, this was a wise precaution.

The corpses of officers killed in battle could not be taken back to the regimental headquarters, but they were, when possible, buried with ceremony, the regiment drawn up in square, the bodies placed on gun carriages, not in coffins but with cloaks or quilts covering their uniforms, the cortege proceeding to the burial tope as the band played the 'Dead March' from Handel's *Saul* (and pipers playing a lament if a Scottish regiment was involved), and then the Anglican service, the Presbyterian prayer and three last volleys fired over the grave.[21] It was almost obligatory to play the 'Dead March' at funerals, for NCOs and private soldiers as well as officers, as the procession made its way to the cemetery, where in due course a tombstone would record that 'The Strife is o'er, the Battle done' or perhaps, in post-Tennysonian times, 'God's finger touched him, and he slept.' After the burial the band would try to dispel the gloomy atmosphere by playing comic songs and light-hearted airs, but the ploy did not always succeed. However beautiful and moving Handel's march may sound in the opera house, listening to the 'continuous drone' several times a day during a cholera epidemic made people even more depressed and terrified, especially the patients in the hospital. In such circumstances sensible COs banned the music; when the colonel and the adjutant of the 62nd died of cholera on the same day, the regimental band decided of its own accord not to play it.[22]

One tomb at the South Park Street Cemetery contains the remains of four children of the Twisden family, who died between 1820 and 1827, none of whom reached the age of two. In the same cemetery are buried seven children of the Hermitage family, who died over the twenty years from 1826, only two of them surviving long enough to become teenagers. Tombstones all over India record a similar toll and reveal little discrimination between classes. At Simla a stone slab commemorates the death of three babies of Fred Roberts, the Old Etonian officer who became the commander-in-chief; Stamford Raffles, the founder of Singapore, lost three children in six months. At the time the infant-mortality rate was also high in Britain, though not so extreme. So was death in childbirth, but it too was exacerbated in India by the heat and a lack of medical facilities and later recorded in countless tombstones erected by a 'disconsolate husband'. Women might survive childbirth but die later, still young, worn out by the climate, the loss of children and other problems caused by living in an alien land. Louisa Broughton survived the loss of four infants and several months under siege in the

Agra Fort during the Rebellion, but eventually her body gave up and she died at the age of twenty-three, leaving one baby alive.[23]

The inscriptions on children's tombstones are poignant and repetitive and almost unbearable to read. Perhaps the easiest to accept are the conventional quotations from the Bible or the prayer book: 'Thy will be done', 'The Lord gave, and the Lord hath taken away', or the most popular one, sometimes abbreviated, 'Suffer little children, and forbid them not, to come unto me, for of such is the kingdom of heaven.' How one feels sympathy for parents who accepted the necessary hypocrisy of such sentimental phrases as 'fell asleep in Jesus' or 'safe in the arms of Jesus' or the ghastly couplet 'God loved her too and thought it best / To take her home with him to rest', and then added something real and heartfelt such as 'Mummy misses baby darling in a hundred different ways.' One can sympathize very readily too with those people who, unable to understand why such tragedies happened, pointedly put in the half-line 'God moves in a mysterious way.'

Death and bereavement were much the same in India as in Britain, but in India there was an added poignancy. In Britain people usually lived near the graves of their relations and so could visit them, tend them and leave flowers there; there was even a certain consolation in having members of the same family buried together in the same churchyard. Such conditions did not exist in India except in those few places where there was a settled community such as Kanpur. Most of the British in India lived shifting lives. Their children died and were buried, but they themselves had to move on to the next station, unable to see the graves and yet unable to forget that they were there, untended and unvisited by anyone connected with the child. Often they had taken with them, together with locks of hair and other mementoes, the dried petals of a flower growing on the grave. Over the years they would send money for repair work and the regilding of the inscription, and they would receive letters assuring them that the memorial was being cared for and the weeds had been cleared away. In most cases they would only see it again if they made a special pilgrimage. On 15 August 1947, Independence Day, Robert Baylis, the district judge at Naini Tal, lowered his flag and, 'after pausing only to visit the grave of a child [he] had lost' in Kanpur, made his way to Bombay and 'a slow and dismal voyage to England'.[24]

REPATRIATES

Officials in India spent a lot of time thinking about their retirement, dreaming about it, worrying about it, and making many plans. Where would they live? How far would their pension stretch? Above all, how would they fit in and what would they *do* in a country they may have seen only three or four times in the last thirty years? Britain in the nineteenth century was changing at least as fast as it has done since, and it was bound to feel strange and rather bewildering to be living there again. A man may have gone to India when rail seemed the ultimate means of travel and then returned to find that everyone wanted to fly in the sky or drive like Toad of Toad Hall along the highways.

Yet anxieties in most cases seem to have taken second place to the pleasures of daydreaming. At the end of his day in camp, when he had closed his Dante and put out his lamp, Joseph Goudge used to think of the actors he would see, the concerts he would go to, and the Italian cities he would visit with his new wife.[25] Men and women naturally dreamed of the things that they most missed in India. How wonderful it would be to experience a proper Christmas, to eat the real roast bird rather than a peacock or tinned turkey, to see robins, to put up a fir tree, to have holly and mistletoe instead of poinsettias and branches of palm trees. It would be fun to go to shops and buy presents rather than make purchases by mail order or from an occasional pedlar.

As the departure date approached, people often had doubts, and feelings became ambiguous. Henry Beveridge had long been torn between a Scottish 'burn dancing down under the hawthorns' and the 'great, turbid, rolling Hooghly'; the problem was that India had truly 'burnt itself into him'. Calcutta may not have burnt itself quite so much into William Hickey, but that amiable character felt 'dejected and gloomy' about leaving his friends and his city and seeing 'the melancholy and desponding countenances' of his favourite servants.[26] Leave-takings are sad moments, and they were prolonged in India – especially if the leaver was eminent – by farewell dinners with toasts and speeches to commemorate a man's work, by public receptions and appreciative 'addresses', and by people from the local community – Indian as well as British – accompanying him to the station to see him board the train to Bombay. 'How sad a business' it was, one official told Lord Elgin before sailing home in 1896, 'to break the chain of the work and associations of one's lifetime'.[27] And if the departures took place at the end of the Raj, there was an extra poignancy that went beyond the personal. In 1947 the boxwallah Wilfrid Russell visited the Residency at Kashmir and was sitting in the drawing room when 'a wave of emotion passed through' him, a sudden 'sadness at the imminent passing of all this', a realization that

> it would all be forgotten in a few years – the accumulated knowledge, experience and sacrifice of generations of Englishmen and women, who had spent their lives far from home serving a cause in which they had believed, even if it was now being questioned by new, perhaps less fortunate, generations of their own people. It was like finding oneself in an old English country house, still full of treasures of past generations, soon to come under the hammer in order to pay death duties.[28]

Farewells were easier for private soldiers, most of whom hadn't been there for long, hadn't wanted to go in the first place, had enjoyed few perks and luxuries while they were there, and were leaving because their time was up or their regiment was being sent elsewhere. Private Clemens of the East Yorkshires, whom we last saw in Lucknow in 1935, returned to England after his six-year term in the same ship he had come out on. He left a brief, unsentimental, matter-of-fact description of his arrival and discharge. He and his mates were transported to the regimental depot at Beverley, where they received their pay and discharge papers in the orderly room, and then went to the barrack room where a van from Burton the tailors had brought them some clothes to try on: 'we were soon dressed in "civvies" again'.[29]

Private Swindlehurst of the Lancashire Fusiliers, whom we last knew in Lahore in 1920, was not sad to leave Bombay with its filth and beggars and 'prowling women'. From being assistant butcher on the way out, he now became chief butcher on the home voyage, but apart from fulfilling that duty he spent the time boxing, wrestling, playing cards and singing songs. When the ship reached the Channel and passed Swanage, the men started singing 'Way down upon the Swanee River', and although it was January and the ship docked in Southampton under a grey sky and a cold wind, Swindlehurst was glad to be back and feel 'a drop of good English rain'. That first evening home he and his mates longed for a 'fish and tatty shop' and roamed the streets asking

Southampton's 'natives' – who could not understand 'broad Lanca-shire' – where they might find one. In the end they settled for a sausage-and-mash shop and a lot of beer, which sent them to bed still singing 'Swanee River'. In a few days they were issued with rifles, which made them wonder if they were about to be sent to Ireland, a dangerous place for a soldier early in 1921. It was soon confirmed that Dublin was indeed the destination, via Crewe and Holyhead, a posting that meant a routine of patrolling streets and curfews. When they reached the Irish city, the ranks were given a lecture about not sleeping with the 'Colleens'.[30]

Private soldiers coming home with their battalion after a few years in India found it less difficult to adjust than men and women who were returning as couples or as individuals after three decades away. From the moment a retired Civilian stepped ashore, he would notice changes and differences: small things usually, such as fashions in facial hair, in beards, whiskers and moustaches, or the replacement of monocles and pince-nez by spectacles. He might descend the gangway in a winged collar and straw boater to find that everyone on shore was wearing soft shirts and caps or homburgs. Such changes might be subtle and unimportant in themselves, but they would remind him that he was in many ways a stranger, that he did not quite 'belong', that his homeland had been changing while he was absent in ways he had been excluded from.

Almost invariably the first thing returning exiles grumbled about was the weather; it is remarkable how many of them happened to dis-embark in fog and drizzle. Further disappointment or disillusionment soon followed. Transport was of course more expensive than in India, and much less dignified, especially on the London Underground. Homes they could afford were a good deal smaller than they were used to, and domestic help, so smiling and abundant in India, was compara-tively scarce and expensive. The feelings of many an officer and official were nicely expressed by a fictitious character, Colonel Dewes in A. E. W. Mason's novel *The Broken Road*: 'one misses more than one thought to miss, and one doesn't find half what one thought to find'. Dewes expressed another feeling that would have been familiar to readers who had lived in India: in England, he said, 'one felt a stranger . . . one had lost one's associations'.[31]

A number of senior officials (to be mentioned later) acquired comparably influential jobs after their retirement. Most of them did not, and in consequence felt impotent and unimportant. They may have fought battles or dug canals or governed millions of people, but their compatriots in Britain seldom wanted to know about their exploits or to help put their skills to some domestic use. When Olaf Caroe returned in 1947, feeling that 'the meaning had gone out of life', he was only fifty-four and in need of some occupation. Yet although he had recently been foreign secretary in Delhi and governor of the north-west, neither the Foreign Office nor any other institution wished to employ this talented individual.[32] Caroe's case was not unusual or limited to the period of Independence. In the nineteenth century G. O. Trevelyan noted what a 'severe trial' it was for a 'leader of Calcutta society' to 'become one of the rank and file in the pump room at a watering-place' and to 'sink . . . from the High Court to the Petty Sessions'. The sense of anonymity did not diminish. When one ICS officer retired to East Anglia after 1947, he expected folk there to mistake him for an employee of the Ipswich Co-operative Society.[33]

Many people soon realized how ill adapted they were to life in Britain. As a woman who returned in 1946 later admitted, India had made her 'a completely useless person', unable to cook a meal, clean her house, wash her clothes or make a fire.[34]* Feelings of inadequacy, combined with lack of recognition and even of interest, led naturally to a loss of self-esteem which in turn sometimes led to self-assertion, a need to tell unwilling listeners what you had been doing in India, memsahibs going on about the grandeur of their lives in the empire, their husbands in clubs repeating Poona yarns and tiger talk and 'little Gurkha' anecdotes. The India bores came in various guises: MPs droning on in the House of Commons, soldiers reminiscing about the frontier, anglers insisting that fishing for mahseer was more exciting than trying to catch salmon. Some returned to their colleges and haunted High

---

* One of the exceptions was the talented Mabel Batten (see above, p. 315) who flourished after her return from India. In England she resumed her musical life, composing songs, playing the piano and performing in concert as a mezzo soprano. Elgar, Fauré, Delius and the young Percy Grainger all wrote songs for her, and a scent made of verbena and white lilac was specially made for her by Atkinsons in Old Bond Street. In her fifties Mabel fell in love with the lesbian writer Radclyffe Hall and, after the death of her much older husband in 1910, they lived together in Cadogan Square. In 1916, while gently reproaching Hall for her sexual infidelities – which drew a furious response from the writer – she suffered an apoplectic fit and died a few days later.[35]

Table for the rest of their lives. In the case of Sir Evelyn Howell, who returned in 1932 and lived to be ninety-four, this meant four decades. The obituarist of Emmanuel College, Cambridge, where Howell became an honorary fellow, was respectful of his subject's knowledge of the frontier and his career as governor of Baghdad, Resident first in Waziristan and then in Kashmir, and foreign secretary of the government of India; he related how (in collaboration with Olaf Caroe) he had translated the poems of Khushal Khan, but he declined to mention, perhaps tactfully, that he was a jackal-hunting enthusiast and author of the 'Peshawar Vale Hunt Song', which was sung to the tune of the 'Eton Boating Song'. Yet a slight sense of exasperation can be felt in the description of him 'discoursing on oriental languages' or quizzing 'a don on an unexpected point of philology or literature', and of the old boy bicycling down the towpath to watch the boat races and behaving as if 'the fortunes' of the rowing eights were 'an index of the health of the whole college'. Revelations that he could 'exchange compliments . . . in Latin hendecasyllables or elegiacs', and that he translated Khushal Khan not only into English but also into Latin Horatian metres, suggest that he was a clever old thing with insufficient opportunities to use his talents. The fellows were grateful to him, however, for revising the college address list.[36]

An Indian judge who visited London in the 1890s was struck by the enthusiasm people showed when they spoke to him about India, of their fondness for its people and the places where they had spent their careers: they seemed to 'pine' for India even more than they had pined for England when they were abroad.[37] The British who went to India certainly did a lot of pining. After living in 'the murk and fog and cold of England', the daughter of one Company officer recorded, 'even the burning plains of India' became 'dear in the memory'.[38] In India, observed Walter Lawrence, one longed for the 'pleasant pastures of England', and when one found them one yearned for the colour, the romance and 'the aromatic breezes of the coral strand'.[39] In India the British had found places that reminded them of Devonshire and had tried to create enclaves of Britishness in the Hills; now, when descending a hill down a lane in Devon, they might be reminded of 'the choicest corners of the old Coonor ghat'.[40] Earlier, Devonshire had been part of Fanny Parkes's disappointment when she returned to England in 1839. The cows were fine, the sheep were fat, and the verdure was rich, but everything after India 'must appear small by comparison', and the county was not as hilly as she remembered.[41]

Many people in Britain seemed to develop a romantic sensibility which they may not have been aware of in India, feeling nostalgic for the twilights and for sleeping under the stars, remembering the scent of frangipani or the smell of smoke from a village by the Ganges, recalling the fall of monsoon rain on parched skin and its smell on parched dust, evoking the sights that again seemed so vivid, fruit bats hanging from the branches of dead mango trees, women in coloured saris plucking tea in bright green fields, cattle being driven back to the villages at sundown, 'cow dust time'. Even such words as 'the Frontier Mail' – like 'the Flying Scotsman' – could bring a lump to the throat. And it was not only a middle-class nostalgia. Our friends Clemens and Swindlehurst may not have experienced the feeling – or at least they did not write about it – but others did, including another we now know well, Private Richards. After his return in 1909 the Welch Fusilier acknowledged that English bacon and other food tasted delicious after India, but his 'delight with home' soon 'wore off', and he was longing to be back with his battalion in the tropics, listening to the 'croaking of the bull-frogs and the buzzing noise made by the tropical insects'; he even missed the 'howling of the jackals' at night. Richards applied to go back, and when informed that, as he was now a reservist, he could not rejoin the Colours, he thought seriously of joining a regiment bound for India under a false name; it was the fear of arrest and the thought of doing a recruit's training all over again that deterred him.[42]*

Bert Rendall of the Somerset Light Infantry was another soldier who could not forget the East. In his nineties his living room at Yeovil was still cluttered with Indian brassware and bric-a-brac, Gurkha kukris, engraved vases and candlesticks in the form of cobras; views of the Khyber Pass, Landi Kotal and other places on the frontier hung on the walls, and a sideboard displayed sepia photographs of Rendall in uniform, the khaki serge he wore in the Murree Hills and the battledress of the later Home Guard.[43] In his novel *Coming Up for Air* George Orwell

---

* Richards did manage to rejoin his regiment at the outbreak of hostilities in 1914. He spent almost the entire world war on the Western Front without being seriously wounded and wrote (with the help of Robert Graves, a fellow fusilier) his account of the conflict, *Old Soldiers Never Die* (1933). Its success encouraged him to write a memoir of his Indian service, *Old Soldier Sahib*, published in 1936.

wrote of lower-middle-class interiors in the 'colony' of British repatriates in Ealing with their carved teak furniture and brass trays and
'photographs of chaps in sun-helmets'. A grade higher in wealth
and class meant the addition of hunting trophies, skins on the floor
and antlers on the walls, the head of a tiger or a panther grimacing in
a glass case, something made from an elephant (an umbrella stand perhaps) or a crocodile (maybe a desk blotter). General Pearse, who retired
in the 1880s, was proud that the head of the biggest sambur he had ever
shot presided over his dining room in Cheltenham; James Best found it
reassuring that his 'big buffalo' should look at him every evening from
the top of his stairs as he went to bed.[44] A few tried to recreate India –
rather than British India – and to do so in a less carnal way: one couple
returning from Kalimpong gave their Cotswold farmhouse a 'distinctly
Tibetan interior'. Olaf Caroe, who had retired jobless to Sussex, tried
to reproduce 'a little piece of Kashmir' in his garden. Regarding the
Mughal Gardens as 'perhaps the ultimate terrestrial paradise', he and
his wife planted some of the same trees, including the chenar and the
deodar, and hoped they had 'won a smile from Nur Jahan', the Mughal
emperor's wife.[45]

In 1787 the *Calcutta Gazette* said it was sorry to hear of 'the great dis-
respect in which East Indians' were held in Britain.[46] The paper was
referring to those nabobs who had survived India and returned to Britain with enormous fortunes. Some of their unpopularity could be
ascribed to envy of their wealth and the power it gave them; some to
their ostentatiousness, the brashness of their manners, their bright
and gaudy coats, the rather vulgar ways of displaying their wealth; and
some of it was the result of snobbery, the attitude of inalienable
landed wealth towards fortunes made 'in trade', especially when accumulated by dubious means. Yet even if these attitudes made them
resentful and encouraged them to stick together socially, nabobs were
successful men, in worldly terms, who in most cases achieved what
they had sought: with their fortunes they could buy houses and estates
and parliamentary seats. Many of them also became directors of the
East India Company.

In subsequent centuries repatriates seldom returned with fortunes or
the ability to exert influence on national affairs. A few senior Civilians
received colonial governorships, and Charles Metcalfe administered

both Jamaica and Canada. Yet none before Independence was given an important diplomatic position except Mortimer Durand, a former foreign secretary in India, and none reached the cabinet, though Anthony MacDonnell, a former lieutenant-governor, became a controversial under-secretary for Ireland (1902–8). Writing before the appointments of Durand and MacDonnell, Alfred Lyall stressed that Metcalfe had been the only man to 'have made any sort of success in any time of life unconnected with India'. Bartle Frere's failure in South Africa had been 'very significant'; although undoubtedly a success as governor of Bombay, he had blundered disastrously as governor of the Cape when he provoked the Zulu War of 1879. Continuing his criticism of the repatriates after India, Lyall pointed out that in 'parliamentary waters' they could 'only just manage to swim'.[47] As these were intelligent men with Indian achievements to their name, the most likely explanation for their failures is that India was so vast an undertaking and so debilitating a place that they were physically and mentally too exhausted to cope with further challenges.

At Independence the Foreign Office opened its doors to younger Civilians and Politicals, men still in their thirties or early forties; a number of them duly became ambassadors, although, apart from Humphrey Trevelyan in Moscow, seldom in the senior embassies. The Colonial Office was also receptive, especially to those who wished to go to Africa: several former officers and officials joined the colonial administration in Kenya, the Sudan and both Rhodesias.

In the late summer of 1947 the boxwallah Wilfrid Russell was up at Gulmarg, playing golf with Politicals and officers in the Indian Army, men who had spent their entire careers in India and who were now enjoying a last holiday in Kashmir 'before departing with their guns, their fishing rods and dogs to Kenya and Rhodesia'.[48] For those who feared Britain might be too small, too constricting – and without much for them to do – Africa seemed an exciting alternative: it had space and opportunities and a role in the empire that in the 1940s looked as if it would last longer than it actually did. One could become a game warden or run safaris or continue soldiering by joining the Sudan Defence Force. Yet most went out to farm, and it was a natural transition for tea planters in Assam to become coffee-growers in Kenya: Ursula Graham Bower settled there because her husband had been a planter before the war. Some of these enterprises were evidently successful: at the Nairobi

Agricultural Show Colonel Terence Conner, formerly of the Burma Military Police, won the cup for the best wheat grown in East Africa six years in a row.[49] Yet many people did not stay in Kenya beyond the Mau-Mau years. Although some also left Rhodesia after the 'unilateral declaration of independence' in 1965, one ex-Indian Army officer stayed. Described by a former colleague as 'an ardent supporter of Ian Smith', he barricaded himself in his farmhouse on the Zambesi border and 'lived there surrounded by dogs, rifles and barbed wire'.[50]

Politicals who had spent their professional lives being transferred from post to post within and beyond the Indian frontier sometimes found it difficult to concentrate on a single country in later life. Jack Bazalgette was one of these restless individuals. After Independence he went to Venezuela as an employee of Shell, then to England to work for Dr Barnardo's Homes, then to Istanbul to work on a refugee project for the World Council of Churches, and later to Beirut for more work among refugees. Restlessness followed him into retirement. Deciding that they did not want a permanent home, he and his wife gave what-ever possessions they had to their children and bought themselves a motor caravan in which to live and travel for the rest of their lives.[51]

Back in Britain there were some natural positions for retired Civil-ians to retire to. One was the Home Office, which in early 1947 sent an official to India to interview possible candidates under the age of forty-five; P. D. Martyn, whom we have met at breakfast,* was one Civilian who made the transfer. Another billet, in earlier times, was the India Office. While it employed only a small number of bureaucrats, distin-guished former Civilians could be appointed to its Council, which supervised the activities of the government of India, congenial and not very exacting work, although Alfred Lyall complained that it had the same savour as 'chewed hay'. A less natural place for them, certainly in the eyes of other MPs, was the House of Commons. Retired Civilians were almost bound to be mediocre election candidates – elderly, out of touch and ill informed about domestic politics – and, if victorious in spite of these drawbacks, they almost invariably became poor parlia-mentarians, long-winded speakers with little understanding of debate. As Curzon unsuccessfully warned one aspiring candidate, the retired Civilian 'inevitably gravitated into a parliamentary bore'.[52]

---

* See above, p. 354.

A more promising second career was in academia, for there at least repatriates would be teaching or writing on subjects they knew about: it was logical for a former jungle wallah to join the Forestry Commission in Britain prior to becoming the professor of forestry at Oxford. As we have seen, several political officers in Assam became distinguished anthropologists at Cambridge and SOAS, and a number of retired Civilians were appointed to the Readership in Indian History at Oxford. Another logical occupation was language teaching, especially at universities preparing students for the ICS. An Oxford probationer going to Madras in the 1920s would be taught Tamil or Telugu by Sydney Roberts, a former judge at Cuddalore, while one aimed for Bombay would be taught by C. N. Sneddon ICS who, according to an Indian probationer, spoke Marathi like 'a dear old Brahmin pandit in Poona'.[53] A less obvious post, which Civilians filled with surprising frequency, was that of bursar of schools and universities: St John's College, Oxford, made a habit of recruiting from this source. Perhaps it was the Civilians' reputation for probity and administrative efficiency that made them so popular. Penderel Moon joined the ICS in 1929 when he was a fellow of All Souls College; he worked in India for many years after Independence and then returned to All Souls as a fellow and bursar in 1965. The principal fruit of his retirement, *The British Conquest and Dominion of India*, is one of the longest books ever written on the subject; it was published in 1989, two years after his death.

At Independence some Indian Army officers managed to get themselves transferred to the British Army. Geoffrey Bamford had gone into the Lancashire Fusiliers in 1927, had subsequently joined the Indian Army, and was welcomed back to his Fusiliers in 1947. Yet there were not many places, especially in the infantry, in an army quickly shrinking in the aftermath of the Second World War. Infantry officers from India who wished to continue soldiering often had to become gunners.[54] In 1947 there were few openings too in the police, though in earlier times two inspector-generals in Bengal had become commissioners of the Metropolitan Police in London. Yet between the wars a number of policemen who worked as successful decrypters and interceptors of Russian radio traffic were brought from India to work in MI5 and the Secret Intelligence Service (MI6).[55] Two of them, Alistair Denniston and John Tiltman, were leading code-breakers at the Government Code and Cypher School at Bletchley Park.

Repatriates from India were returning to a country where there were not enough jobs for them; they had after all gone away in the first place because they thought their prospects were better abroad. On their return some might go into banking or business or the law, but not in large numbers and seldom with great success: they were usually too old-fashioned, too out of touch and insufficiently qualified. Many retired officials knew this and, unless they still had children to educate, did not aim high; some were content to become magistrates or join the county council; others found congenial and fairly undemanding jobs such as handicapper at Newmarket, rowing correspondent of *The Times* and curator of the Ipswich Clock Museum. The commonest dream of the official, sweating in Calcutta or baking in the mofussil, was to acquire a smallholding in England and become a farmer. Raising pigs in Cumberland or Red Poll cattle in Somerset had their attractions, but nothing could compete with the vision of an apple orchard, to live in an old rectory, as F. L. Brayne did in Norfolk, and plant fruit trees in a sixty-acre glebe. Not all such agricultural ventures were successful, fortunately perhaps in some cases. On his retirement from the ICS in 1947, Philip Mason tried to combine writing with farming fifteen acres of marginal land in Dorset. The smallholding took up most of his time but gave little in return, and after a struggle he abandoned it and moved his family to London to concentrate on literary work and a job as director of the Institute of Race Relations. His books on British India (in two cases published under the pseudonym Philip Woodruff) are among the most sensitive and well written of those produced by a former Indian administrator.

Repatriates did not usually decide to live in the places where they had been born and brought up, even if family members still lived in them. Nabobs, needing to be close to East India House and Westminster, often based themselves in Mayfair, in the 'nabobery' around Harley Street, from where they could saunter down to the Haymarket to eat curry dishes at the Norris Street Coffee House. Naturally they wanted to have country houses as well, but they usually bought or built these near London, in Berkshire (sometimes known as 'the English Hindoostan') or in Surrey. Although the nabobs had acquired and retained Indian tastes, they had no wish to build homes inspired by Indian architecture in Britain. Their archetypal house was Basildon Park in

Berkshire, built for Sir Francis Sykes with a Palladian exterior and neo-classical rooms. Among nabob homes only Sezincote in Gloucestershire, bought by Charles Cockerell and remodelled by his brother with the advice of Thomas Daniell in 1805–7, is a recognizably 'oriental' building, with 'Hindoo' and 'Mahomedan' motifs on the exterior and stone Brahmin bulls and a Hindu temple in the garden. Yet even Sezincote's interior is classical and Georgian.

London was also the natural base for repatriates of later eras, especially the more ambitious ones, although these rarely aspired to Mayfair. Most of them settled in the west, in Bayswater (dubbed 'Asia Minor') and South Kensington (sometimes known as 'the Anglo-Indian quarter'). When contemplating his retirement, Alfred Lyall used to worry about being a forgotten 'old fogey' living in a small house in Westbourne Grove; in fact he became a popular figure in society and lived in Kensington in the area around Queensgate and the Cromwell Road, where several former lieutenant-governors of the Punjab also settled. Those who had work in London but wished for less noise and bustle went to suburbs such as Sydenham and Beckenham. There was no particular pattern to suburban settlement except that the most popular places were south of the Thames.

Living in the south of England was the general preference for repatriates, whether in London or in the southern counties. The main exception to this was people working in industry: those from Halifax and Accrington who had gone to run the mills at Kanpur tended to retire to Yorkshire and Lancashire.[56] Most others preferred to be in the south, either because they wished to be in or near London or because they desired the warmer climate and lighter winters of the south coast. A belief in the healthy benefits of sea air and sea-bathing persuaded many to settle on the coast and to form colonies in Eastbourne, Hove and St Leonard's. The favourite retirement counties for retired Civilians were Surrey, because it was close to London, and Devonshire, perhaps for the opposite reason. The last seems to have been a favourite abode for men who did not wish to do much else with their lives except go downhill gently and with dignity, playing a sort of sub-squirearchical role while, as the Civilian Reggie Partridge was described by his granddaughter, 'disliking everything new, modern or complicated'.[57]

A survey of ICS members who had joined the service in the last decades of the nineteenth century reveals that their favourite retirement towns were London, Dublin, Oxford (mainly for work), Cheltenham (mainly for leisure) and Camberley.[58] Few lived in East Anglia, and even fewer had settled anywhere north of Worcestershire. Dublin contained a number of them, especially from Madras, but Edinburgh and Glasgow had very few. Scotland as a whole presents a mixed picture. Its nabobs tended to retire to London but soothe their consciences with donations to ancestral places north of the Border. William Fairlie gave part of his indigo profits to 'good causes' in Kilmarnock; John Forbes built a lunatic asylum in Aberdeen.[59] After fifty-four years in India, General Low retired in 1858 but could not face the idea of living in Scotland: he visited his estate in Fife during the summer and lived in Kensington for the rest of the year until in his eighties he gave up both and settled on Brixton Hill.[60]

Yet that is only part of the story. William Tweedie, a political officer who had served very uncomfortably in Baghdad,* had no difficulty about retiring to his home in Dumfriesshire, where he became a JP. Fraser Noble, who was one of the last members of the ICS, had gone to school in Nairn and decided to retire to that town; he had got a double first at Aberdeen University and decided to return there also, becoming a lecturer and later its vice-chancellor. It was natural too for landowners who had bought or saved estates with money acquired in India to wish to enjoy them in person. John Johnstone, Scotland's richest nabob, bought several estates with the fortune he had made in Bengal; he duly retired to Scotland and died at one of them, Alva in Clackmannanshire. In the next century John Stewart of Ardvorlich returned to India (where he had been born) to make money not to buy new estates but to save his family's ancestral one on Loch Earn. He duly did so, after thirty-five years in Kanpur, and retired there.

STAYING ON

In 1977, a few months before he died of cancer, Paul Scott won the Booker Prize for his novel *Staying On*. Unlike the four volumes of his great quartet, it is a short and humorous work, a tragicomedy about a former Indian Army officer and his wife who after Independence had

* See above, p. 185.

'stayed on' and later retired to a hill station, not because they particularly liked India but because they had got used to it and believed they could live more comfortably there on his salary (from a Bombay commercial firm) and later his pension than they could in Britain. The novel was made into a moving television film, the couple memorably played by Trevor Howard and Celia Johnson, and has helped leave the impression that the 'stayers-on' were a handful of officers and their wives who did not return to Britain in 1947.

In fact the British had been 'staying on' in large numbers since the eighteenth century. Old men in the Company days had made their homes there, often with Indian wives and a sprawling family. For William Gardner 'the summit of happiness' was what he had in India: his beloved begum plus 'new books, a garden, a spade, nobody to obey, pyjamas, grandchildren [and] tranquillity'.[61] Why would he wish to abandon all this for a long and hazardous sea voyage followed by life in a chilly country where he would now feel a stranger? Before the Mediterranean route to India was opened, old generals and colonels often thought it too much trouble to go 'home': in the first third of the nineteenth century many died after living for over fifty years in Bengal without having seen Britain since they were teenagers.[62] Surgeons and civil servants of the EIC also remained in India after their careers were over: W. A. Brooke went out as a Writer in 1768 and died at Benares in 1833 at the age of eighty-one. Even men beyond the Company's radius often found life in India too congenial to abandon. After a career sailing as a 'free mariner' in the East Indies, John Pope returned to Bombay and became the city's sheriff before he died there in 1821. His contemporary, the artist Robert Home, arrived in India in 1791, became the court painter at Lucknow, and retired to Kanpur, where he died in 1834 at the age of eighty-two. Almost all professions contained men who had found their niches in India and did not wish to leave them. We have already met George Faulkner, the canal engineer in Orissa whose culture was English, who spoke no language except English, yet who was determined to live and die at his home in India.[63]

At any time before the twentieth century the majority of Britons who stayed in India consisted of former private soldiers and NCOs, men who at the end of their service would begin a new profession and then retire on their army pension. Of a group of nine former Company soldiers working in Madras in 1787, one was 'in trade', one kept a 'punch-house', one ran a livery stable, two were in the arsenal, another two worked in schools, and a further pair was in the service of the nawab of Arcot. A century later, the range of post-military occupations would have expanded to include work on the railways and in the police.

In the 1840s Captain Hervey observed that 'our old European soldiers' were 'very partial to Bangalore' and that those 'attached to native women' liked to retire there. It seemed to him a sensible system until he went to Cuddalore, another retirement station, where he witnessed the 'poor old fellows' living in an 'abject' state with their 'black or tawny' wives; they had no employment and little to do and, instead of using the circulating library, they clustered around the 'skittle-ground and arrack-shop' where they gambled, squabbled and then went 'reeling home in a disgraceful state of intoxication'.[64]

The East India Company encouraged old soldiers 'attached to native women' to retire to certain designated places, usually in or close to a cantonment. This custom continued long after the Company's demise, and not just for private soldiers with Indian wives. When Harman Luker retired from the Indian police in the 1890s, the family debate was not about which country to go to but which part of India to settle in, whether somewhere in the mountains or in the Plains or along the coast. There was no thought of them living in Britain. Although he came from Gloucestershire, Luker had lived in India for forty years, and his wife Ellen was a 'country-born' English woman who had never been to England. The eventual choice was a 'pukka brick' bungalow at Dinapur on the Ganges, a military station with several friends among the pensioners and potential husbands in the regiments for their three daughters.[65]

In a very different category of stayers-on were officers of the Indian Army who in 1947 remained, often from a sense of duty, to help deal with the chaos and tragedy of Partition. Although sickened by the sectarian massacres and demoralized by the collapse of civil authority, some 2,000 of them chose to remain in their posts. The 'handover' was not abrupt or indeed resentful, and it did not entail the rapid departure of all British personnel; one regiment, the Somerset Light Infantry, did not leave Bombay until 1948. The independent countries of India and Pakistan each appointed a British commander-in-chief, men who had been contemporaries at Sandhurst and who would have been in a

difficult position if war had broken out between the two new states.*
Pakistan also had British officers in charge of its navy and its air force
as well as a British chief of the general staff, who remained at his post
until 1951. While the most senior figures retired or were replaced in the
early 1950s, some younger officers stayed for longer. After Independence Colonel James Bell worked for the Pakistan Army as director of
military training at Rawalpindi and commandant of the Frontier Force
Regimental Centre at Abbottabad. He then became administrative officer of the Pakistan Air Force School and secretary of the Sind Club in
Karachi before he left Pakistan in 1960.⁶⁶

Independent India did not feel the need for so many British officers,
although it employed General Stable as quartermaster-general and it
kept General Lentaigne, a Gurkha officer who had commanded the
Chindits, as the commandant of its Staff College until 1955, when he
died; it also employed a British head of its navy until 1957. As by 1947
the ICS was half Indian, Nehru's administration did not require many
British civil servants except on the north-east frontier. Elsewhere it
invited a number of Civilians to stay on for a while, including Allan
Arthur, a Punjabi district officer who was also asked to work for Pakistan.† Chakravarti Rajagopalachari, the minister of education and the
arts in Nehru's interim government (1946–7), appealed to some civil
servants to remain in their jobs with the argument that India needed
their talent.⁶⁷ One who responded was Peter Gwynn, an Irishman with
Indian nationalist sympathies who served in Madras and Andhra
Pradesh until 1967. Yet the province where the British were most needed
was Assam, whose new government had few qualified administrators,
either as district officers or at a more senior level. Nehru appointed Sir
Ronald Lodge as governor in 1949, and T. S. Hayley was implored to
stay on as secretary to the Assam government in charge of rural development. Political officers for the tribal areas were also in demand, even
if they had retired and returned to Britain. Geoffrey Allen was back in
England, depressed by ration books, a dockers' strike and the difficulty
of finding a job, when the Indian government offered him the post of

---

* In 1948 General Douglas Gracey, Pakistan's second British commander-in-chief,
refused to obey the order of Mohammad Ali Jinnah to send his troops to combat Indian
forces in Kashmir.
† He refused both offers and went to work as a political officer in the Sudan.

political officer for the Balipara Frontier Tract. He did not hesitate. He and his wife went back and worked among the tribals until worries about his lack of pension persuaded him to take a job with the Indian Tea Association. On learning of his resignation, Nehru (who happened to be in Assam just then) tried to persuade him to change his mind by offering him Indian citizenship (with a pension), but Allen stayed with tea, moving to another post at Shillong and remaining there until he retired in 1970.[68]

Pakistan had proportionately fewer 'home-grown' ICS officers than India, and so its desire to retain – or bring back – British Civilians was stronger. It was also the view of the country's first leaders, Jinnah and Liaquat Ali, that British officials were needed to restore order and preserve stability in the aftermath of the vast refugee exoduses. In three of Pakistan's four provinces – West Punjab, East Bengal and the North-West Frontier – Jinnah appointed British former ICS officers as governor: he even cajoled Sir George Cunningham, the ex-rugby international, to come out of retirement in Scotland, where he was now rector of St Andrews University, to resume the governorship of the frontier province which he had held from 1937 to 1946.* If it was unusual for a post-colonial country to appoint officials from the ex-colonial power, at least Jinnah and Liaquat Ali were consistent in the matter. Four Agents to the Governor-General in Quetta – the virtual rulers of Baluchistan – were British, and so were five of the permanent secretaries in the government ministries. Wilfrid Grigson, a remarkable Civilian who had written a book on the Gonds of central India, was brought in as secretary of the Pakistan Refugee Ministry, first in Karachi and then in Lahore, but he was killed in an air crash soon afterwards.

The new civil service of Pakistan was proud to regard itself as the successor of the ICS, and for years its recruiting pamphlet referred to its predecessor as 'the most distinguished Civil Service in the world'.[69] In 1947 the new regime was keen to retain British Civilians at district – as well as gubernatorial – level, and it invited many to stay, even if only for a year or two, to help maintain stability. Liaquat Ali tried to lure Maurice Zinkin to Pakistan, but the brilliant Civilian from Bombay

* After Cunningham's second retirement, the Pakistan government appointed another Scot, Sir Ambrose Dundas, to the post.

was too much in demand: he turned down Liaquat Ali, the Colonial Office and the *Economist* in London in order to work for Unilever in India. Pakistan was more fortunate in its approaches to Alexander MacFarquhar, who served for several years as its commerce and education secretary, to Sidney Ridley, who remained secretary to the government of Sind until 1954, and to Roger Howroyd, who was enticed back from Africa to be a district officer, a revenue commissioner and later chairman of the Lahore Improvement Council. Edward Snelson, who had been called to the Bar before he joined the ICS in 1929, might have stayed in Pakistan indefinitely if he had not fallen out with the country's judiciary. Between 1951 and 1961 he was secretary to the ministries of law and parliamentary affairs and in that capacity was responsible for drafting much of the legislation needed for the new state; he also led the country's delegation to international conferences on the law of the sea. In at least one respect Pakistan must have been good for these four men: their average age when they died was ninety.

British Civilians also chose to stay on in East Bengal, which was about to become East Pakistan. When Stephen Hatch-Barnwell passed the ICS exam he was sent to Bengal (although it had been his last choice) and arrived there in 1933, when political terrorism was at its height. One of his duties was to act as a supplementary bodyguard to his district officer (the extremists' favourite target), walking behind him with his hand in his pocket, clutching a revolver. Yet he grew to love Bengal and wished to stay there after Independence. He could have gone to either side of the partitioned province, but he opted for Pakistan because it had greater need of civil servants and because it would have felt strange working with Congressmen who had spent decades trying to get rid of people like himself.

After he had made his choice, Hatch-Barnwell was transferred to Bakerganj, a delta district that included numerous islands in the Bay of Bengal and which was bound to be included in the new Muslim state. There, on 15 August 1947, this very tall, very thin, very English-looking gentleman lowered the Union Jack and cheerfully hoisted the Pakistani flag before giving an animated speech in Bengali to a crowd celebrating the occasion. Perhaps he felt relieved to be no longer the agent of a colonial power but a senior official of an independent country. As a district officer he began the process by which the mangrove forests of the Sundarbans were eventually protected; he then moved on to become director-general of grain procurement, and he ended up as chairman of the East Pakistan Agricultural Development Corporation, a job he left in 1966 after nineteen years as an employee of the government. He never regretted his decision to stay on, yet from time to time he reflected rather ruefully on the impoverishment it had caused him, especially when he and his wife were living in a 'most miserable little flat' in Dacca. As an officer in the ICS in 1940, he had owned a car, a motor-boat, two horses and a motor bicycle. Some of these he gave up during the war; the car he had to relinquish later because his salary lagged behind the rise in the cost of living in East Pakistan. By the 1960s, although he was earning as much as any other civil servant in the country, he could afford only a pushbike.[70]

In 1947 John Christie chose to remain in India not to continue his civil service career but because he and his wife 'had struck some roots in Delhi', and he wished to go on working there, first in business and later in industry. The independence of India and Pakistan did of course mean a huge change in the political and military structures of the Sub-continent: most of the British soldiers went back to Britain, and so did many of the administrators. Yet in other spheres not a lot changed, at least not for a decade or more. The year 1947 was not like the end of a great military struggle when the invaders are all expelled and their collaborators are rounded up and punished. Even in so sensitive a field as the judiciary, where ex-colonialists might be regarded warily and suspected of bias, judges carried on their careers and reached the top of their profession. Sir Arthur Harries, once a barrister at the Middle Temple, retired as chief justice of the High Court of Calcutta in 1959. William Broome, formerly an ICS officer and district judge, became chief justice of the High Court at Allahabad and remained there till 1972, after which he retired to Bangalore. He had a Hindu wife and, according to his obituarist, 'his commitment to India was complete'.[71]

Most professions were not greatly affected by the changes of regime. Missionaries continued to work in schools and hospitals, and the Oxford Mission and the Cambridge Brotherhood supplied bishops for the various Anglican sees, including the new diocese of Dacca. Both men and women stayed to work in the medical profession. At Independence officers of the IMS were offered the options of retirement or work in Pakistan, but not India, which had enough qualified doctors of its own. E. J. Somerset, professor of ophthalmology at the Calcutta Medical College, considered going to Pakistan but decided against because he 'rather expected it to fold up in chaos' and, if it did, 'bang would go' his pension. He then thought of returning to Britain, but patients he had amassed in his private practice in Calcutta begged him to remain. So he did and, although he was no longer employed by the college, their fees were able to sustain an agreeable life revolving around his clinic, his house, his clubs and his sport – golf on Wednesday and Saturday afternoons at the Royal Calcutta Club, where bearers were placed near the seventh and fourteenth holes to serve orange and lime juice to dehydrated golfers. The business community of the Bengal capital, both British and Indian, prospered in the 1950s, and several of Somerset's ex-IMS colleagues were also able to establish large private practices. He himself used to spend a few months in Britain every third year, and in 1961, in his mid-fifties, he decided to retire there. He had always thought the few old 'dugouts' who remained indefinitely in India 'looked rather pathetic', and he did not wish to become an 'old codger with no contemporaries'. There were also positive reasons to return to Britain: he needed to spend ten years working for the National Health Service before he could qualify for a pension, and he wanted to educate his daughters in a British school.[72]

One profession which in some ways became easier and more interesting after Independence was journalism. During the Raj British journalists often found themselves attacked by 'koi-hais'* for being too liberal and sympathetic to Indians, and by nationalists for being apologists for the empire. Now they could be unbiased commentators and reporters. As editor of the Calcutta *Statesman*, a paper he had joined in 1937, Ian Stephens felt 'specially suited to urge upon the two successor-states the necessity for something like mutual friendliness'. He loved both India and Pakistan although after a while he found it impossible to be impartial between them. Considering the Indians to be 'morally wrong' and the Pakistanis 'in the main right' on the Kashmir issue, he felt obliged to resign and move to Pakistan. He duly became director of the GHQ historical section at Rawalpindi, where he deplored the way

* The most reactionary Britons in Bengal were known as 'koi-hais' or 'qi-his' from the way they summoned servants in their homes or clubs. The phrase means, 'Is anyone there?'

that Pakistan's generals had adopted 'all too British' habits such as dropping in for 'evening whiskies'.[73]

One of his successors at the *Statesman* was Evan Charlton, who went to India in the mid-1930s only because he found the 'journalistic ladder in England . . . desperately over-crowded'; he had had no family connection or personal interest in India. Yet he soon fell 'in love with the colours, patterns and smells of the great northern Indian plains'. After serving in the Indian Army during the war, he returned to the *Statesman*, retiring as its editor in 1967; for him India and journalism had proved to be more interesting than the fate of the British Empire. So were they for C. R. Maundy, another ex-Indian Army officer, who became an editor of the *Illustrated Weekly of India*, a magazine read eagerly by anglicized Indians in the 1950s.

Another job that often seemed easier to perform after Independence was teaching. Leslie Goddard was typical of numerous schoolmasters who took up posts in the Hills in the early 1930s and remained there until they retired in the mid-1960s, in Goddard's case as rector (headmaster) of St Paul's School in Darjeeling. For him, as for others, 1947 was not a crucial moment in his career. J. A. K. Martyn was one of several British teachers who in 1935 helped start the Doon School, a public school for Indian boys at Dehra Dun; he became its second headmaster and remained in the post until 1966, when he retired in the town itself. Far from complicating his life, Independence helped it become 'much pleasanter than before'. Although Indians had never made him 'feel at all unwelcome', they now explicitly made him feel 'very welcome'; and he no longer had to live 'rather uncomfortably . . . in two different social worlds'. Moreover, as the school's prestige grew – and governors and generals came as guests to its Founder's Days – he could feel proud that his institution was now 'playing a more important part in the life of the country'.[74] Another teacher who believed passionately in the importance of his school was Major Geoffrey Langlands, who taught at Aitchison College at Lahore before setting up his own school at Chitral, high in the Hindu Kush. In 2013, at the age of ninety-five, he finally retired as headmaster, but he was so possessive of Langlands College and so resistant to the reforms of his successor, an Englishwoman, that he resumed control two years later and sealed the coup by persuading the interior ministry (headed by one of his former pupils) to cancel her visa. Only after a protest from the governors and the rest of the staff did he back down and allow her to resume her post as headmistress.[75] In October 2017 Queen Elizabeth sent the major congratulations on celebrating his hundredth birthday, ninety-nine years after the death of his father in the flu epidemic at the end of the First World War.

Independence did not provoke a crisis for British firms in India or an exodus of businessmen. There was no rupture. Although in 1946 Congress had threatened to take control of banks and nationalize industries, the party was more conciliatory to capitalism when it came to power. In the old presidency cities businesses flourished in the 1950s, and there were even some new opportunities, especially in Karachi, the first capital of Pakistan. Companies took on young men attracted more to post-colonial India and its low cost of living than to post-war Britain with its rationing and its Labour government. And the perks survived, with the clubs and the golf, the cheap servants and the spacious dwellings. In Bombay you could still go to race meetings or Gilbert and Sullivan concerts at the Gymkhana, though you could no longer drink at the Yacht Club, which lost its liquor licence in 1949 and did not get it back until 1961.[76]

Surprising though the success of British firms may have been in the 1950s, nobody should have been surprised that it did not continue into the 1960s. In the mid-1950s Congress decided to limit the activities of the managing agencies and to adopt a 'socialistic pattern' for its society and its economy. India was after all a poor post-colonial country with a government that believed it should tackle its problems with nationalization, protection, a planned economy and an enormous bureaucracy. The British and their businesses were thus hit by high taxation, work permits for foreigners, a drastic devaluation of the rupee in 1966 and the abolition of the managing agencies in 1969. All forms of British enterprise suffered from the changes. The Kanpur mills passed one by one into Indian hands, and the last of the British owners left India in November 1970. The planters had prospered in the 1950s, but land reforms in the south and government regulations everywhere persuaded them that they had no future. At the High Range Club in Munnar there were still enough planters in 1962 to hold golf tournaments between 'England' and 'Scotland', but most of them left soon afterwards.[77] In 1970 Adam Hare retired after managing tea gardens for thirty-two years in Sylhet in what was still East Pakistan though about to become

Bangladesh. Yet retirement did not always mean repatriation. One small burial ground in the Sylhet district contains the graves of Tam Arthur, a planter from Dundee who died in 1976, his mother-in-law, who had died the year before, and his son, who died in 1983.[78]

According to the British High Commission, the number of British residents in India halved in successive decades, from 28,000 in 1951 to 14,000 ten years later, to some 6,500 in 1971, though these figures presumably include only those who were registered with the High Commission.[79] The 'stayers-on', those who had been there since before 1947, declined (proportionately) more quickly from the 1970s, a consequence of old age and death, and in the early twenty-first century Hugh Purcell went to India to interview and write about some of the last of them. Almost inevitably he found 'eccentrics' and 'legendary figures' such as Bob Wright, once described by the *Hindustan Times* (with some exaggeration) as the 'most influential figure in Calcutta after Mother Teresa', a boxwallah who ran charities, represented the British in West Bengal, and saved the Tollygunge Club from collapse.[80] His wife Anne made a post-colonial career for herself as a passionate conservationist and a trustee of the Indian branch of the World Wide Fund for Nature.

Moving to Bombay, now known as Mumbai, Purcell went to the Yacht Club to meet Major Frank Courtney, who had come to India with the Royal Fusiliers in 1935, had fought with the 4th Indian Division in the Middle East in the Second World War, and had stayed on to work in radio. Although he had a house in Hampshire and a daughter in Monaco, the major preferred to live in Mumbai because he thought Indians were better carers of old people. Another Bombay resident with a home in England was Lieutenant-Colonel Graham Tullet, who was too young to be a stayer-on but who had been elected president of the Yacht Club in 2004 even though its 1,200 members were now all Indians except for himself, Courtney and one other person. Tullet's English home was in Somerset, and during the fox-hunting season he would often spend Friday evening drinking at the Dolphin Bar of the Yacht Club, board the KLM flight to Amsterdam which left at one in the morning, then fly from the Netherlands to Bristol and – with the help of the five-and-a-half-hour time difference – get to his house in time for breakfast before riding to hounds a couple of hours later.[81]

After Independence Paul Scott's fictional colonel, 'Tusker' Smalley, 'took a commercial job' with a British firm in Bombay, and fifteen years later he and his wife, Lucy, retired to a hill station. That was a natural pattern for men who were middle-aged in 1947 and who needed a job. Couples at retirement age – and widows at any age – were more likely to head straight for the Hills. Before hill stations, widows who wished to remain in India had lived in the Plains or in the more salubrious climate of Bangalore. Begum Johnson, whom we have already met, lived long and contentedly in old age in Calcutta. So, a generation later, did Mrs Hannah Ellerton, who, like the 'begum', outlived her husbands, became a matriarchal figure in society, and died at the age of eighty-five.[82]

Many women supplemented their widow's pensions by running boarding houses or renting out rooms in their homes to lodgers or 'paying guests'. From the middle of the nineteenth century, they usually went to the hill stations, though some retired to Kashmir, where they were unkindly known as 'the Yaks' because they wore 'shaggy fur coats of local manufacture'.[83] Some of these ladies were formidable memsahibs and very choosey about their lodgers. One of them, the widow of Major Bateman-Champain, was for a long time the leader of society at the hill station of Lansdowne, where she was accepted as the 'self-appointed guardian of ancient custom'; nobody contested her right to be escorted into dinner in the local Mess (the 3rd Gurkhas) by the senior officer present. Known as 'Mrs Fizzer', Mrs Bateman-Champain let rooms in her bungalow to one or two members of the 'Fishing Fleet' and made it her project to marry them off while they were staying with her, often to officers of the regiment. 'So skilled' was she that, during the years John Morris was with the Gurkhas, 'none of these maidens failed to catch her man'.[84]

Small colonies of stayers-on were established at many of the hill stations, among others Simla, Shillong, Naini Tal, Gulmarg and Darjeeling. Some people liked to retire to Dehra Dun, which had a good climate for gardening, and go up to nearby Mussoorie when the weather became too hot. Yet the most popular retirement stations were in the Nilgiris, where it never snowed. In the early 1920s a group of retired officials and boxwallahs known as the 'Coonor Octogenarians' were 'famous for their skill at Badminton . . . and their readiness to come down to the plains to meet an emergency or fill a gap'.[85] Yet even the claims of Coonor and Kodaikanal were not considered comparable to those of Ooty. Since the middle of the nineteenth century the summer capital of the south had attracted all kinds of pensioners, soldiers, planters, officials and clergymen, as well as widows. One forest officer retired there and was buried at his request in a teak wood he had planted nearby.[86] Funerals at Ooty might generally be small village-type ceremonies, but they could be a lot grander. When General Sir James Charlemagne Dormer died there in 1893, his body lay in state at his residence, and as the cortege made its way to the church to be met by the bishop, it was accompanied by gunfire salutes and the band of the Royal Scots playing the 'Dead March'; behind the coffin walked the general's favourite horse 'in full trappings with the boots reversed in the stirrups' – a custom at military funerals indicating that the deceased will ride no more.[87]

Ooty used to have a retirement colony of about a hundred families. After Independence some of these went to Britain, decided they had made a mistake and came back again, but many more left or died off over the next twenty years. When Molly Panter-Downes visited the place in 1966, she was told that the town still had 'about thirty families', but she soon realized that quite a few of these 'families' consisted of a solitary person. There were no young adults and no children except a few from the tea plantations near Coonor who came for tea at the Club on Sundays. Almost nobody ran a business except Mrs Carter, the wife of a retired tea planter, who made farmhouse cheeses from the milk of cattle grazing in the Nilgiri pastures.[88]

The stayers-on at Ooty may have kept their community alive for a few years after 1947, playing tennis, going to the Club, 'carrying on as normal'. But it became a sad place soon afterwards, inhabited mainly by the old, the lonely and the bereaved, people with nowhere else to go, men and women struggling on small pensions of diminishing value. Some seemed to survive only by adhering to a completely rigid routine, behaving as if the smallest deviation would make them lose their bearings and perhaps crack up. The only permanent resident in the hotel where Panter-Downes stayed was Miss Kathleen Myers, a former principal of St Mary's College in Madras who had retired to Ooty, where she was now the 'honorary secretary' of the Nilgiri Library, a red-brick Gothic edifice. Miss Myers ran her days according to timetables so regular that her fellow resident soon knew at exactly what time she would fold up her napkin, drive to the library, go for her 'constitutional' or set out for the bridge table in her tweed suit. On Tuesday, Thursday and Saturday she strode into the Club on the dot of half-past five to play bridge with the Club secretary and two other ladies; on Monday and Wednesday she played the same game at the Indian Union Club, and on Fridays she returned there for meetings of the Culture Circle, either to attend a lecture or to listen to gramophone records. Sundays had no unalterable schedule, but Miss Myers often went to the Assembly Rooms cinema to see 'some American trash'.[89] It was a routine designed to combat loneliness.

Khushwant Singh, the distinguished writer and journalist, recalled that he had known three types of English persons in India: those who had disliked the country, the dirt, the climate, the smells and indeed the people; those who had liked it for what it gave them – the sport, the servants, the standard of living – but who ignored the Indians; and those who had 'liked everything about India, stayed away from the racist clubs, went out of their way to befriend Indians and maintained contacts with them after returning to England'; some of these had also supported 'the freedom movement and stayed on in India after the country gained independence'. This last group may have been the smallest, but it was not negligible: Khushwant Singh admitted he was 'fortunate in knowing quite a few of this breed'.[90]

We have found numerous examples of people who decided in the course of their Indian careers that they did not want to return to Britain when they retired: India was now their home. A smaller number of men only realized that India should be their home after they had gone back to England. One of these was T. R. Bell, who went to India in the 1880s to work in the forests of the Bombay presidency, where he became chief conservator and pursued his passion for lepidoptery. In retirement he gave his butterfly collection to the Natural History Museum in London and worked there himself, an ideal pensioner's job, one might have thought. In fact Bell could not stand London or England, and he fled back to Karwar, a paradise for lepidopterists, and died there in 1948.[91] A few years younger than Bell, Loftus Tottenham was a Civilian who had spent his career working in the south. According to Humphrey Trevelyan, he was very partial to Malayali women and was 'reputed to have progeny all down the west coast'.[92] Whatever the truth of the report, he was an able and sympathetic civil servant. It was 'torture', observed Trevelyan, for him to retire to

Devon, where his sisters had prepared him a home at Paignton which they renamed Lofthouse. So he returned to India to become diwan or chief minister of the princely state of Pudukottai, where he died in 1946, leaving money for the poor of the place to feast every year on the anniversary of his death. However, according to his godson, Sir Stephen Egerton, the funds were diverted to the family of the executor and were soon exhausted.[93]

Khushwant Singh's third category had its origins more than a century before he was born, with men such as 'Hindoo Stuart' and William Gardner. The species may have become endangered soon after them, but it survived, revived and expanded between the world wars. And after 1947 there was no need for it to be threatened ever again. Rid of the encumbrance of empire, Britons could enjoy and appreciate India without having to apologize for being there. John Grigg, the journalist who renounced his father's title (Baron Altrincham), could become a friend of leading Congress politicians in a way that would have been impossible for his grandfather Harry (an ICS officer who was Resident of Travancore and Cochin) or his father, Edward, a politician who was offered the governorship of Bengal. And there was reciprocal relief on India's side: even its post-colonial historians, however critical of the Raj, were seldom Anglophobes at a personal level. Friendships and love affairs now could – and did – happen naturally, on a basis of equality, with rapidly diminishing disapproval on both sides. Freer from prejudice, sensibilities opened up and flourished. The Australian journalist Philip Knightley went to India in 1960, married an Indian woman and decided that 'everything in India tastes, smells and feels better because with the Indian way of life the senses are more alive'.[94]

No one, no group, no age can be representative of the British presence in India, initiated in the reign of the first Queen Elizabeth and culminating, at any rate officially, just before the reign of the second. This book has anyway been mainly about individuals, and India was a good place for individualism. It was also a good place for eccentrics, so my book ends with one who was very British, very pro-Indian and strongly opposed to the Raj.

J. B. S. Haldane, an Old Etonian Marxist and scientist, was twice wounded in the First World War before he went to India to convalesce. He loved the country, where he ate street food and drank unboiled water, but he decided not to return there until he 'could associate with Indians on a footing of equality'. Thirty-five years later, by now a very famous and versatile biologist, he went back, and in 1957 he and his wife, Helen Spurway (also a biologist), decided to move to India to work at an institute in Calcutta. He was soon learning Sanskrit, wearing Indian clothes, becoming a vegetarian, promoting 'non-violent biological studies' (i.e. without killing animals in experiments) and wishing that 'Gandhism [was] actively preached and practised in Britain'.

Haldane gave several explanations for his move to India, political, scientific and personal. On the political front he thought India was 'doing as much for world peace' as anyone else, and he found Jawaharlal Nehru a more sympathetic politician than any British leader. On the scientific side he felt that, while the West had become obsessed with technique and technology, India's diversity of fauna and flora offered new opportunities for field work and a more human and humane biology. As for the personal, that was the easiest to explain. He had worked for three decades at Oxford, Cambridge and London universities, and now he needed a more congenial climate to retire to and relax in. Above all he wanted to wear fewer clothes: to have spent 'sixty years in socks was enough'.*95

* In 1962 the Haldanes, who now had Indian citizenship, moved to Orissa, where he died two years later at the age of seventy-two. Helen stayed on and died in 1978 after she caught rabies while doing research in the forests of Adilabad.

Envoi

'I am a camera with its shutter open,' wrote the novelist Christopher Isherwood on the opening page of his book *Goodbye to Berlin*; at the moment of writing, the camera was 'recording' a man shaving in a window and a woman in a kimono washing her hair. In this book I have also tried to be a camera with the shutter open, not quite as 'passive [and] not thinking' as Isherwood claimed to be, but one that has allowed the men and women in these pages to come before the lens, to speak their lines and walk about the stage without too much direction from me. I have not tried to put forward a thesis or make a particular argument: this book is a social history rather than a political one, and it is about individuals rather than institutions. Yet as 'the British in India' is a controversial subject, some concluding reflections may be appropriate.

I am not going to attempt to set up scales or produce a balance sheet, to weigh indigo planters who tyrannized Indian peasants against doctors who saved Indian lives, or to balance the undoubted violence of British soldiers against the deeds of a famine worker or a builder of canals. British individuals went to India for many different reasons and did very different things when they got there. Some went out to make money – as businessmen do everywhere – and some went out to do what they could to improve lives, in a spirit of altruism, in a world where there were no United Nations agencies and no World Health Organization.

Imperialism, which usually means the conquest and exploitation of one people by another, involves deaths and injustices, but that does not mean that it did nothing positive during its 3,000-year history. Nor does it mean that all imperialists were bad people, though this has been the view of many distinguished intellectuals and academics of our era. One of these was the late Edward Said, whom I knew, liked and admired – though less so when he wrote about history because then he became dogmatic and a generalizer, rather than a scholar who allowed his research to determine his argument. His insistence that Irish people could never be English any more than Cambodians could be French[1] is refuted by some of the Irishmen in this book, who saw no contradiction in simultaneously being Irish nationalists and British imperialists. More pertinent to India was his assertion that in the nineteenth century 'every European' who wrote about the Orient was 'a racist, an imperialist, and almost totally ethnocentric'.[2]

Such views – and those of Said's many followers – are not only cocksure and sweeping but also fundamentally anti-historical, judging the past from the zeitgeist and morality of the present. If their exponents spent more time in the archives, they might discover Irishmen in India who were indeed very like Englishmen, and find Britons who were not racists and imperialists when they were writing about the place. And even if some Britons were both of these things – which were common to the age – they might not also be wicked human beings.

Complexity of motive is a theme permeating this book. British people might be imperialists yet decide on a course of action because religious, emotional or other factors outweighed their imperialism. Or they might recognize that they had a conjunction of motives which happily encouraged them to act as they did. When in 1911 the civil servant James Mackenna wrote his paper 'The Rhinoceros Beetle . . . and Its Ravages in Burma', he was hoping the work would be satisfying to himself, useful to the Indian government and helpful to the people of Burma. Greed and the quest for adventure are well-attested motives for young Britons setting out for India. Altruism has been largely forgotten, though it too is well recorded, not just in the memoirs of old people trying to justify their careers but also in the letters and diaries of young men and women describing the work they were doing at the time and about which they felt passionate and idealistic.

British officials in India too often pursued reforms with feelings of cultural superiority and a western Christian's scorn for Hinduism, its traditions and its adherents. They were frequently insensitive in their treatment of the Indian people and in their attitudes to local customs and susceptibilities. But was it really wrong of them to aspire to change some of those customs – to campaign against female infanticide, to abolish the burning alive of widows, to prevent Naga tribesmen from scalping the women and children of other tribes and bringing home their trophies in triumph? If an NGO worked for such things in some remote place today, would we not be applauding it?

Apologists for the Raj used to say that the British 'gave' Indians this and 'taught' them that, usually with reference to subjects such as cricket, liberalism, education, the English language, the civil service, the rule of law (and the quality of that law), even parliamentary democracy. The verbs were not well chosen, although 'bequeathed' is a reasonable word to use in two of these examples because the successor states of the Raj adopted the law codes and the civil service of the British with few changes after Independence. Sunil Khilnani has rightly written that 'democracy [was not] a gift of the departing British', but 'a concept of the state' was, and so was 'the principle of representative politics'.[3] Indians may not have received many 'gifts', but of their own accord they *used* British ways and institutions to transform their lives and to create and fashion their new nations. As the Indian sociologist André Béteille has written, the universities established by the Raj 'opened new horizons both intellectually and institutionally in a society that had stood still in a conservative and hierarchical mould for centuries'; these 'open and secular institutions' allowed Indians at last to question, among other things, 'the age-old restrictions of gender and caste'.[4]

The British did not 'teach' Indians liberalism – which had a long-standing, if fitful, tradition in India already – but in the nineteenth century they took certain decisions on matters of law, education and the English language which made it almost inevitable that an Indian version of it would be adopted on the Subcontinent. As the historian C. A. Bayly has written, 'Britain helped liberalism take root in India by institutionalizing it through schools and colleges, newspapers and colonial law courts, and thereby converted an entire generation of Indians to a way of thinking about their own future that led to today's Indian democracy.'[5] A great early leader of Congress, Gopal Krishna Gokhale, was a liberal as a result of his education at Elphinstone College in Bombay. The views of Mohandas Gandhi too owed much to British institutional influences, his years at the Inner Temple in London, his knowledge of English law, as well as his friendship with British liberals. Jawaharlal Nehru, a liberal both in his political sensibility and in his practice of secular democracy, had been a pupil at Harrow and Cambridge. He and his colleagues guided Indian nationalism towards that rare Asian phenomenon, an essentially liberal revolution: not communist, not fascist, not military, not even British – but liberal in an Indian fashion.

I have been visiting India over a period of nearly half a century and have never had a row – scarcely an argument – about the nature of the Raj. I have worked in several other countries, both in Europe and in Asia, but in none have I found it easier to make close and enduring friendships. Writing about the relationship between Britain and India today, the Indian historian Ramachandra Guha has said that it is of course political and economic, but it is social and cultural as well, and also *emotional*, adding that, 'of all relations between former colony and erstwhile empire, this one is the least acrimonious'.[6] No doubt the chief reason for this is the magnanimity of the Indian character, but another might be that British imperialism in India was not always quite so bad as its detractors (especially the home-grown ones) have claimed. There is, I realize, little hope of a consensus on the matter, but the best attempt at one that I have found was made by an Indian economist when he received an honorary degree at Oxford in 2005. His name was Manmohan Singh, and he happened to be his country's prime minister at the time.

Today, with the balance and perspective offered by the passage of time and the benefit of hindsight, it is possible for an Indian prime minister to assert that India's experience with Britain had its beneficial consequences too. Our notions of the rule of law, of a Constitutional government, of a free press, of a professional civil service, of modern universities and research laboratories, have all been fashioned in the crucible where an age-old civilization of India met the dominant Empire of the day. These are all elements which we still value and cherish. Our judiciary, our legal system, our bureaucracy and our police are all great institutions, derived from British-Indian administration, and they have served our country exceedingly well.

Glossary of Indian and Anglo-Indian Words plus Some English Words Used in an Indian Context

ayah – an Indian nanny or nursemaid

baba, baba log – child, child folk

babu – usually employed as a pejorative term for a semi-anglicized Hindu clerk

batta – an allowance for military officers on campaign

bearer – a valet, senior male servant

begum – a Muslim princess, a female ruler of an Indian state

boxwallah – a pedlar in Hindustani, later used to describe a British merchant or businessman

burra memsahib – the wife of a senior officer or official

burra peg – a large measure of alcohol, usually brandy or whisky

cantonment – a military station

chaprasi – a messenger or errand boy

charpoy – a string bed

chee-chee (or *chi-chi*) – disparaging term for the way Eurasians (later called Anglo-Indians) spoke English

chota hazri – a light and very early breakfast

chota peg – a single measure of alcohol, usually brandy or whisky

chowkidar – a night watchman or village policeman

chummery – a house shared by bachelors

Civilian – a member of the Indian Civil Service (ICS)

collector – a revenue officer, chief civil servant in a district

cutchery – a court house, sometimes a magistrate's office

dais – an hereditary midwife in rural India (now known as 'traditional birth attendant')

dak bungalow – a rest-house for officers and other travellers maintained by the Indian government

dandy – a sort of hammock on a pole carried by dandy wallahs

darzi – a tailor

Factor – a fairly junior civil servant in the East India Company

fakir – usually used to describe an ascetic, semi-naked Hindu devotee *furlough* – (from the Dutch *verlof*) long leave, usually first taken after eight years' service in India

ghazi – a Muslim warrior or 'fanatic'

griffin – a newcomer in his first year in India

Hills (the) – generic British name for the Indian uplands

hookah-burdar – a servant in charge of his master's pipe, or hookah

jampan – a sort of sedan chair carried by two pairs of porters, or jampannies

jezail – long-barrelled Afghan musket

jheel – a swamp

jirga – a council of tribal elders in north-western India

khansama – a butler, steward, sometimes cook

khitmutgar – a senior servant who waits at table

maharani – the wife of a maharaja

maidan – an open space in the centre of a town

mali – a gardener

mofussil – rural areas, 'up country'

munshi – a teacher or secretary

nabob – term for an eighteenth-century Briton who had made a fortune in India

nawab – a Muslim nobleman or ruler

palanquin – a covered litter, carried by porters, often used for long journeys

patel – a village headman

patwari – a village accountant and registrar

Plains (the) – generic British name for lowland India

Political – a member of the Indian Political Service (IPS)

punkah – a large cloth fan attached to the ceiling

punkah wallah – the Indian who pulls the rope of the punkah

purdah – the curtain screening women from the sight of male strangers

purdah nashin – a woman who is secluded 'behind the curtain'

raga – the melodic base of Indian classical music

rani – the wife of a raja

Resident – a senior member of the Indian Political Service stationed in a princely state

ryot – a peasant cultivator

sepoy – an Indian soldier in the ranks of the East India Company and later of the Indian Army

shikar – the pursuit of 'game' (e.g. hunting, shooting and fishing)

shikari – a hunter or a hunting guide

sola topi – a lightweight pith hat or sun helmet

sowar – trooper in the Indian Army cavalry

sweeper – the most menial of servants, a cleaner of lavatories

syce – a groom

tahsildar – a revenue officer in charge of a tahsil

tiffin – a midday snack or light early lunch
tonga – a light two-wheeled carriage, usually drawn by ponies
Vedas – the ancient, sacred Hindu books
Writer – a junior civil servant of the East India Company
zemindar – a large landowner and rent collector in Bengal
zenana – the area in a household where women were kept secluded

Notes

INTRODUCTION

1. BBC One, 2 October 2014   2. Matthews, 7   3. Dewey (1993), 14–16
4. Cobb, 17

CHAPTER ONE: NUMBERS

1. Kebbel, 529–34   2. Gilmour (1994), 363   3. Naipaul, 8, 18   4. John Strachey, 390   5. Hunter, 6; letter to *The Times*, 4 January 1878, quoted in Philips,
392; Pottinger, 192   6. From the introduction to Saumarez Smith, xii   7. Randolph Churchill, 332   8. Article by Brendan Lennard, published in Hobart
(Tasmania) in 2015, inserted into the obituaries volumes in the OIOC
9. Davenport-Hines, 67–9   10. Philips, 219   11. Spear (1998), 11, 29; Keay
(1993), 277–8   12. Marshall (1976), 180; Bayly (1991), 186; Yalland (1987),
70   13. Renford, 11, 15   14. *Census of India 1901*, vol. 1, 93   15. Panckridge
and Macalpine, 80   16. McCrae and Friends, 36   17. Griffiths, 189–91
18. Unpublished memoir in Viola Bayley Papers

CHAPTER TWO: MOTIVATIONS

1. Devine, 335   2. *South Park Street Cemetery*, 15   3. Clive Williams, 189–95   4.
Hickey, vol. 3, 328, 350   5. Hickey, vol. 3, 244   6. Hickey, vol. 3, 155   7. Hickey,
vol. 1, 130, 237; Hickey, vol. 3, 210; Hickey, vol. 2, 199–200   8. Tomalin, 282–7,
306–7, 313–14   9. Hansen, 15–16   10. McCrae and Friends, 93   11. Walter
Lawrence, 117–18   12. Monk Papers; Morgan, *passim*   13. Postle, 29–31, 34–7,
40–41, 125–7, 138   14. Margaret Verney, 50, 57–8   15. Grierson, vol.
6, 489   16. Devine, 252   17. Dewey (1993), 106   18. Obituary, *Daily Telegraph*,
13 November 1996; see also McCrae and Friends, *passim*   19. Campbell, vol. 1,
2   20. Rothschild, 18–22   21. Lindsay, vol. 2, 202   22. Yalland (1994), 98,
124   23. Lawson (1905), 28   24. Lawson (1905), 30–31   25. Speech in the
House of Lords, 22 January 1770   26. Jane Austen to Cassandra Austen, 18 April

1811   27. Rothschild, 46–7   28. Hickey, vol. 3, 236–7   29. Marshall (1976), 209   30. See EIC annual lists for the 1820s   31. Hickey, vol. 3, 156   32. Marshall (1976), 202   33. Combermere and Knollys, 215–16   34. Llewellyn-Jones (1985), 51, 66, 69, 80–83, 143, 163–5   35. Jacquemont, 72   36. Jacquemont, 10   37. Robertson, 15–16   38. See *Tribune*, 7 June 1898   39. Martin, 607   40. Symonds (1991), 46   41. Buchan, 93   42. Hunt and Harrison, 7   43. Ex-Civilian, 281   44. Interview with Martin Fearn in Edinburgh, 6 June 2006   45. Unpublished memoir, Hubback Papers   46. Beames, 233   47. Christie, 20–21   48. Macleod, 158   49. Jeffrey Cox, 34–7   50. Pinney (1990), 75   51. Gandhi, 46   52. Quoted in Moon (1989), 368   53. Macduff, 57–8; Fitzgerald, 12–21; Jeffrey Cox, 54   54. Farrington (1988), 182   55. Unpublished memoir, Welch Papers   56. Tyndale-Biscoe (1951), 22, 44–5   57. Bellew, 6–8   58. Dunsterville, 13–14; article in *The Times*, 27 August 2002; Prendergast, 36–7   59. Christie, 7, 17; Halliday, 9–10; *Indo-British Review*, vol. XXII, no. 2, 5; Humphrey Trevelyan, 10   60. Unpublished memoir, Shortt Papers; Tydd, 1; *Daily Telegraph*, 2 April 1988   61. Notes in Campbell and Shuttleworth Papers   62. Battye (1984), 210, 235   63. Draft memoir, in Bailey Papers   64. Note in Rice Papers   65. Rivett-Carnac, 12–13; Lyall to sister, 5 October 1882, Lyall Papers   66. Temple, vol. 1, 46; Elsmie, 55   67. Philip Williams, 3–5, 22   68. Unpublished memoir by A. G. N. Verity   69. John Morris, *passim*   70. R. C. B. Bristow, 18   71. *Chowkidar*, autumn 2007, 95; *FIBIS*, autumn 2013, 3; Wilkinson, 143; unpublished memoir in Meneaud-Lissenburg Papers   72. Information from Hugh Thomas   73. Andrew Roberts, 60   74. Bellasis, *passim*   75. Mount, 16–17   76. Baylis, 25–6   77. E. C. Cox, *passim*   78. C. A . Kincaid, 15; Woodruff, *The Guardians*, 220; Symonds (1991), 193   79. Hook, *passim*; obituary in *The Times*, 17 September 1990   80. *FIBIS*, spring 2016, 49–50   81. Drafts of memoir in Caroe Papers   82. Obituary in *Daily Telegraph*, 2 January 1989   83. Stevenson-Hamilton, 13   84. Birdwood (1941), 36; Dunsterville, 66–7   85. Ian Hamilton, 23   86. Charles Allen (1976), 36; Philip Mason (1978), 31   87. *Indo-British Review*, vol. XXII, no. 2, 138; Pearce, 2; Herbert Thompson, 39; *Indo-British Review*, vol. XXIII, no. 1, 27; Zinkin, 1   88. Currie, 113   89. Vickers, 5–7   90. Unpublished memoir, Porter Papers; Masters, 144   91. Philip Mason (1978), 68; Stevenson-Hamilton, 27   92. Unpublished memoir, Bradfield Papers   93. Robinson, 141–2   94. C. A. Kincaid, 36–7   95. Chazal, 1   96. Diary in Fryer Papers   97. Hansen, 1–2   98. Jennifer Ellis, 40   99. Diver, 11   100. Green Papers; unpublished memoir in Hardy Papers   101. Kaye (1997), 93   102. Renton, 149   103. Gailey, 329   104. Information from Ben Watson   105. *FIBIS*, spring 2016, 11–17   106. Hickey, vol. 3, 320; Hickey, vol. 4, 114   107. Unpublished memoir, Bowring Papers   108. Robb (*Sentiment ...*), note on 236   109. Mount, 230–32   110. Dalrymple (2002), 372n; Hilton Brown (1954), 62   111. Falkland, 94–5   112. Beveridge, 213   113. John Morris, 94   114. Gailey, 268–70   115. Jeffrey Cox, 5, 18   116. Lind, 58   117. Obituary in *Daily Telegraph*, 7 August 1991 118. Obituary in *The Times*, 9 December 1983 119. Yalland (1994), 390; Lind, 54–8 120. Maisie Wright, v, 12, 46, 52 121. Webb, 85 122. Maisie Wright, 41 123. Barr (1989), 129–32, 143–8 124. Beveridge, 213 125. 'Letters from a Governess' (Naida Tierney), BBC radio broadcast, n.d. 126. Barr (1989), 42 127. 'Barmaids in Calcutta', Curzon Papers, F111/280; Ballhatchett, 137–40 128. L/PJ/6/311 file 2082, APAC

CHAPTER THREE: ORIGINS AND IDENTITIES

1. Cohn, 435 2. Unpublished memoir in Meneaud-Lissenburg Papers; Beyts obituaries in *Daily Telegraph*, 12 December 1997 and 22 March 2001 3. Collett, 3–9, 45 4. Ashby and Whately, vii, 6, 19, 141, 153, 297, 311, 380, 386 5. Unpublished ms by Archibald Macnab in Macnabb Papers 6. Obituary in *Daily Telegraph*, 29 November 1997 7. See family notes in Glasfurd Papers 8. 'The Exiles' Line' 9. Holroyd, vol. 1, 29–30 10. Caine, 101 11. Holroyd, vol. 1, 13, 140–41, 228–35 12. Unpublished ms by Archibald Macnab in Macnabb Papers 13. George Birdwood, 9 14. Campbell, vol. 1, 8; Beames, 60; George Birdwood, 9 15. Campbell, vol. 1, 8 16. *Genealogists' Magazine*, vol. 6, 1932–3 17. Dewey (1991), *passim* 18. Dewey (1973), 269; Moore (1966), 90; Symonds (1966), 44 19. Compton, 281–2; Spangenberg, 19, 153 20. Dewey (1993), 163 21. Buettner, 178 22. *India Office List*, 1886 23. *India Office List* 1938; information from Anne Chisholm and the late Martin Fearn ICS; memo in Maynard Papers; Sifton to father, 18 October 1904, Sifton Papers; Dewey (1993), 203 24. See article by Ian Baxter in *FIBIS*, autumn 2013, 23–5; note in Shuttleworth Papers 25. Currie, 15, 113 26. See article by Joan Harris in *FIBIS*, autumn 2015, 18–28 27. Longford (1969), 322 28. John Fraser, 75 29. Wisdom and Hall, 35–57 *passim*; *Norman Wisdom*, a documentary directed and produced by Sally Norris, BBC Productions, 2008 30. Richards, 82; unpublished memoir, Clemens Papers 31. Gilmour (2002), 4 32. Currie, 15, 17 33. Walton, 22; L. Fleming, vol. 1, 117; Tydd, 103 34. Ashby and Whateley, 19 35. Coles, 1 36. 'Miss Youghal's Sais' 37. Coote, 253 38. Harrison, 27–35 39. Berkeley-Hill, 78–80 40. Purcell, 48–50 41. Furbank, vol. 1, 215 42. Panckridge and Macalpine, 52–3, 64 43. Hilton Brown (1954), 156 44. Yalland (1987), 57; Lovatt and de Jong, 15–17, 107–9 45. Slater, 39, 235, 254–5 46. Yalland (1987), 104–5, 228 47. Cook, 515 48. See articles by his granddaughter, Joy Rathbone, in the *Evening Echo*, January and February 1982 49. Brasted, 590 50. Cook, 518–19; Brasted, 398 51. Cook, 518 52. Butler to Francis Scott, 26 June and 21 December 1920, Scott Papers 53. Unpublished memoir in Clough Papers 54. Copley, 165–6 55. R. C. B. Bristow, 68 56. Norris (1996), 99–100 57. Fry, 207–8; J. Muir, 25–7 58. Unpublished memoir by Monica Clough in Clough Papers 59. Fry, 431 60. Powell, 21–7 61. Loch, *passim*

62. Devine, 260   63. May, *passim*   64. Piggin, 103   65. Jeffrey Cox, 235–6   66. Wilkinson, 58; Hickey, vol. 3, 171   67. Evan Cotton, 181–5   68. Campbell to Northbrook, 29 July 1873, Northbrook Papers   69. Pakenham, 20, 22   70. Rotary Club of Kodaikanal, 71; *Hindu*, 27 October 2012   71. Sengoopta, 73–92 *passim*   72. Hardinge to Erskine, 15 May 1934, Erskine Papers   73. Hope to Erskine, undated but spring 1939, Erskine Papers   74. Walter Lawrence diary 1900, Lawrence Papers; correspondence between Curzon and Hamilton, 1901, Curzon Papers   75. Curzon to Hamilton, 26 August 1903, Curzon Papers   76. Correspondence between Curzon and Hamilton, 1903, Curzon Papers   77. Jowett's speech at banquet in honour of Landsdowne, 1888, Jowett Papers; Asquith, 187   78. Wenlock to Elgin, 6 June 1994, Elgin Papers   79. Billy Gladstone to Elgin, 4 June 1894, Elgin Papers   80. Minto, 318

CHAPTER FOUR: IMPERIAL APPRENTICES

1. Danvers, 90   2. 'Languages of India' from the Statistical Office of East India House, 1852   3. Beames, 63   4. Unpublished ms, Bowring Papers; Campbell (1852), 265   5. Grant to mother, March 1856, Charles Grant Papers   6. Beames, 64–7   7. Beames, 64   8. Avril Powell, 53   9. Dispatch to Northbrook, 24 February 1876, L/PJ/6/24, file 1438, APAC   10. Eardley-Wilmot to Cranbrook, 9 January 1880, L/PJ/6/2, file 53, APAC   11. Instructions for the Guidance of Candidates selected in 1863, file E/355/62, APAC   12. Best, 278   13. Unpublished memoir, Hayward Papers   14. Unpublished memoir, Iris Portal Papers   15. Christie, 20–21; Hatch-Barnwell, 5   16. *Oxford* magazine, 15 February 1893   17. Unpublished memoir, Macnabb Papers; Hallam to Butler, 2 August 1886, Harcourt Butler Papers; unpublished memoir, Hayward Papers   18. Potter, 68–71   19. unpublished memoir, Pearse Papers   20. Beames, 91; Montgomery, 9   21. Unpublished memoir in Hayward Papers; unpublished memoir in Harcourt Butler Papers   22. Griffin, 523   23. Bartle Frere in Hilton Brown (1948), 229   24. Fergusson to Hartington letters, 1881–2, Fergusson Papers   25. Gilmour (2005), 65; Wedderburn, 102   26. Grey and Lawrence correspondence, April 1866, John Lawrence Papers   27. Smith to Pinnell, 4 April 1918, Pinnell Papers   28. Gordon, 72   29. Heathcote (1995), 160; Woodruff, *The Founders*, 283   30. Henry Tyler's unpublished memoir, Tyler Papers   31. Buettner, 178   32. Clay, 18, 33   33. Dunsterville, 57   34. Unpublished memoir of Maurice Henry, Henry Papers   35. Unpublished memoir by B. J. Amies, Amies Papers   36. Macduff, 46–9   37. From *Departmental Ditties and Other Verses*   38. Macduff, 49   39. Norris (2004), 42–3; note in Bruce Papers   40. Nigel Hamilton, 35   41. Wilkinson, 74   42. McDonald, 35–6   43. McDonald, 29   44. Anil Kumar, 127–30   45. Beames, 122–3   46. Unpublished memoir by H. E. Shortt, 7–8, Shortt Papers; Berkeley-Hill, 81–4   47. Unpublished memoir in Shortt Papers, 8

CHAPTER FIVE: VOYAGES AND OTHER JOURNEYS

1. Stephens, 15   2. Log of ship in Ms Eng. Misc. b.22, Bodleian   3. Note in biography files, OIOC   4. Evan Cotton, 174–5   5. Sutton, 27, 85–7; Games, 81; Hickey, vol. 4, 420   6. Evan Cotton, 60   7. Hickey, vol. 4, 458, 461; Bellew, vol. 1, 38–40; Evan Cotton, 54, 180   8. Hickey, vol. 4, 419 and vol. 1, 118, 150   9. Bellasis, 231–3   10. Unpublished memoir by Henry Tyler in Tyler Papers; Parkes, 355   11. Unpublished memoir by Henry Tyler in Tyler Papers   12. Evan Cotton, 137   13. Evan Cotton, 134–7; Hickey, vol. 4, 476–8; Millar, 23–7   14. Keay (1993), 167   15. Labey and Brice, *passim*; see also www.hmsconway.org   16. Evan Cotton, 126–8   17. Beames, 77; Woolf, 12; unpublished memoir by Monica Clough in Clough Papers; Furbank, vol. 1, 223   18. Baylis, 54; Chitty, 1   19. Edith Gubbins to sister, January 1903, Gubbins Papers; Furbank, vol. 1, 223   20. Rowan Hamilton, 1–2   21. Reed, 12; Lord Birdwood, 30; MacPherson, 38; Hill, 12; Baden-Powell (1915), 8–9; M. Butler to Isabel, 15 November 1896, Montagu Butler Papers   22. Fryer diary 1864, Fryer Papers; Thompson diary, Thompson Papers; Prendergast, 39   23. Charles Allen (1976), 42   24. Unpublished notes by Lady Chapman, Chapman Papers   25. Stephens, 130   26. Gilmour (1994), 216–17   27. John Morris, 192–3   28. Randolph Churchill, 394–5   29. Albert Hervey, vol. 1, 12; Fryer diary 1864, Fryer Papers   30. Letters from Madge Green to parents, October 1921, Green Papers; MacPherson, 42–5, 50   31. Unpublished memoir in Hayward Papers; Madge Green to parents, October 1921, Green Papers; unpublished memoir in Swindlehurst Papers   32. McMullan and Wilcox, 63–5   33. Edyth Gubbins to sister, January 1903, Gubbins Papers; Madge Green to parents, October 1921, Green Papers; MacPherson, 44   34. Mills, 15, 123   35. Swindlehurst memoir, Swindlehurst Papers   36. Swindlehurst memoir, Swindlehurst Papers   37. Hickey, vol. 1, 164–6; Albert Hervey, vol. 1, 21, 28   38. Beames, 78   39. Unpublished memoir in Clemens Papers; H. Robinson, 17; Swindlehurst memoir, Swindlehurst Papers   40. Maynard to mother, 24 November 1886, Maynard Papers; Stephens, 133; R. Slater in Hunt and Harrison, 18   41. Parkes, 174–8, 185–6, 284–5   42. Pemble, 133–8   43. Dewey (2014), *passim*   44. White, 38, 46, 77   45. Carritt, 116–18; MacPherson, 161; Christie, 42; Saumarez Smith, 10–31 *passim*   46. Ex-Civilian, vol. 2, 100–101   47. John Strachey (1894), 9   48. Lord Roberts, vol. 1, 13   49. Hickey, vol. 3, 171   50. John Morris, 209   51. Gilmour (1994), 211   52. Darling (1966), 19; Percy and Ridley, 283   53. Currie, 90; William Wright, 100   54. Swindlehurst memoir in Swindlehurst Papers; E. Lorimer to parents, 5 January 1912, Overend Lorimer Papers   55. Kerr, 1–2, 85, 105–7, 117   56. Arnold (1983), 149   57. Kerr, 77–8; Barr (1989), 116–18   58. Westwood, 73–4   59. *Indo-British Review*, vol. xxii, no. 2, 126; Christie, 77; Archer 97; note in Boyes Papers   60. E. C. Cox, 11   61. Rowan Hamilton, 38; unpublished memoir in Mrs B. Bayley Papers; unpublished memoir in Meneaud-Lissenburg Papers   62. Masters, 76   63. Baylis, 62–7; Butler to Isabel, 26 December 1891, Harcourt

Butler Papers **64.** Hilton Brown (1954), 276–8; Reid, 123 **65.** Captain Portal diary, October 1925, Captain Portal Papers; E. Colebrook diary, July 1931, Colebrook Papers; letters from Stanley to Erskine, June 1934, Erskine Papers **66.** Baylis, 40; letters from Le Bailly to mother, 1927–8, Le Bailly Papers; Pearce, 463, 480; Crofton, xiii; Fleming, vol. 1, 3 **67.** Note by Noel Tindal Porter, Porter Papers

CHAPTER SIX: WORKING LIVES: INSIDERS

1. Lovat Fraser, 260 **2.** Ex-Civilian, vol. 2, 252 **3.** Maynard lecture in Rawalpindi, 1913, Maynard Papers **4.** Christie, 45–6 **5.** Beames, 223–5 **6.** Ward to Wyndham, 15 September 1903, Ward Papers **7.** Pearce, 245–6 **8.** Sifton to father, 21 May 1903, Sifton Papers **9.** Beames, 122 **10.** Arnold (1993), 208-29, *passim*; Gilmour (2005), 208–10 **11.** Reid, 51; William and Mildred Archer, 38–40 **12.** Wakefield, 91–2 **13.** Horsley to father, 25 May 1890, Horsley Papers; Fryer to Elgin, 11 October 1895, Elgin Papers **14.** Butler to uncle, 11 February 1891, Harcourt Butler Papers **15.** Butler to mother, 20 May 1891, Harcourt Butler Papers **16.** Unpublished recollections in Wingate Papers; Reid, 44–5 **17.** Francis to Phelps, 19 August 1893, Phelps Papers **18.** Maynard to Murray, 20 March 1887, Gilbert Murray Papers **19.** Woolf, 180 **20.** Hunt and Harrison, 135 **21.** Hatch-Barnwell, 28 **22.** Francis to Phelps, 24 September 1893, Phelps Papers **23.** Yeats-Brown (1930), 97 **24.** Whish, 316 **25.** Reid, 135 **26.** Woolf, 247 **27.** Herbert Thompson, 96; Hatch-Barnwell, 83 **28.** Memo on appointments in Wenlock Papers **29.** Hickey, vol. 4, 341 **30.** Aberigh-Mackay, 41 **31.** Maconochie, 90 **32.** Woodruff, *The Guardians*, 196 **33.** Curzon to Cunningham, 23 January 1899, Curzon Papers **34.** Tupper, 315; Hamilton to Curzon, 20 October 1899, Curzon Papers **35.** Hamilton to Curzon, 23 January 1901; Curzon to Hamilton, 13 February 1902, Curzon Papers **36.** Christie, 61, 64 **37.** Christie, 66 **38.** Unpublished memoir, Hayward Papers; Darling (1966), 20 **39.** MacDonnell to the *Englishman*, July 1884, MacDonnell Papers; Kanwar, 45 **40.** Lyall letters to mother and sisters, 1871–4, Lyall Papers **41.** Note in Clerk Papers **42.** Lovat Fraser, 471–2 **43.** Coen, 37 **44.** Herbert Thompson, 46, 124–5 **45.** Walter Lawrence, 66, 73; Durand, 182–3 **46.** Walter Lawrence, 128, 142 **47.** Humphrey Trevelyan, 165 **48.** Humphrey Trevelyan, 154 **49.** Walter Lawrence, 60–62 **50.** Grigg to E. Grigg, 13 February 1893, Grigg Papers **51.** Chenevix Trench (1987), 19 **52.** Malleson to Mayo, 29 August 1869, Argyll Papers **53.** Wakefield 172, 177; Chenevix Trench (1987), 164; Lee-Warner to Durand, 9 May 1887, Durand Papers **54.** Gilmour (2005), 168–71 **55.** Chenevix Trench (1987), 56 **56.** Winston Churchill, 145-6 **57.** Letters from Tweedie to Durand, August 1885, Durand Papers **58.** Letters from E. Lorimer to parents, March–April 1911, Overend Lorimer Papers **59.** Godley to Curzon, 6 January 1899, Curzon Papers **60.** Gilmour

(1994), 269   61. Letters from E. Lorimer to parents, 1911–12, Overend Lorimer Papers   62. Gordon-Alexander, 280   63. Unpublished memoir by H. E. Shortt in Shortt Papers; unpublished memoir by Ernest Bradfield in Bradfield Papers   64. Macleod, 154; unpublished memoir in B. A. Amies in Amies Papers   65. John Morris, 76.   66. Notes in Crichton Papers, and obituary in the *Lancet*, 19 May 1984   67. Notes in Crichton Papers, and obituary in the *Lancet*, 19 May 1984   68. From notes in Leventon Papers   69. Unpublished memoir in Bradfield Papers   70. Unpublished memoir in Shortt Papers   71. Unpublished memoir in Bradfield Papers   72. Unpublished memoir in Bradfield Papers   73. Unpublished memoir in Bradfield Papers   74. Trevelyan, 154–5

CHAPTER SEVEN: WORKING LIVES: THE OPEN AIR

1. Shelden, 13–16   2. Singh, 126   3. *Indo-British Review*, vol. XXIII, no. 1, 28; unpublished recollections in Wingate Papers; Maconochie to Phelps, 4 June 1890, Phelps Papers   4. Christie, 58–9; Best, 127; Butler to uncle, 25 December 1897, and unpublished memoir, Harcourt Butler Papers; Butler to Scott, 15 October 1922, Scott Papers   5. Le Bailly to mother, 18 February 1930, Le Bailly Papers   6. Sifton to father, 25 October 1904, Sifton Papers; Anne Wilson, 52   7. Baylis, 110–11; Dawkins to mother, 4 December 1915, Dawkins Papers   8. Eden, xxi   9. Portal diary in Portal Papers; Colebrook notes in Colebrook Papers   10. Portal notes and diary, Portal Papers   11. Portal diary, Portal Papers   12. W. Lawrence diaries, 11 November 1902, Walter Lawrence Papers   13. Dawkins to mother, 17 November 1917, Dawkins Papers   14. Best, 65; Eardley-Wilmot, 175–6   15. Dawkins, 7–8, 24; Enid to mother, 14 December 1916, Dawkins Papers   16. Letters from Dawkins to mother, 1910, Dawkins Papers   17. Raghavan, 208   18. Talk by Dawkins at Little Baddow, 1937, Dawkins Papers; Best, 77, 312; Eardley-Wilmot, 14, 43, 111–12, 236–7; Currie, 130   19. Eardley-Wilmot, 20, 42; Best, 82, 107, 121, 130, 132   20. Eardley-Wilmot, 166–7   21. Horsley to father, 28 April and 4 May 1873, Horsley Papers   22. Best, 160–62, 184, 206–7   23. Letters from Chenevix Trench to aunt, July 1902 and December 1905, Chenevix Trench Papers   24. Unpublished memoir in Viola Bayley Papers   25. Coles, 16   26. Hansen 4–7, 67; S. M. Edwardes, 39–40, 118; unpublished memoir in Curry Papers   27. S. M. Edwardes, 85–7   28. Bombay Confidential Proceedings, Judicial Department, vol. 25, 1917 (P CONF 25) APAC; see also Chandavarkar, 198–205   29. Tydd, 101–2   30. Gillen, 17–25 *passim*   31. Steven Runciman, quoted in Shelden, 86   32. Crick, 101–2; Shelden, 115–27 *passim*   33. Robertson, 59–61   34. 'Remarks on the Corps of Madras Sappers and Miners', Shaw Stewart Papers   35. Stone, 16–18; Robertson 18–19, 63, 101, 111, 124; Arnold (1988), 113; Guy and Boyden, 184   36. Obituary in *The Times*, November 1918   37. Kerr, 79–80   38. Notes of Cyril Lloyd Jones and memoir by son, Lloyd Jones Papers   39. Robertson, 38, 40, 133; Crooke,

146–7 **40.** Beames, 225–6 **41.** Typescript by Colonel Oatts in Oatts Papers; Ritchie, 320 **42.** Ritchie, 318–21 **43.** Yalland (1987), 194 **44.** Waley-Cohen, 45–6; Yalland (1987), 195–6 **45.** Oatts typescript, Oatts Papers; Carstairs, 57 **46.** Sengoopta, 71; Beames, 148–50, 171–84 *passim* **47.** Renford, 49–50; Reid, 22; *Indo-British Review*, vol. XXII, no. 2, 45 **48.** 'The Tea Assistant in Cachar', 1870 manuscript essay by D. Fowlis in National Library of Scotland; Sanderson, 1; Achaya, 185–6; information on Knighton from Judy Urquhart **49.** Unpublished memoir in Clough Papers; Christie, 124 **50.** Renford, 54 **51.** 'The Tea Assistant in Cachar', 1870 manuscript essay by D. Fowlis in National Library of Scotland; unpublished memoir in Clough Papers **52.** Unpublished memoir in Clough Papers **53.** Beames, 292; Henry Cotton, 85, 157 **54.** Burton 21; Yalland (1987), 198 **55.** Henry Cotton, 157–8 **56.** R. and S. Wilberforce, vol. 4, 11 **57.** Fry, 186 **58.** Reid, 109; Ronald Johnston, 146 **59.** Piggin, 157–71 *passim*, 206, 224–5, 292 **60.** Journal of Beatrice Batty, ms Eng. misc. e. 103 (Bodleian) **61.** Mathews, 127–8 **62.** Welldon, 265, 291 **63.** Mary Lutyens (1961), 38 **64.** Note in Clerk Papers **65.** Beveridge, 44 **66.** Note on Rice family, Rice Papers; Richter, 292 **67.** Richter, 139–40, 290–91 **68.** Macduff, 77–90, *passim* **69.** Macduff, 96–7 **70.** Ward, 90 **71.** Datta, 193–5 **72.** Best, 16 **73.** Ballhatchett, 134–7 **74.** William and Mildred Archer, 72–3; Joan Allen, 124 **75.** Wald, 44–5; Rowan Hamilton, 87 **76.** 9 March 1843 **77.** Maitland, 156–7 **78.** Richter, 281 **79.** Macduff, 99–102 **80.** Beveridge, 360 **81.** Morling, 18 **82.** Morling, 19–21 **83.** Morling, 27, 43–8, 62, 67 **84.** Morling, 43, 49, 74, 140 **85.** Jeffrey Cox, 7–8, 18, 52 **86.** *Wilsonian* 2013–14, Mumbai, vol. 106, 12. **87.** Millar, 155 **88.** Andrew Porter (2004), 179, 260–61, 266; Jeffrey Cox, 189, 214 **89.** *Women's Christian College, Madras*, 1 **90.** Tyndale-Biscoe (1922), 257–9 **91.** Note in McCall Papers; 'Account of non-British Missionary establishments in India 1924–39' by K. M. Mullan (1972) in Roman Catholic Missions Box (CSAS); Reid, 112, 134; unpublished memoir in Shortt Papers **92.** Macduff, 163–4 **93.** Tyndale-Biscoe (1922), 266–70, 277–9, 292; Tyndale-Biscoe (1951), 50, 128 **94.** Tyndale-Biscoe (1922), 281, 296–9; Tyndale-Biscoe (1951), 65–6 **95.** Colyer Sackett, 105–6 **96.** Rosemary Fitzgerald in Pati and Harrison (2001), 111–12, 126, 129 **97.** See appendix in Bradfield Papers **98.** Best, 251–3 **99.** Jeffrey Cox, 67

CHAPTER EIGHT: THE MILITARY LIFE

1. Maurice Henry, unpublished memoir, Tatham Papers; Raghavan, 85 **2.** Candler, vii **3.** Albert Hervey, vol. 1, vi–vii **4.** Marston, 11–12; Staunton to Du Cane, 14 December 1885, Du Cane Papers **5.** Prendergast, 56–7, 62; Dunsterville, 78 **6.** Stevenson-Hamilton, 20–21; John Morris, 118 **7.** Unpublished memoir in Kirke Papers; R. C. B. Bristow, 23 **8.** Masters, 180 **9.** Philip Mason

(1986), 379; Johnston, 7   10. Hamid, 33, 43, 52–3, 130   11. Philip Mason
(1978), 79   12. Magan, 111   13. Lord Birdwood, 41   14. Unpublished memoir
in Meneaud-Lissenburg Papers; Hilton, 15   15. Gilmour (2002), 44–50   16.
Unpublished memoir in Clemens Papers   17. Unpublished memoir in Clemens
Papers; unpublished memoir in Meneaud-Lissenburg Papers; Wisdom, 36–
45   18. John Fraser, 83; Dodwell (1926), 79–80; Richards, 85   19. Unpublished
memoir in Meneaud-Lissenburg Papers   20. Unpublished diary (1919–20) in
Swindlehurst Papers; unpublished memoir in Clemens Papers; Richards, 85–
7   21. Unpublished memoir in Clemens Papers   22. Letters from Dowdall to
family, 1889–90, Dowdall Papers   23. Albert Hervey, vol. 2, 232   24. John
Morris, 82   25. Unpublished diary in Swindlehurst Papers; Dunsterville, 105;
Richards, 192; Wisdom, 56   26. Unpublished memoir in Clemens Papers   27.
ASCB Handbook, 1933   28. John Fraser, 94   29. Curzon to Hamilton, 13 June
1900, Curzon Papers   30. Baden-Powell (1915), 92, 96, 106   31. Richards, 180;
John Fraser, 111, 113; Dowdall to brother, 16 October 1890, Dowdall Papers;
programme in Oppenheimer Papers   32. Albert Hervey, vol. 2, 45, 153, 155,
229–32   33. Mills, 42–4, 47–8, 56   34. R. C. B. Bristow, 80   35. Unpublished
memoir in Clemens Papers   36. Mills, 47–8; Ian Hamilton, 43   37. Ian Hamilton, 43–4; Prendergast, 42; Richards, 223   38. Unpublished diary in Swindlehurst
Papers   39. Parkes, 88   40. Richards, 155–7; Masters, 173–4   41. Dowdall to
mother, 21 December 1890, Dowdall Papers   42. John Fraser, 83   43. Unpublished memoir in Meneaud-Lissenburg Papers   44. Philip Mason (1986), 212;
Baird, 166; Northbrook to Queen Victoria, 13 September 1875, Northbrook
Papers   45. Norris (1996), 89   46. Mills, 122; Richards, 79, 81, 129, 262–
3   47. Wald, 149–52   48. Albert Hervey, vol. 1, 328–35, and vol. 2, 2–3, 65,
114   49. Albert Hervey, vol. 1, 316, 320, 331–5, and vol. 2, 2–3,12, 26, 42   50.
Unpublished diary in Swindlehurst Papers   51. Richards, 110   52. Masters,
125–7   53. Unpublished memoir in Sweeney Papers   54. Courtauld, 265
55. Albert Hervey, vol. 1, viii   56. Dunsterville, 79, 124   57. Omissi, 208–19;
Marston, 37–43   58. Slim, 73–98   59. Ian Hamilton, 172–80   60. Randolph
Churchill, 226, 287–9   61. Randolph Churchill, 368, 372–3, 406   62. Letters
from Dowdall to family, October 1890, Dowdall Papers   63. Letters from Dow-
dall to mother, November–December 1890, Dowdall Papers   64. Memoir of the
expedition in Kirke papers   65. Lord Roberts, vol. 2, 53–7   66. William Wright,
79; Prendergast, 88   67. Prendergast, 70, 74–6, 88, 91; John Morris, 126–7   68.
Curzon to Chamberlain, 28 June 1902, Curzon Papers   69. Prendergast, 80–84;
Chenevix Trench (1985), 51   70. Johnston, 21; obituary of Evelyn Howell in
Emmanuel College magazine, 1971–2; Chenevix Trench (1987), 53, 98   71.
Norris (2004), 56   72. Warburton, 40–41, 107–12   73. Norris (2004), 86;
Cubitt-Smith, 55; Prendergast, 68–9; John Morris, 124   74. Cubitt-Smith, 55;
obituary of Evelyn Howell in Emmanuel College Magazine, 1971–2   75. Pren-
dergast, 82; Hilton, 94–5; Chenevix Trench (1985), 93   76. Masters, 26; Hilton,

104–5; notes in Caroe Papers 77. Webb, 129–30; John Morris, 125, 187, 215 78. John Morris, 125, 187, 215; Webb, 129–30 79. Albert Hervey, vol. 2, 159 80. Dunsterville, 241 81. John Morris, 82 82. Tuker, 1 83. Hamid, 67 84. John Morris, 218 85. Ian Hamilton, 61 86. Ballard, 50 87. R. C. B. Bristow, 68; John Morris, 77; Hamid, 'Passing it On' in 8202-20, National Army Museum 88. Lieutenant Haughton's diary, 1907, in Haughton Papers 89. Unpublished memoir in Pearse Papers 90. Prendergast, 45–6, 108 91. Ian Hamilton, 39, 96, 114 92. Randolph Churchill, 328 93. Chetwode circular, October 1931, Drew Papers 94. Albert Hervey, vol. 1, 69; unpublished memoir in Pearse Papers; Ian Hamilton, 38; Western, 202 95. Nigel Hamilton, 34 96. John Morris, 81 97. William Wright, 62–3; John Morris, 84–5 98. Cubitt-Smith, 122; John Morris, 85 99. John Morris, 86; Burton, 19 100. John Morris, 87; Dunsterville, 60, 65 101. John Morris, 87 102. Rory Muir, 52; Hickey, vol. 4, 190 103. Masters, 109 104. O'Dwyer, 128 105. Winston Churchill, 122 106. Chitty, 28; Cubitt-Smith, 42, 49; Dunsterville, 113; Dennis Kincaid, 209–10 107. Prendergast, 99; Charles Allen (1979), 107; Stephens, 175; Allen (1976), 149

CHAPTER NINE: INTIMACIES

1. Brodie, 51–2 2. Brodie, 51–2 3. Dalrymple (2002), 120–21; Saroop, 22–5 4. MacGregor, 296, 305 5. Nevile, 5 6. Ghosh, 68 7. Notes by Brigadier Bullock in Lady Lloyd Papers 8. Hickey, vol. 3, 213, 276, 327, and vol. 4, 26–7, 133, 140–41 9. Robb, *Sex* ..., 57 10. Robb, *Sex* ..., *passim* 11. Robb, *Sex* ..., *passim* 12. Yalland (1987), 45–6 13. Robb, *Sex* ..., *passim* 14. Hickey, vol. 3, 284–5, and vol. 4, 271–2 15. Notes from Brigadier Bullock in Lady Lloyd Papers; Ghosh, 125–6 16. By Durba Ghosh, cited in Dalrymple (2002), 52 17. Eden, 373; C. A. Kincaid, 5 18. Ghosh, 35–6 19. Sen, chapter 5 20. *Chowkidar*, spring 2012, 8, and autumn 2011, 128–9 21. Bulley, 116–19, 122–3 22. Lee-Warner, 295 23. Collis, 53 24. Hamilton to Curzon, 4 July 1901, Curzon Papers 25. Ballhatchett, 146–54; Crosthwaite to White, 5 October 1888, and Mackenzie note, 3 May 1892, White Papers; Fryer to Curzon, 1 June 1900, Curzon Papers 26. Ballhatchett, 149; Curzon to Fryer, 1 June 1900, Curzon Papers 27. Ballhatchett, 153–4; Hamilton to Curzon, 15 August 1901, Curzon Papers 28. Currie, 95 29. John Fraser, 117, 119 30. Brigid Allen, 16–17; Farwell, 102 31. Ian Hamilton, 40 32. Unpublished memoir in Amies Papers 33. Pamela Edith Condon. Information from her daughter Judy Urquhart 34. John Morris, 97 35. Hose to Phelps, 20 December 1887, Phelps Papers 36. From unpublished manuscript, Verity Papers 37. Beames, 73–6; unpublished memoir in Hayward Papers; unpublished manuscript in Verity Papers 38. Ritchie, 155 39. Martyn, 1 40. T. Zinkin, 6–13; obituary, *Daily Telegraph*, 29 May 2002 41. Hickey, vol. 3, 145–6 42. Information from Xan

Smiley, a grandson of the couple   43. Note in Shaw Stewart Papers   44. Yalland (1994), 130, 346; T. Zinkin, 102–3; Philip Hutchins, 19   45. Chisholm, 69, 77, 80, 183   46. Information from their daughter, Judy Urquhart   47. Berkeley-Hill, 105–6; Eden, 76; note by daughter in Maynard Papers; Tydd, 84   48. Lee, 89; note in Partridge Papers   49. *FIBIS*, spring 2016, 3   50. Unpublished memoir in Verity Papers   51. Townend, 45   52. Information from Ben Watson, son of the couple   53. Fleming, vol. 1, 132–4   54. Yalland (1994), 134   55. Jebb, 19–20   56. Pearce, 88–91   57. Letters to Bertha Tufnell (1901–2) in Gubbins Papers   58. Dunsterville, 157–8   59. Dunsterville 171–2; Prendergast, 106–7; R. C. B. Bristow, 65, 77   60. Unpublished memoir in Hayward Papers   61. Pearce, 417, 422   62. Gibson, 14–24   63. Letters from Lyall to his sisters, 1870s, Lyall Papers   64. Note in Lupton Papers; Butler to sister Isabel, 3 December 1892, Harcourt Butler Papers; information from Judy Urquhart   65. Young, 164   66. Anglesey, 60   67. Young, 165   68. Hickey, vol. 3, 187   69. Unpublished memoir in Hayward Papers   70. Keay (1993), 256–63   71. Edwardes-Stuart, *passim*   72. Hickey, vol. 3, 333   73. Wilkinson, 112   74. Panckridge and Macalpine, 54–5   75. Henry Cotton, 121; Baird-Murray, 41–2; *Chowkidar*, spring 2016, 53   76. 1937 diary in Bradfield Papers; Bolton, 134–5; Guha (1999), 124, 143, 167   77. Guha (1999), 198   78. Berkeley-Hill, 105–6, 109–10, 271, 331   79. Carritt, 73–4; *Indo-British Review*, vol. xxii, no. 2, 142   80. *Chowkidar*, spring 2008, 112   81. Beames, 88   82. Albert Hervey, vol. 1, 199–203; Lyall to sister Sybilla, 6 April 1856, Lyall Papers   83. Arnold (1979), 107, 112; Wald, 26–7   84. Unpublished memoir in Kellie Papers   85. Note by Brigadier Packard in Packard Papers; Richards, 216   86. Unpublished memoir in Clough Papers; Philip Mason (1978), 80   87. Chisholm, 56, 61; Vickers, 6–7   88. Curzon to Hamilton, 11 November 1901, Curzon Papers   89. Kaye (1990), 436   90. Curzon to Scarsdale, 11 November 1903, Curzon Papers   91. Beveridge, 345   92. Pearce, 12; Chenevix Trench (1987), 46   93. Robins, 88–9   94. Owens, 10; Robin Moore, 70   95. Du Cane to father, 3 May 1885, Du Cane Papers   96. Ridley (2012), 180   97. Longford (1979), 152, 162, 427   98. Gilmour (2002), 33   99. Gilmour (2002), 51   100. Civilian, 43–4, 236   101. Welldon, 219   102. Charles Allen (1976), 134; Humphrey Trevelyan, 177   103. Unpublished memoir in Harcourt Butler Papers; Humphrey Trevelyan, 122   104. David Verney, 24   105. Unpublished memoir in Pearse Papers   106. Kaye (1997), 271; Venning, 164–5; Clay, 90–91; Swayne-Thomas, 30–33   107. Masters, 150–51   108. Butler to Scott, 26 June and 1 October 1920, Scott Papers   109. Steel (1929), 124–5   110. Yalland (1994), 187   111. Edyth Tufnell to sister Bertha Tufnell, 16 January 1905, Gubbins Papers; Berkeley-Hill, 181   112. Perham, 61–5   113. Caine, 70–71.   114. Sriran V, 'Of Napier and Mrs Elliot', *Hindu*, 6 June 2013. Additional information from Sriram Venkatakrishnan to the author   115. Robertson, 109–10   116. Caine, 152, 162–8, 278   117. Lambert, 17–18   118. Richings, 2000; Morse, 108–9   119. Bonus to

Phelps, 10 January 1889, Phelps Papers **120**. Gilmour (2005), 151-2 **121**. Bonus to Phelps, 10 January 1889, Phelps Papers **122**. Conchman to Phelps, 30 October 1894, Phelps Papers **123**. Dufferin to Cross, 23 April 1887, Dufferin Papers **124**. Lyall to sister, 22 February 1887, and to brother, 4 October 1885, Lyall Papers **125**. Lyall to sister, 22 February 1887, Lyall Papers **126**. Griffin to Dufferin, 26 March 1887, Dufferin Papers **127**. Richards, 151-2 **128**. Wald, 154-5 **129**. Devereux, *passim* **130**. Sellon, *passim* **131**. McLynn, 32 **132**. Masters, 152 **133**. Berkeley-Hill, 130 **134**. Clark, 101 **135**. T. Zinkin, 10; Stephens, 162-3 **136**. Clark, 92 **137**. Simson, 6, 10, 30 **138**. Wardrop, 2, 53 **139**. Moray Brown, 307-11 **140**. Moray Brown, 322 **141**. Yeats-Brown (1930), 38 **142**. Butler, 98-9, 119, 152, 228-30 **143**. Carritt, 93-4; Martyn, 95; John Morris, 105-6 **144**. Havelock Ellis, 309-11 **145**. Havelock Ellis, 312-15 **146**. Unpublished diary in Swindlehurst Papers **147**. See notes compiled by M. Hardiment in Hardiment Papers **148**. Richards, 114, 184-8 **149**. Unpublished memoir in Meneaud-Lissenburg Papers **150**. Unpublished memoir in Meneaud-Lissenburg papers; S. M. Edwardes, 93-4 **151**. Quoted in *Discover NLS*, summer 2010, National Library of Scotland **152**. Levine, 206-7, 231; Havelock Ellis, 314 **153**. Ballhatchett, 132-3; Richards 277-8; Levine, 231-2; Department Annual Reports V/24/2297, APAC; Public and Judicial Department Annual Files L/PJ/6 1207, APAC **154**. Ballhatchett, 53, 59, 82-3; Hyam, 120-27 **155**. Kitchener memo, October 1905, PRO 30/57 **156**. Brodie, 66-70; McLynn, 40-45 **157**. Hyam, 32-5; Royle, 159; Gilmour (1994), 248 **158**. Carritt, 22-6 **159**. Note by Brigadier Packard in Packard Papers **160**. See notes compiled by M. Hardiment in Hardiment Papers **161**. Havelock Ellis, 311 **162**. Furbank, vol. 1, 224 **163**. Masters, 154 **164**. Hyam, 128-31 **165**. Furbank, vol. 1, 231-2; Hyam, 136 **166**. Furbank, vol. 2, 81-6

CHAPTER TEN: DOMESTICITIES

1. Maitland, 47, 110; Herbert, 31 **2**. Lawson (1905), 269-71 **3**. Curzon to Esher, 12 April and 12 June, 1901, Curzon Papers **4**. Lindsay, 12; Philip Davies, 51-60, 70-72 **5**. Norris (1996), 49-51; Staley, 13-14 **6**. Fleming, vol. 1, 6 **7**. Unpublished memoir in Clough Papers **8**. Charles Allen (1979), 60; unpublished memoir in Clough Papers **9**. Kaye (1997), 9 **10**. Raleigh Trevelyan, 492-3 **11**. Raleigh Trevelyan, 364; unpublished memoir in Clough Papers **12**. Waley-Cohen, 238-9 **13**. 1829 diary in Hannay Papers **14**. Unpublished memoir in Clough Papers **15**. Herbert, 55, 87, 149 **16**. Hattersley, 310-11 **17**. Hickey, vol. 4, 397 **18**. Maitland, 89 **19**. Losty, 41-2; Charles Allen (1976), 79 **20**. Beveridge, 182, 196 **21**. Unpublished memoir in Somerset Papers **22**. Grimwood, 49 **23**. Christie, 38; Tydd, 164; E. Lorimer letters to parents, 1911, Overend Lorimer Papers; Fleming, vol. 1, 149; Lady Lawrence,

368 24. Raleigh Trevelyan, 2 25. Fleming, vol. 2, 232 26. Yalland (1994), 300; Maisie Wright, 3 27. Unpublished memoir by V. Haig in Haig Papers 28. Lady Lawrence, 38; letter from Joseph Goudge in unpublished memoir, Goudge Papers 29. Durand, 318–19 30. Hunt and Harrison, 125 31. See correspondence in Calvocoressi Papers 32. Kenneth Harris, 78 33. Information from Stuart Proffitt to the author 34. Beveridge, 182, 196 35. Unpublished memoir in Davidson Papers 36. Baylis, 114–15 37. Stocqueler, 57 38. Muthiah (1992), 71–2 39. Hilton Brown (1948), 49–50 40. Fay, 181, 189, 234 41. Maitland, 48–9 42. Hilton Brown (1948), 53 43. E. M. Collingham, 68; Burton 17, 27; 'Wyvern', 1 44. Burton, 93–4; Lizzie Collingham, 115, 138–42 45. 'Wyvern', 1–2 46. Unpublished memoir in Somerset Papers 47. Hilton Brown (1948), 54 48. Ramaswami, 13 49. Murphy, *passim* 50. Burton, 102; E. Dawkins to mother, 29 March 1916, Dawkins Papers 51. Saumarez Smith, 34–5 52. Martyn, 116 53. Unpublished memoir in Davidson Papers 54. Prendergast, 94–5, 111 55. Ex-Civilian, 16–17; Philip Hutchins, 45 56. Waley-Cohen, 106–7 57. Moray Brown, 254 58. Albert Hervey, vol. 2, 184–5; Pemble, 183 59. Burton, 101–7; Bellew, 101 60. Letters 1922–3, Green Papers; Bolton, 85; Craig, 162; Fleming, vol. 1, 4 61. Robert Bristow, 114 62. Hickey, vol. 2, 163 63. Hickey, vol. 2, 130, 138 64. Western, 265 65. Woolf, 116 66. Rory Muir, 102 67. Seton-Karr, 38–9 68. Slater, 156 69. Darling (1966), 152–3 70. Advertisement in the *Pioneer*, 1 April 1923 71. Henry Cotton, 85 72. Raleigh Trevelyan, 274; Philip Hutchins, 18; Rivett-Carnac, 91; Prendergast, 51 73. Speech by Sir Patrick Playfair, Calcutta Dinner, 1913 74. Darling (1966), 74–5 75. Lagavulin's advertisement in *Traill's Indian Diary*, 1897 76. Winston Churchill, 140–41 77. Naida Tierney, 'Letters from a Governess' (1920–22), BBC radio broadcast, date unknown 78. Hilton Brown (1954), 294–5 79. Unpublished memoir in Boyes Papers; Alexander McGill 1868 diary, McGill Papers 80. Scudamore, 1–3 81. Information from the Partridge family; documents in Partridge Papers 82. Beames, 185 83. Scudamore, 11–12 84. Walter Lawrence, 58 85. E. M. Collingham (2001), 96; Buettner, 53, 61; Brendon, 165; Fleming, vol. 1, 50 86. Pinney (1999), 583 87. Buettner, 29 88. Fuller, 195 89. Buettner, 29 90. Battye (1997), 20 91. Maitland, 236 92. Dalrymple (2002), 381, 389–90 93. Robb, *Sentiment . . .*, 169 94. Lovatt and de Jong, 104, 109 95. William and Mildred Archer, 112 96. Millar, 95–7 97. Penner, 95–6 98. Elsmie, 352 99. Fleming, vol. 2, 353 100. Shoma Chaudhury, *Tehelka*, 28 February 2004; obituary in the *Guardian*, 2 December 2016 101. Fay, 211; Kaye (1990), 113 102. Lady Wilson, 203–4 103. Shields, 31, 42 104. Venning, 88 105. Henry Cotton, 125 106. Hilton, 203–4 107. Notes in Glasfurd Papers; Stephens, 16 108. Stokes to Mrs Currie, 20 September 1874, Stokes Papers 109. Headington, 13 110. Scudamore, 31–2 111. Raleigh Trevelyan, 1 112. Christie, 7–8 113. Shelden, 28–31 114. Ross, 68 115. Buettner, 148 116. Mangan, 63 117. Letters from Horsley to father 1891–2,

Horsley Papers   118. Arnold (1979), 109   119. Craig, 38, 43; Arnold (1979), 107   120. Craig, 41; Fleming, vol. 1, 259–60   121. Kaye (1990), 195; Fleming, vol. 2, 15; Ross, 68   122. Documents in the Dunphy Papers   123. Craig, 47–50   124. Ashby and Whately, 280–84, 297   125. *Simla Times*, 19 October 1933   126. Brendon, 136, 138   127. Wendy M. Davis, 58   128. Grimwood, 44   129. Bennett (1995), 188–9   130. Herbert, 174   131. Wendy M. Davis, 86–8.   132. Fleming, vol. 2, 251   133. Chisholm, 6–7

CHAPTER ELEVEN: FORMALITIES

1. Wakefield, 2–3   2. Misra, 37   3. Charles Allen (1976), 101; Fleming, vol. 2, xv; Jones, 9   4. Lady Lawrence, 209   5. Tandon, 160   6. Monroe, 32   7. Knightley, 24   8. Dewey (1993), 204   9. Rowan Hamilton, 34   10. MacMillan, 156   11. Randolph Churchill, 301   12. Wakefield, 3   13. Battye (1997), 32; list in Oppenheimer Papers   14. Welldon, 233–4; Lady Lawrence, 292   15. Halliday, 222   16. Bayley to H. Butler, 31 October 1910, Harcourt Butler Papers   17. Programmes in Blakeway Papers   18. Kaye (1997), 47, 68; Stevenson-Hamilton, 53   19. Raleigh Trevelyan, 435; Lyall to sister, 20 July 1883, Lyall Papers   20. Seton-Karr, *passim*   21. Norris (1996), 87–8   22. Hickey, vol. 2, 191; Jacob, 165   23. Stevenson-Hamilton, 39–42   24. Erskine to Hope, 19 April 1939, Erskine Papers   25. Sandeman, 26   26. David Verney, 104; programmes in Colebrook Papers   27. Beames, 128   28. Townend, 108–9; Purcell, 224   29. H. Trevelyan, 111; Wakefield, 7   30. Kipling, (1991), 38   31. Maitland, 48–9   32. Green to mother, 14 November 1921, Green Papers   33. Menus in Allanson Papers   34. Menus in Oppenheimer Papers   35. Menus in Bell Papers and Russell Papers   36. Notes in Thompson Papers; Macleod, 136   37. Gee to Phelps, 29 December 1889, Phelps Papers   38. Humphrey Trevelyan, 112   39. Furbank, vol. 1, 223–4; Dewey (1993), 147; Ackerley, 12, 30; John Morris, 98–9; Dewey (1993), 158   40. Dewey (1993), 158; Spear (1988), 89; Ghose, 252; Falkland, 91; Webb, 183   41. Berkeley-Hill, 354   42. Woolf, 12, 17–18, 24–5, 31–2, 37–46 *passim*, 151   43. Reed, 17–18; Panckridge and Macalpine, 11–12   44. Panckridge and Macalpine, 72, 77   45. Panckridge and Macalpine, 90   46. Civilian, 51   47. Ramaswami, 21   48. Townend, 118; Allen (1976), 105; unpublished memoir in Bradfield Papers; Slater, 46–7   49. Muthiah (1992), 68–70   50. Maconochie, 90; letters from Le Bailly to mother, 1927–8, Le Bailly Papers   51. Fleming, vol. 1, 408, and vol. 2, 70   52. *Letters from an Indian Judge*, 22–3   53. Dennis Kincaid, 215   54. Vickers, 7   55. Carritt, 88; unpublished memoir in Somerset Papers   56. Letter from Lady Bernard, 25 July 1901, White Papers   57. Panckridge and Macalpine, 72–3, 93   58. Prendergast, 112–13   59. Monroe, 38   60. H. Butler to father, 1 December 1891, Harcourt Butler Papers   61. Letters about Balasore Club in MacDonald Papers   62. Reed, 150–52; Robert Bristow, 192; Chazal, 9   63. Documents in Erskine Papers   64. Spear (1998), 130–34   65. Dalrymple (2006),

85–91   66. Margaret Verney, 74   67. See numerous letters from 'griffins' in the Phelps Papers   68. Masani, 144   69. Beveridge, 96   70. Butler to uncle, 29 October 1891, Harcourt Butler Papers   71. Stephens, 334   72. Stephens, 174   73. Stuart, 58, 390–91   74. Nirad Chaudhuri (1967), 88   75. Butler to Phelps, 12 April 1893, Phelps Papers   76. Furbank, vol. 2, 98–9   77. Walter Lawrence, 215   78. Tandon, 204–11   79. Nirad Chaudhuri (1967), 120–27; Nirad Chaudhuri (1987), 363   80. Notes by Temple in Temple Papers   81. Guha (2002), 90   82. Speech at National Educational Conference, Ahmedabad, 2 August 1924   83. Ackerley, 8–9, 128   84. Darling (1966), 146   85. Rowan Hamilton, 99   86. Letter quoted in unpublished memoir in Harcourt Butler Papers   87. Letter quoted in unpublished memoir in Harcourt Butler Papers   88. Moss King, 48   89. Goschen 1924 diary, Goschen Papers   90. Minto, 275; Walter Lawrence, 139–40   91. Butler to father, 2 November 1898, Harcourt Butler Papers   92. Henry Cotton, 66 · 93. Wilfrid Blunt (1909), 216–17; Beveridge, 210–11; Sifton to father, 19 March 1903, Sifton Papers   94. Beames, 247   95. Amit Chaudhuri, 152–4   96. Information from Sunanda Datta-Ray. See also his essay, 'Didima: The Last Ingabanga' in *The Penguin Book of New Writing from India*, vol. 1, New Delhi, 2005   97. Unpublished memoir in Donaldson Papers; Humphrey Trevelyan, 214   98. Furbank, vol. 2, 106   99. Spurling, 136–40, 280–91, 301–2

CHAPTER TWELVE: SINGULARITIES

1. Darling (1966), 31   2. Beames, 103   3. 1940 diary in Dunlop Papers; Woolf, 31–2, 120   4. Darling (1966), 51, 175   5. Lyall to sister, 7 April 1865 and 7 January 1868; Bayly (1999), 360; Elliott to Elgin, 25 April 1895, Elgin Papers   6. Letters of 1916–17 in Goudge Papers; information from Anne Chisholm   7. Hunt and Harrison, 126   8. Darling (1966), 51, 75; Mason (1978), 80, 147; Emily Lorimer to father, 15 April 1911, Overend Lorimer Papers   9. William and Mildred Archer, 82–4; Le Mesurier to Phelps, 10 March 1895, Phelps Papers   10. Bence-Jones (1973), 105   11. Francis to Phelps, 3 May 1896, Phelps Papers   12. Avril Powell, 256–7   13. L/PJ/6/63, file 118, APAC   14. Seal, 135   15. Glancey, 12–13, 105–10   16. Williams and Potts, 5–6; Gopal, 120   17. Francis to Phelps, 24 September 1893, Phelps Papers   18. Saumarez Smith, 41, 50, 71   19. John Morris, 91–2   20. Moon (1989), 428   21. Gilmour (2005), 259–61   22. Guha (2013), 222   23. Carritt, 125–94 *passim*   24. Beveridge, 384   25. Darling (1966), 117–18; William and Mildred Archer, 4–5   26. Appendix C in 'Memorandum drawn up by the ICS Central Association', n.d., EUR F/173/14, APAC   27. Brodie, 274   28. Brendon, 183   29. Unpublished memoir in Clough Papers; Philip Mason (1978), 92   30. Pearce, *passim*   31. Parkes, 293, 311   32. Lady Wilson, 83–4, 155   33. Lady Lawrence, 70, 120, 229   34. Murphy, 139; Dewar, 7   35. Margaret Verney, 97; Macleod, 20   36. Unpublished

memoir in Davidson Papers; letter to mother, 16 April 1923, Green Papers; Lady Lawrence, 56, 161; Walter Lawrence, 50   37. Albert Hervey, vol. 2, 293; Rivett-Carnac, 92–3; letter to mother, 4 January 1922, Green Papers; Falkland, vol. 1, 283   38. Jacob, *passim*   39. From letters to her parents 1911–20, Overend Lorimer Papers   40. Letters from Clinton and Enid Dawkins to their parents, 1909–19, Dawkins Papers   41. Barr (1989), 138–9   42. Letters from Madge Green to her parents, 1921–6, Green Papers   43. William and Mildred Archer, 11   44. Humphrey Trevelyan, 246   45. Gil Harris, 189–211 *passim*   46. Stuart, 295–9   47. Wilkinson, 83–4   48. Jeffrey Cox, 76, 225–9, 237   49. Henry Cotton, 143–4   50. Woolf, 237; Robinson, 65–76 *passim*   51. Norris (2004), 177–8   52. Walter Lawrence, 84, 102   53. Bower (1950), 136; Bower (1953), 4   54. Bower (1950), 231–7, 246–8   55. Bower (1953), 238   56. Guha (1999), 68   57. Guha (1999), 95   58. Guha (1999), 105   59. Guha (1999), 313   60. Walter Lawrence, 101   61. T. E. Lawrence notebook, Houghton Ms Eng 1252 (355)   62. Walter Lawrence, 100–102   63. Spear (1998), 59–60   64. Arnold (1979), 114–17; Bradley-Birt, 232   65. Norris (2004), 36–7; Richards, 251–5   66. Arnold (1979), 114   67. Dilke, 517–18   68. Arnold (1979), 120–23   69. Information in Erskine Papers   70. Sifton to father, 20 August 1903, Sifton Papers   71. Walter Lawrence, 100

CHAPTER THIRTEEN: AT EASE

1. Mildred Archer (1969), 640–41   2. Head, 5–6   3. Desmond (1982), 3–7; Ryan, 47–52; Fabb, 5–7   4. Fay, 192; Seton-Karr, 149   5. Pemble, 37, 42–5, 49–50, 65–6   6. 1924 diary in Goschen Papers   7. Reviews in W. Russell Papers   8. Price, 149–84 *passim*   9. Diver (1909), 23–4   10. Minto, 321   11. Durand to Northbrook, 25 June 1876, Northbrook Papers   12. M. Massey, 5; Audrey Carpenter in *FIBIS*, spring 2015, 4, 9   13. Pemble, 58, 65–6   14. Geoffrey Kendal, 74–84; Felicity Kendal, 4   15. Mount, 362   16. Thompson diary, 1900, Thompson Papers   17. Magan, 150, 206–7; O'Dwyer, 145   18. Maynard to mother, 24 November 1886, Maynard Papers   19. Bonus to Phelps, 27 January 1887, Phelps Papers   20. E. C. Cox, 180–82, 207, 278   21. G. O. Trevelyan, 153   22. Hook, 48   23. Magan, 124; Lord Roberts, vol. 1, 450   24. Unpublished memoir in Shortt Papers   25. Reid, 75; Maconochie to Phelps, 17 September 1890, Phelps Papers   26. Dowdall to mother, 21 April 1893, Dowdall Papers; unpublished memoir in Bowring Papers   27. Lawson (1868), 46; Younghusband diary, 3 March 1894, Younghusband Papers   28. Elsmie, 144   29. Henry Cotton, 115   30. Albert Hervey, vol. 2, 229–32.   31. Fleming, vol. 2, 47   32. Chettur, *passim*   33. Tikekar, 43–4; *Chowkidar*, autumn 2011, 127   34. Ghose, 44–5; Falkland, 142   35. Erskine to George V, 4 May 1935, Erskine Papers   36. Walter Lawrence, 128–9   37. Masters, 248   38. Chazal, 140   39. Kaye (1997), 270–71; Chenevix Trench (1987), 177   40.

David Verney, 120   41. Battye (1997), 24   42. Lady Wilson, 304   43. Currie, 127   44. 'William the Conqueror'; Chitty, 81; Battye (1997), 96   45. Masters, 319   46. *Indian Daily Telegraph*, 24 September 1901   47. Mangan, 33–6   48. *ASCB Handbook*, ii   49. Pearce, 372; information in Green Papers; Chettur, 57   50. *History of the 5th Royal Gurkha Rifles*, 127   51. Lowell Thomas, 267–8   52. Townend, 118; Magan, 33   53. *ASCB Handbook*, 18, 20   54. Norris (1996), 73; Shelden, 115; Christie, 25   55. Guha (2002), 53–9   56. Albert Hervey, vol. 1, 274   57. Battye (1984), 166.   58. Jacob, 87   59. Hatch-Barnwell, 143   60. Le Bailly diary, 21 February 1928, Le Bailly Papers   61. Hatch-Barnwell, 28   62. Unpublished memoir in Hayward Papers; C. A. Kincaid, 52   63. Docker, 115   64. Guha (2002), 48   65. Guha (2002), 220   66. Unpublished memoir in Moore Papers   67. Glasfurd, 313; R. C. B Bristow, 73   68. Edward Blunt, 228–9; Maconochie, 26; Best, 160–61; unpublished memoir in Hayward Papers   69. *The Lahore Guide and Directory*, 1896   70. Minto, 60; Erskine to Brabourne, 2 December 1935, Erskine Papers   71. Moray Brown, 140–41   72. Burke, 166–74, 235–40   73. Christie 25; unpublished diary in Hely-Hutchinson Papers   74. See, for example, letters in the papers of Lord Goschen and Lord Erskine   75. Stanley to Erskine, 27 May 1934, Erskine to George VI, 29 December 1937, Hardinge to Erskine, 3 February 1938 in Erskine Papers   76. Unpublished memoir in Verity Papers; unpublished memoir in Shortt Papers   77. Moray Brown, 225   78. Minto, 60   79. Moray Brown, 109   80. 1908 diary in Haughton Papers; Baden-Powell (1915), 238   81. Moray Brown, 287; Burke, 320–39   82. Sanderson, 183   83. Newall, 236–7; Burke, 270   84. Sanderson, 379   85. Elliott, 38, 80; Moray Brown, 139, 226   86. Unpublished memoir in Frederick Bailey Papers   87. Fleetwood Wilson, 119–23   88. Unpublished memoir in Moore Papers; Woolf, 201; Charles Allen (1976), 116   89. Randolph Churchill, 295   90. Goschen diary, June 1924, Goschen Papers   91. Walter Lawrence, 57   92. Stanley to Erskine, 27 May 1934, Erskine Papers   93. Nair (1983), 175   94. Panckridge and Macalpine, 26   95. Goschen diaries 1924–5, Goschen Papers   96. Ex-Civilian, 114–15   97. Townend, 160–61; Tydd, 21; Shaw Stewart to wife, 3 August n.d. (1880s), Shaw Stewart Papers   98. Magan, 128   99. Randolph Churchill, 428–31; Winston Churchill, 133   100. Albert Hervey, vol. 2, 164–5; unpublished memoir in Bradfield Papers   101. Clark, 49–50   102. Diaries in Goschen Papers; Erskine to Hope, 19 April 1939, Erskine Papers   103. Hook, 23   104. Wardrop, 121–2, 239   105. Baden-Powell (1915), 37–8; Lord Birdwood, 60   106. Yalland (1994), 359–60; Lady Erskine-Crum in the *Field*, 6 September 1930   107. Yeats-Brown (1930), 144–6   108. Simson, 75   109. Wylie to Durand, July 1885, Durand Papers   110. Warburton, 198   111. Scott, 236   112. Warburton, 114–15, 144, 297   113. Newall, 281; Warburton, 137; Calcutta Tent Club rules, APAC   114. Note in Yeats-Brown Papers; Yeats-Brown (1937), 31

CHAPTER FOURTEEN: LAST POSTS

1. Wilkinson, 9   2. Unpublished memoir in Lloyd Jones Papers   3. Marshall (1976), 218–19   4. Nair (1984), 140   5. Dodwell (1926), 109–11   6. Philip Mason (1986), 174   7. Lord Roberts, vol.1, 5   8. Vincent Davies, 23   9. Yalland (1987), 277   10. Butler to father, 2 October 1891, Harcourt Butler Papers   11. Farrington and Radford, 95   12. Wilkinson, 184; Gailey, 117   13. Hewson, 16; Wilkinson, 201   14. Albert Hervey, vol. 1, 298–300   15. Hickey, vol. 4, 221, 230   16. Fleming, vol. 2, 126–7   17. Philip Mason (1978), 78–9   18. *Chowkidar*, spring 2009, 9   19. Harfield, 17; Heathcote (1974), 158   20. Wilkinson, 34–7   21. Captain Oldfield's unpublished memoir, Oldfield Papers; William Wright, 220   22. Jeal, 66; unpublished memoir in Kellie Papers   23. Volkers, 68   24. Robert Baylis in *Indo-British Review*, vol. XXII, no. 2, 136   25. Goudge to Phyllis, 24 August 1917, unpublished memoir in Goudge Papers   26. Beveridge, 231–49 *passim*; Hickey, vol. 4, 382   27. Pritchard to Elgin, 25 February 1896, Elgin Papers   28. Russell, 104–5   29. Unpublished memoir in Clemens Papers   30. Unpublished diary in Swindlehurst Papers   31. A. E. W. Mason, 135–6   32. Unpublished memoir in Caroe Papers   33. *Indo-British Review*, vol. XXII, no. 2, 75   34. Fleming, vol. 2, 274   35. Cline, 61–9; Souhami, 39–42, 57   36. *Emmanuel College Magazine*, 1971–2   37. Buettner, 215–16   38. Unpublished memoir by Flora Holman in Holman Papers   39. Walter Lawrence, 156   40. Lawson (1868), 224   41. Parkes, 359–60   42. Richards, 306–7   43. Mills, 130   44. Unpublished memoir in Pearse Papers; Best, 50   45. John Morris, 153; unpublished memoir in Caroe Papers   46. Seton-Karr, 204   47. Lyall to Grant Duff, 24 June 1887, Lyall Papers   48. Russell, 137   49. Obituary in *Daily Telegraph*, 18 May 1994   50. Cubitt-Smith, 61   51. Bazalgette (1985), *passim*   52. Henry Cotton, 293   53. Halliday, 12   54. Prendergast, 250   55. Walton, 26–7   56. Yalland (1994), 247, 259–62   57. Notes in Partridge Papers   58. Addresses given in 'List of Retired Civilians ...' in Indian Civil Service (Retired) Association Collection   59. Avril Powell, 24; note in Forbes Papers   60. Mount, 630   61. Parkes, xiii   62. Wilkinson, 45   63. Beames, 225–6   64. Albert Hervey, vol. 2, 50, 221–6   65. Ashby and Whately, 139–41   66. Obituary in *Daily Telegraph*, 25 September 1997   67. Hunt and Harrison, 244   68. Joan Allen, 110–51, *passim*   69. Kirk-Greene, 87   70. Hatch-Barnwell, *passim*; obituary in *The Times*, 2 November 1989   71. *Daily Telegraph*, 3 March 1988   72. Unpublished memoir in Somerset Papers   73. Stephens, 290–96, 323, 333   74. Singh, 81–3   75. *The Times*, 25 June 2015; *Guardian*, 15 February 2016   76. Purcell, 215–16   77. Notes in G. W. P. Milne Papers   78. Radford and Farrington, 19, 30   79. Purcell, 15–16   80. Purcell, 38–68 *passim*   81. Purcell, 217–22   82. Bennett (2002), 4, 23, 106   83. Kaye (1997), 385–6   84. John Morris, 93–5   85. Slater, 36–7   86. Currie, 41   87. *Chowkidar*, autumn 2007, 88   88. Spurling, 355; Panter-Downes, 81, 124

89. Panter-Downes, 65–6, 96   90. Singh, vii–viii   91. Lady Lawrence, 108–10   92. Humphrey Trevelyan, 133 93. Egerton to author, 11 February 2006 94. Singh, 122   95. Ramachandra Guha in *Times Literary Supplement*, 16 June 2006

ENVOI

1. Said (1994), 275   2. Said (1978), 204   3. Khilnani, 17–24   4. A. Béteille, 'Universities at the Crossroads', *Current Science*, vol. 92, no. 4, 25 February 2007   5. Cited by Ferdinand Mount in *London Review of Books*, 7 September 2017   6. *London Review of Books*, 20 December 2012

Sources and Bibliography

MANUSCRIPT COLLECTIONS

Abbreviations

CSAS = Centre of South Asian Studies (Cambridge)
NAM = National Army Museum
APAC = Asia, Pacific and Africa Collections, British Library
IWM = Imperial War Museum

Businessmen, Planters, Engineers, etc.

Arthur Atkinson, APAC
Matthew Calvocoressi, private collection
John Forbes, CSAS
D. Fowlis, National Library of Scotland
Cyril Walter Lloyd Jones, APAC
G. W. P. Milne, CSAS
Mauger Monk, APAC
Colonel H. A. Oatts, CSAS
Wilfrid Russell, APAC

East India Company

Paul Benfield, APAC
Robert and John Campbell, APAC
Jameson family, APAC
Ormathwaite Collection (members of the Fowke, Walsh, Clive and Maskelyne
  families), APAC

Governors and Viceroys

Lord (George) Curzon, APAC
Lord (Frederick) Dufferin, APAC
Lord (Victor) Elgin, APAC
Lord (John) Erskine, APAC
Sir James Fergusson, APAC
Lord (George) Goschen, APAC
Sir Mountstuart Grant Duff, APAC
Lord (Henry) Lansdowne, APAC
Sir John Lawrence, APAC
Lord (Gilbert) Minto, National Library of Scotland
Lord (Thomas) Northbrook, APAC
Lord (Beilby) Wenlock, APAC

Indian Army and British Army

Major P. R. Adams, NAM
Colonel B. J. Amies, NAM
William Appleby, CSAS
Private R. Clemens, IWM
Colonel W. A. B. Dennys (in Heaney Papers), APAC
Lieutenant Thomas Dowdall, APAC
Lieutenant-General Robert Drew, IWM
Lieutenant Herbert Du Cane, Bodleian Library
Major Richard Fanshawe, NAM
Major H. Le M. Fellowes, NAM
Captain Richard Gubbins, NAM
Major-General S. Shahid Hamid, NAM
Lieutenant Henry Haughton, APAC
Colonel Maurice Henry, private collection
Brigadier-General Terence Keyes, APAC
General Walter Kirke, APAC
General Herbert Kitchener, National Archives
Sergeant Alexander McGill, CSAS
Captain Dudley Meneaud-Lissenburg, IWM
General Thomas Nicoll, APAC
Major Francis Oldfield, private collection
Brigadier J. J. Packard, CSAS
General George Pearse, APAC
Captain Melville Portal, APAC
Major-General John Shaw Stewart, private collection

Major-General Andrew Skeen, APAC
G. J. Sweeney, CSAS
Private J. P. Swindlehurst, IWM
Lieutenant Henry Tyler, APAC
Captain Henry Van Homrigh, NAM
Colonel E. A. H. Webb, APAC
Major Francis Yeats-Brown, University of Texas, Austin

Indian Civil Service

H. L. L. Allanson, CSAS
Hugh Barnes, Bodleian Library
Charles Stuart Bayley, private collection
Frank Owen Bell, APAC
Augustus Fortunatus Bellasis, APAC
Henry Beveridge, APAC
Lewen Bowring, APAC
Harcourt Butler, APAC (*see also* Lord Francis Scott)
Montagu Butler, APAC
George Campbell, APAC
Olaf Caroe, APAC
Charles Godfrey Chenevix Trench, APAC
George Russell Clerk, APAC
John Clague, APAC
Frederick Graham Cracknell, CSAS
Hugh Dow, APAC
Sidney Dunlop, APAC
Richardson Evans, APAC
Martin Fearn, private collection
William S. Foster, CSAS
Frederick Fryer, APAC
Joseph Goudge, private collection
Charles Grant, APAC
Henry Grigg, private collection
Henry Haig, CSAS
Malcolm Hailey, APAC
Maurice Hayward, APAC
Benjamin Heald, APAC
William Herschel, APAC
Theodore Hope, APAC
William Henry Horsley, APAC
Henry Fraser Howard, APAC
John Hubback, CSAS

H. Knight, CSAS
H. T. Lambrick, APAC
William Lee-Warner, APAC
Havilland Le Mesurier, APAC
Cecil C. Lowis, Bodleian Library
Walter Lupton, APAC
Alfred Lyall, APAC
A. G. McCall, APAC
Ian Hay Macdonald, APAC
Anthony MacDonnell, Bodleian Library
Roderick Henry Macleod, CSAS
John Maynard, APAC (and in Gilbert Murray Papers, Bodleian Library)
Christopher Minns, APAC
William James Money, APAC
George and Reginald Partridge, private collection
James Penny, CSAS
L. G. Pinnell, CSAS
Arthur Platt, APAC
Noel Tindal Porter, CSAS
H. Quinton, CSAS
H. F. Samman, J. C. Moore and E. A. Prinsep, Bodleian Library
A. T. Shuttleworth, CSAS
James Sifton, APAC
Henry Stokes, APAC
John Strachey, APAC
Richard Temple, APAC
John Perronet Thompson, APAC
F. W. Ward, APAC
Herbert Thirkell White, APAC
Andrew Wingate, CSAS
John Woodburn, APAC

Indian Forest Service

Basil Henry Baden-Powell, APAC
Clinton Dawkins, APAC
Herbert Comyn Walker, CSAS

Indian Medical Service

Captain T. W. Barnard, APAC
Lieutenant-General Ernest Bradfield, CSAS
Lieutenant-Colonel Walter Hugh Crichton, CSAS

Colonel George Kellie, NAM
Lieutenant-Colonel Robert Kennedy, APAC
Lieutenant-Colonel Asher Leventon, APAC
Colonel H. E. Shortt, IWM
Major E. J. Somerset, APAC

Indian Police

Edward Hilder Colebrook, APAC
J. C. Curry, CSAS

Indian Political Service

Gordon Hay Anderson, CSAS
Lieutenant-Colonel Frederick Marshman Bailey, APAC
Denys Blakeway, private collection
Major W. M. Cubitt, APAC
Colonel Armine Dew, APAC
Mortimer Durand, APAC
Evelyn Howell, APAC
Walter Lawrence, APAC
Francis Younghusband, APAC
George Yule, APAC

Teachers, Missionaries and Sundry Religious Figures

Anglican Missions in India, CSAS
Beatrice Batty, Bodleian Library
Percy Brown, APAC
Victor Dunphy, CSAS
Gay Hellier, CSAS
Benjamin Jowett, Balliol College, Oxford
L. R. Phelps, Oriel College Oxford
Benjamin Rice, CSAS
Roman Catholic Missions in India, CSAS
H. Welch, CSAS

Women (*see also* Missionaries)

Ruth Barton, CSAS
B. Bayley, CSAS
Viola Bayley, CSAS
Diana F. Boyes, CSAS

P. Cartwright, CSAS
Lady Chapman, CSAS
Monica Francis Clough, CSAS
Decima Curtis, APAC
S. V. Davidson, IWM
Enid Dawkins (Smythies), APAC
Barbara Donaldson, CSAS
Lady Erskine-Crum, CSAS
Yvonne Fitzroy, APAC
Eileen Gage (in Kinsman Papers), CSAS
H. Ghoshal, CSAS
Lucy Grant, CSAS
M. L. (Madge) Green, APAC
V. M. Haig, CSAS
Margaret Campbell Hannay, CSAS
Flora Holman, CSAS
Lady Lloyd, APAC
Constance Maude, CSAS
Lady Maxwell, CSAS
Agnes Moffat, NAM
Phoebe Norton-Griffiths, CSAS
Emily Overend Lorimer, APAC
F. Packard, CSAS
N. E. Parry, CSAS
Alicia Percival, CSAS
Millicent Pilkington, CSAS
Iris Portal, CSAS
Anne Tatham, private collection
Judy Urquhart, private collection
A. G. N. Verity, private collection

Miscellaneous

Frank Herbert Brown, APAC
Richard Isaac Bruce, APAC
Calcutta Tent Club, APAC
Glasfurd family, APAC
Arthur Godley (in Kilbracken Papers), APAC
Lord George Hamilton, APAC
Melville Hardiment, IWM
J. W. Hely-Hutchison, Bodleian Library

Courtenay Ilbert, APAC
Rudyard Kipling, Sussex University
Thomas Henry Digges La Touche, APAC
Macnabb family, APAC
Louis Mallet, Balliol College, Oxford
Gilbert Murray, Bodleian Library, Oxford
Francis Oppenheimer, Balliol College, Oxford
Thomas Walter Powell and family, APAC
Rice family, CSAS
Salmon family, NAM
Lord Francis Scott, private collection
C. M. Scriven, CSAS
Unceremonials Club, APAC

India Office, Government of India and Other Official Files and Publications in the APAC

Bengal Calendar (List of East India Company's civil and military servants)
Bombay Confidential Proceedings, Judicial Department, vol. 25, 1917 (P CONF 25)
Census of India 1871–1931
Civil List of Officers of the Indian Medical Service
Crown Representatives' Records at Indian States' Residencies (R/2)
Department Annual Reports (V/24/2297)
East India College Haileybury Records
East India Company: List of Civil Servants 1771–85
East India Register and Directory 1803–42
History of Services (V/12)
Imperial Gazetteer of India 1881–1909
India List, Civil and Military 1877–1906
India Office List 1886–1947
India Register 1843–60
Indian Army List 1889–1947
Indian Army and Civil Service List 1877–1906
Indian Civil Service (Retired) Association Collection
Indian Home Department, Rules and Regulations (V/27/212/1-5)
Languages of India (Statistical Office, East India House, 1852)
Public and Judicial Department Records and Annual Files (L/PJ/6)
Records of Pensions and Annuities (L/AG/21)
Records of Service (L/F/10)
Thacker's Bengal and Indian Directories
Warrant of Precedence

BOOKS AND ARTICLES

George Aberigh-Mackay, *Twenty-one Days in India*, W. H. Allen & Co., London, 1881

K. T. Achaya, *The Food Industries of British India*, Oxford University Press, Delhi, 1994

J. R. Ackerley, *Hindoo Holiday*, Chatto & Windus, London, 1932

Rafiuddin Ahmed, *The Bengal Muslims 1871–1906: A Quest for Identity*, Oxford University Press, Delhi, 1981

G. T. Alder, *British India's Northern Frontier, 1865–95*, Longmans, London, 1963

Imran Ali, *The Punjab under Imperialism, 1885–1947*, Princeton University Press, 1988

Brigid Allen, 'Indian diaries, 1712–1956: An Introduction', India Office Library and Records Report, London, 1980

Charles Allen, *Duel in the Snows*, John Murray, London, 2004

——, *Plain Tales from the Raj*, Readers Union, Newton Abbot, 1976

——, *Lives of the Indian Princes*, Arrow, London, 1986

——, *Raj: A Scrapbook of British India*, Penguin, London, 1979

——, *Soldier Sahibs*, John Murray, London, 2000

Joan Allen, *'Missy Baba' to 'Burra Mem': The Life of a Planter's Daughter in Northern India, 1913–1970*, BACSA, London, 1998

Marquess of Anglesey (ed.), *Sergeant Pearman's Memoirs*, Jonathan Cape, London, 1968

Mildred Archer, *British Drawings in the India Office Library*, vol. 2, HMSO, London, 1969

William and Mildred Archer, *India Served and Observed*, BACSA, London, 1994

David Arnold, *Colonizing the Body: State Medicine and Epidemic Disease in Nineteenth-century India*, University of California Press, Berkeley, 1993

——, 'European Orphans and Vagrants in India in the Nineteenth Century', *Journal of Imperial and Commonwealth History*, vol. VII, no. 2, January 1979

——, *Famine*, Blackwell, Oxford, 1988

——, 'White Colonization and Labour in Nineteenth-century India', *Journal of Imperial and Commonwealth History*, vol. XI, no. 2, January 1983

Lillian Luker Ashby and Roger Whately, *My India*, Little Brown, Boston, 1937

ASCB Handbook, Army Sport Control Board, India, 1933

S. R. Ashton, *British Policy towards the Indian States, 1905–1939*, Curzon Press, London, 1982

Margot Asquith, *More Memories*, Cassell, London, 1933

George F. Atkinson, *Curry and Rice*, Rupa, Chennai, 2001

Robert Baden-Powell, *Indian Memories*, Herbert Jenkins, London, 1915

——, *Pig-sticking or Hog-hunting*, Herbert Jenkins, London, 1924

J. G. Baird (ed.), *Private Letters of the Marquess of Dalhousie,* Irish University Press, Shannon, 1972

Maureen Baird-Murray, *A World Overturned: A Burmese Childhood,* Constable, London, 1997

C. Ballard, *Smith-Dorrien,* Constable, London, 1931

Kenneth Ballhatchett, *Race, Sex and Class under the Raj,* Weidenfeld & Nicolson, London, 1980

Surendranath Banerjea, *A Nation in Making,* Oxford University Press, Calcutta, 1925

Sarmila Banerjee, *Studies in Administrative History of Bengal,* Rajesh, New Delhi, 1978

Pat Barr, *The Dust in the Balance: British Women in India, 1905–1945,* Hamish Hamilton, London, 1989

——, *The Memsahibs: The Women of Victorian India,* Secker & Warburg, London, 1976

Evelyn Désirée Battye, *The Fighting Ten,* BACSA, London, 1984

——, *The Kashmir Residency,* BACSA, London, 1997

Audrey Baylis, *And Then Garhwal,* BACSA, London, 1981

C. A. Bayly, *Empire and Information,* Cambridge University Press, 1999

——, *Indian Society and the Making of the British Empire,* Cambridge University Press, 1990

——, *The Local Roots of Indian Politics: Allahabad 1880–1920,* Clarendon Press, Oxford, 1975

—— (ed.), *The Raj: India and the British, 1600–1947,* National Portrait Gallery, London, 1991

——, *Recovering Liberties: Indian Thought in the Age of Liberalism and Empire,* Cambridge University Press, 2011

Christopher Bayly and Tim Harper, *Forgotten Armies: The Fall of British Asia, 1941–1945,* Allen Lane, London, 2004

——, *Forgotten Wars: The End of Britain's Asian Empire,* Allen Lane, London, 2007

Jack Bazalgette, *The Captains and the Kings Depart,* Amate Press, Oxford, 1984

——, *Careering On,* Amate Press, Oxford, 1985

John Beames, *Memoirs of a Bengal Civilian,* Eland, London, 1990

M. Bellasis, *Honourable Company,* Hollis & Carter, London, 1952

Captain Bellew, *Memoirs of a Griffin,* vol. 1, W. H. Allen, London, 1843

Mark Bence-Jones, *Palaces of the Raj,* George Allen and Unwin, London, 1973

——, *The Viceroys of India,* Constable, London, 1982

Mary Bennett, *The Ilberts in India,* BACSA, London, 1995

——, *Who Was Dr Jackson?,* BACSA, London, 2002

Owen Berkeley-Hill, *All Too Human,* Peter Davies, London, 1939

James W. Best, *Forest Life in India,* John Murray, London, 1935

Lord Beveridge, *India Called Them*, George Allen, London, 1947

K. C. Bhanja, *Darjeeling at a Glance*, Oxford Book and Stationery Company, Darjeeling, 1941

Raja Bhasin, *Simla*, Penguin, Delhi, 1994

Sidney Bidwell, *Swords for Hire*, John Murray, London, 1971

George C. M. Birdwood, *Competition and the Indian Civil Service*, Henry S. King, London, 1872

Lord Birdwood, *Khaki and Gown*, Ward, Lock & Co., London, 1941

Bindon Blood, *Four Score Years and Ten*, G. Bell, London, 1933

Edward Blunt, *The ICS*, Faber, London, 1937

Wilfrid Scawen Blunt, *Ideas about India*, Kegan Paul, London, 1885

——, *India under Ripon*, Fisher Unwin, London, 1909

Angela Bolton, *The Maturing Sun*, Imperial War Museum, London, 1986

N. B. Bonarjee, *Under Two Masters*, Oxford University Press, 1970

H. V. Bowen, *The Business of Empire: The East India Company and Imperial Britain, 1756–1833*, Cambridge University Press, 2006

Ursula Graham Bower, *Hidden Land*, John Murray, London, 1953

——, *Naga Path*, John Murray, London, 1950

Boxwallah, *An Eastern Backwater*, Andrew Melrose, London, n.d.

F. B. Bradley-Birt, *Chota Nagpore: A Little-known Province of the Empire*, Smith, Elder, London, 1903

Howard V. Brasted, 'Irish Home Rule Politics and India, 1873–1886: Frank Hugh O'Donnell and Other Irish "Friends of India"', Edinburgh University doctoral thesis, 1974

Vyvyen Brendon, *Children of the Raj*, Weidenfeld & Nicolson, London, 2005

R. C. B. Bristow, *Memories of the British Raj*, Johnson, London, 1974

Robert Bristow, *Cochin Saga*, Cassell, London, 1959

Fawn Brodie, *The Devil Drives*, Eland, London, 1986

Hilton Brown, *Parry's of Madras*, Parry and Co., Madras, 1954

—— (ed.), *The Sahibs*, William Hodge, London, 1948

J. Moray Brown, *Shikar Sketches*, Hurst and Blackett, London, 1887

Judith M. Brown, *Windows into the Past*, University of Notre Dame Press, Indiana, 2009

Judith M. Brown and W. M. Roger Louis (eds.), *The Oxford History of the British Empire: The Twentieth Century*, Oxford University Press, 1999

John Buchan, *A Lodge in the Wilderness*, Blackwood, Edinburgh, 1906

Edward J. Buck, *Simla Past and Present*, Times Press, Bombay, 1925

Elizabeth Buettner, *Imperial Families: Britons and Late Imperial India*, Oxford University Press, 2004

Anne Bulley, *Free Mariner: John Adolphus Pope in the East Indies, 1786–1821*, BACSA, London, 1992

W. S. Burke, *The Indian Field Shikar Book*, Thacker, Spink, Calcutta, 1928

David Burton, *The Raj at Table*, Faber and Faber, London, 1994

Iris Butler, *The Eldest Brother: The Marquess Wellesley*, Hodder & Stoughton, 1973

Alex M. Cain, *The Cornchest for Scotland*, National Library for Scotland, Edinburgh, 1986

P. J. Cain and A. G. Hopkins, *British Imperialism: Innovation and Expansion*, Longman, London, 1993

Barbara Caine, *Bombay to Bloomsbury: A Biography of the Strachey Family*, Oxford University Press, 2005

George Campbell, *Memoirs of My Indian Career*, 2 vols., Macmillan, London, 1893

———, *Modern India*, John Murray, London, 1852

Edmund Candler, *The Sepoy*, John Murray, London, 1919

David Cannadine, *Ornamentalism: How the British Saw Their Empire*, Allen Lane, London, 2001

Olaf Caroe, *The Pathans*, Macmillan, London, 1958

Michael Carritt, *A Mole in the Crown*, Michael Carritt, Hove, 1985

R. Carstairs, *The Little World of an Indian District Officer*, Macmillan, London, 1912

Rajnarayan Chandavarkar, *Imperial Power and Popular Politics*, Cambridge University Press, 1998

Sudhir Chandra, *Enslaved Daughters: Colonialism, Law and Women's Rights*, Oxford University Press, Delhi, 1999

Neil Charlesworth, *British Rule and the Indian Economy, 1800–1914*, Macmillan, London, 1982

Amit Chaudhuri, *Calcutta: Two Years in the City*, Union, London, 2013

Nirad C. Chaudhuri, *The Autobiography of an Unknown Indian*, Hogarth Press, London, 1987

———, *The Continent of Circe*, Chatto & Windus, London, 1967

John de Chazal, *Sunset of the Raj*, Wincanton Press, Wincanton, 1987

Sydney Checkland, *The Elgins, 1766–1917*, Aberdeen University Press, 1988

Charles Chenevix Trench, *The Frontier Scouts*, Jonathan Cape, London, 1985

———, *Viceroy's Agent*, Jonathan Cape, London, 1997

S. K. Chettur, *The Steel Frame and I*, Asia Publishing House, London, 1962

Valentine Chirol, *Fifty Years in a Changing World*, Jonathan Cape, London, 1927

Anne Chisholm, *Rumer Godden*, Pan, London, 1999

Anne Chitty, *Musings of a Memsahib*, Belhaven, Lymington, 1988

Chowkidar, 1977–2017, BACSA, London

John Christie, *Morning Drum*, BACSA, London, 1983

P. L. Chudgar, *Indian Princes under British Protection*, William & Norgate, London, 1929

Randolph Churchill, *Winston S. Churchill: Youth, 1874–1900*, Heinemann, London, 1966

Winston S. Churchill, *My Early Life*, Thornton Butterworth, London, 1930

Civilian, *The Civilian's South India*, Bodley Head, London, 1921

Miles Clark, *High Endeavours: The Extraordinary Life and Adventures of Miles and Beryl Smeeton*, Grafton, London, 1991

John Clay, *John Masters*, Michael Joseph, London, 1992

Sally Cline, *Radclyffe Hall*, John Murray, London, 1997

Richard Cobb, *A Second Identity*, Oxford University Press, 1969

Terence C. Coen, *The Indian Political Service*, Chatto & Windus, London, 1971

Bernard S. Cohn, *An Anthropologist among the Historians and Other Essays*, Oxford University Press, Delhi, 1987

C. E. Coles, *Recollections and Reflections*, Saint Catherine Press, London, 1918

Nigel Collett, *The Butcher of Amritsar: General Reginald Dyer*, Hambledon & London Press, London, 2005

Linda Colley, *Britons: Forging the Nation, 1707–1837*, Pimlico, London, 1994

E. M. Collingham, *Imperial Bodies*, Polity, Cambridge, 2001

Lizzie Collingham, *Curry: A Biography*, Chatto & Windus, London, 2005

Maurice Collis, *Trials in Burma*, Faber, London, 1938

Peter Collister, *'Hellfire Jack!'* VC, BACSA, London, 1989

F. Colyer Sackett, *Vision and Venture: A Record of Fifty Years in Hyderabad, 1879–1929*, Cargate, London, 1930

Mary, Viscountess Combermere and Capt. W. W. Knollys, *Memoirs and Correspondence of Field-Marshal Viscount Combermere*, vol. 2, Hurst and Blackett, London, 1866

J. M. Compton, 'Open Competition and the Indian Civil Service, 1854–1876', *English Historical Review*, vol. 83, 1968

Scott B. Cook, 'The Irish Raj: Social Origins and Careers of Irishmen in the Indian Civil Service, 1855–1914', *Journal of Social History*, spring 1987

Stephen Coote, *John Keats: A Life*, Hodder & Stoughton, London, 1995

Ian Copland, *The British Raj and the Indian Princes*, Sangman, Pune, 1982

Antony Copley, *C. Rajagopalachari: Gandhi's Southern Commander*, Indo-British Historical Society, Madras, 1986

Jim Corbett, *My India*, Oxford University Press, New Delhi, 1952

Evan Cotton, *East Indiamen: The East India Company's Maritime Service*, Batchworth Press, London, 1949

Henry Cotton, *Indian & Home Memories*, Fisher Unwin, London, 1911

Anne de Courcy, *The Fishing Fleet*, Weidenfeld & Nicolson, London, 2012

Simon Courtauld, *Footprints in Spain*, Quartet, London, 2017

E. C. Cox, *My Thirty Years in India*, Mills & Boon, London, 1909

Jeffrey Cox, *Imperial Fault Lines: Christianity and Colonial Power in India, 1818–1940*, Stanford University Press, 2002

Hazel Innes Craig, *Under the School Topee*, BACSA, London, 1990

D. G. Crawford, *A History of the Indian Medical Service, 1600–1913*, Thacker & Co., London, 1914

Bernard Crick, *George Orwell*, Secker & Warburg, London, 1980

Denis Hayes Crofton, *Souvenirs of a Competition Wallah*, Volturna, London, 1994

W. Crooke, *The North-Western Provinces of India*, Methuen, London, 1897

Henry Cubitt-Smith, *Yadgari, or, Memories of the Raj*, Cubitt-Smith, Holt, 1987

H. S. Cunningham, *British India and Its Rulers*, W. H. Allen & Co., London, 1881

———, *Chronicles of Dustypore*, Smith, Elder, London, 1885

Mary McDonald Currie, *Forest Families*, British Empire and Commonwealth Museum, Bristol, 2000

George N. Curzon, *British Government in India* (2 vols.), Cassell, London, 1925

William Dalrymple, *City of Djinns*, HarperCollins, London, 1993

———, *The Last Mughal*, Bloomsbury, London, 2006

———, *Return of a King*, Knopf, New York, 2013

———, *White Mughals*, HarperCollins, London, 2002

Thomas and William Daniell, *Oriental Scenery* (6 series), London, 1795–1808

Frederick Danvers, *Memorials of Old Haileybury College*, Constable, London, 1894

Malcolm Darling, *Apprentice to Power: India, 1904–1908*, Hogarth Press, London, 1966

———, *At Freedom's Door*, Oxford University Press, 1949

Neeta Das and Rosie Llewellyn-Jones (eds.), *Murshidabad*, Marg Foundation, Mumbai, 2013

Surendra Kumar Datta, *The Desire of India*, Church Missionary Society, London, 1908

Richard Davenport-Hines, *The Seven Lives of John Maynard Keynes*, William Collins, London, 2015

Saul David, *The Indian Mutiny*, Viking, London, 2002

C. Collin Davies, *The Problem of the North-West Frontier, 1890–1908*, Cambridge University Press, 1932

Philip Davies, *Splendours of the Raj*, John Murray, London, 1985

Vincent Davies, *British Cemeteries of Patna and Dinapore*, BACSA, London, 1989

Wendy M. Davis, *Dal & Rice*, McGill-Queen's University Press, Montreal, 2009

Richard Dawkins, *An Appetite for Wonder*, Bantam Press, London, 2013

Ray Desmond, *The European Discovery of the Indian Flora*, Oxford University Press, 1992

———, *Victorian India in Focus*, HMSO, London, 1982

Charles Devereux, *Venus in India*, Harper Perennial, London, 2009

T. M. Devine, *Scotland's Empire, 1600–1815*, Allen Lane, London, 2003

Douglas Dewar, *Jungle Folk*, John Lane, London, 1912

Clive Dewey, *Anglo-Indian Attitudes: The Mind of the Indian Civil Service*, Hambledon Press, London, 1993

———, 'The Education of a Ruling Caste: The Indian Civil Service in the Era of Competitive Examination', *English Historical Review*, vol. 88, 1973

———, *The Passing of Barchester*, Hambledon Press, London, 1991

———, *Steamboats on the Indus*, Oxford University Press, New Delhi, 2014

Charles Dilke, *Greater Britain*, Macmillan, London, 1869

David Dilks, *Curzon in India*, 2 vols., Hart-Davis, London, 1969–70

Maud Diver, *The Englishwoman in India*, Blackwood, Edinburgh, 1909

Edward Docker, *History of Indian Cricket*, Macmillan, Delhi, 1976

Henry Dodwell, *The Nabobs of Madras*, Williams and Norgate, London and Edinburgh, 1926

E. C. Dozey, *A Concise History of Darjeeling*, Jetsun, Calcutta, 1989

L. C. Dunsterville, *Stalky's Reminiscences*, Jonathan Cape, London, 1928

Mortimer Durand, *Sir Alfred Comyn Lyall*, Blackwood, Edinburgh, 1913

Sainthill Eardley-Wilmot, *Forest Life and Sport in India*, Edward Arnold, London, 1910

Emily Eden, *Up the Country*, Virago, London, 1984

Michael Edwardes, *Bound to Exile*, Sidgwick & Jackson, London, 1969

———, *The Nabobs at Home*, Constable, London, 1991

S. M. Edwardes, *The Bombay City Police*, Oxford University Press, 1923

Ivor Edwardes-Stuart, *The Calcutta of Begum Johnson*, BACSA, London, 1990

DeWitt C. Ellinwood, *Between Two Worlds: A Rajput Officer in the Indian Army, 1905–21*, University Press of America, Lanham, 2005

Havelock Ellis, *Studies in the Psychology of Sex*, vol. 3, F. A. Davis, Philadelphia, 1928

Jennifer Ellis (ed.), *Thatched with Gold: The Memoirs of Mabell, Countess of Airlie*, Hutchinson, London, 1962

G. Elsmie, *Thirty-five Years in the Punjab*, David Douglas, Edinburgh, 1908

Ex-Civilian, *Life in the Mofussil*, 2 vols., Kegan Paul, London, 1878

John Fabb, *The British Empire from Photographs*, Batsford, London, 1986

Geoffrey Faber, *Jowett*, Faber and Faber, 1957

Viscountess Falkland, *Chow-Chow*, vol. 1, Hurst and Blackett, London, 1857

Susan Maria Farrington, *Peshawar Cemetery*, BACSA, London, 1988

Susan Maria Farrington and John A. Radford, *Chittagong Christian Cemeteries*, BACSA, London, 1999

Byron Farwell, *Armies of the Raj*, Viking, London, 1989

Eliza Fay, *Original Letters from India*, Hogarth Press, London, 1986

Niall Ferguson, *Empire: How Britain Made the Modern World*, Allen Lane, London, 2003

FIBIS, 2013–17, Families in British India Society, London

H. Fielding-Hall, *The Passing of Empire*, Hurst and Blackett, London, 1913

Michael Fisher, *Indirect Rule in India: Residents and the Residency System, 1764–1858*, Oxford University Press, Delhi, 1998

Penelope Fitzgerald, *The Knox Brothers*, Flamingo, London, 2002

Laurence Fleming, *Last Children of the Raj*, 2 vols., Dexter Haven, London, 2016

G. W. Forrest, *Cities of India*, Dutton, New York, 1903

Adrian Fort, *Wavell: The Life and Times of an Imperial Servant*, Jonathan Cape, London, 2009

H. L. Fraser, *Among Indian Rajahs and Ryots*, Seeley, London, 1911

John Fraser, *Sixty Years in Uniform*, Stanley Paul, London, 1939

Lovat Fraser, *India after Curzon*, William Heinemann, London, 1911

Patrick French, *Younghusband*, HarperCollins, London, 1994

Michael Fry, *The Scottish Empire*, Birlinn, Edinburgh, 2001

Bampfylde Fuller, *The Empire of India*, Pitman & Sons, London, 1913

P. N. Furbank, *E. M. Forster*, 2 vols., Secker & Warburg, London, 1977

Andrew Gailey, *The Lost Imperialist: Lord Dufferin*, John Murray, London, 2015

Edward Gait, *A History of Assam*, Thacker, Spink, Calcutta, 1926

Alison Games, *The Web of Empire: English Cosmopolitans in an Age of Expansion, 1560–1660*, Oxford University Press, 200.

M. K. Gandhi, *An Autobiography*, Penguin, London, 2001

Akshoy Kumar Ghosal, *Civil Service in India under the East India Company*, University of Calcutta, 1944

Indira Ghose, *Memsahibs Abroad*, Oxford University Press, Delhi, 1996

Durba Ghosh, *Sex and the Family in Colonial India*, Cambridge University Press, 2006

Mary Gibson, *Warneford VC*, Friends of the Fleet Air Arm Museum, Yeovilton, 1979

Charles H. Gillen, *H. H. Munro (Saki)*, Twayne, New York, 1969

Martin Gilbert, *Servant of India: A Study of Imperial Rule from 1905 to 1910*, Longman, London, 1966

David Gilmour, *Curzon*, John Murray, London, 1994

———, *The Long Recessional: The Imperial Life of Rudyard Kipling*, John Murray, London, 2002

———, *The Ruling Caste: Imperial Lives in the Victorian Raj*, John Murray, London, 200

Jonathan Glancey, *Nagaland: A Journey to India's Forgotten Frontier*, Faber and Faber, London, 2011

Captain A. I. R. Glasfurd, *Rifle and Romance in the Indian Jungle*, John Lane, London, 1905

John Glendevon, *The Viceroy at Bay*, Collins, London, 1971

Victoria Glendinning, *Raffles*, Profile, London, 2012

Jon and Rumer Godden, *Two under the Indian Sun*, Macmillan, London, 1966

William Golant, *The Long Afternoon: British India, 1601–1947*, Hamish Hamilton, London, 1975

S. Gopal, *British Policy in India, 1858–1905*, Cambridge University Press, 1965

Iain Gordon, *Soldier of the Raj: The Life of Richard Purvis*, Leo Cooper, London, 2001

W. Gordon-Alexander, *Recollections of a Highland Subaltern*, Edward Arnold, London, 1898

H. J. C. Grierson (ed.), *The Letters of Sir Walter Scott*, 10 vols., Constable, 1932–6

Lepel Griffin, 'The Indian Civil Service Examinations', *Fortnightly Review*, vol. 17, 1875

Percival Griffiths, *To Guard My People: The History of the Indian Police*, Ernest Benn, London, 1971

Ethel St Clair Grimwood, *My Three Years in Manipur*, Richard Bentley, London, 1891

Ramachandra Guha, *An Anthropologist among the Marxists*, Permanent Black, Delhi, 2001

———, *A Corner of a Foreign Field, The Indian History of a British Sport*, Picador, London, 2002

———, *Gandhi Before India*, Allen Lane, London, 2013

———, *Savaging the Civilized: Verrier Elwin, His Tribals and India*, Oxford University Press, Delhi, 1999

Alan J. Guy and Peter B. Boyden, *Soldiers of the Raj: The Indian Army, 1600–1947*, National Army Museum, London, 1997

Catherine Hall, *Macaulay and Son*, Yale University Press, Newhaven and London, 2012

James Halliday, *A Special India*, Chatto & Windus, London, 1968

S. Shahid Hamid, *So They Rode and They Fought*, Midas Books, Tunbridge Wells, 1983

Lord George Hamilton, *Parliamentary Reminiscences and Reflections, 1886–1906*, John Murray, London, 1922

Ian Hamilton, *Listening for the Drums*, Faber and Faber, London, 1944

Nigel Hamilton, *The Full Monty: Montgomery of Alamein*, vol. 1, Allen Lane, London, 2001

August Peter Hansen, *Memoirs of an Adventurous Dane in India, 1904–47*, BACSA, London, 1999

Alan Harfield, *Meerut: The First Sixty Years*, BACSA, London, 1992

Jonathan Gil Harris, *The First Firangis*, Aleph, New Delhi, 2015

Kenneth Harris, *Attlee*, Weidenfeld & Nicolson, London, 1984

Mark Harrison, *Public Health in British India: Anglo-Indian Preventive Medicine, 1859–1914*, Cambridge University Press, 1994

Robert Harvey, *Clive*, Hodder & Stoughton, London, 1998

D. J. Hastings (ed.), *Bombay Buccaneers*, BACSA, London, 1986

Stephen Hatch-Barnwell, *The Last Guardian*, University Press Ltd, Dhaka, 2011

Roy Hattersley, *The Devonshires*, Chatto & Windus, London, 2013

Raymond Head, *Catalogue of Paintings, Drawings, Engravings and Busts*, Royal Asiatic Society, London, 1991

Christopher Headington, *Peter Pears*, Faber, London, 1992

T. A. Heathcote, *The Indian Army*, David & Charles, Newton Abbot, 1974

——, *The Military in British India*, Manchester University Press, 1995

Maurice Hennessy, *The Rajah from Tipperary*, Sidgwick & Jackson, London, 1971

Eugenia W. Herbert, *Flora's Empire: British Gardens in India*, Allen Lane, London, 2011

Albert Hervey, *Ten Years in India or The Life of a Young Officer*, 3 vols., William Shoberl, London, 1850

H. Hervey, *The European in India*, Stanley Paul, London, 1913

Eileen Hewson, *Darjeeling & the Dooars: Christian Cemeteries and Memorials*, BACSA, London, 2006

William Hickey, *Memoirs*, 4 vols., Hurst and Blackett, London, 1919–25

Claude Hill, *India-Stepmother*, Blackwood, Edinburgh, 1929

Richard Hilton, *Nine Lives: The Autobiography of an Old Soldier*, Hollis & Carter, London, 1955

History of the 5th Royal Gurkha Rifles, 1858 to 1928, Gale & Olden, Aldershot

Paul Hockings (ed.), *Blue Mountains: The Ethnography and Biogeography of a South Indian Region*, Oxford University Press, Delhi, 1989

Dennis Holman, *Sikander Sahib: The Life of Colonel James Skinner*, Heinemann, London, 1961

Richard Holmes, *The British Soldier in India*, HarperCollins, London, 2005

Michael Holroyd, *Lytton Strachey*, vol. 1, Heinemann, London, 1967

Hilary Hook, *Home from the Hill*, The Sportsman's Press, London, 1997

Roland Hunt and John Harrison, *The District Officer in India, 1930–1947*, Scolar Press, London, 1980

Tristram Hunt, *Ten Cities That Made an Empire*, Allen Lane, London, 2014

W. W. Hunter, *The Annals of Rural Bengal*, 3 vols., Smith Elder, London, 1868

Francis G. Hutchins, *The Illusion of Permanence: British Imperialism in India*, Princeton University Press, 1967

Philip Hutchins, *An Indian Career, 1858–1908*, private publication, 1927

Ronald Hyam, *Empire and Sexuality*, Manchester University Press, 1991

'The Indian Civil Service: Survivors Remember the Raj', *Indo-British Review*, vol. XXII, no. 2 and vol. XXIII, no. 1., Madras, n.d.

Violet Jacob, *Diaries and Letters from India*, Canongate, Edinburgh, 1990

Victor Jacquemont, *Letters from India, 1829–1832*, Macmillan, London, 1936

Lawrence James, *Raj: The Making and Unmaking of British India*, Little Brown, London, 1997

Maya Jasanoff, *Edge of Empire*, Knopf, New York, 2005

Tim Jeal, *Baden-Powell*, Hutchinson, London, 1989

Miles Jebb, *Patrick Shaw Stewart*, Dovecote Press, Wimborne Minster, 2010

Robin Jeffrey (ed.), *People, Princes and Paramount Power*, Oxford University Press, Delhi, 1978

Ronald Johnston, *One Man's Life*, privately published, n.d.

James Johnstone, *My Experiences in Manipur and the Naga Hills*, Sampson Low, London, 1896

Stephanie Jones, *Merchants of the Raj: British Managing Agency Houses in Calcutta Yesterday and Today*, Macmillan, Basingstoke, 1992

Arnold P. Kaminsky, *The India Office, 1880–1910*, Mansell, London, 1986

Pamela Kanwar, *Imperial Simla*, Oxford University Press, Delhi, 1990

M. M. Kaye, *Golden Afternoon*, Viking, London, 1997

———, *Sun in the Morning*, Viking, London, 1990

John Keay, *The Honourable Company: A History of the East India Company*, HarperCollins, London, 1993

———, *India: A History*, HarperCollins, London, 2000

T. E. Kebbel (ed.), *Selected Speeches of the Earl of Beaconsfield*, vol. 2, Longmans Green, London, 1882

Caroline Keen, *Princely India and the British*, I. B. Tauris, London, 2012

Felicity Kendal, *White Cargo*, Michael Joseph, London, 1998

Geoffrey Kendal (with Clare Colvin), *The Shakespeare Wallah*, Sidgwick & Jackson, London, 1986

R. L. Kennion, *Diversions of an Indian Political*, Blackwood, Edinburgh, 1932

Ian J. Kerr, *Building the Railways of the Raj, 1850–1900*, Oxford University Press, Delhi, 1995

Omar Khalidi, *The British Residency in Hyderabad*, BACSA, London, 2005

Sunil Khilnani, *The Idea of India*, Penguin, London, 2012

C. A. Kincaid, *Forty-four Years a Public Servant*, Blackwood, Edinburgh, 1934

Dennis Kincaid, *British Social Life in India*, George Routledge, London, 1938

Anthony D. King, *The Bungalow*, Oxford University Press, New York, 1995

Mrs Robert Moss King, *The Diary of a Civilian's Wife in India, 1877–1882*, 2 vols., Richard Bentley, London, 1884

Rudyard Kipling, *Barrack-room Ballads and Other Verses*, Methuen, London, 1917

———, *Departmental Ditties and Other Verses*, Methuen, London, 1904

———, *Plain Tales from the Hills*, Macmillan, London, 1931

———, *Something of Myself*, Cambridge University Press, 1991

Anthony Kirk-Greene, *Britain's Imperial Administrators, 1858–1966*, Macmillan, London, 1900

Philip Knightley, *Philby: The Life and Views of the KGB Masterspy*, André Deutsch, London, 1988

Anil Kumar, *Medicine and the Raj: British Medical Policy in India, 1835–1911*, Sage Publications, New Delhi, 1998

Deepak Kumar, *Science and the Raj*, Oxford University Press, Delhi, 1995

G. T. Labey and R. K. H. Brice, 'The Bengal Pilot Service' (unpublished), National Maritime Museum, Greenwich, 1970

Katar Lalvani, *The Making of India*, Bloomsbury, London, 2016

Gavin Lambert, *Mainly about Lindsay Anderson*, Faber, London, 2000

H. T. Lambrick, *John Jacob of Jacobabad*, Cassell, London, 1960

Lady Lawrence, *Indian Embers*, George Ronald, Oxford, n.d.

Walter Lawrence, *The India We Served*, Cassell, London, 1928

Charles A. Lawson, *At Home on Furlough*, Times Press, Madras, 1868

———, *Memories of Madras*, Swan Sonnenschein & Co., London, 1905

Harold Lee, *Brothers in the Raj: The Lives of John and Henry Lawrence*, Oxford University Press, Karachi, 2002

William Lee-Warner, *The Life of the Marquess of Dalhousie*, vol. 1, Irish University Press, Shannon, 1972

———, *The Native States of India*, Macmillan, London, 1910

Peter Levi, *Edward Lear*, Macmillan, London, 1995

Phillipa Levine, *Prostitution, Race, and Politics*, Routledge, London, 2003

Ivor Lewis, *Sahibs, Nabobs and Boxwallahs*, Oxford University Press, Delhi, 1997

Mary Ann Lind, *The Compassionate Memsahibs*, Westport, 1988

Lord Lindsay, *Lives of the Lindsays*, privately published, Wigan, 1840

Rosie Llewellyn-Jones, *Engaging Scoundrels*, Oxford University Press, New Delhi, 2000

———, *A Fatal Friendship: The Nawabs, the British and the City of Lucknow*, Oxford University Press, Delhi, 1985

Gordon Loch, *The Family of Loch*, privately published, Edinburgh, 1934

Elizabeth Longford, *A Pilgrimage of Passion: The Life of Wilfrid Scawen Blunt*, Weidenfeld & Nicolson, London, 1979

———, *Wellington: The Years of the Sword*, Weidenfeld & Nicolson, London, 1969

J. P. Losty, *Calcutta: City of Palaces*, British Library, London, 1990

Heather Lovatt and Peter de Jong, *Above the Heron's Pool*, BACSA, London, 1993

Anabel Loyd, *Picnic Crumbs*, Polperro Heritage Press, Clifton-upon-Teme, 2012

Mary Lutyens (ed.), *Lady Lytton's Court Diary, 1895–1899*, Hart-Davis, London, 1961

Mary Lutyens, *The Lyttons in India*, John Murray, London, 1979

Alfred Lyall, *Verses Written in India*, Kegan Paul, London, 1893

A. R. Macduff, *The Utmost Bound of the Everlasting Hills*, James Nisbet, London, 1902

Arthur MacGregor (ed.), *The Cobbe Cabinet of Curiosities*, Yale University Press, Newhaven and London, 2015

R. D. Macleod, *Impressions of an Indian Civil Servant*, Witherby, London, 1938

Margaret MacMillan, *Women of the Raj*, Thames and Hudson, London, 1988

Evan Maconochie, *Life in the Indian Civil Service*, Chapman & Hall, London, 1926

Donald MacPherson, *The Raj: A Time Remembered*, Pentland Press, Edinburgh, 2000

William Magan, *Soldier of the Raj*, Michael Russell, London, 2002

Julia Charlotte Maitland, *Letters from Madras, during the years 1836–9*, John Murray, London, 1843

J. A. Mangan, *The Games Ethic and Imperialism*, Viking, London, 1986

P. J. Marshall, *Bengal: The British Bridgehead*, Cambridge University Press, 1987

———, *East Indian Fortunes, The British in Bengal in the Eighteenth Century*, Oxford University Press, 1976

P. J. Marshall (ed.), *The Oxford History of the British Empire: The Eighteenth Century*, Oxford University Press, 2001

David Marston, *The Indian Army and the End of the Raj*, Cambridge University Press, 2014

Robert Montgomery Martin (ed.), *The Despatches, Minutes and Correspondence of the Marquess Wellesley*, vol. 2, W. H. Allen, London, 1836

G. D. Martineau, *Controller of Devils*, privately published, n.d.

Margaret Martyn, *Married to the Raj*, BACSA, London, 1992

Zareer Masani, *Macaulay: Britain's Liberal Imperialist*, Bodley Head, London, 2013

A. E. W. Mason, *The Broken Road*, John Murray, London, 1907

Philip Mason, *A Matter of Honour*, Papermac, London, 1986

———, *A Shaft of Sunlight*, André Deutsch, London, 1978

Montague Massey, *Recollections of Calcutta for over Half a Century*, Thacker, Spink, Calcutta, 1918

John Masters, *Bugles and a Tiger*, Michael Joseph, London, 1956

Basil Mathews, *The Secrets of the Raj*, University for Missionary Education, London, 1913

Roderick Matthews, *Flaws in the Jewel: Challenging the Myths of British India*, HarperCollins, Noida, 2010

Andrew J. May, *Welsh Missionaries and Imperialism*, Manchester University Press, 2012

Alister McCrae and Friends, *Tales of Burma*, James Paton, Paisley, 1981

Donald McDonald, *Surgeons Twoe and a Barber*, Heinemann, London, 1950

Martha McLaren, *British India and British Scotland, 1780–1830*, University of Akron Press, Ohio, 2001

Frank McLynn, *Burton: Snow upon the Desert*, John Murray, London, 1993

Gordon McMullan and Zoë Wilcox, *Shakespeare in Ten Acts*, British Library, London, 2016

Thomas R. Metcalf, *Ideologies of the Raj*, Cambridge University Press, 1997

————, *An Imperial Vision: Indian Architecture and the British Raj*, Faber and Faber, London, 1989

A. A. Millar, *Alexander Duff of India*, Canongate, Edinburgh, 1992

C. P. Mills, *A Strange War*, Alan Sutton, Gloucester, 1988

Mary, Countess of Minto, *India, Minto and Morley, 1905–1910*, Macmillan, London, 1934

Maria Misra, *Business, Race, and Politics in British India c. 1850–1960*, Oxford University Press, 1999

Elizabeth Monroe, *Philby of Arabia*, Faber and Faber, London, 1973

Brian Montgomery, *Monty's Grandfather: A Life's Service for the Raj*, Blandford Press, Poole, 1984

Penderell Moon, *The British Conquest and Dominion of India*, Duckworth, London, 1989

————, *Divide and Quit*, Chatto & Windus, London, 1962

Robin Moore, *Paul Scott's Raj*, Heinemann, London, 1990

R. J. Moore, *Sir Charles Wood's Indian Policy*, Manchester University Press, 1966

Geoffrey Moorhouse, *Calcutta*, Penguin, London, 1988

————, *India Britannica*, Harvill, London, 1988

Andrew Morgan (ed.), *Mussoorie Merchant: The Indian Letters of Mauger Fitzhugh Monk*, Pagoda Tree Press, Bath, 2006

David Morling, *Pioneering on the Cauvery*, Marshall Brothers, London, 1924

James Morris, *Farewell the Trumpets: An Imperial Retreat*, Faber, London, 1978

————, *Heaven's Command: An Imperial Progress*, Faber, London, 1973

————, *Pax Britannica: The Climax of Empire*, Faber, London, 1968

Jan Morris, *Stones of Empire*, Oxford University Press, 1987

John Morris, *Hired to Kill*, Hart-Davis, London, 1960

Belinda Morse, *Calamity and Courage: A Heroine of the Raj*, Book Guild Publishing, Brighton, 2008

George Morton-Jack, *The Indian Army on the Western Front*, Cambridge University Press, 2014

Ferdinand Mount, *The Tears of the Rajas: Mutiny, Money and Marriage in India 1805–1905*, Simon & Schuster, London, 2015

J. Muir, *The Indian Civil Service and the Scottish Universities*, W. P. Kennedy, Edinburgh, 1855

Rory Muir, *Wellington: The Path to Victory, 1769–1814*, Yale University Press, Newhaven and London, 2013

Rudrangshu Mukherjee, *Avadh in Revolt, 1857–1858*, Permanent Black, Ranikhet, 2002

Ray Murphy (ed.), *Edward Lear's Indian Journal*, Jarrolds, London, 1953

S. Muthiah, *Madras Discovered*, East-West Press, Madras, 1992

————, *Madras: Its Past and Present*, Affiliated East-West Press Private Limited, Madras, 1995

Naini Tal: A Historical and Descriptive Account, Government Press, Allahabad, 1928

V. S. Naipaul, *India: A Wounded Civilization*, André Deutsch, London, 1977

P. Thankappan Nair (ed.), *British Social Life in Ancient Calcutta, 1750 to 1850*, Sanskrit Pustak Bhandar, Calcutta, 1983

P. Thankappan Nair, *Calcutta in the Eighteenth Century*, Firma KLM, Calcutta, 1984

Pran Nevile, *Rare Glimpses of the Raj*, Somaiya, Mumbai, 1998

Capt. J. T. Newall, *Scottish Moors and Indian Jungles*, Hurst and Blackett, London, 1889

H. A. Newell, *Topee and Turban*, Bodley Head, London, 1921

Beverley Nichols, *Verdict on India*, Jonathan Cape, London, 1944

Paul Byron Norris, *Follow My Bangalorey Man*, BACSA, London, 1996

———, *Ulysses in the Raj*, BACSA, London, 1992

———, *Willingly to War, 1939–1945*, BACSA, London, 2004

C. J. O'Donnell, *The Irish Future and the Lordship of the World*, Cecil Palmer, London, 1929

Michael O'Dwyer, *India as I Knew It*, Constable, London, 1925

L. L. S. O'Malley, *The Indian Civil Service, 1601–1930*, Frank Cass, London, 1965

David Omissi, *The Sepoy and the Raj: The Indian Army, 1860–1940*, Macmillan, Basingstoke, 1998

George Orwell, *Burmese Days*, Secker & Warburg, London, 1949

Roger Owen, *Lord Cromer*, Oxford University Press, 2004

Patricia Owens (ed.), *An American Memsahib in India: The Letters and Diaries of Irene Mott Bose*, BACSA, London, 2006

Valerie Pakenham, *The Noonday Sun: Edwardians in the Tropics*, Methuen, London, 1985

H. R. Packridge and R. I. Macalpine, *The Bengal Club, 1827–1970*, Statesman Press, Calcutta, 1970

Mollie Panter-Downes, *Ooty Preserved*, Hamish Hamilton, London, 1967

Peter Parker, *Ackerley*, Constable, London, 1989

Fanny Parkes, *Begums, Thugs and White Mughals*, Eland, London, 2001

Biswamoy Pati and Mark Harrison (eds.), *Health, Medicine and Empire*, Sangam, London, 2001

———, *The Social History of Health and Medicine in Colonial India*, Routledge, London, 2009

Roger Pearce, *Once a Happy Valley*, Oxford University Press, Karachi, 2001

John Pemble (ed.), *Miss Fane in India*, Alan Sutton, Gloucester, 1985

Clayre Percy and Jane Ridley (eds.), *The Letters of Edwin Lutyens*, Collins, London, 1985

Margery Perham, *Lugard: The Years of Adventure, 1858–1898*, Collins, London, 1956

Jane Pettigrew, *A Social History of Tea*, National Trust, London, 2001

C. H. Philips (ed.), *Historians of India, Pakistan and Ceylon*, Oxford University Press, 1961

Stuart Piggin, *Making Evangelical Missionaries, 1789–1858*, Sutton Courtney Press, 1984

Thomas Pinney (ed.), *The Letters of Rudyard Kipling*, vol. 2, University of Iowa Press, Iowa City, 1990

——, *The Letters of Rudyard Kipling*, vol. 4, Macmillan, Basingstoke, 1999

Andrew Porter, *Religion versus Empire? British Protestant Missionaries and Overseas Expansion, 1700–1914*, Manchester University Press, 2004

Andrew Porter (ed.), *The Oxford History of the British Empire: The Nineteenth Century*, Oxford University Press, 1999

Bernard Porter, *The Absent-Minded Imperialists*, Oxford University Press, 1999

Martin Postle (ed.), *Johann Zoffany RA*, Yale University Press, New Haven and London, 2011

David C. Potter, *India's Political Administrators, 1918–1983*, Oxford University Press, Delhi, 1986

George Pottinger, *Mayo: Disraeli's Viceroy*, Michael Russell, London, 1990

Avril A. Powell, *Scottish Orientalists and India*, Boydell Press, Suffolk, 2010

Violet Powell, *Flora Annie Steel*, Heinemann, London, 1981

John Prendergast, *Prender's Progress: A Soldier in India*, Cassell, London, 1979

Frederick Price, *Ootacamund*, Rupa, Chennai, 2002

Hugh Purcell, *After the Raj*, History Press, Stroud, 2011

John Radford and Susan Maria Farrington, *Tombs in Tea*, BACSA, London, 2001

Srinath Raghavan, *India's War: The Making of Modern South Asia, 1939–1945*, Allen Lane, London, 2016

N. S. Ramaswami, *The Madras Club, 1832–1982*, Chamiers Road, Madras, 1982

S. K. Ratcliffe, *Sir William Wedderburn and the Indian Reform Movement*, George Allen & Unwin, London, 1925

Bharati Ray, *Hyderabad and British Paramountcy, 1858–1883*, Oxford University Press, Delhi, 1988

Stanley Reed, *The India I Knew*, Odhams, London, 1952

Robert Reid, *Years of Change in Bengal and Assam*, Ernest Benn, London, 1966

Raymond K. Renford, *The Non-official British in India to 1920*, Oxford University Press, Delhi, 1987

Claudia Renton, *Those Wild Wyndhams*, Collins, London, 2014

Frank Richards, *Old Soldier Sahib*, Naval & Military Press, Uckfield, 2003

Gordon Richings, 'Charles Bell's Divorce: The Legal Aftermath', *Quarterly Bulletin of the National Library of South Africa*, vol. 54, no. 3, March 2000

Julius Richter, *A History of Missions in India*, Oliphant Anderson, Edinburgh, 1908

Jane Ridley, *Bertie: A Life of Edward VII* Chatto & Windus, London, 2012

——, *Edwin Lutyens*, Pimlico, London, 2003

Gerald Ritchie, *The Ritchies in India*, John Murray, London, 1920

J. H. Rivett-Carnac, *Many Memories*, Blackwood, Edinburgh, 1910

Peter Robb, *Sentiment and Self: Richard Blechynden's Calcutta Diaries, 1791–1822*, Oxford University Press, Delhi, 2011
———, *Sex and Sensibility: Richard Blechynden's Calcutta Diaries, 1790*, Oxford University Press, Delhi, 2011
Andrew Roberts, *Napoleon the Great*, Allen Lane, London, 2014
Lord Roberts, *Forty-one Years in India*, 2 vols., Richard Bentley, London, 1987
Alan Robertson, *Epic Engineering: Great Canals and Barrages of Victorian India*, Beechwood Melrose, Melrose, 2013
Leslie Robins, *Policing the Raj*, Robins, London, 1985
Captain H. R. Robinson, *A Modern De Quincey*, Harrap, 1943
Ronald Robinson and John Gallagher, *Africa and the Victorians*, Macmillan, London, 1961
Alan Ross, *Blindfold Games*, Collins Harvill, London, 1986
Rotary Club of Kodaikanal, 1979
Emma Rothschild, *The Inner Life of Empires*, Princeton University Press, 2011
Norah Rowan Hamilton, *Through Wonderful India and Beyond*, Holden & Harmingham, London, 1915
Jyotirmoy Roy, *History of Manipur*, Firma KLM, Calcutta, 1958
Trevor Royle, *Death before Dishonour: The True Story of Fighting Mac*, Mainstream, Edinburgh 1982
———, *The Last Days of the Raj*, Michael Joseph, London, 1989
Wilfrid Russell, *Indian Summer*, Thacker, Bombay, 1951
James R. Ryan, *Picturing Empire*, Reaktion, London, 1997
Edward Said, *Culture and Imperialism*, Vintage, London, 1994
———, *Orientalism*, Routledge & Kegan Paul, London, 1978
Hugh David Sandeman (ed.), *Selections from Calcutta Gazettes 1816*, Superintendent of Government Printing, Calcutta, 1869
G. P. Sanderson, *Thirteen Years among the Wild Beasts of India*, W. H. Allen, London, 1878
Mahua Sarkar, *Justice in a Gothic Edifice*, Firma KLM, Calcutta, 1997
Narindar Saroop, *A Squire of Hindustan*, Nottingham Court Press, London, 1985
W. H. Saumarez Smith, *A Young Man's Country*, Michael Joseph, London, 1977
Douglas Scott (ed.), *Douglas Haig: Diaries & Letters, 1861–1914*, Pen & Sword, Barnsley, 2006
Pauline Scudamore, *Spike Milligan*, Grafton, London, 1985
Anil Seal, *The Emergence of Indian Nationalism*, Cambridge University Press, 1969
Edward Sellon, *The Ups and Downs of Life*, Wordsworth (Ware), 1966
Sudipta Sen, *Distant Sovereignty: National Imperialism and the Origins of British India*, Routledge, New York, 2002
Chandak Sengoopta, *Imprint of the Raj*, Macmillan, London, 2003
W. S. Seton-Karr (ed.), *Selections from Calcutta Gazettes, 1784–1788*, O. T. Cutter, Calcutta, 1864

Michael Shelden, *Orwell*, Heinemann, London, 1991

Nancy K. Shields, *Birds of Passage: Henrietta Clive's Travels in South India, 1798–1801*, Eland, London, 2009

Frank B. Simson, *Letters on Sport in Eastern Bengal*, R. H. Porter, London, 1886

Khushwant Singh (ed.), *Sahibs Who Loved India*, Penguin India, New Delhi, 2010

F. H. B. Skrine, *Life of Sir William Wilson Hunter*, Longmans, London, 1901

Gilbert Slater, *Southern India*, Allen & Unwin, London, 1936

William Slim, *Unofficial History*, Cassell, London, 1959

Diana Souhami, *The Trials of Radclyffe Hall*, Weidenfeld & Nicolson, London, 1998

The South Park Street Cemetery, 2nd edn, BACSA, London, 1986

Bradford Spangenberg, *British Bureaucracy in India*, South Asia Books, Delhi, 1976

Percival Spear, *A History of India*, vol. 2, Penguin, London, 1990

——, *Master of Bengal: Clive and His India*, Thames and Hudson, London, 1975

——, *The Nabobs*, Oxford University Press, Delhi, 1998

Malcolm Speirs, *Lucknow: Families of the Raj*, Amazon, 2013

Hilary Spurling, *Paul Scott*, Pimlico, London, 1991

Elizabeth Staley, *Monkey Tops: Old Buildings in Bangalore Cantonment*, Tara Books, Bangalore, 1981

Peter Stansky and William Abrahams, *The Unknown Orwell*, Constable, London, 1992

F. A. Steel and G. Gardiner, *The Complete Indian Housekeeper & Cook*, Heinemann, London, 1898

Flora Annie Steel, *The Garden of Fidelity*, Macmillan, London, 1929

Ian Stephens, *Unmade Journey*, Stacey International, London, 1977

G. W. Steevens, *In India*, Blackwood, Edinburgh, 1899

Mary Ann Steggles, *Statues of the Raj*, BACSA, London, 2000

Patrick Hugh Stevenage, *A Railway Family in India*, BACSA, London, 2001

V. E. O. Stevenson-Hamilton, *Yes, Your Excellency*, Thomas Harmsworth, London, 1985

J. H. Stocqueler, *India: Its History, Climate, Productions and Field Sports*, George Routledge and Co., London, 1853

Ian Stone, *Canal Irrigation in India*, Cambridge University Press, 1984

Barbara Strachey, *The Strachey Line*, Gollancz, London, 1985

John Strachey, *India: Its Administration and Progress*, Kegan Paul, London, 1894

Tristram Stuart, *The Bloodless Revolution: Radical Vegetarians and the Discovery of India*, HarperPress, London, 2006

April Swayne-Thomas, *Indian Summer*, New English Library, London, 1981

Richard Symonds, *The British and Their Successors*, Faber and Faber, London, 1966

————, *In the Margins of Independence*, Oxford University Press, Karachi, 2001

————, *Oxford and Empire*, Oxford University Press, 1991

Prakash Tandon, *Punjabi Century, 1857–1947*, Chatto & Windus, London, 1961

Richard Temple, *The Story of My Life*, 2 vols., Cassell, London, 1896

Lowell Thomas, *India: Land of the Black Pagoda*, Garden City, New York, 1930

Edward Thompson, *An Indian Day*, A. A. Knopf, London, 1927

Herbert Thompson, *Icarus Went East*, Justin Woolcott, 2013

Kathryn Tidrick, *Empire and the English Character*, I. B. Tauris, London, 1992

Aroon Tikekar, *The Kincaids*, Promilla, New Delhi, 1992

Claire Tomalin, *Mrs Jordan's Profession*, Viking, London, 1994

Harry Townend, *A History of Shaw Wallace and Co.*, Shaw Wallace and Company Ltd, Calcutta, 1965

G. O. Trevelyan, *Competition Wallah*, Macmillan, London, 1866

Humphrey Trevelyan, *The India We Left*, Macmillan, London, 1972

Raleigh Trevelyan, *The Golden Oriole*, Secker & Warburg, London, 1987

Myna Trustram, *Women of the Regiment: Marriage and the Victorian Army*, Cambridge University Press, 1984

Francis Tuker, *While Memory Serves*, Cassell, London, 1950

Charles Lewis Tupper, *Our Indian Protectorate*, Longmans, Green, London, 1893

Bill Tydd, *Peacock Dreams*, BACSA, London, 1986

C. E. Tyndale-Biscoe, *Kashmir in Sunlight and Shade*, Seeley, Service & Co., London, 1922

————, *Tyndale-Biscoe of Kashmir*, Seeley, Service and Co., London, 1951

Annabel Venning, *Following the Drum: The Lives of Army Wives and Daughters*, Headline, London, 2005

R. C. Vernede (ed.), *British Life in India*, Oxford University Press, Delhi, 1996

David Verney (ed.), *In Viceregal India, 1916–21: The Letters of Ralph Verney*, vol. 2, Tabb House, Padstow, 1994

Margaret M. Verney, *Sir Henry Stewart Cunningham*, John Murray, London, 1923

Colonel H. M. Vibart, *Richard Baird Smith*, Constable, London, 1897

Hugo Vickers, *Vivien Leigh*, Hamish Hamilton, London, 1988

Robin Volkers, *Agra, St Paul's Cemetery*, BACSA, London, 2007

Edward Wakefield, *Past Imperative*, Chatto & Windus, London, 1966

Erica Wald, *Vice in the Barracks: Medicine, the Military and the Making of Colonial India, 1780–1868*, Palgrave Macmillan, London, 2014

Ethel Waley-Cohen (ed.), *A Young Victorian in India: Letters of H. M. Kisch*, Jonathan Cape, London, 1957

Judith E. Walsh, *Growing Up in British India*, Holmes and Meier, New York, 1983

Calder Walton, *Empire of Secrets: British Intelligence, the Cold War and the Twilight of Empire*, HarperPress, London, 2013

Robert Warburton, *Eighteen Years in the Khyber*, John Murray, London, 1900

Andrew Ward, *Our Bones are Scattered*, John Murray, London, 1996

A. E. Wardrop, *Modern Pig-sticking*, Macmillan, London, 1914

Philip Warner, *Auchinleck*, Cassell, London, 2001

Sidney and Beatrice Webb, *Indian Diary*, Oxford University Press, 1990

W. Wedderburn, *Allan Octavian Hume* (new edn by Edward C. Moulton), Oxford University Press, Delhi, 2002

Bishop Welldon, *Recollections and Reflections*, Cassell, London, 1915

J. S. Western, *Reminiscences of an Indian Cavalry Officer*, Allen & Unwin, London, 1922

J. N. Westwood, *Railways of India*, David & Charles, Newton Abbot, 1974

B. C. Whish, *A District Office in Northern India*, Thacker, Spink, Calcutta, 1892

Herbert Thirkell White, *A Civil Servant in Burma*, Edward Arnold, London, 1913

R. and S. Wilberforce, *The Life of William Wilberforce*, 5 vols., John Murray, London, 1839

Antony Wild, *The East India Company*, HarperCollins, London, 1999

Theon Wilkinson, *Two Monsoons: The Life and Death of Europeans in India*, Duckworth, London, 1987

Clive Williams, *The Nabobs of Berkshire*, Goosecroft, Purley on Thames, 2010

Philip M. Williams, *Hugh Gaitskell*, Jonathan Cape, London, 1979

Donovan Williams and E. Daniel Potts, *Essays in Indian History*, Asia Publishing House, London, 1973

W. N. Willis, *Western Men with Eastern Morals*, Stanley Paul, London, 1913

Anne C. Wilson, *Hints for the First Years of Residence in India*, Oxford University Press, 1904

Guy Fleetwood Wilson, *Letters to Nobody, 1908–1913*, John Murray, London, 1921

Jon Wilson, *India Conquered: Britain's Raj and the Conquest of Empire*, Simon and Schuster, London, 2016

Lady Wilson, *Letters from India*, Century, London, 1984

Norman Wisdom (with William Hall), *Don't Laugh at Me*, Century, London, 1992

Women's Christian College Madras, 1915–1935

Philip Woodruff, *The Founders*, Jonathan Cape, London, 1963

——, *The Guardians*, Jonathan Cape, London, 1963

Leonard Woolf, *Growing*, Hogarth Press, London, 1964

Maisie Wright, *Under Malabar Hill*, BACSA, London, 1988

William Wright, *Through the Indian Mutiny: The Memoirs of James Fair-weather*, Three Rivers Publishers, New Delhi, 2011

'Wyvern' (Colonel Kenney-Herbert), *Culinary Jottings from Madras*, Higgin-botham, Madras, 1885

Marianne Young (Mrs Postans), *Western India in 1838*, vol. 1, Saunders and Otley, London, 1839

Zoë Yalland, *Boxwallahs: The British in Cawnpore, 1857–1901*, Michael Russell, London, 1994

——, *Traders and Nabobs: The British in Cawnpore, 1765–1857*, Michael Russell, London, 1987

F. Yeats-Brown, *Bengal Lancer*, Victor Gollancz, London, 1930

——, *Lancer at Large*, Victor Gollancz, London, 1937

Henry Yule and A. C. Burnell, *Hobson Jobson*, Munshiram Manoharlal, New Delhi, 1994

Tanya Zinkin, *French Memsahib*, Thomas Harmsworth, Stoke Abbott, 1989

Index

Balliol College 81, 392, 411
  and Dawkins family 199
  and ICS 116–18, 122
  and viceroys 107–8
Ballygunge 328
Baloo, Palwankar 407
Baluchistan 59, 126, 229, 265
  British deaths in 491
  Sandeman in 184–5
Bambrick, Valentine 44–5
Bamford, Geoffrey 503
Bangalore 1, 125, 245, 436
  architecture of 339
  Churchill in 263–5
  climate of 251, 343, 373
  retirement to 508
  temperance societies in 256
Bangladesh 12
Banham, Philip 87
Bankipore 391
  Beveridges in 345, 349
Barcroft, Robbie 56
Bareilly Tent Club 482–3
Barlow, George Hilario
  sues for divorce 320
Barlow, George Pratt 320
Barnard, Henry 490
Barnes, 'Barney'
  assassination of 268
Baroda 179, 325
Barr, David
  career in IPS 182
  promotion of 192
Barrackpore 147, 343, 381
Barry, Charlotte ('Mrs Hickey')
  134, 285
Basildon Park 505
Basrah Times 427
Bassein 310, 429
Batchelor, Stanley 60
Bateman, Rowland 435
Bateman-Champain, Mrs 517
Bath and West Society 199

Batten, George 315
Batten, Mabel 317
  in Simla 315
  success as singer 497n.
Batty, Beatrice
  missionary intentions of 225
Battye family
  military careers of 46–7
Battye, Richmond
  as reluctant soldier 47
Battye, Warren 466
Bayley, Charles
  as Resident in Hyderabad 387
Bayley, Vernon 205
Bayley, Violet
  experiences in India 21–2
Baylis, Robert 493
Bayly, C. A.
  on liberalism in India 524
Bazalgette, Jack
  post-Indian career of 502
Beale, Edward 261
Beale, Henry 261
Beames, Ellen
  giving birth in India 364
Beames, John 124, 189, 296, 364,
    390, 451
  on Calcutta 145
  debts in India 119
  as district officer 162
  experiences at Haileybury
    111–13
  on George Faulkner 214–15
  on IMS doctors 128
  as linguist 417
  and planters 217–18, 220–22
  resigns as master of lodge 410
  voyage to India 138
Beatson, William 55–6
Becher, Anne
  marriages of 64
Bedford Grammar School 82, 373
Beechey, George Duncan 37